LIBERTY
EQUALITY
POWER

777-874

LIBERTY EQUALITY POWER

A History of the American People

CONCISE SECOND EDITION

VOLUME II: SINCE 1863

JOHN M. MURRIN
Princeton University

PAUL E. JOHNSON
University of South Carolina

JAMES M. MCPHERSON
Princeton University

GARY GERSTLE
University of Maryland

EMILY S. ROSENBERG
Macalester College

NORMAN L. ROSENBERG
Macalester College

HARCOURT COLLEGE PUBLISHERS

Fort Worth   Philadelphia   San Diego   New York   Orlando   Austin   San Antonio
Toronto   Montreal   London   Sydney   Tokyo

Publisher	Earl McPeek
Executive Editor	David C. Tatom
Executive Market Strategist	Steve Drummond
Developmental Editor	Margaret McAndrew Beasley
Project Editor	Charles J. Dierker
Art Director	Brian Salisbury
Production Manager	Diane Gray
Art & Design Coordinator	Florence Fujimoto

Cover Image: *The White Way* © Philadelphia Museum of Art/CORBIS.

ISBN: 0-15-508284-1

Library of Congress Catalog Card Number: 00-103390

Address for Domestic Orders
Harcourt College Publishers, 6277 Sea Harbor Drive, Orlando, FL 32887-6777. 800-782-4479

Address for International Orders
International Customer Service, Harcourt, Inc., 6277 Sea Harbor Drive, Orlando, FL 32887-6777. 407-345-3800. (fax) 407-345-4060. (e-mail) hbintl@harcourt.com

Address for Editorial Correspondence
Harcourt College Publishers, 301 Commerce Street, Suite 3700, Fort Worth, TX 76102

Web Site Address
http://www.harcourtcollege.com

Harcourt College Publishers will provide complimentary supplements or supplement packages to those adopters qualified under our adoption policy. Please contact your sales representative to learn how you qualify. If as an adopter or potential user you receive supplements you do not need, please return them to your sales representative or send them to: Attn: Returns Department, Troy Warehouse, 465 South Lincoln Drive, Troy, MO 63379.

Printed in the United States of America

0 1 2 3 4 5 6 7 8 9 039 10 9 8 7 6 5 4 3 2 1

∾ About the Authors ∾

John M. Murrin, *Princeton University*

John M. Murrin, a specialist in American colonial and revolutionary history, is the author of the first section (Chapters 1–6) of *Liberty, Equality, Power,* Concise Second Edition. He has edited one multivolume series and five books, including *Colonial America: Essays in Politics and Social Development,* Fourth Edition (1993) and *Saints and Revolutionaries* (1984). His many essays on early American history show a diversity of interests that range from ethnic tensions, the early history of trial by jury, and the political culture of Revolutionary America, to the rise of professional baseball and college football. Professor Murrin was elected president of the Society of Historians of the Early American Republic (SHEAR) for 1998–99.

Paul E. Johnson, *University of South Carolina*

Paul E. Johnson authored the second section of the text (Chapters 7–12). A specialist in early national social and religious history, he is also the author of *A Shopkeeper's Millennium: Society and Revivals in Rochester, New York, 1815–1837* (1978); coauthor (with Sean Wilentz), of *The Kingdom of Matthias: Sex and Salvation in 19th-Century America* (1994); and editor of *African-American Christianity: Essays in History* (1994). He has been awarded the Merle Curti Prize of the Organization of American Historians (1980), and a John Simon Guggenheim Memorial Fellowship (1995).

James M. McPherson, *Princeton University*

James M. McPherson is the author of the third section of the text (Chapters 13–19). A distinguished Civil War historian, he won the 1989 Pulitzer Prize for his book *Battle Cry of Freedom: The Civil War Era.* His other publications include *Marching Toward Freedom: Blacks in the Civil War,* Second Edition (1991), *Ordeal by Fire: The Civil War and Reconstruction,* Second Edition (1992), *Abraham Lincoln and the Second American Revolution* (1991), and *For Cause and Comrades: Why Men Fought in the Civil War* (1997). In addition, he is, along with Gary Gerstle, a consulting editor of *American Political Leaders: From Colonial Times to the Present* (1991) and *American Social Leaders: From Colonial Times to the Present* (1993).

Gary Gerstle, *University of Maryland*

Gary Gerstle is the author of the fourth section of the text (Chapters 20–25). A specialist in labor, immigration, and political history, he has published *Working-Class Americanism: The Politics of Labor in a Textile City, 1914–1960* (1989), *The Rise and Fall of the New Deal Order, 1930–1980* (1989) and articles in the *American Historical Review, Journal of American History, American Quarterly,* and many other journals. He is a consulting editor, along with James M. McPherson, of *American Political Leaders: From Colonial Times to the Present* (1991) and *American Social Leaders: From Colonial Times to the Present* (1993). He has been awarded many honors, including a National Endowment for the Humanities Fellowship for University Teachers, an Institute for Advanced Study Membership, and a John Simon Guggenheim Memorial Fellowship.

EMILY S. ROSENBERG, *Macalester College*

Emily S. Rosenberg is the author, along with Norman L. Rosenberg, of the last section of the text (Chapters 26–31). She specializes in United States foreign relations in the 20th century and is the author of the widely used book *Spreading the American Dream: American Economic and Cultural Expansion, 1890–1945* (1982). Her other publications include (with Norman L. Rosenberg) *In Our Times: America Since 1945,* Fifth Edition (1995) and numerous articles on subjects such as international finance, gender issues, and foreign relations. She has served on the board of the Organization of American Historians, on the board of editors of the *Journal of American History,* and as president of the Society for Historians of American Foreign Relations.

NORMAN L. ROSENBERG, *Macalester College*

Norman L. Rosenberg is coauthor, along with Emily S. Rosenberg, of the final section of the text (Chapters 26–31). He specializes in legal history with a particular interest in legal culture and First Amendment issues. His books include *Protecting the "Best Men": An Interpretive History of the Law of Libel* (1990) and (with Emily S. Rosenberg) *In Our Times: America Since 1945,* Fifth Edition (1995). He has published articles in the *Rutgers Law Review, Constitutional Commentary, Law & History Review,* and many other legal journals.

~ PREFACE ~

W hy take a course in American history? This is a question that many college and university students ask. In many respects, students today are like the generations of Americans who have gone before them: optimistic and forward looking, far more eager to imagine where we as a nation might be going than to reflect on where we have been. If anything, this tendency has become more pronounced in recent years, as the Internet revolution has accelerated the pace and excitement of change and made even the recent past seem at best quaint, at worst uninteresting and irrelevant.

But it is precisely in these moments of great change that a sense of the past can be indispensable in terms of guiding our actions in the present and future. We can find in other periods of American history moments, like our own, of dizzying technological change and economic growth, rapid alterations in the concentration of wealth and power, and basic changes in patterns of work, residence, and play. How did Americans at those times create, embrace, and resist these changes? In earlier periods of American history, the United States was home, as it is today, to a remarkably diverse array of ethnic and racial groups. How did earlier generations of Americans respond to the cultural conflicts and misunderstandings that often arise from conditions of diversity? How did immigrants perceive their new land? How and when did they integrate themselves into American society? To study how ordinary Americans of the past struggled with these issues is to gain perspective on the opportunities and problems that we face today.

History also provides an important guide to affairs of state. What should the role of America be in world affairs? Should we participate in international bodies such as the United Nations or insist on our ability to act autonomously and without the consent of other nations? What is the proper role of government in economic and social life? Should the government regulate the economy? To what extent should the government enforce morality regarding religion, sexual practices, drinking and drugs, movies, TV, and other forms of mass culture? And what are our responsibilities as citizens to each other and to the nation? Americans of past generations have debated these issues with verve and conviction. Learning about these debates and how they were resolved will enrich our understanding of the policy possibilities for today and tomorrow.

History, finally, is about stories—stories that we all tell about ourselves, our families, our communities, our ethnicity, race, region, and religion, and our nation. They are stories of triumph and tragedy, of engagement and flight, and of high ideals and high comedy. When telling these stories, "American history" is often the furthest thing from our minds. But, often, an implicit sense of history informs what we say about grandparents who immigrated many years ago, the suburb in which we live, the church, synagogue, or mosque that we attend, or the ethnic or racial group to which we belong. But how well do we really understand these individuals, institutions, and groups? Do we tell the right stories about them, ones that capture the complexities of their past? Or have we wittingly or unwittingly simplified, altered, or flattened them? A study of American history first helps us to ask these questions and then to answer them. In the process, we can engage in a fascinating journey of intellectual and personal discovery and situate ourselves more firmly than we had ever thought possible in relation to those who came before us. We can gain firmer self-knowledge and a greater appreciation for the richness of our nation and, indeed, of all humanity.

THE *LIBERTY EQUALITY POWER* APPROACH

In this book we tell many small stories, and one large one: how America transformed itself, in a relatively brief era of world history, from a land inhabited by hunter-gatherer and agricultural Native American societies into the most powerful industrial nation on earth. This story has been told many times before, and those who have told it in the past have usually emphasized the political experiment in liberty and equality that took root here in the 18th century. We, too, stress the extraordinary and transformative impact that the ideals of liberty and equality exerted on American politics, society, and economics during the American Revolution and after. We show how the creation of a free economic environment—one in which entrepreneurial spirit, technological innovation, and industrial production has flourished—underpinned American industrial might. We have emphasized, too, the successful struggles for freedom that, over the course of the last 225 years, have brought—first to all white men, then to men of color and finally to women—rights and opportunities that they had not previously known.

But we have also identified a third factor in this pantheon of American ideals—that of power. We examine power in many forms: the accumulation of vast economic fortunes that dominated the economy and politics; the dispossession of native Americans from land that they regarded as theirs; the enslavement of millions of Africans and their African American descendants for a period of almost 250 years; the relegation of women and of racial, ethnic, and religious minorities to subordinate places in American society; and the extension of American control over foreign peoples, such as Latin Americans and Filipinos, who would have preferred to have been free and self-governing. We do not mean to suggest that American power has always been turned to these negative purposes. Subordinate groups have themselves marshaled power to combat oppression, as in the abolitionist and civil rights crusades, the campaign for woman's suffrage, and the labor movement. The state has used its power to moderate poverty and to manage the economy in the interests of general prosperity. And it has used its military power to defeat Nazi Germany, World War II Japan, the Cold War Soviet Union, and other enemies of freedom.

The invocation of power as a variable in American history forces us to widen the lens through which we look at the past and to complicate the stories we tell. Ours has been a history of freedom and domination; of progress toward realizing a broadly democratic polity and of delays and reverses; of abundance and poverty; of wars for freedom and justice and for control of foreign markets.

In complicating our master narrative in this way, we think we have rendered American history more exciting and intriguing. Progress has not been automatic, but the product of on-going struggles.

In this book we have also tried to capture the diversity of the American past, both in terms of outcomes and in terms of the variety of groups who have participated in America's making. Native Americans, in this book, are not presented simply as the victims of European aggression but as a people remarkably diverse in their own ranks, with a variety of systems of social organization and cultural expression. We give equal treatment to the industrial titans of American history—the likes of Andrew Carnegie and John D. Rockefeller—and to those, such as small farmers and poor workers, who resisted the corporate reorganization of economic life. We celebrate the great moments of 1863, when African Americans were freed from slavery, and of 1868, when they were made full citizens of the United States. But we also note how a majority of African Americans had to wait another 100 years, until the civil rights movement of the 1960s, to gain full access to American freedoms. We tell similarly complex stories about women, Latinos, and other groups of ethnic Americans.

Political issues, of course, are only part of America's story. Americans have always loved their leisure and have created the world's most vibrant popular culture. They have embraced technological innovations, especially those promising to make their lives easier and more fun. We have, therefore, devoted considerable space to a discussion of American popular culture, from the founding of the first newspapers in the 18th century to the rise of movies, jazz, and the comics in the 20th century, to the cable television and Internet revolutions in recent years. We have pondered, too, how American industry has periodically altered home and personal life by making new products—such as clothing, cars, refrigerators, and computers—available to consumers. In such ways we hope to give our readers a rich portrait of how Americans lived at various points in our history.

This book is a brief version of the much admired, *Liberty, Equality, Power*, second edition. We have reduced the length of that volume the hard way—not by cutting whole sections but by carefully eliminating single phrases, lines, and sentences on every page. Thus readers can be assured that all the topics covered in the longer version are covered here; indeed all the headings and subheadings remained unchanged. And the high quality of the writing in *Liberty Equality Power*, a feature much valued by its users, has been preserved. And yet, the text is significantly shorter, thus giving instructors more flexibility in determining how to use it in their courses. With this brief edition, it becomes easier to give students supplementary reading assignments or to expand a Web-based portion of the course.

In a brief edition of this sort, the art and photography program of the longer edition must inevitably be reduced. Nevertheless, we have included a significant number of visuals, and we have carried over from the larger work its highly popular "American Album" feature. More than half of the chapters include an "American Album," a brief essay illustrated with historic photos or artwork that offers a visual excursion into a fascinating moment of the American past. In addition to the themes of liberty, equality, and power, these features explore subjects especially intriguing to students—sports, the environment, gender roles, religion, popular and material culture, war, and race. They can be easily integrated into lectures and classroom discussion or left for students to discover on their own.

We have also carried over into this work most of the graphs and charts from the second edition as well as the chapter-ending chronologies of major events and movements that users of the comprehensive volume have found so useful.

ACKNOWLEDGMENTS

We recognize the contributions of reviewers who read portions of the manuscript in various stages:

Janet Brantley, *Texarkana College*
Sally Hadden, *Florida State University*
Terry Isaacs, *South Plains College*
Thomas Ott, *University of North Alabama*
Geoffrey Plank, *University of Cincinnati*
Stephen Webre, *Louisiana Tech University*

We also appreciate the comments of students at South Plains College who read selected chapters: Anna-Marie Darden, Samuel Hinojosa, and Gwen W. McEntire.

We have once again benefited from the excellent work of the veteran Harcourt staff, and we would like to thank these individuals in particular: David C. Tatom, executive editor; Margaret McAndrew Beasley, senior developmental editor; Charles Dierker, senior project editor; Diane Gray, production manager; Brian Salisbury, senior art director; Steve Drummond, executive market strategist; and Carolyn D. Smith, freelance manuscript editor. Several of these individuals have probably read the various versions of this textbook almost as many times as we have, and yet their enthusiasm for and commitment to this project remain undiminished. Their skills at editing, production, and promotion, and at keeping a dispersed group of authors focused on the tasks at hand are as sharp as ever. We are deeply in their debt.

John M. Murrin
Paul E. Johnson
James M. McPherson
Gary Gerstle
Emily S. Rosenberg
Norman L. Rosenberg

∾ Contents in Brief ∾

～ Contents in Detail ～

CHAPTER 17

RECONSTRUCTION, 1863–1877   465

Chapter 21
Progressivism   547

CHAPTER 24
THE 1920S   633

CHAPTER 25
THE GREAT DEPRESSION AND THE NEW DEAL, 1929–1939   661

CHAPTER 27
THE AGE OF CONTAINMENT, 1946–1954   727

CHAPTER 30

AMERICA IN TRANSITION: ECONOMICS, CULTURE, AND SOCIAL CHANGE IN THE LATE 20TH CENTURY   815

CHAPTER 31

WINDS OF CHANGE: POLITICS AND FOREIGN POLICY FROM FORD TO CLINTON   845

~ LIST OF MAPS ~

～ AMERICAN ALBUMS ～

RECONSTRUCTION, 1863–1877

WARTIME RECONSTRUCTION

ANDREW JOHNSON AND RECONSTRUCTION

THE ADVENT OF CONGRESSIONAL RECONSTRUCTION

THE IMPEACHMENT OF ANDREW JOHNSON

THE GRANT ADMINISTRATION ~ THE RETREAT FROM RECONSTRUCTION

From the beginning of the Civil War, the North fought to "reconstruct" the Union. At first Lincoln's purpose was to restore the Union as it had existed before 1861. But once the abolition of slavery became a Northern war aim, the Union could never be reconstructed on its old foundations. Instead, it must experience a "new birth of freedom," as Lincoln had said at the dedication of the military cemetery at Gettysburg.

But precisely what did "a new birth of freedom" mean? At the very least it meant the end of slavery. The slave states would be reconstructed on a free-labor basis. But what would be the dimensions of liberty for the 4 million freed slaves? Would they become citizens equal to their former masters in the eyes of the law? And on what terms should the Confederate states return to the Union? What would be the powers of the states and of the national government in a reconstructed Union?

WARTIME RECONSTRUCTION

Lincoln pondered these questions long and hard. At first he feared that whites in the South would never extend equal rights to the freed slaves. In 1862 and 1863, Lincoln encouraged freedpeople to emigrate to all-black countries like Haiti. But black leaders, abolitionists, and many Republicans objected to that policy. Black people were Americans. Why should they not have the rights of American citizens instead of being urged to leave the country?

Lincoln eventually was converted to the logic and justice of that view. But in beginning the process of reconstruction, Lincoln first reached out to southern *whites* whose allegiance to the Confederacy was lukewarm. On December 8, 1863, Lincoln issued his Proclamation of Amnesty and Reconstruction, which offered presidential pardon to southern whites who took an oath of allegiance to the United States and accepted the abolition of slavery. In any state where the number of white males aged 21 or older who took this oath equaled 10 percent of the number of voters in 1860, that nucleus could reestablish a state government to which Lincoln promised presidential recognition.

Because the war was still raging, this policy could be carried out only where Union troops controlled substantial portions of a Confederate state: Louisiana, Arkansas, and Tennessee in early 1864. Nevertheless, Lincoln hoped that once the process had begun in those areas, it might snowball as Union military victories convinced more and more Confederates that their cause was hopeless. As matters turned out, those military victories were long delayed, and reconstruction in most parts of the South did not begin until 1865.

Another problem that slowed the process was growing opposition within Lincoln's own party. Many Republicans believed that white men who had fought *against* the Union should not be rewarded with restoration of their political rights while black men who had fought *for* the Union were denied those rights. The Proclamation of Reconstruction stated that "any provision which may be adopted by [a reconstructed] State government in relation to the freed people of such State, which shall recognize and declare their permanent freedom, provide for their education, and which may yet be consistent, as a temporary arrangement, with their present condition as a laboring, landless, and homeless class, will not be objected to by the national Executive." This seemed to mean that white landowners and former slaveholders could adopt labor regulations and other measures to control former slaves, so long as they recognized their freedom.

RADICAL REPUBLICANS AND RECONSTRUCTION

These were radical advances over slavery, but for many Republicans they were not radical enough. If the freedpeople were landless, they said, provide them with land by confiscating the plantations of leading Confederates as punishment for treason. Radical Republicans also distrusted oaths of allegiance sworn by ex-Confederates. Rather than simply restoring the old ruling class to power, they asked, why not give freed slaves the vote, to provide a genuinely loyal nucleus of supporters in the South?

These radical positions did not command a majority of Congress in 1864. Yet the experience of Louisiana, the first state to reorganize under Lincoln's more moderate policy, convinced even nonradical Republicans to block that policy. Enough white men in the occupied portion of the state took the oath of allegiance to satisfy Lincoln's conditions. They adopted a new state constitution and formed a government that abolished slavery and provided a school system for blacks. But the new government did not grant blacks the right to vote. It also authorized planters to enforce restrictive labor policies on black plantation workers. Louisiana's actions alienated a majority of congressional Republicans, who refused to admit representatives and senators from the "reconstructed" state.

At the same time, though, Congress failed to enact a reconstruction policy of its own. This was not for lack of trying. In fact, both houses passed the Wade-Davis reconstruction bill (named for Senator Benjamin Wade of Ohio and Representative Henry Winter Davis of Maryland) in July 1864. That bill did not enfranchise blacks, but it did impose such stringent loyalty requirements on southern whites that few of them could take the required oath. Lincoln therefore vetoed it.

Lincoln's action infuriated many Republicans. Wade and Davis published a blistering "manifesto" denouncing the president. This bitter squabble threatened for a time to destroy Lincoln's chances of being reelected. But Union military success in the fall of 1864 reunited the Republicans behind Lincoln. The collapse of Confederate military resistance the following spring set the stage for compromise on a policy for the postwar South. Two days after Appomattox, Lincoln promised that he would soon announce such a policy. But three days later he was assassinated.

ANDREW JOHNSON AND RECONSTRUCTION

In 1864 Republicans had adopted the name "Union Party" to attract the votes of War Democrats and border-state Unionists who could not bring themselves to vote Republican. For the same reason, they also nominated Andrew Johnson of Tennessee as Lincoln's running mate.

Of "poor white" heritage, Johnson had clawed his way up in the rough-and-tumble politics of East Tennessee. This was a region of small farms and few slaves, where there was little love for the planters who controlled the state. Johnson denounced the planters as "stuck-up aristocrats" who had no empathy with the southern yeomen for whom Johnson became a self-appointed spokesman. Johnson was the only senator from a seceding state who refused to support the Confederacy. For this, the Republicans rewarded him with the vice presidential nomination, hoping to attract the votes of pro-war Democrats and upper-South Unionists.

Booth's bullet therefore elevated to the presidency a man who still thought of himself as primarily a Democrat and a southerner. The trouble this might cause in a party that was mostly Republican and northern was not immediately apparent, however. In fact, Johnson's enmity toward the "stuck-up aristocrats" whom he blamed for leading the South into secession prompted him to utter dire threats against "traitors." "Traitors must be impoverished," he said. "They must not only be punished, but their social power must be destroyed."

Radical Republicans liked the sound of this. It seemed to promise the type of reconstruction they favored—one that would deny political power to ex-Confederates and would enfranchise blacks. They envisioned a coalition between these new black voters and the small minority of southern whites who had never supported the Confederacy. These men could be expected to vote Republican. Republican governments in southern states would guarantee freedom and would pass laws to provide civil rights and economic opportunity for freed slaves.

JOHNSON'S POLICY

From a combination of pragmatic, partisan, and idealistic motives, therefore, radical Republicans prepared to implement a progressive reconstruction policy. But Johnson unexpectedly refused to cooperate. Instead of calling Congress into special session, he moved ahead on his own. On May 29, Johnson issued two proclamations. The first provided for a blanket amnesty for all but the highest-ranking Confederate officials and military officers, and those ex-Confederates with taxable property worth $20,000 or more. The second named a provisional governor for North Carolina and directed him to call an election of delegates to frame a new state constitution. Only white men who had received amnesty and taken an oath of allegiance could vote. Similar proclamations soon followed for other former Confederate states. Johnson's policy was clear. He would exclude both blacks and upper-class whites from the reconstruction process.

Many Republicans supported Johnson's policy at first. But the radicals feared that restricting the vote to whites would open the door to the restoration of the old power structure in the South. They began to sense that Johnson was as dedicated to white supremacy as any

Confederate. "White men alone must govern the South," he told a Democratic senator. After a tense confrontation with a group of black men led by Frederick Douglass, Johnson told his private secretary: "I know that damned Douglass; he's just like any nigger, and he would sooner cut a white man's throat than not."

Moderate Republicans believed that black men should participate to some degree in the reconstruction process, but in 1865 they were not yet prepared to break with the president. They regarded his policy as an "experiment" that would be modified as time went on. "Loyal negroes must not be put down, while disloyal white men are put up," wrote a moderate Republican. "But I am quite willing to see what will come of Mr. Johnson's experiment."

SOUTHERN DEFIANCE

As it happened, none of the state conventions enfranchised a single black. Some of them even balked at ratifying the Thirteenth Amendment (which abolished slavery). Reports from Unionists and army officers in the South told of neo-Confederate violence against blacks and their white sympathizers. Johnson seemed to encourage such activities by allowing the organization of white militia units in the South. "What can be hatched from such an egg," asked a Republican newspaper, "but another rebellion?"

Then there was the matter of presidential pardons. After talking fiercely about punishing traitors, and after excluding several classes of them from his amnesty proclamation, Johnson began to issue special pardons to many ex-Confederates, restoring to them all property and political rights. Moreover, under the new state constitutions southern voters were electing hundreds of ex-Confederates to state offices. Even more alarming to northerners, who thought they had won the war, was the election to Congress of no fewer than nine ex-Confederate congressmen, seven ex-Confederate state officials, four generals, four colonels, and even the former Confederate vice president, Alexander H. Stephens.

Somehow the aristocrats and traitors Johnson had denounced in April had taken over the reconstruction process. What had happened? Flattery was part of the answer. In applying for pardons, thousands of prominent ex-Confederates or their tearful female relatives had confessed the error of their ways and had appealed for presidential mercy. Reveling in his power, Johnson waxed eloquent on his "love, respect, and confidence" toward southern whites, for whom he now felt "forbearing and forgiving."

More important, perhaps, was the praise and support Johnson received from leading northern Democrats. Though the Republicans had placed him on their presidential ticket in 1864, Johnson was after all a Democrat. That party's leaders enticed Johnson with visions of reelection as a Democrat in 1868 if he could manage to reconstruct the South in a manner that would preserve a Democratic majority there.

THE BLACK CODES

That was just what the Republicans feared. Their concern was confirmed in the fall of 1865 when some state governments enacted "Black Codes."

One of the first tasks of the legislatures of the reconstructed states was to define the rights of 4 million former slaves who were now free. The option of treating them exactly like white citizens was scarcely considered. Instead, the states excluded black people from juries and the ballot box, did not permit them to testify against whites in court, banned interracial marriage, and punished them more severely than whites for certain crimes. Some states defined any un-employed black person as a vagrant and hired him out to a planter, forbade blacks to lease land, and provided for the apprenticing to whites of black youths who did not have adequate parental support.

These Black Codes aroused anger among northern Republicans, who saw them as a brazen attempt to reinstate a quasi-slavery. "We tell the white men of Mississippi," declared the *Chicago Tribune,* "that the men of the North will convert the State of Mississippi into a frog pond before they will allow such laws to disgrace one foot of the soil in which the bones of our soldiers sleep and over which the flag of freedom waves." And, in fact, the Union Army's occu-pation forces did suspend the implementation of Black Codes that discriminated on racial grounds.

Land and Labor in the Postwar South

The Black Codes, though discriminatory, were designed to address a genuine problem. The end of the war had left black-white relations in the South in a state of limbo. The South's economy was in a shambles. Burned-out plantations, fields growing up in weeds, and railroads without tracks, bridges, or rolling stock marked the trail of war. Most tangible assets except the land itself had been destroyed. Law and order broke down in many areas. The war had ended early enough in the spring to allow the planting of at least some food crops. But who would plant and cultivate them? One-quarter of the South's white farmers had been killed in the war; the slaves were slaves no more. "We have nothing left to begin anew with," lamented a South Carolina planter. "I never did a day's work in my life, and I don't know how to begin."

But despite all, life went on. Slaveless planters and their wives, soldiers' widows and their children plowed and planted. Confederate veterans drifted home and went to work. Former slaveowners asked their former slaves to work the land for wages or shares of the crop, and many did so. But others refused, because for them to leave the old place was an essential part of freedom. "You ain't, none o' you, gwinter feel rale free," said a black preacher to his congre-gation, "till you shakes de dus' ob de Ole Plantashun offen yore feet" (dialect in original source).

Thus in the summer of 1865 the roads were alive with freedpeople on the move. Many of them signed on to work at farms just a few miles from their old homes. Others moved into town. Some looked for relatives who had been sold away during slavery or from whom they had been separated during the war. Some wandered aimlessly. Crime increased, and whites or-ganized vigilante groups to discipline blacks and force them to work.

The Freedmen's Bureau

Into this vacuum stepped the United States Army and the Freedmen's Bureau. Tens of thou-sands of troops remained in the South until civil government could be restored. The Freed-men's Bureau (its official title was Bureau of Refugees, Freedmen, and Abandoned Lands), created by Congress in March 1865, became the principal agency for overseeing relations be-tween former slaves and owners. Staffed by army officers, the bureau established posts throughout the South to supervise free-labor wage contracts between landowners and freed-people. The Freedmen's Bureau also issued food rations to 150,000 people daily during 1865, one-third of them to whites.

THE FREEDMEN'S BUREAU   Created in 1865, the Freedmen's Bureau stood between freed slaves and their former masters in the postwar South, charged with the task of protecting freedpeople from injustice and repression. Staffed by officers of the Union Army, the bureau symbolized the military power of the government in its efforts to keep peace in the South.

The Freedmen's Bureau was viewed with hostility by southern whites. But without it, the postwar chaos and devastation in the South would have been much greater. Bureau agents used their influence with black people to encourage them to sign free-labor contracts and return to work.

In negotiating labor contracts, the Bureau tried to establish minimum wages. Because there was so little money in the South, however, many contracts called for share wages—that is, paying workers with shares of the crop. At first, landowners worked their laborers in large groups called gangs. But many black workers resented this system. Thus, a new system evolved, called sharecropping, whereby a black family worked a specific piece of land in return for a share of the crop produced on it.

LAND FOR THE LANDLESS

Freedpeople, of course, would have preferred to farm their own land. "What's de use of being free if you don't own land enough to be buried in?" asked one black sharecropper (dialect in original). Some black farmers did manage to save up enough money to buy small plots of land. Demobilized black soldiers purchased land with their bounty payments, sometimes pooling their money to buy an entire plantation, on which several black families settled. Northern philanthropists helped some freedmen buy land. But for most ex-slaves the purchase of land was impossible. Few of them had money, and even if they did, whites often refused to sell.

Several northern radicals proposed legislation to confiscate ex-Confederate land and redistribute it to freedpeople. But those proposals got nowhere. And the most promising effort to put thousands of slaves on land of their own also failed. In January 1865, after his march through Georgia, General William T. Sherman had issued a military order setting aside thousands of acres of abandoned plantation land in the Georgia and South Carolina low-country for settlement by freed slaves. The army even turned over some of its surplus mules to black farmers. The expectation of "40 acres and a mule" excited freedpeople in 1865. But President Johnson's Amnesty Proclamation and his wholesale issuance of pardons restored most of this property to pardoned ex-Confederates. The same thing happened to white-owned land elsewhere in the South. Placed under the temporary care of the Freedmen's Bureau for subsequent possible distribution to freedpeople, by 1866 nearly all of this land had been restored to its former owners by order of President Johnson.

EDUCATION

Abolitionists were more successful in helping freedpeople get an education. During the war, freedmen's aid societies and missionary societies founded by abolitionists had sent teachers to

A BLACK SCHOOL DURING RECONSTRUCTION   In the antebellum South, teaching slaves to read and write was forbidden. Thus, about 90 percent of the freedpeople were illiterate in 1865. One of their top priorities was education. At first, most of the teachers in the freedmen's schools established by northern missionary societies were northern white women. But as black teachers were trained, they took over the elementary schools, such as this one photographed in the 1870s.

Union-occupied areas of the South to set up schools for freed slaves. After the war, this effort was expanded with the aid of the Freedmen's Bureau. Two thousand northern teachers fanned out into every part of the South to train black teachers. After 1870 missionary societies concentrated on making higher education available to African Americans. They founded many of the black colleges in the South. These efforts reduced the southern black illiteracy rate to 70 percent by 1880 and to 48 percent by 1900.

THE ADVENT OF CONGRESSIONAL RECONSTRUCTION

The civil and political rights of freedpeople would be shaped by the terms of reconstruction. By the time Congress met in December 1865, the Republican majority was determined to take control of the process by which former Confederate states would be restored to full representation. Congress refused to admit the representatives and senators elected by the former Confederate states under Johnson's reconstruction policy, and set up a special committee to formulate new terms. The committee held hearings at which southern Unionists, freedpeople, and U.S. Army officers testified to abuse and terrorism in the South. Their testimony convinced Republicans of the need for stronger federal intervention to define and protect the civil rights of freedpeople. However, because racism was still strong in the North, the special committee decided to draft a constitutional amendment that would encourage southern states to enfranchise blacks but would not require them to do so.

SCHISM BETWEEN PRESIDENT AND CONGRESS

Meanwhile, Congress passed two laws to protect the economic and civil rights of freedpeople. The first extended the life of the Freedmen's Bureau and expanded its powers. The second defined freedpeople as citizens with equal legal rights and gave federal courts appellate jurisdiction to enforce those rights. But to the dismay of moderates who were trying to heal the widening breach between the president and Congress, Johnson vetoed both measures. He followed this action with a speech to Democratic supporters in which he denounced Republican leaders as traitors who did not want to restore the Union except on terms that would degrade white southerners. Democratic newspapers applauded the president for vetoing bills that would "compound our race with niggers, gypsies, and baboons."

THE FOURTEENTH AMENDMENT

Johnson had thrown down the gauntlet to congressional Republicans. But with better than a two-thirds majority in both houses, they passed the Freedmen's Bureau and Civil Rights bills over the president's vetoes. Then on April 30, the special committee submitted to Congress its proposed Fourteenth Amendment to the Constitution. After lengthy debate, the amendment received the required two-thirds majority in Congress on June 13 and went to the states for ratification. Section 1 defined all native-born or naturalized persons, including blacks, as American citizens and prohibited the states from abridging the "privileges and immunities" of citizens, from depriving "any person of life, liberty, or property without due process of law," and from denying to any person "the equal protection of the laws." Section 2 gave states the option of either enfranchising black males or losing a proportionate number of congressional seats and electoral votes. Section 3 disqualified a significant number of ex-Confederates from holding federal or state office. Section 4 guaranteed the national debt and repudiated the Confederate debt. Section 5 empowered Congress to enforce the Fourteenth Amendment by "appropriate legislation."

The Fourteenth Amendment had far-reaching consequences. Section 1 has become the most important provision in the Constitution for defining and enforcing civil rights. It vastly expanded federal powers to prevent state violations of civil rights. It also greatly enlarged the rights of blacks.

THE 1866 ELECTIONS

During the campaign for the 1866 congressional elections Republicans made clear that any ex-Confederate state that ratified the Fourteenth Amendment would be declared "reconstructed" and that its representatives and senators would be seated in Congress. Tennessee ratified the amendment, but Johnson counseled other southern legislatures to reject the amendment, and they did so. Johnson then created a "National Union Party" made up of a few conservative Republicans who disagreed with their party, some border-state Unionists who supported the president, and Democrats.

The inclusion of Democrats doomed the effort from the start. Many northern Democrats still carried the taint of having opposed the war effort, and most northern voters did not trust them. The National Union Party was further damaged by race riots in Memphis and New Orleans. The riots bolstered Republican arguments that national power was necessary to protect "the fruits of victory" in the South. Perhaps the biggest liability was Johnson himself. In a whistle-stop tour through the North, he traded insults with hecklers and embarrassed his supporters.

Republicans swept the election. Having rejected the reconstruction terms embodied in the Fourteenth Amendment, southern Democrats now faced far more stringent terms. "They would not cooperate in rebuilding what they destroyed," wrote an exasperated moderate Republican, so "we must remove the rubbish and rebuild from the bottom."

THE RECONSTRUCTION ACTS OF 1867

In March 1867 the new Congress enacted two laws prescribing new procedures for the full restoration of the former Confederate states to the Union. The Reconstruction acts of 1867 divided the 10 southern states into five military districts, directed army officers to register voters for the election of delegates to new constitutional conventions, and enfranchised males aged 21 and older (including blacks) to vote in those elections. When a state had adopted a new constitution that granted equal civil and political rights regardless of race and had ratified the Fourteenth Amendment, it would be declared reconstructed and its newly elected congressmen would be seated.

These measures embodied a true revolution. Just a few years earlier, southerners had been masters of 4 million slaves and part of an independent Confederate nation. Now they were shorn of political power, with their former slaves not only freed but also politically empowered.

Like most revolutions, the reconstruction process did not go smoothly. Many southern Democrats breathed defiance and refused to cooperate. The presence of the army minimized anti-black violence. But thousands of white southerners who were eligible to vote refused to do so, hoping that their nonparticipation would delay the process long enough for northern voters to come to their senses and elect Democrats to Congress.

Blacks and their white allies organized Union leagues to mobilize the new black voters into the Republican Party. Democrats branded southern white Republicans as "scalawags" and northern settlers as "carpetbaggers." By September 1867, there were 735,000 black voters and only 635,000 white voters registered in the 10 states. At least one-third of the registered white voters were Republicans.

President Johnson did everything he could to block Reconstruction. He replaced several Republican generals with Democrats. He had his attorney general issue a ruling that interpreted the Reconstruction acts narrowly, thereby forcing a special session of Congress to pass a supplementary act in July 1867. And he encouraged southern whites to obstruct the registration of voters and the election of convention delegates.

Johnson's purpose was to slow the process until 1868 in the hope that northern voters would repudiate Reconstruction in the presidential election of that year, when Johnson planned to run as the Democratic candidate. Indeed, in off-year state elections in the fall of 1867 Republicans suffered setbacks in several northern states. "I almost pity the radicals," chortled one of President Johnson's aides after the 1867 elections. "After giving ten states to the negroes, to keep the Democrats from getting them, they will have lost the rest."

THE IMPEACHMENT OF ANDREW JOHNSON

Johnson struck even more boldly against Reconstruction after the 1867 elections. In February 1868, he removed from office Secretary of War Edwin M. Stanton, who had administered the War Department in support of the congressional Reconstruction policy. This appeared to violate the Tenure of Office Act, passed the year before over Johnson's veto, which required Senate consent for such removals. By a vote of 126 to 47 along party lines, the House impeached Johnson on February 24. The official reason for impeachment was that he had violated the Tenure of Office Act, but the real reason was Johnson's stubborn defiance of Congress on Reconstruction.

Under the U.S. Constitution, impeachment by the House does not remove an official from office. It is more like a grand jury indictment that must be tried by a petit jury—in this case, the Senate, which sat as a court to try Johnson on the impeachment charges brought by the House. If convicted by a two-thirds majority of the Senate, he would be removed from office.

The impeachment trial proved to be long and complicated, which worked in Johnson's favor by allowing passions to cool. The Constitution specifies the grounds on which a president can be impeached and removed: "Treason, Bribery, or other high Crimes and Misdemeanors." The issue was whether Johnson was guilty of any of these acts. His able defense counsel exposed technical ambiguities in the Tenure of Office Act that raised doubts about whether Johnson had actually violated it. Behind the scenes, Johnson strengthened his case by promising to appoint the respected General John M. Schofield as secretary of war and to stop obstructing the Reconstruction acts. In the end, seven Republican senators voted for acquittal on May 16, and the final tally fell one vote short of the necessary two-thirds majority.

THE COMPLETION OF FORMAL RECONSTRUCTION

The end of the impeachment trial cleared the poisonous air in Washington. Constitutional conventions met in the South during the winter and spring of 1867–1868. The constitutions they wrote were among the most progressive in the nation. The new state constitutions enacted universal male suffrage. Some disfranchised certain classes of ex-Confederates for several years, but by 1872 all such disqualifications had been removed. The constitutions mandated statewide public schools for both races for the first time in the South. Most states permitted segregated schools, but schools of any kind for blacks represented a great step forward. Most of the constitutions increased the state's responsibility for social welfare.

Violence in some parts of the South marred the voting on ratification of these state constitutions. A night-riding white terrorist organization, the Ku Klux Klan, made its first appearance during the elections. Nevertheless, voters in seven states ratified their constitutions and elected new legislatures that ratified the Fourteenth Amendment in the spring of 1868. That amendment became part of the United States Constitution the following summer, and the newly elected representatives and senators from those seven states, nearly all of them Republicans, took their seats in the House and Senate.

THE FIFTEENTH AMENDMENT

The remaining three southern states completed the reconstruction process in 1869 and 1870. Congress required them to ratify the Fifteenth as well as the Fourteenth Amendment. The Fifteenth Amendment prohibited states from denying the right to vote on grounds of race, color, or previous condition of servitude. Its purpose was not only to prevent any future revocation of black suffrage by the reconstructed states, but also to extend equal suffrage to the border states and to the North. But the challenge of enforcement lay ahead.

THE ELECTION OF 1868

Just as the presidential election of 1864 was a referendum on Lincoln's war policies, so the election of 1868 was a referendum on the reconstruction policy of the Republicans. The Republican nominee was General Ulysses S. Grant. Though he had no political experience, Grant commanded greater authority and prestige than anyone else in the country. Grant agreed to run for the presidency in order to preserve in peace the victory for Union and liberty he had won in war.

The Democrats turned away from Andrew Johnson and nominated Horatio Seymour, the wartime governor of New York. They adopted a militant platform denouncing the Reconstruction acts as "a flagrant usurpation of power . . . unconstitutional, revolutionary, and void." The platform also demanded "the abolition of the Freedmen's Bureau, and all political instrumentalities designed to secure negro supremacy."

The vice presidential candidate, Frank Blair of Missouri, became the point man for the Democrats. In a public letter he proclaimed, "There is but one way to restore the Government and the Constitution, and that is for the President-elect to declare these [Reconstruction] acts null and void, compel the army to undo its usurpations at the South, disperse the carpet-bag State Governments, [and] allow the white people to reorganize their own governments."

The only way to achieve this bold counterrevolutionary goal was to suppress Republican voters in the South. This the Ku Klux Klan tried its best to do. Federal troops had only limited success in preventing the violence. In Louisiana, Georgia, Arkansas, and Tennessee, the Klan or Klan-like groups committed dozens of murders and intimidated thousands of black voters. The violence helped the Democratic cause in the South but probably hurt it in the North, where many voters perceived the Klan as an organization of neo-Confederate paramilitary guerrillas.

Seymour did well in the South, carrying five former slave states and coming close in others despite the solid Republican vote of the newly enfranchised blacks. But Grant swept the electoral vote 214 to 80. Seymour actually won a slight majority of the white voters nationally, so without black enfranchisement, Grant would have had a minority of the popular vote.

THE GRANT ADMINISTRATION

Grant is usually branded a failure as president. His two administrations (1869–1877) were plagued by scandals. His private secretary allegedly became involved in the infamous "Whiskey Ring," a network of distillers and revenue agents that deprived the government of millions of tax dollars; his secretary of war was impeached for selling appointments to army posts and Indian reservations; and his attorney general and secretary of the interior resigned under suspicion of malfeasance in 1875.

Honest himself, Grant was too trusting of subordinates. But not all of the scandals were Grant's fault. This was an era notorious for corruption at all levels of government. The Tammany Hall "Ring" of "Boss" William Marcy Tweed in New York City may have stolen more money from taxpayers than all the federal agencies combined. In Washington, one of the most widely publicized scandals, the Credit Mobilier affair, concerned Congress rather than the Grant administration. Several congressmen had accepted stock in the Credit Mobilier, a construction company for the Union Pacific Railroad, which received loans and land grants from the government in return for ensuring lax congressional supervision, thereby permitting financial manipulations by the company.

What accounted for this explosion of corruption in the postwar decade? The expansion of government contracts and the bureaucracy during the war had created new opportunities for the unscrupulous. Then came a relaxation of tensions and standards following the intense sacrifices of the war years. Rapid postwar economic growth, led by an extraordinary rush of railroad construction, encouraged greed and get-rich-quick schemes of the kind satirized by Mark Twain and Charles Dudley Warner in their 1873 novel *The Gilded Age,* which gave its name to the era.

CIVIL SERVICE REFORM

But some of the increase in corruption during the Gilded Age was more apparent than real. Reformers focused on the dark corners of corruption hitherto unilluminated because of the nation's preoccupation with war and reconstruction. Thus, the actual extent of corruption may have been exaggerated by the publicity that reformers gave it. In reality, during the Grant administration several government agencies made real progress in eliminating abuses that had flourished in earlier administrations.

One area of progress was civil service reform. Its chief target was the "spoils system." With the slogan "To the victor belong the spoils," the victorious party in an election rewarded party workers with appointments as postmasters, customs collectors, and the like. The hope of getting appointed to a government post was the glue that kept the faithful together when a party was out of power. The spoils system politicized the bureaucracy and staffed it with unqualified personnel who spent more time working for their party than for the government.

Civil service reformers wanted to separate the bureaucracy from politics by requiring competitive examinations for the appointment of civil servants. This movement gathered steam during the 1870s and finally achieved success in 1883 with the passage of the Pendleton Act, which established the modern structure of the civil service. When Grant took office, he seemed to share the sentiments of civil service reformers. Grant named a civil service commission headed by George William Curtis, a leading reformer and editor of *Harper's Weekly*. But many congressmen, senators, and other politicians resisted civil service reform because patronage was the grease of the political machines that kept them in office. They managed to subvert reform, sometimes using Grant as an unwitting ally and thus turning many reformers against the president.

FOREIGN POLICY ISSUES

A foreign policy fiasco added to Grant's woes. The irregular procedures by which his private secretary had negotiated a treaty to annex Santo Domingo (now the Dominican Republic) alienated leading Republican senators, who defeated ratification of the treaty. Grant's political inexperience led him to act like a general who needed only to give orders rather than as a president who must cultivate supporters. The fallout from the Santo Domingo affair widened the fissure in the Republican Party.

But the Grant administration had some solid foreign policy achievements to its credit. Hamilton Fish, the able secretary of state, negotiated the Treaty of Washington in 1871 to settle the vexing "Alabama Claims." These were damage claims against Britain for the destruction of American shipping by the C.S.S. *Alabama* and other Confederate commerce raiders built in British shipyards. The treaty established an international tribunal to arbitrate the U.S. claims, resulting in the award of $15.5 million in damages to U.S. shipowners and a British expression of regret.

The events leading to the Treaty of Washington also resolved another long-festering issue between Britain and the United States: the status of Canada. The seven separate British North American colonies were especially vulnerable to U.S. desires for annexation. In 1867 Parliament passed the British North America Act, which united most of the Canadian colonies into a new and largely self-governing Dominion of Canada.

The successful conclusion of the treaty cooled Canadian-American tensions. It also led to the resolution of disputes over American commercial fishing in Canadian waters. American demands for annexation of Canada faded away. These events gave birth to the modern nation of Canada, whose 3,500-mile border with the United States remains the longest unfortified frontier in the world.

RECONSTRUCTION IN THE SOUTH

During Grant's two administrations, the "Southern Question" was the most intractable issue. A phrase in Grant's acceptance of the presidential nomination in 1868 had struck a responsive chord in the North: "Let us have peace." With the ratification of the Fifteenth Amendment, many people breathed a sigh of relief at this apparent resolution of "the last great point that remained to be settled of the issues of the war." It was time to deal with other matters that had been long neglected.

But there was no peace. State governments elected by black and white voters were in place in the South, but Democratic violence protesting Reconstruction and the instability of the Republican coalition that sustained it portended trouble.

BLACKS IN OFFICE

In the North, the Republican Party represented the most prosperous, educated, and influential elements of the population; but in the South, most of its adherents were poor, illiterate, and propertyless. About 80 percent of southern Republican voters were black. Although most black leaders were educated and many had been free before the war, the mass of black voters were illiterate ex-slaves. Neither the leaders nor their constituents, however, were as ignorant as stereotypes have portrayed them. Of 14 black representatives and two black senators elected in the South between 1868 and 1876, all but three had attended secondary school and four had attended college. Several of the blacks elected to state offices were among the best-educated men of their day. For example, Jonathan Gibbs, secretary of state in Florida from 1868 to 1872 and state superintendent of education from 1872 to 1874, was a graduate of Dartmouth College and Princeton Theological Seminary.

It is true that some lower-level black officeholders, as well as their constituents, could not read or write. But illiteracy did not preclude an understanding of political issues for them any more than it did for Irish American voters in the North, many of whom also were illiterate. Southern blacks thirsted for education. Participation in the Union League and the experience of voting were themselves a form of education. Black churches and fraternal organizations proliferated during Reconstruction and tutored African Americans in their rights and responsibilities.

Linked to the myth of black incompetence was the legend of the "Africanization" of southern governments during Reconstruction. The theme of "Negro rule" was a staple of Democratic propaganda. It was enshrined in folk memory and textbooks. In fact, blacks held only 15 to 20 percent of public offices, even at the height of Reconstruction in the early 1870s. There were no black governors and only one black state supreme court justice. Nowhere except in South Carolina did blacks hold office in numbers anywhere near their proportion of the population.

"CARPETBAGGERS"

Next to "Negro rule," carpetbagger corruption and scalawag rascality have been the prevailing myths of Reconstruction. "Carpetbaggers" did hold a disproportionate number of high political offices in southern state governments during Reconstruction. A few did resemble the proverbial adventurer who came south with nothing but a carpetbag in which to stow the loot plundered from a helpless people. But most were Union Army officers who stayed on after the war as Freedmen's Bureau agents, teachers in black schools, or business investors.

Those who settled in the postwar South hoped to rebuild its society in the image of the free-labor North. Many were college graduates. Most brought not empty carpetbags but considerable capital, which they invested in what they hoped would become a new South. They also invested human capital—themselves—in a drive to modernize the region's social structure and democratize its politics. But they underestimated the hostility of southern whites, most of whom regarded them as agents of an alien culture.

"Scalawags"

Most of the native-born whites who joined the southern Republican Party came from the up-country Unionist areas of western North Carolina and Virginia and eastern Tennessee. Others were former Whigs. Republicans, said a North Carolina scalawag, were the "party of progress, of education, of development."

But Democrats were aware that the southern Republican Party they abhorred was a fragile coalition of blacks and whites, Yankees and southerners, hill-country yeomen and low-country entrepreneurs, illiterates and college graduates. The party was weakest along the seams where these disparate elements joined—especially the racial seam. Democrats attacked that weakness with every weapon at their command, including violence.

The Ku Klux Klan

The generic name for the secret groups that terrorized the southern countryside was the Ku Klux Klan. But some went by other names (the Knights of the White Camelia in Louisiana, for example). Part of the Klan's purpose was social control of the black population. Sharecroppers who tried to extract better terms from landowners, or black people who were considered too "uppity," were likely to receive a midnight whipping—or worse—from white-sheeted Klansmen. Scores of black schools, perceived as a particular threat to white supremacy, went up in flames.

But the Klan's main purpose was political: to destroy the Republican Party by terrorizing its voters and, if necessary, murdering its leaders. No one knows the number of politically motivated killings that took place, but it was certainly in the hundreds, probably in the thousands. Nearly all the victims were Republicans; most of them were black. In one notorious incident, the "Colfax Massacre" in Louisiana (April 18, 1873), a clash between black militia and armed whites left three whites and nearly 100 blacks dead.

In some places, notably Tennessee and Arkansas, militias formed by Republicans suppressed and disarmed many Klansmen. But in most areas the militias were outgunned and outmaneuvered by ex-Confederate veterans who had joined the Klan. Some Republican governors were reluctant to use black militia against white guerrillas for fear of sparking a racial bloodbath—as happened at Colfax.

The answer seemed to be federal troops. In 1870 and 1871 Congress enacted three laws intended to enforce the Fourteenth and Fifteenth Amendments. Interference with voting rights became a federal offense, and any attempt to deprive another person of civil or political rights became a felony. The third law, passed on April 20, 1871, and popularly called the Ku Klux Klan Act, gave the president power to suspend the writ of habeas corpus and send in federal troops to suppress armed resistance to federal law.

Armed with these laws, the Grant administration moved against the Klan. But Grant did so with restraint. He suspended the writ of habeas corpus only in nine South Carolina counties. Nevertheless, there and elsewhere federal marshals backed by troops arrested thousands of suspected Klansmen. Federal grand juries indicted more than 3,000, and several

TWO MEMBERS OF THE KU KLUX KLAN   Founded in Pulaski, Tennessee, in 1866 as a social organization similar to a college fraternity, the Klan evolved into a terrorist group whose purpose was intimidation of southern Republicans. The Klan, in which former Confederate soldiers played a prominent part, was responsible for the beating and murder of hundreds of blacks and whites alike from 1868 to 1871.

hundred defendants pleaded guilty in return for suspended sentences; the Justice Department dropped charges against nearly 2,000 others. About 600 Klansmen were convicted. Most of them received fines or light jail sentences, but 65 went to a federal penitentiary for terms of up to five years.

THE ELECTION OF 1872

These measures broke the back of the Klan in time for the 1872 presidential election. A group of dissident Republicans had emerged to challenge Grant's reelection. They believed that conciliation of southern whites rather than continued military intervention was the only way to achieve peace in the South. Calling themselves Liberal Republicans, these dissidents nominated Horace Greeley, the famous editor of the *New York Tribune*. Under the slogan "Anything to beat Grant," the Democratic Party also endorsed Greeley's nomination. On a platform denouncing "bayonet rule" in the South, Greeley urged his fellow northerners to put the issues of the Civil War behind them.

Most voters in the North were still not prepared to trust Democrats or southern whites, however. Anti-Greeley cartoons by Thomas Nast showed Greeley shaking the hand of a Klansman dripping with the blood of a murdered black Republican. On election day Grant swamped Greeley. Republicans carried every northern state and 10 of the 16 southern and border states. But this apparent triumph of Republicanism and Reconstruction would soon unravel.

THE PANIC OF 1873

The U.S. economy had grown at an unprecedented pace since 1867. The first transcontinental railroad had been completed on May 10, 1869, when a golden spike was driven at Promontory Point, Utah Territory, linking the Union Pacific and the Central Pacific. But it was the building of a second transcontinental line, the Northern Pacific, that precipitated a Wall Street panic in 1873 and plunged the economy into a five-year depression.

Jay Cooke's banking firm, fresh from its triumphant marketing of Union war bonds, took over the Northern Pacific in 1869. Cooke pyramided every conceivable kind of equity and loan financing to raise the money to begin laying rails west from Duluth, Minn. Other investment firms did the same as a fever of speculative financing gripped the country. In September 1873 the pyramid of paper collapsed. Cooke's firm was the first to go bankrupt. Like dominoes, hundreds of banks and businesses also collapsed. Unemployment rose to 14 percent and hard times set in.

THE RETREAT FROM RECONSTRUCTION

Democrats made large gains in the congressional elections of 1874, winning a majority in the House for the first time in 18 years. Public opinion also began to turn against Republican policies in the South. Intra-party battles among Republicans in southern states enabled Democrats to regain control of several state governments. Well-publicized corruption scandals also discredited Republican leaders. Although corruption was probably no worse in southern states than in many parts of the North, the postwar poverty of the South made waste and extravagance seem worse. White Democrats scored propaganda points by claiming that corruption proved the incompetence of "Negro-carpetbag" regimes.

Northerners grew increasingly weary of what seemed the endless turmoil of southern politics. Most of them had never had a very strong commitment to racial equality, and they were growing more and more willing to let white supremacy regain sway in the South. "The truth is," confessed a northern Republican, "our people are tired out with this worn out cry of 'Southern outrages'!!!"

By 1875 only four southern states remained under Republican control: South Carolina, Florida, Mississippi, and Louisiana. In those states, white Democrats had revived paramilitary organizations under various names: White Leagues (Louisiana); Rifle Clubs (Mississippi); and Red Shirts (South Carolina). Unlike the Klan, these groups operated openly. In Louisiana, they fought pitched battles with Republican militias in which scores were killed. When the Grant administration sent large numbers of federal troops to Louisiana, people in both North and South cried out against military rule. The protests grew even louder when soldiers marched onto the floor of the Louisiana legislature in January 1875 and expelled several Democratic legislators after a contested election.

THE MISSISSIPPI ELECTION OF 1875

The backlash against the Grant administration affected the Mississippi state election of 1875. Democrats there devised a strategy called the Mississippi Plan. The first step was to "persuade" the 10 to 15 percent of white voters still calling themselves Republicans to switch to the Democrats. Only a handful of carpetbaggers could resist the economic pressures, social ostracism, and threats that made it "too damned hot for [us] to stay out," wrote one white Republican who changed parties.

The second step in the Mississippi Plan was to intimidate black voters, for even with all whites voting Democratic, the party could still be defeated by the 55 percent black majority. Economic coercion against black sharecroppers and workers kept some of them away from the

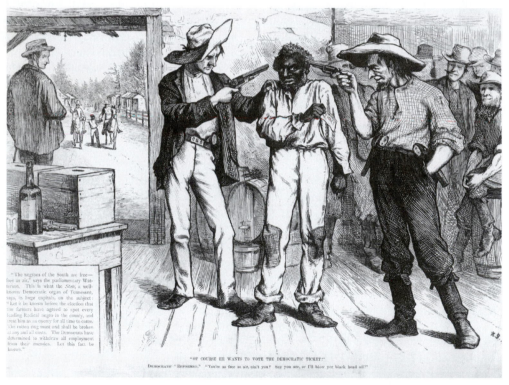

HOW THE MISSISSIPPI PLAN WORKED   This cartoon shows how black counties could report large Democratic majorities in the Mississippi state election of 1875. The black voter holds a Democratic ticket while one of the men, described in the caption as a "Democratic reformer," holds a revolver to his head and says: "You're as free as air, ain't you? Say you are, or I'll blow your black head off!"

polls. But violence was the most effective method. Democratic "rifle clubs" showed up at Republican rallies, provoked riots, and shot down dozens of blacks in the ensuing melees. Governor Adelbert Ames called for federal troops to control the violence. Grant intended to comply, but Ohio Republicans warned him that if he sent troops to Mississippi, the Democrats would exploit the issue of bayonet rule to carry Ohio in that year's state elections. Grant yielded—in effect giving up Mississippi for Ohio.

Governor Ames did try to organize a loyal state militia. But that proved difficult—and in any case, he was reluctant to use a black militia for fear of provoking a race war. "No matter if they are going to carry the State," said Ames with weary resignation, "let them carry it, and let us be at peace and have no more killing." The Mississippi Plan worked like a charm. What had been a Republican majority of 30,000 in 1874 became a Democratic majority of 30,000 in 1875.

THE SUPREME COURT AND RECONSTRUCTION

Even if Grant had been willing to continue intervening in southern state elections, Congress and the courts would have constricted such efforts. The new Democratic majority in the House threatened to cut any appropriations intended for use in the South. And in 1876 the Supreme Court handed down two decisions that declared parts of the 1870 and 1871 laws for enforcement of the Fourteenth and Fifteenth Amendments unconstitutional. In *U.S.* v. *Cruikshank* and *U.S.* v. *Reese,* the Court ruled that the Fourteenth and Fifteenth Amendments apply to actions by *states:* "No State shall . . . deprive any person of life, liberty, or property . . . nor deny to any person . . . equal protection of the laws"; the right to vote "shall not be denied . . . by any State." Therefore, the portions of these laws that empowered the federal government to prosecute *individuals* were unconstitutional. The Court did not say what could be done when states were controlled by white-supremacy Democrats who had no intention of enforcing equal rights.

Meanwhile, in the *Civil Rights Cases* (1883), the Court declared unconstitutional a civil rights law passed by Congress in 1875. That law banned racial discrimination in all forms of public transportation and public accommodations. If enforced, it would have effected a sweeping transformation of race relations—in the North as well as in the South. But even some of the congressmen who voted for the bill doubted its constitutionality, and the Justice Department had made little effort to enforce it. Several cases made their way to the Supreme Court, which in 1883 ruled the law unconstitutional—again on grounds that the Fourteenth Amendment applied only to states, not to individuals. Several states—all in the North—passed their own civil rights laws in the 1870s and 1880s, but less than 10 percent of the black population resided in those states. The mass of African Americans lived a segregated existence.

THE ELECTION OF 1876

In 1876 the Republican state governments that still survived in the South fell victim to the passion for "reform." The mounting revelations of corruption at all levels of government ensured that reform would be the leading issue in the presidential election. Both major parties gave their presidential nominations to governors who had earned reform reputations in their states: Democrat Samuel J. Tilden of New York and Republican Rutherford B. Hayes of Ohio.

Democrats entered the campaign as favorites for the first time in two decades. It seemed likely that they would be able to put together an electoral majority from a "solid South" plus

New York and two or three other northern states. To ensure a solid South, they looked to the lessons of the Mississippi Plan. In 1876 a new word came into use to describe Democratic techniques of intimidation: "bulldozing." To bulldoze black voters meant to trample them down or keep them away from the polls. In South Carolina and Louisiana, the Red Shirts and the White Leagues mobilized for an all-out bulldozing effort.

The most notorious incident, the "Hamburg Massacre," occurred in the village of Hamburg, South Carolina, where a battle between a black militia unit and 200 Red Shirts resulted in the capture of several militiamen, five of whom were shot "while attempting to escape." This time Grant did send in federal troops. He pronounced the Hamburg Massacre "cruel, bloodthirsty, wanton, unprovoked . . . a repetition of the course that has been pursued in other Southern States."

The federal government also put several thousand deputy marshals and election supervisors on duty in the South. Though they kept an uneasy peace at the polls, they could do little to prevent assaults, threats, and economic coercion in backcountry districts, which reduced the potential Republican tally in the former Confederate states by at least 250,000 votes.

DISPUTED RESULTS

When the results were in, Tilden had carried four northern states, including New York with its 35 electoral votes, and all the former slave states except—apparently—Louisiana, South Carolina, and Florida. From those three states came disputed returns. Since Tilden needed only one of them to win the presidency, while Hayes needed all three, and since Tilden seemed to have carried Louisiana and Florida, it appeared initially that he had won the presidency. But frauds and irregularities reported from several bulldozed districts in the three states clouded the issue. The official returns ultimately sent to Washington gave all three states—and therefore the presidency—to Hayes. But the Democrats refused to recognize the results—and they controlled the House.

The country now faced a serious constitutional crisis. Many people feared another civil war. The Constitution offered no clear guidance on how to deal with the matter. It required the concurrence of both houses of Congress in order to count the electoral votes of the states, but with a Democratic House and a Republican Senate such concurrence was not forthcoming. To break the deadlock, Congress created a special electoral commission consisting of five representatives, five senators, and five Supreme Court justices split evenly between the two parties, with one member, a Supreme Court justice, supposedly an independent—but in fact a Republican.

Tilden had won a national majority of 252,000 popular votes, and the raw returns gave him a majority in the three disputed states. But an estimated 250,000 southern Republicans had been bulldozed away from the polls. In a genuinely fair and free election, the Republicans might have carried Mississippi and North Carolina as well as the three disputed states. While the commission agonized, Democrats and Republicans in Louisiana and South Carolina each inaugurated their own separate governors and legislatures. Only federal troops in the capitals at New Orleans and Columbia protected the Republican governments in those states.

THE COMPROMISE OF 1877

In February 1877, three months after voters had gone to the polls, the electoral commission issued its ruling. By a partisan vote of 8 to 7—with the "independent" justice voting with the

CHRONOLOGY

1863	Lincoln issues Proclamation of Amnesty and Reconstruction
1864	Congress passes Wade-Davis bill; Lincoln kills it by pocket veto
1865	Congress establishes Freedmen's Bureau • Andrew Johnson becomes president, announces his reconstruction plan • Southern states enact Black Codes • Congress refuses to seat southern congressmen elected under Johnson's plan
1866	Congress passes civil rights bill and expands Freedmen's Bureau over Johnson's veto • Race riots in Memphis and New Orleans • Congress approves Fourteenth Amendment • Republicans increase congressional majority in fall elections
1867	Congress passes Reconstruction acts over Johnson's vetoes • Congress passes Tenure of Office Act over Johnson's veto
1868	Most southern senators and representatives readmitted to Congress under congressional plan of Reconstruction • Andrew Johnson impeached but not convicted • Ulysses S. Grant elected president • Congress ratifies Fourteenth Amendment
1870	Fifteenth Amendment is ratified
1871	Congress passes Ku Klux Klan Act
1872	Liberal Republicans defect from party • Grant wins reelection
1873	Economic depression begins with the Panic
1874	Democrats win control of House of Representatives
1875	Democrats implement Mississippi Plan • Congress passes civil rights act
1876	Centennial celebration in Philadelphia • Disputed presidential election causes constitutional crisis
1877	Compromise of 1877 installs Rutherford B. Hayes as president • Hayes withdraws troops from South
1883	Supreme Court declares civil rights act of 1875 unconstitutional

Republicans—it awarded all the disputed states to Hayes. The Democrats cried foul and began a filibuster in the House to delay the final electoral count beyond the inauguration date of March 4. But, behind the scenes, a compromise began to take shape. Hayes promised his support as president for federal appropriations to rebuild war-destroyed levees on the lower Mississippi and federal aid for a southern transcontinental railroad. Hayes's lieutenants also hinted at the appointment of a southerner as postmaster general, who would have a considerable amount of patronage at his disposal. Hayes also signaled his intention to end "bayonet rule." He believed that the goodwill and influence of southern moderates would offer better protection for black rights than federal troops could provide. In return for his commitment to withdraw the troops, Hayes asked for—and received—promises of fair treatment of freedpeople and respect for their constitutional rights.

THE END OF RECONSTRUCTION

Such promises were easier to make than to keep, as future years would reveal. In any case, the Democratic filibuster collapsed and Hayes was inaugurated on March 4. He soon fulfilled his part of the Compromise of 1877: ex-Confederate Democrat David Key of Tennessee became postmaster general; the South received more federal money in 1878 for internal improvements than ever before; and federal troops left the capitals of Louisiana and South Carolina. The last two Republican state governments collapsed. Any remaining voices of protest could scarcely be heard above the sighs of relief that the crisis was over.

CONCLUSION

Before the Civil War, most Americans had viewed a powerful government as a threat to individual liberties. That is why the first 10 amendments to the Constitution (the Bill of Rights) imposed strict limits on the powers of the federal government. But during the Civil War and especially during Reconstruction, it became clear that the national government would have to exert an unprecedented amount of power to free the slaves and guarantee their equal rights as free citizens. That is why the Thirteenth, Fourteenth, and Fifteenth Amendments to the Constitution contained clauses stating that "Congress shall have power" to enforce these provisions for liberty and equal rights.

During the post–Civil War decade, Congress passed civil rights laws and enforcement legislation to accomplish this purpose. Federal marshals and troops patrolled the polls to protect black voters, arrested thousands of Klansmen and other violators of black civil rights, and even occupied state capitals to prevent Democratic paramilitary groups from overthrowing legitimately elected Republican state governments. But by 1875 many northerners had grown tired of or alarmed by this continued use of military power to intervene in the internal affairs of states. The Supreme Court stripped the federal government of much of its authority to enforce certain provisions of the Fourteenth and Fifteenth Amendments.

The withdrawal of federal troops from the South in 1877 constituted both a symbolic and a substantive end of the 12-year postwar era known as Reconstruction. Reconstruction had achieved the two great objectives inherited from the Civil War: to reincorporate the former Confederate states into the Union, and to accomplish a transition from slavery to freedom in the South. But that transition was marred by the economic inequity of sharecropping and the social injustice of white supremacy. And a third goal of Reconstruction, enforcement of the equal civil and political rights promised in the Fourteenth and Fifteenth Amendments, was betrayed by the Compromise of 1877. In subsequent decades the freed slaves and their descendants suffered repression into segregated second-class citizenship.

18

FRONTIERS OF CHANGE, POLITICS OF STALEMATE, 1865–1890

AGENCIES OF WESTWARD EXPANSION ⁓ THE LAST INDIAN FRONTIER
THE NEW SOUTH ⁓ THE POLITICS OF STALEMATE

One of the most remarkable developments in the post–Civil War generation was the accelerating westward expansion. From 1865 to 1890 the white population of the West increased five times faster than that of the nation as a whole. Through the Homestead Act, land grants to railroads, the Morrill Act (which turned land over to states to finance "agricultural and mechanical colleges"), and other liberal land laws enacted during and after the Civil War, some 400 million acres passed into private ownership by farmers, ranchers, and other forms of enterprise. The number of American farms more than doubled. Their output of cattle, hogs, and hay more than doubled while the production of corn, wheat, and oats nearly tripled.

This growth enabled American farmers to increase agricultural exports tenfold. These exports were partly fueled by immigration. Many of the 4 million immigrants who came from Germany, the Czech region of the Austro-Hungarian empire, and the Scandinavian countries during this period settled in the Midwest or Far West and became farmers. To them the opportunity to obtain 160 acres in Minnesota or Nebraska seemed miraculous. The power of a generous government to make equality of opportunity available to them underpinned the extraordinary expansion of population and agricultural production after the Civil War.

But that growth and opportunity came at great cost. The Indians were herded onto reservations. Buffalo were hunted almost to extinction. Millions of acres of forest and native grasslands were cut down or plowed up, setting the stage for destructive erosion, floods, and dust bowls in future generations. The overproduction of American agriculture drove prices down and contributed to a worldwide agricultural depression.

AGENCIES OF WESTWARD EXPANSION

One of the main engines of this postwar growth was the railroad. Five transcontinental railroads went into service between 1869 and 1893. At the end of the Civil War, there had been only 3,272 miles of rail west of the Mississippi. By 1890 the total was 72,473 miles. The existence of this infrastructure spurred settlement and economic development.

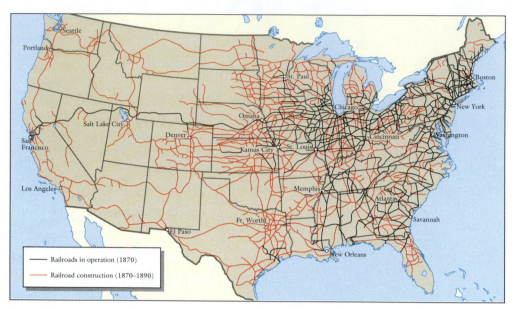

RAILROAD EXPANSION, 1870–1890

No longer did this region appear on maps as "The Great American Desert." There was plenty of desert, to be sure. But during the 1870s and early 1880s precipitation was heavier than normal, giving rise to the erroneous (as it turned out) notion that "rainfall follows the plow"—that settlement and cultivation somehow changed the weather.

This was the age of the "sodbuster," who adapted to the almost treeless prairies and plains by fencing with barbed wire (invented in 1874) and building his first house out of the sod that he broke with his steel plow. It was also the era of "bonanza farms" in the Red River Valley of Dakota Territory and the Central Valley of California—huge wheat farms cultivated with heavy machinery and hired labor.

Perhaps even more important to the growth of the West were the mining and ranching frontiers. This was the West of prospectors and boom towns that became ghost towns, of cowboys and cattle drives, of gold rushes and mother lodes, of stagecoach robbers and rustlers. It is a West so celebrated on stage, screen, radio, and television that it is hard to separate myth from reality—a reality in which thousands of black and Mexican American cowboys rode the Goodnight-Loving Trail, eastern capital and railroads came increasingly to control the mines and the grasslands, and gold or silver miners and cowboys came to resemble more closely the coal miners and farm laborers of the East than the romanticized independent spirits of legend.

THE MINING FRONTIER

Gold discoveries had propelled the first waves of western settlement, but in the 1870s silver eclipsed gold. Other minerals also increased in value. Rich copper mines opened in Montana at about the same time that Alexander Graham Bell's invention of the telephone (1876) and

THE SOD-HOUSE FRONTIER On the prairies and plains of the regions west of the Mississippi, trees were scarce and the cost of lumber was prohibitive until railroads crisscrossed the land. So the settlers built their first houses from the tough prairie sod, which baked in the sun to almost the hardness of bricks.

Thomas A. Edison's invention of the incandescent lightbulb (1879) and construction of a successful electrical generator (1881) created a demand for thousands of tons of copper wire.

Violence was never far from the surface in the mining frontier. In the early days, claim-jumping, robberies, and vigilante justice made life precarious. As placer mining of streams gave out, men ravaged the environment by hydraulic mining, deep bores, and strip-mining. Mining became a highly capitalized and mechanized industry in which the biggest and richest mines were owned by corporations with headquarters in the East. Capital-labor relations were savage. Violent strikes at Coeur d'Alene, Idaho, in 1892, at Cripple Creek, Colorado, in 1894 and again in 1903, and at other places caused western governors to call out the militia 10 times from 1892 to 1904.

THE RANCHING FRONTIER

Of course, the dominant symbol of the Old West is not the prospector or the hard-rock miner: It is the cowboy. The postwar boom in the range cattle industry had its beginnings in southern Texas. The Spaniards had introduced longhorn cattle there in the 18th century. This hardy breed multiplied rapidly; by the 1850s millions of them roamed freely on the Texas plains. Then the Civil War depleted the cattle supply in the older states, where prices rose to the unheard-of sum of $40 a head. The postwar explosion of population and railroads westward brought markets and railheads ever closer to western cattle that were free to anyone who rounded them up and branded them.

Astute Texans were not slow to see that the longhorns represented a fortune on the hoof—if they could be driven northward the 800 miles to the railhead at Sedalia, Missouri. In the spring of 1866, cowboys hit the trail with 260,000 cattle in the first of the great drives. However, disease, stampedes, bad weather, Indians, and irate farmers killed or ran off most of the cattle.

Only a few thousand head made it to Sedalia, but the prices they fetched convinced ranchers that the system would work, if only they could find a better route. By 1867 the rails of the Kansas Pacific had reached Abilene, Kansas, 150 miles closer to Texas, making it possible to drive the herds through a sparsely occupied portion of Indian Territory. About 35,000 longhorns reached Abilene that summer, where they were loaded onto cattle cars for the trip to Kansas City or Chicago. The development of refrigerated rail cars in the 1870s enabled Chicago to ship dressed beef all over the country.

More than a million longhorns bellowed their way north on the Chisholm Trail to Abilene over the next four years while the railhead crept westward to other Kansas towns, chiefly Dodge City, which became the most wide-open and famous of the cow towns. Cattle drives grew shorter as railroads inched forward. Ranchers grazed their cattle for free on millions of acres of open, unfenced government land. But clashes with "grangers" (the ranchers' contemptuous term for farmers) on the one hand and with a growing army of sheep ranchers on the other—not to mention rustlers—led to several "range wars." Most notable was the Johnson County War in Wyoming in 1892. Grangers and small ranchers there defeated the hired guns of the Stock Growers' Association, which represented larger ranchers.

By that time, however, the classic form of open-range grazing was already in decline. The boom years of the early 1880s had overstocked the range and driven down prices. Then came record cold and blizzards on the southern range in the winter of 1885–1886, followed by even

BLACK COWBOYS   Some studies of cowboys estimate that one-quarter of them were black. That estimate is probably too high for all cowboys, but it might be correct for Texas, where this photograph was taken.

worse weather on the northern plains the following winter. Hundreds of thousands of cattle froze or starved to death. These catastrophes spurred reforms that brought an end to open-range grazing.

Ranching and the cowboy survived, but in a form quite different from their Hollywood image. Most cowboys were small, wiry men; the mustangs they rode could not carry large men. In popular literature and movies, one seldom encounters a Mexican cowboy portrayed in a favorable light and even more rarely a black cowboy. But of the 40,000 cowboys who rode the range between 1865 and 1885, several thousand were blacks or Mexicans. Cowboys were tough and hardy, but hardly any of them became gunfighters. The work was hard, the pay was low, and their life was far from glamorous. Nevertheless, the romantic image of the cowboy, which began with the dime novels of the 19th century, has endured as a central myth of American popular culture.

THE LAST INDIAN FRONTIER

The westward expansion of the ranching and farming frontiers after 1865 doomed the free range of the Plains Indians and the buffalo. In the 1830s, the purpose of moving eastern tribes to preserves west of the Mississippi had been to end strife by separating whites and Indians. But in scarcely a decade, white settlers had penetrated these lands. In the 1850s, when the Kansas and Nebraska territories were opened to white settlement, the government forced a dozen of the tribes living there to cede 15 million acres, leaving them on reservations totaling less than 1.5 million acres. Thus began what historian Philip Weeks has called the "policy of concentration."

In the aftermath of the Civil War, the process of concentrating Indian tribes on reservations accelerated. Chiefs of the five "civilized tribes"—Cherokees, Creeks, Choctaws, Chickasaws, and Seminoles—had signed treaties of alliance with the Confederacy. At that time they were living in Indian Territory (most of present-day Oklahoma), where their economy was linked to the South. Many of them, especially members of the mixed-blood upper class, were slaveholders. But siding with the Confederacy proved to be a costly mistake for the "civilized tribes." The U.S. government "reconstructed" Indian Territory more quickly and with less contention than it reconstructed the former Confederate states. Treaties with the five tribes in 1866 required them to grant tribal citizenship to their freed slaves and reduced tribal lands by half.

CONFLICT WITH THE SIOUX

The Civil War had set in motion a generation of Indian warfare more violent and widespread than anything since the 17th century. Herded onto reservations along the Minnesota River by the Treaty of Traverse des Sioux in 1851, the Santee Sioux grew restive in the summer of 1862. Angry braves began to speak openly of reclaiming ancestral hunting grounds. Then on August 17, a robbery in which five white settlers were murdered seemed to open the floodgates. The braves persuaded Chief Little Crow to take them on the warpath, and over the next few weeks, at least 500 white Minnesotans were massacred.

Hastily mobilized militia and army units finally suppressed the uprising. A military court convicted 319 Indians of murder and atrocities and sentenced 303 of them to death. Appalled,

Lincoln personally reviewed the trial transcripts and reduced the number of executions to 38. The government evicted the remaining Sioux from Minnesota to Dakota Territory.

In the meantime, the army's pursuit of fleeing Santee Sioux provoked other Sioux tribes farther west. By 1864 and for a decade afterward, fighting flared between the army and the Sioux across the northern plains. It reached a climax after gold-seekers in 1874 and 1875 poured into the Black Hills of western Dakota, a sacred place to the Sioux. At the battle of Little Big Horn in Montana Territory on June 25, 1876, Sioux warriors led by Sitting Bull and Crazy Horse, along with their Cheyenne allies, wiped out George A. Custer and the 225 men with him in the 7th Cavalry. In retaliation, General Philip Sheridan carried out a winter campaign in which the Sioux and Cheyenne were crushed.

Largest and most warlike of the Plains tribes, the Sioux were confined to a reservation in Dakota Territory where poverty, disease, apathy, and alcoholism reduced this once proud people to desperation. In 1890 a current of hope arrived at the Sioux reservation in the form of a "Ghost Dance." The Ghost Dance expressed the belief that the Indians' god would destroy the whites and return their land. Alarmed by the frenzy of the dance, federal authorities sent soldiers to the Sioux reservation. A confrontation at Wounded Knee in the Dakota badlands led to a shootout that left 25 soldiers and at least 150 Sioux dead. Wounded Knee symbolized the death of 19th century Plains Indian culture.

SUPPRESSION OF OTHER PLAINS INDIANS

Just as the Sioux uprising in Minnesota had triggered war on the northern plains in 1862, a massacre of Cheyennes in Colorado in 1864 sparked a decade of conflict on the southern plains. The discovery of gold near Pike's Peak set off a rush to Colorado in 1858 and 1859. The government responded by calling several Cheyenne and Arapaho chiefs to a council and persuading them to sign a treaty giving up all claims to land in this region in exchange for a reservation at Sand Creek in southeast Colorado.

In 1864 hunger and resentment on the reservation prompted many of the braves to return to their old hunting grounds and to raid white settlements. Skirmishes soon erupted into open warfare. In the fall, Cheyenne Chief Black Kettle, believing that he had concluded peace with the Colorado settlers, returned to the reservation. There, at dawn on November 29, militia commanded by Colonel John Chivington surrounded and attacked Black Kettle's unsuspecting camp, killing 200 Indians.

The notorious Sand Creek massacre set a pattern for several similar attacks on Indian villages in subsequent years. Their purpose was to corral all the Indians onto the reservations that were being created throughout the West. In addition to trying to defeat the Indians in battle, the Army encouraged the extermination of the buffalo herds. Professional hunters slaughtered the large, clumsy animals by the millions for their hides, thus depriving Plains Indians of their principal source of food, shelter, and clothing.

The Indians were left with no alternative but to come into the reservations, and by the 1880s nearly all of them had done so. Chief Joseph of the Nez Percé pronounced the epitaph for their way of life when federal troops blocked the escape of his band from Montana to Canada in 1877:

> I am tired of fighting. Our chiefs are killed. The old men are all dead. It is cold and we have no blankets . . . no food. . . . The little children are freezing to death. . . . Hear me, my chiefs; I am tired; my heart is sick and sad. From where the sun now stands, I will fight no more forever.

The "Peace Policy"

The iron fist of repression was one part of the government's Indian policy. The other was the velvet glove of reform. Reformers believed that Indians must be compelled to give up their nomadic culture and settle down as the first step toward being assimilated into the American polity as citizens. Just as reformers wanted to reconstruct the South by assimilating emancipated slaves into a free-labor society, so they wished to reconstruct Indian culture by means of schools and Christian missions.

President Grant, in his inaugural address in 1869, announced this new "Peace Policy" toward Indians. He urged "their civilization and ultimate citizenship." "Civilization" meant acceptance of white culture, including the English language, Christianity, and individual ownership of property. "Citizenship" meant allegiance to the United States rather than to a tribe. In 1869 Grant established a Board of Indian Commissioners and staffed it with humanitarian reformers. In 1871 Indians became "wards of the nation," to be civilized and prepared for citizenship.

Some Indians accepted this destruction of their culture as inevitable. Others resisted. That resistance fed the flames of frontier wars for nearly a decade after 1869. "I love the land and the buffalo," said the Kiowa Chief Satanta. "I love to roam over the wide prairie, and when I do, I feel free and happy, but when we settle down we grow pale and die."

But with their military power broken and the buffalo gone, most Indians by the 1880s had acquiesced in the "reconstruction" that offered them citizenship. Also in the 1880s, the reformers found themselves in a strange alliance with land-hungry westerners, who greedily eyed the 155 million acres of land tied up in reservations. If part of that land could be allotted directly to individual ownership by Indian families, the remainder would become available for purchase by whites. The Dawes Severalty Act did just that in 1887. This landmark legislation called for the dissolution of Indian tribes as legal entities, offered Indians the opportunity to become citizens, and allotted each head of family 160 acres of farmland or 320 acres of grazing land.

For whites eager to seize reservation land, the Dawes Act brought a bonanza. At noon on April 22, 1889, the government threw open specified parts of the Indian Territory to "Boomers," who descended on the region like locusts and by nightfall had staked claim to nearly 2 million acres. Eventually, whites gained title to 108 million acres of former reservation land.

For Indians, writes historian Philip Weeks, the Dawes Act "proved an unqualified failure." Although many Indians made a successful transition to the new order, others slipped further into depression, destitution, and alcoholism.

Mexican Americans

Mexican Americans in the West were also forced to adjust to a new order. At the hands of Anglo-American settlers, Mexican Americans suffered dispossession of their land, loss of political influence, and suppression of their culture. Even as early as 1849 in the northern California gold fields, resentment of "foreigners" provoked violence against Mexican American miners—and the Foreign Miners Tax of 1850 effectively forced Mexican Americans out of the gold fields. As the 19th century progressed, hordes of Anglo-American "squatters" invaded the expansive holdings of the Mexican American elite, who were forced to seek relief in the courts. Although their claims were generally upheld, these legal proceedings often stretched on for years. After exorbitant legal fees and other expenses were taken into account, a legal triumph

DESTRUCTION OF THE BUFFALO

Historians estimate that as many as 30 million bison (popularly called buffalo) once roamed the grasslands of North America. By the mid-19th century, however, the expansion of European-American settlement, the demand for buffalo robes in the European and eastern U.S. markets, and competition from Indian horses for grazing lands had reduced the herds by many millions. Such pressures intensified after the Civil War—as railroads penetrated the West and new technology enabled tanners to process buffalo hides for leather. Professional hunters flocked to the range and systematically killed the bison; the hides were then shipped out by rail, as shown in the photograph at right. Passengers on trains sometimes shot buffalo from the cars as shown in the magazine illustration. The U.S. Army encouraged this slaughter in order to force the Plains Indians onto reservations by depriving them of their traditional sustenance from hunting bison. By the 1880s the buffalo were almost extinct, leaving behind millions of bones, which were gathered and piled, as in the photograph of buffalo skulls, for shipment to plants that ground them into fertilizer.

was often a Pyrrhic victory. In the end, most Mexican American landholders in northern California were forced to sell the very lands they had fought to keep. Similarly, the ranchers in southern California were forced to sell their lands after devastating droughts in the 1860s virtually destroyed the ranching industry. Forced off the land, California's Mexican Americans increasingly found themselves concentrated in segregated urban *barrios*.

The migration of Anglos into eastern Texas had played a role in fomenting the war for Texas independence and in bringing about the war with Mexico (see Chapter 13). By the latter half of the 19th century, eastern Texas was overwhelmingly Anglo; most Mexican Americans were concentrated in the Rio Grande valley of southern Texas. As in California, Anglos in Texas used force and intimidation to disfranchise the Mexican Americans. The vaunted Texas Rangers often acted as an Anglo vigilante force. Eventually, Mexican Americans in Texas were reduced to a state of peonage, dependent on their Anglo protectors for political and economic security.

Similar patterns prevailed in New Mexico, but the effects of Anglo-American settlement were mitigated somewhat because New Mexicans continued to outnumber Anglo-Americans. Earlier in the 19th century, international trade along the Santa Fe Trail had strengthened the political and economic status of the New Mexican elites. Now these same elites consolidated their position by acting as power brokers between poorer New Mexicans and wealthy Anglos.

Despite all these difficulties, Spanish-speaking peoples in the Southwest and California managed to preserve much of their distinctive culture. Moreover, Mexican American agricultural methods and mining techniques were adopted by Anglo-American immigrants to the region.

THE NEW SOUTH

Southern whites proved more resistant than western Indians to Yankee dominance. Nevertheless, after the North's retreat from Reconstruction, a Yankee presence did remain, in the form of investment and a "New South" ideology.

The Republican Party did not disappear from the South after 1877. Nor was the black vote immediately and totally suppressed. Republican presidential candidates won about 40 percent of the votes in former slave states through the 1880s, and a number of blacks continued to win elections to state legislatures until the 1890s. Down to 1901, every U.S. Congress but one had at least one black representative from the South.

But there was enough "bulldozing" of black voters (Chapter 17) to keep the southern states solid for the Democrats. In 1880 the Democratic Party hoped to build on this foundation to win the presidency. They nominated a Civil War hero, General Winfield Scott Hancock. His opponent was another Civil War general, James A. Garfield, who had served in Congress since the war. In an election with the closest popular vote in American history, Hancock carried every southern state, while Garfield won all but three northern states—and the election.

However, following this political defeat, a new spirit of enterprise quickened southern life in the 1880s. Some southerners even went so far as to acknowledge that the Yankees had shown them the way. And they welcomed northern investment. Henry Grady, editor of the *Atlanta Constitution*, was the leading spokesman for the New South ideology. In an 1886 speech to northern businessmen, Grady boasted of the New South's achievements: "We have sown towns and cities in the place of theories, and put business above politics. . . . We have established thrift in city and country. We have fallen in love with work."

SOUTHERN INDUSTRY

The South's textile industry expanded rapidly during the 1880s. Along the piedmont from Virginia to Alabama, new cotton mills sprang up. The labor force was almost entirely white. About 40 percent of the workers were women, and 25 percent were children aged 16 and younger. These "lintheads" labored long hours for wages about half the level prevailing in New England's mills. This cheap labor gave southern mill owners a competitive advantage. In 1880 the South had only 5 percent of the country's textile-producing capacity; by 1900 it had 23 percent.

Tobacco was another southern industry that developed from a regional crop. Unlike the textile industry, many of the workers in the tobacco factories were black. James B. Duke of North Carolina transformed the tobacco industry when he installed cigarette-making machines at Durham in 1885. In 1890 he created the American Tobacco Company, which controlled 90 percent of the market, with himself at its head.

Railroads and iron were two New South industries that were especially dependent on outside capital. During the 1880s, railroad construction in the South outpaced the national average. In 1886 southern railroads with a 5-foot gauge shifted to the national standard of 4 feet $8\frac{1}{2}$ inches. This change integrated southern lines into the national network and symbolized northern domination of the region's railroads. During those same years, northern capital helped fuel the growth of an iron and steel industry in the South. In 1880, the former slave states produced only 9 percent of the nation's pig iron; by 1890, that proportion had doubled. Most of the growth was concentrated in northern Alabama, where the proximity of coal, limestone, and ore made the new city of Birmingham the "Pittsburgh of the South."

The heavy northern investment in these industries meant that the South had less control over economic decisions that affected its welfare. Some historians have referred to the South's "colonial" relationship to the North in the late 19th century. And because of the low wages prevailing in the South, the economic benefits that accrued from industrial growth were inequitably distributed. Average southern per capita income remained only two-fifths of the average in the rest of the country well into the 20th century.

SOUTHERN AGRICULTURE

The main reason for this relative poverty, however, was the weakness of the region's agriculture. A crucial reason for this retardation was the low level of investment in farming. One-crop specialization, overproduction, declining prices, and an exploitative credit system also contributed to the problem. The basic institution of the southern rural economy was the crop lien system, which came into being because of the shortage of money and credit. Few banks had survived the war, and land values had plummeted, so it was impossible for farmers to get a bank loan with their land as collateral. Instead, merchants provided farmers with supplies and groceries in return for a lien on their next crop.

This system might have worked well if the merchants had charged reasonable interest rates and if cotton and tobacco prices had remained high enough for the farmer to pay off his debts after harvest with a little left over. But the country storekeeper charged a credit price 50 or 60 percent above the cash price. And crop prices, especially for cotton, were dropping steadily. Cotton prices declined from an average of 12 cents a pound in the 1870s to 6 cents in the 1890s. As prices fell, many farmers went deeper and deeper into debt to the merchants. Sharecroppers and tenants incurred a double indebtedness: to the land-owner, whose land they sharecropped or rented, and to the merchant, who furnished them supplies on credit. Many sharecroppers, particularly blacks, fell into virtual peonage.

One reason for the fall of cotton prices was overproduction. Britain had encouraged the expansion of cotton growing in Egypt and India during the Civil War to make up for the loss of American cotton. So after the war, southern growers had to face international competition. From 1878 to 1898 output doubled. This overproduction drove prices ever lower. To get credit, farmers had to plant every acre with the most marketable cash crop—cotton. This practice exhausted the soil, required ever-increasing amounts of expensive fertilizer, and fed the cycle of overproduction and declining prices.

It also reduced the amount of land that could be used to grow food crops. Farmers who might otherwise have produced their own cornmeal and raised their own hogs for bacon became dependent on merchants for these supplies. By the 1890s they had to import nearly half their food at a price 50 percent higher than it would have cost to grow their own. Many southerners recognized that only diversification could break this dependency. But the crop lien system locked them into it.

RACE RELATIONS IN THE NEW SOUTH

The downward spiral of the rural southern economy caused frustration and bitterness in which blacks became the scapegoats of white rage. Lynching rose to an all-time high in the 1890s, averaging 188 per year. The viciousness of racist propaganda reached an all-time low. Serious antiblack riots broke out at Wilmington, North Carolina, in 1898 and in Atlanta in 1906. Several states adopted new constitutions that disfranchised most black voters by means of literacy or property qualifications (or both), poll taxes, and other clauses implicitly aimed at black voters. The new constitutions contained "understanding clauses" or "grandfather clauses" that enabled registrars to register white voters who were unable to meet the new requirements. In *Williams* v. *Mississippi* (1898), the U.S. Supreme Court upheld these disfranchisement clauses on the grounds that they did not discriminate "on their face" against blacks. State Democratic parties then established primary elections in which only whites could vote.

It was during these same years that most southern states passed "Jim Crow" laws, which mandated racial segregation in public facilities of all kinds. In the landmark case of *Plessy* v. *Ferguson* (1896), the Supreme Court sanctioned such laws so long as the separate facilities for blacks were equal to those for whites—which, in practice, they never were.

One of the worst features of race relations in the New South was the convict leasing system. The southern prison system was inadequate to accommodate the increase in convicted criminals after emancipation. Most states began leasing convicts to private contractors—coal-mining firms, railroad construction companies, planters, and so on. The state not only saved the cost of housing and feeding the prisoners but also received an income for leasing them; the lessees obtained cheap labor whom they could work like slaves. The cruelty and exploitation suffered by the convicts became a national scandal. Ninety percent of the convicts were black, the result in part of discriminatory law enforcement practices. The convicts were ill fed, ill clothed, victimized by sadistic guards, and worked to death. Annual mortality rates among convicts in several states ranged up to 25 percent.

Northern reformers condemned what they called "this newest and most revolting form of slavery." Thoughtful southerners agreed; reform groups, many of them led by white women, sprang up in the South to work for the abolition of convict leasing.

In 1895 a new black leader emerged. Booker T. Washington, a 39-year-old educator who had founded Tuskegee Institute in Alabama, gave a speech at the Atlanta Exposition that made him famous. In effect, Washington accepted segregation as a temporary accommodation between the races in return for white support of black efforts for education, social uplift, and economic progress. "In all things that are purely social we can be as separate as the fingers," said Washington, "yet one as the hand in all things essential to mutual progress."

Washington's goal was not permanent second-class citizenship for blacks, but improvement through self-help and uplift until they earned white acceptance as equals. Yet to his black critics, Washington's strategy and rhetoric seemed to play into the hands of white supremacists.

THE POLITICS OF STALEMATE

During the years between the Panic of 1873 and the Panic of 1893, serious economic and social issues beset the American polity. As described in the next chapter, the strains of rapid industrialization, an inadequate monetary system, agricultural distress, and labor protest built up to potentially explosive force. But the two mainstream political parties seemed indifferent to these problems. Paralysis gripped the national government as the Civil War continued to cast its shadow into the future.

KNIFE-EDGE ELECTORAL BALANCE

The five presidential elections from 1876 through 1892, taken together, were the most closely contested elections in American history. No more than 1 percent separated the popular vote of the two major candidates in any of these contests except 1892, when the margin was 3 percent. The Democratic candidate won twice (Grover Cleveland in 1884 and 1892), and in two other elections carried a tiny plurality of popular votes (Tilden in 1876 and Cleveland in 1888) but lost narrowly in the Electoral College. During only six of those 20 years did the same party control the presidency and both houses, and then by razor-thin margins.

The few pieces of major legislation during these years—the Pendleton Civil Service Act of 1883, the Interstate Commerce Act of 1887, and the Sherman Antitrust Act of 1890—could be enacted only by bipartisan majorities, and only after they had been watered down by numerous compromises. Politicians often debated the tariff, but the tariff laws they passed had little real impact on the economy.

Divided government and the even balance between the two major parties accounted for the political stalemate. Neither party had the power to enact a bold legislative program; both parties avoided taking firm stands on controversial issues. Both parties practiced the politics of the past rather than the politics of the present. At election time, Republican candidates "waved the bloody shirt" to keep alive the memory of the Civil War. They castigated Democrats as former rebels or Copperheads who could not be trusted with the nation's destiny. Democrats, in turn, especially in the South, denounced racial equality and branded Republicans as the party of "Negro rule." From 1876 almost into the 20th century scarcely anyone but a Confederate veteran could be elected governor or senator in the South.

Availability rather than ability or a strong stand on issues became the prime requisite for presidential and vice presidential nominees. Geographical "availability" was particularly important. The solid Democratic South and the rather less solid Republican North gave each party a firm bloc of electoral votes in every election. But in three large northern states—New York, Ohio, and Indiana—the two parties were so closely balanced that the shift of a few thousand votes would determine the margin of victory for one or the other party in the state's electoral votes. And these three states alone represented 74 electoral votes, fully one-third of the total necessary for victory.

So it is not surprising that of 20 nominees for president and vice president by the two parties in five elections, 16 of them were from these three states. Only once did each party nominate a presidential candidate from outside these three states: Democrat Winfield Scott Hancock of Pennsylvania in 1880 and Republican James G. Blaine of Maine in 1884. Both lost.

CIVIL SERVICE REFORM

The most salient issue of national politics in the early 1880s was civil service reform. The Republicans split into three factions known as Mugwumps (the reformers), Stalwarts (who opposed reform), and Half-Breeds (who supported halfway reforms). Mugwumps and Half-Breeds combined to nominate James A. Garfield for president in 1880; Chester A. Arthur was nominated for vice president. Four months after Garfield took office, a man named Charles Guiteau approached the president at the railroad station in Washington and shot him. Garfield lingered for two months before dying on September 19, 1881.

Described by psychiatrists as a paranoid schizophrenic, Guiteau had been a government clerk and a supporter of the Stalwart faction of the Republican Party; he had lost his job under the new administration. As he shot Garfield he shouted: "I am a Stalwart and Arthur is president now!" This tragedy gave a final impetus to civil service reform. In 1883 Congress passed the Pendleton Act, which established a category of civil service jobs that were to be filled by competitive examinations. At first, only a tenth of government positions fell within that category, but a succession of presidential orders gradually expanded the list to about half by 1897. State and local governments began to emulate federal civil service reform in the 1880s and 1890s.

Like the other vice presidents who had succeeded presidents who died in office (John Tyler, Millard Fillmore, and Andrew Johnson), Arthur failed to achieve nomination for president in his own right. The Republicans in 1884 turned instead to Speaker of the House James G. Blaine of Maine. Blaine had made enemies over the years, however, especially among Mugwumps, who felt that his cozy relationship with railroad lobbyists while Speaker disqualified him for the presidency.

The Mugwumps had a tendency toward self-righteousness in their self-appointed role as spokesmen for political probity. They were small in number but large in influence. Many were editors, authors, lawyers, college professors, or clergymen. Concentrated in the Northeast, they admired the Democratic governor of New York, Grover Cleveland, who had gained a reputation as an advocate of reform and "good government." When Blaine won the Republican nomination, the Mugwumps defected to Cleveland.

In such a closely balanced state as New York, that shift could make a decisive difference. But Blaine hoped to neutralize it by appealing to the Irish vote. He made the most of his Irish ancestry on the maternal side. But that effort was rendered futile late in the campaign when a Protestant clergyman characterized the Democrats as the party of "Rum, Romanism, and Rebellion." Though Blaine was present when the Reverend Samuel Burchard made this remark, he failed to repudiate it. When the incident hit the newspapers, Blaine's hope for Irish support faded. Cleveland carried New York State by 1,149 votes (a margin of one-tenth of 1 percent) and thus became the first Democrat to be elected president in 28 years.

THE TARIFF ISSUE

Ignoring a rising tide of farmer and labor discontent, Cleveland decided to make or break his presidency on the tariff issue. He devoted his annual State of the Union message in December 1887 entirely to the tariff, maintaining that lower import duties would help all Americans by reducing the cost of consumer goods and expanding American exports. Republicans responded that low tariffs would flood the country with products from low-wage industries abroad, forcing American factories to close and throwing American workers out on the streets. The following year, the Republican nominee for president, Benjamin Harrison, pledged to retain the protective tariff. To reduce the budget surplus that had built up during the 1880s, the Republicans also promised more generous pensions for Union veterans.

The voters' response was ambiguous. Cleveland's popular-vote plurality actually increased from 29,000 in 1884 to 90,000 in 1888. But a shift of six-tenths of 1 percent put New York in

CHRONOLOGY

1862	Sioux uprising in Minnesota; 38 Sioux executed
1864	Colorado militia massacres Cheyenne in village at Sand Creek, Colorado
1866	Cowboys conduct first cattle drive north from Texas
1869	President Grant announces his "peace policy" toward Indians
1876	Sioux and Cheyenne defeat Custer at Little Big Horn
1880	James A. Garfield elected president
1881	Garfield assassinated; Chester A. Arthur becomes president
1883	Pendleton Act begins reform of civil service
1884	Grover Cleveland elected president
1887	Dawes Severalty Act dissolves Indian tribal units and implements individual ownership of tribal lands
1888	Benjamin Harrison elected president
1889	Government opens Indian Territory (Oklahoma) to white settlement
1890	Wounded Knee massacre • New Mississippi constitution pioneers black disfranchisement in South • Republicans try but fail to enact federal elections bill to protect black voting rights • Congress enacts McKinley Tariff
1892	Grover Cleveland again elected president
1895	Booker T. Washington makes his "Atlanta Compromise" address
1896	*Plessy* v. *Ferguson* legalizes "separate but equal" state racial segregation laws
1898	*Williams* v. *Mississippi* condones use of literacy tests and similar measures to restrict voting rights

the Republican column and Harrison in the White House. Republicans also gained control of both houses of Congress. They promptly made good on their campaign pledges by passing legislation that almost doubled Union pensions and by enacting the McKinley Tariff of 1890. Named for Congressman William McKinley of Ohio, this law raised duties on a large range of products to an average of almost 50 percent.

In the midterm congressional elections, the voters handed the Republicans a decisive defeat, converting a House Republican majority of six to a Democratic majority of 147, and a Senate Republican majority of eight to a Democratic majority of six. Nominated for a third time in 1892, Cleveland built on this momentum to win the presidency by the largest margin in 20 years. But this outcome was deceptive. On March 4, 1893, when Cleveland took the oath of office for the second time, he stood atop a social and economic volcano that would soon erupt.

CONCLUSION

In 1890 the superintendent of the U.S. Census made a sober announcement of dramatic import: "Up to and including 1880 the country had a frontier of settlement, but at present the unsettled area has been so broken into by isolated bodies of settlement that there can hardly be said to be a frontier line . . . any longer."

This statement prompted a young historian at the University of Wisconsin, Frederick Jackson Turner, to deliver a paper in 1893 that became the single most influential essay ever published by an American historian. For nearly 300 years, said Turner, the existence of a frontier of European-American settlement advancing relentlessly westward had shaped American character. To the frontier Americans owed their upward mobility, their high standard of living, and the rough equality of opportunity that made liberty and democracy possible. "American social development has been continually beginning over again on the frontier," declared Turner.

For many decades Turner's insight dominated Americans' perceptions of themselves and their history. Today, however, the Turner thesis is largely discredited as failing to explain the experiences of the great majority of people who lived and worked in older cities and towns or on plantations hundreds of miles or more from any frontier, and whose culture and institutions were molded more by their place of origin than by a "frontier."

But the significance of Turner's remarks is not whether he was right; in the 1890s he expressed a widely-shared belief among white Americans. They *believed* that liberty and equality were at least partly the product of the frontier, of the chance to go west and start a new life. And now that opportunity seemed to be coming to an end—at the same time that the Panic of 1893 was launching another depression, the worst that the American economy had yet experienced. This depression caused the social and economic tinder that had been accumulating during the two preceding decades to burst into flame.

ECONOMIC CHANGE AND THE CRISIS OF THE 1890S

ECONOMIC GROWTH ∽ LABOR STRIFE ∽ FARMERS' MOVEMENTS

THE RISE AND FALL OF THE PEOPLE'S PARTY

Alexis de Tocqueville visited the United States in 1831 and published his famous analysis, *Democracy in America,* in 1835. At that time more than two-thirds of all Americans lived on farms and only 10 percent lived in towns or cities with populations larger than 2,500. The overwhelming majority of white males owned property and worked for themselves rather than for wages. What impressed Tocqueville most was the relative absence of both great wealth and great poverty; the modest prosperity of the broad middle class created the impression of equality.

During the next generation the North began to industrialize, cities grew much faster than rural areas, and inequality of wealth and income grew larger. The country's preoccupation with sectional issues prior to the Civil War and the gnawing problems of Reconstruction after the war diverted attention from the economic and social problems associated with industrialism and class inequality. With the depression that followed the Panic of 1873, however, these problems burst spectacularly into public view.

ECONOMIC GROWTH

During the 15 years between recovery from one depression in 1878 and the onset of another in 1893, the American economy grew at one of the fastest rates in its history. All sectors of the economy were expanding. The most spectacular growth was in manufacturing, which increased by 180 percent, while agriculture grew by 26 percent.

RAILROADS

The railroad was the single most important agent of economic growth during these years. Track mileage increased from 103,649 to 221,864 miles; the number of locomotives and revenue cars (freight and passenger) increased by a similar amount. Railroads converted from iron to steel rails and wheels, boosting steel production. Railroads were the largest consumers of coal, the largest carriers of goods and people, the largest single employer of labor.

The power wielded by the railroads inevitably aroused hostility. Companies often charged less for long hauls than for short hauls in areas with little or no competition. The rapid proliferation of tracks produced overcapacity in some areas. This caused rate-cutting wars that

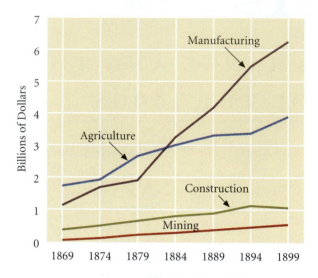

VALUE ADDED BY
ECONOMIC SECTOR,
1869–1899 (IN 1879 PRICES)

benefited some shippers at the expense of others—usually small ones. To avoid "ruinous competition" (as the railroads viewed it), companies formed "pools" by which they divided traffic and fixed their rates. Some of these practices made sound economic sense; others appeared discriminatory and exploitative. Railroads kept rates higher in areas with no competition (most farmers lived in areas served by only one line) than in regions with competition. Grain elevators, many of which were owned by railroad companies, came under attack for cheating farmers.

Farmers responded by organizing cooperatives to sell crops and buy supplies. The umbrella organization for many of these cooperatives was the Patrons of Husbandry, known as the Grange, founded in 1867. But farmers could not build their own railroads. So they organized "antimonopoly" parties and elected state legislators who enacted "Granger laws" in several states. These laws established railroad commissions that fixed maximum freight rates and warehouse charges. Railroads challenged the laws in court. Eight challenges made their way to the U.S. Supreme Court, which in *Munn* v. *Illinois* (1877) ruled that states could regulate businesses clothed with a "public interest"—including railroads.

The welter of different and sometimes conflicting state laws, plus rulings by the U.S. Supreme Court in the 1880s that states could not regulate interstate railroad traffic, brought a drive for federal regulation. After years of discussion, Congress passed the Interstate Commerce Act in 1887. This act, like most such laws, was a compromise that reflected the varying viewpoints of shippers, railroads, and other pressure groups. It outlawed pools, discriminatory rates, long-haul versus short-haul differentials, and rebates to favored shippers. It required that freight and passenger rates must be "reasonable and just." What that meant was not entirely clear, but the law created the Interstate Commerce Commission (ICC) to define it on a case-by-case basis. Because the ICC had minimal enforcement powers, however, federal courts frequently refused to issue the orders it requested. Nevertheless, the ICC had some effect on railroad practices. And freight rates continued to decline during this period as railroad operating efficiency improved.

The outstanding example of the railroads' impact on everyday life was the creation of standard time zones. Before 1883 many localities and cities kept their own time, derived from the sun's meridian in each locality. When it was noon in Chicago, it was 11:27 A.M. in Omaha, 11:56 A.M. in St. Louis, 12:09 P.M. in Louisville, and 12:17 P.M. in Toledo. This played havoc with railroad timetables. In 1883 a consortium of railroads established four standard time zones and put new timetables into effect for these zones. There was some grumbling about the arrogance of railroad presidents changing "God's time." For the most part, however, the public accepted the change, and Congress finally got around to sanctioning standard time zones in 1918.

TECHNOLOGY

Technological advances during this era had an enormous impact: automatic signals, air brakes, and knuckle couplers on the railroads; the Bessemer and then the open-hearth process in the steel mills; the telephone, electric light, and typewriter (all in the 1870s); the phonograph and motion pictures (1890s); the elevator and structural steel for buildings, which made possible the first "skyscrapers" (1880s); the electric dynamo (generator), which not only laid the basis for such household items as refrigerators and washing machines but also provided a new source of industrial power that gradually replaced water power and the steam engine; and the internal combustion engine, which made possible the first automobiles (1890s) and the first airplane flight by the Wright brothers in 1903.

WEALTH AND INEQUALITY

All these wonders of economic growth and technological change were not accomplished without human cost. One such cost was a widening gulf between rich and poor. While the average per capita income of all Americans increased by 35 percent from 1878 to 1893, real wages advanced only 20 percent. And that advance masked sharp inequalities of wages by skill, region, race, and gender. Many unskilled and semiskilled workers made barely enough to support themselves, much less a family.

The perception of class inequality was even greater than the reality. Many wealthy people practiced what Thorstein Veblen described in his book *The Theory of the Leisure Class* (1899) as "conspicuous consumption." They sent agents to Europe to buy up paintings and tapestries from impoverished aristocrats. In their mansions on Fifth Avenue and their summer homes at Newport they entertained lavishly. These extravagant habits gave substance to the labeling of this era as the Gilded Age and sharpened the growing sense of class consciousness.

Some of the newly rich made their money by methods that critics considered predatory, and were labeled "robber barons." They included William Vanderbilt, Jay Gould, Jim Fisk, and Collis P. Huntington in railroading; John D. Rockefeller in oil; Andrew Carnegie and Henry Clay Frick in steel; James B. Duke in tobacco; and John Pierpont Morgan in banking.

Criticism of the "robber barons" sometimes focused more on the immense power commanded by their wealth than on the wealth itself. Fisk and Gould bribed legislators, manipulated the stock market, exploited workers, and cheated stockholders. Rockefeller either bought out or ruined his competitors, obtained rebates and drawbacks on rail shipments of oil, and created a monopoly in his determined efforts to gain control of oil refining. Carnegie and Frick pushed laborers to the limit in 72-hour workweeks, redefined skill levels and changed work rules, and sped up the pace in steel mills in a ceaseless quest for greater efficiency and lower labor costs. Morgan's banking firm built an empire of leveraged financing and interlocking corporate directorates.

These activities could be—and were—defended on grounds of entrepreneurial innovation and efficiency, and the enterprises these men created did enable the United States to leap ahead of Britain as an industrial power. By 1913 American manufacturing output equaled that of the next three industrial nations combined—Germany, Britain, and France. The "robber barons" created wealth for all Americans. And not all of them practiced conspicuous consumption. Professing a gospel of stewardship, Carnegie, Rockefeller, and others gave away much of their wealth to educational and philanthropic institutions.

THE ANTITRUST MOVEMENT

Nevertheless, many Americans feared the power wielded by these tycoons. Their monopoly or near-monopoly share of the market in oil, steel, tobacco, sugar, transportation, and other products seemed to violate the ideal of fair competition. To curb that power, an "antitrust" movement emerged in the 1880s. The word "trust" derived from an investment strategy in which the stockholders of several refining companies turned over their shares to Rockefeller's Standard Oil in return for so-called trust certificates. The term came to be applied to all large corporations that controlled a substantial share of any given market. In response to pressures to curb such "trusts," several states passed antitrust laws in the 1880s.

But because the larger corporations operated across state lines, reformers turned to Congress, which responded in 1890 by passing the Sherman Antitrust Act. The act stated that "Every contract, combination in the form of trust or otherwise, or conspiracy, in restraint of trade or commerce among the several States is hereby declared to be illegal." But what constituted "restraint of trade"? For that matter, what constituted a trust? Of eight cases against corporations brought before federal courts from 1890 to 1893, the government lost seven. In 1895 the Supreme Court dealt the Sherman Act a crippling blow in *U.S. v. E. C. Knight Company,* in which it ruled that manufacturing was not commerce and therefore did not fall under jurisdiction of the law.

LABOR STRIFE

The drive for even greater speed and productivity on railroads and in factories gave the United States the unhappy distinction of having the world's highest rate of industrial accidents. Many families were impoverished by workplace accidents that killed or maimed their chief breadwinner. This was one source of a rising tide of labor discontent. Another was the erosion of worker autonomy in factories, where managers made decisions about procedures and pace of operations that were once made by workers themselves. Many crafts that had once been a source of pride to those who practiced them became just a job that could be performed by anyone. Labor became increasingly a commodity to be bought for wages rather than a craft whereby the worker sold the product of his labor rather than the labor itself.

For skilled artisans, this was an alarming trend. In 1866 the leaders of several craft unions had formed the National Labor Union. Labor parties sprang up in several states, and several states established bureaus or departments of labor that had little substantive power but did begin to gather and report data. These pressures filtered up to Washington, where Congress created the

THE RAILROAD STRIKES OF 1877   This illustration shows striking workers on the Baltimore and Ohio Railroad forcing the engineer and fireman from a freight train at Martinsburg, West Virginia, on July 17, 1877.

Bureau of Labor in 1884 and elevated it to cabinet rank in 1903. In 1894 Congress also made the first Monday in September an official holiday—Labor Day—to honor working people.

The National Labor Union withered away in the depression of the 1870s. But industrial violence escalated. In the anthracite coal fields of eastern Pennsylvania, the Molly Maguires carried out guerrilla warfare against mine owners. In the later 1870s, the Greenbackers (a group that urged currency expansion) and labor reformers formed a coalition that elected several local and state officials plus 14 congressmen in 1878.

THE GREAT RAILROAD STRIKE OF 1877

Railroads became an early focal point of labor strife. Citing declining revenues during the depression that followed the Panic of 1873, several railroads cut wages by as much as 35 percent between 1874 and 1877. When the Baltimore and Ohio Railroad announced its third 10 percent wage cut on July 16, 1877, workers struck. The strike spread rapidly to other lines, and traffic from St. Louis to the East Coast came to a halt. Ten states called out their militias. Strikers and militia fired on each other, and workers set fire to rolling stock and roundhouses. By the time federal troops brought things under control in the first week of August, at least 100 strikers, militiamen, and bystanders had been killed, hundreds more had been injured, and uncounted millions of dollars of property had gone up in smoke.

THE KNIGHTS OF LABOR

The principal labor organization that emerged in the 1880s was the Knights of Labor. Founded in Philadelphia in 1869, the Knights were at first a secret fraternal society. But under the leadership of Terence V. Powderly, the Knights abandoned secrecy in 1879 and emerged as a potent national federation of unions. The Knights of Labor departed in several respects from the norm of labor organization at that time. Most of its unions were organized by industry rather than by craft, giving many unskilled and semiskilled workers union representation for the first time. Some admitted women; some also admitted blacks.

The goal of most members of the Knights was to improve their lot within the existing system through higher wages, shorter hours, and better working conditions. This meant collective bargaining with employers; it also meant strikes. But Powderly and the Knights' national leadership discouraged the members from calling strikes. One reason they did so was practical: A losing strike often destroyed a union as employers replaced strikers with strikebreakers, or "scabs."

Another reason was philosophical. Strikes constituted a tacit recognition of the legitimacy of the wage system. In Powderly's view, wages siphoned off to capital a part of the wealth created by labor. The Knights, Powderly said, intended "to secure to the workers the full enjoyment of the wealth they create." This was a goal grounded both in the past independence of skilled workers and in a radical vision of the future—a vision in which workers' cooperatives would own the means of production.

The Knights did sponsor several modest workers' cooperatives. Their success was limited, partly because of a lack of capital and of management experience and partly because even the most skilled craftsmen found it difficult to compete with machines. Ironically, the Knights gained their greatest triumphs through strikes. In 1884 and 1885 successful strikes against the Union Pacific and Missouri Pacific railroads won enormous prestige and a rush of new members, which by 1886 totaled 700,000. But defeat in a second strike against the two railroads in the spring of 1886 was a serious blow. Then came the Haymarket bombing in Chicago.

HAYMARKET

Chicago was a hotbed of labor radicalism. Anarchists infiltrated some trade unions in Chicago and leaped aboard the bandwagon of a national movement centered in that city for a general strike on May 1, 1886, to achieve the eight-hour workday. Chicago police were notoriously hostile to labor organizers and strikers, so the scene was set for a violent confrontation.

The May 1 showdown coincided with a strike at the McCormick farm machinery plant in Chicago. A fight outside the gates on May 3 brought a police attack on the strikers. Anarchists then organized a protest meeting at Haymarket Square on May 4. Toward the end of the meeting, the police suddenly arrived in force. When someone threw a bomb into their midst, the police opened fire. When the wild melee was over, 50 people lay wounded and 10 dead—six of them policemen.

This affair set off a wave of hysteria against labor radicals. Police in Chicago rounded up hundreds of labor leaders. Eight anarchists went on trial for conspiracy to commit murder—though no evidence turned up to prove that any of them had thrown the bomb. All eight were convicted; four were hanged on November 11, 1887. The case bitterly divided the country.

Many workers, civil libertarians, and members of the middle class branded the verdicts judicial murder. But the majority of Americans applauded them.

The Knights of Labor were caught in this antilabor backlash. Although the Knights had nothing to do with the Haymarket affair, Powderly's opposition to the wage system sounded suspiciously like anarchism. Membership in the Knights plummeted from 700,000 in the spring of 1886 to fewer than 100,000 by 1890.

As the Knights of Labor waned, a new national labor organization waxed. Founded in 1886, the American Federation of Labor (AFL) was a loosely affiliated association of unions organized by trade or craft: cigar-makers, machinists, carpenters, and so on. Under the leadership of Samuel Gompers, an immigrant cigar-maker, the AFL accepted capitalism and the wage system and worked for better conditions, higher wages, shorter hours, and occupational safety. Most of the members of the AFL unions were skilled workers. Its membership grew from 140,000 in 1886 to nearly a million by 1900.

HENRY GEORGE

Labor militancy did not die in the wake of Haymarket, however. Two best-selling books helped keep alive the vision of a more equalitarian social order. The first seemed an unlikely candidate for best-seller status. It was a book on economics titled *Progress and Poverty* (1879). Henry George, the self-educated author, had spent 15 years working as a sailor, printer, and prospector before becoming a newspaper editor in California. In his travels, George had been struck by the appalling contrast between wealth and poverty. He fixed on "land monopoly" as the cause: the control of land and resources by the few at the expense of the many. His solution was 100 percent taxation on the "unearned increment" in the value of land—that is, on the difference between the initial purchase price and the eventual market value (minus improvements), or what today we would call capital gains.

Progress and Poverty achieved astonishing success. By 1905 it had sold 2 million copies and been translated into several languages. However, few economists endorsed the single tax and the idea made little headway. The real impact of George's book came from its portrayal of the injustice of poverty in the midst of plenty. George became a hero to labor. He joined the Knights of Labor, moved to New York City, and ran for mayor as the candidate of the United Labor Party in 1886. He narrowly lost, but his campaign dramatized the grievances of labor and alerted the major parties to the power of that constituency.

EDWARD BELLAMY

The other book that found a wide audience was a novel, *Looking Backward,* by Edward Bellamy. Bellamy was a New England writer imbued with the tenets of Christian reform. *Looking Backward* takes place in the year 2000 and contrasts the America of that year with the America of 1887. In 2000 all industry is controlled by the national government, everyone works for equal pay, there are no rich and no poor, no strikes, no class conflict. Bellamy was not a Marxian socialist, and he preferred to call his collectivist order "Nationalism." His vision of a world without social strife appealed to middle-class Americans, who bought half a million copies of *Looking Backward* every year for several years in the early 1890s. More than 160 Nationalist clubs sprang up to support the idea of public ownership, if not of all industries, at least of public utilities.

Some of Bellamy's followers called themselves Christian Socialists. They formed the left wing of a broader movement, the Social Gospel, that deeply affected mainstream Protestant denominations in the rapidly growing cities of the Gilded Age. Shocked by poverty and over-crowding in the sprawling tenement districts, clergymen and laypeople associated with the Social Gospel embraced a theology which held that ameliorating the plight of the poor was as important as saving souls. They supported the settlement houses that were being established in many cities during the 1890s (see Chapter 21) and pressed for legislation to curb the ex-ploitation of the poor and provide them with opportunities for betterment.

THE HOMESTEAD STRIKE

Plenty of evidence was at hand to feed middle-class fears that America was falling apart. Strikes occurred with a frequency and a fierceness that made 1877 and 1886 look like mere preludes to the main event. The most dramatic confrontation took place in 1892 at the Homestead plant (near Pittsburgh) of the Carnegie Steel Company. Carnegie and his plant manager, Henry Clay Frick, were determined to break the power of the country's strongest union, the Amalgamated Association of Iron, Steel, and Tin Workers. Frick used a dispute over wages and work rules as an opportunity to close the plant (a "lockout") preparatory to reopening it with nonunion workers. When the union called a strike and refused to leave the plant (a "sitdown"), Frick called in 300 Pinkerton guards to oust them. A full-scale gun battle between strikers and Pinkertons erupted on July 6, leaving nine strikers and seven Pinkertons dead and scores wounded. Frick persuaded the governor to send in 8,000 militia to protect the strikebreakers, and the plant reopened.

PENNSYLVANIA MILITIA AT CARNEGIE'S HOMESTEAD STEEL MILL, 1892   After the shoot-out between striking workers and Pinkerton guards, the Pennsylvania militia reopened the mills and pro-tected strikebreakers from striking workers. This photograph shows the militia using steel beams manu-factured by the mill as a makeshift barricade.

THE DEPRESSION OF 1893–1897

By the 1890s the use of state militias to protect strikebreakers had become common. Events after 1893 brought an escalation of conflict. The most serious economic crisis since the depression of 1873–1878 was triggered by the Panic of 1893, a collapse of the stock market that plunged the economy into a severe four-year depression. The bankruptcy of the Reading Railroad and the National Cordage Company in early 1893 set off a process that by the end of the year had caused 491 banks and 15,000 other businesses to fail. By mid-1894 the unemployment rate had risen to more than 15 percent.

In Ohio, a reformer named Jacob Coxey conceived the idea of sending Congress a "living petition" of unemployed workers to press for appropriations to put them to work on road building and other public works. "Coxey's army" inspired other groups to hit the road and ride the rails to Washington during 1894. This descent of the unemployed on the capital provoked arrests by federal marshals and troops, and ended when Coxey and others were arrested for trespassing on the Capitol grounds.

THE PULLMAN STRIKE

Even more alarming to middle-class Americans was the Pullman strike of 1894. George M. Pullman had made a fortune in the manufacture of sleeping cars and other rolling stock for railroads. Workers in his large factory complex lived in the company town of Pullman just south of Chicago, where they enjoyed paved streets, clean parks, and decent houses rented from the company. But Pullman controlled every aspect of their lives, banned liquor from the town, and punished workers whose behavior did not suit his ideas of decorum. When the Panic of 1893 caused a sharp drop in orders for Pullman cars, the company laid off a third of its work force and cut wages for the rest by 30 percent. But it did not reduce rents in company houses or prices in company stores. Pullman refused to negotiate with a workers' committee, which called a strike and appealed to the American Railway Union (ARU) for help.

The Railway Union had been founded the year before by Eugene V. Debs. A native of Indiana, Debs had been elected secretary of the Brotherhood of Locomotive Firemen in 1875. By 1893 he had become convinced that the conservative stance of the railroad craft unions was contrary to the best interests of labor. So he formed the ARU to include all railroad workers in one union. When Pullman refused the ARU's offer to arbitrate the strike of Pullman workers, Debs launched a boycott by which ARU members would refuse to run any trains that included Pullman cars. When the railroads attempted to fire the ARU sympathizers, whole train crews went on strike. Rail traffic was paralyzed.

Over the protests of Governor John P. Altgeld of Illinois, President Grover Cleveland sent in federal troops. The U.S. attorney general also obtained a federal injunction against Debs under the Sherman Antitrust Act on grounds that the boycott and the strike were a conspiracy in restraint of trade. This creative use of the Sherman Act was upheld by the Supreme Court in 1895 and became a powerful weapon against labor unions.

For a week in July 1894 the Chicago railroad yards resembled a war zone. Millions of dollars of equipment went up in smoke. Thirty-four people were killed. Finally, state militia and federal troops restored order and broke the strike. Debs went to jail for six months.

The Pullman strike was only the most dramatic event of a year in which 750,000 workers went on strike and another 3 million were unemployed. But it was a surge of discontent from down on the farm that wrenched American politics off its foundations in the 1890s.

RETURNING TO ILLINOIS, 1894   This photograph shows one of the thousands of farm families who had moved into Kansas, Nebraska, and other plains states in the wet years of the 1870s and 1880s, only to give up during the dry years of the 1890s. Their plight added fuel to the fire of rural unrest and protest during those years.

FARMERS' MOVEMENTS

After the Civil War, farmers from the older states and immigrants from northern Europe poured into the territories and states of Dakota, Nebraska, Kansas, Texas, and—after 1889— Indian Territory. Some went on to the Pacific Coast states or stopped in the cattle-grazing and mining territories in between. This wave of settlement brought nine new states into the Union between 1867 and 1896 that almost equaled in total size all the states east of the Mississippi.

The vagaries of nature and weather were magnified in the West. Grasshopper plagues wiped out crops several times in the 1870s. Dry, searing summer winds alternated with violent hailstorms to scorch or level whole fields of wheat and corn. Winter blizzards intensified the isolation of farm families. Adding to these woes, the relatively wet years of the 1870s and early 1880s gave way to an abnormally dry cycle the following decade, causing many farmers to give up and return east.

Despite these problems, American grain production soared, increasing three times as fast as the American population from 1870 to 1890. Only rising exports could sustain such expansion in farm production. But by the 1880s the improved efficiency of large farms in eastern Europe brought intensifying competition and consequent price declines, especially for wheat. Prices on the world market fell about 60 percent from 1870 to 1895, while the wholesale price index for all commodities declined by 45 percent during the same period.

CREDIT AND MONEY

Victims of a world market largely beyond their control, farmers lashed out at targets nearer home: banks, commission merchants, railroads, and the monetary system. In truth, these institutions did victimize farmers, though not always intentionally. The long period of price deflation from 1865 to 1897, unique in American history, exacerbated the problem of credit. A price decline of 1 or 2 percent a year added that many points cumulatively to the nominal interest rate. If a farmer's main crop was wheat or cotton, whose prices declined even further, his real interest rate was that much greater.

The federal government's monetary policies worsened the problems of deflation. After the Civil War the Treasury's policy was to bring the greenback dollar to par with gold by reducing the amount of greenbacks in circulation. This limitation of the money supply produced deflationary pressures. Western farmers, who suffered from downward pressure on crop prices, were particularly vociferous in their protests against this situation, which introduced a new sectional conflict into politics—not North against South, but East against West. However, parity between greenbacks and gold would not be reached until 1879.

The benefits of parity were sharply debated then and remain controversial today. On the one hand, it strengthened the dollar, placed government credit on a firm footing, and helped create a financial structure for the remarkable economic growth that tripled the gross national product during the last quarter of the 19th century. On the other hand, the restraints on money supply hurt the rural economy in the South and West; they hurt debtors who found that deflation enlarged their debts by increasing the value of greenbacks; and they probably worsened the two major depressions of the era (1873–1878 and 1893–1897) by constraining credit.

THE GREENBACK AND SILVER MOVEMENTS

Many farmers in 1876 and 1880 supported the Greenback Party, whose platform called for the issuance of more U.S. Treasury notes (greenbacks). Even more popular was the movement for "free silver." Until 1873 government mints had coined both silver and gold dollars at a ratio of 16 to 1—that is, 16 ounces of silver were equal in value to one ounce of gold. However, when new discoveries of gold in the West after 1848 placed more gold in circulation relative to silver, that ratio undervalued silver, so that little was being sold for coinage. In 1873 Congress enacted a law, branded as "the Crime of 1873," that ended the coinage of silver dollars.

Soon after the law was passed, the production of new silver mines began to increase dramatically, which soon brought the price of silver below the old ratio of 16 to 1. Silver miners joined with farmers to demand remonetization of silver. In 1878 Congress responded by passing the Bland-Allison Act requiring the Treasury to purchase and coin not less than $2 million nor more than $4 million of silver monthly. Once again, silver dollars flowed from the mint. But the amounts issued did not absorb the increasing production of silver and did little, if anything, to slow deflation. The market price of silver dropped to a ratio of 20 to 1.

Pressure for "free silver"—that is, for government purchase of all silver offered for sale at a price of 16 to 1 and its coinage into silver dollars—continued through the 1880s. The admission of five new western states in 1889 and 1890 contributed to the passage of the Sherman Silver Purchase Act in 1890. That act increased the amount of silver coinage, but not at the 16-to-1 ratio. Even so, it went too far to suit the "gold bugs," who wanted to keep the United States on the international gold standard. President Cleveland blamed the Panic of 1893 on the Sherman

Silver Purchase Act, which caused a run on the Treasury's gold reserves triggered by uncertainty over the future of the gold standard. Cleveland called a special session of Congress in 1893 and persuaded it to repeal the Sherman Silver Purchase Act, setting the stage for the most bitter political contest in a generation.

THE FARMERS' ALLIANCE

Agrarian reformers supported the free silver movement, but many had additional grievances concerning problems of credit, railroad rates, and the exploitation of workers and farmers by the "money power." A new farmers' organization emerged in the 1880s. Starting in Texas as the Southern Farmers' Alliance, it expanded into other southern states and then into the North as well. By 1890 it had evolved into the National Farmers' Alliance and Industrial Union.

Reaching out to 2 million farm families, the Alliance set up marketing cooperatives. It served the social needs of farm families by bringing them together, especially in the sparsely settled regions of the West. It also gave farmers a sense of pride and solidarity to counter the image of "hick" and "hayseed."

The Farmers' Alliance developed a comprehensive political agenda. At a national convention in Ocala, Florida, in December 1890, it set forth these objectives: a graduated income tax; direct election of U.S. senators; free and unlimited coinage of silver at a ratio of 16 to 1; effective government control and, if necessary, ownership of railroad, telegraph, and telephone companies; and the establishment of "subtreasuries" (federal warehouses) for the storage of crops, with government loans at 2 percent interest on those crops. Of these goals, the most important was the setting up of "subtreasuries." Government storage would allow farmers to hold their crops until market prices were more favorable. Low-interest government loans on the value of these crops would enable farmers to pay their annual debts and thus escape the ruinous interest rates of the crop lien system in the South and bank mortgages in the West.

These were radical demands for the time. Nevertheless, most of them eventually became law: the income tax and the direct election of senators by constitutional amendments in 1913; government control of transportation and communications by various laws in the 20th century; and the "subtreasuries" in the form of the Commodity Credit Corporation in the 1930s.

Anticipating that the Republicans and the Democrats would resist these demands, many Alliancemen were eager to form a third party. In Kansas they had already done so, launching the People's Party (whose members were known as Populists) in 1890. But southerners opposed the idea of a third party. Most of them were Democrats who feared that a third party might open the way for the return of the Republican Party to power.

In 1890 farmers helped elect numerous state legislators and congressmen who pledged to support their cause. But the legislative results were thin. By 1892 many Alliance members were ready to take the third-party plunge.

THE RISE AND FALL OF THE PEOPLE'S PARTY

By 1892 the discontent of farmers in the West and South had reached the fever stage. Enthusiasm for a third party was particularly strong in the plains and mountain states. The most prominent leader of the Farmers' Alliance was Leonidas L. Polk of North Carolina. A Confederate veteran, Polk commanded support in the West as well as in the South. He undoubtedly would have been nominated for president by the newly organized People's Party had not death cut short his career in June 1892.

The first nominating convention of the People's Party met at Omaha a month later. The preamble of their platform expressed the grim mood of delegates. "We meet in the midst of a nation brought to the verge of moral, political, and material ruin," it declared. "The fruits of the toil of millions are boldly stolen to build up colossal fortunes for a few. . . . From the same prolific womb of governmental injustice we breed the two great classes—tramps and millionaires." The platform itself called for unlimited coinage of silver at 16 to 1; creation of the "subtreasury" program for crop storage and farm loans; government ownership of railroad, telegraph, and telephone companies; a graduated income tax; direct election of senators; and laws to protect labor unions against prosecution for strikes and boycotts. To ease the lingering tension between southern and western farmers, the party nominated Union veteran James B. Weaver of Iowa for president and Confederate veteran James G. Field of Virginia for vice president.

Despite winning 9 percent of the popular vote and 22 electoral votes, Populist leaders were shaken by the outcome. In the South most of the black farmers who were allowed to vote stayed with the Republicans. Democratic bosses in several southern states kept white farmers loyal to the party of white supremacy. Only in Alabama and Texas, among southern states, did the Populists get more than 20 percent of the vote. They did even less well in the older agricultural states of the Midwest, where the largest vote share they gained was 11 percent in Minnesota. Only in distressed wheat states like Kansas, Nebraska, and the Dakotas and in the silver states of the West did the Populists do well, carrying Kansas, Colorado, Idaho, and Nevada.

The party remained alive, however, and the anguish caused by the Panic of 1893 seemed to boost its prospects. In several western states, Populists or a Populist-Democratic coalition controlled state governments for a time, and a Populist-Republican coalition won the state elections of 1894 in North Carolina.

President Cleveland's success in getting the Sherman Silver Purchase Act repealed in 1893 drove a wedge into the Democratic Party. Southern and western Democrats turned against Cleveland. Senator Benjamin Tillman of South Carolina told his constituents: "When Judas betrayed Christ, his heart was not blacker than this scoundrel, Cleveland, in deceiving the Democracy. He is an old bag of beef and I am going to Washington with a pitchfork and prod him in his fat ribs."

THE SILVER ISSUE

Democratic dissidents stood poised to take over the party in 1896. They adopted free silver as the centerpiece of their program, raising the possibility of fusion with the Populists. Meanwhile, out of the West came a new and charismatic figure, a silver-tongued orator named William Jennings Bryan. Only 36 years old, Bryan came to the Democratic convention in 1896 as a delegate. Given the opportunity to make the closing speech in the debate on silver, he brought the house to its feet in a frenzy of cheering with his peroration: "You shall not press down upon the brow of labor this crown of thorns, you shall not crucify mankind upon a cross of gold."

This speech catapulted Bryan into the presidential nomination. He ran on a platform that not only endorsed free silver but also embraced the idea of an income tax, condemned trusts, and opposed the use of injunctions against labor. Bryan's nomination created turmoil in the People's Party. Though some Populists wanted to continue as a third party, most of them saw

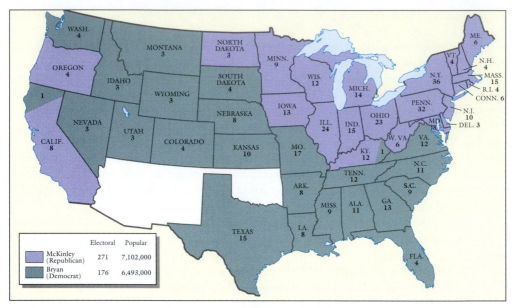

	Electoral	Popular
McKinley (Republican)	271	7,102,000
Bryan (Democrat)	176	6,493,000

PRESIDENTIAL ELECTION OF 1896

fusion with silver Democrats as the road to victory. At the Populist convention, the fusionists got their way and endorsed Bryan's nomination.

THE ELECTION OF 1896

The Republicans nominated William McKinley, who would have preferred to campaign on his specialty, the tariff. But Bryan made that impossible. Crisscrossing the country, Bryan gave as many as 30 speeches a day, focusing almost exclusively on the free silver issue. Republicans responded by denouncing the Democrats as irresponsible inflationists. Free silver, they said, would demolish the workingman's gains in real wages achieved over the preceding 30 years.

Under the skillful leadership of Mark Hanna, an Ohio businessman who became chairman of the Republican National Committee, McKinley waged a "front-porch campaign" in which various delegations visited his home in Canton, Ohio, to hear carefully crafted speeches that were widely publicized in the mostly Republican press. Hanna sent out an army of speakers and printed pamphlets in more than a dozen languages to reach immigrant voters. His propaganda portrayed Bryan as a wild man from the prairie whose monetary schemes would further wreck an economy that had been plunged into depression during a Democratic administration. McKinley's election, by contrast, would maintain the gold standard, revive business confidence, and end the depression.

The 1896 election was the most impassioned and exciting in a generation. Many Americans believed that the fate of the nation hinged on the outcome. The number of voters jumped by 15 percent over 1892. Republicans won a substantial share of the urban, immigrant, and labor vote with the slogan of McKinley as "the advance agent of prosperity." McKinley rode to a convincing victory by carrying every state in the northeast quadrant of the country. Bryan carried

CHRONOLOGY

1869	Knights of Labor founded
1873	"Crime of 1873" demonetizes silver
1877	Railroad strikes cost 100 lives and millions of dollars in damage
1878	Bland-Allison Act to remonetize silver passed over Hayes's veto
1879	Henry George publishes *Progress and Poverty*
1883	Railroads establish four standard time zones
1886	Knights of Labor membership crests at 700,000 • Haymarket riot causes antilabor backlash • American Federation of Labor founded
1887	Edward Bellamy publishes *Looking Backward* • Interstate Commerce Act creates the first federal regulatory agency
1890	Congress passes Sherman Antitrust Act • Congress passes Sherman Silver Purchase Act
1892	Homestead strike fails • Populists organize the People's Party
1893	Financial panic begins economic depression • Congress repeals Sherman Silver Purchase Act
1894	"Coxey's army" of the unemployed marches on Washington • Pullman strike paralyzes the railroads and provokes federal intervention
1896	William McKinley defeats William Jennings Bryan for the presidency

most of the rest. Republicans won decisive control of Congress as well as the presidency. They would maintain control for the next 14 years.

Whether by luck or by design, McKinley did prove to be the advance agent of prosperity. The economy pulled out of the depression during his first year in office and entered into a long period of growth—not because of anything the new administration did but because of the mysterious workings of the business cycle. With the discovery of rich new gold fields in the Yukon, in Alaska, and in South Africa, the silver issue lost potency and a cascade of gold poured into the world economy. The long deflationary trend since 1865 reversed itself in 1897. Farmers entered a new era of prosperity. Bryan ran against McKinley again in 1900 but lost even more emphatically. The nation seemed embarked on a placid sea of plenty. But below the surface, the currents of protest and reform still ran strong.

CONCLUSION

The 1890s were a major watershed in American history. On one side of that divide lay a largely rural society and agricultural economy. But the future belonged to the cities and to a commercial-industrial economy. Before the 1890s most immigrants had come from northern and western Europe and many became farmers. Then the principal origin of immigrants shifted to eastern and southern Europe and nearly all of them settled in cities. Before the 1890s the old sectional issues associated with slavery, the Civil War, and Reconstruction remained important forces in American politics; after 1900 racial issues would not play an important part in national politics for another 60 years. The election of 1896 ended 20 years of even balance between the two major parties and led to more than a generation of Republican dominance.

Most important of all, the social and political upheavals of the 1890s shocked many people into recognition that the liberty and equality they had taken for granted as part of the American dream was in danger of disappearing before the onslaught of wrenching economic changes. The strikes and violence and third-party protests of the decade were a wake-up call. As the forces of urbanization and industrialism continued to grow during the ensuing two decades, many middle-class Americans supported the enlargement of government power to carry out progressive reforms to cure the ills of an industrializing society.

AN INDUSTRIAL SOCIETY, 1890–1920

SOURCES OF ECONOMIC GROWTH ∼ "ROBBER BARONS" NO MORE

OBSESSION WITH PHYSICAL AND RACIAL FITNESS

IMMIGRATION ∼ BUILDING ETHNIC COMMUNITIES

AFRICAN AMERICAN LABOR AND COMMUNITY ∼ WORKERS AND UNIONS

THE JOYS OF THE CITY ∼ THE NEW SEXUALITY AND THE NEW WOMAN

With the collapse of populism in 1896 and the end of the depression in 1897, the American economy embarked on a remarkable stretch of growth. By 1910 America was unquestionably the world's greatest industrial power.

Corporations were changing the face of America. Their factories employed millions. Their production and management techniques became the envy of the industrialized world. A new kind of building—the skyscraper—came to symbolize America's corporate power. These modern towers were made possible by the use of steel rather than stone framework and by the invention of electrically powered elevators. Impelled upward by rising real estate values, they were intended to evoke the same sense of grandeur as Europe's medieval cathedrals. But these monuments celebrated man, not God; material wealth, not spiritual riches; science, not faith.

This chapter explores how the newly powerful corporations transformed America: how the jobs they generated attracted millions of European immigrants, southern blacks, and young single women to northern cities; and how they triggered an urban cultural revolution that made amusement parks, dance halls, vaudeville theater, and movies integral features of American life.

The power of the corporations dwarfed that of individual wage earners. But wage earners sought to limit corporate power through labor unions and strikes, or by organizing institutions of collective self-help within their own ethnic or racial communities. And significant numbers found opportunities and liberties they had not known before: Immigrant entrepreneurs invented ways to make money through legal and illegal enterprise; young, single, working-class women pioneered a sexual revolution; and radicals dared to imagine building a new society where no one suffered from poverty, inequality, and powerlessness.

SOURCES OF ECONOMIC GROWTH

A series of technological innovations in the late 19th century ignited the nation's economic engine. But technological breakthroughs alone do not fully explain the nation's spectacular economic boom. New corporate structures and new management techniques—in combination with the new technology—created the conditions that powered economic growth.

TECHNOLOGY

Two of the most important new technologies were the harnessing of electric power and the invention of the gasoline-powered internal combustion engine. Scientists had long been fascinated by electricity, but only in the late 19th century, through the work of Thomas Edison, George Westinghouse, and Nikola Tesla, did they produce the incandescent bulb that made electric lighting practical in homes and offices, and the alternating current (AC) that made electric transmission possible over long distances. Older industries switched from expensive and cumbersome steam power to more efficient and cleaner electrical power. The demand for electric generators and

INDUSTRIAL AMERICA, 1900–1920

related equipment brought into being new sectors of metalworking and machine-tool industries. Between 1900 and 1920 virtually every major city built electric-powered transit systems to replace horse-drawn trolleys and carriages. In New York City electricity made possible the construction of the first subways. Electric lighting gave cities a new allure. The public also fell in love with the movies, which depended on electricity for the projection of images onto a screen.

The first gasoline engine was patented in the United States in 1878, and the first "horseless carriages" began appearing on European and American roads in the 1890s. But few thought of them as serious rivals to trains and horses; rather, they were seen as playthings for the wealthy. Then, in 1908, Henry Ford unveiled his Model T: an unadorned, even homely car, but reliable enough to travel hundreds of miles without servicing and cheap enough to be affordable to most working Americans. In the ensuing 20 years, Americans bought Model T vehicles by the millions. The stimulus this insatiable demand gave to the economy can scarcely be exaggerated. Millions of cars required millions of pounds of steel alloys, glass, rubber, petroleum, and other material. Millions of jobs in coal and iron-ore mining, oil refining and rubber manufacturing, steelmaking and machine tooling, road construction and service stations came to depend on automobile manufacturing.

CORPORATE GROWTH

Successful inventions such as the automobile required more than the mechanical ingenuity and social vision of inventors like Henry Ford. Corporations with sophisticated organizational

CHANGE IN DISTRIBUTION OF THE AMERICAN WORKFORCE, 1870–1920

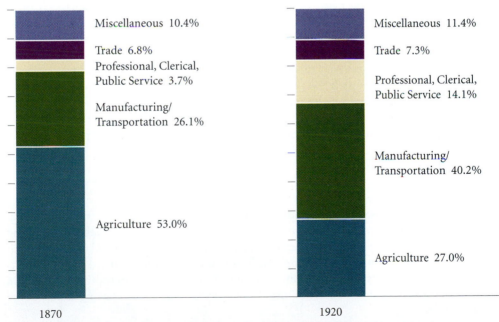

Miscellaneous 10.4%

Trade 6.8%

Professional, Clerical, Public Service 3.7%

Manufacturing/ Transportation 26.1%

Agriculture 53.0%

1870

Miscellaneous 11.4%

Trade 7.3%

Professional, Clerical, Public Service 14.1%

Manufacturing/ Transportation 40.2%

Agriculture 27.0%

1920

Source: Data from Alba Edwards, *Comparative Occupational Statistics for the United States 1870–1940*, U.S. Bureau of the Census, *Sixteenth Census of the United States, 1940, Population* (Washington, D.C., 1943).

and technical know-how were also required to mass-produce and mass-distribute the newly invented products. Corporations had played an important role in the nation's economic life since the 1840s, but in the late 19th and early 20th centuries they underwent significant changes.

The most obvious change was in their size. Delaware's DuPont Corporation, a munitions and chemical manufacturer, employed 1,500 workers in 1902 and 31,000 workers in 1920. Founded with a few hundred employees in 1903, the Ford Motor Company employed 33,000 at its Detroit Highland Park plant by 1916 and 42,000 by 1924.

This growth in scale was in part a response to the enormous size of the domestic market. By 1900 railroads provided the country with an efficient transportation system that allowed corporations to ship goods virtually anywhere in the United States. A national network of telegraph lines made it possible for buyers and sellers separated by thousands of miles to stay in constant communication. And the population, which was expanding rapidly, demonstrated an ever-growing appetite for goods and services.

Mass Production and Distribution

The size of this domestic market encouraged manufacturers to perfect mass-production techniques that increased the speed of production and lowered unit costs. Mass production required the coordination of machines to permit high-speed, uninterrupted production at every stage of the manufacturing process. Mass-production techniques had become widespread in basic steel manufacturing and sugar refining by the 1890s, and spread to the machine-tool industry and automobile manufacturing in the first two decades of the 20th century.

For such production techniques to be profitable, large quantities of output had to be sold. And although the domestic market offered a vast potential for sales, manufacturers often found that distribution systems were inadequate. This was the case with the North Carolina manufacturer of smoking tobacco, James Buchanan Duke. In 1885, Duke invested in several Bonsack cigarette machines, each of which manufactured 120,000 cigarettes a day. Then he advertised his product aggressively throughout the country. He also established regional sales offices so that his sales representatives could keep in touch with local jobbers and retailers. As the sales of cigarettes skyrocketed, more and more corporations sought to emulate Duke's techniques. Over the course of the next 20 years, the characteristics of American "big business" came to be defined by the corporations that were able to integrate mass production and mass distribution.

Corporate Consolidation

Corporate expansion also reflected a desire to avoid market instability. The rapid industrial growth of the late 19th century had proved deeply unsettling to industrialists. As promising economic opportunities arose, more and more industrialists sought to take advantage of them. But overexpansion and increasingly furious competition often turned rosy prospects into less-than-rosy results. Buoyant booms were quickly followed by bankrupting busts. Soon, corporations began looking for ways to insulate themselves from the harrowing course of the business cycle.

In tackling this problem, the railroads led the way. Rather than engaging in ruinous rate wars, railroads began cooperating. They shared information on costs and profits, established standardized rates, and allocated discrete portions of the freight business among themselves. These cooperative arrangements were variously called "pools," "cartels," or "trusts." The 1890 Sherman Antitrust Act declared such cartel-like practices illegal, but the law's enforcement proved to be short-lived (see Chapter 19). Still, the railroads' efforts rarely succeeded for long because they depended heavily on voluntary compliance.

Efforts by corporations to restrain competition and inject order into the economic environment continued unabated, however. Mergers now emerged as the favored instrument of control. By the 1890s powerful and sophisticated investment bankers, such as J. P. Morgan, possessed both the capital and the financial skills to engineer the complicated stock transfers and ownership renegotiations that mergers required. James Duke again led the way in 1890 when he and four competitors merged to form the American Tobacco Company.

The merger movement intensified as the depression of the 1890s lifted. In the years from 1898 to 1904, many of the corporations that would dominate American business throughout most of the 20th century acquired their modern form. The largest merger occurred in steel in 1901, when Andrew Carnegie and J. P. Morgan together fashioned the U.S. Steel Corporation from 200 separate iron and steel companies. U.S. Steel controlled 60 percent of the country's steelmaking capacity. Moreover, its ownership of 78 iron-ore boats and 1,000 miles of railroad gave it substantial control over the procurement of raw materials and the distribution of finished steel products.

REVOLUTION IN MANAGEMENT

The dramatic growth in the number and size of corporations revolutionized corporate management. The ranks of managers mushroomed, as elaborate corporate hierarchies defined both the status and the duties of individual managers. Increasingly, senior managers took over from owners the responsibility for long-term planning. Day-to-day operations were then placed in the hands of numerous middle managers who oversaw particular departments (purchasing, research, production, labor) in corporate headquarters, or who supervised regional sales offices, or directed particular factories. Middle managers also managed the people—accountants, clerks, foremen, engineers, salesmen—in these departments, offices, or factories. The rapid expansion within corporate managerial ranks created a new middle class, intensely loyal to their employers but at odds both with blue-collar workers and with the older middle class of shopkeepers, small businessmen, and independent craftsmen.

As management grew in importance, companies tried to make it more scientific. Firms introduced rigorous cost-accounting methods into departments (such as purchasing) charged with controlling the inflow of materials and the outflow of goods. Many corporations began requiring college or university training in science, engineering, or accounting for entry into middle management. Corporations that had built their success on a profitable invention or discovery sought to maintain their competitive edge by creating research departments and hiring professional scientists—those with Ph.D.'s from American or European universities—to come up with new technological and scientific breakthroughs.

SCIENTIFIC MANAGEMENT ON THE FACTORY FLOOR

The most controversial and, in some respects, the most ambitious effort to introduce scientific practices into management occurred in production. Managers sought optimal arrangements

THE WORLD'S FIRST AUTOMOBILE ASSEMBLY LINE   Introduced by Henry Ford at his Highland Park plant in 1913, this innovation cut production time on Ford Model Ts by an astounding 90 percent, allowing Ford to reduce the price of his cars by more than half and to double the hourly wages of his workers.

of machines and deployments of workers that would achieve the highest speed in production with the fewest human or mechanical interruptions. Some of these managers, such as Frederick Winslow Taylor, methodically examined every human task and mechanical movement involved in each production process. In "time-and-motion studies," they recorded every distinct movement a worker made in performing his or her job, how long it took, and how often it was performed. They hoped thereby to identify and eliminate wasted human energy. Eliminating waste might mean reorganizing an entire floor of machinery so as to reduce "down time" between production steps; it might mean instructing workers to perform their tasks differently; or it might mean replacing uncooperative skilled workers with machines tended by unskilled, low-wage laborers. Regardless of the method chosen, the goal was the same: to make human labor emulate the smooth and apparently effortless operation of an automatic, perfectly calibrated piece of machinery.

Taylor shared his vision widely in the early 20th century, first through speeches to fellow engineers and managers, and then through his writings. By the time he published *The Principles of Scientific Management* (1911), his ideas had already captivated countless corporate managers and engineers, many of whom sought to introduce "Taylorism" into their own production systems.

But the introduction of scientific management practices rarely proceeded easily. Time-and-motion studies were costly, and Taylor's formulas for increasing efficiency and reducing waste

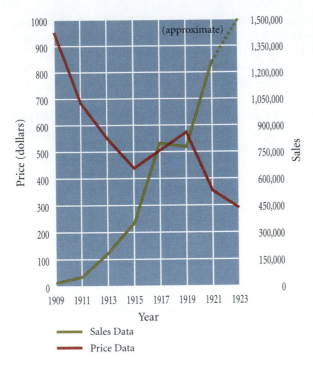

MODEL T PRICES AND SALES, 1909–1923

Source: From Alfred D. Chandler Jr., ed., *Giant Enterprise: Ford, General Motors, and the Automobile Industry* (New York: Harcourt, Brace and World, 1964), pp. 32–33.

were often far less scientific than he claimed. Taylor also overestimated the willingness of workers to play the mechanical role he assigned them. And the skilled workers and general foremen, whom Taylor sought to eliminate, used every available means of resistance. For these reasons, those managers and engineers who persisted in their efforts to apply scientific management invariably modified Taylor's principles.

Henry Ford led the way. His engineers initially adopted Taylorism wholeheartedly, with apparent success. By 1910 they had broken down automobile manufacturing into a series of simple, sequential tasks. Each worker performed only one task—adding a carburetor to an engine, inserting a windshield, mounting tires onto wheels. Then, in 1913 Ford's engineers introduced the first moving assembly line, a continuously moving conveyor belt that carried cars-in-production through each workstation. This innovation eliminated precious time previously wasted in transporting car parts (or partially built cars) by crane or truck from one work area to another. It also sharply limited the time available to workers to perform their assigned tasks.

The continuous assembly line allowed the potential of the factory's many other organizational and mechanical innovations to be fully realized. By 1913 the Ford Motor Company's new Highland Park plant was the most tightly integrated and continuously moving production system in manufacturing. The pace of production exceeded all expectations. A thousand Model Ts began rolling off the assembly line each day. This striking increase in the rate of production enabled Ford to slash the price of a Model T from $950 in 1909 to only $295 in 1923. The assembly line quickly became the most admired—and most feared—symbol of American mass production.

Problems immediately beset the system, however. Repeating a single motion all day long induced mental stupor, and managerial efforts to speed up the line produced physical exhaustion—both of which increased the incidence of error and injury. Some workers tried to organize a union to gain a voice in production matters. But most Ford workers expressed their dissatisfaction simply by quitting. By 1913 employee turnover at Highland Park had reached the astounding rate of 370 percent a year.

A problem of that magnitude demanded a dramatic solution. Ford provided it in 1914 by raising the wage he paid his assembly-line workers to $5 a day, double the average manufacturing wage then prevalent in American industry. The result: Workers, especially young and single men, flocked to Detroit.

Taylor himself had believed that improved efficiency would lead to dramatic wage gains. With his decision to raise wages, Ford was being true to Taylor's principles. But Ford went even further in his innovations. He set up a sociology department, forerunner of the personnel department, to collect job, family, and other information about his employees. He offered his employees housing subsidies, medical care, and other benefits. In short, Ford recognized that workers were more complex than Taylor had allowed, and that high wages alone would not transform them into the perfectly functioning parts of the mass-production system that Taylor had envisioned.

Ford's success impelled others to move in his direction. But it would take time for modern management to come of age. Not until the 1920s did a substantial number of corporations establish personnel departments, institute welfare and recreational programs for employees, and hire psychologists to improve human relations in the workplace.

"ROBBER BARONS" NO MORE

Innovations in corporate management were part of a broader effort among elite industrialists to shed their "robber baron" image. The swashbuckling entrepreneurs of the 19th century—men like Cornelius Vanderbilt, Jay Gould, and Leland Stanford—had wielded their economic power brashly and ruthlessly, while lavishing money on European-style palaces, private yachts, personal art collections, and extravagant entertainments. But the depression of the 1890s shook the confidence of the members of this elite. The anarchist Alexander Berkman's 1892 attempt to assassinate Henry Clay Frick, Andrew Carnegie's right-hand man, by marching into his office and shooting him at point-blank range (Frick survived), terrified industrialists. Although such physical assaults were rare, anger over ill-gotten and ill-spent wealth was widespread.

Seeking a more favorable image, some industrialists began to restrain their displays of wealth and use their private fortunes to advance the public welfare. As early as 1889 Andrew Carnegie had advocated a "gospel of wealth." The wealthy, he believed, should consider all income in excess of their needs as a "trust fund" for their communities. By the time he died in 1919, he had given away or entrusted to several Carnegie foundations 90 percent of his fortune. Among the projects he funded were New York's Carnegie Hall, Pittsburgh's Carnegie Institute (now Carnegie-Mellon University), and 2,500 public libraries throughout the country.

Other industrialists, including John D. Rockefeller, soon followed Carnegie's lead. Rockefeller's ruthless business methods in assembling the Standard Oil Company and in crushing his competition made him one of the most reviled of the robber barons. In the wake of the federal

Leading Industrialist Philanthropic Foundations, 1905–1930

Foundation	Date of Origin	Original Endowment
Buhl Foundation	1927	$10,951,157
Carnegie Corporation of New York	1911	125,000,000
Carnegie Endowment for International Peace	1910	10,000,000
Carnegie Foundation for the Advancement of Teaching	1905	10,000,000
Carnegie Institution of Washington	1902	10,000,000
Duke Endowment	1924	40,000,000
John Simon Guggenheim Memorial Foundation	1925	3,000,000
W. K. Kellogg Foundation	1930	21,600,000
Rockefeller Foundation	1913	100,000,000
Rosenwald Fund	1917	20,000,000
Russell Sage Foundation	1907	10,000,000

Source: Joseph C. Kiger, *Operating Principles of the Larger Foundations* (New York: Russell Sage Foundation, 1957), p. 122.

government's prosecution of Standard Oil for monopolistic practices in 1906, Rockefeller transformed himself into a public-spirited philanthropist. Through the Rockefeller Foundation, which was officially incorporated in 1913, he had dispersed an estimated $500 million by 1919. His most significant gifts included money to establish the University of Chicago and the Rockefeller Institute for Medical Research (later renamed Rockefeller University).

Obsession with Physical and Racial Fitness

The fractious events of the 1890s also induced many wealthy Americans to engage in what Theodore Roosevelt dubbed "the strenuous life." In an 1899 essay with that title, Roosevelt exhorted Americans to live vigorously, to test their physical strength and endurance in competitive athletics, and to experience nature through hiking, hunting, and mountain climbing. He articulated a way of life that influenced countless Americans from a variety of classes and cultures.

The 1890s were indeed a time of heightened enthusiasm for competitive sports, physical fitness, and outdoor recreation. Millions of Americans began riding bicycles and eating healthier foods. A passion for athletic competition gripped American universities. The power and violence of football helped make it the sport of choice at the nation's elite campuses. In athletic competition, as in nature, one could discover and recapture one's manhood, one's virility. The words "sissy" and "pussyfoot" entered common usage in the 1890s as insults hurled at men whose masculinity was found wanting.

Ironically, this quest for masculinity had a liberating effect on women. In the vigorous new climate of the 1890s, young women began to engage in sports and other activities long considered too manly for "the fragile sex." They put away their corsets and long dresses and began wearing simple skirts, shirtwaists, and other clothing that gave them more comfort and freedom of movement.

In the country at large the new enthusiasm for athletics and the outdoor life reflected a widespread dissatisfaction with the growing regimentation of industrial society. But among wealthy Americans, the quest for physical superiority reflected a deeper and more ambiguous anxiety: These Americans worried about their *racial* fitness. Most of them were native-born Americans whose families had lived in the United States for several generations and whose ancestors had come from the British Isles, the Netherlands, or some other region of northwestern Europe. They liked to attribute their success and good fortune to their "racial superiority." They saw themselves as "natural" leaders, members of a noble Anglo-Saxon race endowed with uncommon intelligence, imagination, and discipline. But events of the 1890s had challenged the legitimacy of the elite's wealth and authority, and the ensuing depression mocked their ability to exert economic leadership. The immigrant masses laboring in factories, despite their poverty and alleged racial inferiority, seemed to possess a vitality that the "superior" Anglo-Saxons lacked.

Some rich Americans reacted to the immigrants' vigor and industry by calling for a halt to further immigration. But that would not do for the ebullient Roosevelt, who argued instead for a return to fitness, superiority, and numerical predominance of the Anglo-Saxon race. He called on American men to live the strenuous life and on women to devote themselves to reproduction. The only way to avoid "race suicide," he declared, was for every Anglo-Saxon mother to have at least four children.

Such racialist thought was not limited to wealthy elites. Many other Americans, from a variety of classes and regions, also thought that all people demonstrated the characteristics of their race. Racial stereotypes were used to describe not only blacks, Asians, and Hispanics, but Italians ("violent"), Jews ("nervous"), and Slavs and Poles ("slow"). Such aspersions flowed as easily from the pens of compassionate reformers, such as Jacob Riis, who wanted to help the immigrants, as from the pens of bitter reactionaries, such as Madison Grant, who argued in *The Passing of the Great Race* (1916) that America should rid itself of inferior races.

SOCIAL DARWINISM

Racialist thinking even received "scientific" sanction from distinguished biologists and anthropologists, who believed that racially inherited traits explained variations in the economic, social, and cultural lives of ethnic and racial groups. For a large number of the nation's intellectuals, human society developed according to the "survival of the fittest" principle articulated by the English naturalist Charles Darwin to describe plant and animal evolution. Human history could be understood in terms of an ongoing struggle among races, with the strongest and the fittest invariably triumphing. The wealth and power of the Anglo-Saxon race was ample testimony, in this view, to its superior fitness.

This view, which would become known as "Social Darwinism," was rooted in two developments of the late 19th century, one intellectual and one socioeconomic. Intellectually, it reflected a widely shared belief that human society operated according to principles every bit as scientific as those governing the natural world. The social sciences—economics, political science, anthropology, sociology, psychology—took shape in the late 19th century, each trying to discover the scientific laws governing individual and group behavior. Awed by the accomplishments of natural scientists, social scientists were prone to exaggerate the degree to which social life mimicked natural life; hence the appeal of Social Darwinism.

Social Darwinism was also rooted in the unprecedented interpenetration of the world's economies and peoples. Cheap and rapid ocean travel had bound together continents as never before. International trade, immigration, and imperial conquest made Americans more conscious of the variety of peoples inhabiting the earth. Although awareness of diversity sometimes encourages tolerance and cooperation, in the economically depressed years of the late 19th century, it encouraged intolerance and suspicion, fertile soil for the cultivation of Social Darwinism.

IMMIGRATION

Perhaps the most dramatic evidence of the nation's growing involvement in the international economy was the high rate of immigration. The United States had always been a nation of immigrants, but never had so many come in so short a time. Between 1880 and 1920, some 23 million immigrants came to a country that numbered only 76 million in 1900. In many cities of the Northeast and Midwest, immigrants and their children comprised a majority of the population. Everywhere in the country, except in the South, the working class was overwhelmingly ethnic.

European immigration accounted for approximately three-fourths of the total. Some states received significant numbers of non-European immigrants—Chinese, Japanese, and Filipinos in California; Mexicans in California and the Southwest; and French Canadians in New England—whose presence profoundly affected regional economies, politics, and culture. But their numbers, relative to the number of European immigrants, were small.

Most of the European immigrants who arrived between 1880 and 1914 came from eastern and southern Europe. Among them were 3 to 4 million Italians, 2 million Russian and Polish Jews, 2 million Hungarians, an estimated 4 million Slavs (including Poles, Bohemians, Slovaks, Russians, Ukrainians, Bulgarians, Serbians, Croatians, Slovenians, Montenegrins, and Macedonians), and 1 million from Lithuania, Greece, and Portugal. Hundreds of thousands came as well from Turkey, Armenia, Lebanon, Syria, and other Near Eastern lands abutting the European continent.

These post-1880 arrivals were called "new immigrants" to underscore the cultural gap separating them from the "old immigrants," who had come from northwestern Europe—Great Britain, Scandinavia, and Germany. "Old immigrants" were regarded as racially fit, culturally sophisticated, and politically mature. The "new immigrants," by contrast, were often regarded as racially inferior, culturally impoverished, and incapable of assimilating American values and traditions. This negative view of the "new immigrants" reflected in part a fear of their alien languages, religions, and economic backgrounds. Few spoke English. Most adhered to Catholicism, Greek Orthodoxy, or Judaism rather than Protestantism. And most, with the exception of the Jews, were peasants, unaccustomed to urban industrial life.

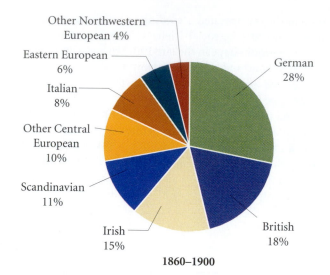

Other Northwestern European 4%
Eastern European 6%
Italian 8%
Other Central European 10%
Scandinavian 11%
Irish 15%
British 18%
German 28%

1860–1900

SOURCES OF IMMIGRATION

Source: Data from *Historical Statistics of the United States, Colonial Times to 1970* (White Plains, N.Y.: Kraus International, 1989), pp. 105–109.

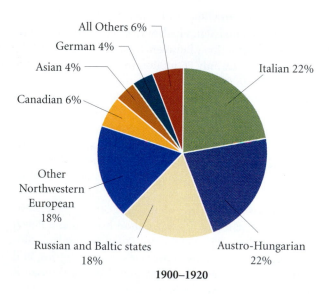

All Others 6%
German 4%
Asian 4%
Canadian 6%
Other Northwestern European 18%
Russian and Baltic states 18%
Austro-Hungarian 22%
Italian 22%

1900–1920

CAUSES OF IMMIGRATION

In fact, the "old" and "new" European immigrants were more similar than different. Both came to America for the same reasons: either to flee religious or political persecution or to escape economic hardship. It is true that the United States attracted a small but steady stream of political refugees throughout the 19th century. Many of these people possessed unusual talents as skilled workers, labor organizers, political agitators, and newspaper editors and thus exercised considerable influence in their ethnic communities. However, only the anti-Semitic policies of Russia in the late 19th and early 20th centuries triggered a mass emigration (in this case Jewish) of political refugees.

Most mass immigration was propelled instead by economic hardship. Europe's rural population was growing at a faster rate than the land could support. European factories absorbed some, but not all, of the rural surplus. And industrialization and urbanization were affecting the European countryside in ways that disrupted rural ways of life. As railroads penetrated the countryside, village artisans found themselves unable to compete with the cheap manufactured goods that arrived from city factories. These handicraftsmen were among the first to emigrate. Meanwhile, rising demand for food in the cities accelerated the growth of commercial agriculture in the hinterland. Some peasant families lost their land. Others turned to producing crops for the market, only to discover that they could not compete with larger, more efficient producers. In addition, by the last third of the 19th century, peasants faced competition from North American farmers. Prices for agricultural commodities plummeted everywhere. The economic squeeze that spread distress among American farmers in the 1880s and 1890s caused even more hardship among Europe's peasantry. These were the circumstances that triggered mass emigration.

PATTERNS OF IMMIGRATION

An individual's or family's decision to emigrate often depended on having a contact—a family member, relative, or fellow villager—already established in an American city. These were people who provided immigrants with a destination, with inspiration (they were examples of success in America), with advice about jobs, and with financial aid. Sometimes whole villages in southern Italy or western Russia—or at least all the young men—seemed to disappear, only to reappear in a certain section of Chicago, Pittsburgh, or New York.

A majority of immigrants viewed their trip to the United States as a temporary sojourn. They came not in search of permanent settlement but in search of the high wages that would enable them to improve their economic standing in their homeland. For them, America was a land of economic opportunity, not a land to call home. This attitude explains why men vastly outnumbered women and children in the migration stream. Some had left wives and children behind; more were single. Most wanted merely to make enough money to buy a farm in their native land. And, true to their dream, many did return home.

The rate of return was negligible among certain groups, however. Jews had little desire to return to the religious persecution they had fled. Most came as families, intending to make America their permanent home. Only 5 percent of them returned home. The rate of return was also low among the Irish, who saw few opportunities in their long-suffering (though much-loved) Emerald Isle. But in the early 20th century, such groups were exceptional. Most immigrants looked forward to returning to Europe.

Immigration tended to move in rhythm with the U.S. business cycle. It rose in boom years and fell off during depressions. It remained at a high level during the first 14 years of the new century when the U.S. economy was experiencing a period of sustained growth, broken only by the brief Panic of 1907–1908.

IMMIGRANT LABOR

In the first decade of the 20th century, immigrant men and their male children built the nation's railroads and tunnels; mined its coal, iron ore, and other minerals; stoked its hot and sometimes deadly steel furnaces; and slaughtered and packed its meat in Chicago's putrid packinghouses. In 1909 first- and second-generation immigrants comprised more than 96 percent of the labor force that built and maintained the nation's railroads. Of the 750,000 Slovaks who arrived in America before 1913, at least 600,000 headed for the coal mines and steel mills of western Pennsylvania. The steel mills of Pittsburgh, Buffalo, Cleveland, and Chicago attracted disproportionately large numbers of Poles and other Slavs as well.

Immigrants also performed "lighter" but no less arduous work. Jews and Italians predominated in garment manufacturing shops. In 1900 French Canadian immigrants and their children held one of every two jobs in New England's cotton textile industry. By 1920 the prosperity of California's rapidly growing agricultural industry depended primarily on Mexican and Filipino labor. In these industries, immigrant women and children, who worked for lower wages than men, formed a large part of the labor force.

Immigrants were as essential as fossil fuels to the smooth operation of the American economic machine. Sometimes, however, the "machine" consumed workers as well as coal and oil. Those who worked in heavy industry, mining, or railroading were especially vulnerable to accident and injury. Between the years 1906 and 1911, almost one-quarter of the recent immigrants employed at the U.S. Steel Corporation's South Works (Pittsburgh) were injured or killed on the job. Lax attention to safety rendered even light industry hazardous and sometimes fatal. In 1911 a fire broke out on an upper floor of the Triangle Shirtwaist Company, a New York City garment factory. The building had no fire escapes. The owners of the factory, moreover, had locked the entrances to each floor as a way of keeping their employees at work. A total of 146 workers perished in the fire or from desperate nine-story leaps to the pavement below.

Chronic fatigue and inadequate nourishment increased the risk of accident and injury. Workweeks averaged 60 hours—10 hours every day except Sunday. Workers who were granted

TRIANGLE SHIRTWAIST COMPANY FIRE   In 1911, a fire at the Triangle Shirtwaist Company in New York City claimed the lives of 146 workers, most of them young Jewish and Italian women. Many died because they could not escape the flames. There were no fire escapes and their employer had locked the entrances to each floor. The tragedy spurred the growth of unions and the movement for factory reform in New York.

Saturday afternoons off considered themselves fortunate. Steelworkers were not so lucky. They labored from 72 to 89 hours a week, and were required to work one 24-hour shift every two weeks.

Most workers had to labor long hours simply to eke out a meager living. In 1900 the annual earnings of American manufacturing workers averaged only $400 to $500 a year. Skilled workers who held higher-paying jobs earned far more than those doing comparable work in Europe. In theory, such well-paid work offered immigrants their greatest opportunities. But most of these jobs were held by Yankees and by the Germans, Irish, Welsh, and other Europeans who had come as part of the "old immigration." Through their unions, workers of northern European extraction also controlled access to new jobs that opened up and usually managed to fill them with a son, relative, or fellow countryman. Consequently, relatively few of the "new immigrants" rose into the prosperous ranks of skilled labor.

From the 1870s to 1910 real wages paid to factory workers and common laborers did rise, but not steadily. Wages fell sharply during depressions. And the hope for sharp increases during periods of recovery collapsed under the weight of renewed mass immigration, which brought hundreds of thousands of new job seekers into the labor market.

Most working families required two or three wage earners to survive. If a mother could not go out to work because there were small children at home, she might rent rooms to some of the many single men who had recently immigrated. But economic security was hard to attain. In his book, *Poverty,* published in 1904, the social investigator Robert Hunter conservatively estimated that 20 percent of the industrial population of the North lived in poverty.

LIVING CONDITIONS

Strained economic circumstances confined many working-class families to cramped and dilapidated living quarters. Many of them lived in two- or three-room apartments, with several sleeping in each room. The lack of windows in city tenements allowed little light or air into these apartments, and few had their own toilets or running water. Crowding was endemic. Overcrowding and poor sanitation resulted in high rates of deadly infectious diseases, especially diphtheria, typhoid fever, and pneumonia.

By 1900 this crisis in urban living had begun to yield to the insistence of urban reformers that cities adopt housing codes and improve sanitation. Between 1880 and 1900, housing inspectors condemned the worst of the tenements and ordered landlords to make certain minimal improvements. City governments built reservoirs, pipes, and sewers to carry clean water to the tenements and to carry away human waste. Newly paved roads lessened the dirt, mud, and stagnant pools of water and thus further curtailed the spread of disease. As a result, urban mortality rates fell in the 1880s and 1890s. Nevertheless, improvements came far more slowly to the urban poor than they did to the middle and upper classes.

BUILDING ETHNIC COMMUNITIES

The immigrants may have been poor, but they were not helpless. Migration itself had required a good deal of resourcefulness, self-help, and mutual aid—assets that survived in the new surroundings of American cities.

A NETWORK OF INSTITUTIONS

Each ethnic group quickly established a network of institutions that gave it a sense of community and multiplied the sources of communal assistance. Some people simply reproduced those institutions that had been important to them in the "Old Country." The devout established churches and synagogues. Lithuanian, Jewish, and Italian radicals reestablished Old World socialist and anarchist organizations. Irish nationalists set up clandestine chapters of the Clan Na Gael to keep alive the struggle to free Ireland from the English. Germans felt at home in their traditional *Turnevereins* (athletic clubs) and musical societies.

Immigrants developed new institutions as well. In the larger cities, foreign-language newspapers disseminated news, advice, and culture. Each ethnic group created fraternal societies to bring together immigrants who had known each other in the Old Country, or who shared the same craft, or who had come from the same town or region. Most of these societies provided members with a death benefit (ranging from a few hundred to a thousand dollars) that guaranteed the deceased a decent burial and the family a bit of cash. Some fraternal societies made small loans as well. Among those ethnic groups that prized home ownership, especially the Slavic groups, the fraternal societies also provided mortgage money. And all of them served as centers of sociability—places to have a drink, play cards, or simply relax with fellow countrymen.

THE EMERGENCE OF AN ETHNIC MIDDLE CLASS

Within each ethnic group, a sizable minority directed their talents and ambitions to economic gain. Some of these entrepreneurs first addressed their communities' needs for basic goods and services. Immigrants preferred to buy from fellow countrymen with whom they shared a language, a history, and presumably a bond of trust. Enterprising individuals responded by opening dry goods stores, food shops, butcher shops, and saloons in their ethnic neighborhoods. Those who could not afford to rent a store hawked their fruit, clothing, or dry goods from portable stands, wagons, or sacks carried on their back. The work was endless, the competition tough. Although many of these small businesses failed, enough survived to give some immigrants and their children a toehold in the middle class.

Other immigrants turned to industry, particularly the garment industry, truck farming, and construction. A clothing manufacturer needed only a few sewing machines to become competitive. Many Jewish immigrants, having been tailors in Russia and Poland, opened such facilities. Competition among these small manufacturers was fierce, and work environments were condemned by critics as "sweatshops": inadequate lighting, heat, and ventilation; 12-hour workdays and 70-hour workweeks during peak seasons, with every hour spent bent over a sewing machine; poor pay and no employment security, especially for the women and children who made up a large part of this labor force. Even at this level of exploitation, many small manufacturers failed. But over time, a good many of them managed to firm up their position as manufacturers and to evolve into stable, responsible employers. Their success contributed to the emergence of a Jewish middle class.

The story was much the same in urban construction, where Italians who had established themselves as labor contractors, or *padroni,* went into business for themselves to take advantage of the rapid expansion of American cities. Though few became general contractors on major downtown projects, many of them did well building family residences or serving as subcontractors on larger buildings.

Japanese Farmers on a Texas Seed Rice Farm, circa 1910 Unlike most immigrants of the early 20th century, Japanese immigrants found a niche in agriculture and used it as a route to middle-class status and income.

In southern California, Japanese immigrants chose agriculture as their route to the middle class. Working as agricultural laborers in the 1890s, they began to acquire their own land in the early years of the 20th century. Altogether, they owned only 1 percent of California's total farm acreage, but their specialization in fresh vegetables and fruits (particularly strawberries), combined with their labor-intensive agricultural methods (with family members supplying the labor), was yielding $67 million in annual revenues by 1919. That was one-tenth of the total revenue generated by California agriculture that year. Japanese farmers sold their produce to Japanese fruit and vegetable wholesalers in Los Angeles, who had chosen a mercantile route to middle-class status.

Each ethnic group created its own history of economic success and social mobility. From the emerging middle classes came many leaders who would provide their ethnic groups with identity, legitimacy, and power and would lead the way toward Americanization and assimilation. Their children tended to do better in school than the children of working-class ethnics, and academic success served as a ticket to upward social mobility in a society that depended more and more on university-trained engineers, managers, lawyers, doctors, and other professionals.

Political Machines and Organized Crime

The underside of this success story could be seen in the rise of government corruption and organized crime. Some ethnic entrepreneurs looked beyond their usual support networks and accepted the help of those who promised to ensure their economic survival. Sometimes the help came from honest unions and upright government officials, but sometimes it did not. Unions were generally weak, and some government officials were susceptible to bribery. Economic necessity became a breeding ground for government corruption and greed. A contractor eager to win a city contract would find it necessary to "pay off" government officials who could throw the contract his way. By 1900 such payments, referred to as graft, had become essential to the day-to-day operation of government in most large cities. The graft, in turn, made local officeholding a rich source of economic gain. Politicians began building political organizations called machines to guarantee their success in municipal elections. The machine "bosses" won the loyalty of urban voters—especially immigrants—by providing poor neighborhoods with paved roads and sewer systems. They helped newly arrived immigrants to get jobs (often on city payrolls) and occasionally provided food, fuel, or clothing to families in dire need.

The bosses who ran the political machines—including "King Richard" Croker in New York, James Michael Curley in Boston, Tom Pendergast in Kansas City, Martin Behrman in New Orleans, and Abe Ruef in San Francisco—served their own needs first. They saw to it that construction contracts went to those who offered the most graft, not to those who were likely to do the best job. They protected gamblers, pimps, and other purveyors of urban vice who contributed large amounts to their machine coffers. And they engaged in widespread election fraud: rounding up truckloads of newly arrived immigrants and paying them to vote a certain way; having their supporters vote two or three times; and stuffing ballot boxes with the votes of phantom citizens who had died, moved away, or never been born.

Big city machines, then, were both a positive and negative force in urban life. Reformers despised them for disregarding election laws and encouraging vice. Immigrants valued them for providing social welfare services and for creating opportunities for upward mobility.

The history of President John F. Kennedy's family offers a compelling example of the economic and political opportunities opened up by machine politics. Both of Kennedy's grandfathers, John Francis ("Honey Fitz") Fitzgerald and Patrick Joseph Kennedy, were the children of penniless Irish immigrants who arrived in Boston in the 1840s. Fitzgerald was the more talented of the two, excelling at academics and winning a coveted place in Harvard's Medical School. But Fitzgerald left Harvard that same year, choosing a career in politics instead. Between 1891 and 1905 he served as a Boston city councillor, Massachusetts state congressman and senator, U.S. congressman, and mayor of Boston. For much of this period, he derived considerable income and power from his position as the North End ward boss.

Patrick Kennedy, a tavern owner and liquor merchant in East Boston, became an equally important figure behind the scenes in Boston city politics. In addition to running the Democratic Party's affairs in Ward Two, he served on the Strategy Board, a secret council of Boston's machine politicians that met regularly to devise policies, settle disputes, and divide up the week's graft. Both Fitzgerald and Kennedy derived a substantial income from their political work and used it to lift their families into middle-class prosperity. Kennedy's son (and the future president's father), Joseph P. Kennedy, would go on to make a fortune as a Wall Street speculator and liquor distributor. But his rapid economic and social ascent had been made possible by his father's and father-in-law's earlier success in Boston machine politics.

Underworld figures, too, influenced urban life. In the early years of the 20th century, gangsterism was a scourge of Italian neighborhoods, where Sicilian immigrants had established outposts of the notorious Mafia, and in Irish, Jewish, Chinese, and other ethnic communities as well. Favorite targets of these gangsters were small-scale manufacturers and contractors, who were threatened with violence and economic ruin if they did not pay a gang for "protection." Gangsters enforced their demands with physical force, beating up or killing those who failed to abide by the "rules." By the 1920s petty extortion had escalated in urban areas, and underworld crime had become big business. Al Capone, the ruthless Chicago mobster who made a fortune from gambling, prostitution, and bootleg liquor during Prohibition, once claimed: "Prohibition is a business. All I do is to supply a public demand. I do it in the best and least harmful way I can." Mobsters like Capone were charismatic figures, both in their ethnic communities and in the nation at large. Few immigrants, however, followed their criminal path to economic success.

AFRICAN AMERICAN LABOR AND COMMUNITY

Unlike immigrants, African Americans remained a predominately rural and southern people in the early 20th century. Most blacks were sharecroppers and tenant farmers. The markets for cotton and other southern crops had stabilized in the early 20th century, but black farmers remained vulnerable to exploitation. Landowners often forced sharecroppers to accept artificially low prices for their crops. At the same time, they charged high prices for seed, tools, and groceries at the local stores that they controlled. Few rural areas generated enough business to support more than one store, or to create a competitive climate that might force prices down. Those sharecroppers who traveled elsewhere to sell their crops or purchase their necessities risked retaliation. Thus, most remained beholden to their landowners, mired in poverty and debt.

Some African Americans sought a better life by migrating to industrial areas of the South and the North. In the South, they worked in iron and coal mines, in furniture and cigarette manufacture, as railroad track layers and longshoremen, and as laborers in the steel mills of Birmingham, Alabama. By the early 20th century, their presence was growing in the urban North as well, where they worked as janitors, elevator operators, teamsters, longshoremen, and servants of various kinds. Altogether, about 200,000 blacks left the South for the North and West between 1890 and 1910.

In southern industries, blacks were subjected to hardships and indignities that even the newest immigrants were not expected to endure. Railroad contractors in the South, for example, treated their black track layers like prisoners. Armed guards marched them to work in the morning and back at night. Track layers were paid only once a month and forced to purchase food at the company commissary, where the high prices claimed most of what they earned. Other employers of black laborers in the South usually did not discipline their workers so severely, but they did isolate them in the dirtiest and most grueling jobs. The "Jim Crow" laws passed by every southern state legislature in the 1890s legalized this rigid separation of the black and white races (see Chapter 18).

Although northern states did not pass Jim Crow laws, the nation's worsening racial climate adversely affected southern blacks who had come north. Industrialists generally refused to hire black migrants for manufacturing jobs, preferring the labor of European immigrants. Only when those immigrants went on strike did employers turn to African Americans.

African Americans who had long resided in northern urban areas also experienced intensifying discrimination in the late 19th and early 20th centuries. In 1870 about a third of the black men in many northern cities had been skilled tradesmen: blacksmiths, painters, shoemakers, and carpenters. But by 1910 only 10 percent of black men made a living in this way. In many cities, the number of barber shops and food catering businesses owned by blacks also went into sharp decline, as did black representation in the ranks of restaurant and hotel waiters. These barbers, food caterers, and waiters had formed a black middle class whose livelihood depended on the patronage of white clients. By the early 20th century, this middle class had been dissipated, the victim of growing racism. Whites were no longer willing to engage the services of blacks, preferring to have their hair cut, beards shaved, food prepared and served by European immigrants. The residential segregation of northern blacks also rose in these years.

Thus, blacks in the North at the turn of the 20th century had to cope with a marked deterioration in their working and living conditions. But they did not lack for resourcefulness. Urban blacks laced their communities with the same array of institutions—churches, fraternal societies, political organizations—that solidified ethnic neighborhoods. A new black middle class arose, comprised of ministers, professionals, and businesspeople who serviced the needs of their racial group. Black-owned realties, funeral homes, doctors' offices, newspapers, groceries, restaurants, and bars opened for business on the commercial thoroughfares of African American neighborhoods. Nevertheless, community-building remained a tougher task among African Americans than among immigrants. Black communities were often smaller and poorer than their white ethnic counterparts; economic opportunities were fewer, and the chance of gaining power or wealth through municipal politics almost nonexistent. Yet, some black entrepreneurs succeeded despite these odds. Madame C. J. Walker, for example, built a lucrative business from the hair and skin lotions she devised and sold to black customers throughout the country. In many cities, African American real estate agents achieved significant wealth and power. Still, most black businessmen could not overcome the obstacles posed by racial prejudice. Thus, the African American middle class remained smaller and more precarious than did its counterpart in ethnic communities, less able to lead the way toward affluence and assimilation.

WORKERS AND UNIONS

Middle-class success eluded most immigrants and blacks in the years prior to the First World War. Even among Jews, whose rate of social mobility was rapid, most immigrants were working class. For most workers, the path toward a better life lay in the improvement of working conditions, not in escape from the working class. Henry Ford's offering of the $5-a-day wage in 1914, double the average manufacturing wage, raised the hopes of many. But in the early decades of the century few other manufacturers were prepared to follow Ford's lead, and most factory workers remained in a fragile economic state.

SAMUEL F. GOMPERS AND THE AFL

For those workers, the only hope for economic improvement lay in organizing unions powerful enough to wrest wage concessions from reluctant employers. This was not an easy task. Federal and state governments, time and again, had shown themselves ready to use military force to break strikes. The courts, following the lead of the U.S. Supreme Court, repeatedly found unions in violation of the Sherman Antitrust Act, even though that act had been intended to control corporations, not unions. Judges in most states usually granted employer requests for injunctions—court orders that barred striking workers from picketing their place of employment (and thus from obstructing employer efforts to hire replacement workers). And prior to 1916 no federal laws protected the right of workers to organize or required employers to bargain with the unions to which their workers belonged.

This hostile legal environment retarded the growth of unions from the 1890s through the 1930s. It also made the major labor organization of those years, the American Federation of

Labor (AFL), more timid and conservative than it had been prior to the depression of the 1890s. In the aftermath of that depression, the AFL poured most of its energy into organizing craft, or skilled, workers such as carpenters, typographers, plumbers, painters, and machinists. Because of their skills, these workers commanded more respect from employers than did the unskilled. Employers negotiated contracts, or trade agreements, with craft unions that stipulated the wages workers were to be paid, the hours they were to work, and the rules under which new workers would be accepted into the trade. These agreements were accorded the same legal protection that American law bestowed on other commercial contracts.

As the AFL focused on these "bread-and-butter" issues, it withdrew from the political activism that had once occupied its attention. It no longer agitated for governmental regulation of the economy and the workplace. This "business" unionism was given its most forceful expression by the AFL's president, Samuel F. Gompers. A onetime Marxist and cigar-maker who had helped found the AFL in 1886, Gompers was reelected to the AFL presidency every year from 1896 until his death in 1924. The AFL showed considerable vitality under his leadership. Aware of the AFL's growing significance and conservatism, the National Civic Federation, a newly formed council of corporate executives, agreed to meet periodically with the organization's leaders to discuss the nation's industrial and labor policies.

Nevertheless, the AFL's success was limited. Its 2 million members represented only a small portion of the total industrial workforce. Its concentration among craft workers, moreover, distanced it from the majority of workers. Unskilled and semiskilled workers could only be organized into an industrial union that offered membership to *all* workers in a particular industry. Gompers understood the importance of such unions and allowed several of them to participate in the AFL. The most significant in the early 20th century were the United Mine Workers (UMW), the United Textile Workers, and the International Ladies Garment Workers Union (ILGWU). Within the AFL, these unions received support from socialist members, who were trying to make the organization more responsive to the needs of the unskilled and semiskilled. But members of the conservative craft unions resisted the socialists' efforts. Craftsmen's feelings of superiority over the unskilled were intensified by their ethnic background. Most were from "old immigrant" stock, and they shared the common prejudice against immigrants from southern and eastern Europe.

The prejudice demonstrated by AFL members toward black workers was even worse. In the early 20th century, nine AFL unions explicitly excluded African Americans from membership, while several others accomplished the same goal by declaring blacks ineligible for union initiation rituals. National unions that did not officially discriminate often permitted their union locals to segregate African American workers in Jim Crow locals or to bar them from membership altogether.

Nevertheless, white and black workers sometimes managed to set aside their suspicions of each other and cooperate. The UMW allowed black workers to join and to rise to positions of leadership. In New Orleans, black and white dockworkers constructed a remarkable experiment in biracial unionism that flourished from the 1890s through the early 1920s. Their unity gave them leverage in negotiations with their employers and allowed them to exercise a great deal of control over the conditions of work. But these moments of cooperation were rare.

Although blacks made up too small a percentage of the working class to build alternative labor organizations that would counteract the influence of the AFL, the "new immigrants" from eastern and southern Europe were too numerous to be ignored. Their participation in the UMW enabled that union to grow from only 14,000 in 1897 to more than 300,000 in 1914.

"BIG BILL" HAYWOOD AND THE IWW

When the AFL failed to help them organize, immigrants turned to other unions. The most important was the Industrial Workers of the World (IWW), led by the charismatic William "Big Bill" Haywood. The IWW rejected the principle of craft organization, hoping instead to organize all workers into "one big union." It scorned the notion that only a conservative union could survive in American society, declaring its commitment to revolution instead. The IWW refused to sign collective bargaining agreements with employers, arguing that such agreements only trapped workers in capitalist property relations. Capitalism had to be overthrown through struggles between workers and their employers at the point of production.

The IWW was too radical and reckless ever to attract a mass membership. Nevertheless, few organizations inspired as much awe and fear. The IWW organized the poorest and most isolated workers—lumbermen, miners, and trackmen in the West, textile workers and longshoremen in the East. Emboldened by IWW leaders, these workers waged strikes against employers who were not accustomed to having their authority challenged. Violence lurked beneath the surface of these strikes and occasionally erupted in bloody skirmishes between

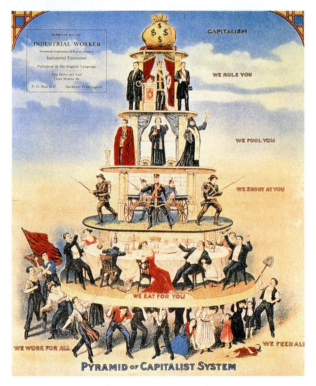

THE RADICAL CRITIQUE OF CAPITALISM   This "Pyramid of the Capitalist System" humorously illustrates how radicals analyzed capitalism—as an economic system that oppressed workers, rewarded the wealthy, and worshipped money. In this pyramid, the police, political leaders, and clerics are all depicted as the servants of capital and the opponents of workers.

strikers and police, National Guardsmen, or the private security forces hired by employers. Some blamed the IWW for the violence, seeing it as a direct outgrowth of calls for a "class war." But others understood that the IWW was not solely responsible. Employers had shown themselves quite willing to resort to violence to enforce their will on employees. In 1913, for example, at Ludlow, Colorado, the Colorado Fuel and Iron Company brought in a private security force and then the local militia to break up a UMW strike. When the company evicted strikers and their families from their homes, the union set up 13 tent colonies to obstruct the entrances to the mines. The standoff came to a bloody conclusion in April 1914 when company police, firing randomly into one colony of tents, killed 66 men, women, and children.

The "Ludlow massacre" outraged and shamed the nation. The massacre revealed yet again what the IWW strikes had repeatedly demonstrated: that many American workers felt abused by their low wages and poor working conditions; that neither the government nor employers offered workers a mechanism that would allow their grievances to be openly discussed and peacefully settled; and that workers, as a result, felt compelled to protest through joining unions and waging strikes, even if it meant risking their lives.

THE JOYS OF THE CITY

Industrial workers might not have been getting their fair share of the nation's prosperity, but they were crowding the dance halls, vaudeville theaters, amusement parks, and ballparks offered by the new world of commercial entertainment. Above all, they were flocking to the movies.

Movies were well suited to poor city dwellers with little money, little free time, and little English. Initially, they cost only a nickel. The "nickelodeons" where they were shown were usually converted storefronts in working-class neighborhoods. Movies did not require much leisure time, for at first they lasted only 15 minutes on average. Those with more time on their hands could stay for a cycle of two or three films. And moviegoers needed no knowledge of English to understand what was happening on the "silent screen," a circumstance that made movies especially attractive to immigrants. By 1910, at least 20,000 nickelodeons dotted northern cities.

Every aspect of these early "moving pictures" was primitive by today's standards. But they were thrilling just the same. The figures appearing on the screen were realistic, yet "larger than life." Moviegoers could transport themselves to parts of the world they otherwise would never see, encounter people they would otherwise never meet, and watch boxing matches they could otherwise not afford to attend. The darkened theater provided a setting in which secret desires, especially sexual ones, could be explored.

No easy generalizations are possible about the content of these early films, more than half of which came from France, Germany, and Italy. Among those produced in the United States, slapstick comedies were common, as were adventure stories and romances. The Hollywood formula of happy endings had yet to be worked out. In 1914 the movies' first sex symbol, Theda Bara, debuted in a movie that showed her tempting an upstanding American ambassador into infidelity and then into ruin. She would be the first of the big screen's many "vamps," so-called because the characters they portrayed, like vampires, thrived on the blood (and death) of men.

NICKELODEONS IN MAJOR AMERICAN CITIES, 1910

CITIES	POPULATION	NICKELODEONS (ESTIMATE)	SEATING CAPACITY	POPULATION PER SEAT
New York	4,338,322	450	150,000	29
Chicago	2,000,000	310	93,000	22
Philadelphia	1,491,082	160	57,000	26
St. Louis	824,000	142	50,410	16
Cleveland	600,000	75	22,500	27
Baltimore	600,000	83	24,900	24
San Francisco	400,000	68	32,400	12
Cincinnati	350,000	75	22,500	16
New Orleans	325,000	28	5,600	58

Source: Garth Jowett, *Film: The Democratic Art* (Boston: Little, Brown, 1976), p. 46.

THE NEW SEXUALITY AND THE NEW WOMAN

The introduction of movies was closely bound up with a sexual revolution in American life. For most of the 19th century, the idea of "separate spheres" had dominated relations between the sexes. The male sphere was one of work, politics, and sexual passion. The female sphere, by contrast, was one of domesticity, moral education, and sexual reproduction. Men and women were not supposed to intrude into each other's spheres. It was "unnatural" for women to work, or to enter the corrupting world of politics, or to engage in pleasurable sex. It was equally "unnatural" for men to devote themselves to child-rearing, or to "idle" themselves with domestic chores, or to live a life bereft of sexual passion. Not only did this doctrine of separate spheres discriminate against women, it also meant that men and women spent substantial portions of their daily lives apart from each other. The ceremonial occasions, meals, and leisure activities that brought them together tended to be closely regulated. The lives of the young, in particular, were closely watched, guided, and supervised by parents, teachers, and ministers.

Although this doctrine, often referred to as Victorianism, never worked as well in practice as it did in theory, throughout the 1880s and 1890s it had a profound influence on gender identity and sexual practice. Then a revolt set in. That revolt came from many sources: from middle-class men who were tiring of a life devoted to regimented work with no time for play; from middle-class women who, after achieving first-rate educations at elite women's colleges, were told they could not participate in the nation's economic, governmental, or professional enterprises; from immigrants, blacks, and other groups who had never been fully socialized into the Victorian world; and from the ready availability of leisure activities far removed from parental supervision.

Among the most influential rebels in the new century were the young, single, working-class women who were entering the workforce in large numbers. The economy's voracious appetite

THEDA BARA AS CLEOPATRA (1917)   Bara was the first movie actress to gain fame for her roles as a "vamp"—a woman whose irresistible sexual charm led men to ruin. Because little effort was made to censor movies prior to the early 1920s, movie directors were able to explore sexual themes and to film their female stars in erotic, and partially nude, poses.

for labor was drawing women out of the home and into factories and offices. Men who would have preferred to keep their wives and daughters at home were forced, given their own low wages, to allow them to go to work. Women's employment doubled between 1880 and 1900, and increased by 50 percent from 1900 to 1920. Meanwhile, the nature of female employment was undergoing a radical change. Domestic service had been the most common occupation for women during the 19th century. Female servants generally worked alone, or with one or two other servants. They worked long hours cooking, cleaning, and caring for their masters' children and received only part of their wages in cash, the rest being "paid" in the form of room and board. Their jobs offered them little personal or financial independence.

Now, women were taking different kinds of jobs. The jobs tended to be either industrial or clerical. In both cases, women worked both with one another and in proximity to men. Their places of work were distant from their homes and from parental supervision. They received all their pay in the form of wages, which, though low, heightened their sense of economic independence. Their ranks, however, included few black women, who, like black men, were largely excluded from the expanding job opportunities in the economy's manufacturing and clerical sectors.

Once the barriers against white women in the workforce had fallen, other barriers also began to weaken—especially the Victorian ban on close associations with men outside of marriage. Young women and men flocked to the dance halls that were opening in every major city. They rejected the stiff formality of earlier ballroom dances like the cotillion or the waltz for the freedom and intimacy of newer forms, like the fox trot, tango, and bunny-hug. They went to movies and to amusement parks together, and they engaged, far more than their parents had, in premarital sex. It is estimated that the proportion of women having sex before marriage rose from 10 percent to 25 percent in the generation that was coming of age between 1910 and 1920.

THE RISE OF FEMINISM

This movement toward sexual equality was one expression of women's dissatisfaction with their subordinate place in society. By the second decade of the 20th century, eloquent spokeswomen had emerged to make the case for full female equality. The writer Charlotte Perkins Gilman called for the release of women from domestic chores through the collectivization of housekeeping. Social activist Margaret Sanger insisted, in her lectures on birth control, that women should be free to enjoy sexual relations without having to worry about unwanted motherhood. The anarchist Emma Goldman denounced marriage as a kind of prostitution and embraced the ideal of "free love"—love unburdened by contractual commitment. Alice Paul, founder of the National Women's Party, brought a new militancy to the campaign for woman suffrage (see Chapter 21).

These women were among the first to use the term "feminism" to describe their desire for complete equality with men. Some of them came together in Greenwich Village, a community of radical artists and writers in lower Manhattan, where they found a supportive environment in which to express and live by their feminist ideals. Crystal Eastman, a leader of the feminist Greenwich Village group called Heterodoxy, defined the feminist challenge as "how to arrange the world so that women can be human beings, with a chance to exercise their infinitely varied gifts in infinitely varied ways, instead of being destined by the accident of their sex to one field of activity."

The movement for sexual and gender equality aroused considerable anxiety in the more conservative sectors of American society. Parents worried about the promiscuity of their children. Conservatives were certain that the "new women" would transform American cities into dens of iniquity. Vice commissions sprang up in every major city to clamp down on prostitution, drunkenness, and pornography. The campaign for prohibition—a ban on the sale of alcoholic beverages—gathered steam. Movie theater owners were pressured into excluding "indecent" films from their screens.

Cultural conservatism was strongest in those areas of the country least involved in the ongoing industrial and sexual revolutions—in farming communities and small towns; in the South, where industrialization and urbanization were proceeding at a slower rate than elsewhere; and among old social elites, who felt pushed aside by the new corporate men of power.

What conservatives shared with radicals was a conviction that the country could not afford to ignore its social problems—the power of the corporations; the poverty and powerlessness of wage earners; the role of women and African Americans. Conservatives were as determined to restore a Victorian morality as radicals were determined to achieve working-class emancipation and women's equality. But in politics, neither would become the dominant force. That role

CHRONOLOGY

1897	Depression ends; prosperity returns
1899	Theodore Roosevelt urges Americans to live the "strenuous life"
1890s	Football becomes sport-of-choice in Ivy League • Young women put away their corsets
1900–1914	Immigration averages more than 1 million per year
1901	U.S. Steel is formed from 200 separate companies • Andrew Carnegie devotes himself to philanthropic pursuits • 1 of every 400 railroad workers dies on the job
1904	20 percent of the North's industrial population lives below poverty line
1905	Industrial Workers of World (IWW) founded
1908	Henry Ford unveils his Model T
1909	Immigrants and their children comprise more than 96 percent of labor force building and maintaining railroads
1910	Black skilled tradesmen in northern cities reduced to 10 percent of total skilled trades workforce • 20,000 nickelodeons dot northern cities
1911	Triangle Shirtwaist Company fire kills 146 workers • Frederick Winslow Taylor publishes *The Principles of Scientific Management*
1913	Henry Ford introduces the first moving assembly line; employee turnover reaches 370 percent a year • John D. Rockefeller establishes Rockefeller Foundation
1914	Henry Ford introduces the $5-a-day wage • 66 men, women, and children killed in "Ludlow massacre" • Theda Bara, movies' first sex symbol, debuts
1919	Japanese farmers in California sell $67 million in agricultural goods, 10 percent of state's total
1920	Nation's urban population outstrips rural population for first time

would fall to the so-called progressives, a widely diverse group of reformers who confidently and optimistically believed that they could bring both order and justice to the new society.

CONCLUSION

Between 1890 and 1920, corporate power, innovation, and demands had stimulated the growth of cities, attracted millions of immigrants from southern and eastern Europe, enhanced commercial opportunities, and created the conditions for a vibrant urban culture. Many Americans thrived in this new environment, taking advantage of business opportunities or, as in the case of women, discovering liberties for dress, employment, dating, and sex that they had not known. But millions of Americans were impoverished, unable to rise in the social order or to earn enough in wages to support their families. African Americans who had migrated to the North in search of economic opportunity suffered more than any other single group, as they found themselves shut out of most industrial and commercial employment.

Henry Ford, whose generous $5-a-day wage drew tens of thousands to his Detroit factories, was an exceptional employer. Although other employers had learned to restrain their crass displays of wealth and had turned toward philanthropy in search of a better public image, they were reluctant to follow Ford's lead.

Working-class Americans proved resourceful in creating self-help institutions to attend to their own and each other's needs. In some cities, they gained a measure of power through the establishment of political machines. Labor unions arose and fought for a society of greater equality and justice. But it remained unclear how successful these institutions would be in their efforts to inject greater equality and opportunity into an industrial society in which the gap between rich and poor had reached alarming proportions.

21

PROGRESSIVISM

PROGRESSIVISM AND THE PROTESTANT SPIRIT

MUCKRAKERS, MAGAZINES, AND THE TURN TOWARD "REALISM"

SETTLEMENT HOUSES AND WOMEN'S ACTIVISM

SOCIALISM AND PROGRESSIVISM ~ MUNICIPAL REFORM

POLITICAL REFORM IN THE STATES

ECONOMIC AND SOCIAL REFORM IN THE STATES

A RENEWED CAMPAIGN FOR CIVIL RIGHTS ~ NATIONAL REFORM

THE TAFT PRESIDENCY ~ ROOSEVELT'S RETURN

THE RISE OF WOODROW WILSON ~ THE ELECTION OF 1912

THE WILSON PRESIDENCY

Progressivism was a reform movement that took its name from individuals who left the Republican Party in 1912 to join Theodore Roosevelt's new party, the Progressive Party. But the term "progressive" refers to a much larger and more varied group of reformers than those who gathered around Roosevelt in 1912. Progressives wanted to cleanse politics of corruption, tame the power of the "trusts" and, in the process, inject more liberty into American life. They fought against prostitution, gambling, drinking, and other forms of vice. They first appeared in municipal politics, organizing movements to oust crooked mayors and to break up local gas or streetcar monopolies. They then carried their fights to the states and finally to the nation.

Progressivism was popular among a variety of groups who brought to the movement distinct, and often conflicting, aims. But on one issue most progressives agreed: the need for an activist government to right political, economic, and social wrongs. Some progressives wanted government to become active only long enough to clean up the political process, end drinking, upgrade the electorate, and break up trusts. But these problems were so difficult to solve that many progressives endorsed the notion of a permanently active government—with the power to tax income, regulate industry, protect consumers from fraud, safeguard the environment, and provide social welfare. Progressives, in other words, came to see the federal government as the institution best equipped to solve social problems.

Such positive attitudes toward government power marked an important change in American politics. Americans had long been suspicious of centralized government, viewing it as the enemy of liberty. The Populists had broken with that view (see Chapter 19), but they had been defeated. So the progressives had to build a new case for strong government as the protector of liberty and equality.

PROGRESSIVISM AND THE PROTESTANT SPIRIT

Progressivism emerged first and most strongly among young, mainly Protestant, middle-class Americans who felt alienated from their society. Many had been raised in devout Protestant homes in which religious conviction had often been a spur to social action. They were expected to become ministers or missionaries or to serve their church in some other way. They had abandoned this path, but they never lost their zeal for righting moral wrongs and for uplifting the human spirit. They were distressed by the immorality and corruption rampant in American politics, and by the gap that separated rich from poor. They became, in the words of one historian, "ministers of reform."

Other Protestant reformers retained their faith. This was true of William Jennings Bryan, the former Populist leader who became an ardent progressive and a prominent evangelical. Throughout his political career, Bryan always insisted that Christian piety and American democracy were integrally related. Billy Sunday, a former major league baseball player who became the most theatrical evangelical preacher of his day, elevated opposition to saloons and the "liquor trust" into a righteous crusade. And Walter Rauschenbusch led a movement known as the Social Gospel, which emphasized the duty of Christians to work for the social good.

Protestants, of course, formed a diverse population, large sections of which showed little interest in reform. Thus, it is important to identify smaller and more cohesive groups of reformers. Of the many that arose, three were of particular importance, especially in the early years: investigative journalists, who were called "muckrakers"; the founders and supporters of settlement houses; and socialists.

MUCKRAKERS, MAGAZINES, AND THE TURN TOWARD "REALISM"

The term "muckraker" was coined by Theodore Roosevelt, who had intended it as a criticism of newspaper and magazine reporters who wrote stories about scandalous situations. But it became a badge of honor among journalists who were determined to expose the seedy, sordid side of life in the United States. During the first decade of the 20th century, they presented the public with one startling revelation after another. Ida Tarbell revealed the shady practices by which John D. Rockefeller had transformed his Standard Oil Company into a monopoly. Lincoln Steffens unraveled the webs of bribery and corruption that were strangling local governments in the nation's great cities. George Kibbe Turner documented the extent of prostitution and family disintegration in the ethnic ghettos of those cities. These muckrakers wanted to shock the public into recognizing the shameful state of political, economic, and social affairs and to prompt "the people" to take action.

The tradition of investigative journalism reached back at least to the 1870s, when newspaper and magazine writers exposed the corrupt practices of New York City's Boss Tweed and his well-oiled Tammany Hall machine. But the rise of the muckrakers reflected two factors, one economic and the other intellectual, which transformed investigative reporting into something of national importance.

INCREASED NEWSPAPER AND MAGAZINE CIRCULATION

A dramatic expansion in newspaper and magazine circulation was the economic factor underlying the rise of the muckrakers. From 1870 to 1909 the number of daily newspapers rose from 574 to 2,600, and their circulation increased from less than 3 million to more than 24 million. During the 1890s magazines also underwent a revolution. Cheap, 10-cent periodicals such as *McClure's Magazine* and *Ladies Home Journal,* with circulations of 400,000 to 1 million, displaced genteel and relatively expensive 35-cent publications such as *Harper's* and *The Atlantic Monthly*. The expanded readership brought journalists considerably more money and prestige and attracted many talented and ambitious men and women to the profession. It also made magazine publishers more receptive to stories that might appeal to their newly acquired millions of readers.

THE TURN TOWARD "REALISM"

The intellectual factor favoring the muckrakers was the turn toward "realism" among the nation's middle class. "Realism" was a way of thinking that prized detachment, objectivity, and skepticism. Many people, for example, felt that constitutional theory had little to do with the way government in the United States actually worked. What could one learn about bosses, machines, and graft from studying the Constitution? There was also a sense that the nation's glorification of the "self-made man" and of "individualism" was preventing Americans from coping effectively with the sudden centrality of large-scale organizations—corporations, banks, labor unions—to the nation's economy and to society.

In the 1890s this impatience reached a crisis point. Intellectuals and artists of all sorts set about creating truer, more realistic ways of representing and analyzing American society. Many of them were inspired by the work of investigative journalists; some had themselves been newspapermen. Years of firsthand observation enabled them to describe American society as it "truly was." They brought shadowy figures vividly to life. They pictured for Americans the captain of industry who ruthlessly destroyed his competitors; the con artist who tricked young people new to city life; the innocent immigrant girl who fell prey to the white slave traders; the corrupt policeman under whose protection urban vice flourished.

A vast middle class, uneasy about the state of American society, applauded the muckrakers for telling these stories, and became interested in reform. Members of this class put pressure on city and state governments to send crooked government officials to jail and to stamp out the sources of corruption and vice. Between 1902 and 1916 more than 100 cities launched investigations of the prostitution trade. At the federal level, all three branches of government felt compelled to address the question of "the trusts"—the concentration of power in the hands of a few industrialists and financiers. Progressivism began to crystallize around the abuses the muckrakers had exposed.

SETTLEMENT HOUSES AND WOMEN'S ACTIVISM

Settlement houses, too, played a crucial role in fashioning the progressive agenda. Established by middle-class reformers, these institutions were intended to help the largely immigrant poor cope with the harsh conditions of city life. Much of the inspiration for them came from young, college-educated, Protestant women from comfortable but not particularly wealthy backgrounds. Highly educated and talented, these women rebelled against being relegated solely to the roles of wife and mother. For them, the settlement houses provided a way to assert their independence and apply their talents in socially useful ways.

HULL HOUSE

Jane Addams and Ellen Gates Starr established the nation's first settlement house, in Chicago, in 1889. The two women had been inspired by a visit the year before to London's Toynbee Hall, where a small group of middle-class men had been living and working with

JANE ADDAMS The founder of the settlement house movement, Addams was the most famous woman reformer of the Progressive Era. This photograph (1930) shows her late in her career, by which time she had dedicated more than 40 years to helping immigrant children and their families.

that city's poor since 1884. Addams and Starr bought a decaying mansion that had once been the country home of a prominent Chicagoan, Charles J. Hull. By 1889 "Hull House" had been surrounded by factories, churches, saloons, and tenements inhabited by very poor, largely foreign-born working-class families.

Addams quickly emerged as the guiding spirit of Hull House. She moved into the building and demanded that all workers there do the same. She and Starr enlisted extraordinary women such as Florence Kelley, Alice Hamilton, and Julia Lathrop. They set up a nursery for the children of working mothers, a penny savings bank, and an employment bureau, soon followed by a baby clinic, a neighborhood playground, and social clubs. Determined to minister to cultural as well as economic needs, Hull House sponsored an orchestra, reading groups, and a lecture series. Members of Chicago's widening circle of reform-minded intellectuals, artists, and politicians contributed their energies to the enterprise. In 1893 Illinois Governor John P. Altgeld named Hull House's Florence Kelley as the state's chief factory inspector. Her investigations led to Illinois's first factory law, which prohibited child labor, limited the employment of women to eight hours a day, and authorized the state to hire inspectors to enforce the law.

There seemed to be no limit to the energy, imagination, and commitment of the Hull House principals. Julia Lathrop used her appointment to the State Board of Charities to agitate for improvements in the care of the poor, the handicapped, and the delinquent. With Edith Abbott and Sophonisba Breckinridge, she established the Department of Social Research at the University of Chicago.

The Hull House leaders did not command the instant fame accorded the muckrakers. Nevertheless, they were steadily drawn into the public arena. Thousands of women across the country were inspired to build their own settlement houses on the Hull House model. By 1910 Jane Addams had become one of the nation's most famous women.

THE CULTURAL CONSERVATISM OF PROGRESSIVE REFORMERS

In general, settlement house workers were much more sympathetic toward the poor, the illiterate, and the downtrodden than the muckrakers were. Jane Addams, though she disapproved of machine politics, saw firsthand the benefits machine politicians delivered to their constituents. She respected the cultural inheritance of the immigrants and admired their resourcefulness. Although she wanted them to become Americans, she encouraged them to preserve their "immigrant gifts" in their new identity. Those attitudes were more liberal than the attitudes of other reformers, who considered most immigrants culturally, even racially, inferior.

But there were limits even to Addams's sympathy for the immigrants. In particular, she disapproved of the new working-class entertainments that gave adolescents extensive and unregulated opportunities for intimate association. She was also troubled by the emergence of the "new woman" and her frank sexuality (see Chapter 20). Addams tended to equate female sexuality with prostitution. Such attitudes revealed the extent to which she still adhered to Victorian notions of "pure," asexual womanhood.

In fact, a good many champions of progressive reform were cultural conservatives. In addition to their position on women's sexuality, their conservatism was evident in their attitudes toward alcohol. Drinking was a serious problem in poor, working-class areas. Settlement house workers were well aware of the ill-effects of alcoholism and sought to combat it. They called on working people to refrain from drink and worked for legislation that would shut

WOMEN ENROLLED IN INSTITUTIONS OF HIGHER EDUCATION, 1870–1930

YEAR	WOMEN'S COLLEGES (THOUSANDS OF STUDENTS)	COED INSTITUTIONS (THOUSANDS OF STUDENTS)	TOTAL (THOUSANDS OF STUDENTS)	PERCENTAGE OF ALL STUDENTS ENROLLED
1870	6.5	4.6	11.1	21.0%
1880	15.7	23.9	39.6	33.4
1890	16.8	39.5	56.3	35.9
1900	24.4	61.0	85.4	36.8
1910	34.1	106.5	140.6	39.6
1920	52.9	230.0	282.9	47.3
1930	82.1	398.7	480.8	43.7

Source: From Mabel Newcomer, *A Century of Higher Education for American Women* (New York: Harper and Row, 1959), p. 46.

down the saloons. The progressives joined forces with the Women's Christian Temperance Union and the Anti-Saloon League. By 1916, through their collective efforts, these groups had won prohibition of the sale and manufacture of alcoholic beverages in 16 states. In 1919 their crowning achievement was the Eighteenth Amendment to the U.S. Constitution, making Prohibition the law of the land (see Chapter 23).

In depicting alcohol and saloons as unmitigated evils, however, the prohibition movement ignored the role saloons played in ethnic, working-class communities. On Chicago's South Side, for example, saloons provided tens of thousands of packinghouse workers with the only decent place to eat lunch. Some saloons catered to particular ethnic groups: They served traditional foods and drinks, provided meeting space for fraternal organizations, and offered camaraderie to men longing to speak in their native tongue. Saloonkeepers sometimes functioned as informal bankers, cashing checks and making small loans.

Alcohol figured in ethnic life in other ways, too. For Catholics, wine was central to Communion. Jews greeted each Sabbath and religious festival with a blessing over wine. For both groups, the sharing of wine or beer marked the celebration of births, marriages, deaths, and other major family events. Understandably, many of the nation's immigrants shunned the prohibition movement. Here was a gulf separating the immigrant masses from the Protestant middle class that even compassionate reformers such as Jane Addams could not bridge.

A NATION OF CLUBWOMEN

Settlement house workers comprised only one part of a vast network of female reformers. Hundreds of thousands of women belonged to local women's clubs. Conceived as self-help organizations in which women would be encouraged to sharpen their minds, refine their domestic skills, and strengthen their moral faculties, these clubs began taking on tasks of social reform. Clubwomen typically focused their energies on improving schools, building libraries and playgrounds, expanding educational and vocational opportunities for girls, and securing fire and sanitation codes for tenement houses. In so doing, they transformed traditional female concerns into questions of public policy and significantly increased public awareness of the problems afflicting children and families.

SOCIALISM AND PROGRESSIVISM

While issues such as women's sexuality and men's alcoholism drew progressives in a conservative direction, other issues drew them to socialism. In the early part of the 20th century, socialism stood for the transfer of control over industry from a few industrialists to the laboring masses. Socialists believed that such a transfer, usually defined in terms of government ownership and operation of economic institutions, would make it impossible for wealthy elites to control society.

The Socialist Party of America, founded in 1901, became a political force during the first 16 years of the century, and socialist ideas influenced progressivism. In 1912, at the peak of its influence, the party's presidential candidate, the charismatic Eugene Victor Debs, attracted almost 1 million votes—6 percent of the total votes cast that year. In that same year, 1,200 Socialists held elective office in 340 different municipalities. More than 300 newspapers and periodicals spread the socialist gospel. The most important socialist publication was *Appeal to Reason*, published by the Kansan Julius Wayland and sent out each week to 750,000 subscribers. In 1905 Wayland published, in serial form, a novel by an obscure muckraker named Upton Sinclair, which depicted the scandalous working conditions in Chicago's meatpacking industry. When it was later published in book form in 1906, *The Jungle* created such an outcry that the federal government was forced to regulate the meat industry.

THE MANY FACES OF SOCIALISM

Socialists came in many varieties. In Milwaukee, they consisted of predominantly German working-class immigrants and their descendants; in New York City, their numbers were strongest among Jewish immigrants from eastern Europe. In the Southwest, tens of thousands of disgruntled native-born farmers who had been Populists in the 1890s now flocked to the socialist banner. In the West, socialism was popular among miners, timber cutters, and others who labored in isolated areas where industrialists enjoyed extraordinary power. These radicals gravitated to the militant labor union, the Industrial Workers of the World (IWW) (Chapter 20), which from 1905 to 1913 found a home in the Socialist Party.

Socialists differed not only in their occupations and ethnic origins but also in their politics. The IWW was the most radical socialist group, with its incessant calls for revolution. By contrast, mainstream socialism was more respectful of American political, cultural, and religious traditions. Mainstream socialists saw themselves as the saviors rather than the destroyers of the American republic. Their confidence that the nation could be redeemed through conventional politics—through the election of Debs as president—is evidence of their affection for American democracy. Evolutionary socialists, led by Victor Berger of Milwaukee, abandoned talk of revolution altogether and chose instead an aggressive brand of reform

CITIES AND TOWNS ELECTING SOCIALIST MAYORS OR OTHER MAJOR MUNICIPAL OFFICERS, 1911–1920

politics. They were dubbed "gas and water socialists" because of their interest in improving city services.

These differences would, after 1912, fragment the socialist movement. But for a decade or so, all these divergent groups managed to coexist in a single political party. That was due in no small measure to the eloquence of Debs. When he was released from a Chicago jail in 1895, where he had been imprisoned for his role in leading the strike against the Pullman Company (see Chapter 19), Debs declared to the 100,000 admirers who had gathered to celebrate his release: "Manifestly the spirit of '76 still survives. The fires of liberty and noble aspirations are not yet extinguished. . . . The vindication and glorification of American principles of government, as proclaimed to the world in the Declaration of Independence, is the high purpose of this convocation."

SOCIALISTS AND PROGRESSIVES

Debs's speeches both attracted and disturbed progressives. On the one hand, he spoke compellingly about the economic threats that concerned progressives. And his confidence that a strong state could bring the economic system under control mirrored the progressives' own faith in the positive uses of government. Indeed, progressives often worked hand-in-hand with socialists to win economic and political reforms, especially at the municipal and state lev-

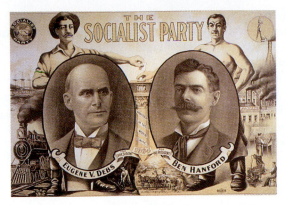

THE RISE OF SOCIALISM   The socialists hoped to bring economic security and dignity to working men and women. Under the leadership of Eugene V. Debs, pictured on the left in this 1904 campaign poster, they became a significant force in American politics. Their influence crested in the election of 1912, when Debs received nearly a million votes.

els, and many intellectuals and reformers moved easily back and forth between socialism and progressivism. Walter Lippmann, who would become a close adviser to President Wilson during the First World War, began his political career in 1912 as an assistant to the Socialist mayor of Schenectady. Several of the era's outstanding intellectuals, including John Dewey, Richard Ely, and Thorstein Veblen, also traveled back and forth between the socialist and progressive camps. So did Helen Keller, the country's leading spokesperson for the disabled.

On the other hand, Debs's talk of revolution scared progressives, as did his efforts to organize a working-class political movement independent of middle-class involvement or control. Although progressives wanted to tame capitalism, they did not want to eliminate it altogether. They wanted to improve the working and living conditions of the masses but not cede political control to them. The progressives hoped to offer a political program with enough socialist elements to counter the appeal of Debs's more radical movement. In this, they were successful.

MUNICIPAL REFORM

Progressive reform arose first in the cities. Early battles were over control of municipal transportation networks and utilities. Street railways were typically owned and operated by private corporations, as were electrical and gas systems. Many of the corporations used their monopoly power to charge exorbitant fares and rates, and often they won that power by bribing city officials who belonged to one of the political machines. Corporations achieved generous reductions in real estate taxes in the same way.

The assault on private utilities and their protectors in city government gained momentum in the mid-1890s. In Detroit, reform-minded Mayor Hazen S. Pingree led successful fights to control the city's gas, telephone, and trolley companies. In Chicago in 1896 and 1897, a group of middle-class reformers ousted a corrupt city council and elected a mayor, Carter Harrison Jr., who promised to protect Chicago's streetcar riders from exploitation. In St. Louis in 1900, middle-class consumers and small businessmen joined hands with striking workers to challenge the "streetcar trust." In Cleveland, the crusading reformer Tom Johnson won election as mayor in 1901, curbed the power of the streetcar interests, and brought honest and efficient government to the city.

Occasionally, a reform politician of Johnson's caliber would rise to power through one of the regular political parties. But this path to power was a difficult one, especially in cities where the political parties were controlled by machines. Consequently, progressives worked for reforms that would strip the parties of their power. Two of their favorite reforms were the city commission and the city manager forms of government.

The City Commission Plan

First introduced in Galveston, Texas, in 1900, the city commission shifted municipal power from the mayor and his aldermen to five city commissioners, each responsible for a different department of city government. In Galveston and elsewhere, the impetus for this reform came from civic-minded businessmen determined to rebuild government on the same principles of efficient and scientific management that had energized the private sector. The results were often impressive. The Galveston commissioners restored the city's credit after a close brush with bankruptcy, improved the city's harbor, and built a massive seawall to protect the city from floods. And they accomplished all that on budgets only two-thirds the size of what they had been in the past. In Houston, Texas; Des Moines, Iowa; Dayton, Ohio; Oakland, California; and elsewhere, commissioners similarly improved urban infrastructures, expanded city services, and strengthened the financial health of the cities.

The City Manager Plan

The city commission system did not always work to perfection, however. Sometimes the commissioners used their position to reward electoral supporters with jobs and contracts; at other times, they pursued power and prestige for their respective departments. The city manager plan was meant to overcome such problems. Under this plan, the commissioners continued to set policy, but the implementation of policy now rested with a "chief executive." This official, who was appointed by the commissioners, was to be insulated from the pressures of running for office. The city manager would curtail rivalries between commissioners and ensure that no outside influences interfered with the expert, businesslike management of the city. The job of city manager was explicitly modeled after that of a corporation executive. First introduced in Sumter, South Carolina, in 1911 and then in Dayton, Ohio, in 1913, by 1919 the city manager plan had been adopted in 130 cities.

The Costs of Reform

Although these reforms limited corruption and improved services, they were not universally popular. Poor and minority voters, in particular, found that their influence in local affairs was weakened by the shift to city commissioners and city managers. Previously, candidates for municipal office (other than the mayor) competed in ward elections rather than in citywide elections. Voters in working-class wards commonly elected workingmen to represent them, and voters in immigrant wards made sure that fellow ethnics represented their interests on city councils. Citywide elections diluted the strength of these constituencies. Candidates from poor districts often lacked the money needed to mount a citywide campaign, and they were further hampered by the nonpartisan nature of such elections. Denied the support of a political party or platform, they had to make themselves personally known to voters throughout the city. That was a much easier task for the city's "leading citizens"—manufacturers, merchants, and lawyers—than it was for workingmen.

POLITICAL REFORM IN THE STATES

Political reform in the cities quickly spread to the states. As at the local level, political parties at the state level were often dominated by corrupt, incompetent politicians who did the bidding of powerful private lobbies. In New Jersey in 1903, for example, large industrial and financial interests, working through the Republican Party machine, controlled numerous appointments to state government, including the chief justice of the state supreme court, the attorney general, and the commissioner of banking and insurance. Such webs of influence ensured that New Jersey would provide large corporations such as the railroads with favorable political and economic legislation.

RESTORING SOVEREIGNTY TO "THE PEOPLE"

Progressives introduced reforms designed to undermine the power of party bosses, restore sovereignty to "the people," and encourage honest, talented individuals to enter politics. One such reform was the direct primary, a mechanism that enabled voters themselves, rather than party bosses, to choose party candidates. By 1916 all but three states had adopted the direct primary. Closely related was a movement to strip state legislatures of their power to choose U.S. senators. State after state enacted legislation that permitted voters to choose senate candidates in primary elections. In 1912 a reluctant U.S. Senate was obliged to approve the Seventeenth Amendment to the Constitution, mandating the direct election of senators.

The direct election of U.S. senators had first been proposed by the Populists back in the 1890s; so too had two other reforms, the initiative and the referendum, both of which were adopted first by Oregon in 1902 and then by 18 other states between 1902 and 1915. The initiative allowed reformers to put before voters in general elections legislation that state legislatures had yet to approve. The referendum gave voters the right in general elections to repeal an unpopular act that a state legislature had passed. Less widely adopted but important nevertheless was the recall, a device that allowed voters to remove from office any public servant who had betrayed their trust. As a further control over the behavior of elected officials, numerous states enacted laws that regulated corporate campaign contributions and restricted lobbying activities in state legislatures.

These laws did not eliminate corporate privilege or destroy the power of machine politicians. Nevertheless, they made politics more honest and strengthened the influence of ordinary voters.

CREATING A VIRTUOUS ELECTORATE

Progressive reformers focused as well on creating a responsible electorate that understood the importance of the vote and that resisted efforts to manipulate elections. To create this ideal electorate, reformers had to see to it that all those citizens who were deemed virtuous could cast their votes free of coercion and intimidation. At the same time, reformers sought to disfranchise all citizens who were considered irresponsible and corruptible. In pursuing these goals, progressives substantially altered the composition of the electorate and strengthened government regulation of voting. The results were contradictory. On the one hand, progressives enlarged the electorate by extending the right to vote to women; on the other hand, they either initiated or tolerated laws that barred large numbers of minority and poor voters from the polls.

THE AUSTRALIAN BALLOT

Government regulation of voting had begun back in the 1890s when virtually every state adopted the Australian, or secret, ballot. This reform required voters to vote in private rather than in public. It also required the government, rather than political parties, to print the ballots and supervise the voting. Prior to this time, each political party had printed its own ballot with only its candidates listed. At election time, each party mobilized its loyal supporters. Party workers offered liquor, free meals, and other bribes to get voters to the polls and to "persuade" them to cast the right ballot. Because the ballots were cast in public, few voters who had accepted gifts of liquor and food dared to cross watchful party officials. Critics argued that the system corrupted the electoral process. They also pointed out that it made "ticket-splitting"— dividing one's vote between candidates of two or more parties—virtually impossible.

The Australian ballot solved these problems. Although it predated progressivism, it reflected the progressives' determination to use government power to encourage citizens to cast their votes responsibly and wisely.

PERSONAL REGISTRATION LAWS

That same determination was apparent in the progressives' support for the personal registration laws that virtually every state passed between 1890 and 1920. These laws required prospective voters to appear at a designated government office with proper identification; only then would they be allowed to register to vote. Frequently, these laws also mandated a certain period of residence in the state prior to registration and a certain interval between registration and actual voting.

Personal registration laws were meant to disfranchise citizens who showed no interest in voting until election day when a party worker arrived with a few dollars and offered a free ride to the polls. They also excluded, however, many hard-working, responsible, poor people who wanted to vote but had failed to register, either because their work schedules made it impossible or because they were intimidated by the complex regulations. The laws were particularly frustrating for immigrants whose knowledge of American government and of the English language were limited.

DISFRANCHISEMENT

Some election laws promoted by the progressives were expressly designed to keep noncitizen immigrants from voting. In the 1880s, 18 states had passed laws allowing immigrants to vote without first becoming citizens. Progressives reversed this trend. At the same time, the newly formed Bureau of Immigration and Naturalization (1906) made it more difficult to become a citizen. Applicants for citizenship now had to appear before a judge who interrogated them, in the English language, on American history and civics. In addition, immigrants were required to provide two witnesses to vouch for their "moral character" and their "attachment to the principles of the Constitution." Finally, immigrants had to swear (and, if necessary, prove) that they were not anarchists or polygamists and that they had resided continuously in the United States for five years.

Most progressives defended the new rigor of the process. U.S. citizenship, they believed, carried great responsibilities; it was not to be bestowed lightly. This position was understandable, given the electoral abuses progressives had exposed. Nevertheless, the reforms also had the effect of denying the vote to a large proportion of the population. Nowhere was exclusion more startling than in the South, where between 1890 and 1904 every ex-Confederate state passed laws designed to strip blacks of their right to vote. Because laws explicitly barring blacks from voting would have violated the Fifteenth Amendment, this exclusion had to be accomplished indirectly—through literacy tests, property qualifications, and poll taxes. Any citizen who failed a reading test, or who could not sign his name, or who did not own a minimum amount of property, or who could not pay a poll tax, lost his right to vote. The citizens who failed these tests most frequently were blacks, who formed the poorest and least educated segment of the southern population, but a large portion of the region's poor whites also failed the tests.

Many progressives in the North bitterly criticized southern disfranchisement. Others joined in 1910 with the black intellectual W. E. B. Du Bois to found the National Association for the Advancement of Colored People (NAACP), an interracial political organization that made the struggle for black equality its primary goal. But in the South, white progressives rarely challenged disfranchisement. They had little difficulty using progressive ideology to justify disfranchisement. Because progressives everywhere believed that the franchise was a precious gift that was to be granted only to those who could handle its responsibilities, it obviously had to be withheld from any who were deemed racially or culturally unfit. Progressives in the North

LYNCHING   This grim photo records the death of five of the approximately 1,000 African Americans who were lynched between 1901 and 1914. The increase in lynching was one measure of the virulence of white racism in the early years of the 20th century.

VOTER PARTICIPATION IN 13 SOUTHERN STATES, 1876, 1892, 1900, 1912

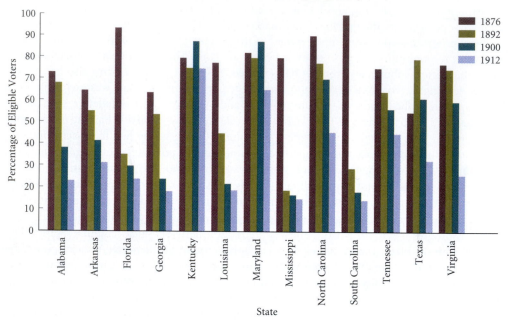

Source: Data from *Historical Statistics of the United States, Colonial Times to 1970* (White Plains, N.Y.: Kraus International, 1989).

excluded many immigrants on just those grounds. Progressives in the South saw the disfranchisement of African Americans in the same light.

DISILLUSIONMENT WITH THE ELECTORATE

In the process of identifying those groups "unfit" to hold the franchise, some progressives soured on the electoral process altogether. The more they looked for rational and virtuous voters, the fewer they found. In *Drift and Mastery* (1914), Walter Lippmann developed a theory that ordinary people had been overwhelmed by industrial and social changes. Because these changes seemed beyond their comprehension or control, they "drifted," unable to "master" the circumstances of modern life or take charge of their own destiny. Lippmann did not suggest that such ordinary people should be barred from voting. But he did argue that more political responsibility should be placed in the hands of appointed officials with the training and knowledge necessary to make government effective and just. The growing disillusionment with the electorate, in combination with intensifying restrictions on the franchise, created an environment in which fewer and fewer Americans actually went to the polls. Voting participation rates fell from 79 percent in 1896 to only 49 percent in 1920.

WOMAN SUFFRAGE

The major exception to this trend was the enfranchisement of women. This momentous reform was embraced by several states during the 1890s and the first two decades of the 20th

SUFFRAGISTS After faltering in the 1870s and 1880s, the campaign for woman suffrage revived during the Progressive Era. Here suffragists campaign for the vote in New York City in 1912. By this time, women had already won the vote in many western states but in few eastern states.

century and then became federal law with the ratification of the Nineteenth Amendment to the Constitution in 1920.

Launched in 1848 at the famous Seneca Falls convention (see Chapter 11), the women's rights movement had floundered in the 1870s and 1880s. In 1890 suffragists came together in a new organization, the National American Woman Suffrage Association (NAWSA). Thousands of young, college-educated women campaigned door-to-door, held impromptu rallies, and pressured state legislators.

Wyoming, which attained statehood in 1890, became the first state to grant women the right to vote, followed in 1893 by Colorado and in 1896 by Idaho and Utah. The main reason for success in these sparsely populated western states was not egalitarianism but rather the conviction that women's supposedly gentler and more nurturing nature would tame and civilize the rawness of the frontier.

This notion reflected a subtle but important change in the thrust of the suffrage movement. Earlier generations had insisted that women were fundamentally equal to men, but the new suffragists argued that women were different from men. Women, they stressed, possessed a moral sense and a nurturing quality that men lacked. Consequently, they understood the civic obligations implied by the franchise and could be trusted to vote virtuously. Their experience as mothers and household managers, moreover, would enable them to guide local and state governments in efforts to improve education, sanitation, and the condition of women and children in the workforce.

Suffragists were slow to ally themselves with blacks, Asians, and other disfranchised groups. In fact, many suffragists, especially those in the South and West, vehemently opposed the franchise for Americans of color. They, like their male counterparts, believed that members of these groups lacked moral strength and thus did not deserve the franchise.

Washington, California, Kansas, Oregon, and Arizona followed the lead of the other western states by enfranchising women in the years from 1910 to 1912. After a series of setbacks in eastern and midwestern states, the movement regained momentum under the leadership of the strategically astute Carrie Chapman Catt, who became president of NAWSA in 1915, and the radical Alice Paul, who founded the militant National Women's Party in 1916. Aided by a heightened enthusiasm for democracy generated by America's participation in the First World War (see Chapter 23) and by the decision to shift the movement's focus from individual states to the nation at large, the suffragists achieved their goal of universal woman suffrage in 1920.

Predictions that suffrage for women would radically alter politics turned out to be false. Although the numbers of voters increased after 1920, voter participation rates continued to decline. Still, the extension of the vote to women, 144 years after the founding of the nation, was a great political achievement.

ECONOMIC AND SOCIAL REFORM IN THE STATES

In some states, progressive reform extended well beyond political parties and the electorate. Progressives also wanted to limit the power of the corporations, strengthen organized labor, and offer social welfare protection to the weak. State governments were pressured into passing such legislation by progressive alliances of middle-class and working-class reformers, and by dynamic state governors.

ROBERT LA FOLLETTE AND WISCONSIN PROGRESSIVISM

Nowhere else did the progressives' campaign for social reform flourish as it did in Wisconsin. The movement arose first in the 1890s as citizens began to mobilize against the state's corrupt Republican Party. These reform-minded citizens came from varied backgrounds. They were middle-class and working-class, urban and rural, male and female, intellectual and evangelical. Wisconsin progressivism had already gained considerable momentum by 1897, when Robert La Follette assumed its leadership.

La Follette was born into a prosperous farming family in 1855. He entered politics as a Republican in the 1880s and embraced reform in the late 1890s. Elected governor in 1900, he secured for Wisconsin both a direct primary and a tax law that stripped the railroad corporations of tax exemptions they had long enjoyed. In 1905 he pushed through a civil service law mandating that every state employee had to meet a certain level of competence.

A tireless campaigner and a spellbinding speaker, "Fighting Bob" won election to the U.S. Senate in 1906. Meanwhile, the growing strength of Wisconsin's labor and socialist movements forced progressive reformers to focus their legislative efforts on issues of corporate greed and social welfare. By 1910 reformers had passed state laws that regulated railroad and utility rates, instituted the nation's first state income tax, and provided workers with compensation for injuries, limitations on work hours, restrictions on child labor, and minimum wages for women.

Many of these laws were written by social scientists at the University of Wisconsin, with whom reformers had close ties. In the first decade of the 20th century, John R. Commons, University of Wisconsin economist, drafted Wisconsin's civil service and public utilities laws. In 1911 Commons designed and won legislative approval for the Wisconsin Industrial Commission, which brought together employers, trade unionists, and professionals and gave them broad powers to investigate and regulate relations between industry and labor throughout the state. Never before had a state government so plainly committed itself to the cause of industrial justice. For the first time, the rights of labor would be treated with the same respect as the rights of industry. Equally important was the responsibility the commission delegated to non-elected professionals: social scientists, lawyers, engineers, and others.

The "Wisconsin idea" was quickly adopted in Ohio, Indiana, New York, and Colorado; and in 1913 the federal government established its own Industrial Relations Commission and hired Commons to direct its investigative staff. In other areas, too, reformers began urging state and federal governments to shift the policymaking initiative away from political parties and toward administrative agencies staffed by professionals.

Progressive Reform in New York

New York was probably second only to Wisconsin in the vigor and breadth of its Progressive movement. As in Wisconsin, progressives in New York focused first on fighting political corruption. Startling revelations of close ties between leading Republican politicians and life insurance companies vaulted the reform lawyer Charles Evans Hughes into the governor's mansion in 1907. Hughes immediately established several public service commissions to regulate railroads and utility companies. As in Wisconsin, the growing strength of labor had an effect. Successful strikes by New York City's garment workers forced state legislators to treat the condition of workers more seriously than they might have otherwise. With the establishment of the Factory Investigating Committee, New York, like Wisconsin, became a pioneer in labor and social welfare policy.

New York state legislators also were being pressured by middle-class reformers whose work with the poor had convinced them that laws were needed to promote social justice. This combined pressure from working-class and middle-class constituencies impelled some state Democrats to convert from machine to reform politics. While they opposed prohibition, city commissions, voter registration laws, and other reforms whose intent seemed anti-immigrant and anti-Catholic, they now agitated for a minimum wage, factory safety, workmen's compensation, the right of workers to join unions, and the regulation of excessively powerful corporations. Their participation in progressivism accelerated the movement's shift away from a preoccupation with political reform and toward questions of economic justice and social welfare.

A Renewed Campaign for Civil Rights

As state legislators in New York and elsewhere were refocusing progressivism on economic and social issues, a new generation of African American activists began insisting that the issue of racial equality also be placed on the reform agenda.

The Failure of Accommodationism

Booker T. Washington's message—that blacks should accept segregation and disfranchisement as unavoidable and focus their energies instead on self-help and self-improvement—was increasingly criticized by black activists. Washington's accommodationist leadership (see Chapter 18), in their eyes, brought blacks in the South no reprieve from racism. More than 100 blacks had been lynched in 1900 alone; between 1901 and 1914 at least 1,000 others would be hanged. Increasingly, unsubstantiated rumors of black assaults on whites became occasions for white mobs to rampage through black neighborhoods and indiscriminately destroy life and property. In 1908 a mob in Springfield, Illinois, attacked black businesses and individuals; a force of 5,000 state militia was required to restore order. The troops were too late, however, to stop the lynching of two innocent black men.

Washington had long believed that blacks who educated themselves or who succeeded in business would be accepted as equals by whites and welcomed into their society. But as militants observed, white rioters made no distinction between rich blacks and poor, or between solid citizens and petty criminals. All that had seemed to matter was the color of one's skin. Similarly, many black militants knew from personal experience that individual accomplishment was not enough to overcome racial prejudice.

FROM THE NIAGARA MOVEMENT TO THE NAACP

Seeing no future in accommodation, W. E. B. Du Bois and other young black activists came together at Niagara Falls in 1905 to fashion their own aggressive political agenda. They demanded that African Americans be given the right to vote in states where it had been taken away; that segregation be abolished; and that the many discriminatory barriers placed in the path of black advancement be removed. They declared their commitment to freedom of speech, the brotherhood of all men, and respect for the working man.

The 1908 Springfield riot had shaken a sizable number of whites. Some, especially those already involved in matters of social and economic reform, now joined in common cause with the Niagara movement. A conference was planned for Lincoln's birthday in 1909 to revive, in the words of the writer William English Walling, "the spirit of the abolitionists" and to "treat the Negro on a plane of absolute political and social equality." The conference brought together a number of distinguished progressives, white and black. They drew up plans to establish an organization dedicated to fighting racial discrimination and prejudice. In May 1910 the National Association for the Advancement of Colored People (NAACP) was officially launched, with Moorfield Storey of Boston as president, Walling as chairman of the executive committee, and Du Bois as the director of publicity and research.

The formation of the NAACP marked the beginning of the modern civil rights movement. The organization immediately launched a magazine, *The Crisis,* edited by Du Bois, to publicize and protest the lynchings, riots, and other abuses directed against black citizens. Equally important was the Legal Redress Committee, which initiated lawsuits against city and state governments for violating the constitutional rights of African Americans. The committee scored its first major success in 1915, when the U.S. Supreme Court ruled that the so-called "grandfather" clauses of the Oklahoma and Maryland constitutions violated the Fifteenth Amendment. (These clauses allowed poor, uneducated whites—but not poor, uneducated blacks—to vote, even if they failed to pay their state's poll tax or to pass its literacy test, by exempting the descendants of men who had voted prior to 1867.)

By 1914, the NAACP had enrolled thousands of members in scores of branches throughout the United States. The organization's success also stimulated the formation of other groups committed to the advancement of blacks. Thus, the National Urban League, founded in 1911, worked to improve the economic and social conditions of blacks in cities. The Urban League pressured employers to hire blacks, distributed lists of available jobs and housing in African American communities, and developed social programs to ease the adjustment of rural black migrants to city life.

Attacking segregation and discrimination through lawsuits was, by its nature, a snail-paced strategy that would take decades to complete. The growing membership of the NAACP, although impressive, was not large enough to qualify it as a mass movement. And its interracial character made the organization seem dangerously radical to millions of whites. White NAACP leaders responded to this hostility by limiting the number and power of African Americans who worked for the organization. This conciliatory policy, in turn, outraged black militants, who argued that a civil rights organization should not be in the business of appeasing white racists.

Despite its limitations, the early work of the NAACP was significant. The NAACP gave Du Bois the security and visibility he needed to carry on his fight against Booker T. Washington's accommodationism. Even before his death in 1915, Washington's enormous influence in black and white communities had begun to recede. The NAACP, more than any other organization, was responsible for resurrecting the issue of racial equality at a time when many white Americans had accepted as normal the practices of racial segregation and discrimination.

NATIONAL REFORM

The more progressives focused on economic and social matters, the more they sought to increase their influence in national politics. Certain problems demanded national solutions. A patchwork of state regulations, for example, was not enough to curtail the power of the trusts, protect workers, or monitor the quality of consumer goods. Moreover, state and federal courts were often hostile toward progressive goals: They repeatedly struck down as unconstitutional reform laws regulating working hours or setting minimum wages, on the grounds that they impinged on the freedom of contract and trade. With a national movement, progressives could force the passage of laws less vulnerable to judicial veto or elect a president who could overhaul the federal judiciary through the appointment and confirmation of progressive-minded judges.

National leadership was not going to emerge from Congress. The Democratic Party had been badly scarred by the Populist challenge of the 1890s. Divided between the radical Bryanites and the conservative followers of Grover Cleveland, and consequently unable to speak with one voice on questions of social and economic policy, after 1896 the Democrats seemed incapable of winning a national election or offering a national agenda. The Republican Party was more unified and popular, but it was controlled by a conservative "Old Guard" that was resolutely pro-business and devoted to a 19th century style of backroom patronage.

National progressive leadership came from the executive rather than the legislative branch, and from two presidents in particular, the Republican Theodore Roosevelt and the Democrat Woodrow Wilson. These two presidents sponsored reforms that profoundly affected the lives of Americans.

THE ROOSEVELT PRESIDENCY

As governor of New York, Roosevelt had shown himself to be a moderate reformer. But even his modest efforts to rid the state's Republican Party of corruption and to institute civil service reform were too much for the state party machine, led by Thomas C. Platt. Consigning Roosevelt to the vice presidency seemed like a safe solution. McKinley was a young, vigorous

Theodore Roosevelt Campaigning for the Presidency in 1912   This photograph captures some of the strength and exuberance that were central features of Roosevelt's public persona and critical to his popular appeal. Note the stuffed deer, eagle, and moosehead adorning the platform: These reminded voters of Roosevelt's love of the outdoors and of the "strenuous life."

politician, fully in control of his party and his presidency. Then in September 1901, less than a year into his second term, McKinley was shot by an anarchist assassin. The president clung to life for nine days, and then died. Upon succeeding McKinley, Theodore Roosevelt, aged 42, became the youngest chief executive in the nation's history.

Born to an aristocratic New York family, Roosevelt nevertheless developed an uncommon affection for "the people." Asthmatic, sickly, and nearsighted as a boy, he remade himself into a vigorous adult. With an insatiable appetite for high-risk adventure, he was also a voracious reader and an accomplished writer. Aggressive and swaggering in his public rhetoric, he was a skilled, patient negotiator in private. A devout believer in the superiority of his Anglo-Saxon race, he nevertheless appointed members of "inferior" races to important posts in his administration. Rarely has a president's personality so enthralled the American public.

Regulating the Trusts

It did not take long for Roosevelt to reveal his flair for the dramatic. In 1902 he ordered the Justice Department to prosecute the Northern Securities Company, a $400 million monopoly that had been set up by leading financiers and railroad tycoons to control all railroad lines and traffic in the Northwest from Chicago to Washington state. Never before had an American president sought to use the Sherman Antitrust Act to break up a monopoly. In 1903 a federal court ordered Northern Securities dissolved, and the U.S. Supreme Court upheld the decision the next year. Roosevelt was hailed as the nation's "trust-buster."

But Roosevelt did not believe in breaking up all, or even most, large corporations. Industrial concentration, he believed, brought the United States wealth, productivity, and a rising standard of living. The role of government should be to regulate these industrial giants, to punish those that used their power improperly, and to protect citizens who were at a disadvantage in their dealings with industry. This new role would require the federal government to expand its powers. The *strengthening* of the federal government—not a return to small-scale industry—was the true aim of Roosevelt's antitrust campaign.

Toward a "Square Deal"

Roosevelt displayed his willingness to use government power to protect the economically weak in a long and bitter 1902 coal miners' strike. Miners in the anthracite fields of eastern Pennsylvania wanted recognition for their union, the United Mine Workers (UMW). They also wanted a 10 to 20 percent increase in wages and an eight-hour day. When their employers, led by the uncompromising George F. Baer of the Reading Railroad, refused to negotiate, they went on strike. In October, the fifth month of the strike, Roosevelt summoned the mine owners and John Mitchell, the UMW president, to the White House. Baer expected Roosevelt to threaten the striking workers with arrest by federal troops if they failed to return to work. Instead, Roosevelt supported Mitchell's request for arbitration and warned the mine owners that if they refused to go along, 10,000 federal troops would seize their property. Stunned, the mine owners agreed to submit the dispute to arbitrators, who awarded the unionists a 10 percent wage increase and a nine-hour day.

The mere fact that the federal government had ordered employers to compromise with their workers carried great symbolic weight. Roosevelt enjoyed a surge of support from ordinary Americans convinced that he shared their dislike for ill-gotten wealth and privilege. He also raised the hopes of African Americans when, only a month into his presidency, he dined with Booker T. Washington at the White House. Blacks were impressed, too, by how easily Roosevelt brushed off the bitter protests of white southerners who accused him of striking a blow against segregation.

In his 1904 election campaign, Roosevelt promised that, if reelected, he would offer every American a "square deal." The slogan resonated with voters and helped carry Roosevelt to a victory over the lackluster, conservative Democrat Alton B. Parker. To the surprise of many observers, Roosevelt had aligned the Republican Party with the cause of reform.

Expanding Government Power: The Economy

Emboldened by his victory, the president intensified his efforts to extend government regulation of economic affairs. His most important proposal was to give the government power to set railroad shipping rates and thereby to eliminate the industry's discriminatory marketing practices. The government, in theory, already possessed this power through the Interstate Commerce Commission (ICC), a national regulatory body established by Congress in 1887. But the courts had so weakened the oversight and regulatory functions of the ICC as to render it virtually powerless. Roosevelt achieved his goal in 1906. Congress passed the Hepburn Act, which significantly increased the ICC's powers of rate review and enforcement. Roosevelt supported the Pure Food and Drug Act, passed by Congress that same year, which protected the public from fraudulently marketed and dangerous foods and medications. The uproar created by the publication of Sinclair's *The Jungle* in 1906 prompted Roosevelt to order a government investigation of conditions in the meatpacking industry. When the investigation corroborated Sinclair's findings, Roosevelt supported the Meat Inspection Act (1906), which committed the government to monitoring the quality and safety of meat being sold to American consumers.

EXPANDING GOVERNMENT POWER: THE ENVIRONMENT

Roosevelt also did more than any previous president to extend federal control over the nation's physical environment. Roosevelt was not a "preservationist" in the manner of John Muir, founder of the Sierra Club, who insisted that the beauty of the land and the well-being of its wildlife should be protected from all human interference. Roosevelt viewed the wilderness as a place to live strenuously, to test oneself against rough natural elements, and to match wits against strong and clever game. Roosevelt further believed that in the West—that land of ancient forests, lofty mountain peaks, and magnificent canyons—Americans could learn something important about their nation's roots and destiny. To preserve this West, Roosevelt oversaw the creation of 5 new national parks, 16 national monuments, and 53 wildlife reserves. The work of his administration led directly to the formation of the National Park Service in 1916.

Roosevelt also emerged a strong supporter of the "conservationist" movement. Conservationists cared little for national parks or grand canyons. They wanted to manage the environment, so as to ensure the most efficient use of the nation's resources for economic development. Roosevelt shared the conservationists' belief that the plundering of western timberlands, grazing areas, water resources, and minerals had reached crisis proportions. Only the institution of broad regulatory controls would restore the West's economic potential.

To that end, Roosevelt appointed a Public Lands Commission in 1903 to survey public lands, inventory them, and establish permit systems to regulate the kinds and numbers of users. Soon after, the Departments of Interior and Agriculture decreed that certain western lands rich in natural resources and waterpower could not be used for agricultural purposes. Government officials also limited waterpower development by requiring companies to acquire permits and then to pay fees for the right to generate electricity on their sites. When political favoritism and corruption within the Departments of the Interior and Agriculture threatened these efforts at regulation, Roosevelt authorized the hiring of university-trained bureaucrats to replace state and local politicians. Scientific expertise, rather than political connections, would now determine the distribution and use of western lands.

Gifford Pinchot, a specialist in forestry management, led the drive for expert and scientific management of natural resources. In 1905 he persuaded Roosevelt to relocate jurisdiction for the national forests from the Department of the Interior to the Department of Agriculture. The newly created National Forest Service quickly instituted a system of competitive bidding for the right to harvest timber on national forest lands. Pinchot and his expanding staff of college-educated foresters also implemented a new policy that exacted user fees from livestock ranchers who had previously used national forest grazing lands for free. Armed with new legislation and bureaucratic authority, Pinchot and fellow conservationists in the Roosevelt administration also declared vast stretches of federal land in the West off-limits to mining and dam construction.

The Old Guard in the Republican Party did not take kindly to these initiatives. When Roosevelt recommended the prosecution of cattlemen and lumbermen who were illegally using federal land for private gain, congressional conservatives struck back with legislation (in 1907) that curtailed the president's power to create new government land reserves. Roosevelt responded by seizing another 17 million acres for national forest reserves before the new law went into effect. To his conservative opponents, excluding commercial activity from public land was bad enough. But flouting the will of Congress with a 17-million-acre land grab was a violation of hallowed constitutional principles governing the separation of powers. Yet, to millions of American voters, Roosevelt's willingness to defy western cattle barons, mining tycoons, and other "malefactors of great wealth" added to his popularity.

Progressivism: A Movement for the People?

Historians have long debated how much Roosevelt's economic and environmental reforms altered the balance of power between the "interests" and the people. Some have demonstrated that many corporations were eager for federal government regulation—that railroad corporations wanted relief from the ruinous rate wars that were driving them to the brink of bankruptcy, for example, and that the larger meatpackers believed that the costs of government food inspections would drive smaller meatpackers out of business. So, too, historians have shown that large agribusinesses, timber companies, and mining corporations in the West believed that government regulation would aid them and hurt smaller competitors. According to this view, government regulation benefited the corporations more than it benefited workers, consumers, and small businessmen.

This view has much to commend it. These early reforms did not go far enough in curtailing corporate power. Corporations fought with some success to turn the final versions of the reform laws to their advantage. But that does not mean that the corporations were the sponsors of reform, or that they dictated the content of reform measures.

Popular anger over the power of the corporations and over political corruption remained a driving force of progressivism. After 1906, the presence in the Senate of La Follette, Albert Beveridge of Indiana, and other anticorporate Republicans gave that anger a powerful national voice. Before he left office in 1909, Roosevelt would expand his reform program to include income and inheritance taxes, a national workmen's compensation law, abolition of child labor, and the eight-hour workday. Those proposals widened the rift between Roosevelt and the Old Guard. In 1907 the progressive program was still evolving. Whether the corporations or the people would benefit most remained unclear.

The Republicans: A Divided Party

The financial panic of 1907 further strained relations between Roosevelt reformers and Old Guard conservatives. A failed speculative effort by several New York banks to corner the copper market triggered a run on banks, a short but severe dip in industrial production, and widespread layoffs. Everywhere, people worried that a devastating depression was in the offing. Indeed, only the timely decision of J. P. Morgan and his fellow bankers to pour huge amounts of private cash into the collapsing banks saved the nation from a disastrous economic crisis. Prosperity quickly returned, but the jitters caused by the panic lingered. Conservatives blamed Roosevelt's "radical" economic policies for the fiasco. To Roosevelt and his fellow progressives, however, the panic merely pointed up how little impact their reforms had actually made on the reign of "speculation, corruption, and fraud."

Roosevelt now committed himself even more strongly to a reform agenda that included a drastic overhaul of the banking system and the stock market. The Republican Old Guard, meanwhile, was more determined than ever to run the "radical" Roosevelt out of the White House. Sensing that he might fail to win his party's nomination, and mindful of a rash promise he had made in 1904 not to run again in 1908, Roosevelt decided not to seek reelection. It was a decision that would soon come back to haunt him. Barely 50, he was too young and energetic to end his political career. And much of his reform program had yet to win Congressional approval.

THE TAFT PRESIDENCY

Roosevelt thought he had found in William Howard Taft, his secretary of war, an ideal successor. Taft had worked closely with Roosevelt on foreign and domestic policies. He had supported Roosevelt's progressive reforms and offered him shrewd advice on countless occasions. Roosevelt believed he possessed both the ideas and the skills to complete the reform Republican program.

To reach that conclusion, however, Roosevelt had to ignore some obvious differences between Taft and himself. Taft neither liked nor was particularly adept at politics. With the exception of a judgeship in an Ohio superior court, he had never held elective office. His greatest political asset was an ability to debate thorny constitutional questions. His respect for the Constitution and its separation of powers made him suspicious of the powers that Roosevelt had arrogated to the presidency. He was by nature a cautious and conservative man. As Roosevelt's anointed successor, Taft easily won the election of 1908, defeating the Democrat William Jennings Bryan with 52 percent of the vote. But his conservatism soon revealed itself in his choice of staid corporation lawyers, rather than freethinking reformers, for cabinet positions.

TAFT'S BATTLES WITH CONGRESS

Taft's troubles began when he appeared to side against progressives in two acrimonious congressional battles. The first was over tariff legislation, the second over the dictatorial powers of House Speaker "Uncle Joe" Cannon.

Progressives had long desired tariff reduction, believing that competition from foreign manufacturers would benefit American consumers and check the economic power of American manufacturers. Taft himself had raised expectations for tariff reduction when he called Congress into special session to consider a reform bill that called for a modest reduction of tariffs and an inheritance tax. The bill passed the House but was gutted in the Senate. When congressional progressives pleaded with Taft to use his power to whip conservative senators into line, he pressured the Old Guard into including a 2 percent corporate income tax in their version of the bill, but he did not insist on the tariff reductions. As a result, the Payne-Aldrich Tariff he signed into law on August 5, 1909, did nothing to encourage foreign imports. Progressive Republicans, bitterly disappointed, held Taft responsible.

They were further angered when Taft withdrew his support of their efforts to strip Speaker Cannon of his legislative powers, which (they felt) he was putting to improper use. By 1910

Republican insurgents no longer looked to Taft for leadership; instead they entered into an alliance with reform-minded congressional Democrats. This bipartisan coalition of insurgents first curbed Cannon's powers and then, over Taft's objections, diluted the pro-business nature of a railroad regulation bill. Relations between Taft and the progressive Republicans then all but collapsed in a bruising controversy over Taft's conservation policies.

THE BALLINGER-PINCHOT CONTROVERSY

Richard A. Ballinger, secretary of the interior, had aroused progressives' suspicions by reopening for private commercial use 1 million acres of land that the Roosevelt administration had previously brought under federal protection. Then, Gifford Pinchot, still head of the National Forest Service, obtained information implicating Ballinger in the sale of Alaskan coal deposits. Pinchot showed the information, including an allegation that Ballinger had personally profited from the sale, to Taft. When Taft defended Ballinger, Pinchot leaked the story to the press and publicly called on Congress to investigate the matter. Pinchot's insubordination cost him his job, but it riveted the nation's attention once again on corporate greed and government corruption. Taft's Old Guard allies controlled the investigation that followed, and Congress exonerated Ballinger. But Louis D. Brandeis, lawyer for the congressional reformers, kept the controversy alive by accusing Taft and his attorney general of tampering with information that had been sent to congressional investigators. Whatever hope Taft may have had of escaping political damage disappeared when Roosevelt, returning from an African hunting trip by way of Europe in the spring of 1910, staged a highly publicized rendezvous with Pinchot in England. In so doing, Roosevelt signaled his continuing support for his old friend Pinchot and his sharp displeasure with Taft.

ROOSEVELT'S RETURN

When Roosevelt arrived in the United States later that summer, he was still insisting that his political career was over. But his craving for the public eye and his conviction that the reform insurgency needed his leadership prompted a quick return from retirement. In September, Roosevelt embarked on a speaking tour, the high point of which was his elaboration at Osawatomie, Kansas, of his "New Nationalism," a far-reaching reform program that called for a strong federal government to stabilize the economy, protect the weak, and restore social harmony.

The 1910 congressional elections confirmed the popularity of Roosevelt's positions. Insurgent Republicans trounced conservative Republicans in primary after primary, and the embrace of reform by the Democrats brought them a majority in the House of Representatives. When Robert La Follette, who was challenging Taft for the Republican presidential nomination, seemed to suffer a nervous breakdown in February 1912, Roosevelt announced his own candidacy.

Although La Follette quickly recovered his health and resumed his campaign, there was little chance that he could beat Roosevelt in the fight for the Republican nomination. Taft, too, would have lost to Roosevelt had the decision been in the hands of rank-and-file Republicans. In the 13 states sponsoring preferential primaries, Roosevelt won nearly 75 percent of the delegates. But the party's national leadership remained in the hands of the Old Guard, and they were determined to deny Roosevelt the Republican nomination. Taft, angered by Roosevelt's

behavior, refused to step aside. At the Republican convention in Chicago, Taft won renomina-
tion on the first ballot.

THE BULL MOOSE CAMPAIGN

Roosevelt had expected this outcome. The night before the convention opened, he had told a
spirited assembly of 5,000 supporters that the party leaders would not succeed in derailing
their movement. The next day, Roosevelt and his supporters withdrew from the convention
and from the Republican Party. In August, the reformers reassembled as the new Progressive
Party, nominated Roosevelt for president and the California governor Hiram W. Johnson for
vice president, and hammered out the far-reaching reform platform they had long envisioned:
sweeping regulation of the corporations, extensive protections for workers, a sharply graduated income tax, and woman suffrage. The new party constituted a remarkable assemblage of
reformers, exhilarated by their defiance of party bosses. "I am as strong as a bull moose," Roosevelt roared as he readied for combat; his proud followers took to calling themselves "Bull
Moosers."

Some of them, however, probably including Roosevelt himself, knew that their mission was
futile. They had failed to enroll many of the Republican insurgents who had supported Roosevelt in the primaries but who now refused to abandon the GOP. Consequently, the Republican vote would be split between Roosevelt and Taft. And Roosevelt could not even be assured
of a united progressive vote. The Democrats had nominated a powerful reform candidate of
their own.

THE RISE OF WOODROW WILSON

Few would have predicted in 1908 that the distinguished president of Princeton University,
Woodrow Wilson, would be the 1912 Democratic nominee for president of the United States.
The son of a Presbyterian minister from Virginia, Wilson had practiced law for a short time
after graduating from Princeton before settling on an academic career. Earning his doctorate
in political science from Johns Hopkins in 1886, he taught history and political science at Bryn
Mawr and Wesleyan (Connecticut) before returning to Princeton in 1890. He became presi-
dent of Princeton in 1902, a post he held until he successfully ran for the governorship of New
Jersey in 1910.

Throughout his almost 30 years in academia, however, Wilson had aspired to a career in
politics. In 1885 he published *Congressional Government,* a brilliant analysis and critique of
Congress. He had long admired the powerful leadership style of such British parliamentary
giants as Benjamin Disraeli and William Gladstone. "I feel like a new prime minister getting
ready to address his constituents," he remarked to his wife as he prepared for the Princeton
presidency in 1902. The national reputation he won in that office rested less on his originality
as an educator than on the leadership he displayed in transforming the humdrum College of
New Jersey into a world-class university.

Wilson's public stature as a university president afforded him new opportunities to com-
ment on political as well as educational matters. Identifying himself with the anti-Bryan wing
of the Democratic Party, he attracted the attention of wealthy conservatives, who saw him as a
potential presidential candidate. They convinced the bosses of the New Jersey Democratic ma-

WOODROW WILSON   Wilson entered politics after a long career in academia, where he had been a distinguished political scientist, historian, and university president. Here he strides across the Princeton campus in 1910, the last year of his college presidency.

chine to nominate Wilson for governor in 1910. Beset by growing opposition to his aggressive style of leadership from trustees and faculty members at Princeton, and eager to test his talents in a new arena, Wilson accepted the nomination and won the governorship handily. He then shocked his conservative backers by declaring his independence from the state's Democratic machine and moving New Jersey into the forefront of reform.

THE UNEXPECTED PROGRESSIVE

Wilson's Presbyterian upbringing had instilled in him a strong sense that society should be governed by God's moral law. As a young man in the 1880s, he had come to believe that the social consequences of unregulated industrialization were repugnant to Christian ethical principles. "The modern industrial organization," he wrote at the time, had "so distorted competition as to put it into the power of some to tyrannize over many, as to enable the rich and strong to combine against the poor and weak." And therefore, Wilson asked, "must not government lay aside all timid scruple and boldly make itself an agency for social reform as well as political control?" Wilson wanted reform to occur in an orderly, peaceful way; he recoiled from the labor and populist agitators who, in his eyes, showed no respect for existing social and political institutions. The more Wilson stressed the values of order, harmony, and tradition in his public speeches as president of Princeton, the more he attracted the attention of conservatives. But although Wilson's reform impulses had receded, they had not disappeared. Their presence in his thought helps to explain his emergence in 1911 and 1912 as one of the most outspoken progressives in the nation.

THE ELECTION OF 1912

At the Democratic convention of 1912, Wilson was something of a dark horse, running a distant second to House Speaker Champ Clark of Missouri. When the New York delegation gave Clark a simple majority of delegates, virtually everyone assumed that he would soon command the two-thirds majority needed to win the nomination. But Wilson's managers held onto Wilson's delegates and began chipping away at Clark's lead. On the fourth day, on the 46th ballot, Wilson finally won the nomination. The exhausted Democrats then closed ranks behind a candidate who pledged to renew the national campaign for reform.

The stage was now set for the momentous 1912 election. Given the split in Republican ranks, Democrats had their best chance in 20 years of regaining the White House. A Wilson victory, moreover, would give the country its first southern-born president in almost 50 years. Finally, whatever its outcome, the election promised to deliver a hefty vote for reform. Both Roosevelt and Wilson were running on reform platforms, and the Socialist Party candidate, Eugene V. Debs, was attracting larger crowds and generating greater enthusiasm than had been expected.

Debate among the candidates focused on the trusts. All three reform candidates agreed that corporations had acquired too much economic power. Debs argued that the only way to ensure popular control of that power was for the federal government to assume ownership of the trusts. Roosevelt called for the establishment of a powerful government that would regulate and, if necessary, curb the power of the trusts. This was the essence of his New Nationalism, the program he had been advocating since 1910.

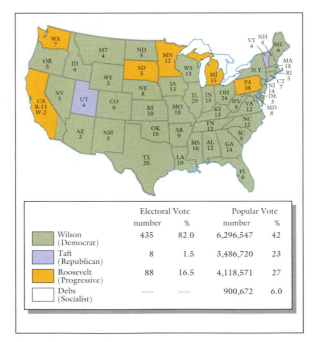

		Electoral Vote		Popular Vote	
		number	%	number	%
▮	Wilson (Democrat)	435	82.0	6,296,547	42
▮	Taft (Republican)	8	1.5	3,486,720	23
▮	Roosevelt (Progressive)	88	16.5	4,118,571	27
▯	Debs (Socialist)	----	----	900,672	6.0

PRESIDENTIAL ELECTION, 1912

Wilson, however, was too suspicious of centralized government to countenance such a program. Rather than regulate the trusts, he wanted to break them up. He wanted to reverse the tendency toward economic concentration and thus restore opportunity to the people. This philosophy, which Wilson labeled the "New Freedom," called for a temporary concentration of governmental power in order to dismantle the trusts. But once that was accomplished, Wilson promised, the government would relinquish its power.

Wilson won the November election with 42 percent of the popular vote to Roosevelt's 27 percent and Taft's 23 percent; Debs made a strong showing with 6 percent, the largest in his party's history. The three candidates who had pledged themselves to sweeping reform programs—Wilson, Roosevelt, and Debs—together won a remarkable 75 percent of the vote.

THE WILSON PRESIDENCY

The new president immediately put into practice the parliamentary-style leadership he had long admired. He assembled a cabinet of talented men who could be counted on for wise counsel, loyalty, and influence over vital Democratic constituencies. He cultivated a public image of himself as a president firmly in charge of his party and as a faithful tribune of the people.

TARIFF REFORM AND A PROGRESSIVE INCOME TAX

Like his predecessor, Wilson first turned his attention to tariff reform. Immediately after his inauguration, he called Congress into special session to consider the matter. The House passed a tariff reduction bill within a month. But the bill ran into trouble in the Senate, chiefly because of the pressure that protectionist lobbyists applied to key Democratic senators. Wilson outflanked them by appealing directly to the American people to destroy the influence of private interests on lawmakers. Wilson's plea to the public, together with an ensuing investigation of senator-lobbyist relations, humbled the Senate into complying with the president's wishes.

The resulting Underwood-Simmons Tariff of 1913 achieved the long-sought progressive aim of significantly reducing tariff barriers (from approximately 40 to 25 percent). Then, partly as a matter of expediency (new funds had to be found to make up for revenue lost to tariff reductions), another progressive ambition was achieved with passage of a law calling for an income tax. The Sixteenth Amendment to the Constitution, ratified by the states in 1913, had already given the government the right to impose an income tax; the income tax law passed by Congress made good on the progressive pledge to reduce the power and privileges of wealthy Americans by requiring them to pay taxes on a greater *percentage* of their income than the poor.

THE FEDERAL RESERVE ACT

Wilson continued to demonstrate his leadership by keeping Congress in session through the summer to consider various plans to overhaul the nation's financial system. Virtually everyone in both parties agreed on the need for greater federal regulation of banks and currency, but there were sharp differences over how to proceed. The banking interests and their congressional supporters wanted the government to give the authority to regulate credit and currency flows either to a single bank or to several regional banks. Progressives opposed the vesting of so much financial power in private hands and insisted that any reformed financial system must be publicly controlled. Wilson worked out a compromise plan that included both private and public controls and marshaled the votes to push it through both the House and the Senate. By the end of 1913 Wilson had signed the Federal Reserve Act, the most important law passed in his first administration.

The Federal Reserve Act established 12 regional banks, each controlled by the private banks in its region. Every private bank in the country was required to deposit an average of 6 percent of its assets in its regional Federal Reserve bank. The reserve would be used to make loans to member banks and to issue paper currency (Federal Reserve notes) to facilitate financial transactions. The regional banks were also instructed to use their funds to shore up member banks in distress and to respond to sudden changes in credit demands by easing or tightening the flow of credit. A Federal Reserve Board appointed by the president and responsible to the public rather than to private bankers would set policy and oversee activities within the 12 reserve banks.

The Federal Reserve system did a great deal to strengthen the nation's financial structure and was in most respects an impressive political achievement for Wilson. In its final form, however, it revealed that Wilson was retreating from his New Freedom pledge. The Federal Reserve Board was a less powerful and less centralized federal authority than a national bank would have been, but it nevertheless represented a substantial increase in government control of banking. Moreover, the bill authorizing the system made no attempt to break up private financial institutions that had grown too powerful. Because it sought to work with large banks rather than to break them up, the Federal Reserve system seemed more consonant with the principles of Roosevelt's New Nationalism than with those of Wilson's New Freedom.

FROM THE NEW FREEDOM TO THE NEW NATIONALISM

Wilson's failure to mount a vigorous antitrust campaign confirmed his drift toward the New Nationalism. For example, in 1914 Wilson swung his full support behind the Federal Trade Commission Act, which created a government agency by that name to regulate business practices. Because the act gave the Federal Trade Commission (FTC) wide powers to collect information on corporate pricing policies and on cooperation and competition among businesses, the FTC might have been used to prosecute trusts for "unfair trade practices." But the Senate stripped the FTC Act's companion legislation, the Clayton Antitrust Act, of virtually all provisions that would have allowed vigorous government prosecution of the trusts. Wilson supported this weakening of the Clayton Act, having decided that the breakup of large-scale industry was no longer practical or preferable. The purpose of the FTC, in Wilson's eyes, was to help businesses, large and small, to regulate themselves in ways that contributed to national well-being.

But would Wilson use government merely to assist businessmen and bankers to regulate themselves? Or would he use government to balance the claims of industry and finance against the claims of labor, farmers, and other disadvantaged groups?

In 1914 and 1915 Wilson favored the first approach: He intended the FTC to become as much a friend to business as a policeman. At this time, Wilson usually refused to use government powers to aid organized groups of workers and farmers. Nor did Wilson, at this time, view with any greater sympathy the campaign for African Americans' political equality. He

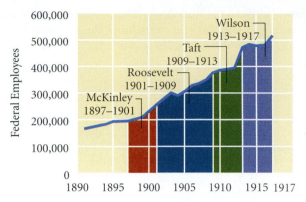

GROWTH IN FEDERAL EMPLOYEES, 1891–1917

Source: Reprinted by permission from *The Federal Government Service,* ed. W. S. Sayre (Englewood Cliffs, N.J.: Prentice-Hall, 1965), p. 41, The American Assembly.

supported efforts by white southerners in his cabinet to segregate their government departments, and he ignored pleas from the NAACP to involve the federal government in a campaign against lynching.

In late 1915, however, Wilson changed his tune, in part because he feared losing his reelection in 1916. The Bull Moosers of 1912 were retreating back to the Republican Party. To halt the progressives' rapprochement with the GOP, he made a stunning bid for their support. In January 1916 he nominated Louis Brandeis to the Supreme Court. Not only was Brandeis one of the country's most respected progressives, he was also the first Jew nominated to serve on the country's highest court. Congressional conservatives did everything they could to block the confirmation of a man they regarded as dangerously radical. But Wilson, as usual, was better organized, and by June his forces in the Senate had emerged victorious.

Wilson followed up this victory by pushing through Congress the first federal workmen's compensation law (the Kern-McGillicuddy Act, which covered federal employees), the first federal law outlawing child labor (the Keating-Owen Act), and the first federal law guaranteeing workers an eight-hour day (the Adamson Act, which covered the nation's 400,000 railway workers). The number of Americans affected by these acts was in fact rather small; nevertheless, Wilson had reoriented the Democratic Party to a New Nationalism that cared as much about the interests of the powerless as the interests of the powerful.

Trade unionists flocked to Wilson, as did most of the prominent progressives who had followed the Bull Moose in 1912. Meanwhile, Wilson had appealed to the supporters of William Jennings Bryan by supporting legislation that made large amounts of federal credit available to farmers in need. He had put together a reform coalition capable of winning a majority at the polls. In the process, he had transformed the Democratic Party. From 1916 on, the Democrats, rather than the Republicans, became the chief guardians of the American reform tradition.

That Wilson did so is a sign of the strength of the reform and radical forces in American society. By 1916 the ranks of middle-class progressives had grown broad and deep. Working-class protest had also accelerated in scope and intensity. In Lawrence, Massachusetts, in 1912, and in Paterson, New Jersey, in 1913, for example, the IWW organized strikes of textile workers that drew national attention, as did the 1914 strike by Colorado mine workers that ended with the infamous Ludlow massacre (see Chapter 20). These protests reflected the mobilization of those working-class constituencies—immigrants, women, the unskilled—long considered inconsequential both to American labor and party politics. Assisted by radicals, these groups had begun to fashion a more inclusive and politically contentious labor movement.

CHRONOLOGY

1889	Hull House established
1890–1904	All ex-Confederate states pass laws designed to disfranchise black voters • Virtually all states adopt the Australian (secret) ballot
1900	La Follette elected governor of Wisconsin • City commission plan introduced in Galveston, Texas
1901–1914	More than 1,000 African Americans lynched
1901	Johnson elected reform mayor of Cleveland • McKinley assassinated; Roosevelt becomes president
1902	Initiative and referendum introduced in Oregon • Roosevelt sides with workers in coal strike
1903	Federal court dissolves Northern Securities Company
1904	Roosevelt defeats Parker for presidency
1905	National Forest Service established
1906	La Follette elected to U.S. Senate • Congress passes Hepburn Act • Upton Sinclair publishes *The Jungle* • Congress passes Pure Food and Drug Act and Meat Inspection Act
1907	Reformer Hughes elected New York governor • Financial panic shakes economy
1908	Taft defeats Bryan for presidency
1909	Congress passes Payne-Aldrich tariff bill
1910	Ballinger-Pinchot controversy • NAACP founded • Wilson elected governor of New Jersey
1911	National Urban League founded • City manager plan introduced in Sumter, South Carolina • Wisconsin Industrial Commission established
1912	Roosevelt forms Progressive Party • Wilson defeats Roosevelt, Taft, and Debs for presidency
1913	Sixteenth and Seventeenth Amendments ratified • Congress passes Underwood-Simmons Tariff • Congress establishes Federal Reserve system
1914	Congress establishes Federal Trade Commission • Congress passes Clayton Antitrust Act
1916	Louis Brandeis appointed to Supreme Court • Kern-McGillicuddy Act, Keating-Owen Act, and Adamson Act passed • National Park Service formed • National Women's Party founded
1919	Eighteenth Amendment ratified
1920	Nineteenth Amendment ratified

Conclusion

By 1916, the progressives had accomplished a great deal. They exposed and curbed some of the worst abuses of the American political system. They enfranchised women and took steps to protect the environment. They broke the hold of laissez-faire economic policies on national politics and replaced it with the idea of a strong federal government committed to economic regulation and social justice. They enlarged the executive branch by establishing new commissions and agencies charged with administering government policies.

The progressives, in short, had presided over the emergence of a new national state, one in which power increasingly flowed away from municipalities and states and toward the federal government. There was a compelling logic to this reorientation: A national government stood a better chance of solving the problems of economic inequality, mismanagement of natural resources, and consumer fraud than did local and state governments.

The promise of effective remedies, however, brought new dangers. In particular, the new national state was giving rise to a bureaucratic elite whose power rested on federal authority rather than private wealth or political machines. The university-educated experts who staffed the new federal agencies, progressives argued, would bring to the political process the very qualities that party politicians allegedly lacked: knowledge, dedication, and honesty. But many of these new public servants were not entirely disinterested and unassuming. Some had close ties to the corporations and businesses that their agencies were expected to regulate. Others allowed their prejudices against women, immigrants, and minorities to shape social policy. Still others believed that "the people" could not be trusted to evaluate the government's work intelligently. For these reasons, the progressive state did not always enhance democracy or secure the people's sovereignty.

BECOMING A WORLD POWER, 1898–1917

THE UNITED STATES LOOKS ABROAD

THE SPANISH-AMERICAN WAR

THE UNITED STATES BECOMES A WORLD POWER

THEODORE ROOSEVELT, GEOPOLITICIAN

WILLIAM HOWARD TAFT, DOLLAR DIPLOMAT

WOODROW WILSON, STRUGGLING IDEALIST

For much of the 19th century, most Americans were preoccupied by continental expansion. Elections rarely turned on international events, and presidents rarely made their reputations as statesmen in the world arena. The diplomatic corps was small and inexperienced. The government projected its limited military power westward and possessed virtually no capacity or desire for involvement overseas.

The nation's rapid industrial growth in the late 19th century forced a turn away from such continentalism. Technological advances, especially the laying of transoceanic cables and the introduction of steamship travel, diminished America's physical isolation. The babel of languages one could hear in American cities testified to how much the Old World had penetrated the New. Then, too, Americans watched anxiously as England, Germany, Russia, Japan, and other industrial powers intensified their competition for overseas markets and colonies, and some believed America also needed to enter this contest.

A war with Spain in 1898 gave the United States an opportunity to upgrade its military and acquire colonies and influence in the Western Hemisphere and Asia. Under Presidents William McKinley and Theodore Roosevelt, the United States pursued these initiatives, with impressive results. But subjugating the peoples of Cuba, Puerto Rico, and the Philippines did not sit well with all Americans. It seemed as though the United States was becoming the kind of nation that many Americans had long despised—one that valued power more than liberty. Exercising imperial power did not trouble Roosevelt, who wanted to create an international system in which a handful of industrial nations pursued their global economic interests, dominated world trade, and kept the world at peace. It did concern Woodrow Wilson, however, who sought to devise a policy toward postrevolutionary Mexico that restrained American might and respected Mexican desires for liberty.

THE UNITED STATES LOOKS ABROAD

By the late 19th century, sizable numbers of Americans had become interested in extending their country's influence abroad. The most important groups were Protestant missionaries, businessmen, and imperialists.

PROTESTANT MISSIONARIES

Protestant missionaries were among the most active promoters of American interests abroad. Integration of the world economy made evangelical Protestants more conscious of the diversity of the world's peoples. Overseas missionary activity grew quickly between 1870 and 1900, most of it directed toward China. Convinced of the superiority of the Anglo-Saxon race, Protestant missionaries considered it their Christian duty to teach the Gospel to the "ignorant" Asian masses and save their souls. Missionaries also believed that their efforts would free those masses from their racial destiny, enabling them to become "civilized."

BUSINESSMEN

For different reasons, industrialists, traders, and investors also began to look overseas, sensing that they could make fortunes in foreign lands. Exports of American manufactured goods rose substantially after 1880. By 1914 American foreign investment equaled 7 percent of the nation's gross national product. Companies such as Kodak Camera, Singer Sewing Machine, Standard Oil, American Tobacco, and International Harvester had become multinational corporations with overseas branch offices.

Some industrialists became entranced by the prospect of clothing, feeding, and housing the 400 million people of China. James B. Duke, who headed American Tobacco, was selling 1 billion cigarettes a year in East Asian markets. Looking for ways to fill empty boxcars heading west from Minnesota to Tacoma, Washington, the railroad tycoon James J. Hill imagined stuffing them with wheat and steel destined for China and Japan. Although export trade with East Asia during this period never fulfilled the expectations of Hill and other industrialists, their talk about the "wealth of the Orient" convinced politicians that this part of the world was important to national well-being.

Events of the 1890s only intensified the appeal of foreign markets. First, the 1890 U.S. census announced that the frontier had disappeared; America had completed the task of westward expansion. Then, in 1893 a young historian named Frederick Jackson Turner published an essay, "The Significance of the Frontier in American History," that articulated what many Americans feared: that the frontier had been essential to the growth of the economy and to the cultivation of democracy. It was the wilderness, Turner argued, that had transformed the Europeans who settled the New World into Americans. They shed their European clothes, tools, social customs, and political beliefs, and acquired distinctively "American" characteristics— rugged individualism, egalitarianism, and a democratic faith. How, Turner wondered, could the nation continue to prosper now that the frontier had gone?

In recent years, historians of the American West have criticized Turner's "frontier thesis." They have argued that the very idea of the frontier as uninhabited wilderness overlooked the tens of thousands of Indians who occupied the region and that much else of what Americans believe about the West is based more on myth than on reality.

LEADING U.S. EXPORTS, 1875 AND 1915

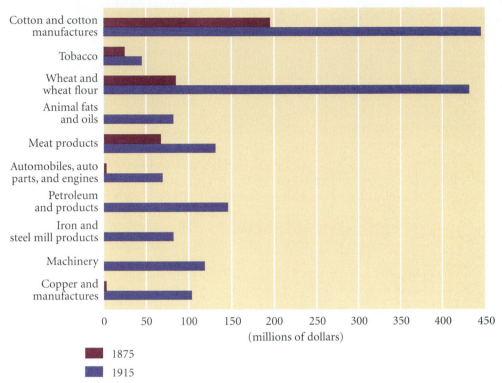

1875
1915

Source: Data from *Historical Statistics of the United States, Colonial Times to 1970* (White Plains, N.Y.: Kraus International, 1989).

Even though these points are valid, they would have meant little to Americans living in Turner's time. For them, as for Turner, concern about the disappearing frontier expressed a fear that the increasingly urbanized and industrialized nation had lost its way. Turner's essay appeared just as the country was entering the deepest, longest, and most conflict-ridden depression in its history (see Chapter 19). What could the republic do to regain its economic prosperity and political stability? Where would it find its new frontiers? One answer to these questions focused on the pursuit of overseas expansion.

IMPERIALISTS

Eager to assist in the drive for overseas economic expansion was a group of politicians, intellectuals, and military strategists who viewed such expansion as a key ingredient in the pursuit of world power. They believed that the United States should build a strong navy, solidify a sphere of influence in the Caribbean, and extend markets into Asia. Their desire to control ports and territories beyond the continental borders of their own country made them imperialists. Many of them were also Social Darwinists, who believed that America's destiny required that it prove itself supreme in international affairs.

Perhaps the most influential imperialist was Admiral Alfred Thayer Mahan. In the 1880s Mahan had become convinced that all the world's great empires, beginning with Rome, had relied on their capacity to control the seas. In an influential book, *The Influence of Sea Power upon History, 1660–1783* (1890), Mahan called for the construction of a first-class navy with enough ships and firepower to make its presence felt everywhere in the world. To be effective, that global fleet would require a canal across Central America. It would also require a string of far-flung service bases. Mahan wanted the U.S. government to take possession of Hawaii and other strategically located Pacific islands with superior harbor facilities.

Presidents William McKinley and Theodore Roosevelt would eventually make almost the whole of Mahan's vision a reality. But in the early 1890s Mahan doubted that Americans would accept the responsibility and costs of empire. Many Americans still insisted that the United States should not aspire to world power by acquiring overseas bases and colonizing foreign peoples.

Mahan underestimated the government's alarm over the scramble of Europeans to extend their imperial control. Every administration from the 1880s on committed itself to a "big navy" policy. Already in 1878, the United States had secured rights to Pago Pago, a superb deep-water harbor in Samoa (a collection of islands in the southwest Pacific inhabited by Polynesians), and in 1885 it had leased Pearl Harbor from the Hawaiians. Both harbors were expected to serve as fueling stations for the growing U.S. fleet.

These attempts to project U.S. power overseas had already deepened the government's involvement in the affairs of distant lands. In 1889, the United States established a protectorate over part of Samoa. In the early 1890s, President Grover Cleveland's administration was increasingly drawn into Hawaiian affairs, as tensions between American sugar plantation owners and native Hawaiians upset the islands' economic and political stability. In 1891 the plantation owners succeeded in deposing the Hawaiian king and putting into power Queen Liliuokalani. But when Liliuokalani strove to establish her independence, the planters, assisted by U.S. sailors, overthrew her too. Cleveland declared Hawaii a protectorate in 1893, but he resisted the imperialists in Congress who wanted to annex the islands.

THE U.S. NAVY, 1890–1914: EXPENDITURES AND BATTLESHIP SIZE

FISCAL YEAR	TOTAL FEDERAL EXPENDITURES	NAVAL EXPENDITURES	NAVAL EXPENDITURES AS PERCENT OF TOTAL FEDERAL EXPENDITURES	SIZE OF BATTLESHIPS (AVERAGE TONS DISPLACED)
1890	$318,040,711	$22,006,206	6.9%	11,000
1900	520,860,847	55,953,078	10.7	12,000
1901	524,616,925	60,506,978	11.5	16,000
1905	657,278,914	117,550,308	20.7	16,000
1909	693,743,885	115,546,011	16.7	27,000 (1910)
1914	735,081,431	139,682,186	19.0	32,000

Sources: (for expenditures) E. B. Potter, *Sea Power: A Naval History* (Annapolis: Naval Institute Press, 1982), p. 187; (for size of ships) Harold Sprout, *Toward a New Order of Sea Power* (New York: Greenwood Press, 1976), p. 52.

By this time, imperialist sentiment in Congress and throughout the nation was being fueled by "jingoism." Jingoists were nationalists who thought that a swaggering foreign policy and a willingness to go to war would enhance their nation's glory. This predatory brand of nationalism emerged not only in the United States, but in Britain, France, Germany, and Japan as well. The anti-imperialist editor of *The Nation*, E. L. Godkin, exclaimed in 1894: "The number of men and officials of this country who are now mad to fight somebody is appalling." Spain's behavior in Cuba in the 1890s gave those men and officials the war they sought.

THE SPANISH-AMERICAN WAR

Relations between the Cubans and their Spanish rulers had long been deteriorating. A revolt in 1868 had taken the Spanish 10 years to subdue. In 1895 the Cubans staged another revolt. The fighting was brutal. Cuban forces destroyed large areas of the island to make it uninhabitable by the Spanish. The Spanish army, led by General Valeriano Weyler, responded in kind, forcing large numbers of Cubans into concentration camps. Denied adequate food, shelter, and sanitation, an estimated 200,000 Cubans died of starvation and disease.

Such tactics inflamed American opinion. Many Americans sympathized with the Cubans. Americans were kept well informed about the atrocities by accounts in the *New York Journal*, owned by William Randolph Hearst, and the *New York World*, owned by Joseph Pulitzer. Hearst and Pulitzer were transforming newspaper publishing in much the same way that other publishers had revolutionized the magazine business (see Chapter 21). To boost circulation they sought out the most sensational and shocking stories and then described them in lurid detail. They were accused of engaging in "yellow journalism"—embellishing stories with titillating details when the true reports did not seem dramatic enough.

The sensationalism of the yellow press and its frequently jingoistic accounts were not sufficient to bring about American intervention in Cuba, however. In the final days of his administration, President Cleveland resisted mounting pressure to intervene. William McKinley, who succeeded him in 1897, harshly denounced the Spanish, with the aim of forcing Spain into concessions that would satisfy the Cuban rebels and bring an end to the conflict. Initially, this strategy seemed to be working: Spain relieved "Butcher" Weyler of his command, stopped incarcerating Cubans in concentration camps, and granted Cuba limited autonomy. But the Spaniards who lived on the island refused to be ruled by a Cuban government, and the Cuban rebels continued to demand full independence. Late in 1897, when riots broke out in Havana, McKinley ordered the battleship *Maine* into Havana harbor to protect U.S. citizens and their property. Two unexpected events then set off a war.

The first was the February 9, 1898, publication in Hearst's *New York Journal* of a letter stolen from Depuy de Lôme, the Spanish minister to Washington, in which he described McKinley as "a cheap politician" and a "bidder for the admiration of the crowd." The de Lôme letter also implied that the Spanish were not serious about resolving the Cuban crisis through negotiation and reform. The news embarrassed Spanish officials and outraged U.S. public opinion. Then, only six days later, the *Maine* exploded in Havana harbor, killing 260 American sailors. Although subsequent investigations revealed that the most probable cause of the explosion was a malfunctioning boiler, Americans were certain that it had been the work of Spanish agents. "Remember the Maine!" screamed the headlines in the yellow press. On March 8, Congress responded to the clamor for war by authorizing $50 million to mobilize U.S. forces. In the meantime, McKinley

"REMEMBER THE *MAINE!*"   The explosion of the battleship *Maine* in Havana harbor on February 16, 1898, killed 260 American sailors and helped to drive the United States into war with Spain.

notified Spain of his conditions for avoiding war: Spain would pay an indemnity for the *Maine,* abandon its concentration camps, end the fighting with the rebels, and commit itself to Cuban independence. On April 9, Spain accepted all the demands but the last. Nevertheless, on April 11, McKinley asked Congress for authority to go to war. Three days later Congress approved a war resolution, which included a declaration (spelled out in the Teller Amendment) that the United States would not use the war as an opportunity to acquire territory in Cuba. On April 24, Spain responded with a formal declaration of war against the United States.

"A SPLENDID LITTLE WAR"

Secretary of State John Hay called the fight with Spain "a splendid little war." Begun in April, it ended in August. More than 1 million men volunteered to fight, while fewer than 500 were killed or wounded in combat. The American victory over Spain was complete, not just in Cuba but in the neighboring island of Puerto Rico and in the Philippines, Spain's strategic possession in the Pacific.

Actually, the war was more complicated than it seemed. The main reason for the easy victory was U.S. naval superiority. In the war's first major battle, a naval engagement in Manila harbor in the Philippines on May 1, a U.S. fleet commanded by Commodore George Dewey destroyed an entire Spanish fleet. On land, the story was different. On the eve of war the U.S. Army consisted of only 26,000 troops. A force of 80,000 Spanish regulars awaited them in Cuba. Congress immediately increased the Army to 62,000 and called for an additional 125,000 volunteers. The response to this call was astounding, but outfitting, training, and transporting the new recruits overwhelmed the Army's capacities. Its standard-issue, blue flannel uniforms proved too heavy for fighting in Cuba. Most of the volunteers had to make

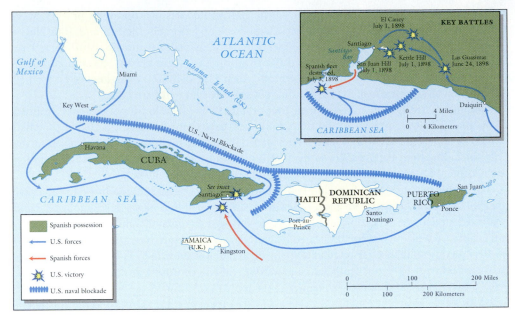

SPANISH-AMERICAN WAR IN CUBA, 1898

do with ancient Civil War rifles that still used black, rather than smokeless, powder. Moreover, the Army was unprepared for the effects of malaria and other tropical diseases.

That the Cuban revolutionaries were predominantly black also came as a shock to the U.S. forces. In their attempts to arouse support for the Cuban cause, U.S. newspapers had portrayed the Cuban rebels as fundamentally similar to white Americans, with an "Anglo-Saxon tenacity of purpose." The Spanish oppressors, by contrast, were depicted as dark complexioned and as possessing the characteristics of their "dark race": barbarism, cruelty, and indolence. The U.S. troops' first encounters with Cuban and Spanish forces dispelled these myths. Their Cuban allies appeared poorly outfitted, rough in their manners, and primarily black-skinned. The Spanish soldiers appeared well-disciplined, tough in battle, and light-complexioned.

The Cuban rebels were actually skilled guerrilla fighters, but racial prejudice prevented most U.S. soldiers and reporters from crediting their military accomplishments. Instead, they judged the Cubans harshly—as primitive, savage, and incapable of self-control or self-government. White U.S. troops preferred not to fight alongside the Cubans; increasingly, they refused to co-ordinate strategy with them.

At first, the U.S. Army's ineptitude and its racial misconceptions did little to diminish the soldiers' hunger for a good fight. No one was more eager for battle than Theodore Roosevelt who, along with Colonel Leonard Wood, led a volunteer cavalry unit comprised of Ivy League gentlemen, western cowboys, sheriffs, prospectors, Indians, and small numbers of Hispanics and ethnic European Americans. Roosevelt's "Rough Riders," as the unit came to be known, landed with the invasion force and played an active role in the three battles fought in the hills surrounding Santiago. Their most famous action was a furious charge up Kettle Hill into the teeth of Spanish defenses. Roosevelt's bravery was stunning, though his judgment was faulty.

Nearly 100 men were killed or wounded in the charge. Reports of Roosevelt's bravery over-shadowed the equally brave performance of other troops, notably the 9th and 10th Negro Cavalries, which played a pivotal role in clearing away Spanish fortifications on Kettle Hill. One Rough Rider commented: "If it had not been for the Negro cavalry, the Rough Riders would have been exterminated." The 24th and 25th Negro Infantry Regiments performed equally vital tasks in the U.S. Army's conquest of the adjacent San Juan Hill.

African American soldiers risked their lives despite the segregationist policies that confined them to all-black regiments. At the time, Roosevelt gave them full credit for what they had done. But soon after returning home, he began minimizing their contributions, even to the point of calling their behavior cowardly. Like most white American officers and enlisted men of the time, Roosevelt had difficulty believing that blacks could fight well.

The taking of Kettle Hill, San Juan Hill, and other high ground surrounding Santiago gave the U.S. forces a substantial advantage over the Spanish defenders. Nevertheless, logistical and medical problems nearly did them in. The troops were short of food, ammunition, and medical facilities. Their ranks were devastated by malaria, typhoid, and dysentery; more than 5,000 soldiers died from disease. Fortunately, the Spanish had lost the will to fight. On July 3 Spain's Atlantic fleet tried to retreat from Santiago harbor and was promptly destroyed by a U.S. fleet. The Spanish army in Santiago surrendered on July 16; on July 18 the Spanish government asked for peace. While negotiations for an armistice proceeded, U.S. forces overran the neighboring island of Puerto Rico. On August 12 the U.S. and Spanish governments agreed to an armistice. But before the news could reach the Philippines, the United States had captured Manila and had taken prisoner 13,000 Spanish soldiers.

The armistice required Spain to relinquish its claim to Cuba, cede Puerto Rico and the Pacific island of Guam to the United States, and tolerate the American occupation of Manila until a peace conference could be convened in Paris on October 1, 1898. At that conference, American diplomats startled their Spanish counterparts by demanding that Spain also cede the Philippines to the United States. After two months of stalling, the Spanish government agreed to relinquish its coveted Pacific colony for $20 million, and the transaction was sealed by the Treaty of Paris on December 10, 1898.

THE UNITED STATES BECOMES A WORLD POWER

America's initial war aim had been to oust the Spanish from Cuba—an aim supported by both imperialists and anti-imperialists, but for different reasons. Imperialists hoped to incorporate Cuba into a new American empire; anti-imperialists hoped to see the Cubans gain their independence. But only the imperialists condoned the U.S. acquisition of Puerto Rico, Guam, and particularly the Philippines. Soon after the war began, President McKinley had cast his lot with the imperialists. First, he annexed Hawaii, giving the United States permanent control of Pearl Harbor. Then, he set his sights on establishing a U.S. naval base at Manila. Never before had the United States sought such a large military presence outside the Western Hemisphere.

In a departure of equal importance, McKinley announced his intent to administer much of this newly acquired territory as U.S. colonies. Virtually all the territory previously acquired by the United States had been settled by Americans, who had eventually petitioned for statehood and been admitted to the Union with the same rights as existing states. In the case of these new territories, however, only Hawaii would be allowed to follow a traditional path toward

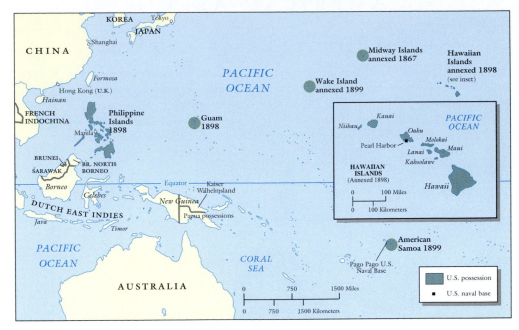

AMERICAN SOUTH PACIFIC EMPIRE, 1900

statehood. There, the powerful American sugar plantation owners prevailed on Congress to pass an act in 1900 extending U.S. citizenship to all Hawaiian citizens and putting Hawaii on the road to statehood. But no influential group of Americans resided in the Philippines. The decision to make the country an American colony was taken mainly to prevent other powers, such as Japan and Germany, from gaining a foothold somewhere in the 400-island archipelago and launching attacks on the American naval base in Manila.

The McKinley administration might have taken a different course. It might have negotiated a deal with Emilio Aguinaldo, the leader of the anticolonial movement, that would have given the Philippines independence in exchange for a U.S. naval base at Manila. An American fleet stationed there would have been able to protect both American interests and the fledgling Philippine nation from predatory assaults by Japan, Germany, or Britain. Alternatively, the United States might have annexed the Philippines outright and offered Filipinos U.S. citizenship as the first step toward statehood. But McKinley believed that self-government was beyond the capacity of the "inferior" Filipino people. The United States would undertake a solemn mission to "civilize" the Filipinos and thereby prepare them for independence. But until that mission was complete, the Philippines would be ruled by American governors appointed by the president.

THE DEBATE OVER THE TREATY OF PARIS

The proposed acquisition of the Philippines aroused opposition both in the United States and in the Philippines. The Anti-Imperialist League enlisted the support of several elder statesmen in McKinley's own party, as well as the former Democratic President Grover Cleveland, the industrialist Andrew Carnegie, and the labor leader Samuel Gompers. William Jennings Bryan,

KETTLE HILL IN BLACK AND WHITE

Theodore Roosevelt believed that the "Rough Rider" regiment that he commanded in the Spanish-American War (pictured below) was a melting pot of southwesterners, Ivy Leaguers, and Indians, with a smattering of Hispanics and ethnic European Americans. Combat, he further believed, would forge these many groups into one, as war had always done in the American past. African Americans and Asian immigrants were the two groups conspicuously absent from this mix.

meanwhile, marshaled a vigorous anti-imperialist protest among Democrats in the South and West. Some anti-imperialists believed that the subjugation of the Filipinos would violate the nation's most precious principle: the right of all people to independence and self-government.

Other anti-imperialists were motivated more by self-interest than by democratic ideals. U.S. sugar producers, for example, feared competition from Filipino producers. Trade unionists worried that poor Filipinos would flood the U.S. labor market and depress wage rates. Some businessmen warned that the costs of maintaining an imperial outpost would exceed

Yet the success of Roosevelt's charge up Kettle Hill and San Juan Hill had depended on the assistance of four regiments of regular Army troops, the 9th and 10th Cavalry and the 24th and 25th Infantry, which happened to be black. Some members of the 10th Cavalry who took part in the battle are pictured below. The fury of the fighting damaged the cohesion of the different regiments to the extent that by the time the troops reached the San Juan summit, they were all intermixed: Ivy Leaguers and southwesterners, Hispanics and European immigrants, even blacks and whites, all fighting side by side. Combat had brought blacks into the great American melting pot, a phenomenon that Roosevelt celebrated at the time by praising the black troops.

But Roosevelt did not truly believe that blacks were the equals of whites, or that they could be absorbed into the American nation. So, over time, he downplayed the role of black troops and questioned their ability to fight. The heroic role of black soldiers not only disappeared from Roosevelt's own memory, but from most paintings and other commemorations of the great charge.

any economic benefits that the colony might produce. Still other anti-imperialists feared the contaminating effects of contact with "inferior" Asian races.

The anti-imperialists almost dealt McKinley and his fellow imperialists a defeat in the U.S. Senate, where the Treaty of Paris had to be ratified. On February 6, 1899, the Senate voted 57 to 27 in favor of the treaty, only one vote beyond the minimum two-thirds majority required for ratification. Two last-minute developments may have brought victory. First, William Jennings Bryan, in the days just before the vote, abandoned his opposition and announced his support for the treaty. Second, on the eve of the vote, Filipinos rose in revolt against the U.S. army of occupation. With another war looming and the lives of American soldiers imperiled, a few senators who had been reluctant to vote for the treaty may have felt obligated to support the president.

THE AMERICAN-FILIPINO WAR

The acquisition of the Philippines immediately embroiled the United States in a long, brutal war to subdue the Filipino rebels. In four years of fighting, more than 120,000 American soldiers served in the Philippines and more than 4,200 of them died. The war brought Americans face-to-face with an unpleasant truth: that American actions in the Philippines were virtually indistinguishable from Spain's actions in Cuba. Like Spain, the United States refused to acknowledge a people's aspiration for self-rule. Like "Butcher" Weyler, American generals permitted their soldiers to use savage tactics. Whole communities suspected of harboring guerrillas were driven into concentration camps, while their houses, farms, and livestock were destroyed. American soldiers executed so many Filipino rebels that the ratio of Filipino dead to wounded reached 15 to 1. One New York infantryman wrote home that his unit had killed 1,000 Filipinos in retaliation for the murder of a single American soldier. Estimates of total Filipino deaths from gunfire, starvation, and disease range from 50,000 to 200,000.

The United States finally gained the upper hand after General Arthur MacArthur (father of Douglas) was appointed commander of the islands in 1900. MacArthur did not lessen the war's ferocity, but he understood that it could not be won by guns alone. He offered amnesty to Filipino guerrillas who agreed to surrender, and he cultivated close relations with the islands' wealthy elites. McKinley supported this effort to build a Filipino constituency sympathetic to the U.S. presence. To that end, he sent William Howard Taft to the islands in 1900 to establish a civilian government. In 1901 Taft became the colony's first "governor-general." He transferred many governmental functions to Filipino control and sponsored a vigorous program of public works (roads, bridges, schools) that would give the Philippines the infrastructure necessary for economic development and political independence. By 1902 this dual strategy of ruthless war against those who had taken up arms and concessions to those who were willing to live under benevolent American rule had crushed the revolt, though sporadic fighting continued until 1913.

CONTROLLING CUBA AND PUERTO RICO

Helping the Cubans achieve independence had been one of the major rationalizations for the war against Spain. But in 1900, when General Leonard Wood, now commander of American forces in Cuba, authorized a constitutional convention to write the laws for a Cuban republic, the McKinley administration made clear it would not easily relinquish control of the island. At McKinley's urging, the U.S. Congress attached to a 1901 army appropriations bill the Platt Amendment delineating three conditions for Cuban independence. First, Cuba would not be permitted to make treaties with foreign powers. Second, the United States would have broad authority to intervene in Cuban political and economic affairs. Third, Cuba would sell or lease land to the United States for naval stations. The delegates to Cuba's constitutional convention were so outraged by these conditions that they refused even to vote on them. But the dependence of Cuba's vital sugar industry on the U.S. market and the continuing presence of a U.S. army on Cuban soil rendered resistance futile. In 1901, by a vote of 15 to 11, the delegates reluctantly wrote the Platt conditions into their constitution.

Cuba's status differed little from that of the Philippines. Both were colonies of the United States. In the case of Cuba, economic dependence closely followed political subjugation. Between 1898 and 1914, American trade with Cuba increased more than tenfold, while investments more than quadrupled. The United States intervened in Cuban political affairs a total of five times between 1906 and 1921 to protect its economic interests and those of the indigenous ruling class with whom it had become closely allied. The economic, political, and military control that the United States imposed on Cuba would fuel anti-American sentiment there for years to come.

Puerto Rico received somewhat different treatment. The United States did not think independence appropriate. Nor did it follow its Cuban strategy by granting Puerto Rico nominal independence under informal economic and political controls. Instead, it annexed the island outright with the Foraker Act (1900). This act contained no provision for making the inhabitants citizens of the United States. Puerto Rico was designated an "unincorporated" territory, which meant that Congress would dictate the island's government and specify the rights of its inhabitants. Puerto Ricans were allowed no role in designing their government, nor was their consent requested. With the Foraker Act, Congress had, in effect, invented a new, imperial mechanism for ensuring sovereignty over lands deemed vital to U.S. economic and military security. The U.S. Supreme Court upheld the constitutionality of this mechanism in a series of historic decisions, known as the Insular Cases, in the years from 1901 to 1904.

In some respects Puerto Rico fared better than "independent" Cuba. Puerto Ricans were granted U.S. citizenship in 1917 and won the right to elect their own governor in 1947. Still, Puerto Ricans enjoyed fewer political rights than Americans in the 48 states. Moreover, throughout the 20th century they endured a poverty rate far exceeding that of the mainland.

The subjugation of Cuba and the annexation of Puerto Rico troubled Americans far less than the U.S. takeover in the Philippines. Since the first articulation of the Monroe Doctrine in 1823, the United States had, in effect, claimed the Western Hemisphere as its sphere of influence. Within that sphere, many Americans believed, the United States possessed the right to act unilaterally to protect its interests. Before 1900 most of its actions (with the exception of the Mexican War) had been designed to limit the influence of European powers. After 1900, however, it assumed a more aggressive role, seizing land, overturning governments it did not like, and forcing its economic and political policies on weaker neighbors.

CHINA AND THE "OPEN DOOR"

Except for the Philippines and Guam, the United States made no effort to take control of Asian lands. Such a policy might well have triggered war with other world powers already well established in the area. The United States opted for a diplomatic rather than a military strategy to achieve its foreign policy objectives. In China, in 1899 and 1900, it proposed the policy of the "Open Door."

The United States was concerned that the actions of the other world powers in China would block its own efforts to open up China's markets to American goods. Britain, Germany, Japan, Russia, and France—each coveted their own chunk of China, where they could monopolize trade, exploit cheap labor, and establish military bases. By the 1890s each of these powers was building a sphere of influence, either by wringing economic and territorial concessions from the weak Chinese government or by seizing outright the land and trading privileges they desired.

To prevent China's breakup and to preserve American economic access to the whole of China, McKinley's secretary of state, John Hay, sent "Open Door" notes to the major world powers. The notes asked each power to open its Chinese sphere of influence to the merchants of other nations and to grant them reasonable harbor fees and railroad rates. Hay also asked each power to respect China's sovereignty by enforcing Chinese tariff duties in the territory it controlled.

None of the world powers was eager to endorse either of Hay's requests, though Britain and Japan gave provisional assent. France, Germany, Russia, and Italy responded evasively, indicating their support for the Open Door policy in theory but insisting that they could not implement it until all the other powers had done so. Hay then put the best face on their responses by declaring that all the powers had agreed to observe his Open Door principles and that he regarded their assent as "final and definitive." The rival powers may have been impressed by Hay's diplomacy, but whether they intended to uphold the United States' Open Door policy was not at all clear.

The first challenge to Hay's policy came from the Chinese themselves. In May 1900 a nationalist Chinese organization, colloquially known as the "Boxers," sparked an uprising to rid China of all "foreign devils" and foreign influences. Hundreds of Europeans were killed, as were many Chinese men and women who had converted to Christianity. When the Boxers laid siege to the foreign legations in Beijing and cut off communication between that city and the outside world, the imperial powers raised an expeditionary force to rescue the diplomats and punish the Chinese rebels. The force broke the Beijing siege in August, and ended the Boxer Rebellion soon thereafter.

Hay now sent out a second round of Open Door notes, asking each power to respect China's political independence and territorial integrity, in addition to guaranteeing unrestricted access to its markets. Worried that the Chinese rebels might strike again, the imperialist rivals responded more favorably. Britain, France, and Germany endorsed Hay's policy outright. With that support, Hay was able to check Russian and Japanese designs on Chinese territory. Significantly, when the powers decided that the Chinese government should pay them reparations for their property and personnel losses during the Boxer Rebellion, Hay convinced them to accept payment in cash rather than in territory. By keeping China intact and open to free trade, the United States had achieved a major foreign policy victory.

DANCE WITH DEATH?   America's acquisition of the Philippines and other colonies in 1898 generated bitter debate at home. This anti-imperialist cartoon from 1899 portrays U.S. expansion as a dangerous dance with "Death." In the background is a spurned and forlorn "Lady Liberty" who is powerless to stop Uncle Sam's infatuation with war and empire.

THEODORE ROOSEVELT, GEOPOLITICIAN

Roosevelt had been a driving force in the transformation of U.S. foreign policy during the McKinley administration. As assistant secretary of the navy, as a military hero, as a vigorous speaker and writer, and then as vice president, Roosevelt worked tirelessly to remake the country into one of the world's great powers. He fervently believed that the Anglo-Saxon character of the nation destined it for supremacy in both economic and political affairs. He did not assume, however, that international supremacy would automatically accrue to the United States. A nation, like an individual, had to strive for greatness. It had to build a military force that could convincingly project power overseas. And it had to be prepared to fight.

Roosevelt's appetite for a good fight caused many people to rue the ascension of this "cowboy" to the White House after McKinley's assassination in 1901. But behind his blustery exterior was a shrewd analyst of international relations. As much as he craved power for himself and the nation, he understood that the United States could not rule every portion of the globe through military or economic means. Consequently, he sought to bring about a balance of power among the great industrial nations through negotiation rather than war. Such a balance would enable each imperial power to safeguard its key interests and contribute to world peace and progress.

Absent from Roosevelt's geopolitical thinking was concern for the interests of less powerful nations. Roosevelt had little patience with the claims to sovereignty of small countries or the human rights of weak peoples. In his eyes, the peoples of Latin America, Asia (with the exception of Japan), and Africa were racially inferior and thus incapable of self-government or industrial progress.

UNITED STATES PRESENCE IN LATIN AMERICA, 1895–1934

THE ROOSEVELT COROLLARY

Ensuring U.S. dominance in the Western Hemisphere ranked high on Roosevelt's list of foreign policy objectives. In 1904 he issued a "corollary" to the Monroe Doctrine, which had asserted the right of the United States to keep European powers from meddling in hemispheric affairs. In his corollary Roosevelt declared that the United States possessed a further right: the right to intervene in the domestic affairs of hemispheric nations to quell disorder and forestall European intervention. The Roosevelt corollary formalized a policy that the United States had already deployed against Cuba and Puerto Rico in 1900 and 1901. Subsequent events in Venezuela and the Dominican Republic had further convinced Roosevelt of the need to expand the scope of U.S. intervention in hemispheric affairs.

The governments of both Venezuela and the Dominican Republic were controlled by corrupt dictators. Both had defaulted on debts owed to European banks. Their delinquency prompted a German-led European naval blockade and bombardment of Venezuela in 1902 and a threatened invasion of the Dominican Republic by Italy and France in 1903. The United States forced the German navy to retreat from the Venezuelan coast in 1903. In the Dominican Republic, after a revolution had chased the dictator from power, the United States assumed control of the nation's customs collections in 1905 and refinanced the Dominican national debt through U.S. bankers.

The prevalence of corrupt, dictatorial regimes in Latin America and the willingness of European bankers to loan these regimes money had provided ideal conditions for bankruptcy, social turmoil, and foreign intervention. The United States now took aggressive actions to correct those conditions. But rarely in Roosevelt's tenure did the United States show a willingness to help the people who had suffered under these regimes to establish democratic institutions or achieve social justice. When Cubans seeking genuine national independence rebelled against their puppet government in 1906, the United States sent in the Marines to silence them.

THE PANAMA CANAL

In addition to maintaining order, Roosevelt's interest in Latin America also embraced the building of a canal across Central America. Central America's narrow width, especially in its southern half, made it the logical place to build a canal. In fact, a French company had obtained land rights and had begun construction of a canal across the Colombian province of Panama in the 1880s. But even though a "mere" 40 miles of land separated the two oceans, the French were stymied by technological difficulties and financial costs of literally moving mountains. Moreover, French doctors found they were unable to check the spread of malaria and yellow fever among their workers. By the time Roosevelt entered the White House in 1901, the French Panama Company had gone bankrupt.

Roosevelt was not deterred by the French failure. He first presided over the signing of the Hay-Pauncefote Treaty with Great Britain in 1901, releasing the United States from an 1850 agreement that prohibited either country from building a Central American canal without the other's participation. He then instructed his advisers to develop plans for a canal across Nicaragua. The Panamanian route chosen by the French was shorter than the proposed Nicaraguan route and the canal begun by the French was 40 percent complete, but the company that possessed the rights to it wanted $109 million for it, more than the United States was willing to pay. In 1902, however, the company reduced the price to $40 million, a sum that Congress approved. Secretary of State Hay quickly negotiated an agreement with Tomas Herran, the

PANAMA CANAL ZONE, 1914

Colombian chargé d'affaires in Washington. The agreement, formalized in the Hay-Herran Treaty, accorded the United States a 6-mile-wide strip across Panama on which to build the canal. Colombia was to receive a onetime $10 million payment and annual rent of $250,000.

The Colombian legislature, however, rejected the proposed payment as insufficient and sent a new ambassador to the United States with instructions to ask for a onetime payment of $20 million and a share of the $40 million being paid to the French company. Actually, the Colombians (not unreasonably) were hoping to stall negotiations until 1904, when they would regain the rights to the canal zone and consequently to the $40 million sale price promised to the French company.

Although Colombia was acting within its rights, Roosevelt would not tolerate the delay. Unable to get what he wanted through diplomatic means, he encouraged the Panamanians to revolt against Colombian rule. The Panamanians had staged several rebellions in the previous 25 years, all of which had failed. But the 1903 rebellion succeeded, mainly because a U.S. naval force prevented Colombian troops from landing in Panama. Meanwhile, the U.S.S. *Nashville* put U.S. troops ashore to help the new nation secure its independence. The United States formally recognized Panama as a sovereign state only two days after the rebellion against Colombia began.

Philippe Bunau-Varilla, a director of the French company from which the United States had bought the rights to the canal, declared himself the new state's diplomatic representative. Even as the duly appointed Panamanian delegation embarked for the United States for negotiations over the canal, Bunau-Varilla rushed to Washington, where he and Secretary of State Hay signed the Hay–Bunau-Varilla Treaty (1903). It granted the United States a 10-mile-wide canal zone in return for $10 million down and $250,000 annually. Thus, the United States secured its

THE PANAMA CANAL UNDER CONSTRUCTION   This illustration shows the combination of machine and human labor that was used to move millions of tons of earth in the building of the Panama Canal, an undertaking that the British Ambassador James Bryce called "the greatest liberty Man has ever taken with Nature."

canal, not by dealing with the newly installed Panamanian government, but with Bunau-Varilla's French company. When the Panamanian delegation arrived in Washington, its hands were tied. If it objected to the counterfeit treaty, the United States might withdraw its troops from Panama, leaving the new country at the mercy of Colombia.

Roosevelt's severing of Panama from Colombia prompted angry protests in Congress. But Roosevelt was not perturbed. He later gloated, "I took the Canal Zone and let Congress debate!"

Roosevelt turned the building of the canal into a test of American ingenuity and willpower. Engineers overcame every obstacle; doctors developed drugs to combat malaria and yellow fever; armies of construction workers "made the dirt fly." The canal remains a testament to the labor of some 30,000 workers, imported mainly from the West Indies, who, over a 10-year period, labored 10 hours a day, six days a week, for 10 cents an hour. Completed in 1914, the canal shortened the voyage from San Francisco to New York by more than 8,000 miles and significantly enhanced the international prestige of the United States.

In 1921 the United States paid the Colombian government $25 million as compensation for its loss of Panama. It took Panama more than 70 years, however, to regain control of the 10-mile-wide strip of land that Bunau-Varilla, in connivance with the U.S. government, had bargained away in 1902. President Jimmy Carter signed a treaty in 1977 providing for the reintegration of the Canal Zone into Panama, and the canal itself was transferred to Panama in 2000.

KEEPING THE PEACE IN EAST ASIA

In Asia, Roosevelt's main objective was to preserve the Open Door policy in China and the balance of power throughout East Asia. The chief threats came from Russia and Japan, both of whom wanted to seize large chunks of China. At first, Russian expansion into Manchuria and Korea prompted Roosevelt to support Japan when in 1904 it launched a devastating attack on the Russian Pacific fleet anchored at Port Arthur, China. But once the ruinous effects of the war on Russia became clear, Roosevelt entered into secret negotiations to arrange a peace. He invited representatives of Japan and Russia to Portsmouth, New Hampshire, and prevailed on them to negotiate a compromise. The settlement, reached in 1905, favored Japan by perpetuating its control over most of the territories it had won during the brief Russo-Japanese War. Its chief prize was Korea, which became a protectorate of Japan, but Japan also acquired the southern part of Sakhalin Island, Port Arthur, and the South Manchurian Railroad. Russia avoided having to pay Japan a huge indemnity and it retained Siberia, thus preserving its role as an East Asian power. Finally, Roosevelt protected China's territorial integrity by inducing the armies of both Russia and Japan to leave Manchuria. Roosevelt's success in ending the Russo-Japanese War won him the Nobel Prize for Peace in 1906.

Although Roosevelt succeeded in negotiating a peace between these two world powers, he subsequently ignored, and even encouraged, challenges to the sovereignty of weaker Asian nations. In a secret agreement with Japan (the Taft-Katsura Agreement of 1905), for example, the United States agreed that Japan could dominate Korea in return for a Japanese promise not to attack the Philippines. And in the Root-Takahira Agreement of 1908, the United States recognized Japanese expansion into southern Manchuria.

In Roosevelt's eyes the overriding need to maintain peace with Japan justified ignoring the claims of Korea and, increasingly, of China. Roosevelt admired Japan's industrial and military might and regarded Japanese expansion into East Asia as a natural expression of its imperial ambition. The task of American diplomacy, he believed, was first to allow the Japanese to build a secure sphere of influence in East Asia and second to encourage them to join the United States in pursuing peace rather than war. This was a delicate diplomatic task that required both sensitivity and strength, especially when anti-Japanese agitation broke out in California in 1906.

White Californians had long feared the presence of Asian immigrants. They had pressured Congress into passing the Chinese Exclusion Act of 1882, which ended most Chinese immigration to the United States. Then they turned their racism on Japanese immigrants. In 1906 the San Francisco school board ordered the segregation of Asian schoolchildren so that they would not "contaminate" white children. In 1907 the California legislature debated a law to bar any more Japanese immigrants from entering the state. Anti-Asian riots erupted in San Francisco and Los Angeles, encouraged in part by hysterical stories in the press about the "Yellow Peril."

Militarists in Japan began talking of a possible war with the United States. Roosevelt assured the Japanese government that he too was appalled by the Californians' behavior. In 1907 he reached a "gentlemen's agreement" by which the Tokyo government promised to halt the immigration of Japanese adult male laborers to the United States in return for Roosevelt's pledge to end anti-Japanese discrimination. Roosevelt did his part by persuading the San Francisco school board to rescind its segregation ordinance.

At the same time, Roosevelt worried that the Tokyo government would interpret his sensitivity to Japanese honor as weakness. So he ordered the main part of the U.S. fleet to embark on a 45,000-mile world tour, including a splashy stop in Tokyo Bay. Many Americans deplored

ANTI-ASIAN HYSTERIA IN SAN FRANCISCO   In 1906, in the midst of a wave of anti-Asian prejudice in California, the San Francisco school board ordered the segregation of all Asian schoolchildren. Here, a 9-year-old Japanese student submits an application for admission to a public primary school and is refused by the principal, Miss M. E. Dean.

the cost of the tour and feared that the appearance of the U.S. Navy in a Japanese port would provoke military retaliation. But Roosevelt brushed his critics aside, and, true to his prediction, the Japanese were impressed by the "Great White Fleet's" show of strength. Their response seemed to lend validity to the African proverb Roosevelt often invoked: "Speak softly and carry a big stick." Roosevelt's policies lessened the prospect of a war with Japan while preserving a strong U.S. presence in East Asia.

WILLIAM HOWARD TAFT, DOLLAR DIPLOMAT

William Howard Taft brought impressive credentials to the job of president. He had gained valuable experience in colonial administration as the first governor-general of the Philippines. As Roosevelt's secretary of war and chief negotiator for the delicate Taft-Katsura agreement of 1905, he had learned a great deal about conducting diplomacy with imperialist rivals. Yet Taft lacked Roosevelt's grasp of balance-of-power politics and capacity for leadership in foreign affairs. Further, Taft's secretary of state, Philander C. Knox, a corporation lawyer from Pittsburgh, was without diplomatic expertise. Knox's conduct of foreign policy seemed to be

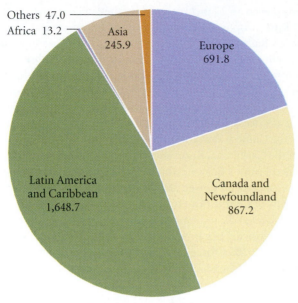

Others 47.0
Africa 13.2
Asia 245.9
Europe 691.8
Latin America and Caribbean 1,648.7
Canada and Newfoundland 867.2

U.S. GLOBAL INVESTMENTS AND INVESTMENTS IN LATIN AMERICA, 1914

Source: From Cleona Lewis, *America's Stake in International Investments* (Washington, D.C.: The Brookings Institute, 1938), pp. 576–606.

Global investments (millions of dollars)

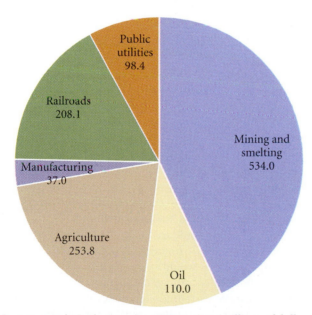

Public utilities 98.4
Railroads 208.1
Manufacturing 37.0
Agriculture 253.8
Oil 110.0
Mining and smelting 534.0

Investments in Latin American Enterprises (millions of dollars)

directed almost entirely toward expanding opportunities for corporate investment overseas, a disposition that prompted critics to deride his policies as "dollar diplomacy."

The inability of Taft and Knox to grasp the complexities of power politics led to a diplomatic reversal in East Asia. Knox, prodded by his banker friends, sought to expand American economic activities throughout China—even in Manchuria, where they encroached on the Japanese sphere of influence. In 1911 Knox proposed that a syndicate of European and American bankers buy the South Manchurian Railroad (then under Japanese control) to open up North China to international trade. Japan reacted by signing a friendship treaty with Russia, its former enemy, which signaled their joint determination to exclude American, British, and French goods from Manchurian markets. Knox's plans for a syndicate collapsed. Similar efforts by Knox to increase American trade with Central and South China triggered further hostile responses from the Japanese and the Russians and contributed to the collapse of the Chinese government and the onset of the Chinese Revolution in 1912.

Dollar diplomacy worked better in the Caribbean. Knox encouraged American investment in the region. Companies such as United Fruit of Boston, which established extensive banana plantations in Costa Rica and Honduras, grew so powerful that they were able to influence both the economies and the governments of Central American countries. When political turmoil threatened their investments, the United States simply sent in its troops. Thus, when Nicaraguan dictator José Santos Zelaya reportedly began negotiating with a European country to build a second trans-Isthmian canal in 1910, a force of U.S. Marines toppled his regime. Marines landed again in 1912 when Zelaya's successor, Adolfo Diaz, angered Nicaraguans with his pro-American policies. This time the Marines were instructed to keep the Diaz regime in power. Except for a brief period in 1925, U.S. troops would remain in Nicaragua continuously from 1912 until 1933.

WOODROW WILSON, STRUGGLING IDEALIST

Woodrow Wilson's foreign policy in the Caribbean initially appeared to be no different from that of his Republican predecessors. In 1915 the United States sent troops to Haiti to put down a revolution; they remained as an army of occupation for 21 years. In 1916, when the people of the Dominican Republic refused to accept a treaty making them more or less a protectorate of the United States, Wilson forced them to accept the rule of a U.S. military government. When German influence in the Danish West Indies began to expand, Wilson purchased the islands from Denmark, renamed them the Virgin Islands, and added them to the U.S. Caribbean empire.

But Wilson's relationship with Mexico in the wake of its revolution reveals that he was troubled by a foreign policy that took no account of a less powerful nation's right to determine its own future. In his dealings with Mexico, however, he was not motivated solely by his fondness for democracy. He also feared that political unrest could lead to violence, social disorder, and revolutionary governments hostile to U.S. economic interests. If a democratic government could be put in place in Mexico, property rights would be respected and U.S. investments would remain secure. Wilson's desire both to encourage democracy and to limit the extent of social change made it difficult to devise a consistent foreign policy toward Mexico.

The Mexican Revolution broke out in 1910 when dictator Porfirio Diaz was overthrown by democratic forces led by Francisco Madero. Madero's talk of democratic reform frightened many foreign investors. Thus, when Madero himself was overthrown early in 1913 by Victoriano Huerta, a conservative general who promised to protect foreign investments, the dollar diplomatists breathed a sigh of relief. Henry Lane Wilson, the U.S. ambassador to Mexico, had helped to engineer Huerta's coup. Before close relations between the United States and Huerta could be worked out, however, Huerta's men murdered Madero.

Woodrow Wilson, who became president shortly after Madero's assassination in 1913, might have overlooked it and entered into close ties with Huerta on condition that he protect American property. Instead, Wilson refused to recognize Huerta's "government of butchers" and demanded that Mexico hold democratic elections. Wilson favored Venustiano Carranza and Francisco ("Pancho") Villa, two enemies of Huerta who commanded rebel armies and who claimed to be democrats. In April 1914 Wilson seized upon the arrest of several U.S. sailors by Huerta's troops to send a fleet into Mexican waters. He then ordered the U.S. Marines to occupy the Mexican port city of Veracruz and to prevent a German ship there from unloading munitions meant for Huerta's army. In the resulting action between U.S. and Mexican forces, 19 Americans and 126 Mexicans were killed. The battle brought the two countries dangerously close to war. Eventually, however, American control over Veracruz weakened and embarrassed Huerta's regime to the point where Carranza was able to take power.

But Carranza did not behave as Wilson had expected. He rejected Wilson's efforts to shape a new Mexican government and announced a bold land-reform program. If the program went into effect, U.S. petroleum companies would lose control of their Mexican properties, a loss that Wilson deemed unacceptable. So Wilson now threw his support to Pancho Villa, who seemed more

CHRONOLOGY

1893	Frederick Jackson Turner publishes an essay announcing the end of the frontier
1898	Spanish-American War (April 14–August 12) • Treaty of Paris signed (December 10), giving U.S. control of Philippines, Guam, and Puerto Rico • U.S. annexes Hawaii
1899–1902	American-Filipino War
1899–1900	U.S. pursues "Open Door" policy toward China
1900	U.S. annexes Puerto Rico • U.S. and other imperial powers put down Chinese Boxer Rebellion
1901	U.S. forces Cuba to adopt constitution favorable to U.S. interests
1903	Hay–Bunau-Varilla Treaty signed, giving U.S. control of Panama Canal Zone
1904	"Roosevelt corollary" to Monroe Doctrine proclaimed
1905	Roosevelt negotiates end to Russo-Japanese War
1906–1917	U.S. intervenes in Cuba, Nicaragua, Haiti, Dominican Republic, and Mexico
1907	Roosevelt and Japanese government reach a "Gentlemen's Agreement" restricting Japanese immigration to U.S. and ending discrimination against Japanese schoolchildren in California
1907–1909	Great White Fleet circles the earth
1909–1913	William Howard Taft conducts "dollar diplomacy"
1910	Mexican Revolution
1914	Panama Canal opens
1914–1917	Wilson struggles to develop a policy toward Mexico
1917	U.S. purchases Virgin Islands from Denmark

willing to protect U.S. oil interests. When Carranza's forces defeated Villa's forces in 1915, Wilson reluctantly withdrew his support of Villa and prepared to recognize the Carranza government.

Furious that Wilson had abandoned him, Villa and his soldiers pulled 18 U.S. citizens from a train in northern Mexico and murdered them, along with another 17 in an attack on Columbus, New Mexico. Determined to punish Villa, Wilson got permission from Carranza to send a U.S. expeditionary force under General John J. Pershing into Mexico. Pershing's troops pursued Villa's forces 300 miles into Mexico but failed to catch them. The U.S. troops did, however, clash twice with Mexican troops under Carranza's command, bringing the countries to the brink of war once again. Because the United States was about to enter the First World War, Wilson could not afford a fight with Mexico. So, in 1917, he quietly ordered Pershing's troops home and grudgingly recognized the Carranza government.

Wilson's policies toward Mexico in the years from 1913 to 1917 seemed to have produced few concrete results, except to reinforce an already deep antagonism among Mexicans toward the United States. His repeated changes in strategy, moreover, seemed to indicate a lack of skill and decisiveness in foreign affairs. Actually, however, Wilson recognized something that Roosevelt and Taft had not: that more and more peoples of the world were determined to control their own destinies. Somehow the nation had to find a way to support their democratic aspirations while also safeguarding its own economic interests.

CONCLUSION

We can assess the dramatic turn in U.S. foreign policy after 1898 either in relation to the foreign policies of rival world powers or against America's own democratic ideals. By the first standard, U.S. foreign policy looks impressive. The United States achieved its major objectives in world affairs: It tightened its control over the Western Hemisphere and projected its military and economic power into Asia. It did so while sacrificing relatively few American lives and while constraining the jingoistic appetite for truly extensive military adventure and conquest. Relatively few foreigners were subjected to American colonial rule. By contrast, in 1900 the British Empire extended over 12 million square miles and embraced one-fourth of the world's population. At times, American rule could be brutal, but on the whole it was no more severe than British rule and significantly less severe than that of the French, German, Belgian, or Japanese imperialists. McKinley, Roosevelt, Taft, and Wilson all placed limits on American expansion and avoided, prior to 1917, extensive foreign entanglements and wars.

If measured against the standard of America's own democratic ideals, however, U.S. foreign policy after 1898 must be judged more harshly. It demeaned the peoples of the Philippines, Puerto Rico, Guam, Cuba, and Colombia as inferior, primitive, and barbaric and denied them the right to govern themselves. In choosing to behave like the imperialist powers of Europe, the United States abandoned its long-standing claim that it was a different kind of nation— one that valued liberty more than power.

Many Americans of the time judged their nation by both standards and thus faced a dilemma. On the one hand, they believed that the size, economic strength, and honor of the United States required it to accept the role of world power and policeman. On the other hand, they continued to believe that they had a mission to spread the values of 1776 to the farthest reaches of the earth. The Mexico example demonstrates how hard it was for the United States to reconcile these two very different approaches to world affairs.

WAR AND SOCIETY, 1914–1920

The First World War broke out in Europe in August 1914. The Triple Alliance of Germany, Austria-Hungary, and the Ottoman Empire squared off against the Triple Entente of Great Britain, France, and Russia. The United States entered the war on the side of the Entente (the Allies, or Allied Powers, as they came to be called) in 1917. Over the next year and a half, the United States converted its immense and sprawling economy into a disciplined war production machine, raised a 5-million-man army, and provided both the war matériel and troops that helped propel the Allies to victory.

But the war also convulsed American society more deeply than any event since the Civil War. This war was the first "total" war, meaning that it required combatants to devote virtually all their resources to the fight. Thus the United States government had no choice but to pursue a degree of industrial control and social regimentation without precedent in American history. Needless to say, this drastic government buildup was itself a controversial measure in a society that had long distrusted state power. Moreover, significant numbers of Americans from a variety of constituencies opposed the war. To overcome this opposition, Wilson couched American war aims in disinterested and idealistic terms: The United States, he claimed, wanted a "peace without victory," a "war for democracy," and liberty for the world's oppressed peoples.

Many people in the United States and abroad responded enthusiastically to Wilson's ideals. But Wilson could not deliver a "peace without victory" without the support of the other victors (England and France), and this support was never forthcoming. At home, disadvantaged groups stirred up trouble by declaring that American society had failed to live up to its democratic and egalitarian ideals. Wilson supported repressive policies to silence these rebels and to enforce unity and conformity on the American people. In the process, he tarnished the ideals for which America had been fighting.

EUROPE'S DESCENT INTO WAR

Europe began its descent into war on June 28, 1914, in Sarajevo, Bosnia, when a Bosnian nationalist assassinated Archduke Franz Ferdinand, heir to the Austro-Hungarian throne. This

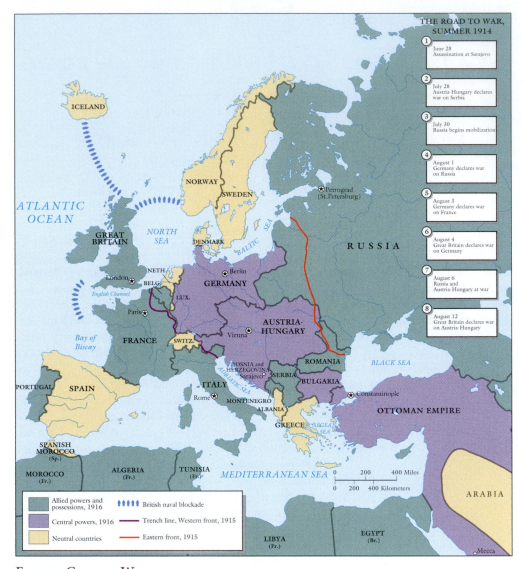

	THE ROAD TO WAR, SUMMER 1914
①	June 28 Assassination at Sarajevo
②	July 28 Austria-Hungary declares war on Serbia
③	July 30 Russia begins mobilization
④	August 1 Germany declares war on Russia
⑤	August 3 Germany declares war on France
⑥	August 4 Great Britain declares war on Germany
⑦	August 6 Russia and Austria-Hungary at war
⑧	August 12 Great Britain declares war on Austria-Hungary

▨	Allied powers and possessions, 1916
▨	Central powers, 1916
▨	Neutral countries
ꜛꜛꜛꜛꜛ	British naval blockade
▬	Trench line, Western front, 1915
▬	Eastern front, 1915

EUROPE GOES TO WAR

act was meant to protest the Austro-Hungarian imperial presence in the Balkans, and to encourage the Bosnians, Croatians, and other Balkan peoples to join the Serbs in establishing independent nations. Austria-Hungary responded to this provocation on July 28 by declaring
war on Serbia, holding it responsible for the archduke's murder.

The conflict might have remained local had not an intricate series of treaties divided Europe into two hostile camps. Germany, Austria-Hungary, and Italy, the so-called Triple Alliance, had promised to come to each other's aid if attacked. Italy would soon opt out of this
alliance, to be replaced by the Ottoman Empire. Arrayed against the nations of the Triple

Alliance were Britain, France, and Russia in the Triple Entente. Russia was obligated by another treaty to defend Serbia against Austria-Hungary, and consequently on July 30 it mobilized its armed forces to go to Serbia's aid. That brought Germany into the conflict to protect Austria-Hungary from Russian attack. On August 3 German troops struck not at Russia itself but at France, Russia's western ally. To reach France, German troops had marched through neutral Belgium. On August 4 Britain reacted by declaring war on Germany.

Complicated alliances and defense treaties of the European nations undoubtedly hastened the rush toward war. But equally important was the fierce competition that existed among the major powers to build the strongest economies, the largest armies and navies, and the grandest colonial empires. Britain and Germany, in particular, were engaged in a bitter struggle for European and world supremacy. Historians now believe that several advisers close to the German emperor, Kaiser Wilhelm II, were actually eager to engage Russia and France in a fight for supremacy on the European continent. They expected that a European war would be swift and decisive—in Germany's favor.

But there was to be no quick victory. The two camps were evenly matched. Moreover, the first wartime use of machine guns and barbed wire made it easier to defend against attack than to go on the offensive. On the western front, after the initial German attack narrowly failed to take Paris in 1914, the two opposing armies confronted each other along a battle line stretching from Belgium in the north to the Swiss border in the south. Troops dug trenches to protect themselves from artillery bombardment and poison gas attacks. Commanders on both sides mounted suicidal ground assaults on the enemy by sending tens of thousands of infantry, armed only with rifles, bayonets, and grenades, out of the trenches and directly into enemy fire. Barbed wire further retarded forward progress, enabling enemy artillery and machine guns to cut down appalling numbers of men. Many of those who were not killed in combat succumbed to disease that spread rapidly in the cold, wet, and rat-infested trenches. In eastern Europe the armies of Germany and Austria-Hungary squared off against those of Russia and Serbia. Though trench warfare was not employed there, the combat was no less lethal. By the time the First World War ended, total casualties, both military and civilian, had reached 37 million.

AMERICAN NEUTRALITY

Soon after the fighting began, Woodrow Wilson told Americans that this was a European war; neither side was threatening a vital American interest. The United States would therefore proclaim its neutrality and maintain normal relations with both sides. Normal relations meant that the United States would continue trading with both camps. Wilson's neutrality policy was greeted by lively opposition, but a majority of Americans applauded Wilson's determination to keep the country out of war.

It was easier to proclaim neutrality than it was to achieve it, however. Many Americans, especially those with economic and political power, identified culturally more with Britain than with Germany. They shared with the English a language, a common ancestry, and a commitment to liberty. Germany had no such attraction for U.S. policymakers. On the contrary, Germany's acceptance of monarchical rule, the prominence of militarists in German politics, and the weakness of democratic traditions inclined U.S. officials to judge Germany harshly.

The United States was tied to Great Britain by economics as well as culture. In 1914 the United States exported more than $800 million in goods to Britain and its allies, compared with $170 million to Germany and Austria-Hungary (which came to be known as the Central Powers). As soon as the war began, the British and then the French turned to the United States for food, clothing, munitions, and other war supplies. The U.S. economy, which had been languishing in 1914, enjoyed a great boom. Bankers began to issue loans to the Allied Powers, further knitting together the American and British economies and giving American investors a direct stake in an Allied victory. Moreover, the British navy had blockaded German ports, which further limited U.S. trade with Germany.

The British blockade of German ports clearly violated American neutrality. The Wilson administration vigorously protested the search and occasional seizure of American merchant ships by the British navy. But it never suspended loans or the export of goods to Great Britain in retaliation for the blockade. To do so would have plunged the U.S. economy into a severe recession. In failing to protect its right to trade with Germany, however, the United States compromised its neutrality and allowed itself to be drawn slowly into war.

SUBMARINE WARFARE

To combat British control of the seas, Germany unveiled a terrifying new weapon, the *Unterseeboot,* or U-boat, the first militarily effective submarine. On May 7, 1915, without warning, a German U-boat torpedoed the British passenger liner *Lusitania,* en route from New York to London. The ship sank in 22 minutes, killing 1,198 men, women, and children, 128 of them U.S. citizens. Americans were shocked by the sinking. The attack appeared to confirm what anti-German agitators were saying: that the Germans were by nature barbaric and uncivilized. The circumstances surrounding the sinking of the *Lusitania,* however, were more complicated than most Americans realized.

Prior to its sailing, the Germans had alleged that the *Lusitania* was secretly carrying a large store of munitions to Great Britain (a charge later shown to have been true) and that it therefore was subject to U-boat attack. Germany had explicitly warned American passengers not to travel on British passenger ships that carried munitions. Moreover, Germany claimed, with some justification, that the purpose of the U-boat attacks—the disruption of Allied supply lines—was no different from Britain's purpose in blockading German ports.

Wilson denounced the sinking of the *Lusitania* in harsh, threatening terms and demanded that Germany pledge never to launch another attack on the citizens of neutral nations, even when they were traveling in British or French ships. Germany acquiesced to Wilson's demand. The resulting lull in submarine warfare was short-lived, however. In early 1916 the Allies began to arm their merchant vessels with guns and depth charges capable of destroying German U-boats. Considering this a provocation, Germany renewed its campaign of surprise submarine attacks. In March 1916 a German submarine torpedoed the French passenger liner *Sussex,* causing a heavy loss of life and injuring several Americans. Again Wilson demanded that Germany spare civilians from attack. In the so-called *Sussex* pledge, Germany once again relented but warned that it might resume unrestricted submarine warfare if the United States did not prevail upon Great Britain to permit neutral ships to pass through the naval blockade.

THE SINKING OF THE *LUSITANIA* On May 7, 1915, a German U-boat torpedoed and sank the British passenger liner *Lusitania,* killing 1,198 people, 128 of them Americans. The event turned U.S. opinion sharply against the Germans, especially because the civilians on board had been given no chance to escape or surrender. Few Americans knew that the ship was secretly transporting a large munitions cache to the British.

The German submarine attacks strengthened the hand of Theodore Roosevelt and others who had been arguing that war with Germany was inevitable and that the United States must prepare itself to fight. By 1916 Wilson could no longer ignore these critics. Between January and September of that year, he sought and won congressional approval for bills to increase the size of the Army and Navy, tighten federal control over National Guard forces, and authorize the building of a merchant fleet. But although Wilson had conceded ground to the pro-war agitators, he did not share their belief that war with Germany was either inevitable or desirable. To the contrary, he accelerated his diplomatic initiatives to forestall the necessity of American military involvement. He dispatched his closest foreign policy adviser, Colonel Edward M. House, to London in January 1916 to draw up a peace plan with the British foreign secretary, Lord Grey. This initiative resulted in the House-Grey memorandum of February 22, 1916, in which Britain agreed to ask the United States to negotiate a settlement between the Allies and the Central Powers. The British believed that the terms of such a peace settlement would be favorable to the Allies. They were furious when Wilson revealed that he wanted an impartial, honestly negotiated peace in which the claims of the Allies and Central Powers would be treated with equal respect and consideration. Britain now rejected U.S. peace overtures, and relations between the two countries grew unexpectedly tense.

THE PEACE MOVEMENT

Underlying Wilson's 1916 peace initiative was a vision of a new world order in which relations between nations would be governed by negotiation rather than war and in which justice would replace power as the fundamental principle of diplomacy. In a major foreign policy address on May 27, 1916, Wilson formally declared his support for an international parliament dedicated to the pursuit of peace, security, and justice for all the world's peoples.

In his effort to keep the United States out of war and to commit national prestige to the cause of international peace rather than conquest, Wilson enjoyed the support of a large number of Americans. In 1915 an international women's peace conference at The Hague (in the Netherlands) had drawn many participants from the United States. A substantial pacifist group emerged among the nation's Protestant clergy. Influential midwestern progressives urged that the United States steer clear of this European conflict, as did prominent socialists. In April 1916 many of the country's most prominent progressives and socialists joined hands in the American Union Against Militarism and pressured Wilson to continue pursuing the path of peace. Wilson's peace campaign also attracted support from the country's sizable Irish and German ethnic populations, who were determined to block any formal military alliance with Great Britain.

WILSON'S VISION: "PEACE WITHOUT VICTORY"

The 1916 presidential election revealed the breadth of peace sentiment. At the Democratic convention, Governor Martin Glynn of New York, the keynote speaker, praised the president for keeping the United States out of war. His portrayal of Wilson as the "peace president" electrified the convention and made "He kept us out of war" a campaign slogan. The slogan proved particularly effective against Wilson's Republican opponent, Charles Evans Hughes, whose close ties to Theodore Roosevelt seemed to place him in the pro-war camp. Combining the promise of peace with a pledge to push ahead with progressive reform, Wilson won a narrow victory.

Emboldened by his electoral triumph, Wilson intensified his quest for peace. On December 16, 1916, he sent a peace note to the belligerent governments, entreating them to consider ending the conflict and, to that end, to state their terms for peace. Although Germany refused to specify its terms and Britain and France announced a set of conditions too extreme for Germany ever to accept, Wilson pressed ahead, initiating secret peace negotiations with both sides. To prepare the American people for what he hoped would be a new era of international relations, Wilson appeared before the Senate on January 22, 1917, to outline his plans for peace. In his speech, he reaffirmed his commitment to an international parliament or League of Nations. But for such a league to succeed, Wilson argued, it would have to be handed a sturdy peace settlement. This entailed a "peace without victory." A peace settlement that did not favor the winners or losers would ensure the equality of the combatants, and "only a peace between equals can last."

Wilson then listed the crucial principles of a lasting peace: freedom of the seas; disarmament; and the right of every people to self-determination, democratic self-government, and security against aggression. Wilson was advocating a revolutionary change in world order, one that would allow all the earth's peoples, regardless of their size or strength, to achieve political independence and to participate as equals in world affairs. These were uncommon views coming from the leader of a world power, and they stirred the despairing masses of Europe and elsewhere who were caught in a deadly conflict.

GERMAN ESCALATION

But Wilson's oratory came too late to serve the cause of peace. Sensing the imminent collapse of Russian forces on the eastern front, Germany had decided to throw its full military might at France and Britain. On land it planned to launch a massive assault on the trenches, and at sea it prepared to unleash its submarines to attack all vessels heading for British ports. Germany knew that this last action would compel the United States to enter the war, but it was gambling on being able to strangle the British economy and leave France isolated before significant numbers of American troops could reach European shores.

On February 1 the United States broke off diplomatic relations with Germany. Wilson continued to hope for a negotiated settlement, however, until February 25, when the British intercepted and passed on to the president a telegram from Germany's foreign secretary, Arthur Zimmermann, to the German minister in Mexico. The infamous "Zimmermann telegram" instructed the minister to ask the Mexican government to attack the United States in the event of war between Germany and the United States. In return, Germany would pay the Mexicans a large fee and regain for them the "lost provinces" of Texas, New Mexico, and Arizona. Wilson, Congress, and the American public were outraged.

In March news arrived that Tsar Nicholas II's autocratic regime in Russia had collapsed and had been replaced by a liberal-democratic government under the leadership of Alexander Kerensky. As long as the tsar ruled Russia and stood to benefit from the Central Powers' defeat, Wilson could not honestly claim that America's going to war against Germany would bring democracy to Europe. Russia's fledgling democratic government's need for support gave Wilson the rationale he needed to justify American intervention.

Appearing before a joint session of Congress on April 2, Wilson declared that the United States must enter the war because "the world must be made safe for democracy." Inspired by his words, Congress broke into thunderous applause. On April 6, Congress voted to declare war by a vote of 373 to 50 in the House and 82 to 6 in the Senate.

The United States thus embarked on a grand experiment to reshape the world. Wilson had given millions of people around the world reason to hope. Although he was taking America to war on the side of the Allies, he stressed that America would fight as an "Associated Power," a phrase meant to underscore America's determination to keep its war aims pure and disinterested.

Still, there was ample cause to worry. Wilson himself understood all too well the risks of his undertaking. If the American people went to war, he predicted, "they'll forget there ever was such a thing as tolerance. To fight you must be brutal and ruthless, and the spirit of ruthless brutality will enter into the very fibre of our national life, infecting Congress, the courts, the policeman on the beat, the man in the street."

AMERICAN INTERVENTION

The entry of the United States into the war gave the Allies the muscle they needed to defeat the Central Powers, but it almost came too late. Germany's resumption of unrestricted submarine warfare took a frightful toll on Allied shipping. From February through July 1917, German subs sank almost 4 million tons of shipping. American intervention ended Britain's vulnerability in dramatic fashion. U.S. and British naval commanders now grouped merchant ships into convoys and provided them with warship escorts through the most dangerous stretches of the North Atlantic. Destroyers armed with depth charges were particularly effective as escorts. Their shallow draft made them invulnerable to torpedoes, and their great acceleration and speed allowed them to pursue slow-moving U-boats. The U.S. and British navies had begun to use sound waves (later called "sonar") to pinpoint the location of underwater craft, and this new technology increased the effectiveness of destroyer attacks. By the end of 1917, the tonnage of Allied shipping lost each month to U-boat attacks had declined by two-thirds. The increased flow of supplies stiffened the resolve of the exhausted British and French troops.

The French and British armies had bled themselves white by taking the offensive in 1916 and 1917 and had scarcely budged the trench lines. The Germans had been content in those years simply to hold their trench position in the West, for they were engaged in a huge offensive against the Russians in the East. The Germans intended first to defeat Russia and then to shift their eastern armies to the West for a final assault on the weakened British and French lines. Their opportunity came in the winter and spring of 1918.

A second Russian revolution in November 1917 had overthrown Kerensky's liberal-democratic government and had brought to power a revolutionary socialist government under Vladimir Lenin and his Bolshevik Party. Believing that the war was not in the best interests of the working classes, Lenin pulled Russia out of the war. In March 1918 he signed a treaty at Brest-Litovsk that added to Germany's territory and resources and enabled Germany to shift its eastern forces to the western front.

Russia's exit from the war hurt the Allies. Not only did it expose French and British troops to a much larger German force, it also challenged the Allied claim that they were fighting a just war against German aggression. Lenin had published the texts of secret Allied treaties showing that Britain and France, like Germany, had plotted to enlarge their nations and empires through war. The revelation that the Allies were fighting for land and riches rather than democratic principles outraged large numbers of people in France and Great Britain, demoralized Allied troops, and threw the French and British governments into disarray. The treaties also embarrassed Wilson, who had brought America into the war to fight for democracy, not territory. But Wilson quickly restored the Allies' credibility by unveiling, in January 1918, a concrete program for peace, the Fourteen Points, that removed territorial aggrandizement as a legitimate war aim.

In March and April 1918, Germany launched its huge offensive against British and French positions, sending Allied troops reeling. A ferocious assault against French lines on May 27 met with little resistance; German troops advanced 10 miles a day until they reached the Marne River, within striking distance of Paris. The French government prepared to evacuate the city. At this perilous moment, a large American army arrived to reinforce what remained of the French lines.

In fact, these American troops, part of the American Expeditionary Force (AEF) commanded by General John J. Pershing, had begun landing in France almost a year earlier. But it took many months to build up a sizable and disciplined force. The United States had had to create a modern army from scratch. Men had to be drafted, trained, supplied with food and equipment; ships for transporting them to Europe had to be found or built. In France, Pershing put his troops through additional training before committing them to battle. He was determined that the American soldiers—or "doughboys," as they were called—should acquit themselves well on the battlefield. The army he ordered into battle to counter the German spring offensive of 1918 fought well. Many American soldiers fell, but Paris was saved, and Germany's best chance for victory slipped from its grasp.

Buttressed by this show of AEF strength, the Allied troops staged a major offensive of their own in late September. Millions of Allied troops advanced across the 200-mile-wide Argonne forest in France, cutting German supply lines. By late October, they had reached the German border. Faced with an invasion of their homeland and with rapidly mounting popular dissatisfaction with the war, German leaders asked for an armistice, to be followed by peace negotiations based on Wilson's Fourteen Points. Having forced the Germans to agree to numerous concessions, the Allies ended the war on November 11, 1918.

Mobilizing for "Total" War

Compared to Europe, the United States suffered little from the war. The deaths of 112,000 American soldiers paled in comparison to European losses: 900,000 by Great Britain, 1.2 million by Austria-Hungary, 1.4 million by France, 1.7 million by Russia, and 2 million by Germany. The U.S. civilian population was also spared most of the war's ravages—the destruction of homes and industries, the shortages of food and medicine, the spread of disease—that afflicted millions of Europeans. Only with the flu epidemic that swept across the Atlantic from Europe in 1919 to claim approximately 500,000 American lives did Americans briefly experience wholesale suffering and death.

Still, the war had a profound effect on American society. Every military engagement the United States had fought since the Civil War had been limited in scope. The First World War was different. It was a "total" war to which every combatant had committed virtually all its resources. The scale of the effort for the United States became apparent early in 1917 when Wilson asked Congress for a conscription law that would permit the federal government to raise a multimillion-man army. The United States would also have to devote much of its agricultural, transportation, industrial, and population resources to the war effort if it wished to end the European stalemate. Who would organize this massive effort? Who would pay for it?

Organizing Industry

Southern and midwestern Democrats, fearing the centralization of governmental authority, pushed for a decentralized approach to mobilization. Northeastern progressives, on the other hand, saw the war as an opportunity to realize their dream of establishing a strong state to regulate the economy, boost efficiency, and achieve social harmony. At first Wilson pursued decentralization, delegating the chore of mobilization to local defense councils throughout the country. When that effort failed, however, Wilson created several centralized federal agencies, each charged with supervising nationwide activity in its assigned economic sector.

The agencies exhibited varying success. The Food Administration, headed by mining engineer Herbert Hoover, was able to increase production of basic foodstuffs substantially through the use of economic incentives. Hoover also put in place an efficient distribution system that delivered food to millions of troops and European civilians. Treasury Secretary William McAdoo, as head of the U.S. Railroad Administration, also performed well in shifting the rail system from private to public control, coordinating dense train traffic, and making capital improvements that allowed goods to move rapidly to eastern ports, where they were loaded onto ships and sent to Europe. At the other extreme, the Aircraft Production Board and Emergency Fleet Corporation did a poor job of supplying the Allies with combat aircraft and merchant vessels. On balance, the U.S. economy performed wonders in supplying troops with uniforms, food, rifles, munitions, and other basic items; it failed badly, however, in producing more sophisticated weapons and machines such as artillery, aircraft, and ships.

At the time, the new government war agencies were thought to possess awesome power over the nation's economy. But most of them were more powerful on paper than in fact. Consider, for example, the War Industries Board (WIB). The WIB floundered for the first nine months of its existence, as it lacked the statutory authority to force manufacturers and the military to adopt its plans. Only the appointment of Wall Street investment banker Bernard Baruch as WIB chairman in March 1918 turned the agency around. Rather than attempting to force manufacturers to do the government's bidding, Baruch permitted industrialists to charge high prices for their products. He won exemptions from antitrust laws for corporations that complied with his requests. In general, he made war production too lucrative an activity to resist. However, he did not hesitate to unleash his wrath upon corporations that resisted WIB enticements.

Baruch's forceful leadership worked reasonably well throughout his nine months in office. War production increased substantially, and manufacturers discovered the financial benefits of cooperation between the public and private sectors. But Baruch's approach created problems, too. His favoritism toward the large corporations hurt smaller competitors. Moreover, the cozy relationship between government and corporate America violated the progressive pledge to protect the people against the "interests."

Organizing Civilian Labor

The government worried as much about labor's cooperation as about industry's compliance. The outbreak of war in 1914 had strengthened the market power of workers, because war orders from Europe prompted manufacturers to expand their production facilities and workforces. Meanwhile, the number of European immigrants plummeted—from more than 1 million in 1914, to 200,000 in 1915, to 31,000 in 1918. That meant that 3 million potential workers were lost to U.S. industry. The economy lost another 5 million workers to military service in 1917 and 1918.

Manufacturers responded to the shortage by encouraging potential workers around the country to come to their factories in the North. From the rural South, 500,000 African Americans migrated to northern cities between 1916 and 1920. Another half-million white southerners followed the same path during that period. Hundreds of thousands of Mexicans fled their homeland for jobs in the Southwest and Midwest. Approximately 40,000 northern women found work as streetcar conductors, railroad workers, metalworkers, munitions makers, and in other jobs customarily reserved for men. The number of female clerical workers doubled between 1910 and 1920, with many of these women finding work in the government war bureaucracies.

These workers alleviated but did not eliminate the nation's acute labor shortage. Workers were quick to recognize the benefits to be won from the tight labor market. White male workers quit jobs they did not like, confident that they could do better. Workers took part in strikes and other collective actions in unprecedented numbers. Union membership almost doubled, from 2.6 million in 1915 to 5.1 million in 1920. Workers commonly sought higher wages and shorter hours through strikes and unionization. Workers also struck in response to managerial attempts to speed up production and tighten discipline. As time passed, increasing numbers of workers began to wonder why the war for democracy in Europe was not being matched by democratization of power in their factories at home. "Industrial democracy" became the battle cry of an awakened labor movement.

Wilson's willingness to include labor in his 1916 progressive coalition reflected his awareness of labor's potential power (see Chapter 21). In 1918 he bestowed prestige on the newly formed National War Labor Board (NWLB) by appointing former president William Howard Taft as one of its two cochairmen. The NWLB brought together representatives of labor, industry, and the public to resolve labor disputes. The presence of Samuel Gompers, president of the American Federation of Labor, on the board gave unions a strong national voice in government affairs. In return for his appointment, Gompers was expected to mobilize workers behind Wilson, discredit socialists who criticized the war, and discourage strikes that threatened war production. Although, like most other federal wartime agencies, the NWLB lacked the ability to impose its will, it managed to pressure many manufacturers into improving wages and hours, reducing wage discrimination, and allowing their workers to join unions.

OCCUPATIONS WITH LARGEST INCREASE IN WOMEN, 1910–1920

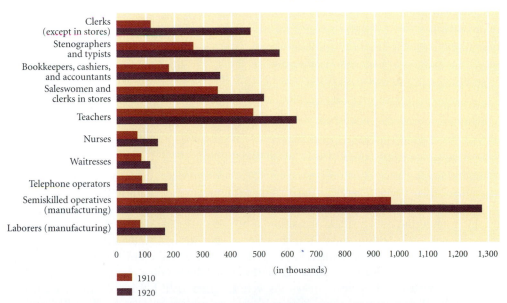

Source: Joseph A. Hill, *Women in Gainful Occupations, 1870–1920*, U.S. Bureau of the Census, Monograph no. 9 (Washington, D.C.: Government Printing Office, 1929), p. 33.

WOMEN DOING "MEN'S" WORK   Labor shortages during the war years allowed thousands of women to take industrial jobs customarily reserved for men. The two female lathe operators in this photograph (taken in an industrial plant in Portland, Oregon) had been schoolteachers before the war.

ORGANIZING MILITARY LABOR

Only when it came to raising an army did the federal government use its full power without hesitation. The Wilson administration committed itself to conscription—to the drafting of most men of a certain age, irrespective of their family's wealth, ethnic background, or social standing. The Selective Service Act of May 1917 empowered the administration to do just that. By war's end, local Selective Service boards had registered 24 million young men age 18 and older, and had drafted nearly 3 million of them into the military. Another 2 million volunteered for service.

There was relatively little resistance to the draft, even among recently arrived immigrants. Foreign-born men constituted 18 percent of the armed forces—a percentage greater than their share of the total male population. Almost 400,000 African Americans served, representing approximately 10 percent, the same as the percentage of African Americans in the total population.

The U.S. Army, under the command of Chief of Staff Peyton March and General John J. Pershing, faced the difficult task of fashioning these ethnically and racially diverse millions into a professional fighting force. Teaching raw recruits to fight was hard enough, Pershing and March observed; teaching them to put aside their racial and ethnic prejudices was a task they refused to tackle. Rather than integrate the armed forces, they segregated black soldiers from white. Virtually all African Americans were assigned to all-black units that were barred from combat. Being stripped of a combat role was particularly galling to blacks, who, in previous wars, had proven themselves to be among the best American fighters.

For a time, the military justified its intensified discrimination against blacks by referring to the results of rudimentary "IQ" (intelligence quotient) tests administered by psychologists to 2 million AEF soldiers. These tests allegedly "proved" that native-born Americans and immigrants from the British Isles, Germany, and Scandinavia were well endowed with intelligence, while African Americans and immigrants from southern and eastern Europe were poorly endowed. But these tests were scientifically so ill-conceived that their findings revealed nothing about the true distribution of intelligence in the population. In 1919 the military discontinued the IQ testing program.

Given the sharp racial and ethnic differences among American troops and the short time Pershing and his staff had to train recruits, the performance of the AEF was impressive. The most decorated soldier in the AEF was Sergeant Alvin C. York of Tennessee, who captured 35 machine guns and 132 prisoners and who killed 17 German soldiers with 17 bullets. York had learned his marksmanship hunting wild turkeys in the Tennessee hills. "Of course, it weren't no trouble nohow for me to hit them big [German] army targets," he later commented. "They were so much bigger than turkeys' heads."

One of the most decorated AEF units was New York's 369th Regiment, a black unit recruited in Harlem. Bowing to pressure from civil rights groups like the NAACP that some black troops be allowed to fight, Pershing had offered the 369th to the French army. The 369th entered the French front line and scored one major success after another. In gratitude for its service, the French government decorated the entire unit with one of its highest honors—the *Croix de Guerre.*

PAYING THE BILLS

As chief purchaser of food, uniforms, munitions, weapons, vehicles, and sundry other items for the U.S. military, the government incurred huge debts. To help pay its bills, it sharply increased tax rates. The new taxes hit the wealthiest Americans the hardest: The richest were slapped with a 67 percent income tax and a 25 percent inheritance tax. Corporations were ordered to pay an "excess profits" tax. The revenues brought in by the taxes, however, provided only about one-third of the $33 billion that the government ultimately spent on the war. The rest came from the sale of "Liberty Bonds." These were 30-year bonds the government sold to individuals with a return of 3½ percent in annual interest.

The government offered five bond issues between 1917 and 1920 and all were quickly sold out. Their success was due in no small measure to a high-powered sales pitch, orchestrated by Treasury Secretary William G. McAdoo, that equated bond purchases with patriotic duty. McAdoo's agents blanketed the country with posters, sent bond "salesmen" into virtually every American community, enlisted Boy Scouts to go door-to-door, and staged rallies at which movie stars such as Mary Pickford, Douglas Fairbanks, and Charlie Chaplin stumped for the war.

AROUSING PATRIOTIC ARDOR

The Treasury's bond campaign was only one aspect of an extraordinary government effort to arouse public support for the war. In 1917 Wilson set up a new agency, the Committee on Public Information (CPI), to publicize and popularize the war. Under the chairmanship of George Creel, a midwestern progressive and a muckraker, the CPI conducted an unprecedented propaganda campaign. It distributed 75 million copies of pamphlets explaining U.S. war aims in several languages. It trained a force of 75,000 "Four Minute Men" to deliver succinct, uplifting war speeches to numerous groups in their home cities and towns. It papered the walls of virtually every public institution (and many private ones) with posters, placed advertisements in mass-circulation magazines, sponsored exhibitions, and peppered newspaper editors with thousands of press releases on the progress of the war.

Faithful to his muckraking past, Creel wanted to give the people "the facts" of the war, believing that well-informed citizens would see the wisdom of Wilson's policies. He also felt his work gave him an opportunity to achieve the progressive goal of uniting all Americans into a single moral community. Americans everywhere were told that the United States had entered the war "to make the world safe for democracy," to help the world's weaker peoples achieve self-determination, to bring a measure of social justice into the conduct of international affairs. Americans were asked to affirm those ideals by doing everything they could to support the war.

This uplifting message had a profound effect on the American people. It imparted to many a deep love of country and a sense of participation in a grand democratic experiment. Workers, women, European ethnics, and African Americans began demanding that America live up to its democratic ideals at home as well as abroad. Workers rallied to the cry of "industrial democracy." Women seized upon the democratic fervor to bring their fight for suffrage to a successful conclusion (see Chapter 21). African Americans began to dream that the war might deliver them from second-class citizenship. European ethnics believed that Wilson's support of their countrymen's rights abroad would improve their own chances for success in the United States.

Although the CPI had helped to unleash it, this new democratic enthusiasm troubled Creel and others in the Wilson administration. The United States, after all, was still deeply divided along class, ethnic, and racial lines. Workers and industrialists regarded each other with suspicion. Cultural differences compounded this class division, for the working class was overwhelmingly ethnic in composition, while the industrial and political elites consisted mainly of the native-born whose families had been "Americans" for generations. Progressives had fought hard to overcome these divisions. They had tamed the power of capitalists, improved the condition of workers, encouraged the Americanization of immigrants, and articulated a new, more inclusive idea of American nationhood. But their work was far from complete when the war broke out, and the war itself opened up new social and cultural divisions. The decision to authorize the CPI's massive unity campaign is evidence that the progressives understood how widespread the discord was. Still, they had not anticipated that the promotion of democratic ideals at home would exacerbate, rather than lessen, existing social and cultural conflicts.

WARTIME REPRESSION

By early 1918 the CPI's campaign had developed a darker, more coercive side. Inflammatory advertisements called on patriots to report on neighbors, coworkers, and ethnics whom they suspected of subverting the war effort. Propagandists called on immigrants to repudiate all ties to their homeland, native language, and ethnic customs. The CPI aroused hostility to Germans by spreading lurid tales of German atrocities and encouraging the

RENAMED GERMAN AMERICAN WORDS

ORIGINAL	"PATRIOTIC" NAME

hamburger	salisbury steak,
	    liberty steak,
	    liberty sandwich

sauerkraut	liberty cabbage
Hamburg Avenue, Brooklyn, New York	Wilson Avenue, Brooklyn, New York
Germantown, Nebraska	Garland, Nebraska
East Germantown, Indiana	Pershing, Indiana
Berlin, Iowa	Lincoln, Iowa
pinochle	liberty
German shepherd	Alsatian shepherd
Deutsches Hans of Indianapolis	Athenaeum of Indiana
Germania Maennerchor of Chicago	Lincoln Club
Kaiser Street	Maine Way

Source: From La Vern J. Rippley, *The German Americans* (Boston: Twayne Publishers, 1976), p. 186; and Robert H. Ferrell, *Woodrow Wilson and World War I, 1917–1921* (New York: Harper and Row, 1985), pp. 205–206.

public to see movies like *The Prussian Cur* and *The Beast of Berlin*. The Department of Justice arrested thousands of German and Austrian immigrants whom it suspected of subversive activities. Congress passed the Trading with the Enemy Act, which required foreign-language publications to submit all war-related stories to post office censors for approval.

German Americans became the objects of popular hatred. American patriots sought to expunge every trace of German influence from American culture. In Boston, performances of Beethoven's symphonies were banned. Libraries removed works of German literature from their shelves, while Theodore Roosevelt and others urged school districts to prohibit the teaching of the German language. Patriotic school boards burned the German books in their districts.

German Americans were at risk of being fired from work, losing their businesses, and being assaulted on the street. A St. Louis mob lynched an innocent German immigrant whom they suspected of subversion. After only 25 minutes of deliberation, a St. Louis jury acquitted the mob leaders, who had brazenly defended their crime as an act of patriotism. German Americans began hiding their ethnic identity, changing their names, speaking German only in the privacy of their homes, celebrating their holidays only with trusted friends.

The anti-German campaign escalated into a general anti-immigrant crusade. Congress passed the Immigration Restriction Act of 1917, which declared that all adult immigrants who

TURNING ENEMIES INTO APES

From the mid-19th to the mid-20th century, Americans frequently drew on simian imagery to describe and demean their enemies, both internal and external. Blacks and Asians were the groups most commonly depicted as apelike, a reflection in part of popular and pseudo-scientific notions that human beings belonged to a series of distinct and unequal "races" with varying capacities for intelligence, morality, and achievement. Africans and Asians often were thought to be the most primitive human races, closest to the apes, and northwest Europeans the most civilized.

But simian imagery was sometimes used against northwest and west Europeans themselves, as the images shown here demonstrate: one portrays Germany in the First World War; the other represents Spain as a brute who cruelly sank the battleship *Maine* in 1898. Both enemies were turned into "brutes" who were alleged to possess no self-control, no knowledge of right from wrong, and no respect for human life, pure womanhood, or law and order. To depict enemies in these terms was to justify America's obligation to use force against them. Brutes, like animals, could only be killed or beaten into submission; they would not respond—as would civilized peoples (such as Americans)—to reason or negotiation. In the case of the Spanish and the Germans, using force meant war.

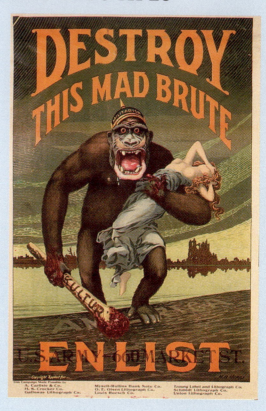

The Spanish Brute Adds Mutilation to Murder

failed a reading test would be denied admission to the United States. The act also banned the immigration of laborers from India, Indochina, Afghanistan, Arabia, the East Indies, and several other countries within an "Asiatic Barred Zone." Congress also passed the Eighteenth Amendment to the Constitution, which prohibited the manufacture and distribution of alcoholic beverages (see Chapter 21). The crusade for Prohibition was not new, but anti-immigrant feelings generated by the war gave it added impetus. Prohibitionists pictured the nation's urban ethnic ghettos as scenes of drunkenness, immorality, and disloyalty. The Eighteenth Amendment was quickly ratified by the states, and in 1919 Prohibition became the law of the land.

More and more, the Wilson administration relied on repression to achieve domestic unity. In the Espionage, Sabotage, and Sedition Acts passed in 1917 and 1918, Congress gave the administration sweeping powers to silence and even imprison dissenters. These acts went far beyond outlawing behavior such as spying for the enemy, sabotaging war production, and calling for the enemy's victory. By making it illegal to write or utter any statement that could be construed as profaning the flag, the Constitution, or the military, they constituted the most drastic restriction of free speech at the national level since enactment of the Alien and Sedition Acts of 1798 (see Chapter 8).

Government repression fell most heavily on the IWW and the Socialist Party. Both groups had opposed intervention before 1917. Although they subsequently muted their opposition, they continued to insist that the true enemies of American workers were to be found in the ranks of American employers, not in Germany or Austria-Hungary. The government responded by banning many socialist materials from the mails and by disrupting socialist and IWW meetings. By the spring of 1918 government agents had arrested 2,000 IWW members, including its entire executive board. Many of those arrested would be sentenced to long jail terms. Eugene V. Debs, the head of the Socialist Party, received a 10-year jail term for making an antiwar speech in Canton, Ohio, in the summer of 1918.

Citizens organized groups to enforce patriotism. The largest of these, the American Protective League, routinely spied on fellow workers and neighbors, opened the mail and tapped the phones of those suspected of disloyalty, and harassed young men who were thought to be evading the draft. Attorney General Thomas Gregory publicly endorsed the group and sought federal funds to support its "police" work.

The spirit of coercion even infected institutions that had long prided themselves on tolerance. In July 1917 Columbia University fired two professors for speaking out against U.S. intervention in the war. The National Americanization Committee, which prior to 1917 had pioneered a humane approach to the problem of integrating immigrants into American life, now supported surveillance, internment, and deportation of aliens suspected of anti-American sentiments.

Wilson himself bore significant responsibility for this climate of repression. On the one hand, he did attempt to block certain pieces of repressive legislation; for example, he vetoed both the Immigration Restriction Act and the Volstead Act (the act passed by Congress to enforce Prohibition), only to be overridden by Congress. But on the other hand Wilson did little to halt Attorney General Gregory's prosecution of radicals or Postmaster General Burleson's campaign to exclude Socialist Party publications from the mail. He ignored pleas from progressives that he intervene in the Debs case. His acquiescence in these matters cost him dearly among progressives and socialists. Wilson believed , however, that once the Allies won the war and arranged a just peace in accordance with the Fourteen

Points, his administration's wartime actions would be forgiven and the progressive coalition would be restored.

THE FAILURE OF THE INTERNATIONAL PEACE

In the month following Germany's surrender on November 11, 1918, Wilson was confident about the prospects of achieving a just peace. Both Germany and the Allies had publicly accepted the Fourteen Points as the basis for negotiations. Wilson's international prestige was enormous. To capitalize on his fame, Wilson broke sharply with diplomatic precedent and decided to head the American delegation to the Paris Peace Conference in January 1919 himself. Some 2 million French citizens lined the parade route in Paris to catch a glimpse of "Wilson, *le juste* [the just]."

In the Fourteen Points, Wilson had translated his principles for a new world order into specific proposals for world peace and justice. The first group of points called for all nations to abide by a code of conduct that embraced free trade, freedom of the seas, open diplomacy, disarmament, and the resolution of disputes through mediation. A second group, based on the principle of self-determination, proposed redrawing the map of Europe to give the subjugated peoples of the Austro-Hungarian, Ottoman, and Russian empires national sovereignty. The last point called for establishing a League of Nations, an assembly in which all nations would be represented and in which all international disputes would be given a fair hearing and an opportunity for peaceful solutions.

"THE SAVIOR OF HUMANITY" Wherever he went in Europe, Wilson was greeted by huge, delirious crowds eager to thank him for ending Europe's terrible war and to endorse his vision of a peaceful, democratic world. Here millions of Italians greet Wilson's arrival in Milan.

THE PARIS PEACE CONFERENCE AND THE TREATY OF VERSAILLES

Although representatives of 27 nations began meeting in Paris on January 12, 1919, to discuss Wilson's Fourteen Points, negotiations were controlled by the "Big Four": Wilson, Prime Minister David Lloyd George of Great Britain, Premier Georges Clemenceau of France, and Prime Minister Vittorio Orlando of Italy. When Orlando quit the conference after a dispute with Wilson, the Big Four became the Big Three. Wilson quickly learned that his negotiating partners' support for the Fourteen Points was much weaker than he had believed. Indeed, Clemenceau and Lloyd George refused to include most of Wilson's points in the peace treaty. The points having to do with freedom of the seas and free trade were omitted, as were the proposals for open diplomacy and Allied disarmament. Wilson won partial endorsement of the

EUROPE AND THE NEAR EAST AFTER THE FIRST WORLD WAR

principle of self-determination: Belgian sovereignty was restored, Poland's status as a nation was affirmed, and the new nations of Czechoslovakia, Yugoslavia, Finland, Lithuania, Latvia, and Estonia were created. Some lands of the former Ottoman Empire—Armenia, Palestine, Mesopotamia, and Syria—were to be placed under League of Nations' trusteeships with the understanding that they would some day gain their independence. But Wilson failed in his efforts to block a British plan to transfer former German colonies in Asia to Japanese control, an Italian plan to annex territory inhabited by 200,000 Austrians, and a French plan to take from Germany its valuable Saar coal mines.

Nor was Wilson able to blunt the drive to punish Germany for its wartime aggression. In addition to awarding the Saar basin to France, the Allies gave portions of northern Germany to Denmark and portions of eastern Germany to Poland and Czechoslovakia. Germany was stripped of virtually its entire navy and air force, and forbidden to place soldiers or fortifications in western Germany along the Rhine. In addition, Germany was forced to admit its responsibility for the war. In accepting this "war guilt," Germany was, in effect, agreeing to compensate the victors in cash ("reparations") for the pain and suffering it had inflicted on them.

Lloyd George and Clemenceau brushed off the protests of those who viewed this desire to prostrate Germany as a cruel and vengeful act. That the German people, after their nation's 1918 defeat, had overthrown the monarch (Kaiser Wilhelm II) who had taken them to war, and had reconstituted their nation as a democratic republic won them no leniency. In 1921 an Allied commission notified the Germans that they were to pay the victors $33 billion, a sum well beyond what a defeated and economically ruined Germany could muster. The Treaty of Versailles was signed by Great Britain, France, the United States, Germany, and other European nations on June 28, 1919.

THE LEAGUE OF NATIONS

The Allies' single-minded pursuit of self-interest disillusioned many liberals and socialists in the United States. But Wilson seemed not to be dismayed, for he had won approval of the most important of his Fourteen Points—the point that called for the creation of the League of Nations. The League, whose structure and responsibilities were set forth in the Covenant attached to the peace treaty, would usher in Wilson's new world order. Drawing its membership from the signatories to the Treaty of Versailles (except, for the time being, Germany), the League would function as an international parliament and judiciary, establishing rules of international behavior and resolving disputes between nations through rational and peaceful means.

The League, Wilson believed, would redeem the failures of the Paris Peace Conference. Under its auspices, free trade and freedom of the seas would be achieved, reparations against Germany would be reduced or eliminated, disarmament of the Allies would proceed, and the principle of self-determination would be extended to peoples outside Europe. Moreover, the League would have the power to punish aggressor nations, which would be subject to economic isolation and military retaliation.

WILSON VERSUS LODGE: THE FIGHT OVER RATIFICATION

For the League to succeed, however, Wilson had to convince the U.S. Senate to ratify the Treaty of Versailles. Wilson knew that this would be no easy task. The Republicans had gained a majority in the Senate in 1918, and two groups within their ranks were determined to frustrate Wilson's ambitions. One group was a caucus of 14 midwesterners and westerners known as the "irreconcilables." Most of them were conservative isolationists who wanted the United States to preserve its separation from Europe, but a few were prominent progressives who had voted against the declaration of war in 1917. Under no circumstances would they support a plan that would embroil the United States in European affairs.

The second opposition group was led by Senator Henry Cabot Lodge of Massachusetts. Its members did not subscribe to Wilson's belief that every group of people on earth had a right to form their own nation; that every state, regardless of its size, should have a voice in world affairs; and that disputes between nations could be settled in open, democratic forums. They subscribed instead to Theodore Roosevelt's vision of a world controlled by a few great nations, each militarily strong, secure in its own sphere of influence, and determined to avoid war through a carefully negotiated balance of power. These Republicans preferred to let Europe return to the power politics that had prevailed before the war rather than experiment with a new world order that might constrain and compromise U.S. power and autonomy.

Of particular importance in the Republican critique were the questions it raised about the power given the League by Article X to undertake military actions against aggressor nations. Did Americans want to authorize an international organization to decide when the United States would go to war? Was this not a violation of the Constitution, which vested war-making power solely in Congress? Even if the constitutional problem could be solved, how could the United States ensure that it would not be forced into a military action that might damage its national interest?

It soon became clear, however, that a number of the Republicans, especially Lodge, were more interested in humiliating Wilson than in engaging in debate. They accused him of promoting socialism through his wartime expansion of government power. They were angry that he had failed to include any distinguished Republicans on the Paris peace delegation. And they were still bitter about the 1918 congressional elections, when Wilson had argued that a Republican victory would embarrass the nation abroad in a critical moment in world affairs. Though Wilson's electioneering had failed to sway the voters (the Republicans won a majority in both Houses), his suggestion that a Republican victory would injure national honor had infuriated Theodore Roosevelt and his supporters. Roosevelt died in 1919, but his close friend Lodge kept his rage alive.

As chairman of the Senate Foreign Relations Committee, which was charged with considering the treaty before reporting it to the Senate floor, Lodge had considerable power, and he did everything possible to obstruct ratification. When his committee finally reported the treaty to the full Senate, it came encumbered with nearly 50 amendments whose adoption Lodge made a precondition of his support. Some of the amendments expressed reasonable concerns—namely, that participation in the League not diminish the role of Congress in determining foreign policy, or compromise the sovereignty of the nation, or involve the nation in an unjust or ill-advised war. But many were meant only to complicate the task of ratification.

Despite Lodge's obstructionism, the treaty's chances for ratification by the required two-thirds majority of the Senate were still good. Many Republicans were prepared to vote for ratification if Wilson indicated his willingness to accept some of the proposed amendments.

Wilson possessed the political savvy to salvage the treaty and, along with it, U.S. participation in the League of Nations. But at this crucial moment in national and world history, he refused to compromise and announced that he would carry his case directly to the people. In September 1919 he undertook a whirlwind cross-country tour in which he addressed as many crowds as he could reach, sometimes speaking for an hour at a time, four times a day. However, in thinking that this "appeal to the country" would force Republican senators to change their votes, Wilson had gravely miscalculated. All he achieved was his own physical exhaustion.

On September 25, after giving a speech at Pueblo, Colorado, Wilson suffered excruciating headaches throughout the night. His physician ordered him back to Washington, where on October 2 he suffered a near-fatal stroke. Wilson hovered near death for two weeks and remained seriously disabled for another six. Wilson's wife, Edith Bolling Wilson, and his doctor isolated him from Congress and the press, withholding news they thought might upset him and preventing the public from learning how much his body and mind had deteriorated.

Many historians believe that the stroke impaired Wilson's political judgment. If so, that may explain his refusal to consider any of the Republican amendments to the treaty, even after it had become clear that compromise offered the only chance of winning U.S. participation in the League of Nations. When Lodge presented an amended treaty for a ratification vote on November 19, Wilson ordered Senate Democrats to vote against it; 42 (of 47) Democratic senators complied, and with the aid of 13 Republican irreconcilables, the Lodge version was defeated. Only moments later, the unamended version of the treaty—Wilson's version—received only 38 votes.

THE TREATY'S FINAL DEFEAT

As the magnitude of the calamity became apparent, supporters of the League in Congress, the nation, and the world urged the Senate and the president to reconsider. Wilson would not budge. A bipartisan group of senators desperately tried to work out a compromise without consulting him. When that effort failed, the Senate put to a vote, one more time, the Lodge version of the treaty. Because 23 Democrats, most of them southerners, still refused to break with Wilson, this last-ditch effort at ratification failed.

The judgment of history lies heavily upon these events, for the flawed treaty and the failure of the League are thought by many to have contributed to Adolf Hitler's rise and the outbreak of a second world war even more terrifying than the first. It is necessary to ask, then, whether American participation in the League would have significantly altered the course of world history.

The mere fact of U.S. membership in the League would not have magically solved Europe's postwar problems. The U.S. government was inexperienced in diplomacy and prone to mistakes. Its freedom to negotiate solutions to international disputes would have been limited by the large number of American voters who remained strongly opposed to American entanglement in European affairs. Even if such opposition could have been overcome, the United States would still have confronted European countries determined to go their own way.

Nevertheless, one thing is clear: No stable international order could have arisen after the First World War without the full involvement of the United States. The League of Nations required American authority and prestige in order to operate effectively as an international parliament. We cannot know whether the League, with American involvement, would have

WOODROW WILSON'S FOURTEEN POINTS, 1918: RECORD OF IMPLEMENTATION

1. Open covenants of peace openly arrived at	Not fulfilled
2. Absolute freedom of navigation upon the seas in peace and war	Not fulfilled
3. Removal of all economic barriers to the equality of trade among nations	Not fulfilled
4. Reduction of armaments to the level needed only for domestic safety	Not fulfilled
5. Impartial adjustments of colonial claims	Not fulfilled
6. Evacuation of all Russian territory; Russia to be welcomed into the society of free nations	Not fulfilled
7. Evacuation and restoration of Belgium	Fulfilled
8. Evacuation and restoration of all French lands; return of Alsace-Lorraine to France	Fulfilled
9. Readjustment of Italy's frontiers along lines of Italian nationality	Compromised
10. Self-determination for the former subjects of the Austro-Hungarian Empire	Compromised
11. Evacuation of Romania, Serbia, and Montenegro; free access to the sea for Serbia	Compromised
12. Self-determination for the former subjects of the Ottoman Empire; secure sovereignty for Turkish portion	Compromised
13. Establishment of an independent Poland with free and secure access to the sea	Fulfilled
14. Establishment of a League of Nations affording mutual guarantees of independence and territorial integrity	Compromised

Source: From G. M. Gathorne-Hardy, *The Fourteen Points and the Treaty of Versailles*, Oxford Pamphlets on World Affairs, no. 6 (1939), pp. 8–34; and Thomas G. Paterson et al., *American Foreign Policy: A History*, 2nd ed. (Lexington, Mass.: D. C. Heath, 1983), vol. 2, pp. 282–293.

offered the Germans a less humiliating peace, allowing them to rehabilitate their economy and salvage their national pride; nor whether an American-led League would have stopped Hitler's expansionism before it escalated into full-scale war in 1939. Still, it seems fair to suggest that American participation would have strengthened the League and improved its ability to bring a lasting peace to Europe.

THE POSTWAR PERIOD: A SOCIETY IN CONVULSION

The end of the war brought no respite from the forces that were convulsing American society. Workers were determined to regain the purchasing power they had lost to inflation. Employers were determined to halt or reverse the wartime gains labor had made. Radicals saw in this conflict between capital and labor the possibility of a socialist revolution. Conservatives were certain that the revolution had already begun. Returning white servicemen were nervous about regaining their civilian jobs and looked with hostility on the black, Hispanic, and female workers who had been recruited to take their places. Black veterans were in no mood to return to segregation and subordination.

LABOR-CAPITAL CONFLICT

Nowhere was the escalation of conflict more evident than in the workplace. In 1919, 4 million workers—one-fifth of the nation's manufacturing workforce—went on strike. In January 1919, a general strike paralyzed the city of Seattle when 60,000 workers walked off their jobs. By August, walkouts had been staged by 400,000 eastern and midwestern coal miners, 120,000 New England textile workers, and 50,000 New York City garment workers. Then came two strikes that turned public opinion sharply against labor. In September, Boston policemen walked off their jobs after the police commissioner refused to negotiate with their newly formed union. Rioting and looting soon broke out. Massachusetts Governor Calvin Coolidge, outraged by the policemen's betrayal of their sworn public duty, refused to negotiate with them, called out the National Guard to restore order, and then fired the entire police force.

Hard on the heels of the policemen's strike came a strike by more than 300,000 steelwork-ers in the Midwest. No union had established a footing in the steel industry since the 1890s, when Andrew Carnegie had ousted the ironworkers' union from his Homestead, Pennsylva-nia, mills. Most steelworkers labored long hours (the 12-hour shift was still standard) for low wages in workplaces where they were exposed to serious injury. The organizers of the 1919 strike had somehow managed to persuade steelworkers with varied skill levels and ethnic backgrounds to put aside their differences and demand an eight-hour day and union recogni-tion. When the employers rejected those demands, the workers walked off their jobs. The em-ployers responded by procuring armed guards to beat up the strikers and by hiring nonunion labor to keep the plants running. In many areas, local and state police prohibited union meet-ings, ran strikers out of town, and opened fire on those who disobeyed orders. In Gary, Indi-ana, a confrontation between unionists and armed guards left 18 strikers dead. To arouse public support for their antiunion campaign, industry leaders painted the strike leaders as dangerous and violent radicals bent on the destruction of political liberty and economic free-dom. They succeeded in arousing public opinion against the steelworkers, and the strike col-lapsed in January 1920.

RADICALS AND THE RED SCARE

The steel companies succeeded in putting down the strike by fanning the public's fear that rev-olutionary sentiment was spreading among the workers. Radical sentiment was indeed on the rise. Mine workers and railroad workers had begun calling for the permanent nationalization of coal mines and railroads. Longshoremen in San Francisco and Seattle refused to load ships carrying supplies to the White Russians who had taken up arms against Lenin's Bolshevik gov-ernment. Socialist trade unionists mounted the most serious challenge to Gompers' control of the AFL in 25 years. In 1920, nearly a million Americans voted for the Socialist presidential candidate Debs.

This radical surge did not mean, however, that leftists had fashioned themselves into a sin-gle movement or political party. On the contrary, the Russian Revolution had split the Ameri-can Socialist Party. One faction, which would keep the name Socialist and would continue to be led by Debs, insisted that radicals follow a democratic path to socialism. The other group, which would take the name Communist, wanted to establish a Lenin-style "dictatorship of the proletariat." Small groups of anarchists, some of whom advocated campaigns of terror to speed the revolution, represented yet a third radical tendency.

The fact that the radical camp was in such disarray escaped the notice of most Americans, who assumed that radicalism was a single, coordinated movement bent on establishing a communist government on American soil. Beginning in 1919, this perceived "Red Scare" prompted government officials and private citizens to embark on yet another campaign of repression.

The postwar repression of radicalism closely resembled the wartime repression of dissent. Thirty states passed sedition laws to punish people who advocated revolution. Numerous public and private groups intensified Americanization campaigns designed to strip foreigners of their "subversive" ways and remake them into loyal citizens. A newly formed veterans' organization, the American Legion, took on the American Protective League's role of identifying seditious individuals and organizations and making sure that the public's devotion to "100 percent Americanism" did not abate.

The Red Scare reached its climax on New Year's Day 1920 when federal agents broke into the homes and meeting places of thousands of suspected revolutionaries in 33 cities. Directed by Attorney General A. Mitchell Palmer, these widely publicized "Palmer raids" were meant to expose the extent of revolutionary activity. Palmer's agents uncovered three pistols, no rifles, and no explosives. Nevertheless, they arrested 6,000 people and kept many of them in jail for weeks without formally charging them with a crime. Finally, those who were not citizens (approximately 500) were deported and the rest were released.

As Palmer's exaggerations of the Red threat became known, many Americans began to reconsider their near-hysterical fear of dissent and subversion. But the political atmosphere remained hostile to radicals, as the Sacco and Vanzetti case revealed. In May 1920, two Italian-born anarchists, Nicola Sacco and Bartolomeo Vanzetti, were arrested in Brockton, Massachusetts, and charged with armed robbery and murder. Both men proclaimed their innocence and insisted that they were being punished for their political beliefs. Indeed, their foreign accents and their defiant espousal of anarchist doctrines in the courtroom inclined many Americans, including the judge who presided at their trial, to view them harshly. Although the case against them was weak, they were convicted of first-degree murder and sentenced to death. Their lawyers attempted numerous appeals, all of which failed. Anger over the verdicts began to build, first among Italian Americans, then among radicals, and finally among liberal intellectuals. Protests compelled the governor of Massachusetts to appoint a commission to review the case, but no new trial was ordered. On August 23, 1927, Sacco and Vanzetti were executed, still insisting that they were innocent.

RACIAL CONFLICT AND THE RISE OF BLACK NATIONALISM

The more than 400,000 blacks who served in the armed forces believed that a victory for democracy abroad would help them achieve democracy for themselves at home. At first, the discrimination they encountered in the military did not weaken their conviction that they would be treated as full-fledged citizens upon their return. Thousands joined the NAACP, which was at the forefront of the fight for racial equality. By 1918, there were 100,000 African Americans subscribing to the NAACP's magazine, *The Crisis*, whose editor, W. E. B. Du Bois, had urged them to support the war.

MARCUS GARVEY, BLACK NATIONALIST   Marcus Garvey participates in a black nationalist parade in Harlem. Garvey wears a plumed hat and is seated on the right, in the car's back seat. He often appeared in public as he does here—in a showy military-style uniform complete with epaulets and an admiral's hat.

That wartime optimism made the discrimination and hatred African Americans encountered after the war hard to endure. Many black workers who had found jobs in the North were fired to make way for returning white veterans. Returning black servicemen, meanwhile, had to scrounge for poorly paid jobs as unskilled laborers. In the South, lynch mobs targeted black veterans who were no longer willing to tolerate the usual insults and indignities.

The worst antiblack violence that year occurred in the North, however. Crowded conditions during the war had forced black and white ethnic city dwellers into uncomfortably close proximity. Many ethnic whites regarded blacks with a mixture of fear and prejudice. These racial tensions escalated into race riots. The deadliest explosion occurred in Chicago in July 1919, when a black teenager who had been swimming in Lake Michigan was killed by whites after coming too close to a whites-only beach. Rioting soon broke out throughout the city, with white mobs invading black neighborhoods, torching homes and stores, and attacking innocent residents. Led by war veterans, some of whom were armed, the blacks fought back, turning the border areas between white and black neighborhoods into battle zones. Fighting raged for five days, leaving 38 dead (23 black, 15 white) and more than 500 injured. Race rioting in other cities pushed the death total to 120 before the summer of 1919 ended.

The riots made it clear to blacks that the North was not the Promised Land. Confined to unskilled jobs and to segregated neighborhoods with substandard housing and exorbitant rents, black migrants in Chicago, New York, and other northern cities suffered severe economic hardship throughout the 1920s. The NAACP carried on its campaign for civil rights and racial equality, but many blacks no longer shared its belief that they would one day be accepted as first-class citizens. They turned instead to a compelling leader from Jamaica, Marcus Garvey. Garvey called on blacks to give up their hopes for integration and to set about forging a separate black nation. He reminded blacks that they possessed a rich culture stretching back over the centuries that would enable them to achieve greatness as a nation. Garvey's grand vision was to build a black nation in Africa that would bring together all the world's people of African descent. In the short term, he wanted to help American and Caribbean blacks to achieve economic and cultural independence.

Garvey's call for black separatism and self-sufficiency—or, black nationalism, as it came to be called—elicited a remarkable response among blacks in the United States. In the early 1920s, the Universal Negro Improvement Association (UNIA), which Garvey had founded, enrolled millions of members. His newspaper, *The Negro World,* reached a circulation of 200,000. Garvey's most visible economic venture was the Black Star Line, a shipping company with three ships that proudly flew the UNIA flag from their masts.

This black nationalist movement did not endure for long, however. Garvey entered into bitter disputes with other black leaders, including W. E. B. Du Bois, who regarded him as a flamboyant, self-serving demagogue. Garvey sometimes showed poor judgment, as when he expressed support for the Ku Klux Klan on the grounds that it shared his pessimism about the possibility of racial integration. Inexperienced in economic matters as well, Garvey squandered a great deal of UNIA money on abortive business ventures. In 1923 he was convicted of mail fraud involving the sale of Black Star stocks and was sentenced to five years in jail. In 1927 he was deported to Jamaica and the UNIA folded. But Garvey's philosophy of black nationalism endured.

CHRONOLOGY

1914	First World War breaks out (July–August)
1915	German submarine sinks *Lusitania* (May 7)
1916	Woodrow Wilson unveils peace initiative • Wilson reelected as "peace president"
1917	Germany resumes unrestricted submarine warfare (February) • Tsar Nicholas II overthrown in Russia (March) • U.S. enters the war (April 6) • Committee on Public Information established • Congress passes Selective Service Act, Espionage Act, Immigration Restriction Act • War Industries Board established • Lenin's Bolsheviks come to power in Russia (Nov.)
1918	Lenin signs treaty with Germany, pulls Russia out of war (March) • Germany launches offensive on western front (March–April) • Congress passes Sabotage Act and Sedition Act • French, British, and U.S. troops repel Germans, advance toward Germany (April–October) • Eugene V. Debs jailed for making antiwar speech • Germany signs armistice (Nov. 11)
1919	Treaty of Versailles signed (June 28) • Chicago race riot (July) • Wilson suffers stroke (September 25) • Police strike in Boston
1919–1920	Steelworkers strike in Midwest • Red Scare prompts "Palmer raids" • Senate refuses to ratify Treaty of Versailles • Universal Negro Improvement Association grows under Marcus Garvey's leadership
1920	Anarchists Sacco and Vanzetti convicted of murder
1923	Marcus Garvey convicted of mail fraud
1924	Woodrow Wilson dies
1927	Sacco and Vanzetti executed

CONCLUSION

The resurgence of racism in 1919 and the consequent turn to black nationalism among African Americans were signs of how the high hopes of the war years had been dashed. Industrial workers, immigrants, and radicals also learned through bitter experience that the fear, intolerance, and repression unleashed by the war interrupted their pursuit of liberty and equality. Of the reform groups, only woman suffragists made enduring gains—especially the right to vote—but, for the feminists in their ranks, these steps forward did not compensate for the collapse of the progressive movement and, with it, their program of achieving equal rights for women across the board.

A similar disappointment engulfed those who had embraced and fought for Wilson's dream of creating a new and democratic world order. The world in 1919 appeared as volatile as it had been in 1914. More and more Americans—perhaps even a majority—were coming to believe that U.S. intervention had been a colossal mistake.

In other ways, the United States benefited a great deal from the war. By 1919, the American economy was by far the world's strongest. The nation's economic strength triggered an extraordinary burst of growth in the 1920s, and millions of Americans rushed to take advantage of the prosperity that this "people's capitalism" had put within their grasp. But the joy generated by affluence did not dissolve the class, ethnic, and racial tensions that the war had exposed. And the failure of the peace process added to Europe's problems, delayed the emergence of the United States as a leader in world affairs, and created the preconditions for another world war.

24

THE 1920S

PROSPERITY ∼ THE POLITICS OF BUSINESS

FARMERS, SMALL-TOWN PROTESTANTS, AND MORAL TRADITIONALISTS

ETHNIC AND RACIAL COMMUNITIES

THE "LOST GENERATION" AND DISILLUSIONED INTELLECTUALS

In 1920 Americans elected a president, Warren G. Harding, who could not have been more different from his predecessor, Woodrow Wilson. A Republican, Harding presented himself as a common man with common desires. In his 1920 campaign he called for a "return to normalcy." Although he died in office in 1923, his carefree spirit is thought to characterize the 1920s.

To many Americans, indeed, the decade was one of fun rather than reform, of good times rather than high ideals. It was, in the words of novelist F. Scott Fitzgerald, the "Jazz Age," a time when the quest for personal gratification seemed to replace the quest for public welfare.

CULTURE SHOCK   This photo juxtaposes the short dresses and dance steps of young women alongside the longer dresses and formal bearing of the older generation. Here, older women seem enchanted with the young women, but many others of their generation were discomfited by the revolution in dance and female demeanor that they were witnessing.

Despite Harding's call for a return to a familiar past, America seemed to be rushing head-long into the future. The word "modern" began appearing everywhere: modern times, modern women, modern technology, the modern home, modern marriage. Although the word was rarely defined, it connoted certain beliefs: that science was a better guide to life than religion; that people should be free to choose their own lifestyles; that sex should be a source of plea-sure for women as well as men; that women and minorities should be equal to and enjoy the same rights as white men.

Many other Americans, however, reaffirmed their belief that God's word transcended sci-ence; that people should obey the moral code set forth in the Bible; that women were not equal to men; and that blacks, Mexicans, and eastern European immigrants were inferior to Anglo-Saxon whites. They made their voices heard in a resurgent Ku Klux Klan and the fun-damentalist movement, and on issues such as evolution and immigration.

Modernists and traditionalists confronted each other in party politics, in legislatures, in courtrooms, and in the press. Their battles make it impossible to think of the 1920s merely as a time for the pursuit of leisure. Nor were the 1920s free of economic and social problems that had troubled Americans for decades.

PROSPERITY

Despite the strains placed on the U.S. economy after the First World War, it remained strong and innovative during the 1920s. Its industries had emerged intact, even strength-ened, from the war. The war needs of the Allies had created an insatiable demand for American goods and capital. Manufacturers and bankers had exported so many goods and extended so many loans to the Allies that by war's end the United States was the world's leading creditor nation.

For a time after the war ended, the country did experience economic turmoil and depres-sion. From 1919 to 1921, it struggled to redirect industry from wartime production to civilian production. Workers went on strike to protest wage reductions or increases in the workweek. Farmers were hit by a severe depression as the overseas demand for American foodstuffs fell from its peak of 1918 and 1919. Disgruntled workers and farmers even joined forces to form statewide farmer-labor parties. In 1924 the two groups formed a national Farmer-Labor Party. Robert La Follette, their presidential candidate, received an impressive 16 percent of the vote that year. But then the third-party movement fell apart.

Its collapse reflected a rising public awareness of how vigorous and productive the econ-omy had become. Beginning in 1922, the nation embarked on a period of remarkable growth. From 1922 to 1929, gross national product grew at an annual rate of 5.5 percent. The unem-ployment rate never exceeded 5 percent—and real wages rose about 15 percent.

A CONSUMER SOCIETY

The rate of economic growth was matched by the variety of products being produced. In the 19th century economic growth had rested primarily on the production of capital goods, such as factory machinery and railroad tracks. In the 1920s, however, growth rested more on the proliferation of consumer goods. Some products, such as cars and telephones, had been available since the early 1900s, but in the 1920s their sales reached new levels. Other consumer goods became available for the first time—tractors, washing machines, refrigerators, electric irons, radios, and vacuum cleaners. The term "consumer durable" was coined to describe such goods, which, unlike food, clothing, and other "perishables," were meant to last. Even "perishables" took on new allure. Scientists had discovered the importance of vitamins in the diet and began urging Americans to consume more fresh fruits and vegetables. Improvements in refrigeration and in packaging, meanwhile, made it possible to transport fresh produce long distances and to extend its shelf life in grocery stores. And more and more stores were being operated by large grocery chains that could afford the latest refrigeration and packaging technology.

The public responded to these innovations with excitement. American industry had made fresh food and stylish clothes available to the masses. Refrigerators, vacuum cleaners, and washing machines would spare women much of the drudgery of housework. Radios would expand the public's cultural horizons. Automobiles, asphalt roads, service stations, hot dog stands, "tourist cabins" (the forerunners of motels), and traffic lights seemed to herald a wholly new civilization. By the middle of the decade the country was a network of paved roads. Camping trips and long-distance vacations became routine. Farmers and their families could now hop into their cars and head for the nearest town with its stores, movies, amusement parks, and sporting events. Suburbs proliferated, billed as the perfect mix of urban and rural life. Young men and women everywhere discovered that cars were a place where they could "make out," and even make love, without fear of reproach by prudish parents or prying neighbors.

In the 1920s Americans also discovered the benefits of owning stocks. The number of stockholders in AT&T, the nation's largest corporation, rose from 140,000 to 568,000. By 1929, as many as 7 million Americans owned stock, most of them people of ordinary, middle-class means.

A PEOPLE'S CAPITALISM

Capitalists boasted that they had created a "people's capitalism" in which virtually all Americans could participate. Now, everyone could have a share of luxuries and amenities. Poverty, capitalists claimed, had been banished, and the gap between rich and poor had been closed. If every American could own a car and house, buy quality clothes, own stock, take vacations, and go to the movies, then clearly there was no longer any significant inequality in society.

Actually, although wages were rising, millions of Americans still did not earn enough income to partake fully of the marketplace. Robert and Helen Lynd were social scientists who studied the people of Muncie, Indiana, a small industrial city of 35,000, and published their findings in a classic study entitled *Middletown*. They discovered that working-class families who bought a car often did not have enough money left for other goods. One housewife admitted, "We don't have no fancy clothes when we have the car to pay for. . . . The car is the only pleasure we have." But many industrialists were reluctant to increase wages, and workers lacked the organizational strength to force them to pay more.

One solution came with the introduction of consumer credit. Car dealers, home appliance salesmen, and other merchants began to offer installment plans that enabled consumers to purchase a product by making a down payment and promising to pay the rest in installments. By 1930, 15 percent of all purchases were made on the installment plan.

Even so, many poor Americans benefited little from the consumer revolution. Middle-class Americans acquired a disproportionate share of consumer durables. They also were the main consumers of fresh vegetables and the main buyers of stock.

THE RISE OF ADVERTISING AND MASS MARKETING

But even middle-class consumers had to be wooed. How could they be persuaded to buy another car only a few years after they had bought their first one? General Motors had the answer. In 1926 it introduced the concept of the annual model change. Its cars were given a different look every year as GM engineers changed headlights and chassis colors, streamlined bodies, and added new features. The strategy worked. GM leaped past Ford and became the world's largest car manufacturer.

Henry Ford reluctantly introduced his Model A in 1927 to provide customers with a colorful alternative to the drab Model T. Having spent his lifetime selling a product renowned for its utility and reliability, Ford could not believe that sales could be increased by appealing to the intangible hopes and fears of consumers. He was wrong. The desire to be beautiful, handsome, or sexually attractive; to exercise power and control; to demonstrate competence and success; to escape anonymity, loneliness, and boredom; to experience pleasure—all such desires, once activated, could motivate a consumer to buy a new car at a time when the old one was still serviceable, or to spend money on goods that might have once seemed frivolous to some.

Arousing such desires required more than bright colors, sleek lines, and attractive packaging. It called for advertising campaigns intended to make a product seem to be the answer to the consumer's desires. To create those campaigns, corporations turned to a new kind of company: professional advertising firms. The new advertising entrepreneurs believed that many Americans were bewildered by bureaucratic workplaces and the anonymity of urban living. This modern anomie, they argued, left consumers susceptible to suggestion.

In their campaigns, advertisers played upon the emotions and vulnerabilities of their target audiences. One cosmetics ad decreed: "Unless you are one woman in a thousand, you must use powder and rouge. Modern living has robbed women of much of their natural color." A mouthwash ad warned about one unsuspecting gentleman's bad breath—"the truth that his friends had been too delicate to mention"—while a tobacco ad matter-of-factly declared: "Men at the top are apt to be pipe-smokers. . . . It's no coincidence—pipe-smoking is a calm and deliberate habit—restful, stimulating. His pipe helps a man think straight. A pipe is back of most big ideas."

Advertising professionals believed they were helping people to manage their lives in ways that would increase their satisfaction and pleasure. By enhancing one's appearance and personality with the help of goods to be found in the marketplace, one would have a better chance of achieving success and happiness.

American consumers responded enthusiastically. The most enthusiastic of all were middle-class Americans, who could afford to buy what the advertisers were selling. Many of them were newcomers to middle-class ranks, searching for ways to affirm—or even create—their new identity. The aforementioned ad for pipe tobacco, for example, was certainly targeted at the new middle-class man—who held a salaried position in a corporate office or bank, or worked as a commission salesman.

As male wage earners moved into the new middle class, their wives were freed from the necessity of outside work. Advertisers appealed to the new middle-class woman, too, as she refocused her attention toward dressing in the latest fashion, managing the household, and raising the children. Vacuum cleaners and other consumer durables would make her more efficient. Cosmetics would aid women in their "first duty"—to be beautiful for the men in their lives—a beauty that would lead to sexual arousal and fulfillment for both men and women.

CHANGING ATTITUDES TOWARD MARRIAGE AND SEXUALITY

That husbands and wives were encouraged to pursue sexual satisfaction together was one sign of how much prescriptions for married life had changed since the 19th century, when women were thought to lack sexual passion and men were tacitly expected to satisfy their drives through extramarital liaisons. Modern husbands and wives were expected to share other leisure activities as well—dining out, playing cards with friends, going to the movies, attending concerts, and discussing the latest selection from the newly formed Book-of-the-Month Club.

The public pursuit of pleasure was also noticeable among young and single middle-class women. The so-called "flappers" of the 1920s donned short dresses, rolled their stockings down, wore red lipstick, and smoked in public. Flappers were signaling their desire for independence and equality; but they had no thought of achieving those goals through politics, as had their middle-class predecessors in the woman suffrage movement. Rather, those goals were to be achieved through the creation of a new female personality endowed with self-reliance, outspokenness, and a new appreciation for the pleasures of life.

CELEBRATING A BUSINESS CIVILIZATION

Industrialists, advertisers, and merchandisers now began to claim that what they were doing was at the heart of American civilization. In 1924 President Calvin Coolidge declared that "the business of America is business." Even religion became a business. Bruce Barton, in his best-seller *The Man That Nobody Knows* (1925), depicted Jesus as a business executive "who picked up twelve men from the bottom ranks of business and forged them into an organization that conquered the world."

Some employers set up employee cafeterias, hired doctors and nurses to staff on-site medical clinics, and engaged psychologists to counsel troubled employees. They built ball fields and encouraged employees to join industry-sponsored leagues. They published employee newsletters and gave awards to employees who did their jobs well and with good spirit. Some even gave employees a voice in determining working conditions. The real purpose of these measures—collectively known as welfare capitalism—was to encourage employee loyalty to the firm and to the capitalist system.

INDUSTRIAL WORKERS

Many industrial workers benefited from the nation's prosperity. A majority of them enjoyed rising wages and a reasonably steady income. Skilled craftsmen in the older industries of construction, railroad transportation, and printing fared especially well. The several million workers employed in the large mass-production industries also did well. Their wages were relatively high, and they enjoyed unprecedented benefits—paid sick leave, paid vacations, life insurance, stock options, subsidized mortgages, and retirement pensions. Although all workers in companies with these programs were eligible for such benefits, skilled workers were in the best position to claim them.

Semiskilled and unskilled industrial workers had to contend with a labor surplus throughout the decade. As employers replaced workers with machines, the aggregate demand for industrial labor increased at a lower rate than it had in the preceding 20 years. Despite a weakening demand for labor, rural whites, rural blacks, and Mexicans continued their migration to the cities, stiffening the competition for factory jobs. Employers could hire and fire as they saw fit and were therefore able to keep wage increases lagging behind increases in productivity.

This softening demand for labor helps to explain why many working-class families did not benefit much from the decade's prosperity or from its consumer revolution. An estimated 40 percent of workers remained mired in poverty, unable to afford a healthy diet or adequate housing, much less any of the more costly consumer goods.

The million or more workers who labored in the nation's two largest industries, coal and textiles, suffered the most during the 1920s. Throughout the decade, both industries experienced severe overcapacity. By 1926 only half of the coal mined each year was being sold. New England textile cities experienced levels of unemployment that sometimes approached 50 percent. One reason was that many textile industrialists had shifted their operations to the South, where taxes and wages were lower. But the southern textile industry also suffered from excess capacity, and prices and wages continued to fall. Plant managers put constant pressure on their workers to speed up production. Workers loathed the frequent "speed-ups" of machines and the "stretch-outs" in the number of spinning or weaving machines each worker was expected to tend. By the late 1920s, labor strife and calls for unionization were rising sharply among disgruntled workers in both the South and the North.

Unionization of textiles and coal, and of more prosperous industries as well, would have brought workers a larger share of the decade's prosperity. Moreover, progressive labor leaders, such as Sidney Hillman of the Amalgamated Clothing Workers, argued that unionization would actually increase corporate profits by compelling employers to observe uniform wage and hour schedules that would restrain ruinous competition. Hillman pointed out that rising wages would enable workers to purchase more consumer goods and thus increase corporate sales and revenues. But Hillman's views were ignored outside the garment industry.

Elsewhere, unions lost ground as business and government remained hostile to labor organization. A conservative Supreme Court whittled away at labor's legal protections. In 1921 it ruled that lower courts could issue injunctions against union members, prohibiting them from striking or picketing an employer. State courts also enforced what union members called "yellow dog" contracts, written pledges by which employees promised not to join a union while they were employed. Any employee who violated that pledge was subject to immediate dismissal. These measures crippled efforts to organize trade unions. Membership fell from a high of 5 million in 1920 to less than 3 million in 1929, a mere 10 percent of the nation's industrial workforce. Not all of the decline was the result of the hostile political climate, though. Many workers, especially those who were benefiting from welfare capitalist programs, decided they no longer needed trade unions. And the labor movement hurt itself by moving too slowly to open its ranks to semiskilled and unskilled factory workers.

THE POLITICS OF BUSINESS

Republican presidents governed the country from 1921 to 1933. In some respects, their administrations resembled those of the Gilded Age, when presidents were mediocre, corruption was rampant, and the government's chief objective was to remove obstacles to capitalist development. But in other respects, the state-building tradition of Theodore Roosevelt lived on, although in somewhat altered form.

HARDING AND THE POLITICS OF PERSONAL GAIN

Warren Gamaliel Harding defeated the Democrat James M. Cox for the presidency in 1920. From modest origins as a newspaper editor in the small town of Marion, Ohio, Harding had risen to the U.S. Senate chiefly because the powerful Ohio Republican machine knew it could count on him to do its bidding. His election to the presidency occurred for the same reason. The Republican Party bosses believed that almost anyone they nominated in 1920 could defeat the Democratic opponent; they chose Harding because they could control him. Harding's good looks and geniality made him a favorite with voters, and he swept into office with 61 percent of the popular vote.

Aware of his own intellectual limitations, Harding included talented men in his cabinet. But he did not possess the will to alter his ingrained political habits. He had built his political career on a willingness to please the lobbyists who came to his Senate office asking for favors and deals. He had long followed Ohio boss Harry M. Daugherty's advice and would continue to do so, now that he had made Daugherty his attorney general. Harding apparently did not think of men such as Daugherty as self-serving or corrupt. They were his friends; they had been with him since the beginning of his political career. He made sure the "boys" had jobs in his administration, and he continued to socialize with them.

It seems that Harding kept himself blind to the widespread use of public office for private gain that characterized his administration. His old friends, the "Ohio gang," got rich selling government appointments, judicial pardons, and police protection to bootleggers. By 1923 the corruption could no longer be concealed. Journalists and senators began to focus public attention on the actions of Secretary of the Interior Albert Fall, who had persuaded Harding to transfer control of large government oil reserves at Teapot Dome, Wyoming, and Elk Hills, California, from the Navy to the Department of the Interior. Fall had then immediately leased the deposits to two oil tycoons, Harry F. Sinclair and Edward L. Doheny, who were allowed to pump oil from the wells in exchange for providing the Navy with a system of fuel tank reserves. Fall had issued the leases secretly, without allowing other oil corporations to compete for them, and he had accepted almost $400,000 from Sinclair and Doheny.

Fall would pay for this shady deal with a year in jail. He was not the only Harding appointee to do so. Charles R. Forbes, head of the Veterans' Bureau, would go to Leavenworth Prison for swindling the government out of $200 million in hospital supplies. The exposure of Forbes's theft prompted his lawyer, Charles Cramer, to commit suicide; Jesse Smith, Attorney General Daugherty's close friend and housemate, also killed himself, apparently to avoid being indicted and brought to trial. Daugherty himself managed to escape conviction and incarceration for bribery by burning incriminating documents held by his brother's Ohio bank. Still, Daugherty was forced to leave government service in disgrace.

Harding grew depressed when he finally realized what had been going on. In the summer of 1923, in poor spirits, he left Washington for a West Coast tour. He fell ill in Seattle and died from a heart attack in San Francisco. The train returning his body to Washington attracted crowds of grief-stricken mourners who little suspected the web of corruption and bribery in which Harding had been caught.

COOLIDGE AND THE POLITICS OF LAISSEZ-FAIRE

Harding's successor, Vice President Calvin Coolidge, never socialized with the "boys." He believed that the best government was the government that governed least, and he took a nap every afternoon. The welfare of the country hinged on the character of its people—their willingness to work hard, to be honest, to live within their means. Coolidge quickly put to rest the anxiety aroused by the Harding scandals.

Born in Vermont and raised in Massachusetts, he gained national visibility in September 1919, when as governor of Massachusetts he took a firm stand against Boston's striking policemen (see Chapter 23). His reputation as a man who battled labor radicals earned him a place

A STERN YANKEE   In sharp contrast to Harding, President Calvin Coolidge did not enjoy informality, banter, or carousing. Here he fishes alone and in formal attire.

on the 1920 national Republican ticket. His image as an ordinary man helped convince voters in 1920 that the Republican Party would return the country to its commonsensical ways after eight years of reckless reforms. Coolidge won his party's presidential nomination handily in 1924 and easily defeated his Democratic opponent, John W. Davis. Coolidge's popularity remained strong throughout his first full term, and he probably would have been renominated and reelected in 1928. But he chose not to run.

Coolidge took greatest pride in those measures that reduced the government's control over the economy. The Revenue Act of 1926 slashed the high income and estate taxes that progressives had pushed through Congress during the First World War. Coolidge twice vetoed the McNary-Haugen Bill, which would have compelled the government to pay subsidies to farmers when domestic farm prices fell below certain levels. He stripped the Federal Trade Commission of the powers it needed to regulate business affairs. And he supported Supreme Court decisions invalidating Progressive Era laws that had strengthened organized labor and protected children and women from exploitation.

HOOVER AND THE POLITICS OF "ASSOCIATIONALISM"

Republicans in the 1920s did more than simply lift government restraints and regulations from the economy. Some Republicans, led by Secretary of Commerce Herbert Hoover, conceived of government as a dynamic, even progressive, economic force. Hoover did not want government to control industry, but he did want government to persuade private corporations to abandon their wasteful, selfish ways and turn to cooperation and public service. Hoover envisioned an economy built on the principle of association. Industrialists, wholesalers, retailers, operators of railroad and shipping lines, small businessmen, farmers, workers, doctors—each of these groups would form a trade association whose members would share economic information, discuss problems of production and distribution, and seek ways of achieving greater efficiency and profit. Hoover believed that the very act of associating in this way—an approach that historian Ellis Hawley has called "associationalism"—would convince participants of the superiority of cooperation over competition, of negotiation over conflict, of public service over selfishness.

During the war, Hoover had directed the government's Food Administration and had made it an outstanding example of public management. From that experience, he had come to appreciate the advantages of coordinating the activities of thousands of producers and distributors scattered across the country. Hoover's ambition as secretary of commerce was to make the department the grand orchestrator of economic cooperation. During his eight years in that post, from 1921 to 1929, he organized over 250 conferences around such themes as unemployment or the problems of a particular industry or economic sector. He brought together government officials, representatives of business, policymakers, and others who had a stake in strengthening the economy.

Hoover achieved some notable successes. He convinced steel executives to abandon the 12-hour day. His support of labor's right to organize contributed to the passage of the 1926 Railway Labor Act, one of the few acts of the 1920s that endorsed labor's right to bargain collectively. His efforts to persuade farmers to join together in marketing cooperatives, which he believed would solve problems of inefficiency and overproduction, led to the Cooperative Marketing Act of 1926. He worked to standardize the size and shape of a great variety of products so as to increase their usefulness and strengthen their sales. When the Mississippi River overflowed its banks in 1927, Hoover was the man Coolidge appointed to organize the relief effort. Hoover used this disaster as an opportunity to place credit operations in flood-affected areas on a sounder footing and to organize local banks into associations with adequate resources and expertise.

Hoover's dynamic conception of government brought him into conflict with Republicans whose economic philosophy began and ended with laissez-faire. Hoover found himself increasingly at odds with Coolidge, who declared in 1927: "That man has offered me unsolicited advice for six years, all of it bad."

THE POLITICS OF BUSINESS ABROAD

Republican domestic policy disagreements between laissez-faire and associationalism spilled over into foreign policy as well. Hoover had accepted the post of secretary of commerce thinking he would represent the United States in negotiations with foreign companies and governments. In fact, he intended to apply his concept of "associationalism" to international relations. He wanted the world's leading nations to meet regularly in conferences, to limit military buildups and to foster an international environment in which capitalism could flourish. Aware that the United States would have to contribute to the creation of such an environment, Hoover hoped to persuade American bankers to adopt investment and loan policies that would aid European recovery. If they refused to do so, he was prepared to urge the government to take an activist, supervisory role in foreign investment.

In 1921 and 1922 Hoover had some influence on the design of the Washington Conference on the Limitation of Armaments. Although he did not serve as a negotiator at the conference—Secretary of State Charles Evans Hughes reserved that role for himself and his subordinates—he did supply Hughes's team with a wealth of economic information. And he helped Hughes to use that information to design forceful, detailed proposals for disarmament. Those proposals gave U.S. negotiators a decided advantage over their European and Asian counterparts and helped them win a stunning accord, the Five-Power Treaty, by which the United States, Britain, Japan, France, and Italy agreed to scrap more than 2 million tons of their warships. Hughes also obtained pledges from all the signatories that they would respect the "Open Door" in China, long a U.S. foreign policy objective (see Chapter 22).

These triumphs redounded to Hughes's credit but not to Hoover's, and Hughes used it to consolidate his control over foreign policy. He rebuffed Hoover's efforts to put international economic affairs under the direction of the Commerce Department and rejected Hoover's suggestion to intervene in the international activities of U.S. banks. In so doing, Hughes revealed his affinity for the laissez-faire rather than the associational school of Republican politics. Hughes was willing to urge bankers to participate in Europe's economic recovery, and he was willing to use the power of government to protect their investments once they were made, but the bankers would be free to decide which loans would be appropriate.

Hughes put his policy into action in 1923 to resolve a crisis in Franco-German relations. The victorious Allies had imposed on Germany an obligation to pay $33 billion in war reparations (see Chapter 23). In 1923, when the impoverished German government suspended its payments, France sent troops to occupy the Ruhr valley, whose industry was vital to the German economy. German workers retaliated by going on strike, and the crisis threatened to undermine Europe's precarious economic recovery.

Hughes understood that the only way to relieve the situation was to convince the French to reduce German reparations to a reasonable level. To help them come to that decision, he demanded that France repay in full the money it had borrowed from the United States during the First World War. The only way France could pay off those loans was to get additional credit from U.S. bankers, but Hughes made it clear that this would not happen until France had agreed to reduce German reparations. At last France relented and sent representatives to a U.S.-sponsored conference in 1924 to restructure Germany's obligation.

At this point, Hughes suddenly withdrew the government from the conference proceedings and turned over negotiations to a group of American bankers. The conference produced the Dawes Plan (after the Chicago banker and chief negotiator, Charles G. Dawes), which sharply reduced German reparations from $542 million to $250 million annually and called on U.S. and foreign banks to stimulate the German economy with a quick infusion of $200 million in loans. Within a matter of days, banker J. P. Morgan Jr. raised more than $1 billion from eager American investors. Money poured into German financial markets, and the German economy was apparently stabilized.

The Dawes Plan won applause on both sides of the Atlantic. But it soon became apparent that the U.S. money flooding into Germany was creating its own problems. American investors were so eager to lend to Germany that their investments became speculative and unsound. At this point, a stronger effort by the U.S. government to direct loans to sound investments might have helped. But Hughes's successor as secretary of state, Frank Kellogg, was interested in no such initiatives; nor was Secretary of the Treasury Mellon.

In only two areas did Republicans depart from their hands-off approach to foreign affairs. The first was in their pursuit of disarmament and world peace. The Five-Power Treaty, negotiated by Hughes in 1921 and 1922, was a major success. Secretary of State Kellogg drew up a treaty with Aristide Briand, the French foreign minister, outlawing war as a tool of national policy. In 1928, representatives of the United States, France, and 13 other nations met in Paris to sign the Kellogg-Briand pact. Hailed as a great stride toward world peace, the pact soon attracted the support of 48 other nations.

Coolidge viewed the treaty as an opportunity to further reduce the size of the U.S. government. With the threat of war removed, the United States could scale back its military forces and eliminate much of the bureaucracy needed to support a large standing army and navy. Unfortunately, the pact contained no enforcement mechanism. It would do nothing to slow the next decade's descent into militarism and war.

The other area in which the Republican administrations of the 1920s took a hands-on approach was Latin America. U.S. investments in the region more than doubled from 1917 to 1929, and the U.S. government continued its policy of intervening in the internal affairs of Latin America to protect U.S. interests. Republican administrations did attempt to curtail American military involvement in the Caribbean. The Coolidge administration pulled American troops out of the Dominican Republic in 1924 and Nicaragua in 1925. But, in the case of Nicaragua, U.S. Marines were sent back in 1926 to end a war between liberal and conservative Nicaraguans and to protect American property; this time they stayed until 1934. U.S. troops, meanwhile, occupied Haiti continuously between 1919 and 1934, keeping in power governments friendly to U.S. interests.

FARMERS, SMALL-TOWN PROTESTANTS, AND MORAL TRADITIONALISTS

Although many Americans benefited from the prosperity of the 1920s, others did not. Over-production was impoverishing substantial numbers of farmers. Beyond economic hardship, many white Protestants, especially those in rural areas and small towns, believed that the country was being overrun by racially inferior and morally suspect foreigners.

AGRICULTURAL DEPRESSION

The 1920s brought hard times to the nation's farmers after the boom period of the war years. During the war, domestic demand for farm products had risen steadily, and foreign demand had exploded as the war disrupted agricultural production in France, Ukraine, and other European food-producing regions. Soon after the war, however, Europe's farmers quickly resumed their customary levels of production. Foreign demand for American foodstuffs fell precipitously, creating an oversupply and depressing prices in the United States.

Contributing further to the plight of U.S. farmers was the sharp rise in agricultural productivity made possible by the tractor, which greatly increased the acreage that each farmer could cultivate. Produce flooded the market. Prices fell even further, as did farm incomes. By 1929, the annual per capita income of rural Americans was only $223, one-quarter that of the non-farm population. Millions were forced to sell their farms. Their choices were then to scrape together a living as tenants or to abandon farming altogether.

Those who stayed on the land grew increasingly vociferous in their demands. In the first half of the decade, radical farmers working through such organizations as the Nonpartisan League of North Dakota and farmer-labor parties in Minnesota, Wisconsin, and other midwestern states led the movement. By the second half of the decade, however, leadership of the farm movement had passed from farming radicals to farming moderates, and from small farmers in danger of dispossession to larger farmers and agribusinesses seeking to extend their holdings. By lobbying through such organizations as the Farm Bureau Federation, the more powerful agricultural interests brought pressure on Congress to set up economic controls that would protect them from failure. Their proposals, embodied in the McNary-Haugen Bill, called on the government to erect high tariffs on foreign produce and to purchase surplus U.S. crops at prices that enabled farmers to cover their production costs. The government would then sell the surplus crops in the world market for whatever prices they fetched. Any money lost in international sales would be absorbed by the government rather than by the farmers. The McNary-Haugen Bill passed Congress in 1926 and in 1928, only to be vetoed by President Coolidge both times.

CULTURAL DISLOCATION

Added to the economic plight of the farmers was a sense of cultural dislocation. Farmers had long perceived themselves as the backbone of the nation—hardworking, honest, God-fearing yeomen, guardians of independence and liberty.

The 1920 census challenged the validity of that view. For the first time, a slight majority of Americans now lived in urban areas. That finding did not in itself signify very much, for the census classified as "urban" those towns with a population as small as 2,500. But the census figures did reinforce the widespread perception that both the economic and cultural vitality of the nation had shifted from the countryside to the metropolis. Industry, the chief engine of prosperity, was an urban phenomenon. Leisure—the world of amusement parks, department stores, professional sports, movies, cabarets, and theaters—was to be enjoyed in cities; so too were flashy fashions and open sexuality. Cities also were the home of secular intellectuals who had scrapped their belief in Scripture and in God and had embraced science as their new, unimpeachable authority.

All through the Progressive Era rural Americans had believed that the cities could be redeemed, that city dwellers could be reformed, that the Protestant values of rural America would triumph. War had crushed that confidence and had replaced it with the fear that urban culture and urban people would undermine all that "true" Americans held dear.

These fears grew even more intense with the changes brought by prosperity. Urban-industrial America was obviously the most prosperous sector of society; its consumer culture and its commodities were penetrating the countryside as never before. Even small towns now sported movie theaters and automobile dealerships. Radio waves carried news of city life into isolated farmhouses. The growth in the circulation of national magazines also broke down the wall separating country from city.

Rural Americans were ambivalent about this cultural invasion. On the one hand, country dwellers were eager to participate in the consumer marketplace. On the other, they worried that by doing so they would expose the countryside to atheism, immorality, and radicalism. Their determination to protect their imperiled way of life was manifested by their support of Prohibition, the Ku Klux Klan, immigration restriction, and religious fundamentalism.

PROHIBITION

The Eighteenth Amendment to the Constitution, which prohibited the manufacture and sale of alcohol, went into effect in January 1920. At its inception it was supported by a large and varied constituency that included farmers, middle-class city dwellers, feminists, and progressive reformers. It soon became apparent, however, that Prohibition was doing more to encourage law-breaking than abstinence. With only 1,500 federal agents to enforce the law, the government could not possibly police the drinking habits of 110 million people. With little fear of punishment, those who wanted to drink did so, either brewing liquor at home or buying it from speakeasies and bootleggers. Because the law prevented legitimate businesses from manufacturing liquor, organized crime simply added alcohol to its business portfolio. Mobsters procured much of their liquor from Canadian manufacturers, smuggled it across the border, protected it in warehouses, and distributed it to speakeasies. Al Capone's Chicago-based mob alone employed 1,000 men to protect its liquor trafficking, which was so lucrative that Capone became the richest (and most feared) gangster in America.

These unexpected consequences caused many early advocates of Prohibition, especially in the cities, to withdraw their support. That was not the response of Prohibition's rural, Protestant supporters, however. The violence spawned by liquor trafficking confirmed their view that alcohol was an agent of evil that had to be eradicated. The high-profile participation of Italian, Irish, and Jewish gangsters in the bootleg trade merely reinforced their view that Catholics and Jews were threats to law and morality. Many rural Protestants became more, not less, determined to rid the country of liquor once and for all; many resolved to rid the country of Jews and Catholics as well.

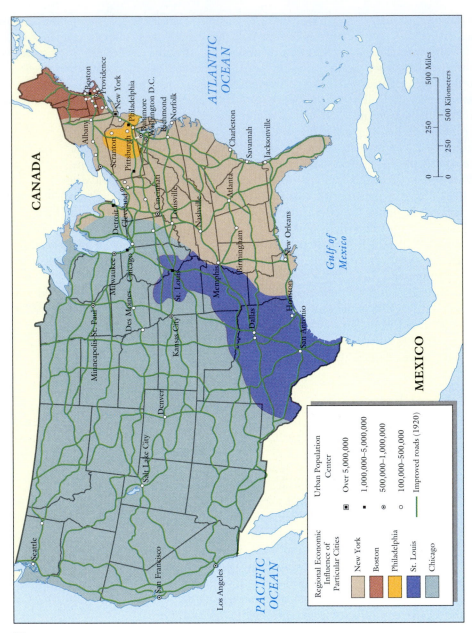

URBANIZATION, 1920

The Ku Klux Klan

The original Ku Klux Klan, formed in the South in the late 1860s, had died out with the defeat of Reconstruction and the reestablishment of white supremacy (see Chapter 17). The new Klan was created in 1915 by William Simmons, a white southerner who had been inspired by D. W. Griffith's racist film, *Birth of a Nation*, in which the early Klan was depicted as having saved the nation (and especially its white women) from predatory blacks. By the 1920s control of the Klan had passed from Simmons to a Texas dentist, Hiram Evans, and its ideological focus had expanded from a loathing of blacks to a hatred of Jews and Catholics as well. Evans's Klan propagated a nativist message that the country should contain—or better yet, eliminate—the influence of Jews and Catholics and restore "Anglo-Saxon" racial purity, Protestant supremacy, and traditional morality to national life. Evans's message swelled Klan ranks and expanded its visibility and influence in the North and South alike. By 1924, as many as 4 million Americans are thought to have belonged to the Klan, including the half-million members of its female auxiliary, Women of the Ku Klux Klan.

In some respects, the Klan functioned just as many other fraternal organizations did. It offered members friendship networks, social services, and conviviality. Its rituals, regalia, and mock-medieval language (the Imperial Wizard, Exalted Cyclops, Grand Dragons, etc.) gave initiates the same sense of superiority, valor, and mystery that so many other fraternal societies imparted to their members. But the Klan also stirred up hate. It thrived on lurid

Women of the Ku Klux Klan Women comprised a substantial portion of the Klan's membership in the 1920s. Here a group marches in an "America First" parade in Binghamton, New York.

tales of financial extortion by Jewish bankers and sexual exploitation by Catholic priests. The accusations were sometimes general, as in the claim that an international conspiracy of Jewish bankers had caused the agricultural depression. More common, and more incendiary, however, were the seemingly plausible, yet totally manufactured, tales of Jewish or Catholic depravity. For example, Catholic priests and nuns were said to prey on Protestant girls and boys who had been forced into convents and Catholic orphanages. These outrageous stories sometimes provoked attacks on individual Jews and Catholics. More commonly, they prompted campaigns to boycott Jewish businesses and Catholic institutions, and to ruin reputations.

The emphasis on sexual exploitation in these stories reveals the anxiety Klan members felt about modern society's acceptance of sexual openness and sexual gratification. Many Klanspeople lived in towns like Muncie, Indiana, where, as the Lynds reported, life was suffused with modern attitudes. That such attitudes might reflect the yearnings of Protestant youth rather than the manipulation of deceitful Jews and Catholics was a truth some Protestant parents found difficult to accept.

IMMIGRATION RESTRICTION

Although the vast majority of Protestant Americans never joined the Klan, many of them did respond to the Klan's nativist argument that the country and its values would best be served by limiting the entry of outsiders. That was the purpose of the Johnson-Reed Immigration Restriction Act of 1924.

By the early 1920s most Americans believed that the country could no longer accommodate the million immigrants who had been arriving each year prior to the war and the more than 800,000 who arrived in 1921. Industrialists no longer needed unskilled European laborers to operate their factories, their places having been taken either by machines or by African American and Mexican workers. And most of the leaders of the labor movement were convinced that the influx of workers unfamiliar with English and with trade unions was weakening labor solidarity. Progressive reformers no longer believed that immigrants could be easily Americanized or that harmony between the native-born and the foreign-born could be readily achieved. Congress responded to constituents' concerns by passing an immigration restriction act in 1921. Then, in 1924, the more comprehensive Johnson-Reed Act imposed a yearly quota of 165,000 immigrants from countries outside the Western Hemisphere.

The sponsors of the 1924 act believed that certain groups—British, Germans, and Scandinavians, in particular—were racially superior and that, consequently, these groups should be allowed to enter the United States in greater numbers. However, because the Constitution prohibits the enactment of explicitly racist laws, Congress had to achieve this racist aim through subterfuge. Lawmakers established a formula to determine the annual immigrant quota for each foreign country, which was to be computed at 2 percent of the total number of immigrants from that country already resident in the United States in the year 1890. In 1890, immigrant ranks had been dominated by the British, Germans, and Scandinavians, so the new quotas would thus allow for a relatively larger cohort of immigrants from those countries. Immigrant groups that were poorly represented in the 1890 population—Italians, Greeks, Poles, Slavs, and eastern European Jews—were effectively locked out. The Johnson-Reed Act also reaffirmed the long-standing policy of excluding Chinese immigrants, and it added Japanese and other Asians to the list of groups that were altogether barred from entry. The act did not

ANNUAL IMMIGRANT QUOTAS UNDER THE JOHNSON-REED ACT, 1925–1927

NORTHWEST EUROPE AND SCANDINAVIA		EASTERN AND SOUTHERN EUROPE		OTHER COUNTRIES	
Country	*Quota*	*Country*	*Quota*	*Country*	*Quota*
Germany	51,227	Poland	5,982	Africa (other than Egypt)	1,100
Great Britain and Northern Ireland	34,007	Italy	3,845	Armenia	124
		Czechoslovakia	3,073		
Irish Free State (Ireland)	28,567	Russia	2,248	Australia	121
				Palestine	100
Sweden	9,561	Yugoslavia	671	Syria	100
		Romania	603		
Norway	6,453	Portugal	503	Turkey	100
France	3,954	Hungary	473	New Zealand and Pacific Islands	100
Denmark	2,789	Lithuania	344		
Switzerland	2,081	Latvia	142	All others	1,900
Netherlands	1,648	Spain	131		
Austria	785	Estonia	124		
Belgium	512	Albania	100		
Finland	471	Bulgaria	100		
Free City of Danzig	228	Greece	100		
Iceland	100				
Luxembourg	100				
Total (number)	142,483	Total (number)	18,439	Total (number)	3,745
Total (%)	86.5%	Total (%)	11.2%	Total (%)	2.3%

Note: Total annual immigrant quota was 164,667

Source: From *Statistical Abstract of the United States* (Washington, D.C.: Government Printing Office, 1929), p. 100.

officially limit immigration from nations in the Western Hemisphere, chiefly because agribusiness interests in Texas and California had convinced Congress that cheap Mexican laborers were indispensable to their industry's prosperity. Still, the establishment of a Border Patrol along the U.S.-Mexican border and the imposition of a $10 head tax on all prospective Mexican immigrants made entry into the United States more difficult for Mexicans than it had been.

The Johnson-Reed Act accomplished Congress's underlying goal. Annual immigration from transoceanic nations fell by 80 percent. The large number of available slots for English and German immigrants regularly went unfilled, while the smaller number of available slots for Italians, Poles, Russian Jews, and others prevented hundreds of thousands of them from entering the country. A "national origins" system put in place in 1927 reduced the total annual quota further, to 150,000, and reserved more than 120,000 of these slots for immigrants from northwestern Europe.

Remarkably few Americans, outside of the ethnic groups that were being discriminated against, objected to these laws at the time they were passed—an indication of how broadly acceptable racism and nativism had become.

FUNDAMENTALISM

Of all the forces reacting against urban life, Protestant fundamentalism was perhaps the most enduring. Fundamentalists regard the Bible as God's word and thus the source of all "fundamental" truth. They believe that every event depicted in the Bible, from the creation of the world in six days to the resurrection of Christ, happened exactly as the Bible describes it. For fundamentalists, God is a deity who intervenes directly in the lives of individuals and communities.

The rise of the fundamentalist movement from the 1870s through the 1920s roughly paralleled the rise of urban-industrial society. Fundamentalists recoiled from the "evils" of the city—from what they perceived as its poverty, its moral degeneracy, its irreligion, and its crass materialism. Fundamentalism took shape in reaction against two additional aspects of urban society: the growth of liberal Protestantism and the revelations of science.

Liberal Protestants believed that religion had to be adapted to the skeptical and scientific temper of the modern age. The Bible was to be mined for its ethical values rather than for its literal truth. Liberal Protestants removed God from his active role in history and refashioned him into a distant and benign deity who watches over the world but does not intervene to punish or to redeem. They turned religion away from the quest for salvation and toward the pursuit of good deeds, social conscience, and love for one's neighbor. Fundamentalism arose in part to counter the "heretical" claims of the liberal Protestants.

Liberal Protestants and fundamentalists both understood that science was the source of most challenges to Christianity. Scientists believed that rational inquiry was a better guide to the past and to the future than prayer and revelation. Scientists even challenged the ideas that God had created the world and had fashioned mankind in his own image. These were beliefs that many religious peoples, particularly fundamentalists, simply could not accept. Conflict was inevitable. It came in 1925, in Dayton, Tennessee.

THE SCOPES TRIAL

No aspect of science aroused more anger among fundamentalists than Charles Darwin's theory of evolution. There was no greater blasphemy than to suggest that man emerged from lower forms of life instead of being created by God himself. In Tennessee in 1925, fundamentalists succeeded in getting a law passed forbidding the teaching of "any theory that denies the story of the divine creation of man as taught in the Bible."

For Americans who accepted the authority of science, denying the truth of evolution was as ludicrous as insisting that the sun revolved around the earth. They ridiculed the fundamentalists, but they worried that the passage of the Tennessee law might signal the onset of a campaign to undermine First Amendment guarantees of free speech. The American Civil Liberties Union began searching for a teacher who would be willing to challenge the constitutionality of the Tennessee law. They found their man in John T. Scopes, a 24-year-old biology teacher in Dayton. After confessing that he had taught evolution to his students, Scopes was arrested. The case quickly attracted national attention. William Jennings Bryan announced that he would help to prosecute Scopes, and the famous liberal trial lawyer Clarence Darrow rushed to Dayton to lead Scopes's defense. That Bryan and Darrow had once been allies in the progressive movement only heightened the drama. A small army of journalists, led by H. L. Mencken, descended on Dayton.

The trial dragged on, and most of the observers expected Scopes to be convicted. (He was.) But it took an unexpected turn when Darrow persuaded the judge to let Bryan testify as an "expert on the Bible." Darrow knew that Bryan's testimony would have no bearing on the question of Scopes's innocence or guilt. His aim was to expose Bryan as a fool for believing that the Bible was a source of literal truth and thus to embarrass the fundamentalists. In a brilliant confrontation, Darrow made Bryan's defense of the Bible look silly, and he then led Bryan to admit that the "truth" of the Bible was not always easy to accept. In that case, Darrow asked, how could fundamentalists be so sure that everything in the Bible was literally true?

In his account of the trial, Mencken portrayed Bryan as a pathetic figure who had been devastated by his humiliating experience on the witness stand, a view popularized in the 1960 movie, *Inherit the Wind*. When Bryan died only a week after the trial ended, Mencken claimed that the trial had broken Bryan's heart.

Bryan deserved a better epitaph than the one Mencken had given him. Diabetes caused his death, not a broken heart. Nor was Bryan the innocent fool that Mencken made him out to be. He remembered when social conservatives had used Darwin's phrase "survival of the fittest" to prove that the wealthy and politically powerful were racially superior to the poor and powerless (see Chapter 20). His rejection of Darwinism evidenced his democratic faith that all human beings were creatures of God and thus capable of striving for perfection and equality.

The public ridicule attendant on the Scopes trial did take its toll on fundamentalists. Many of them retreated from politics and refocused their attention on purging sin from their own hearts rather than from the hearts of others. In the end, the fundamentalists were able to prevail on three more states to prohibit the teaching of evolution. But the controversy had even more far-reaching effects. Worried about losing sales, publishers quietly removed references to Darwin from their science textbooks, a policy that would remain in force until the 1960s.

ETHNIC AND RACIAL COMMUNITIES

The 1920s were a decade of change for ethnic and racial minorities. Some minorities benefited from the prosperity of the decade; others created and sustained vibrant subcultures. All, however, experienced a surge in religious and racial discrimination that made them uneasy in Jazz Age America.

EUROPEAN AMERICANS

European American immigrants were concentrated in the cities of the Northeast and Midwest. A large number were semiskilled and unskilled industrial laborers and suffered economic

DEMOCRATIC PRESIDENTIAL VOTING IN CHICAGO BY ETHNIC GROUPS, 1924 AND 1928

	PERCENT DEMOCRATIC	
	1924	*1928*
Czechoslovaks	40%	73%
Poles	35	71
Lithuanians	48	77
Yugoslavs	20	54
Italians	31	63
Germans	14	58
Jews	19	60

Source: From John M. Allswang, *A House for All Peoples: Ethnic Politics in Chicago, 1890–1936* (Lexington: University Press of Kentucky), p. 42.

insecurity as a result. In addition, they faced cultural discrimination. Catholics generally opposed Prohibition, viewing it as a crude attempt by Protestants to control their behavior. Southern and eastern Europeans, particularly Jews and Italians, resented immigration restriction and the implication that they were unworthy of citizenship. Many Italians were outraged by the execution of Nicola Sacco and Bartolomeo Vanzetti in 1927 (Chapter 23). Had the two men been native-born Protestants, Italians argued, their lives would have been spared.

Southern and eastern Europeans everywhere were the objects of intensive Americanization campaigns. State after state passed laws requiring public schools to instruct children in the essentials of citizenship. Several states, including Rhode Island, extended these laws to private schools as well, convinced that immigrants' children who attended Catholic parochial schools were spending too much time learning about their native religion, language, and country. An Oregon law tried to eliminate Catholic schools altogether by ordering all children aged 8 to 16 to enroll in public schools. But attending a public school was no guarantee of acceptance, either—a lesson learned by Jewish children who had excelled in their studies only to be barred from Harvard, Columbia, and other elite universities.

Southern and eastern European Americans responded to these insults and attacks by strengthening the very institutions and customs Americanizers were trying to undermine. Ethnic associations flourished in the 1920s. Children learned their native languages and customs at home and at church if not at school, and joined with their parents to celebrate their ethnic heritage.

These immigrants and their children were not oblivious to the new consumer culture, however. They flocked to movies and amusement parks, to baseball games and boxing matches. Children usually entered more enthusiastically into the world of American mass culture than did their immigrant parents. Many ethnics found it possible to reconcile their own culture with American culture. Youngsters who went to the movies did so with friends from within their community. Ethnics also played sandlot baseball, but their leagues were customarily organized around churches or ethnic associations. In these early days of radio, ethnics living in large cities could always find programs in their native language and music from their native lands.

European American ethnics also resolved to develop the political muscle needed to defeat the forces of nativism and to turn government policy in a more favorable direction. One sign of this determination was a sharp rise in the number of immigrants who became U.S. citizens. Armed with the vote, ethnics turned out on election day to defeat unsympathetic city councilmen, mayors, state representatives, and even an occasional governor. Their growing national strength first became apparent at the Democratic national convention of 1924, when urban-ethnic delegates almost won approval of planks calling for the repeal of Prohibition and condemnation of the Klan. Then, after denying the presidential nomination to William G. McAdoo, they nearly secured it for their candidate, Alfred E. Smith, the Irish American governor of New York. McAdoo represented the rural and southern constituencies of the Democratic Party. His forces ended up battling Smith's urban-ethnic forces for 103 ballots, until the two men gave up and supporters from each camp switched their votes to a compromise candidate, the corporate lawyer John W. Davis.

The nomination fight devastated the Democratic Party in the short term, and the popular Coolidge easily defeated the little-known Davis. But the convention upheaval of 1924 also marked an important milestone in the bid by European Americans for political power. They would achieve a second milestone at the Democratic national convention of 1928 when, after another bitter nomination struggle, they were finally successful in securing the presidential nomination for Al Smith. Never before had a major political party nominated a Catholic for that high office. Herbert Hoover crushed Smith in the general election, as nativists stirred up anti-Catholic prejudice yet again, and as large numbers of southern Democrats either stayed home or voted Republican. But there were encouraging signs in the campaign, none more so than Smith's beating Hoover in the nation's 12 largest cities. European Americans would yet have their day.

AFRICAN AMERICANS

Despite the urban race riots of 1919 (see Chapter 23), African Americans continued to leave their rural homes for the industrial centers of the South and the North. In New York City and Chicago, their numbers grew so large that they formed cities unto themselves. Within these black metropolises, complex societies emerged consisting of workers, businessmen, professionals, intellectuals, artists, and entertainers. Social differentiation intensified as various groups—long-resident northerners and newly arrived southerners, religious conservatives and cultural radicals, African Americans and African Caribbeans—found reason to disapprove of one another's ways. Still, the diversity and complexity of urban black America were thrilling, nowhere more so than in Harlem, the "Negro capital."

Not even the glamour of Harlem could erase the reality of racial discrimination, however. Most African Americans could find work only in New York City's least-desired and lowest-paying jobs. Because they could rent apartments only in areas that real estate agents and banks had designated as "colored," African Americans suffered the highest rate of residential segregation of any minority group. Harlem became a black ghetto, an area set apart from the rest of the city by the skin color of its inhabitants, by its higher population density and poverty rate, by its higher incidence of infectious diseases, and by the lower life expectancy of its people. At the same time, substantial numbers of New York City's European

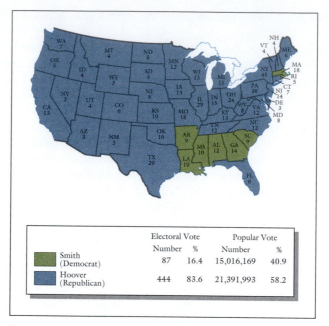

		Electoral Vote		Popular Vote	
		Number	%	Number	%
🟩	Smith (Democrat)	87	16.4	15,016,169	40.9
🟦	Hoover (Republican)	444	83.6	21,391,993	58.2

PRESIDENTIAL ELECTION, 1928

ethnics were leaving their lower Manhattan ghettos for the "greener" pastures of Brooklyn and the Bronx.

Blacks did enjoy some important economic breakthroughs in the 1920s. Henry Ford, for example, hired large numbers of African Americans to work in his Detroit auto factories. But even here a racist logic was operating, for Ford believed that black and white workers, divided along racial lines, would not challenge his authority.

African Americans grew pessimistic about achieving racial equality. After Marcus Garvey's black nationalist movement collapsed in the mid-1920s (see Chapter 23), no comparable organization arose to take its place. The NAACP continued to fight racial discrimination, and the Urban League carried on quiet negotiations with industrial elites to open up jobs to African Americans. But the victories were small; white allies were scarce. The political initiatives emerging among European ethnics had no counterpart in the African American community.

In terms of black culture, however, the 1920s were remarkably vigorous and productive. Black musicians coming north to Chicago and New York brought with them their distinctive musical styles, most notably the blues and ragtime. Influenced by the harmonies and techniques of European classical music, these southern styles metamorphosed into jazz. Urban audiences found this new music irresistible. In Chicago, Detroit, New York, New Orleans, and elsewhere, jazz musicians came together in cramped apartments, cabarets, and nightclubs to jam, compete, and entertain. Jazz seemed to express something quintessentially modern. Jazz musicians broke free of convention, improvised, and produced new sounds that gave rise to new sensations. Both blacks and whites found in jazz an escape from the routine, the predictability, and the conventions of their everyday lives.

DEATH RATES FROM SELECTED CAUSES FOR NEW YORK CITY RESIDENTS, 1925

CAUSE OF DEATH	TOTAL POPULATION	AFRICAN AMERICAN POPULATION
General death rate (per 1,000 population)	11.4	16.5
Pneumonia	132.8	282.4
Pulmonary tuberculosis	75.5	258.4
Infant mortality (per 1,000 live births)	64.6	118.4
Maternal mortality (per 1,000 total births)	5.3	10.2
Stillbirths (per 1,000 births)	47.6	82.7
Homicide	5.3	19.5
Suicide	14.8	9.7

Note: Rate is per 100,000 population, unless noted

Source: Cheryl Lynn Greenberg, *"Or Does It Explode?" Black Harlem in the Great Depression* (New York: Oxford University Press, 1991), p. 32.

THE HARLEM RENAISSANCE

Paralleling the emergence of jazz was a black literary and artistic awakening known as the Harlem Renaissance. Black novelists, poets, painters, sculptors, and playwrights set about creating works rooted in their own culture instead of imitating the styles of white Europeans and Americans. The movement had begun during the war, when blacks sensed that they might at last be advancing to full equality. It was symbolized by the image of the "New Negro," who would no longer be deferential to whites but who would display his or her independence through talent and determination. As racial discrimination intensified after the war, cultural activities took on special significance. The world of culture was the one place where blacks could express their racial pride and demonstrate their talent.

Langston Hughes, a young black poet, said of the Harlem Renaissance: "We younger Negro artists who create now intend to express our individual dark-skinned selves without fear or shame. If white people are pleased, we are glad. If they are not, it doesn't matter. We know we are beautiful. And ugly, too." In 1925, *Survey Graphic*, a white liberal magazine, devoted an entire issue to "Harlem—the Mecca of the New Negro."

But even these cultural advances did not escape white prejudice. The most popular jazz nightclubs in Harlem, most of which were owned and operated by whites, refused to admit black customers. The only African Americans who were permitted inside were the jazz musicians, singers and dancers, prostitutes, and kitchen help. Moreover, the musicians had to play what the white patrons wanted to hear. Duke Ellington, for example, featured "jungle music," which for whites revealed the "true" African soul—sensual, innocent, primitive.

Artists and writers experienced similar pressures. Many of them depended for their sustenance on the support of wealthy white patrons. Those patrons were generous, but they wanted a return on their investment. Charlotte Mason, the New York City matron who supported Hughes and another black writer, Zora Neale Hurston, for example, felt free to judge their work and expected them to entertain her friends by demonstrating "authentic Negritude."

MEXICAN AMERICANS

After the Johnson-Reed Act of 1924, Mexicans became the country's chief source of immigrant labor. A total of 500,000 Mexicans came north in the 1920s. Most settled in the Southwest. In Texas three of every four construction workers and eight of every 10 migrant farm workers were Mexicans. In California, Mexican immigrants made up 75 percent of the state's agricultural workforce.

Mexican farm laborers in Texas worked long hours for little money. They were usually barred from becoming machine operators or assuming other skilled positions. Forced to follow the crops, they had little opportunity to develop settled homes and communities. Farm

"LOS MADRUGADORES" Led by Pedro J. Gonzalez (seated, on left), this popular Mexican group sang *corridos* in live performances and on KMPC, a Spanish-language radio station in 1920s Los Angeles.

owners rarely required the services of Mexican workers for more than several days or weeks, and few were willing to spend the money required to provide decent homes and schools. Houses typically lacked even wooden floors or indoor plumbing. Mexican laborers found it difficult to protest these conditions. Their knowledge of English and American law was limited. Many were in debt to employers who had advanced them money and who threatened them with jail if they failed to fulfill the terms of their contract. Others feared deportation; they lacked visas, having slipped into the United States illegally rather than pay the immigrant tax or endure harassment from the Border Patrol.

Increasing numbers of Mexican immigrants, however, found their way to California. Some escaped agricultural labor altogether for construction and manufacturing jobs. Mexican men in Los Angeles worked in the city's large railroad yards, at the city's numerous construction sites, as unskilled workers in local factories, and as agricultural workers in the fruit and vegetable fields of Los Angeles County. Mexican women labored in the city's garment shops, fish canneries, and food processing plants.

The Los Angeles Mexican American community increased in complexity as it grew in size. By the mid-1920s it included a growing professional class, a proud group of *californios* (Spanish-speakers who had been resident in California for generations), a large number of musicians and entertainers, a small but energetic band of entrepreneurs and businessmen, conservative clerics and intellectuals who had fled or been expelled from revolutionary Mexico, and Mexican government officials who had been sent to counter the influence of the conservative exiles and to strengthen the ties of the immigrants to their homeland. This diverse mix gave rise to much internal conflict, but it also generated considerable cultural vitality. Indeed, Los Angeles became the same kind of magnet for Mexican Americans that Harlem had become for African Americans. Mexican musicians flocked to Los Angeles, as did Mexican playwrights. The city supported a vigorous Spanish-language theater. Mexican musicians performed on street corners, at ethnic festivals and weddings, at cabarets, and on the radio. Especially popular were folk ballads, called *corridos*, that spoke to the experiences of Mexican immigrants.

This flowering of Mexican American culture in Los Angeles could not erase the low wages, high rates of infant mortality, racial discrimination, and other hardships Mexicans faced; nor did it encourage Mexicans to mobilize themselves as a political force. Unlike European immigrants, Mexican immigrants showed little interest in becoming American citizens and acquiring the vote. Yet, the cultural vibrancy of the Mexican immigrant community did sustain many individuals who were struggling to survive in a strange, and often hostile, environment.

THE "LOST GENERATION" AND DISILLUSIONED INTELLECTUALS

Many native-born, white artists and intellectuals also felt uneasy in America in the 1920s. Their unease arose not from poverty or discrimination but from alienation. They despaired of American culture and regarded the average American as anti-intellectual, small-minded, materialistic, and puritanical. The novelist Sinclair Lewis ridiculed small-town Americans in *Main Street* (1920), "sophisticated" city dwellers in *Babbitt* (1922), physicians in *Arrowsmith* (1925), and evangelicals in *Elmer Gantry* (1927).

Before the First World War intellectuals and artists had been deeply engaged with "the people." Although they were critical of many aspects of American society, they believed that they could help bring about a new politics and improve social conditions. Some of them joined the war effort before the United States had officially intervened. Ernest Hemingway, John Dos Passos, and e. e. cummings, among others, sailed to Europe and volunteered their services to the Allies, usually as ambulance drivers carrying wounded soldiers from the front.

America's intellectuals were shocked by the effect the war had on American society. The wartime push for consensus created intolerance of radicals, immigrants, and blacks. Not only had many Americans embraced conformity for themselves, but they seemed determined to force conformity on others. The young critic Harold Stearns wrote in 1921 that "the most moving and pathetic fact in the social life of America today is emotional and aesthetic starvation." Before these words were published, Stearns had sailed for France. So many alienated young men like Stearns showed up in Paris that Gertrude Stein, an American writer whose Paris apartment became a gathering place for them, took to calling them the "Lost Generation."

These writers and intellectuals managed to convert their disillusionment into a new literary sensibility. The finest works of the decade focused on the psychological toll of living in what the poet T. S. Eliot referred to as *The Waste Land* (1922). F. Scott Fitzgerald's novel *The Great Gatsby* (1925) told of a man destroyed by his desire to be accepted into a world of wealth, fancy cars, and fast women. In the novel *A Farewell to Arms* (1929), Ernest Hemingway wrote of an American soldier overwhelmed by the senselessness and brutality of war who deserts the army for the company of a woman he loves. The playwright Eugene O'Neill created characters haunted by despair, loneliness, and unfulfilled longing. Writers created innovations in style as well as in content. Sherwood Anderson, in his novel *Winesburg, Ohio* (1919), blended fiction and autobiography. John Dos Passos, in *Manhattan Transfer* (1925), mixed journalism with more traditional literary methods. Hemingway wrote in an understated, laconic prose that somehow drew attention to his characters' rage and vulnerability.

White southern writers found a tragic sensibility surviving from the South's defeat in the Civil War that spoke to their own loss of hope. One group of writers, calling themselves "the Agrarians," argued that the enduring agricultural character of their region offered a more hopeful path to the future than did the mass-production and mass-consumption regime that had overtaken the North. In 1929 William Faulkner published *The Sound and the Fury,* the first in a series of novels set in northern Mississippi's fictional Yoknapatawpha County. Faulkner explored the violence and terror that marked relationships among family members and townspeople, while at the same time maintaining compassion and understanding.

DEMOCRACY ON THE DEFENSIVE

Their disdain for the masses led many intellectuals to question democracy itself. If ordinary people were as stupid, prejudiced, and easily manipulated as they seemed, how could they be entrusted with the fate of the nation? Walter Lippmann, a former radical and progressive, declared that modern society had rendered democracy obsolete. In his view, average citizens, buffeted by propaganda emanating from powerful opinion-makers, could no longer make the kind of informed, rational judgments that were needed to make democracy work. Lippmann's solution, and that of many other political commentators, was to shift government power from the people to educated elites. Those elites, who would be appointed rather than elected, would conduct foreign and domestic policy in an informed, intelligent way.

These antidemocratic views did not go uncontested. The philosopher John Dewey was the most articulate spokesman for the "prodemocracy" position. He acknowledged that the concentration of power in a few giant organizations had eroded the authority of Congress, the presidency, and other democratic institutions. But democracy was not doomed, he insisted. The people could reclaim their freedom by making big business subject to government control. The government could then use its power to democratize corporations and to regulate the communications industry to ensure that every citizen had access to the facts needed to make reasonable, informed political decisions.

Dewey's views attracted the support of a wide range of liberal intellectuals and reformers, including Robert and Helen Lynd, the authors of *Middletown;* Rexford Tugwell, professor of economics at Columbia; and Felix Frankfurter, a rising star at Harvard Law School. Some of these activists had ties to labor leaders and to New York Governor Franklin D. Roosevelt. They formed the vanguard of a new liberal movement that was committed to taking up the work the progressives had left unfinished.

But these reformers were utterly without power, except in a few states. The Republican Party had driven reformers from its ranks. The Democratic Party was a fallen giant, crippled by a split between its principal constituencies—rural Protestants and urban ethnics—over Prohibition, immigration restriction, and the Ku Klux Klan. The labor movement was moribund. The Socialist Party had never recovered from the trauma of war and Bolshevism.

CHRONOLOGY

1920	Prohibition goes into effect • Warren G. Harding defeats James M. Fox for presidency • Census reveals a majority of Americans live in urban areas • 8 million cars on road
1922	United States, Britain, Japan, France, and Italy sign Five-Power Treaty, agreeing to reduce size of their navies
1923	Teapot Dome scandal lands Secretary of the Interior Albert Fall in jail • Harding dies in office; Calvin Coolidge becomes president
1924	Dawes Plan to restructure Germany's war debt put in effect • Coolidge defeats John W. Davis for presidency • Ku Klux Klan membership approaches 4 million • Immigration Restriction Act cuts immigration by 80 percent and discriminates against Asians and southern and eastern Europeans
1925	Scopes trial upholds right of Tennessee to bar teaching of evolution in public schools • *Survey Graphic* publishes a special issue, *The New Negro,* announcing the Harlem Renaissance • F. Scott Fitzgerald publishes *The Great Gatsby* • U.S. withdraws Marines from Nicaragua
1926	Revenue Act cuts income and estate taxes • Coolidge vetoes McNary-Haugen bill, legislation meant to relieve agricultural distress • U.S. sends Marines back to Nicaragua to end civil war and protect U.S. property
1928	15 nations sign Kellogg-Briand pact, pledging to avoid war • Coolidge vetoes McNary-Haugen bill again • Herbert Hoover defeats Alfred E. Smith for presidency
1929	Union membership drops to 3 million • 27 million cars on road • William Faulkner publishes *The Sound and the Fury*
1930	Los Angeles's Mexican population reaches 100,000

La Follette's Farmer-Labor Party, after a promising debut, had stalled. John Dewey and his friends tried to launch yet another third party, but they failed to raise money or arouse mass support.

Reformers took little comfort in the presidential election of 1928. Hoover's smashing victory suggested that the trends of the 1920s—the dominance of the Republicans, the centrality of Prohibition to political debate, the paralysis of the Democrats, the growing economic might of capitalism, and the pervasive influence of the consumer culture—would continue unabated.

CONCLUSION

Signs abounded in the 1920s that Americans were creating a new and bountiful society. The increased accessibility of cars and other consumer durables; rising real wages, low unemployment, and installment buying; and the spread of welfare capitalism—all these pointed to an economy that had become more prosperous, more consumer-oriented, even somewhat more egalitarian. Moves to greater equality within marriage and to enhanced liberty for single women suggested that economic change was propelling social change as well.

But many working-class and rural Americans benefited little from the decade's prosperity. And the changes aroused resistance, especially from farmers and small-town Americans who feared that the rapid growth of cities was rendering their white, Protestant America unrecognizable.

In the Democratic Party, farmers, small-town Americans, and moral traditionalists fought bitterly against the growing power of urban, ethnic constituencies. Elsewhere, the traditionalists battled hard to protect religion's authority against the inroads of science and to purge the nation of "inferior" population streams. In the process they arrayed themselves against American traditions of liberty and equality.

Their resistance to change caused many of the nation's most talented artists and writers to turn away from their fellow Americans in disgust. Meanwhile, although ethnic and racial minorities experienced high levels of discrimination, they nevertheless found enough freedom to create vibrant ethnic and racial communities and to launch projects of cultural renaissance.

The Republican Party, having largely shed its reputation for reform, took credit for engineering the new economy of consumer plenty. It looked forward to years of political dominance. A steep and unexpected economic depression, however, would soon dash that expectation, revive the Democratic Party, and destroy Republican political power for a generation.

The Great Depression and the New Deal, 1929–1939

The Great Depression began on October 29, 1929—"Black Tuesday"—with a spectacular stock market crash. On that one day, the value of stocks plummeted $14 billion. By the end of that year, stock prices had fallen 50 percent from their September highs. By 1932, the worst year of the depression, they had fallen another 30 percent. Meanwhile the unemployment rate had soared to 25 percent.

Many Americans who lived through the Great Depression were never able to forget the scenes of misery that they saw on every hand. In cities, the poor meekly awaited their turn at ill-funded soup kitchens. Scavengers poked through garbage cans for food, scoured railroad tracks for coal that had fallen from trains, and sometimes ripped up railroad ties for fuel. Hundreds of thousands of Americans built makeshift shelters out of cardboard, scrap metal, and whatever else they could find in the city dump. They called their towns "Hoovervilles," after the president whom they despised for his apparent refusal to help them.

The Great Depression brought cultural crisis as well as economic crisis. In the 1920s the leaders of American business had successfully redefined the national culture in business terms, as Americans' values became synonymous with the values of business: economic growth, freedom of enterprise and acquisitiveness. But with the prestige of business and business values in decline, how could Americans regain their hope and recover their confidence in the future?

The gloom broke in early 1933 when Franklin Delano Roosevelt became president and unleashed the power of government to regulate capitalist enterprises, to restore the economy to health, and to guarantee the social welfare of Americans unable to help themselves. Roosevelt called his pro-government program a "new deal for the American people." In the short term, the New Deal did not restore prosperity to America. But the "liberalism" that the New Deal championed found acceptance among millions, who agreed with Roosevelt that only a large and powerful government could guarantee Americans their liberty.

CAUSES OF THE GREAT DEPRESSION

There had been other depressions, or "panics," in American history, and no one would have been surprised had the boom of the 1920s been followed by an economic downturn lasting a year or two. No one was prepared, however, for the economic catastrophe of the 1930s.

STOCK MARKET SPECULATION

In 1928 and 1929 the New York Stock Exchange had undergone a remarkable run-up in prices. Money had poured into the market. But many investors were buying on 10 percent "margin"—putting up only 10 percent of the price of a stock and borrowing the rest from brokers or banks. They expected to be able to resell their shares within a few months at dramatically higher prices, pay back their loans from the proceeds, and still clear a handsome profit. And, for a while, that is exactly what they did. But the possibility of making a fortune with an investment of only a few thousand dollars only intensified investors' greed. Money flowed indiscriminately into all kinds of risky enterprises, as speculation became rampant. The stock market spiraled upward, out of control. When confidence in future earnings finally faltered, in October 1929, creditors began demanding that investors who had bought stocks on margin repay their loans. The market crashed from its dizzying heights.

Still, the crash, by itself, does not explain why the Great Depression lasted as long as it did. Poor decision making by the Federal Reserve Board, an ill-advised tariff that took effect soon after the depression hit, and a lopsided concentration of wealth in the hands of the rich deepened the economic collapse and made recovery more difficult.

MISTAKES BY THE FEDERAL RESERVE BOARD

In 1930 and 1931, the Federal Reserve curtailed the amount of money in circulation and raised interest rates, thereby making credit more difficult for the public to secure. This tight money policy was disastrous. What the economy needed was an expanded money supply, lower interest rates, and easier credit. Such a course would have enabled debtors to pay their creditors. Instead, by choosing the opposite course, the Federal Reserve plunged an economy starved for credit deeper into depression.

AN ILL-ADVISED TARIFF

The Tariff Act of 1930, also known as the Hawley-Smoot Tariff, accelerated economic decline abroad and at home. It not only raised tariffs on 75 agricultural goods; it also raised tariffs on 925 manufactured products. Industrialists had convinced their supporters in the Republican-controlled Congress that such protection would give American industry much needed assistance. But the legislation was a disaster. Angry foreign governments retaliated by raising their own tariff rates to keep out American goods. International trade, already weakened by the tight credit policies of the Federal Reserve, was dealt another blow at the very moment when it desperately needed a boost.

A Maldistribution of Wealth

A serious maldistribution in the nation's wealth that had developed in the 1920s also stymied economic recovery. Between 1918 and 1929 the share of the national income that went to the wealthiest 20 percent of the population rose by more than 10 percent, while the share that went to the poorest 60 percent fell by almost 13 percent. The Coolidge administration contributed to this maldistribution by lowering taxes on the wealthy. The deepening inequality of income distribution slowed consumption and held back the growth of consumer-oriented industries. Even when the rich spent their money lavishly, they still spent a smaller proportion of their total incomes on consumption than wage earners did. Had more of the total increase in national income found its way into the pockets of average Americans during the 1920s, the demand for consumer goods would have been steadier and the newer consumer industries would have been correspondingly stronger. Such an economy might have recovered relatively quickly from the stock market crash of 1929. But recovery from the Great Depression did not come until 1941, more than a decade later.

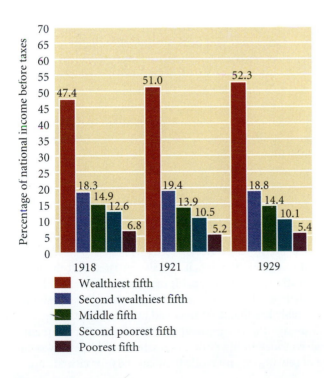

Income Distribution before the Great Depression

Source: From Gabriel Kolko, *Wealth and Power in America: An Analysis of Social Class and Income Distribution* (New York: Praeger, 1962), p. 14.

HOOVER: THE FALL OF A SELF-MADE MAN

In 1928 Herbert Hoover seemed to represent living proof that the American dream could be realized by anyone who was willing to work for it. At Stanford University he majored in geology. After graduation, he took part in mining expeditions to many parts of the world. As he rose quickly through corporate ranks, Hoover's managerial skills brought him more demanding and more handsomely rewarded tasks. Hoover's government service began during the First World War, when he won an international reputation for his expert management of agricultural production in the United States and his success in feeding millions of European soldiers and civilians. Then, in the 1920s, he served as an active and influential secretary of commerce (see Chapters 23 and 24). As the decade wound down, no American seemed better qualified to become president of the United States, an office that Hoover assumed in March 1929. Hoover was certain he could make prosperity a permanent feature of American life. "We in America today are nearer to the final triumph over poverty than ever before in the history of any land," he declared in August 1928. A little more than a year later, the Great Depression struck.

HOOVER'S PROGRAM

Within a short time after the stock market collapse, the depression had spread to nearly every sector of the economy. To cope with the crisis, Hoover first turned to the "associational" principles he had followed as secretary of commerce (see Chapter 24). He encouraged organizations of farmers, industrialists, and bankers to share information, bolster one another's spirits, and devise policies to aid economic recovery. Farmers would restrict output, industrialists would hold wages at predepression levels, and bankers would help each other remain solvent.

Hoover, to his credit, pursued a more aggressive set of economic policies once he realized that associationalism had failed to improve economic conditions. To ease a concurrent European crisis, Hoover secured a one-year moratorium on loan payments that European governments owed American banks. He steered through Congress the Glass-Steagall Act of 1932, intended to help American banks meet the demands of European depositors who wished to convert their dollars to gold. And to ease the crisis at home he began to expand the government's economic role. The Reconstruction Finance Corporation (RFC), created in 1932, made $2 billion available in loans to ailing banks and to corporations willing to build low-cost housing, bridges, and other public works. The Home Loan Bank Board, set up that same year, offered funds to savings and loans, mortgage companies, and other financial institutions that lent money for home construction.

Despite this new government activism, Hoover was uncomfortable with the idea that the government was responsible for restoring the nation's economic welfare. In 1932 RFC expenditures gave rise to the largest peacetime deficit in U.S. history, prompting Hoover to try to balance the federal budget. He supported the Revenue Act of 1932, which tried to increase government revenues by raising taxes, thus erasing the deficit. He also insisted that the RFC issue loans only to relatively healthy institutions that were capable of repaying them and that it favor public works, such as toll bridges, that were likely to become self-financing. As a result of these constraints, the RFC spent considerably less than Congress had mandated.

Hoover was especially reluctant to engage the government in providing relief to unemployed and homeless Americans. To give money to the poor, he insisted, would destroy their desire to work, undermine their sense of self-worth, and erode their capacity for citizenship.

THE BONUS ARMY

In the spring of 1932 a group of army veterans mounted a particularly emotional challenge to Hoover's policies. In 1924 Congress had authorized a $1,000 bonus for First World War veterans in the form of compensation certificates that would mature in 1945. Now the veterans were demanding that the government pay the bonus immediately. A group of them from Portland, Oregon, decided to take action. Calling themselves the Bonus Expeditionary Force, they hopped onto empty boxcars of freight trains heading east, determined to stage a march on Washington. As the impoverished "army" moved eastward their ranks multiplied, so that by the time they reached Washington their number had swelled to 20,000. The so-called Bonus Army set up camp in the Anacostia Flats, southeast of the Capitol, and petitioned Congress for early payment of the promised bonus. The House of Representatives agreed, but the Senate turned them down. Hoover refused to meet with them. In July, federal troops led by Army Chief of Staff Douglas MacArthur and 3rd Cavalry Commander George Patton attacked the veterans' Anacostia encampment, set the tents and shacks ablaze, and dispersed the protestors. In the process, more than 100 veterans were wounded and one infant was killed.

News that veterans and their families had been attacked in the nation's capital served only to harden anti-Hoover opinion. In the 1932 elections, Hoover received only 39.6 percent of the popular vote and just 59 (of 531) electoral votes. When he left the presidency in 1933 Hoover was a bewildered man, reviled by Americans for what they took to be his indifference to suffering and his ineptitude in dealing with the economy's collapse.

THE BONUS ARMY'S ENCAMPMENT SET ABLAZE   U.S. troops under the command of General Douglas MacArthur torched the tents and shacks that housed thousands of First World War veterans who had come to Washington to demand financial assistance from the government.

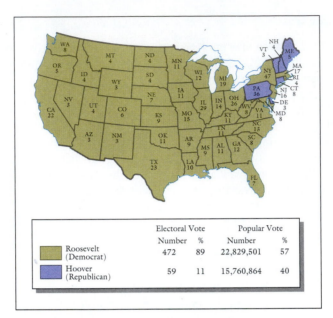

	Electoral Vote		Popular Vote	
	Number	%	Number	%
Roosevelt (Democrat)	472	89	22,829,501	57
Hoover (Republican)	59	11	15,760,864	40

PRESIDENTIAL ELECTION, 1932

THE DEMOCRATIC ROOSEVELT

The man who defeated Hoover, Franklin D. Roosevelt, was born in 1882 into a patrician family. On his father's side, Roosevelt was descended from Dutch gentry who in the 17th century had built large estates on the fertile land along the Hudson River. His mother's family—the Delanos—traced their ancestors back to the Mayflower. In short, Roosevelt was raised among people who were convinced of their superiority. His education at Groton, Harvard College, and Columbia Law School was typical of the path followed by the sons of America's elite.

The Roosevelt family was wealthy, although not spectacularly so by the standards of the late 19th century. His parents' net worth of more than $1 million was relatively small in comparison to the fortunes being amassed by the rising class of industrialists and railroad tycoons, many of whom commanded fortunes of $50 to $100 million or more. This widening gap in wealth disturbed families like the Roosevelts, who were concerned that the new industrial elite would dislodge them from their social position. Moreover, they were offended by the newcomers' vulgar displays of wealth, lack of taste and etiquette, and hostility toward those less fortunate than themselves. In 1899 Theodore Roosevelt, an older cousin of Franklin Roosevelt, had remarked that such people were "sunk in a scrambling commercialism, heedless of the higher life."

In 1921, at the age of 39, Franklin Roosevelt was stricken by polio and permanently lost the use of his legs. Before becoming paralyzed, Roosevelt had not distinguished himself either at school or in the practice of law, nor could he point to many significant political achievements. He owed his political ascent more to his famous name than to actual accomplishments or hard work. He was charming, gregarious, and popular among his associates in the New York Democratic Party. He enjoyed a good time and devoted a great deal of energy to sailing, partying, and enjoying the company of women other than his wife, Eleanor. After his illness, Roosevelt spent the next two years bedridden, and he seemed to acquire a new determination and seriousness.

Roosevelt's physical debilitation also transformed his relationship with Eleanor, with whom he had shared a testy and increasingly loveless marriage. Eleanor's dedication to nursing Franklin back to health forged a new bond between them. More conscious of his dependence on others, he now welcomed her as a partner in his career. Eleanor soon displayed a talent for political organization and public speaking. She would become an active, eloquent First Lady and an architect of American liberlism.

ROOSEVELT LIBERALISM

As governor of New York for four years (1929–1933), Roosevelt had initiated various reform programs, and his success made him the front-runner in the contest for the 1932 Democratic presidential nomination. It was by no means certain, however, that he would be the party's choice. Since 1924 the Democrats had been sharply divided between southern and midwestern agrarians on the one hand and northeastern ethnics on the other. The agrarians favored government regulation—both of the nation's economy and of the private affairs of its citizens. Their support of government intervention in the pursuit of social justice marked them as economic progressives, while their advocacy of Prohibition revealed a deep cultural conservatism as well as a nativistic strain. By contrast, urban ethnics opposed Prohibition and other forms of government interference in the private lives of its citizens. On the issue of whether the government should regulate the economy, urban ethnics were divided, with former New York governor Al Smith increasingly committed to a policy of laissez-faire and Senator Robert Wagner of New York and others supporting more federal control.

Roosevelt understood the need to carve out a middle ground. As governor of New York, and then as a presidential candidate in 1932, he surrounded himself with men and women who embraced the new reform movement called liberalism. Liberals shared with the agrarians and Wagner's supporters a desire to regulate capitalism, but agreed with Al Smith that the government had no business telling people how to behave.

But Roosevelt was by no means assured of the presidential nomination in 1932. At the Democratic convention in July, Smith worked to secure the nomination of the more conservative Newton Baker. William Gibbs McAdoo, hoping to deadlock the convention so that he could take the nomination himself, initially supported Speaker of the House John Nance Garner. As the balloting entered its third round, Roosevelt began to fall behind. At that point, however, McAdoo and Garner reevaluated their strategy. Recognizing that party unity and a victory in the general election might be more important than their own ambitions, they swung their support to Roosevelt, putting him over the top. Roosevelt, in gratitude, chose Garner as his vice presidential running mate. In a rousing call to action, he declared: "Ours must be the party of liberal thought, of planned action, of enlightened international outlook, and of the greatest good for the greatest number of citizens." He promised "a new deal for the American people."

In his campaign, Roosevelt sometimes spoke of using government programs to stabilize the economy, but he also spent much of his time wooing conservative Democrats. In point of fact, Roosevelt only made two outright promises during his presidential campaign: to repeal Prohibition and to balance the budget. Thus, the nation had to wait until March 4, 1933—the day Roosevelt was sworn in as president—to learn what the New Deal would bring.

THE FIRST NEW DEAL, 1933–1935

By the time Roosevelt assumed office, the economy lay in shambles. From 1929 to 1932 industrial production fell by 50 percent, while new investment declined from $16 billion to a mere fraction of $1 billion. The nation's banking system was on the verge of collapse. In 1931 alone, more than 2,000 banks had shut their doors. The unemployment rate was soaring. Some Americans feared that the opportunity for reform had already passed.

But not Roosevelt. "This nation asks for action, and action now," Roosevelt declared in his inaugural address. Roosevelt was true to his word. In his first "Hundred Days," from early March through early June 1933, Roosevelt persuaded Congress to pass 15 major pieces of legislation to help bankers, farmers, industrialists, workers, homeowners, the unemployed, and the hungry. He also prevailed on Congress to repeal Prohibition. Not all the new laws helped to relieve distress and promote recovery. But, in the short term, that seemed not to matter. Roosevelt had brought excitement and hope to the nation. He was confident, decisive, and defiantly cheery. "The only thing we have to fear is fear itself," he declared. He used the radio to reach out to ordinary Americans. On the second Sunday after his inaugural, he launched a series of radio addresses known as "fireside chats," speaking in a plain, friendly, and direct voice to the forlorn and discouraged.

DELIVERING A FIRESIDE CHAT   Soon after taking office, Roosevelt began using the radio airwaves to speak to the American people in an informal and friendly manner. His "fireside chats" substantially boosted his popularity.

To hear the president speaking warmly and conversationally—as though he were actually there in the room—was riveting. An estimated 500,000 Americans wrote letters to Roosevelt within days of his inaugural address. Millions more would write to him and to Eleanor Roosevelt over the next few years. Many of the letters were simply addressed to "Mr. or Mrs. Roosevelt, Washington, D.C."

Roosevelt was never the benign father figure he made himself out to be. His public image was skillfully crafted. Compliant news photographers agreed not to show him in a wheelchair. For his part, Roosevelt often sought to hide the true content of legislation he proposed with diverting rhetoric.

To his credit, Roosevelt used his popularity and executive power to strengthen American democracy at a time when democracy was crumbling in Europe. During his long tenure in office, however, he set in motion tendencies that would long plague American politics: a drift of power to the executive branch, a steady expansion of the size and reach of federal bureaucracies, and a widening gap between political appearance and political reality.

SAVING THE BANKS

Roosevelt's first order of business was to save the nation's financial system. By inauguration day, several states had already shut their banks. Roosevelt immediately ordered all the nation's banks closed—a bold move he brazenly called a "bank holiday." He then had Congress rush through an Emergency Banking Act (EBA) that made federal loans available to private bankers. He followed that with an Economy Act (EA) that committed the government to balancing the budget.

Both the EBA and the EA were fiscally conservative programs that Hoover had proposed earlier. The EBA made it possible for private bankers to retain financial control of their institutions, and the EA announced the government's intention of pursuing a fiscally prudent course. Only after the financial crisis had eased did Roosevelt turn to the structural reform of banking. A second Glass-Steagall Act (1933) separated commercial banking from investment banking. It also created the Federal Deposit Insurance Corporation (FDIC), which assured

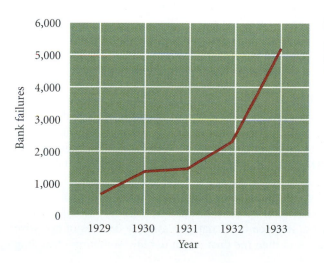

BANK FAILURES, 1929–1933

Source: From C. D. Bremer, *American Bank Failures* (New York: Columbia University Press, 1935), p. 42.

depositors that the government would protect up to $5,000 of their savings. The Securities Act (1933) and the Securities Exchange Act (1934) imposed long overdue regulation on the New York Stock Exchange, both by reining in buying on the margin and by establishing the Securities and Exchange Commission to enforce federal law.

SAVING THE PEOPLE

Roosevelt understood the need to temper financial prudence with compassion. Congress responded swiftly in 1933 to Roosevelt's request to establish the Federal Emergency Relief Administration (FERA), granting it $500 million for relief to the poor. To head it, Roosevelt appointed a brash young reformer, Harry Hopkins. Roosevelt then won congressional approval for the Civilian Conservation Corps (CCC), which put more than 2 million single young men to work planting trees, halting erosion, and otherwise improving the environment. The following winter, Roosevelt launched the Civil Works Administration (CWA), an ambitious work-relief program, also under Harry Hopkins's direction, that hired 4 million unemployed at $15 a week and put them to work on 400,000 small-scale government projects. For middle-class Americans threatened with the loss of their homes, Roosevelt won congressional approval for the Homeowners' Loan Corporation (1933) to refinance mortgages. These direct subsidies to millions of jobless and home-owning Americans lent credibility to Roosevelt's claim that the New Deal would set the country on a new course.

REPAIRING THE ECONOMY: AGRICULTURE

In 1933 Roosevelt expected economic recovery to come not from relief, but through agricultural and industrial cooperation. He regarded the Agricultural Adjustment Act, passed in May, and the National Industrial Recovery Act (NIRA), passed in June, as the most important legislation of his Hundred Days. Both were based on the idea that curtailing production would trigger economic recovery. By shrinking the supply of agricultural and manufactured goods, Roosevelt's economists reasoned, they could restore the balance of normal market forces. Then, as demand for scarce goods exceeded supply, prices would rise and revenues would climb. Farmers and industrialists, earning a profit once again, would increase their investment in new technology and hire more workers.

To curtail farm production, the Agricultural Adjustment Administration (AAA), set up by the Agricultural Adjustment Act, began paying farmers to keep a portion of their land out of cultivation and to reduce the size of their herds. The program was controversial, as many farmers did not readily accept the idea that they were to be paid more money for working less land and husbanding fewer livestock. But few refused to accept government payments.

The AAA had made no provision, however, for the countless tenant farmers and farm laborers who would be thrown out of work by the reduction in acreage. In the South, the victims were disproportionately black. A Georgia sharecropper wrote Harry Hopkins of his misery: "I have Bin farming all my life But the man I live with Has Turned me loose taking my mule [and] all my feed. . . . I can't get a Job so Some one said Rite you."

The programs of the AAA also proved inadequate to Great Plains farmers, whose economic problems had been compounded by ecological crisis. Just as the depression rolled in, the rain stopped falling on the plains. The land, stripped of its native grasses by decades of excessive plowing, dried up and turned to dust. And then the dust began to blow, sometimes traveling

Legislation Enacted during the "Hundred Days," March 9–June 16, 1933

Date	Legislation	Purpose
March 9	Emergency Banking Act	Provide federal loans to private bankers
March 20	Economy Act	Balance the federal budget
March 22	Beer-Wine Revenue Act	Repeal Prohibition
March 31	Unemployment Relief Act	Create the Civilian Conservation Corps
May 12	Agricultural Adjustment Act	Establish a national agricultural policy
May 12	Emergency Farm Mortgage Act	Provide refinancing of farm mortgages
May 12	Federal Emergency Relief Act	Establish a national relief system, including the Civil Works Administration
May 18	Tennessee Valley Authority Act	Promote economic development of the Tennessee Valley
May 27	Securities Act	Regulate the purchase and sale of new securities
June 5	Gold Repeal Joint Resolution	Cancel the gold clause in public and private contracts
June 13	Home Owners Loan Act	Provide refinancing of home mortgages
June 16	National Industrial Recovery Act	Set up a national system of industrial self-government and establish the Public Works Administration
June 16	Glass-Steagall Banking Act	Create Federal Deposit Insurance Corporation; separate commercial and investment banking
June 16	Farm Credit Act	Reorganize agricultural credit programs
June 16	Railroad Coordination Act	Appoint federal coordinator of transportation

Source: Arthur M. Schlesinger Jr., *The Coming of the New Deal* (Boston: Houghton Mifflin, 1959), pp. 20–21.

1,000 miles across open prairie. Dust became a fixed feature of daily life on the plains (which soon became known as the "Dust Bowl"), covering furniture, floors, and stoves, and penetrating people's hair and lungs.

The government responded to this calamity by establishing the Soil Conservation Service (SCS) in 1935. Recognizing that the soil problems of the Great Plains could not be solved simply by taking land out of production, SCS experts urged plains farmers to plant soil-conserving grasses and legumes in place of wheat. They taught them how to plow along contour lines and how to build terraces. Plains farmers were open to these suggestions, especially when the government offered to subsidize those willing to implement them. Bolstered by the new assistance, plains agriculture began to recover.

Still, the government offered little to the rural poor—the tenant farmers and sharecroppers. Nearly 1 million had left their homes by 1935, and another 2.5 million would leave after 1935. Most headed west, piling their belongings onto their jalopies, snaking along Route 66 until they reached California. They became known as Okies, because many, although not all, had come from Oklahoma.

In 1936 the Supreme Court ruled that AAA-mandated limits on farm production constituted illegal restraints of trade. Congress responded by passing the Soil Conservation and Domestic Allotment Act, which justified the removal of land from cultivation for reasons of conservation rather than economics. This new act also called upon landowners to share their government subsidies with sharecroppers and tenant farmers, although landowners managed to evade this and subsequent laws that required them to share federal funds.

The use of subsidies, begun by the AAA, did eventually bring stability and prosperity to agriculture. But the costs were high. Agriculture became the most heavily subsidized sector of the U.S. economy, and the Department of Agriculture grew into one of the government's largest bureaucracies. And the rural poor, black and white, never received a fair share of federal benefits.

REPAIRING THE ECONOMY: INDUSTRY

American industry was so vast that paying individual manufacturers direct subsidies to reduce, or even halt, production was never contemplated. Instead, the government decided to limit production through persuasion and association. To head the National Recovery Administration (NRA), authorized under the National Industrial Recovery Act, Roosevelt chose General Hugh Johnson. Johnson's first task was to persuade industrialists and businessmen to agree to raise employee wages to a minimum of 30 to 40 cents an hour and to limit employee hours to a maximum of 30 to 40 hours a week. The intent was to reduce the quantity of goods that any factory or business could produce.

Johnson launched a high-powered publicity campaign. He distributed pamphlets and pins throughout the country. He used the radio to exhort all Americans to do their part. He staged an elaborate NRA celebration in Yankee Stadium and organized a massive parade down New York City's Fifth Avenue. He sent letters to millions of employers asking them to place a "blue eagle"—the logo of the NRA—on storefronts, at factory entrances, and on company stationery to signal their participation in the campaign to limit production and restore prosperity. Blue eagles soon sprouted everywhere, usually accompanied by the slogan "We Do Our Part."

Johnson understood, however, that his propaganda campaign could not by itself guarantee recovery. So he brought together the largest producers in every sector of manufacturing and asked each group (or conference) to work out a code of fair competition that would specify prices, wages, and hours throughout the sector. He also asked each conference to restrict production.

In the summer and fall of 1933, the NRA codes drawn up for steel, textiles, coal mining, rubber, garment manufacture, and other industries seemed to be working. The economy picked up and people began to hope that an end to the depression might be near. But in the winter and spring of 1934, economic indicators plunged downward once again and manufacturers began to evade the provisions of the codes. Government committees set up to enforce the codes were powerless to punish violators. By the fall of 1934, it was clear that the NRA had failed. When the Supreme Court declared the NRA codes unconstitutional in May 1935, the Roosevelt administration allowed the agency to die.

REBUILDING THE NATION

In addition to establishing the NRA, the National Industrial Recovery Act launched the Public Works Administration (PWA). The PWA was given a $3.3 billion budget to sponsor internal improvements that would strengthen the nation's infrastructure of roads, bridges, sewage systems, hospitals, airports, and schools. The PWA authorized the building of three major dams in the West—the Grand Coulee, Boulder, and Bonneville—that opened up large stretches of Arizona, California, and Washington to industrial and agricultural development. It funded the construction of the Triborough Bridge in New York City and the 100-mile causeway linking Florida to Key West. It also appropriated money for the construction of thousands of new schools between 1933 and 1939.

The TVA Alternative

One piece of legislation passed during Roosevelt's First New Deal specified a strategy for economic recovery very different from the one promoted by the NRA. The Tennessee Valley Authority Act (1933) called for the government itself—rather than private corporations—to promote economic development throughout the Tennessee Valley, a vast river basin winding through parts of Kentucky, Tennessee, Mississippi, Alabama, Georgia, and North Carolina. The act created the Tennessee Valley Authority (TVA) to control flooding on the Tennessee River, harness its water power to generate electricity, develop local industry (such as fertilizer production), and improve river transportation. The extent of its control over economic development reflected the influence of Rexford Tugwell and other New Dealers

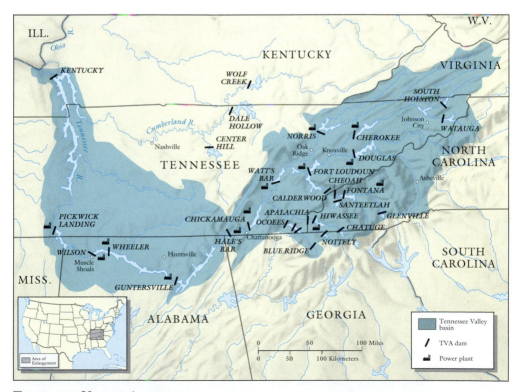

Tennessee Valley Authority

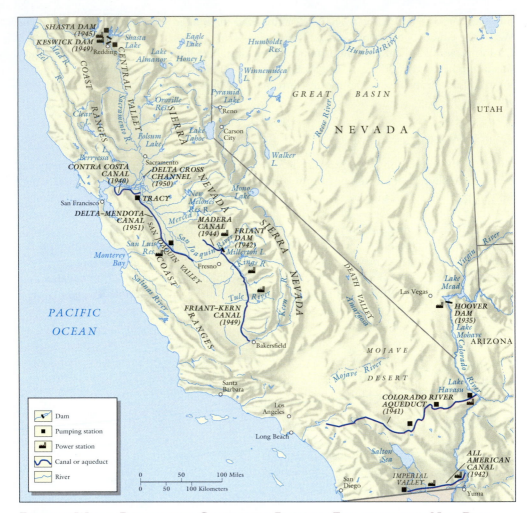

FEDERAL WATER PROJECTS IN CALIFORNIA BUILT OR FUNDED BY THE NEW DEAL

who were committed to a government-planned and government-operated economy. Although they rarely said so, these reformers were drawn to socialism.

The accomplishments of the TVA were many. It built, completed, or improved more than 20 dams. At several of the dam sites, the TVA built hydroelectric generators and soon became the nation's largest producer of electricity. Its low rates compelled private utility companies to reduce their rates as well. The TVA also constructed waterways to bypass unnavigable stretches of the river, reduced the danger of flooding, and taught farmers how to prevent soil erosion and use fertilizers.

Although the TVA was one of the New Deal's most celebrated successes, it generated little support for more ambitious experiments in national planning. For the government to have assumed control of established industries and banks would have been quite a different matter from bringing prosperity to an impoverished region. Like Roosevelt, few members of Congress or the public favored the radical growth of governmental power that such programs would entail. Thus, the New Deal never embraced the idea of the federal government as a substitute for private enterprise.

THE NEW DEAL AND WESTERN DEVELOPMENT

As the example of the TVA suggests, New Deal programs could make an enormous difference to a particular region's welfare. The region that benefited most from the New Deal was the West. Between 1933 and 1939, per capita payments for public works projects, welfare, and federal loans in the Rocky Mountain and Pacific Coast states outstripped those of any other region.

Central to this western focus was the program of western dam building. Western real estate and agricultural interests wanted to dam the West's major rivers to provide water and electricity for urban and agricultural development. They found a government ally in the Bureau of Reclamation, a hitherto small federal agency that became, under the New Deal, a prime dispenser of infrastructural funds. Drawing on PWA monies, the bureau oversaw the building of the Boulder Dam (later renamed Hoover Dam), which provided drinking water for southern California, irrigation water for California's Imperial Valley, and electricity for Los Angeles and southern Arizona. It also authorized the Central Valley Project and the All-American Canal, vast water-harnessing projects in central and southern California meant to provide irrigation, drinking water, and electricity to California farmers and towns. The greatest construction project of all was the Grand Coulee Dam on the Columbia River in Washington, which created a lake 150 miles long. Together with the Bonneville Dam (also on the Columbia), the Grand Coulee gave the Pacific Northwest the cheapest electricity in the country and created the potential for huge economic and population growth.

These developments did not attract as much attention in the 1930s as did the TVA. The benefits of this dam building program were not fully realized until after the Second World War. Also, dam building in the West was not seen as a radical experiment in government planning and management. Unlike the TVA, the Bureau of Reclamation hired private contractors to do the work and made them rich. Moreover, the benefits of these dams were intended to flow first to large agricultural and real estate interests, not to the poor; they were intended to aid private enterprise, rather than bypass it. In political terms, then, dam building in the West was more conservative than it was in the Tennessee Valley.

POLITICAL MOBILIZATION, POLITICAL UNREST, 1934–1935

Although Roosevelt and the New Dealers quickly dismantled the NRA in 1935, they could not stop the political forces it had set it in motion. Americans now believed that they themselves could make a difference. If the New Dealers could not achieve economic recovery, the people would find others who could.

POPULIST CRITICS OF THE NEW DEAL

Some critics were disturbed by what they perceived as the conservative bent of New Deal programs. Banking reforms, the AAA, and the NRA, they alleged, all seemed to favor large economic interests. Ordinary people had been ignored.

In the South and Midwest, millions listened regularly to the radio addresses of Louisiana Senator Huey Long, a former governor of that state and a spellbinding orator. In attacks on New Deal programs, he alleged that "not a single thin dime of concentrated, bloated, pompous wealth, massed in the hands of a few people has been raked down to relieve the masses." Long offered a simple alternative: "Break up the swollen fortunes of America and . . . spread the wealth among all our people."

Long's rhetoric inspired hundreds of thousands of Americans to join the Share the Wealth clubs his supporters organized. A majority came from middle-class ranks, worried that the big business orientation of New Deal programs might undermine their economic and social status. Substantial numbers of Share the Wealth club members also came from highly skilled and white-collar sections of the working class. By 1935 Roosevelt regarded Long as the man most likely to unseat him in the presidential election of 1936. But before that campaign began, Long was murdered by an assassin.

Meanwhile, in the Midwest, Father Charles Coughlin, the "radio priest," delivered a message similar to Long's. Like Long, Coughlin appealed to anxious middle-class Americans and to privileged groups of workers who believed that middle-class status was slipping from their grasp. A devoted Roosevelt supporter at first, Coughlin had become a harsh critic. The New Deal was run by bankers, he claimed. The NRA was a program to resuscitate corporate profits. Coughlin called for a strong government to compel capital, labor, agriculture, professionals, and other interest groups to do its bidding. He founded the National Union of Social Justice (NUSJ) in 1934 as a precursor to a political party that would challenge the Democrats in 1936. Coughlin admired leaders, such as Italy's Benito Mussolini, who built strong states through decree rather than through democratic consent.

As Coughlin's disillusionment with the New Deal deepened, a strain of anti-Semitism became apparent in his radio talks, as in his accusation that Jewish bankers were masterminding a world conspiracy to dispossess the toiling masses. Although Coughlin was a compelling speaker, he failed to build the NUSJ into an effective force. Its successor, the Union Party, attracted only a tiny percentage of voters in 1936. Embittered, Coughlin moved further and further to the political right. By 1939 his denunciations of democracy and Jews had become so extreme that some radio stations refused to carry his addresses. But millions of ordinary Americans continued to believe that the "radio priest" was their savior.

Another popular figure was Francis E. Townsend, a California doctor who claimed that the way to end the depression was to give every senior citizen $200 a month. The Townsend Plan briefly garnered the support of an estimated 20 million Americans.

None of these self-styled reformers—Long, Coughlin, and Townsend—showed much skill at transforming his popularity into disciplined political parties that could compete in elections. Still, their attacks on New Deal programs deepened popular discontent and helped to legitimate other insurgent movements. The most important of them was the labor movement.

LABOR'S REBIRTH

The ranks of the working class were diverse: immigrant radicals and ethnic conservatives, northerners and southerners, blacks and whites, skilled and unskilled, factory workers and farm workers, men and women. But labor's diversity was not as great as it had been during the Progressive Era. Mass immigration had ended in 1921, and the trend toward Americanization

JOHN L. LEWIS   The president of the United Mine Workers and principal founder of the CIO, Lewis was the most famous and charismatic labor leader of the 1930s. Lewis's large frame, dramatic features, and deep voice gave him a powerful and compelling presence, which he used to good effect. In this fresco, the artist Ben Shahn celebrates Lewis's physical power and appeal.

at school, at work, and in popular entertainment had broadened throughout the decade. The Great Depression itself further heightened the sense of shared experience.

This commonality of working-class sentiment first became apparent in 1932, when many workers voted for Roosevelt. Following his election, the NRA helped to transform their despair into hope. It set guidelines for wages and work hours that, if implemented by employers, would improve working conditions. Moreover, Clause 7(a) of the National Industrial Recovery Act granted workers the right to join labor unions of their own choosing, and obligated employers to recognize unions and bargain with them in good faith.

Millions of workers joined labor unions in 1933 and early 1934, encouraged by John L. Lewis, president of the United Mine Workers, who often declared in his rousing speeches and radio addresses: "The president wants you to join a union." Actually, Roosevelt did not favor the rapid growth of unions. But Lewis believed that by repeatedly invoking the president's name he could transform working-class support for Roosevelt into union strength.

The demands of union members were quite modest at first. They wanted employers to observe the provisions of the NRA codes. They wanted to be treated fairly by their foremen. And they wanted employers to recognize their unions. But few employers were willing to grant them any say in their working conditions. Many ignored the NRA's wage and hour guidelines altogether, and even used their influence over NRA code authorities to get worker requests for wage increases and union recognition rejected.

Workers flooded Washington with letters addressed to President Roosevelt, Labor Secretary Frances Perkins, and General Hugh Johnson asking them to force employers to comply with the law. When their pleas went unanswered, workers began to take matters into their own hands. In 1934 they staged 2,000 strikes in virtually every industry and region of the country. A few of those strikes escalated into armed confrontations between workers and police that shocked the nation. In Toledo in May, 10,000 workers surrounded the Electric Auto-Lite plant, declaring that they would block all exits and entrances until the company agreed to shut down operations and negotiate a union contract. A seven-hour pitched battle between strikers and police waged with water hoses, tear gas, and gunfire failed to dislodge the strikers. Ultimately, the National Guard was summoned, and two strikers were killed in an exchange of gunfire. In San Francisco in July, longshoremen fought employers and police in street skirmishes in which two were killed and scores wounded. Employers there had hoped that the use of force would break a two-month-old strike, but the violence provoked more than 100,000 additional workers in the transportation, construction, and service industries to walk off their jobs in a general strike. From July 5 to July 19, the city of San Francisco was virtually shut down.

The largest and most violent confrontation began on September 1, 1934, with the strike of 400,000 textile workers at mills from Maine to Alabama. Workers who had never acknowledged a common bond with their fellows now joined hands. They insisted that they were Americans bound together by class and national loyalties that transcended ethnic and religious differences. In the first two weeks of September, the strikers brought cotton production to a virtual standstill. Employers recruited replacement workers and hired private security forces to protect them. At many of the mills, the arrival of strikebreakers prompted violent confrontations between strikers and police. In northern communities, such as Saylesville and Woonsocket, Rhode Island, full-scale riots erupted. The result was several deaths, hundreds of injuries, and millions of dollars in property damage. Similar confrontations took place throughout the South.

ANGER AT THE POLLS

By late September, textile union leaders had lost their nerve and called off the strike. But workers took their anger to the polls. In Rhode Island, they broke the Republican Party's 30-year domination of state politics. In the country as a whole, Democrats won 70 percent of the contested seats in the Senate and House. The Democrats increased their majority, from 310 to 319 (out of 432) in the House, and from 60 to 69 (out of 96) in the Senate.

But the victory was not an unqualified one for Roosevelt and the First New Deal. The 74th Congress would include the largest contingent of radicals ever sent to Washington. Their support for the New Deal depended on whether Roosevelt delivered more relief, more income security, and more political power to farmers, workers, the unemployed, and the poor.

THE RISE OF RADICAL THIRD PARTIES

Radical critics of the New Deal also made an impressive showing in state politics in 1934 and 1936. They were particularly strong in states gripped by labor unrest. In Wisconsin, for example, Philip La Follette, the son of Robert La Follette (see Chapter 21), was elected governor in 1934 and 1936 as the candidate of the radical Wisconsin Progressive Party. In Minnesota, discontented agrarians and urban workers organized the Minnesota Farmer-Labor (MFL) Party and elected their candidate to the governorship in 1930, 1932, 1934, and 1936. And in California, the socialist and novelist Upton Sinclair and his organization, End Poverty in California (EPIC), came closer to winning the governorship than anyone had expected.

These impressive showings made it clear that many voters were prepared to abandon Democrats who refused to endorse a more comprehensive program of reform. A widespread movement to form local labor parties offered further evidence of voter volatility, as did the growing appeal of the Communist Party.

The American Communist Party (CP) had emerged in the early 1920s with the support of radicals who wanted to adopt the Soviet Union's path to socialism. They began to attract attention in the early 1930s. Confident that the Great Depression signaled the death throes of capitalism, party members dedicated themselves to marshaling the forces of socialism.

CP organizers spread out among the poorest and most vulnerable populations in America—homeless urban blacks in the North, black and white sharecroppers in the South, Chicano and Filipino agricultural workers in the West—and mobilized them in unions and unemployment leagues. CP members also played significant roles in the strikes described earlier, and they were influential in the Minnesota Farmer-Labor Party. Once they stopped preaching world revolution in 1935 and began calling instead for a "popular front" of democratic forces against fascism, their ranks grew even more. By 1938, approximately 80,000 Americans were thought to have been members of the Communist Party.

Although the Communist Party proclaimed its allegiance to democratic principles beginning in 1935, it nevertheless remained a dictatorial organization that took its orders from the Soviet Union. Many Americans feared the growing strength of the CP and began to call for its suppression. Actually, the CP was never strong enough to pose a real political threat. Membership turnover was high, as many left the party after learning about its undemocratic character. Its chief role in 1930s politics was to channel popular discontent into unions and political parties that would, in turn, force New Dealers to respond to the demands of the nation's dispossessed.

THE SECOND NEW DEAL, 1935–1937

The labor unrest of 1934 had taken Roosevelt by surprise, and for a time he kept his distance from the masses mobilizing in his name. But in the spring of 1935, with the presidential election coming up in 1936, he decided to place himself at their head. He called for the "abolition of evil holding companies," attacked the wealthy for their profligate ways, and called for new programs to aid the poor and downtrodden. Roosevelt had not become a socialist, as his critics have charged. Rather, he sought to reinvigorate his appeal among poorer Americans and turn them away from radical solutions.

PHILOSOPHICAL UNDERPINNINGS

To point the New Deal in a more populist direction, Roosevelt turned increasingly to a relatively new economic theory, underconsumptionism. Advocates of this theory held that a chronic weakness in consumer demand had caused the Great Depression. The path to recovery lay, therefore, not in restricting the output of producers but in boosting consumer expenditures through government support for strong labor unions (to force up wages), higher social welfare expenditures (to put more money in the hands of the poor), and vast public works projects (to create hundreds of thousands of new jobs).

Underconsumptionists did not worry that new welfare and public works programs might strain the federal budget. If the government found itself short of revenue, it could always borrow additional funds from private sources. Government borrowing, in fact, was viewed as a crucial antidepression tool. Those who lent the government money would receive a return on their investment; those who received government assistance would have additional income to spend on consumer goods; and manufacturers would profit from increases in consumer spending. Government borrowing, in short, would stimulate the circulation of money throughout the economy and would put an end to the depression.

Many politicians and economists rejected the notion that increased government spending and the deliberate buildup of federal deficits would lead to prosperity. Roosevelt himself remained committed to fiscal restraint and balanced budgets. But in 1935, as the nation entered its sixth year of the depression, he was willing to give the new ideas a try. Reform-minded members of the 1934 Congress were themselves eager for a new round of legislation directed more to the needs of ordinary Americans than to the needs of big business.

LEGISLATION OF THE SECOND NEW DEAL

Much of that legislation was passed by Congress from January to June 1935—a period that came to be known as the Second New Deal. Two of the acts were of historic importance. The Social Security Act, passed in May, required the states to set up welfare funds from which money would be disbursed to the elderly poor, the unemployed, unmarried mothers with dependent children, and the disabled. It also enrolled a majority of working Americans in a pension program that guaranteed them a steady income upon retirement. A federal system of employer and employee taxation was set up to fund the pensions.

Equally historic was the passage, in June, of the National Labor Relations Act (NLRA). This act delivered what the NRA had only promised: the right of every worker to join a union of his or her own choosing, and the obligation of employers to bargain with that union in good faith. The NLRA, also called the Wagner Act after its sponsor in the Senate, Robert Wagner of New York, set up a National Labor Relations Board (NLRB) to supervise union elections and to investigate claims of unfair labor practices. The NLRB was to be staffed by federal appointees, who would have the power to impose fines on employers who violated the law.

Congress also passed the Holding Company Act to break up the 13 utility companies that controlled 75 percent of the nation's electric power. It passed the Wealth Tax Act, which increased tax rates on the wealthy from 59 to 75 percent, and on corporations from 13¾ to 15 percent; and it passed the Banking Act, which strengthened the power of the Federal Reserve Board over its member banks. It created the Rural Electrification Administration (REA) to bring electric power to rural households. Finally, it passed the $5 billion Emergency Relief Appropriation Act. Roosevelt funneled part of this sum to the PWA and the CCC and used another part to create the National Youth Administration (NYA), which provided work and guidance to the nation's youth.

SELECTED WPA PROJECTS IN NEW YORK CITY, 1938

CONSTRUCTION AND RENOVATION	EDUCATION, HEALTH, AND ART	RESEARCH AND RECORDS
East River Drive	Adult education: homemaking, trade and technical skills, and art and culture	Sewage treatment, community health, labor relations, and employment trends surveys
Henrik Hudson Parkway		
Bronx sewers	Children's education: remedial reading, lip reading, and field trips	Museum and library catalogs and exhibits
Glendale and Queens public libraries		Municipal office clerical support
King's County Hospital	Prisoners' vocational training, recreation, and nutrition	Government forms standardization
Williamsburg housing project		
School buildings, prisons, and firehouses	Dental clinics	
	Tuberculosis examination clinics	
Coney Island and Brighton Beach boardwalks	Syphilis and gonorrhea treatment clinics	
Orchard Beach	City hospital kitchen help, orderlies, laboratory technicians, nurses, doctors	
Swimming pools, playgrounds, parks, drinking fountains		
	Subsistence gardens	
	Sewing rooms	
	Central Park sculpture shop	

Source: John David Millet, *The Works Progress Administration in New York City* (Chicago: Public Administration Service, 1938), pp. 95–126.

Roosevelt directed most of the new relief money, however, to the Works Progress Administration (WPA). The WPA built or improved thousands of schools, playgrounds, airports, and hospitals. WPA crews were put to work raking leaves, cleaning streets, and landscaping cities. In the process, the WPA provided jobs to approximately 30 percent of the nation's jobless.

By the time the decade ended, the WPA, in association with an expanded Reconstruction Finance Corporation, PWA, and other agencies, had brought about the building of 500,000 miles of roads, 100,000 bridges, 100,000 public buildings, and 600 airports. The New Deal had transformed America's urban and rural landscapes. The awe generated by those great public works projects helped Roosevelt retain popular support at a time when the success of the New Deal's economic policies was uncertain. The WPA also funded a vast program of public art, supporting the work of thousands of painters, architects, writers, playwrights, actors, and intellectuals. Beyond extending relief to struggling artists, it fostered the creation of art that spoke to the concerns of ordinary Americans, adorned public buildings with colorful murals, and boosted public morale.

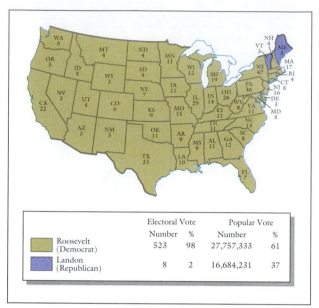

	Electoral Vote		Popular Vote	
	Number	%	Number	%
Roosevelt (Democrat)	523	98	27,757,333	61
Landon (Republican)	8	2	16,684,231	37

PRESIDENTIAL ELECTION, 1936

VICTORY IN 1936: THE NEW DEMOCRATIC COALITION

Roosevelt described his Second New Deal as a program to limit the power and privilege of the wealthy few and to increase the security and welfare of ordinary citizens. He called on voters to strip the corporations of their power and "save a great and precious form of government for ourselves and the world." American voters responded by handing Roosevelt a landslide victory. He received 61 percent of the popular vote; Alf Landon of Kansas, his Republican opponent, received only 37 percent.

The 1936 election won for the Democratic Party its reputation as the party of reform and the party of the "forgotten American." Of the 6 million Americans who went to the polls for the first time, 5 million voted for Roosevelt. Among the poorest Americans, Roosevelt received 80 percent of the vote. Black voters in the North deserted the Republican Party, calculating that their interests would best be served by the "Party of the Common Man." Roosevelt also did well among white middle-class voters, many of whom were grateful to him for pushing through the Social Security Act. These constituencies would constitute the "Roosevelt coalition" for most of the next 40 years.

RHETORIC VERSUS REALITY

Roosevelt's anticorporate rhetoric in 1935 and 1936 was more radical than the laws he supported. The Wealth Tax Act took considerably less out of wealthy incomes and estates than was advertised, and the utility companies that were to have been broken up by the Holding Company Act remained largely intact. Moreover, Roosevelt promised more than he delivered to the nation's poor. Farm workers, for example, were not covered by the Social Secu-

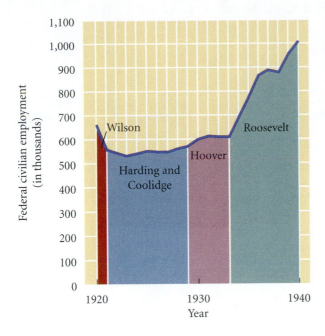

GROWTH IN FEDERAL CIVILIAN EMPLOYMENT, 1920–1940

Source: Data from *Historical Statistics of the United States, Colonial Times to 1970* (White Plains, N.Y.: Kraus International, 1989), p. 1102

rity Act or by the National Labor Relations Act. Consequently, thousands of African American sharecroppers in the South, along with substantial numbers of Chicano farm workers in the Southwest, were excluded from their protections and benefits. Moreover, the New Deal made little effort to restore voting rights to southern blacks or to protect their basic civil rights.

Roosevelt's populist stance in 1935 and 1936 also obscured the enthusiastic support that some capitalists were according the Second New Deal. In the West, Henry J. Kaiser headed a consortium of six companies that built the Hoover, Bonneville, and Grand Coulee dams. In the Midwest and the East, Roosevelt's corporate supporters included real estate developers, mass merchandisers, clothing manufacturers, and the like. These firms, in turn, had financial connections with recently established investment banks and with consumer-oriented banks such as the Bank of America. They were willing to tolerate strong labor unions, welfare programs, and high levels of government spending. But they had no intention of surrendering their wealth or power. The Democratic Party had become, in effect, the party of the masses and one section of big business. The conflicting interests of these two constituencies would create tensions within the Democratic Party throughout all the years of its political domination.

New Deal Men, New Deal Women

For the academics, policymakers, and bureaucrats who designed and administered the rapidly growing roster of New Deal programs and agencies, 1936 and 1937 were exciting years. Fired by idealism and dedication, they were confident they could make the New Deal work. They planned and won congressional approval for the Farm Security Administration (FSA),

IMAGES OF MEN AND WOMEN IN THE GREAT DEPRESSION

Women played an important role in the New Deal. Eleanor Roosevelt set the tone through her visible involvement in numerous reform activities. She met with many different groups of Americans, including the miners depicted in the photo here, seeking to learn more about their condition and ways that the New Deal might assist them. But women also found their activism limited by a widespread hostility toward working women, who were thought to be taking scarce jobs away from men. In the popular movie, *Mr. Smith Goes to Washington* (1939), Jefferson Smith (Jimmy Stewart) helps a hardboiled career secretary, Clarissa Saunders (Jean Arthur), to realize that work has dam-

an agency designed to improve the economic lot of tenant farmers, sharecroppers, and farm laborers. They drafted and got passed laws that outlawed child labor, set minimum wages and maximum hours for adult workers, and committed the federal government to building low-cost housing. They investigated and tried to regulate concentrations of corporate power.

aged her sweet, womanly soul. By movie's end, Saunders is ready to leave her job and become Smith's wife and home-maker. Many other movies of the period also conveyed the sentiment that women belonged in the home.

Men, for their part, responded enthusiastically to the hypermasculinism that characterized much of the decade's mass culture. Images of strong, muscled work-ers were popular with trade unionists who feared that the Depression would strip them of their manly roles as workers and breadwinners. Boys and male adolescents, meanwhile, found a new hero in Superman, the "man-of-steel" comic-book hero who debuted in 1938. Super-man's strength, unlike that of so many men in the 1930s, could not be taken away—except by Kryptonite and Lois Lane, that "dangerous" working woman.

Although they worked on behalf of "the people," the New Dealers themselves constituted a new class of technocrats. But they did have noble aspirations. What fired their imagination was the prospect of building a strong state committed to prosperity and justice. They did not welcome interference from those they regarded as less intelligent or motivated by outworn ideologies.

This was particularly true of the men. Many had earned advanced degrees in law and economics at elite universities such as Harvard, Columbia, and Wisconsin. Not all had been raised among wealth and privilege, however, as was generally the case with earlier generations of reformers. To his credit, Franklin Roosevelt was the first president since his cousin Theodore Roosevelt to welcome Jews and Catholics into his administration. These were men who had to struggle to make their way, first on the streets and then in school and at work. They brought to the New Deal intellectual aggressiveness, quick minds, and mental toughness.

The profile of New Deal women was different. Although a few, notably Eleanor Roosevelt and Secretary of Labor Frances Perkins, were more visible than women in previous administrations had been, many of the female New Dealers worked in relative obscurity, in agencies like the Women's Bureau or the Children's Bureau (both in the Department of Labor). And women who worked on major legislation or directed major programs received less credit than men in comparable positions. Moreover, female New Dealers tended to be a generation older than their male colleagues and were more likely to be Protestant than Catholic or Jewish.

The New Deal offered these women little opportunity, however, to advance the cause of women's equality. Demands for greater economic opportunity, sexual freedom, and full equality for women and men were heard less often in the 1930s than they had been in the preceding two decades. One reason was that the women's movement had fragmented after suffrage had been achieved. Another was that prominent New Deal women did not vigorously pursue a campaign for equal rights. They concentrated instead on "protective legislation"—laws that safeguarded female workers, who were thought to be more fragile than men. Those who in-

RATES OF UNEMPLOYMENT IN SELECTED MALE AND FEMALE OCCUPATIONS, 1930

MALE OCCUPATIONS	PERCENTAGE MALE	PERCENTAGE UNEMPLOYED
Iron and steel	96%	13%
Forestry and fishing	99	10
Mining	99	18
Heavy manufacturing	86	13
Carpentry	100	19
Laborers (road and street)	100	13

FEMALE OCCUPATIONS	PERCENTAGE FEMALE	PERCENTAGE UNEMPLOYED
Stenographers and typists	96%	5%
Laundresses	99	3
Trained nurses	98	4
Housekeepers	92	3
Telephone operators	95	3
Dressmakers	100	4

Source: U.S. Department of Commerce, Bureau of the Census, *Fifteenth Census of the United States, 1930, Population* (Washington, D.C.: Government Printing Office, 1931).

sisted that women needed special protections could not easily argue that women were the equal of men in all respects.

But feminism was hemmed in on all sides by a male hostility that the depression had only intensified. Men had built their male identities on the value of hard work and the ability to provide economic security for their families. For them, the loss of work unleashed feelings of inadequacy. That the unemployment rates of men tended to be higher than those of women exacerbated male vulnerability. Many fathers and husbands resented wives and daughters who had taken over their breadwinning roles.

This male anxiety had political and social consequence. Several states passed laws outlawing the hiring of married women. The labor movement made the protection of the male wage earner one of its principal goals. The Social Security pension system did not cover waitresses, domestic servants, and other largely female occupations.

Many artists introduced a strident masculinism into their painting and sculpture. Mighty Superman, the new comic-strip hero of 1938, reflected the spirit of the times. Superman was depicted as a working-class hero who, on several occasions, saved workers from coal mine explosions and other disasters caused by the greed and negligence of villainous employers.

Superman's greatest vulnerability, however, other than kryptonite, was his attraction to the sexy and aggressive *working* woman, Lois Lane. He was never able to resolve his dilemma by marrying Lois and tucking her away in a safe domestic sphere, because the continuation of the comic strip demanded that Superman repeatedly be exposed to kryptonite and female danger. But the producers of male and female images in other mass media, like the movies, faced no such technical obstacles. Anxious men could take comfort from the conclusion of the movie *Woman of the Year,* in which Spencer Tracy persuades the ambitious Katharine Hepburn to exchange her successful newspaper career for the bliss of motherhood and homemaking.

LABOR ASCENDANT

In 1935 John L. Lewis of the United Mine Workers, Sidney Hillman of the Amalgamated Clothing Workers, and the leaders of six other unions that had seceded from the American Federation of Labor (AFL) cobbled together a new labor organization. The Committee for Industrial Organization (CIO—later renamed the Congress of Industrial Organizations) took as its goal the organization of millions of nonunion workers into effective unions that would strengthen labor's influence in the workplace. In 1936 Lewis and Hillman created a second organization, Labor's Non-Partisan League (LNPL), to develop a labor strategy for the 1936 elections. Although professing the league's nonpartisanship, Lewis intended from the start that LNPL's role would be to channel labor's money, energy, and talent into Roosevelt's reelection campaign. Roosevelt welcomed the league's help, and labor would become one of the most important constituencies of the new Democratic coalition. The passage of the Wagner Act and the creation of the NLRB in 1935 enhanced the labor movement's status and credibility. Membership in labor unions climbed steadily, and in short order union members began flexing their new muscles.

In late 1936 the United Auto Workers (UAW) took on General Motors, widely regarded as the mightiest corporation in the world. Workers occupied key GM factories in Flint, Michigan, declaring that their "sit-down" strike would continue until GM agreed to recognize the UAW and negotiate a collective bargaining agreement. Frank Murphy, the pro-labor governor of Michigan, refused to use National Guard troops to evict the strikers, and Roosevelt declined to send federal

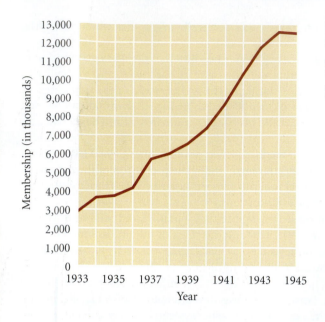

LABOR UNION MEMBERSHIP, 1933–1945

Source: From Christopher Tomlins, "AFL Unions in the 1930s," in Melvyn Dubofsky and Stephen Burwood, eds., *Labor* (New York: Garland, 1990), p. 1023.

troops. General Motors capitulated after a month of resistance. Soon, the U.S. Steel Corporation, which had defeated unionists in the bloody strike of 1919 (see Chapter 23), announced that it was ready to negotiate a contract with the newly formed CIO steelworkers union.

The labor movement's public stature grew along with its size. Many writers and artists depicted the labor movement as the voice of the people and the embodiment of the nation's values. Murals sprang up in post offices and other public buildings featuring portraits of blue-collar Americans at work. Broadway's most celebrated play in 1935 was Clifford Odets's *Waiting for Lefty,* a raw drama about taxi drivers who confront their bosses and organize an honest union. Audiences were so moved by the play that they often spontaneously joined in the final chorus of "Strike, Strike, Strike."

Similarly, many of the most popular novels and movies of the 1930s celebrated the decency, honesty, and patriotism of ordinary Americans. In *Mr. Deeds Goes to Town* (1936) and *Mr. Smith Goes to Washington* (1939) Frank Capra delighted movie audiences with fables of simple, small-town heroes vanquishing the evil forces of wealth and decadence. Likewise, in *The Grapes of Wrath,* the best-selling novel of 1939, John Steinbeck told an epic tale of an Oklahoma family's fortitude in surviving eviction from their land, migrating westward, and suffering exploitation in the "promised land" of California. In themselves and in one another, Americans seemed to discover the resolve they needed to rebuild a culture that had surrendered its identity to corporations and business.

AMERICA'S MINORITIES AND THE NEW DEAL

Reformers generally believed that issues of capitalism's viability, economic recovery, and the inequality of wealth and power outweighed problems of racial and ethnic discrimination. Because they were disproportionately poor, most minority groups did profit from the populist

and pro-labor character of New Deal reforms. But the gains were distributed unevenly. Eastern and southern European ethnics benefited the most while African Americans and Mexican Americans advanced the least.

EASTERN AND SOUTHERN EUROPEAN ETHNICS

Eastern and southern European immigrants and their children had begun mobilizing politically in the 1920s in response to religious and racial discrimination (see Chapter 24). By the early 1930s, they had made themselves into a formidable political force in the Democratic Party. Roosevelt understood their importance well. He made sure that a significant portion of New Deal monies for welfare, infrastructural improvements, and unemployment relief reached the urban areas where most European ethnics lived. As a result, Jewish and Catholic Americans voted for Roosevelt in overwhelming numbers. The New Deal did not eliminate anti-Semitism and anti-Catholicism from American society, but it did allow millions of European ethnics to believe, for the first time, that they would overcome the second-class status they had long endured.

Southern and eastern European ethnics also benefited from their strong presence in the working-class. Forming one of the largest groups in the mass-production industries of the Northeast, Midwest, and West, they made crucial contributions to the labor movement's rebirth. Roosevelt accommodated himself to their wishes because he understood and feared the power they wielded through their labor organizations.

AFRICAN AMERICANS

The New Deal did more to reproduce patterns of racial discrimination than to advance the cause of racial equality. African Americans who belonged to CIO unions or who lived in northern cities benefited from New Deal programs, but the vast majority of blacks lived in rural areas of the South where they were barred from voting, largely excluded from AAA programs, and denied federal protection in their efforts to form agricultural unions. The TVA hired few blacks. Those enrolled in the CWA and other work-relief programs frequently received less pay than whites doing the same jobs. Roosevelt consistently refused to support legislation to make lynching a federal crime.

This failure to push a strong civil rights agenda did not mean that New Dealers were themselves racist. Eleanor Roosevelt spoke out frequently against racial injustice. In 1939 she resigned from the Daughters of the American Revolution when the organization refused to allow black opera singer Marian Anderson to perform in its concert hall. She then pressured the federal government into granting Anderson permission to sing from the steps of the Lincoln Memorial. On Easter Sunday, 75,000 people gathered to hear Anderson and to demonstrate their support for racial equality.

Franklin Roosevelt eliminated segregationist practices in the federal government that had been in place since Woodrow Wilson's presidency. He appointed African Americans to important second-level posts in his administration. Working closely with each other in what came to be known as the "Black Cabinet," these officials fought hard against discrimination in New Deal programs.

But Roosevelt was never willing to make the fight for racial justice a priority. He refused to support his black cabinet if it meant alienating white southern senators who controlled key congressional committees. This refusal revealed Roosevelt's belief that economic issues were more important than racial ones. It revealed, too, Roosevelt's pragmatism. His decisions to support particular policies often depended on his calculation of their potential political cost or gain. Roosevelt believed that pushing for civil rights would cost him the support of the white South. Meanwhile, African Americans and their suppporters were not yet strong enough as an electoral constituency or as a reform movement to force Roosevelt to accede to their wishes.

MEXICAN AMERICANS

The experience of Mexicans during the Great Depression was particularly harsh. In 1931, Hoover's secretary of labor, William N. Doak, announced a plan for repatriating illegal aliens (returning them to their land of origin) and giving their jobs to American citizens. The federal campaign quickly focused on Mexican immigrants in California and the Southwest. The U.S. Immigration Service staged a number of highly publicized raids, rounded up large numbers of Mexicans and Mexican Americans, and demanded that each detainee prove his or her legal status. Those who failed to produce the necessary documentation were deported.

Local governments pressured many more into leaving. Los Angeles County officials, for example, "persuaded" 12,000 unemployed Mexicans to leave by threatening to remove them from the relief rolls and offering them free railroad tickets to Mexico; Colorado officials secured the departure of 20,000 Mexicans through the use of similar techniques. The combined efforts of federal, state, and local governments created a climate of fear in Mexican communities that prompted 500,000 to return to Mexico by 1935. This total equaled the number of Mexicans who had come to the United States in the 1920s. Included in repatriate ranks were a significant number of legal immigrants who were unable to produce their immigration papers, the American-born children of illegals, and some Mexican Americans who had lived in the Southwest for generations.

The advent of the New Deal in 1933 eased but did not eliminate pressure on Chicano communities. New Deal agencies made more money available for relief, thereby lightening the burden on state and local governments. Some federal programs, moreover, prohibited the removal of illegal aliens from relief rolls. But federal laws, more often than not, failed to dissuade local officials from continuing their campaign against Mexican immigrants. Where Mexicans gained access to relief rolls, they received payments lower than those given to "Anglos" (whites) or were compelled to accept tough agricultural jobs that did not pay living wages.

Life grew harder in other ways for Mexicans who stayed in the United States. The Mexican cultural renaissance that had arisen in 1920s Los Angeles (see Chapter 24) could not continue. Hounded by government officials, Mexicans everywhere sought to escape public attention and scrutiny. In Los Angeles, where their influence had been felt throughout the city in the 1920s, they retreated into the separate community of East Los Angeles.

Mexicans and Mexican Americans who lived in urban areas and worked in blue-collar industries did benefit from New Deal programs. In Los Angeles, for example, Chicanos responded to the New Deal's pro-labor legislation by joining unions in large numbers and winning concessions from their employers. These Mexicans and Mexican Americans shared the belief of southern and eastern Europeans that the New Deal would bring them economic improvement and cultural acceptance. But most Chicanos lived in rural areas and labored in agricultural jobs. The National Labor Relations Act did not protect their right to organize unions, while the Social Security Act excluded them from the new federal welfare system.

NATIVE AMERICANS

From the 1880s until the early 1930s, federal policy had contributed to the elimination of Native Americans as a distinctive population. The Dawes Act of 1887 (see Chapter 18) had called for tribal lands to be broken up and allotted to individual owners in the hope that Indians would adopt the work habits of white farmers. But Native Americans had proved stubbornly loyal to their languages, religions, and cultures. Few of them succeeded as farmers, and many of them lost land to white speculators.

The shrinking land base in combination with a growing population deepened Native American poverty. The assimilationist pressures on Native Americans, meanwhile, reached a climax in the intolerant 1920s when the Bureau of Indian Affairs (BIA) outlawed Indian religious ceremonies, forced children from tribal communities into federal boarding schools, banned polygamy, and imposed limits on the length of men's hair.

Government officials working in the Hoover administration began to question this draconian policy, but its reversal had to await the New Deal and Roosevelt's appointment of John Collier as the commissioner of the BIA. Collier pressured the CCC, AAA, and other New Deal agencies to employ Indians on projects that improved reservation land and trained Indians in land conservation methods. He prevailed on Congress to pass the Pueblo Relief Act of 1933, which compensated Pueblos for land taken from them in the 1920s, and the Johnson-O'Malley Act of 1934, which funded states to provide for Indian health care, welfare, and education.

Collier also took steps to abolish federal boarding schools, encourage enrollment in local public schools, and establish community day schools. He insisted that Native Americans be allowed to practice their traditional religions, and he created the Indian Arts and Crafts Board in 1935 to nurture traditional Indian artists and to help them market their works.

The centerpiece of Collier's reform strategy was the Indian Reorganization Act (IRA, also known as the Wheeler-Howard Act) of 1934, which revoked the allotment provisions of the Dawes Act. The IRA restored land to tribes, granted Indians the right to establish constitutions and bylaws for self-government, and provided support for new tribal corporations that would regulate the use of communal lands. This was a landmark act that signaled the government's recognition that Native American tribes possessed the right to chart their own political, cultural, and economic futures. It reflected Collier's commitment to "cultural pluralism," a doctrine that celebrated the diversity of peoples and cultures in American society and sought to protect that diversity against the pressures of assimilation.

Collier encountered opposition everywhere: from Protestant missionaries and cultural conservatives who wanted to continue an assimilationist policy; from white farmers and businessmen who feared that the new legislation would restrict their access to Native American land; and even from a sizable number of Indian groups, some of which had embraced assimilation while others viewed the IRA as one more attempt by the federal government to impose "the white man's will" on the Indian peoples.

A vocal minority of Indians continued to oppose the act even after its passage. The most crushing blow came when the Navajo Indians voted to reject its terms. For a variety of reasons,

76 other tribes joined the Navajo in opposition. Still, a large majority of tribes supported Collier's reform and began organizing new governments under the IRA. Although their quest for independence would suffer setbacks, as Congress and the BIA continued to interfere with their economic and political affairs, these tribes gained significant measures of freedom and autonomy.

THE NEW DEAL ABROAD

When he first entered office, Roosevelt seemed to favor a nationalist approach to international relations. The United States, he believed, should pursue foreign policies to benefit its domestic affairs, without regard for the effects of those policies on world trade and international stability. Thus, in June 1933, Roosevelt abruptly pulled the United States out of the World Economic Conference in London, a meeting called by leading nations to strengthen the gold standard and thereby stabilize the value of their currencies. Roosevelt feared that the other nations would force the United States into an agreement designed to keep the gold content of the dollar high and commodity prices in the United States low. This would then frustrate the efforts of just-established New Deal agencies to inflate the prices of agricultural and industrial goods.

Soon after his withdrawal from the London conference, however, Roosevelt put the United States on a more internationalist course. In November 1933, he became the first president to recognize the Soviet Union and to establish diplomatic ties with its Communist rulers. In December 1933, he inaugurated a "Good Neighbor Policy" toward Latin America by formally renouncing the right of the United States to intervene in the affairs of Latin American nations. To back up his pledge, Roosevelt ordered home the Marines stationed in Haiti and Nicaragua, scuttled the Platt Amendment that had given the United States control over the Cuban government since 1901, and granted Panama more political autonomy and a greater administrative role in operating the Panama Canal.

None of this, however, meant that the United States had given up its influence over Latin America. When a 1934 revolution brought a radical government to power in Cuba, the United States ambassador there worked with conservative Cubans to put a regime more favorable to U.S. interests in its place. The United States did refrain from sending its troops to Cuba. It also kept its troops at home in 1936 when a radical government in Mexico nationalized a number of U.S.-owned and British-owned petroleum companies. The United States merely demanded that the new Mexican government compensate the oil companies for their lost property—a demand that Mexico eventually met.

The Roosevelt administration's recognition of the Soviet Union and embrace of the Good Neighbor Policy can be seen as an international expression of the liberal principles that guided its domestic policies. But these diplomatic initiatives also reflected Roosevelt's interest in stimulating international trade. American businessmen wanted access to the Soviet Union's market. Latin America was already a huge market for the United States, but one in need of greater stability.

Roosevelt's interest in building international trade was also evident in his support for the Reciprocal Trade Agreement, passed by Congress in 1934. This act allowed his administration to lower U.S. tariffs by as much as 50 percent in exchange for similar reductions by other nations. By the end of 1935, the United States had negotiated reciprocal trade agreements with

14 countries. Roosevelt's turn to free trade further solidified support for the New Deal in parts of the business community.

Actually increasing the volume of international trade turned out to be more difficult than passing legislation to encourage it. The supporters of free trade encountered vociferous opposition to tariff reduction both within the United States and abroad. In Germany and Italy, belligerent nationalists Adolf Hitler and Benito Mussolini told their people that the solution to their ills lay not in trade but in military strength and conquest. Throughout the world, similar appeals to national pride proved to be more popular than calls for tariff reductions and international trade.

STALEMATE, 1937–1940

By 1937 and 1938 the New Deal had begun to lose momentum. One reason was an emerging split between working-class and middle-class Democrats. After the UAW's victory over General Motors in 1937, other workers began to imitate the successful tactics pioneered by the Flint militants. The sit-down strike became ubiquitous across the nation. Many middle-class Americans, meanwhile, were becoming disturbed by labor's growing power.

THE COURT-PACKING FIASCO

The president's proposal on February 5, 1937, to alter the makeup of the Supreme Court exacerbated middle-class fears. Roosevelt asked Congress to give him the power to appoint one new Supreme Court justice for every member of the court who was over the age of 70 and who had served for at least 10 years. His stated reason was that the current justices were too old and feeble to handle the large volume of cases coming before them. But his real purpose was to prevent the conservative justices on the court from dismantling his New Deal. Roosevelt had not minded when, in 1935, the court had declared the NRA unconstitutional, but he was not willing to see the Wagner Act and the Social Security Act invalidated. His proposal, if accepted, would have given him the authority to appoint six additional justices, thereby securing a pro–New Deal majority.

What seems remarkable about this episode is Roosevelt's willingness to tamper with an institution that many Americans considered sacred. The president seemed genuinely surprised by the storm of indignation that greeted his "court-packing" proposal. Roosevelt's political acumen had apparently been dulled by the victory he had won in 1936. His inflated sense of power infuriated many who had previously been New Deal enthusiasts. Although working-class support for Roosevelt remained strong, many middle-class voters turned away from the New Deal. In 1937 and 1938 a conservative opposition took shape, uniting Republicans, conservative Democrats, and civil libertarians determined to protect private property and government integrity.

Ironically, Roosevelt's court-packing scheme may not have been necessary. In March 1937, just one month after he proposed his plan, Supreme Court Justice Owen J. Roberts, who had formerly opposed New Deal programs, decided to support them. In April and May, the Court upheld the constitutionality of the Wagner Act and Social Security Act, both by a 5-to-4 margin. Roosevelt allowed his court-reform proposal to die in Congress that summer. Within three years, five of the aging justices had retired, giving Roosevelt the

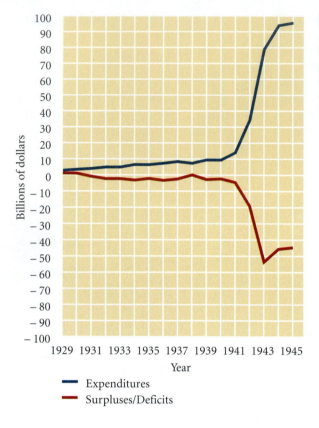

FEDERAL EXPENDITURES AND SURPLUSES/DEFICITS, 1929–1945

Source: Data from *Historical Statistics of the United States, Colonial Times to 1970* (White Plains, N.Y.: Kraus International, 1989), p. 1105.

Expenditures

Surpluses/Deficits

opportunity to fashion a court more to his liking. But nonetheless, Roosevelt's reputation had suffered.

THE RECESSION OF 1937–1938

Whatever hope Roosevelt may have had for a quick recovery from the court-packing fiasco was dashed by a sharp recession that struck the country in late 1937 and 1938. The New Deal programs of 1935 had stimulated the economy. In 1937 production surpassed the highest level of 1929, and unemployment fell to 14 percent. Believing that the depression was easing at last, Roosevelt began to scale back relief programs. New payroll taxes took $2 billion dollars from wage earners' salaries to finance the Social Security pension fund. That withdrawal would not have hurt the economy had the money been returned to circulation as pensions for retirees. But no Social Security pensions were scheduled to be paid until 1941. Once again, the economy became starved for money, and once again the stock market crashed. By March 1938, the unemployment rate had soared to 20 percent. In the off-year elections later that year, voters elected many conservative Democrats and Republicans opposed to the New Deal. These conservatives were not strong enough to dismantle the New Deal reforms already in place, but they were able to block the passage of new programs.

CHRONOLOGY

1929	Herbert Hoover assumes the presidency • Stock market crashes on "Black Tuesday"
1930	Tariff Act (Hawley-Smoot) raises tariffs
1932	Unemployment rate reaches 25 percent • Reconstruction Finance Corporation established • Bonus Army marches on Washington • Roosevelt defeats Hoover for presidency
1933	Roosevelt assumes presidency • "Hundred Days" legislation defines First New Deal (March–June) • Roosevelt administration recognizes the Soviet Union • "Good Neighbor Policy" toward Latin America launched • Reciprocal Trade Agreement lowers tariffs
1934	Father Charles Coughlin and Huey Long challenge conservatism of First New Deal • 2,000 strikes staged across country • Democrats overwhelm Republicans in off-year election • Radical political movements emerge in Wisconsin, Minnesota, Washington, and California • Indian Reorganization Act restores tribal land, provides funds, and grants limited right of self-government to Native Americans
1935	Committee for Industrial Organization (CIO) formed • Supreme Court declares NRA unconstitutional • Roosevelt unveils his Second New Deal • Congress passes Social Security Act • National Labor Relations Act (Wagner Act) guarantees workers' right to join unions • Holding Company Act breaks up utilities' near-monopoly • Congress passes Wealth Tax Act • Emergency Relief Administration Act passed; funds Works Progress Administration and other projects • Rural Electrification Administration established • Number of Mexican immigrants returning to Mexico reaches 500,000
1936	Roosevelt defeats Alf Landon for second term • Supreme Court declares AAA unconstitutional • Congress passes Soil Conservation and Domestic Allotment Act to replace AAA • Farm Security Administration established
1937	United Auto Workers defeat General Motors in sit-down strike • Roosevelt attempts to "pack" the Supreme Court • Supreme Court upholds constitutionality of Social Security and National Labor Relations Acts • Severe recession hits
1938	Conservative opposition to New Deal does well in off-year election • Superman comic debuts
1939	75,000 gather to hear Marian Anderson sing at Lincoln Memorial

CONCLUSION

The New Deal reinvigorated American democracy. Some feared that Roosevelt, by accumulating more power into the hands of the federal government than had ever been done in peacetime, aspired to autocratic rule. But nothing of the sort happened. The New Dealers inspired millions of Americans who had never before voted to go to the polls. Groups that had been marginalized now felt that their political activism could make a difference.

Not everyone benefited to the same degree from the broadening of American democracy. Northern factory workers, farm owners, European ethnics, and middle-class consumers were among the groups who benefited most. In contrast, the socialist and communist elements of the labor movement failed to achieve their radical demands. Southern industrial workers, black and white, benefited little from New Deal reforms; so did farm laborers. Feminists made no headway. African Americans and Mexican Americans gained meager influence over public policy.

Of course, New Deal reforms might not have mattered to any group had not the Second World War rescued the New Deal economic program. With government war orders flooding factories from 1941 on, the economy grew vigorously, unemployment vanished, and prosperity finally returned. The architects of the Second New Deal, who had argued that large government expenditures would stimulate consumer demand and trigger economic recovery, were vindicated.

The war also solidified the political reforms of the 1930s: an increased role for the government in regulating the economy and in ensuring the social welfare of those unable to help themselves; strong state support of unionization, agricultural subsidies, and progressive tax policies; the use of government power and money to develop the West and Southwest. Voters returned Roosevelt to office for unprecedented third and fourth terms. And these same voters remained wedded for the next 40 years to Roosevelt's central idea: that a powerful state would enhance the pursuit of liberty and equality.

AMERICA DURING THE SECOND WORLD WAR

THE ROAD TO WAR: AGGRESSION AND RESPONSE

FIGHTING THE WAR IN EUROPE ∼ THE PACIFIC THEATER

THE WAR AT HOME: THE ECONOMY

THE WAR AT HOME: SOCIAL ISSUES ∼ SHAPING THE PEACE

The Second World War, a struggle of unprecedented destruction, vastly changed American life. The United States abandoned isolationism, moved toward military engagement on the side of the Allies, and emerged triumphant in a global war in which U.S. forces fought and died in North Africa, Europe, and Asia.

The mobilization for war finally brought the United States out of the Great Depression and produced significant economic and social change. The nation's productive capacity—spurred by new technologies and by a new working relationship among government, business, labor, and scientific researchers—dwarfed that of every other nation and provided the economic basis for military victory.

At home, citizens considered the meaning of liberty and equality both in the international order and in their own lives. Although a massive propaganda effort heralded the war as a struggle to protect and preserve "the American way of life," the war inevitably raised significant questions. How would America, while striving for victory, reorder its economy, its culture, and the social patterns that had shaped racial, ethnic, and gender relationships during the 1930s? What process of international reconstruction might be required to build a prosperous and lasting peace?

THE ROAD TO WAR: AGGRESSION AND RESPONSE

The road to the Second World War began at least a decade before U.S. entry in 1941. In Japan, Italy, and Germany, economic collapse and rising unemployment created political conditions that nurtured ultranationalistic movements. Elsewhere in Europe and in the United States itself, economic problems made governments turn inward, concentrating upon domestic recovery and avoiding expensive foreign entanglements.

THE RISE OF AGGRESSOR STATES

On September 18, 1931, Japanese military forces seized Manchuria and created a puppet state called Manchukuo. This action violated the League of Nations charter, the Washington treaties, and the Kellogg-Briand Pact (see Chapter 24). Japanese military leaders won their gamble: The international community was too preoccupied with domestic economic ills to counter Japan's move. In the United States, the Hoover-Stimson Doctrine declared a policy of "nonrecognition" of Manchukuo, and the League of Nations also condemned Japan's action; but these stands were not backed by force, and Japan ignored them.

Meanwhile, ultranationalist states in Europe also sought to alleviate domestic ills through military aggression. Adolf Hitler's National Socialist (Nazi) Party came to power in Germany in 1933, instituting a fascist regime, a one-party dictatorial state. Hitler denounced the Versailles peace settlement of 1919, blamed Germany's plight on a Jewish conspiracy, claimed a genetic superiority for the "Aryan" race of German-speaking peoples, and promised to build a new empire (the "Third Reich"). The regime withdrew from the League of Nations and reinstituted compulsory military service. Another fascist government in Italy, headed by Benito Mussolini, also launched a military buildup and dreamed of empire. In October 1935 Mussolini's armies invaded Ethiopia. After meeting fierce resistance, Italy prevailed over Ethiopian forces.

ISOLATIONIST SENTIMENT AND AMERICAN NEUTRALITY

Many Americans wished to isolate their country from these foreign troubles. Antiwar movies, such as *All Quiet on the Western Front* and *The Big Parade,* popularized the notion that war was a power game played by business and governmental elites who used appeals to nationalism to dupe common people into serving as cannon fodder. Between 1934 and 1936 a Senate investigating committee headed by Republican Gerald P. Nye of North Dakota held well-publicized hearings. The Nye committee underscored claims that the nation had been maneuvered into the First World War to preserve the profits of American bankers and munitions makers. By 1935 public opinion polls suggested that Americans overwhelmingly opposed involvement in foreign conflicts.

To prevent a repetition of the circumstances that had supposedly drawn the United States into the First World War, Congress enacted neutrality legislation. The Neutrality Acts of 1935 and 1936 mandated an arms embargo against belligerents, prohibited loans to them, and curtailed Americans' travel on ships belonging to nations at war. The Neutrality Act of 1937 further broadened the embargo to cover all trade with belligerents, unless the nation at war paid in cash and carried the products away in its own ships.

The isolationist mood in the United States, matched by British policies of noninvolvement, encouraged Hitler's expansionist designs. In March 1936 Nazi troops seized the Rhineland. And a few months later, Hitler and Mussolini extended aid to General Francisco Franco, a fellow fascist who was seeking to overthrow Spain's republican government. Republicans in Spain appealed to antifascist nations for assistance, but only the Soviet Union responded. Britain, France, and the United States, fearing that the conflict would flare into world war if more nations took sides, adopted policies of noninvolvement.

GROWING INTERVENTIONIST SENTIMENT

Although the United States remained officially uninvolved, the Spanish Civil War did precipitate a major debate over foreign policy. Many conservative groups in the United States applauded Franco as a strong anticommunist whose fascist state would support religion and a stable social order in Spain. In contrast, the political left championed the cause of republican Spain and denounced the fascist repression that was sweeping Europe. Cadres of Americans, including the famed "Abraham Lincoln battalion," crossed the Atlantic and joined Soviet-organized, international brigades, which fought alongside republican forces. American peace groups split over how to respond. Some continued to advocate neutrality and isolation, but others argued for a strong stand against fascist militarism and aggression.

In October 1937 President Franklin Roosevelt called for international cooperation to "quarantine" aggressor states, and he gingerly suggested some modification of America's neutrality legislation. But congressional leaders were adamant in maintaining the policy of noninvolvement.

JAPAN'S INVASION OF CHINA

As Americans were debating strict neutrality versus cautious engagement, Japan launched an attack against China. In the summer of 1937, after an exchange of gunfire between Japanese and Chinese troops at the Marco Polo Bridge southwest of Beijing, Japanese armies invaded southward, capturing Beijing, Shanghai, Nanjing, and Shandong. The Japanese government demanded that China become subservient politically and economically to Tokyo. It also announced a plan for a greater East Asia Co-Prosperity Sphere, which would supposedly liberate peoples throughout Asia from Western colonialism and create a self-sufficient economic zone under Japanese leadership. Toward the end of 1937 Japanese planes sank the *Panay*, an American gunboat that was evacuating American officials from Nanjing, but Japan's quick apology defused the potential crisis. Even so, the *Panay* incident and Japanese brutality in occupying Nanjing alarmed Roosevelt.

Further aggression heightened the sense of alarm among interventionists in the United States. In October 1936 Germany and Italy agreed to cooperate as the "Axis Powers," and Japan joined them to form an alliance against the Soviet Union in November 1936. Italy followed Japan and Germany in withdrawing from the League of Nations. In March 1938 Hitler annexed Austria to the Third Reich and then announced his intention to annex the Sudetenland, a portion of Czechoslovakia inhabited by 3.5 million people of German descent.

THE OUTBREAK OF WAR IN EUROPE

The leaders of France and Britain, wishing to avoid a confrontation with Germany, met with Hitler in Munich in September of 1938. They acquiesced to Germany's seizure of the Sudetenland in return for Hitler's promise to seek no more territory. However, the promise of peace did not last. In March 1939 Germans marched into Prague and, within a few months, annexed the rest of Czechoslovakia. In August 1939 Hitler signed a nonaggression pact with the Soviet Union. In a secret protocol Stalin and Hitler plotted to divide Poland and the Baltic states. By the fall of 1939 Germany was clearly preparing for an attack on Poland.

Britain and France pledged to defend Poland, and on September 1, 1939, Hitler's invasion forced them into action. Two days after Hitler's armies stormed into Poland, Britain and France declared war on Germany. The Allies, however, were unable to mobilize in time to help the Poles, who were outnumbered and outgunned. With Soviet troops moving in simultaneously from the east, Poland fell within weeks. Once the occupation of Poland was completed, Hitler's troops waited out the winter of 1939–1940.

The lull proved only temporary. In April 1940 a German *blitzkrieg,* or "lightning war," began moving swiftly and suddenly, overrunning Denmark, Norway, the Netherlands, Belgium, Luxembourg, and then France. The speed with which Hitler's army moved shocked Allied leaders

ICELAND

NORTH
SEA

German submarine attacks
in North Atlantic

NORWAY
Oslo

SWEDEN
Stockholm

FINLAND

Helsinki

Leningrad

UNION OF SOVIET
SOCIALIST REPUBLICS

Moscow

Denmark and Norway
occupied, April 1940   5

Poland invaded,
September 1939.
World War II begins   4

ESTONIA
Tallinn

Riga
LATVIA

DENMARK

IRELAND
Dublin

UNITED
KINGDOM

Belgium, the Netherlands
occupied, May 1940   6

Copenhagen

LITHUANIA
Kaunas

Battle of Britain
Fall, 1940   9

London

NETH.
Amsterdam

GERMANY
Berlin

EAST
PRUSSIA

POLAND
Warsaw

Western Soviet Union and
Eastern Europe occupied,
1941–1942   10

ATLANTIC
OCEAN

Allied evacuation from
Dunkirk, May 1940   7

Dunkirk
BELG.
Brussels

Germany demands annexation of
Sudetenland, September 1938   2

Czechoslovakia seized,
August 1939   3

Stalingrad

Paris
LUX.

Prague

CZECHOSLOVAKIA

France surrenders, June 1940,
and Vichy government
installed, June 1940   8

FRANCE

Germany effects *Anschluss*
with Austria, March 1938   1

Vienna

Berne
Munich
SWITZ.

Vichy

AUSTRIA

Budapest

HUNGARY

ROMANIA
Bucharest

BLACK SEA

YUGOSLAVIA
Belgrade

Lisbon

PORTUGAL

Madrid

SPAIN

ITALY

Corsica
(Vichy Fr.)

ADRIATIC SEA

Rome

BULGARIA
Sofia

Ankara

Tirana

GIBRALTAR
(U.K.)

Sardinia

AEGEAN
SEA

TURKEY

SP. MOROCCO

Algiers

Tunis

Sicily

GREECE
Athens

SYRIA

FR. MOROCCO
(Vichy Fr.)

ALGERIA
(Vichy Fr.)

TUNISIA
(Vichy Fr.)

Malta (U.K.)

Dodecanese Is.
(It.)

Rhodes
(It.)

Cyprus
(U.K.)

LEBANON
Beirut

Damascus

Crete
(Gr.)

MEDITERRANEAN SEA

Suez
Canal

PALESTINE
(BR. MANDATE)
Jerusalem

Amman

TRANS
JORDAN
(BR. MANDATE)

■ Axis Powers, Germany and Italy, 1938	■ Neutral nations
■ Axis satellites and areas brought under Axis control	- - - German advance up to December 1941
■ Areas controlled by Allies, as of November 1942	— German advance up to November 1942

Cairo

LIBYA
(It.)

EGYPT

RED SEA

GERMAN EXPANSION AT ITS HEIGHT

in Paris and London; Britain barely managed to evacuate its troops, but not its equipment, from the French coastal town of Dunkirk, just before it fell to the German onslaught that began in late May. Early in June, Italy joined Germany by declaring war on the Allies. In June 1940, France fell, and Hitler installed a pro-Nazi government at Vichy in southern France. In only six weeks, Hitler's army had seized complete control of Europe's Atlantic coastline, from the North Sea south to Spain, where Franco remained officially neutral but decidedly pro-Axis.

AMERICA'S RESPONSE TO WAR IN EUROPE

From 1939 to 1941 Roosevelt tried to mobilize public opinion against Congress's Neutrality Acts and in favor of what he called "measures short of war" that would bolster the Allied fight against the Axis. At Roosevelt's urging, late in 1939 Congress lifted the Neutrality Act's ban on selling arms to either side and substituted a "cash-and-carry" provision that permitted arms sales to belligerents who could pay cash for their purchases and carry them away in their own ships. Because Britain and France controlled the Atlantic sea lanes, they clearly benefited from this change in U.S. policy. Congress also passed the Selective Training and Service Act of 1940, the first peacetime draft in U.S. history. Abandoning any further pretense of neutrality, the United States began supplying war matériel directly to Great Britain.

Meanwhile, from August through October 1940 Germany's *Luftwaffe* subjected British air bases to daily raids, coming close to knocking Britain's Royal Air Force (RAF) out of the war. Just as he was on the verge of success, however, Hitler lost patience with this strategy and ordered instead the bombing of London and other cities. The bombing of Britain's cities aroused a sense of urgency about the war in the United States. The use of airpower against civilians in the Battle of Britain, as it was called, shocked Americans, who heard the news in dramatic radio broadcasts from London.

In September 1940 the president agreed to transfer 50 First World War–era naval destroyers to the British navy. In return, the United States gained the right to build eight naval bases in British territory in the Western Hemisphere. This "destroyers-for-bases" deal infuriated isolationist members of Congress. Even within the president's own party, opposition was strong. The opposition extended beyond Congress. The most formidable opposition came from the America First Committee, organized by General Robert E. Wood, head of Sears, Roebuck and Company.

Although the people who tried to keep the United States out of the war were generally lumped together as "isolationists," this single term obscures their ideological diversity. Some pacifists opposed all wars as immoral, even those against evil regimes. Some political progressives disliked fascism but feared even more the growth of centralized power that the conduct of war would require in the United States. On the other hand, some conservatives sympathized with fascism, and some Americans opposed Roosevelt's pro-Allied policies because they shared Hitler's anti-Semitism.

A current of anti-Semitism existed in the country at large. In 1939 congressional leaders had quashed the Wagner-Rogers Bill, which would have boosted immigration quotas in order to allow for the entry of 20,000 Jewish children otherwise slated for Hitler's concentration camps. Bowing to anti-Semitic prejudices, the United States adopted a restrictive refugee policy that did not permit even the legal quota of Jewish immigrants from eastern Europe to enter the country during the Second World War. The consequences of these policies became even graver after June of 1941, when Hitler established the death camps that would systematically exterminate millions of Jews, gypsies, homosexuals, and anyone else whom the Nazis deemed "unfit" for life in the Third Reich and its occupied territories.

To counteract the isolationists, those who favored supporting the Allies also organized. The Military Training Camps Association, for example, lobbied on behalf of the Selective Service Act. The Committee to Defend America by Aiding the Allies, headed by William Allen White, a well-known Republican newspaper editor, organized more than 300 local chapters in just a few weeks. Like the isolationists, interventionist organizations drew from an ideologically diverse group of supporters. All, however, sounded alarms about the dangerous possibility that fascist brutality, militarism, and racism might overrun Europe as Americans watched passively.

Presidential election politics in 1940 forced Roosevelt to tone down his pro-Allied rhetoric. The Republicans nominated Wendell Willkie, a lawyer and business executive with ties to the party's liberal, internationalist wing. The Democrats nominated Roosevelt for a third term. To differentiate his policies from Willkie's, the president played to the popular opposition to war. He promised not to send American boys to fight in "foreign wars." Once he had won an unprecedented third term, however, Roosevelt produced his most ambitious plan yet to support Britain's war effort.

AN "ARSENAL OF DEMOCRACY"

Britain was nearly out of money, so the president proposed an additional provision to the Neutrality Act. The United States would now loan, or "lend-lease," rather than sell munitions to the Allies. By making the United States a "great arsenal of democracy," FDR assured Americans, he would "keep war away from our country and our people." But not everyone in Congress felt as Roosevelt did, and debate over the Lend-Lease Act was bitter. Nevertheless, House Resolution 1776 was passed by Congress on March 11, 1941. When Germany turned its attention away from Britain and suddenly attacked its recent ally the Soviet Union in June, Roosevelt extended lend-lease to Joseph Stalin's communist regime, even though it had earlier cooperated with Hitler.

In September 1941 Senator Burton K. Wheeler of Montana created a special Senate committee to investigate whether Hollywood movies were being used to sway people in a pro-war direction. Some isolationists, pointing out that many Hollywood producers were Jewish, expressed blatantly anti-Semitic opinions.

Roosevelt next took steps to coordinate military strategy with Britain. Should the United States be drawn into a two-front war against both Germany and Japan, the president pledged to follow a Europe-first strategy. And to back up his promise, Roosevelt deployed thousands of marines to Greenland and Iceland to relieve British troops, which had occupied these strategic Danish possessions after Germany's seizure of Denmark.

Then, in August 1941, Roosevelt and British Prime Minister Winston Churchill, meeting on the high seas off the coast of Newfoundland, worked out the basis of what would shortly become a formal wartime alliance. An eight-point declaration of common principles, the so-called Atlantic Charter, disavowed territorial expansion, endorsed free trade and self-determination, and pledged the postwar creation of a new world organization that would ensure "general security." Roosevelt agreed to Churchill's request that the U.S. Navy convoy American goods as far as Iceland. This step, aimed at ensuring the safe delivery of lend-lease supplies to Britain, inched the United States even closer to belligerence. Soon, in an undeclared naval war, Germany was using its formidable submarine "wolfpacks" to attack U.S. ships.

By this time, Roosevelt and his advisers understood that in order to defeat Hitler the United States would have to enter the war, but public support for such a move was still lacking. The president urged Congress to repeal the Neutrality Act altogether to allow U.S. merchant ships to carry munitions directly to Britain. Privately, he may have hoped that Germany would commit some provocative act in the North Atlantic that would move public opinion toward further involvement. The October 1941 sinking of the U.S. destroyer *Reuben James* did just that, and Congress did repeal the Neutrality Act—but the vote was so close and the debate so bitter that Roosevelt knew he could not yet seek a formal declaration of war.

THE ATTACK AT PEARL HARBOR

As it turned out, America's formal entry into the war came about as a result of escalating tensions with Japan rather than Germany. In response to Japan's invasion of China in 1937, the

United States extended economic credits to China to bolster its efforts to defend itself. Then, in 1939 the United States abrogated its Treaty of Commerce and Navigation with Japan.

These measures did little to deter Japanese aggression, and by 1940 Germany's successes in Europe had further raised the stakes in Asia. Japan quickly mobilized to exploit the vacuum created by a weakened Europe. Japanese expansionists called for the incorporation of Southeast Asia into their East Asian Co-Prosperity Sphere.

The president hoped that a 1940 ban on the sale of aviation fuel and high-grade scrap iron to Japan would slow Japan's imminent military advance into Southeast Asia. But this act only intensified Japanese militancy. After joining the Axis alliance in September 1940, Japan pushed deeper into Indochina. When its occupation of French Indochina went unopposed, its military forces prepared to launch attacks on Singapore, the Netherlands East Indies (Indonesia), and the Philippines. Roosevelt expanded the trade embargo against Japan, promised further assistance to China, and accelerated the U.S. military buildup in the Pacific. Then, in mid-1941, Roosevelt froze Japanese assets in the United States, effectively bringing under presidential control all commerce between the two countries. With this action, Roosevelt hoped to bring Japan to the bargaining table. But faced with impending economic strangulation, the leaders of Japan began planning for a preemptive attack on the United States.

On December 7, 1941, nearly the entire U.S. Pacific fleet, stationed at Pearl Harbor in Hawaii, was destroyed by Japanese bombers. Only the fleet's aircraft carriers, which were out to sea at the time, were spared. Altogether, 19 ships were sunk or severely damaged; 188 planes were destroyed on the ground; and more than 2,200 Americans were killed. In a war message broadcast by radio on December 8, Roosevelt decried the Japanese attack and labeled December 7 "a date which will live in infamy," a phrase that served as a rallying cry throughout the war.

For the Japanese, the attack on Pearl Harbor was an act of desperation. With limited supplies of raw materials, Japan had little hope of winning a prolonged war. Japanese military strategists gambled that a crippling blow would so weaken U.S. military power that a long war would be avoided. Japanese leaders decided to risk a surprise attack.

A few Americans charged that Roosevelt had intentionally provoked Japan in order to open a "backdoor" to war. They pointed out that the fleet at Pearl Harbor lay vulnerable at its docks, not even in a state of full alert. In actuality, the American actions and inactions that led to Pearl Harbor were more confused than they were devious. Beginning in 1934 the United States had gradually enlarged its Pacific fleet, and Roosevelt had also increased the number of B-17 bombers based in the Philippines. The president hoped that the possibility of aerial attacks would intimidate Japan and slow its expansion. But the strategy of deterrence failed. It may also have contributed to the lack of vigilance at Pearl Harbor. American leaders doubted that Japan would risk a direct attack, and intelligence experts expected Japan to move toward Singapore or other British or Dutch possessions. Intercepted messages, along with visual sightings of Japanese transports, seemed to confirm preparations for a strike in Southeast Asia (a strike that did occur). A warning that Japan might also be targeting Pearl Harbor was not sent with sufficient urgency and was lost under a mountain of intelligence reports.

On December 8, 1941, Congress declared war against Japan. Japan's allies, Germany and Italy, declared war on the United States three days later. Hitler mistakenly assumed that war with Japan would keep the United States preoccupied in the Pacific. The three Axis Powers drastically underestimated America's ability to mobilize swiftly and effectively.

FIGHTING THE WAR IN EUROPE

The first few months after America's entry into the war proved to be discouraging. German forces already controlled most of Europe from Norway to Greece and had pushed rapidly eastward into the Soviet Union. Now they were rolling across North Africa. In the Atlantic, German submarines were endangering Allied supply lines. Japan seemed unstoppable in the Pacific. Japanese forces overran Malaya, the Dutch East Indies, and the Philippines and drove against the British in Burma and the Australians in New Guinea.

Long before December 7, 1941, the Roosevelt administration had expected war and had vainly tried to prepare for it. When war came, Army morale was low, industrial production was still on a peacetime footing, and labor-management relations were contentious. As the country faced the need for rapid economic and military mobilization, new government bureaucracies began to spring up everywhere.

The wartime growth in the size of government transformed American foreign policymaking. Military priorities superseded all other demands. The administration was being forced to settle on new policies overnight and then implement them on a global scale the following day. The newly formed Joint Chiefs of Staff, consisting of representatives from each of the armed services, became Roosevelt's major source of guidance on military strategy. The War Department's new Pentagon complex dwarfed the State Department's cramped quarters at "Foggy Bottom." The giant five-story, five-sided building was completed in January 1943, after 16 months of round-the-clock work.

In the Atlantic, German submarines sank 7 million tons of Allied shipping in the first 16 months after Pearl Harbor. In 1942 aircraft equipped with radar, a new technology developed in collaboration with Britain, proved effective against submarines. During 1943 Germany's submarine capability faded "from menace to problem," in the words of Admiral Ernest King.

CAMPAIGNS IN NORTH AFRICA AND ITALY

Military strategy became a contentious issue among the Allied Powers. All advisers agreed that their primary focus would be on Europe, and Roosevelt and his military strategists immediately established a unified command with the British. The Soviet Union pleaded with Roosevelt and Churchill to open a second front in western Europe to relieve Germany's pressure on the USSR. Many of Roosevelt's advisers agreed. They feared that if German troops forced the Soviet Union out of the war, Germany would then turn its full attention to defeating Britain. Churchill, however, urged instead the invasion of French North Africa, in order to peck away at the edges of enemy power rather than strike at its heart. At a meeting between Roosevelt and Stalin at Casablanca, Morocco, in January 1943, Roosevelt sided with Churchill, and the promised invasion of France was postponed. To assuage Stalin's fears that his two allies might sign a separate peace with Hitler, the two leaders did announce that they would stay in the fight until Germany agreed to an unconditional surrender.

The North African operation, code-named TORCH, began with Anglo-American landings in Morocco and Algeria in November 1942. To ease resistance against the Allies' North African invasion, U.S. General Dwight D. Eisenhower struck a deal with French Admiral Jean Darlan, the Vichy officer who controlled France's colonies in North Africa. Darlan agreed to break with the Vichy regime in return for Eisenhower's pledge that the United States would support him. The deal outraged some Americans who believed that it compromised the moral purpose of the war. Darlan's assassination in December 1942 put an end to the embarrassment. But the antagonism that Eisenhower's action had created between Americans and the Free French movement, led by General Charles de Gaulle, had lasting consequences after the war.

As TORCH progressed, the Soviets managed to turn the tide of battle at Stalingrad. Despite this defeat in the East, Hitler poured reinforcements into North Africa, but could not stop either TORCH or the British, who were driving west from Egypt. In the summer of 1943 Allied troops followed up the successful North African campaign by overrunning the island of Sicily and then fighting their way slowly north through Italy's mountains.

Some American officials increasingly worried about the postwar implications of wartime strategy. Secretary of War Henry Stimson, for example, warned that the peripheral campaigns through Africa and Italy might leave the Soviets dominating central Europe. Acting on their advice, Roosevelt finally agreed to set a date for the cross-Channel invasion that Stalin had long been promised.

Operation OVERLORD

Operation OVERLORD finally began on June 6, 1944, D-Day. During the months preceding D-Day, probably the largest invasion force in history had been assembled in England. Disinformation and diversionary tactics had led the Germans to expect a landing at the narrowest part of the English Channel rather than in the Normandy region. Allied intelligence officers knew from monitoring the cables sent to Tokyo by Japan's ambassador in Berlin that their ruse had worked. After several delays, due to the Channel's unpredictable weather, nervous commanders finally ordered the daring plan to begin. The night before, as naval guns pounded the Normandy shore, three divisions of paratroopers were dropped behind enemy lines to disrupt German communications. Then, at dawn, more than 4,000 Allied ships landed troops and supplies on Normandy's beaches. The first American troops to land at Omaha Beach met especially heavy German fire and took enormous casualties. But the waves of invading troops continued. Within three weeks, over 1 million people had landed, secured the Normandy coast, and opened the long-awaited second front.

Just as the Battle of Stalingrad had reversed the tide of the war in the East, so operation OVERLORD turned the tide in the West. Within three months, U.S., British, and Free French troops entered Paris. After turning back a desperate German counteroffensive in Belgium, at the Battle of the Bulge in December and January, Allied armies swept eastward, crossing the Rhine and heading toward Berlin.

The Allies disagreed on how the defeat of Germany should be orchestrated. British strategists favored a swift drive, so as to meet up with Soviet armies in Berlin or even farther east. General Eisenhower favored a strategy that was militarily less risky and politically less provocative to the Soviets. He was also eager to end the war on a note of trust and believed that racing the Soviets to Berlin would undermine the basis for postwar Soviet-American cooperation. In the end, Eisenhower's views prevailed. He moved cautiously along a broad front, halting his troops at the Elbe River, west of Berlin, and allowing Soviet troops to roll into the German capital.

As the war in Europe drew to a close, the horrors perpetrated by the Third Reich became visible to the world. Although only a military victory could put an end to German death camps, the Allies could have saved thousands of Jews by encouraging them to emigrate and helping them to escape. Allied leaders, however, worried about the impact large numbers of Jewish refugees would have on their countries, and they were also reluctant to use scarce ships to transport Jews to

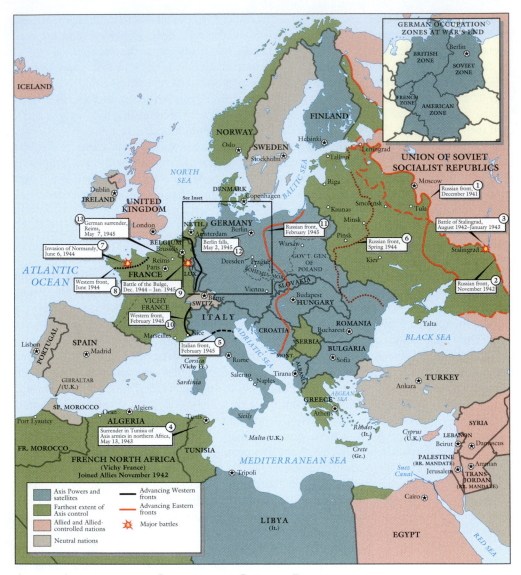

ALLIED ADVANCES AND COLLAPSE OF GERMAN POWER

neutral sanctuaries. In 1943, after Romania proposed permitting an evacuation of 70,000 Jews from its territory, Allied leaders avoided any serious discussion of the plan. The United States even refused to relax its strict policy on visas to admit Jews who might have escaped on their own.

Hitler's campaign of extermination, now called the Holocaust, killed between 5 and 6 million Jews out of Europe's prewar population of 10 million; hundreds of thousands more from various other groups were also murdered, especially gypsies, homosexuals, intellectuals, communists, and the physically and mentally handicapped. The Allies would, in 1945 and 1946, bring 24 high German officials to trial at Nuremburg for "crimes against humanity." Large quantities of money, gold, and jewelry that Nazi leaders stole from victims of the Holocaust and deposited in Swiss banks remained largely hidden from view for more than 50 years. Not until 1997 did Jewish groups and the U.S. government begin to force investigations of the Swiss banking industry and its relationship to stolen "Nazi gold."

With Hitler's suicide in April and Germany's surrender on May 8, 1945, the military foundations for peace in Europe were complete. Soviet armies controlled eastern Europe; British and U.S. forces predominated in Italy and the rest of the Mediterranean; Germany and Austria fell under divided occupation. Governmental leaders now needed to work out a plan for transforming these military arrangements into a comprehensive political settlement for the postwar era. Meanwhile, the war in the Pacific was still far from over.

THE PACIFIC THEATER

For six months after Pearl Harbor, nearly everything in the Pacific went Japan's way. Singapore fell easily. American naval garrisons in the Philippines and on Guam and Wake islands were overwhelmed, and American and Filipino armies were forced to surrender at Bataan and Corregidor in the Philippines. Other Japanese forces steamed southward to menace Australia. Then the tide turned.

SEIZING THE INITIATIVE IN THE PACIFIC

When Japan finally suffered its first naval defeat at the Battle of the Coral Sea in May 1942, Japanese naval commanders decided to hit back hard. They amassed 200 ships and 600 planes to destroy what remained of the U.S. Pacific fleet and to take Midway Island. U.S. intelligence, however, was monitoring Japanese codes and warned Admiral Chester W. Nimitz of the plan. Surprising the Japanese navy, U.S. planes sank four Japanese carriers and destroyed a total of 322 planes.

Two months later, American forces splashed ashore at Guadalcanal in the Solomon Islands. The bloody engagements in the Solomons continued for months on both land and sea, but they accomplished one major objective: seizing the initiative against Japan. This success, combined with the delay in opening a second front in Europe, also affected grand strategy. According to prewar plans, the war in Europe was to have received highest priority. But by 1943 the two theaters were receiving roughly equal resources.

The bloody engagements in the Pacific dramatically illustrated that the war was one in which racial prejudices reinforced brutality. For Japan, the Pacific conflict was a war to establish forever the superiority of the divine Yamato race. Prisoners taken by the Japanese were brutalized in unimaginable ways. The Japanese army's Unit 731 tested bacteriological weapons in China and conducted horrifying medical experiments on live subjects. American propaganda images also played upon themes of racial superiority, portraying the Japanese as animalistic subhumans. American troops often rivaled Japan's forces in their disrespect for the enemy dead and sometimes killed the enemy rather than take prisoners.

CHINA POLICY

U.S. policymakers hoped that China would fight Japan more effectively and then emerge after the war as a strong and united nation. Neither hope was realized.

General Joseph W. Stilwell undertook the job of turning China into an effective military force. Jiang Jieshi (formerly spelled Chiang Kai-shek) headed China's government and appointed Stilwell his chief of staff. But frictions between "Vinegar Joe" Stilwell and Jiang became so intense that in May 1943 Roosevelt bowed to Jiang's demand for Stilwell's dismissal. Meanwhile, Japan's advance into China continued, and in 1944 its forces captured seven of the principal U.S. air bases in China.

During the same period China was beset by civil war. Jiang's Nationalist government was incompetent, corrupt, and unpopular. It avoided engaging the Japanese invaders and still made extravagant demands for U.S. assistance. Meanwhile, a growing communist movement led by Mao Zedong was fighting effectively against the Japanese and enjoyed widespread support among Chinese peasants. Stilwell urged Roosevelt to cut off support to Jiang unless he fought with more determination. Roosevelt, however, feared that such actions would create even greater chaos. He continued to provide moral support and matériel to Jiang's armies. Moreover, pressed by a powerful "China lobby" of domestic conservatives, he insisted that Jiang's China be permitted to stand with the major powers after victory had been won. By tying U.S. policy to Jiang's leadership, Roosevelt and the "China lobby" prepared the way for great difficulties in forging a China policy in the postwar period.

PACIFIC STRATEGY

In contrast to the war in Europe, there was no unified command to guide the war in the Pacific; consequently, military actions often emerged from compromise. General Douglas MacArthur, commander of the army in the South Pacific, favored an offensive launched from his headquarters in Australia through New Guinea and the Philippines and on to Japan. After Japan drove him out of the Philippines in May 1942, he promised to return. Admiral Nimitz disagreed. He favored an advance across the smaller islands of the central Pacific, which would provide more direct access to Japan. Unable to decide between the two strategies, the Joint Chiefs of Staff authorized both.

Marked by fierce fighting and heavy casualties, both offensives moved forward. MacArthur took New Guinea, and Nimitz's forces liberated the Marshall Islands and the Marianas in 1943 and 1944. At about this point, an effective radio communication system conducted by a Marine platoon of Navajo Indians made a unique contribution to the war effort. Navajo, a language unfamiliar to both the Japanese and the Germans, provided a secure medium for sensitive communications. In late 1944 the fall of Saipan brought American bombers within range of Japan. The capture of the islands of Iwo Jima and Okinawa further shortened that distance during the spring of 1945.

As the seaborne offensive proceeded, the United States brought its airpower into play. In February 1944 General Henry Harley ("Hap") Arnold presented Roosevelt with a plan for strategic air assaults on Japanese cities. His proposal included a systematic campaign of destruction through the firebombing of urban targets. Roosevelt approved the plan. In the month before bombing began, the Office of War Information lifted its ban on atrocity stories about Japan's treatment of American prisoners. As grisly reports and racist anti-Japanese propaganda swept across the country, it was thought the public would become more accepting of the killing of Japanese civilians. Arnold's original air campaign, operating from bases in China, turned out to be cumbersome and ineffective; it was replaced by an even more lethal operation, running from Saipan, under the aegis of General Curtis LeMay.

NAVAJO SIGNAL CORPS   Sending messages in their native language, which was unfamiliar to the Japanese, Navajo Indians in the Signal Corps made a unique contribution to preserving the secrecy of U.S. intelligence.

The official position on the incendiary raids on Japanese cities was that they constituted "precision" rather than "area" bombing. In actuality, the success of a mission was measured in terms of the number of square miles that had been left scorched and useless. The number of Japanese civilians killed in the raids is estimated to have been greater than the number of Japanese soldiers killed in battle. An attack on Tokyo on the night of March 9–10, 1945, inaugurated the new policy, inflicting 185,000 casualties.

By the winter of 1944–1945, a combined sea and air strategy had emerged: The United States would seek "unconditional surrender" by blockading Japan's seaports, continuing its bombardment of Japanese cities from the air, and perhaps invading Japan itself. Later critics of the policy of unconditional surrender have suggested that it may have hardened the determination with which Japan fought the war after its inevitable defeat had become obvious. With the unconditional surrender policy in place and Japan's determination to fight even in the face of certain defeat, the strategy of American leaders seemed to require massive destruction to achieve victory.

ATOMIC POWER AND JAPANESE SURRENDER

At Los Alamos, New Mexico, scientists from all across the United States had been secretly working on a weapon that promised just such massive destruction. Advances in theoretical

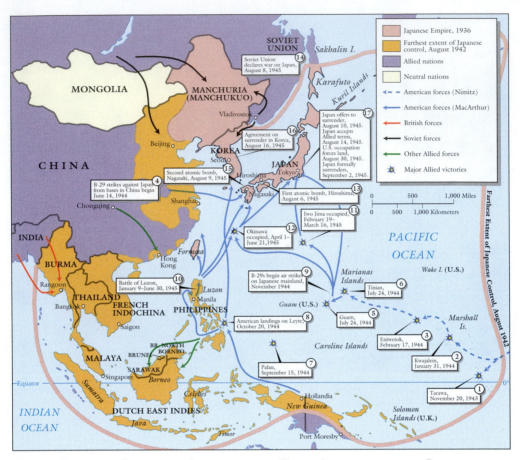

PACIFIC THEATER OFFENSIVE STRATEGY AND FINAL ASSAULT AGAINST JAPAN

physics during the 1930s had suggested that splitting the atom (fission) would release a tremendous amount of energy. Fearful that Germany was racing ahead in this effort, Albert Einstein, a Jewish refugee from Germany, urged President Roosevelt to launch a secret program to build a bomb based on atomic research. The government subsequently enlisted top scientists in the Manhattan Project, the largest and most secretive military project yet undertaken. On July 16, 1945, the first atomic weapon was successfully tested at Trinity Site, near Alamagordo, New Mexico. The researchers then notified the new president, Harry Truman, that the terrifying new weapon was ready.

Truman and his top policymakers assumed that the weapon should be put to immediate military use. They were eager to end the war, both because a possible land invasion of Japan might have cost so many American lives and also because the Soviet Union was planning to enter the Pacific theater, and Truman wished to limit Soviet power in that region. Churchill called the bomb a "miracle of deliverance" and a peace-giver. Truman later said that he had never lost a night's sleep over its use.

TOTAL WAR: DRESDEN AND HIROSHIMA   The effects of "total war" are graphically illustrated in these photographs—of the devastation of Dresden, Germany (top), by the British Bomber Command and the U.S. 8th Air Force on February 13 and 14, 1945, and that of Hiroshima, Japan (bottom), by the U.S. 509th Composite Group on August 6, 1945. In the initial attack on Dresden, 786 aircraft dropped 5,824,000 pounds (2,600 long tons) of bombs on the city, killing an estimated 60,000 people and injuring another 30,000. An area of more than 2.5 square miles in the town center was demolished, and some 37,000 buildings were destroyed. To critics, the bombing of Dresden, a target that many argued was of little strategic value, exemplified the excessive use of airpower.

In sobering comparison, the devastation of Hiroshima was created by one bomb weighing only 10,000 pounds (4.4 long tons)—an atomic bomb—which was dropped from one aircraft. The single U-235 bomb killed 68,000 people outright, injured another 30,000, and left 10,000 missing. (These figures do not include those who later developed diseases from deadly gamma rays.) Almost 5 square miles of the city's center was obliterated, and 40,653 buildings were destroyed. Truman reported the strike as "an overwhelming success." Many hailed the atomic bomb as a necessary step toward military victory; others worried about the dawn of the "nuclear age."

Other advisers had more qualms, and there was some disagreement over where and how the bomb should be deployed. A commission of atomic scientists recommended a "demonstration" that would impress Japan with the bomb's power yet cause no loss of life. But most of Truman's advisers agreed that simply demonstrating the bomb's power might not be enough. They believed that it would take massive destruction to bring unconditional surrender.

In the context of the earlier brutal aerial bombardment of Japanese cities, dropping atomic bombs on the previously unbombed cities of Hiroshima and Nagasaki on August 6 and 9, 1945, seemed simply an acceleration of existing policy rather than a departure from it. "Fat Man" and "Little Boy," as the two bombs were nicknamed, were merely viewed as bigger, more effective firebombs. Of course, atomic weapons did produce yet a new level of violence. Colonel Paul Tibbets, who piloted the plane that dropped the first bomb, reported that "the shimmering city became an ugly smudge . . . a pot of bubbling hot tar." Teams of U.S. observers who entered the cities in the aftermath were stunned at the immediate devastation, including the instantaneous incineration of both human beings and man-made structures, as well as the longer-lasting horror of radiation disease. The mushroom clouds over Hiroshima and Nagasaki would inaugurate a new "atomic age," in which dreams of peace were mingled with nightmares of Armageddon. But in those late summer days of 1945, most Americans sighed with relief. News reports on August 15 proclaimed Japan's surrender, VJ Day.

THE WAR AT HOME: THE ECONOMY

The success of the U.S. military effort in both Europe and Asia depended on mobilization at home. Ultimately, it was this mobilization that finally brought the depression of the 1930s to an end. But the war did more than restore prosperity. It transformed the nation's entire political economy—its government, its business and financial institutions, and its labor force.

GOVERNMENT'S ROLE IN THE ECONOMY

The federal bureaucracy nearly quadrupled in size during the war, as new economic agencies proliferated. The most powerful of these, the War Production Board, oversaw the conversion and expansion of factories, allocated resources, and enforced production priorities and schedules. The War Labor Board had jurisdiction over labor-management disputes, and the War Manpower Commission allocated labor to various industries. The Office of Price Administration regulated prices to control inflation and rationed such scarce commodities as gasoline, rubber, steel, shoes, coffee, sugar, and meat. Although most of the controls were abandoned after the war, the concept of greater governmental regulation of the economy survived.

From 1940 to 1945 the U.S. economy expanded rapidly. In each year of the war, GNP rose by 15 percent or more. When Roosevelt called for the production of 60,000 planes, shortly after Pearl Harbor, skeptics jeered. Yet within the next few years the nation produced nearly 300,000 planes. The Maritime Commission oversaw construction of more than 53 million tons of shipping. The previously stagnant economy spewed out prodigious quantities of other supplies, including 2.5 million trucks and 50 million pairs of shoes.

Striving to increase production, industry entered into an unprecedented relationship with government to promote scientific and technological research and development, "R&D." Government money subsidized new industries, such as electronics, and enabled others, such as rubber and chemicals, to transform their processes and products. The newly established Office of Scientific Research and Development entered into contracts for a variety of projects with universities and scientists. Under this program, radar, penicillin, rocket engines, and other new products were rapidly perfected for wartime use.

BUSINESS AND FINANCE

To finance the war effort, government spending rose from $9 billion in 1940 to $98 billion in 1944. In 1941 the national debt stood at $48 billion; by VJ Day it was $280 billion. With few goods to buy, Americans invested in war bonds, turning their savings into tanks and planes. Although war bonds provided a relatively insignificant contribution to defense spending, they did help drive the level of personal saving up to 25 percent of consumer income.

WOMEN ARE ENLISTED IN THE WAR EFFORT This picture of a Jeep assembly line at Willys-Overland in Toledo, Ohio, illustrates the extent to which women during the Second World War took over manufacturing jobs traditionally held by men. It was usually stressed, however, that the trend would be merely temporary. Photographs such as this, in which carefully groomed women are attired in dresses and aprons, conveyed a double message: Women needed to fill in for men who were away during the war, but they should retain their traditional symbols of femininity and be ready to resume more traditional roles after victory.

CHILDREN ARE ENLISTED IN THE WAR EFFORT   These children, flashing the "V-for-Victory" sign, stand atop a pile of scrap metal. Collecting scrap of all kinds for war production helped to engage millions of Americans on the home front.

As production shifted from autos to tanks, from refrigerators to guns, many consumer goods became scarce. Essentials such as food, fabrics, and gasoline were rationed and, consequently, were shared more equitably than they had been before the war. Higher taxes on wealthier Americans tended to redistribute income and narrow the gap between the poor and the well-to-do. War bonds, rationing, and progressive taxation gave Americans a sense of shared sacrifice and helped ease the class tensions of the 1930s.

As the war fostered an increase in personal savings and promoted a measure of income redistribution, however, it also facilitated the dismantling of many of the New Deal agencies most concerned with the interests of the poor. A Republican surge in the off-year elections of 1942—the GOP gained 44 seats in the House and 7 new senators—helped strengthen an anti–New Deal, conservative coalition in Congress. In 1943 Congress abolished the job creation programs run by the Works Progress Administration (WPA), the Civilian Conservation Corps (CCC), and the National Youth Administration (NYA) (see Chapter 25). It also shut down the Rural Electrification Administration (REA) and Farm Security Administration (FSA), agencies that had assisted impoverished rural areas. As business executives flocked to Washington to run the new wartime bureaus, the Roosevelt administration shifted its attitude toward big business from one of guarded hostility to one of cooperation.

Social programs withered as big businesses that were considered essential to victory flourished under government subsidies. What was "essential," of course, became a matter of definition. Coca-Cola and Wrigley's chewing gum won precious sugar allotments by arguing that GIs overseas "needed" to enjoy their products. Both companies prospered. The Kaiser Corporation, whose spectacular growth in the 1930s had been spurred by federal dam contracts, now turned its attention to the building of ships, aircraft, and military vehicles. Federal subsidies, low-interest loans, and tax breaks enabled factories to expand and retool.

The war concentrated power in the largest corporations. The enforcement of antitrust laws was postponed at Roosevelt's request. Legal challenges that had been years in preparation, such as the case against America's great oil cartel, were now tucked away. Congressional efforts to investigate alleged collusion in the awarding of government contracts and to increase assistance to small businesses made little progress in Washington's crisis atmosphere. The top 100 companies, which had provided 30 percent of the nation's total manufacturing output in 1940, were providing 70 percent by 1943.

The Workforce

During the first two years of military buildup, many workers who had been idled during the Depression were called back to work. Employment in heavy industry invariably went to men, and most of the skilled jobs went to whites. But as military service drained the supply of white male workers, women and minorities became more attractive as candidates for production jobs. Soon, both private employers and government were encouraging women to go to work, southern African Americans to move to northern industrial cities, and Mexicans to enter the United States under the *bracero* guest worker program.

Women were hired for jobs that had never been open to them before. They became welders, shipbuilders, lumberjacks, miners. As major league baseball languished from a lack of players, female teams sprang up to give new life to the national pastime. Many employers hired married women, who, before the war, were often banned even from such traditionally female occupations as teaching. Minority women moved into clerical or secretarial jobs, where they had not previously been welcome. Most workplaces, however, continued to be segregated by sex.

The character of unpaid labor, long provided mostly by women, also underwent significant change. Volunteer activities such as Red Cross projects, civil defense work, and recycling drives claimed more and more of the time of women, children, and older people. In the home, conservation was emphasized. Government propaganda exhorted homemakers: "Wear it out, use it up, make it do, or do without." Both in the home and in the factory, women's responsibilities and workloads increased.

The new labor market improved the economic position of African Americans generally. By executive order in June 1941, the president created the Fair Employment Practices Commission (FEPC), which tried to ban discrimination in hiring. In 1943 the government announced that it would not recognize as collective bargaining agents any unions that denied admittance to minorities. The War Labor Board outlawed the practice of paying different wages to whites and nonwhites doing the same job. Before the war, the African American population had been mainly southern, rural, and agricultural; within a few years, a substantial percentage of African Americans had become northern, urban, and industrial. Although employment discrimination was hardly eliminated, twice as many African Americans held skilled jobs at the end of the war as at the beginning.

For both men and women, the war brought higher wages and longer work hours. Although in 1943 the government got labor unions to limit demands for wage increases to 15 percent, overtime often raised paychecks far more. During the war, average weekly earnings rose nearly 70 percent. Farmers, who had suffered through many years of low prices and overproduction, doubled their income and then doubled it again.

LABOR UNIONS

The scarcity of labor during the war substantially strengthened the labor union movement. Union membership rose by 50 percent. Women and minority workers joined unions in unprecedented numbers, but the main beneficiaries of labor's new power were white males.

Especially on the national level, the commitment of organized labor to female workers was weak. Not a single woman served on the executive boards of either the AFL or the CIO. The International Brotherhood of Teamsters even required women to sign a statement that their union membership could be revoked when the war was over. Unions did fight for contracts stipulating equal pay for men and women in the same job, but these benefited women only as long as they held "male" jobs. The unions' primary purpose in advocating equal pay was to maintain wage levels for the men who would return to their jobs after the war. During the first year of peace, as employers trimmed their workforces, both business and unions gave special consideration to returning veterans and worked to ease women out of the labor force. Unions based their wage demands on the goal of securing male workers a "family wage," one that would be sufficient to support an entire family.

Some unions, reflecting the interests of their white male members, also supported racial discrimination. Union members believed that the hiring of lower-paid, nonwhite workers would jeopardize their own, better-paid positions. Early in the war, most AFL affiliates in the aircraft and shipbuilding industries had refused to accept African Americans as members. They quarreled with the FEPC over this policy throughout the war. As growing numbers of African Americans were hired, racial tensions in the workplace increased. In various factories across the country white workers walked off the job to protest the hiring of African Americans. Beyond revealing deep-seated racism, such incidents reflected the union leaders' fears of losing the organizing gains and recognition they had fought so hard to win during the 1930s.

The labor militancy of the 1930s was muted by a wartime no-strike pledge, but it nonetheless persisted. Despite no-strike assurances, for example, the United Mine Workers union called a strike in the bituminous coal fields in 1943. When the War Labor Board took a hard line against the union's demands, the strike was prolonged. In Detroit, disgruntled aircraft workers roamed the factory floors, cutting off the neckties of their supervisors; wildcat strikes erupted in St. Louis, Detroit, and Philadelphia. Congress responded by passing the Smith-Connally Act of 1943, which empowered the president to seize plants or mines if strikes interrupted war production. Even so, the war helped to strengthen organized labor's place in American life.

ASSESSING ECONOMIC CHANGE

Overall, the impact of the war on America's political economy was significant. During the war, the workplace became more inclusive in terms of gender and race than ever before, and so did labor unions. More people entered the paid labor force, and many of them earned more money than rationing restrictions allowed them to spend. Although some of these changes proved to be short-lived, the new precedents and expectations arising from the wartime experience could not be entirely effaced at war's end.

More than anything else, the institutional scale of American life was transformed. Big government, big business, and big labor all grew even bigger during the war years. Science and technology forged new links of mutual interest among these three sectors. The old America of small farms, small businesses, and small towns did not disappear. But urban-based, bureaucratized institutions increasingly organized life in postwar America.

THE WAR AT HOME: SOCIAL ISSUES

Dramatic social changes accompanied the wartime mobilization. Ordered by military service or attracted by employment, many people moved away from the communities where they had grown up. Even on the home front, the war involved constant sacrifice. The war, most Americans believed, was being fought to preserve democracy and individual freedom. Yet for many, wartime ideals highlighted everyday inequalities.

WARTIME PROPAGANDA

During the First World War, government propagandists had asked Americans to fight for a more democratic world and a permanent peace. But such idealistic goals had little appeal for the skeptical generation of the 1930s and 1940s. Sensitive to popular attitudes, the Roosevelt administration asked Americans to fight to preserve the "American way of life"—not to save the world.

Hollywood studios and directors eagerly answered the government's call by shaping inspiring and sentimental representations of American life. Called to make a series of government films entitled *Why We Fight,* Frank Capra contrasted Norman Rockwell–type characters with harrowing portrayals of the mass obedience and militarism in Germany, Italy, and Japan. A hundred or so Hollywood personalities received commissions to make films for the Army's Pictorial Division.

Print advertising also contributed to the wartime propaganda effort. Roosevelt encouraged advertisers to sell the benefits of freedom. Most obliged, and "freedom" often appeared in the guise of new washing machines, ingenious kitchen appliances, improved automobiles, a wider range of lipstick hues, and automation in a hundred forms. As soon as the war was over, the ads promised, American technological know-how would usher in a consumer's paradise.

In the spring of 1942, Roosevelt created the Office of War Information (OWI) to coordinate policies related to propaganda and censorship. Liberals charged that the OWI was dominated by advertising professionals who dealt in slogans rather than substance.

Freedom from Want

Conservatives blasted it as a purveyor of crass political advertisements for causes favored by Roosevelt and liberal Democrats. Despite such sniping, the OWI established branches throughout the world, published a magazine called *Victory,* and produced hundreds of films, posters, and radio broadcasts.

GENDER EQUALITY

As women took over jobs traditionally held by men, many people began to take more seriously the idea of gender equality. Some 350,000 women volunteered for military duty during the war; more than 1,000 women served as civilian pilots with the WASPs (Women's Airforce Service Pilots). Not everyone approved. But most in Congress came to support a women's corps, with full status, for each branch of the military, a step that had been thwarted during the First World War.

The military service of women, together with their new importance in the labor market, strengthened arguments for laws to guarantee equal treatment. But women's organizations themselves disagreed over how to advance women's opportunities. Organizations representing middle-class women strongly backed passage of an Equal Rights Amendment (ERA), but other groups, more responsive to the problems of poor women, opposed its passage. They saw it as a threat to the protective legislation, regulating hours and hazardous conditions, that women's rights crusaders had struggled to win earlier in the century. Should women continue to be accorded "protected" status in view of their vulnerability to exploitation in a male-directed workplace? Or should they fight for "equal" status?

Even as the war temporarily narrowed gender differences in employment, government policies and propaganda frequently framed changes in women's roles in highly traditional terms. Women's expanded participation in the workplace was often portrayed as a short-term sacrifice. Feminine stereotypes abounded. A typical ad suggesting that women take on farm work declared: "A woman can do anything if she knows she looks beautiful doing it." Despite the acceptance of women into the armed services, most were assigned to stateside clerical and supply jobs; only a relatively few women served overseas. Day care programs for mothers working outside their homes received reluctant and inadequate funding. The 3,000 centers set up during the war filled only a fraction of the need and were swiftly shut down after the war. Leading social scientists and welfare experts, mostly male, blamed working mothers for the apparent rise in juvenile delinquency and in the divorce rate during the war years.

The war also widened the symbolic gap between "femininity" and "masculinity." Military culture encouraged men to adopt a "pin-up" mentality toward women. Tanks and planes were decorated with symbols of female sexuality, and wartime fiction often associated manliness with brutality and casual sex. After the war, tough-guy fiction with a violent and misogynist edge, like Mickey Spillane's "Mike Hammer" series of detective novels, became one of the most successful formulas of popular culture.

RACIAL EQUALITY

Messages about race were as ambiguous as those related to gender. Before the Second World War, America had been a sharply segregated society. African Americans, disfranchised in the South and only beginning to achieve voting power in the North, had only limited access to the political, legal, or economic systems. The fight against fascism, however, challenged this old order in a number of ways.

Nazism, a philosophy based on the idea of racial inequality, exposed the racist underpinnings of much of 20th century social science theory. The view that racial difference was not a

"UNITED WE WIN"   Government posters created during the Second World War attempted to mute class and racial divisions and to offer images of all Americans united against fascism.

function of biology but a function of culture gained wider popular acceptance during the war. The implication was that a democratic and pluralistic society could accommodate racial difference. This new thinking helped to lay the foundation for the postwar struggle against discrimination.

The northward migration of African Americans accelerated demands for equality. Drawn by the promise of wartime jobs, nearly 750,000 African Americans relocated to northern cities, where many sensed the possibility of political power for the first time in their lives. They found an outspoken advocate of civil rights within the White House itself. First Lady Eleanor Roosevelt repeatedly antagonized southern Democrats and members of her husband's administration by her advocacy of civil rights and her participation in integrated social functions.

African Americans understood the irony of fighting for a country that denied them equality and challenged the government to live up to its own rhetoric about freedom and democracy. The *Amsterdam News,* a Harlem newspaper, called for a "Double V" campaign—victory at home as well as abroad. In January 1941 labor leader A. Philip Randolph threatened to lead tens of thousands of frustrated black workers in a march on Washington to demand more defense jobs and integration of the military forces. President Roosevelt viewed the march as potentially embarrassing to his administration and urged that it be canceled. Randolph's persistence, however, forced Roosevelt to make concessions. In return for Randolph's canceling the march, the president created the FEPC in June of that year. The FEPC initially seemed a victory for equal rights, but Roosevelt gave the agency little power over discriminatory employers.

Roosevelt also let stand the policy of segregation in the armed forces. "A jim crow army cannot fight for a free world," proclaimed the NAACP newspaper *The Crisis*. Yet General George C. Marshall, Secretary of War Stimson, and others remained opposed to change. African Americans were relegated to inferior jobs in the military and excluded from combat status. Toward the end of the war, when manpower shortages forced the administration to put African American troops into combat, they performed with distinction.

RACIAL TENSIONS

In industrial cities, the wartime boom threw already overcrowded, working-class neighborhoods into turmoil. Many of the residents of these neighborhoods came from European immigrant backgrounds or had migrated from rural areas. Wartime work provided their first real opportunity to escape from poverty, and they viewed the minority newcomers as unwelcome rivals for jobs and housing. In 1943, for example, it was estimated that between 6,000 and 10,000 African Americans arrived in Los Angeles every month. Once there, their living options were effectively limited to a few overcrowded neighborhoods segregated by landlords' practices and by California's restrictive housing covenants—legal agreements prohibiting the sale of homes to certain religious or racial groups.

Around the country, public housing projects presented a particularly explosive dilemma to federal officials charged with administering the supply of desperately needed housing. Whites resisted the forced integration of public housing; nonwhites denounced the government for vacillating. In Buffalo, New York, threats of violence caused the cancellation of one housing project. In Detroit in June 1943, when police escorted African American tenants into a new complex, a full-scale race riot erupted.

Racial disturbances were not restricted to confrontations between whites and blacks. In Los Angeles, the so-called "zoot suit" incidents of 1943 pitted whites against Mexican Americans. Minor incidents between young Mexican American men wearing "zoot suits"—flamboyant outfits that featured oversized coats and trousers—and soldiers and sailors from nearby military bases escalated into virtual warfare between the zoot-suiters and local police. The Roosevelt administration feared that the zoot suit violence might have a negative effect on the Good Neighbor Policy in Latin America. The president's Coordinator of Inter-American Affairs, therefore, allocated federal money to train Spanish-speaking Americans for wartime jobs, to improve education in barrios, and to open up more opportunities in colleges throughout the American Southwest.

American Indians comprised a significant group of new migrants to urban areas during the war. The war introduced powerful pressures for migration and assimilation. By the end of the war, approximately 25,000 Indian men and several hundred Indian women had served in the armed forces, where Indians were fully integrated with whites. Some 40,000 other Indians found war work in nearby cities, many leaving their reservation for the first time. For Indians, the white-dominated towns and cities tended to be strange and hostile places. Many Indians moved back and forth between city and reservation, holding their urban jobs for only a few months at a time while seeking to live between two quite different worlds.

For African Americans, Latinos, and Indians, fighting for the "American way of life" represented a commitment not to the past but to the future. Increasingly, Americans of all backgrounds were realizing that racial grievances had to be addressed. In Detroit, for example, the local NAACP chapter emerged from the wartime years with a strong base from which to fight for jobs and political power. The Committee (later, Congress) on Racial Equality (CORE), an organization founded in 1942 and composed of whites and blacks who advocated nonviolent resistance to segregation, devised new strategies during the war. CORE activists staged sit-ins to integrate restaurants, theaters, and even prison dining halls in Washington, D.C.

However, of all the minority groups in the United States, Japanese Americans suffered most grievously during the war. In the two months following the attack on Pearl Harbor, West Coast communities became engulfed in hysteria against people of Japanese descent. One military report concluded that a "large, unassimilated, tightly knit racial group, bound to an enemy nation by strong ties of race, culture, custom, and religion . . . constituted a menace" that justified extraordinary action.

Despite lack of evidence of disloyalty, government officials in February 1942 issued Executive Order 9066, directing the relocation and internment of first- and second-generation Japanese Americans (called Issei and Nisei, respectively) at inland camps. Forced to abandon their possessions or sell them for a pittance, nearly 130,000 Japanese Americans were confined in flimsy barracks, enclosed by barbed wire and under armed guard. Two-thirds of the detainees were native-born U.S. citizens. Many had been substantial landowners in California's agricultural industries. In December 1944 a divided Supreme Court upheld the constitutionality of Japanese relocation in *Korematsu* v. *U.S.* (In 1988, however, Congress officially apologized for the injustice and authorized the payment of a cash indemnity to any affected person who was still living.)

Despite the internment, the suffering and sacrifice of Japanese American soldiers became legendary: The 100th Battalion, comprised of Nisei from Hawaii, was nearly wiped out; 57 percent of the famed 442nd Regimental Combat Team were killed or wounded in the mountains of Italy; and 6,000 members of the Military Intelligence Service provided invaluable service in the Pacific theater.

Racial hostilities reflected the underlying strains in America's social fabric, but there were other tensions pulling at Americans as well. Rifts developed between city dwellers and migrants from rural areas. Californians derided the "Okies," people who had fled the Dust Bowl of Oklahoma, as ignorant and dirty. In Chicago, migrants from Appalachia were met with a similar reception. Many ethnic communities, by preserving the language and culture of their homelands, also reflected social rivalries and divisions.

Despite the underlying fragmentation of American society, the symbol of the "melting pot," together with appeals to nationalism, remained powerful. Wartime propaganda stressed the theme of national unity. The Second World War was called a "people's war," and America's "melting pot" was purposefully contrasted with the German and Japanese obsessions with racial purity. Wartime movies, plays, and music reinforced a sense of national community by building on cultural nationalism and expressing pride in American historical themes.

The great movements of population during the war eroded geographical distinctions, and wartime demands for additional labor weakened the barriers to many occupations. As each of America's racial and ethnic minorities established records of distinguished military service, the claim of equality—"Americans All," in the words of a wartime slogan—took on greater moral force. The possibility for more equitable participation in the mainstream of American life, together with rhetoric extolling social solidarity and freedom, provided a foundation for the civil rights movements of the decades ahead.

SHAPING THE PEACE

On April 13, 1945, newspaper headlines across the country mourned, "President Roosevelt Dead." Sorrow and shock were widespread and profound—in the armed forces, in diplomatic conference halls, and among factory workers, farmers, and bureaucrats. Roosevelt had accumulated a host of critics and enemies, yet he had been the most popular president in modern history, and he left an enduring imprint on American life.

Compared with the legacy of Roosevelt, Vice President Harry Truman's stature seemed impossibly small. Born on a farm near Independence, Missouri, Harry Truman had served in France during the First World War. After the war, he went into politics in Kansas City. He was elected to the Senate in 1934 and was chosen as Roosevelt's running mate in 1944. Truman was poorly prepared for the job of president. He knew little about international affairs or about any informal understandings that Roosevelt may have made with foreign leaders.

Despite his inexperience, Truman built on Roosevelt's many wartime conferences and agreements to shape the framework of international relations for the next half-century.

THE UNITED NATIONS AND INTERNATIONAL ECONOMIC ORGANIZATIONS

In the Atlantic Charter of 1941 and at a conference in Moscow in October 1943, the Allies had already pledged to create an international organization to replace the defunct League of Nations. The new United Nations (UN) fulfilled Woodrow Wilson's vision of an international body to deter aggressor nations. At the Dumbarton Oaks Conference in Washington in August 1944 and a subsequent meeting in San Francisco in April 1945, the Allies worked out the organizational structure of the UN. It would have a General Assembly, in which each member nation would be represented and have one vote. And it would have a Security Council, whose makeup would include five permanent members—the United States, Great Britain, the Soviet Union, France, and China—and six rotating members. The Security Council would have primary responsibility for maintaining peace, but any individual member of the council could exercise an absolute veto over any council decision. Finally, a UN Secretariat would handle day-to-day business, and an Economic and Social Council would promote social and economic advancement throughout the world.

The U.S. Senate accepted the UN charter in July 1945 with only two dissenting votes. This resounding victory for internationalism contrasted sharply with the Senate's rejection of membership in the League of Nations after the First World War. Americans of an earlier generation had worried that internationalist policies might impinge on their country's ability to follow its own national interests. But following the Second World War, because U.S. power clearly dominated emerging organizations such as the UN, Americans thought it less likely that decisions of international bodies would clash with their nation's own foreign policies. In addition, Americans recognized that the war had partly resulted from the lack of a coordinated, international response to aggression during the 1930s.

Postwar economic settlements also illustrated a growing acceptance of new international organizations. In dealing with the world economy, U.S. policymakers endeavored to establish stable exchange rates for currency, create an international lending authority, and eliminate discriminatory trade practices.

At the Bretton Woods (New Hampshire) Conference of 1944, Americans had worked toward these objectives. The agreements reached at Bretton Woods created the International Monetary Fund (IMF), designed to maintain a stable system of international exchange by ensuring that each national currency could be converted into any other currency at a fixed rate. Exchange rates could be altered only with the agreement of the fund. The International Bank for Reconstruction and Development, later renamed the World Bank, was also created to provide loans to war-battered countries and to promote the resumption of world trade. In 1947 a General Agreement on Tariffs and Trade (GATT) created the institutional structure for implementing free and fair trade agreements.

SPHERES OF INTEREST AND POSTWAR POLITICAL SETTLEMENTS

In wartime conversations, Stalin, Churchill, and Roosevelt all had assumed that powerful nations would have special "spheres of influence" in the postwar world. As early as January 1942 the Soviet ambassador to the United States reported to Stalin that Roosevelt had tacitly assented to Soviet postwar control over the Baltic states of Lithuania, Latvia, and Estonia. In 1944 Stalin and Churchill agreed informally and secretly that Britain would continue its dominance in Greece and that the Soviets could dominate Romania and Bulgaria. Roosevelt understood why the Soviets wanted friendly states on their vulnerable western border, but, at the Teheran Conference of November 1943, he told Stalin that American voters of Polish, Latvian, Lithuanian, and Estonian descent expected their homelands to be independent after the war.

Precisely how Roosevelt intended to handle the issue of Soviet influence in the postwar world will never be known. As long as Soviet armies were essential to Germany's defeat, Roosevelt cooperated with Stalin whenever possible. After Roosevelt's death, however, the military results of the war, particularly the USSR's powerful position in eastern Europe, strongly influenced postwar settlements regarding territory. On issues of governance—particularly in Germany, Poland, and Korea—splits between U.S. and Soviet interests widened. Germany, especially, became a focus and a symbol of bipolar tensions.

Early in the war, both the United States and the Soviet Union had urged the dismemberment and deindustrialization of Nazi Germany after its defeat. At a conference held at Yalta, in Ukraine, in early February 1945, the three Allied powers agreed to divide Germany into four zones of occupation (with France as the fourth occupation force). Later, as relations among the victors cooled, this temporary division of Germany permanently solidified into a Soviet-dominated zone in the East and the three Allied zones in the West. Berlin, the German capital, also was divided, even though it lay totally within the Soviet zone.

Postwar rivalries also centered on Poland. At Yalta, the Soviets agreed to permit free elections in Poland after the war and to create a government "responsible to the will of the people," but Stalin also believed that the other Allied leaders had tacitly accepted the idea that Poland would fall within the Soviet's postwar sphere of influence. The agreement at Yalta was ambiguous at best. The war was still at a critical stage, and the western Allies chose to sacrifice clarity over the Polish issue in order to encourage cooperation with the Soviets. After Yalta, the Soviets assumed that Poland would be in their sphere of influence, but many Americans charged the Soviets with bad faith for failing to hold free elections and for not relinquishing control.

In Asia, military realities also influenced postwar settlements. At Teheran in November 1943 and again at Yalta, Stalin pledged to send troops to Asia as soon as Germany had been defeated. But when U.S. policymakers learned that the atomic bomb was ready for use against Japan, they became eager to limit Soviet involvement in the Pacific theater. The first atomic bomb fell on Hiroshima just one day before the Soviets were to enter the war against Japan, and the United States took sole charge of the occupation and postwar reorganization of Japan. The Soviet Union and the United States split Korea, which had been occupied by Japan, into separate zones of occupation. Here, as in Germany, the zones later emerged as two antagonistic states (see Chapter 27).

The fate of the European colonies that had been seized by Japan in Southeast Asia was another issue that remained unresolved in the planning for peace. The United States would have preferred to see the former British and French colonies become independent nations, but U.S. policymakers also worried about the left-leaning politics of many anticolonial nationalist movements. As the United States developed an anticommunist foreign policy, it moved to support Britain and France in their efforts to reassemble their colonial empires.

In the Philippines, the United States honored its long-standing pledge to grant independence. A friendly government that agreed to respect U.S. economic interests and military bases took power in 1946 and enlisted American advisers to help deal with leftist rebels. The Mariana, the Caroline, and the Marshall Islands, all of which had been captured by Japan during the war, were designated Trust Territories of the Pacific by the United Nations and placed under U.S. administration in 1947.

Although the countries of Latin America had not been very directly involved in the war or the peace settlements, U.S. relations with them were also profoundly affected by the war. During the 1930s Roosevelt's Good Neighbor Policy had helped to improve U.S.–Latin American relations. The Office of Inter-American Affairs (OIAA), created in 1937, began an aggressive and successful policy of expanding cultural and economic ties. Just weeks after the German invasion of Poland in 1939, at the Pan American Conference in Panama City, Latin American leaders showed that the hemisphere was nearly united on the side of the Allies. The conferees declared a 300-mile-wide band of neutrality in waters around the hemisphere (excepting Canada). After U.S. entry into the war, at a January 1942 conference in Rio de Janeiro, all the Latin American countries except Chile and Argentina broke off diplomatic ties with the Axis governments. When naval warfare in the Atlantic severed commercial connections between Latin America and Europe, Latin American countries became critical suppliers of raw materials to the United States, to the benefit of both.

Wartime conferences and settlements avoided clear decisions about creating a Jewish homeland in the Middle East. The Second World War prompted survivors of the Holocaust and Jews from around the world to take direct action. Zionism, the movement to found a Jewish state in their ancient homeland, drew thousands of Jews to Palestine, where they began to carve out the new state of Israel. Middle Eastern affairs, which had been of small concern to U.S. policymakers before 1941, would take on greater urgency after 1948, when the Truman administration recognized the new state of Israel.

CHRONOLOGY

1931	Japanese forces seize Manchuria
1933	Hitler takes power in Germany
1936	Spanish Civil War begins • Germany and Italy agree to cooperate as the Axis Powers
1937	Neutrality Act broadens provisions of Neutrality Acts of 1935 and 1936 • Roosevelt makes "Quarantine" speech • Japan invades China
1938	France and Britain appease Hitler at Munich
1939	Hitler and Stalin sign Soviet-German nonaggression pact • Hitler invades Poland; war breaks out in Europe • Congress amends Neutrality Act to assist Allies
1940	Paris falls after German *blitzkreig* (June) • Battle of Britain carried to U.S. by radio broadcasts • Roosevelt makes "destroyers-for-bases" deal with Britain • Selective Service Act passed • Roosevelt wins third term
1941	Lend-Lease established • Roosevelt creates Fair Employment Practices Commission • Atlantic Charter proclaimed by Roosevelt and Churchill • U.S. engages in undeclared naval war in North Atlantic • Congress narrowly repeals Neutrality Act • Japanese forces attack Pearl Harbor (December 7)
1942	Rio de Janeiro Conference (January) • President signs Executive Order 9066 for internment of Japanese Americans (February) • General MacArthur driven from Philippines (May) • U.S. victorious in Battle of Midway (June) • German army defeated at Battle of Stalingrad (August) • Operation TORCH begins (November)
1943	Axis armies in North Africa surrender (May) • Allies invade Sicily (July) and Italy (September) • "Zoot suit" incidents in Los Angeles; racial violence in Detroit • Allies begin drive toward Japan through South Pacific islands
1944	Allies land at Normandy (D-Day, June 6) • Allied armies reach Paris (August) • Allies turn back Germans at Battle of the Bulge (September) • Roosevelt reelected to fourth term • Bretton Woods Conference creates IMF and World Bank • Dumbarton Oaks Conference establishes plan for UN
1945	U.S. firebombs Japan • Yalta Conference (February) • Roosevelt dies; Truman becomes president (April) • Germany surrenders (May) • Potsdam Conference (July) • Hiroshima and Nagasaki hit with atomic bombs (August) • Japan signs terms of surrender (September) • United Nations established (December)

CONCLUSION

The world changed dramatically during the Second World War. Wartime mobilization ended the Great Depression and shifted the New Deal's focus away from domestic social reform and toward international concerns. It brought a historic victory over dictatorial, brutal regimes, and the United States emerged as the world's preeminent power.

At home, the war brought significant change. A more powerful national government, concerned with preserving national security, assumed nearly complete power over the nation's economy. New, cooperative ties were forged among government, business, labor, and scientific researchers. All sectors worked together to provide the seemingly miraculous growth in productivity that ultimately won the war.

The early 1940s sharpened debates over the nature of liberty and equality. Many Americans saw the Second World War as a struggle to protect and preserve the power and liberties they already enjoyed. Others, inspired by a struggle against racism and injustice abroad, insisted that a war for freedom should help expand equal rights at home.

News of Japan's surrender prompted the largest celebration in the nation's history. International conferences established a structure for the United Nations and for new, global economic institutions. Still, Americans remained uncertain about post-war reconstruction of former enemies and about future relations with wartime allies, particularly the Soviet Union. Domestically, the wrenching dislocations of war took their toll. And, of course, the nation now faced the future without the charismatic leadership of Franklin D. Roosevelt.

THE AGE OF CONTAINMENT, 1946–1954

The Second World War, heralded as an effort to preserve and protect the fabric of American life, had ended up transforming it. The struggle against fascism had brought foreign policy issues to the center of political debate, and the international struggles of the postwar period kept them there. As the Second World War gave way to a "Cold War" between the United States and the Soviet Union, Washington adopted global policies to "contain" the Soviet Union and to enhance America's economic and military security. Preoccupation with national security abroad, however, raised calls for limiting dissent at home.

The Cold War years from 1946 to 1954 also produced questions about government power. What role should Washington play in planning the postwar economy? What should be its relationship to social policymaking, especially efforts to achieve equality? These broad questions first emerged during the presidency of Democrat Harry Truman, from 1945 to 1953. They would remain central concerns during the administration of his Republican successor, Dwight David Eisenhower.

CREATING A NATIONAL SECURITY STATE, 1945–1949

The wartime alliance between the United States and the Soviet Union had never been anything but a marriage of convenience. Defeat of the Axis Powers had demanded that the two governments cooperate, but collaboration scarcely lasted beyond VE Day. Relations between the United States and the Soviet Union steadily degenerated into a Cold War of suspicion and growing tension.

ONSET OF THE COLD WAR

Historians have discussed the origins of the Cold War from many different perspectives. The traditional interpretation focuses on Soviet expansionism, stressing a traditional Russian appetite for new territory, or an ideological zeal to spread international communism, or some interplay between the two. According to this view, the United States needed to take as hard a line as possible. Other historians—generally called revisionists—argue that the Soviet Union's obsession with securing its borders was an understandable response to the invasion of its territory during both world wars. The United States, in this view, should have tried to reassure the Soviets by seeking accommodation, instead of pursuing policies that intensified Stalin's fears. Still other scholars maintain that assigning blame obscures the clash of deep-seated rival interests that made postwar tensions between the two superpowers inevitable.

In any view, the role of Harry Truman proved important. Truman initially hoped that he could somehow cut a deal with Soviet Premier Joseph Stalin. However, as disagreements between the two former allies mounted, Truman came to rely on advisers hostile to Stalin's Soviet Union.

The atomic bomb provided an immediate source of friction. At the Potsdam Conference of July 1945, Truman had casually remarked to Stalin, "We have a new weapon of unusual destructive force." Stalin immediately ordered a crash program to develop atomic weapons of his own. Truman hoped that the bomb would scare the Soviets, and it did. Historians still debate whether it frightened the Soviets into more cautious behavior or made them more fearful and aggressive.

In 1946 Truman authorized Bernard Baruch, a presidential adviser and special representative to the United Nations, to offer a plan for the international control of atomic power. The Baruch plan called for full disclosure by all UN member nations of nuclear research and materials, creation of an international authority to ensure compliance, and destruction of all U.S. atomic weapons once these first steps were completed. Andrei A. Gromyko, the Soviet ambassador to the UN, countered by proposing that the United States unilaterally destroy its atomic weapons first, with international disclosure and control to follow. The United States refused. Both sides used this deadlock to justify a stepped-up arms race.

Other sources of Soviet-American friction involved U.S. loan policies and the Soviet sphere of influence in Eastern Europe. Truman abruptly suspended lend-lease assistance to the Soviet Union in early September 1945. Subsequently, Truman's administration linked extension of U.S. reconstruction loans to its goal of rolling back Soviet power in Eastern Europe. However, lack of capital and signs of Western hostility provided the Soviets with excuses for tightening their grip. A Soviet sphere of influence, which Stalin called defensive and Truman labeled proof of communist expansionism, emerged in Eastern Europe. Suspicion steadily widened into mutual distrust.

From 1947 on, Harry Truman placed his personal stamp on the presidency by focusing on the fight against the Soviet Union. The menace of an "international communist conspiracy" was said to justify extraordinary measures to ensure U.S. national security. The claim of protecting "national security" allowed Truman to justify policy initiatives, in both foreign and domestic affairs, that extended the reach and power of the executive branch of government.

CONTAINMENT ABROAD: THE TRUMAN DOCTRINE

In March 1947, the president announced what became known as the Truman Doctrine when he addressed Congress on the civil war in Greece, a conflict in which communist-led insurgents were trying to topple a corrupt but pro-Western government. Historically, Greece had fallen within Great Britain's sphere of influence. But Britain could no longer maintain its formerly strong presence there or in the Middle East. A leftist victory in Greece, Truman's advisers claimed, would open neighboring Turkey to Soviet subversion. Seeking to justify U.S. aid to Greece and Turkey, Truman addressed Congress on March 12, 1947, in dramatic terms.

U.S. security interests, according to this Truman Doctrine, were now worldwide. Truman declared that the fate of "free peoples" everywhere hung in the balance. Unless the United

States unilaterally aided countries "who are resisting attempted subversion by armed minorities or by outside pressures," totalitarian communism would spread around the world and threaten the security of the United States itself.

Initially, the Truman Doctrine's global vision of national security encountered skepticism. Henry Wallace, the president's most visible Democratic critic, chided Truman for exaggerating the expansive nature of Soviet foreign policy and its threat to the United States. Conservative Republicans looked suspiciously at the increase of executive power and the vast expenditures that the Truman Doctrine seemed to imply. If Truman wanted to win support for his position, Republican Senator Arthur Vandenberg had already advised, he would need to "scare hell" out of people, something that Truman proved quite willing to do.

The rhetorical strategy worked. With backing from both Republicans and Democrats, Truman's request for $400 million in assistance to Greece and Turkey, most of it in military aid, was passed by Congress in the spring of 1947. This vote signaled broad, bipartisan support for a national security policy that came to be called "containment."

The term "containment" was first used in a 1947 article in the influential journal *Foreign Affairs*, written under the pseudonym "X" by George Kennan, the State Department's leading expert on Soviet affairs. Kennan argued that the "main element" in any U.S. policy "must be that of a long-term, patient but firm and vigilant containment of Russian expansive tendencies." The article quickly became associated with the alarmist tone of the Truman Doctrine.

Containment thus became the catchphrase for a global, anticommunist, national security policy. In the popular view, containment linked all leftist insurgencies, wherever they occurred, to a totalitarian movement controlled from Moscow that directly threatened the United States. Although foreign policy debates regularly included sharp disagreements over precisely *how* to pursue the goal of containment, few Americans dared to question *why* the country needed a far-flung, activist foreign policy.

TRUMAN'S LOYALTY PROGRAM

Nine days after proclaiming the Truman Doctrine, the president issued Executive Order 9835, which called for a system of loyalty boards empowered to determine whether there were "reasonable grounds" for believing that any government employee belonged to an organization or held political ideas that might pose a "security risk" to the United States. People judged to be security risks would lose their government jobs. The Truman loyalty program also authorized the attorney general's office to identify organizations it considered subversive, and in December 1947 the first Attorney General's List was released.

In developing the loyalty program, the Truman administration needed to gauge the extent of Soviet espionage activities in the United States. Although few historians ever doubted that the Soviets carried on spy operations, scholars have disagreed about their scope and success. Were Soviet agents operating only at the fringes or had they penetrated the top levels of the U.S. government? Were they supplying information that might have been obtained almost anywhere or were they stealing vital national secrets? As early as 1943, an Army counterintelligence unit had begun secretly intercepting transmissions between Moscow and the United States. Collected (and finally released to the public in 1995) as the "Venona files," these intercepted messages suggested that the USSR had several agents in wartime government agencies, including the Office of War Information and the top-secret OSS. Moscow began obtaining secret information about U.S. atomic work in 1944. The issue of Soviet spies, in short, was a legitimate cause of concern.

Curiously, the national security bureaucrats who intercepted the Soviet messages seem to have told neither the president nor his attorney general anything about their own super-secret operation or the intelligence being gathered. Truman's apparent lack of clear information may help to explain his inconsistent justification for the loyalty program. On the one hand, the president claimed that there were only a few security risks in the government but that their potential to do harm demanded a response that was unprecedented in peacetime. On the other hand, the president's program also clashed with the argument that a limited internal security threat logically demanded a limited, carefully crafted governmental response. Truman's approach angered both civil libertarians, who charged the president with going too far, and staunch anticommunists, who accused him of doing too little to fight the Red Menace at home.

The National Security Act, the Marshall Plan, and the Berlin Crisis

The National Security Act of 1947 created several new bureaucracies. It began the process that transformed the old Navy and War departments into a new Department of Defense, finally established in 1949. It instituted another new arm of the executive branch, the National Security Council (NSC), with broad authority over the planning of foreign policy. It established the Air Force as a separate service equal to the Army and Navy. And it created the Central Intelligence Agency (CIA) to gather information and to undertake covert activities in support of the nation's newly defined security interests.

The CIA proved the most flexible arm of the national security bureaucracy. Shrouded from public scrutiny, it used its secret funds to finance and encourage anticommunist activities around the globe. The CIA cultivated ties with anti-Soviet groups in Eastern Europe and even within the Soviet Union itself. It helped finance pro-U.S. labor unions in Western Europe to curtail the influence of leftist organizations. It orchestrated covert campaigns to prevent the Italian Communist Party from winning an electoral victory in 1948 and to bolster anticommunist parties in France, Japan, and elsewhere.

Truman's administration also linked economic policies in Western Europe to the doctrine of containment. Concerned that the region's severe economic problems might embolden leftist, pro-Soviet political movements, Secretary of State George Marshall sought to strengthen the economies of Western Europe. Shortly after Congress approved funding for the Truman Doctrine, the secretary proposed the Marshall Plan, under which governments in Western Europe would coordinate their plans for postwar economic reconstruction with the help of funds provided by the United States. Between 1946 and 1951, nearly $13 billion in U.S. assistance was distributed to 17 Western European nations.

The Marshall Plan proved a stunning success. In response to charges that it was a "giveaway" program, the administration pointed out that it opened up both markets and investment opportunities in Western Europe to American businesses. Moreover, it helped stabilize the European economy by quadrupling industrial production within its first few years. Improved standards of living enhanced political stability and helped undermine left-wing political parties in Europe.

American policymakers believed that to revitalize Europe under the Marshall Plan they would first have to restore the economy of Germany, which was still divided into zones of occupation. In June 1948 the United States, Great Britain, and France announced a plan for currency reform that would be the first step in merging their sectors of occupation into a federal German republic. Soviet leaders were alarmed. Having twice been invaded by Germany during the preceding 35 years, they wanted a reunited but weak Germany. Hoping to sidetrack Western plans for Germany, in June 1948 the Soviets cut off all highways, railroads, and water routes linking West Berlin to West Germany.

This Soviet blockade of Berlin failed. Air routes to the city remained open, and American and British pilots, in what became known as the Berlin Airlift, delivered tons of supplies to the city's beleaguered residents. Truman reinstated the draft and sent two squadrons of B-29 bombers to Britain. Recognizing his defeat, Stalin abandoned the blockade in May 1949. The Soviets then created the German Democratic Republic out of their East German sector, and West Berlin survived as an enclave tied to the West.

THE ELECTION OF 1948

National security issues helped Harry Truman win the 1948 election, a victory that capped a remarkable political comeback. Truman had been losing the support of some Democrats, led by Henry A. Wallace, who thought his containment policies too militant. In the off-year national election of 1946, voters had given the Republicans control of Congress for the first time since 1928. Although his standing in public opinion polls had risen slowly in 1947 and 1948, most political pundits thought Truman had little chance to win the presidency in his own right in 1948. Challenged from the left by a new Progressive Party, which nominated Wallace, and from the right by both the Republican nominee, Thomas E. Dewey, and Strom Thurmond, the candidate of the States' Rights Party, or "Dixiecrats," Truman waged a vigorous campaign. He called Congress into special session, presented it with domestic policy proposals that were

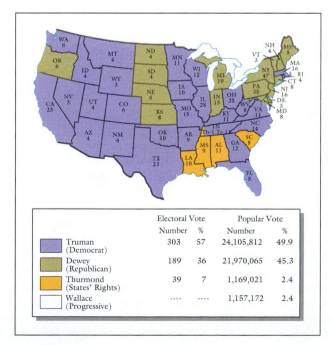

		Electoral Vote		Popular Vote	
		Number	%	Number	%
	Truman (Democrat)	303	57	24,105,812	49.9
	Dewey (Republican)	189	36	21,970,065	45.3
	Thurmond (States' Rights)	39	7	1,169,021	2.4
	Wallace (Progressive)	----	----	1,157,172	2.4

PRESIDENTIAL ELECTION, 1948

DEWEY DEFEATS TRUMAN?   Contrary to the predictions that had led to this newspaper headline, Harry Truman defeated Thomas Dewey in the close election of 1948. The "little man from Missouri" would continue to pursue containment abroad.

anathema to the GOP, and then denounced the "Republican Eightieth Congress, that do-nothing, good-for-nothing, worst Congress."

Thomas Dewey proved a cautious, lackluster campaigner. A pro-Democratic newspaper caricatured Dewey's standard speech as four "historic sentences: Agriculture is important. Our rivers are full of fish. You cannot have freedom without liberty. The future lies ahead." Truman, for his part, conducted an old-style campaign. He moved from town to town, stopping to denounce Dewey and Henry Wallace from the back of a railroad car. Dewey was plotting "a real hatchet job on the New Deal," and the Republican Party was controlled by a cabal of "cunning men" who were planning "a return of the Wall Street economic dictatorship," Truman charged. "Give 'em hell, Harry!" shouted enthusiastic crowds. In November, Truman won only 49.9 percent of the popular vote but gained a solid majority in the electoral college.

Truman's victory now seems less surprising to historians than it did to political analysts in 1948. Despite Republican electoral gains in the congressional elections of 1946, the Democratic Party was far from enfeebled. Indeed, the Democrats running for Congress in 1948, who identified themselves with Roosevelt rather than with Truman, generally polled a higher percentage of the popular vote in their districts than did Truman himself. Still, the loyalty of voters to the memory of Franklin Roosevelt and to his New Deal coalition helped Truman.

Meanwhile, Truman commanded a constituency of his own by virtue of his anticommunist policies. In this sense, Truman's presidency established a pattern that would persist for several decades: If Democratic candidates could avoid appearing "soft" or "weak" on national security issues, they stood a good chance of being elected president. Truman's hard-line national security credentials proved especially effective against Henry Wallace. Hampered by his refusal to reject the support of Communist Party members, Wallace failed to win a single electoral vote and received less than 3 percent of the popular tally.

THE ERA OF THE KOREAN WAR, 1949–1952

To carry out the containment policy, the Truman administration marshaled the nation's economic and military resources. A series of Cold War crises in 1949 heightened its anti-communist fervor and deepened its focus on national security issues.

NATO, CHINA, AND THE BOMB

In April 1949 the United States, Canada, and 10 European nations formed the North Atlantic Treaty Organization (NATO). Members of NATO pledged that an attack against one would

The Cold War split Europe into two opposing alliances. Germany was divided into two countries: The Federal Republic of Germany (West Germany) and the German Democratic Republic (East Germany). Berlin, the former capital of Germany, was also divided. In 1949 NATO was formed, and in 1955 the Warsaw Pact came into existence.

THE DIVISION OF BERLIN

American Zone
British Zone
French Zone
Soviet Zone

(The American, British, and French zones were consolidated as West Berlin)

NATO Countries
Warsaw Pact Countries
Nonaligned Countries

DIVIDED GERMANY AND THE NATO ALLIANCE

automatically be considered an attack against all. Some U.S. leaders worried about the implications of NATO. Republican Senator Robert Taft of Ohio declared that it was a provocation to the Soviet Union and an "entangling alliance" that defied common sense, violated the traditional U.S. foreign policy of nonentanglement, and threatened constitutional government by eclipsing Congress's power to declare war. But the NATO concept prevailed, and the idea of pursuing containment through such "collective security" pacts expanded during the 1950s.

Meanwhile, events in China elevated Cold War tensions. Between 1945 and 1948 the United States extended to Jiang Jieshi's government a billion dollars in military aid and another billion in economic assistance. But Jiang steadily lost ground to the communist forces of Mao Zedong. Experienced U.S. diplomats privately predicted that Jiang's downfall was inevitable, but the Truman administration continued publicly to portray Jiang as a respected leader of "free China" and to prop up his regime.

In 1949, when Mao's armies forced Jiang off the mainland to the offshore island of Formosa (Taiwan), many Americans wondered how communist forces could have triumphed. Financed by conservative business leaders, a powerful "China lobby" excoriated Truman and his new secretary of state, Dean Acheson, for being "soft" on communism and spoke of a global communist conspiracy directed from Moscow. Responding to the criticism, Acheson and Truman escalated their anticommunist rhetoric. For more than 20 years, even after friction between China and the Soviet Union became evident, the United States refused to recognize or deal with Mao's "Red China."

Late in 1949 the threat became even more alarming. Word reached Washington in September that the Soviets had exploded a crude atomic device, marking the end of the U.S. nuclear monopoly. Already besieged by critics who saw a world filled with Soviet gains and American defeats, Truman authorized the development of a new bomb based upon the still unproven concept of nuclear fusion. The decision to build this "hydrogen bomb" wedded the doctrine of containment to the creation of ever more deadly nuclear technology.

NSC-68

Prompted by events of 1949, the Truman administration reviewed its foreign policy assumptions. The task of conducting this review fell to Paul Nitze, a hard-liner who produced a top-secret policy paper officially identified as National Security Council document number 68 (NSC-68). It opened with an emotional account of a global ideological clash between "freedom," spread by U.S. power, and "slavery," promoted by the Soviet Union as the center of "international communism." Warning against any negotiations with the Soviets, the report urged a full-scale offensive to enlarge U.S. power. It endorsed covert action, economic pressure, more vigorous propaganda efforts, and a massive military buildup. Because Americans might oppose larger military spending and budget deficits, the report warned, U.S. actions should be labeled as "defensive" and be presented as a stimulus to the economy rather than as a drain on national resources.

THE KOREAN WAR

The dire warnings of NSC-68 seemed confirmed in June 1950 when communist North Korea attacked South Korea. The Truman administration portrayed the move as a simple case of Soviet-inspired aggression against a "free" state. Truman invoked once again the policy of containment: "If aggression is successful in Korea, we can expect it to spread through Asia and Europe to this hemisphere." The Korean situation, however, defied such simplistic analysis. Korea had been occupied by Japan between 1905 and 1945, and after Japan's defeat in the Second World War, Koreans had expected to establish their own independent state. Instead, the Soviet and U.S. zones of occupation resulting from the war were transformed into political entities. Korea became two states, split at the 38th parallel. The Soviet Union supported a communist government in the North under the dictatorial Kim Il-sung; the United States backed Syngman Rhee to head the unsteady yet autocratic government in the South.

But Korea could not be easily split along an arbitrary geographic line. It remained a single society, though it was riven by political factions as well as by ethnic and religious divisions. Rhee's oppressive regime generated opposition in the South. As discontent spread, Kim moved troops across the 38th parallel on June 25, 1950, to attempt unification. Earlier, he had consulted both Soviet and Chinese leaders about his plans and received their support, after assuring them that a U.S. military response was highly unlikely.

The fighting in Korea soon escalated into an international conflict. The Soviets were boycotting the United Nations on the day the invasion was launched. Consequently, they were not present to veto a U.S. proposal to send a peacekeeping force to Korea. Under UN auspices, the United States rushed assistance to the dictatorial Rhee, who moved to eliminate disloyal civilians in the South as well as to repel the invading armies of the North.

U.S. goals in Korea were unclear. Should the United States seek to "contain" communism by driving the North Koreans back over the 38th parallel? Or should it try to reunify the country under Rhee's leadership? At first, that decision could be postponed because the war was going so badly. North Korean troops pushed their Soviet-made tanks rapidly southward; within three months, they took Seoul and reached the southern tip of the Korean peninsula. American troops seemed unprepared and, unaccustomed to the unusually hot Korean weather during these first months, fell sick. But American firepower gradually took its toll on the elite troops who had spearheaded North Korea's rapid move southward. North Korea had to send fresh, untrained recruits to replace seasoned fighters.

General Douglas MacArthur then devised a plan that most other commanders considered crazy: an amphibious landing behind enemy lines at Inchon. Those stunned by the riskiness of his proposed invasion were even more astounded by its results. On September 15, 1950, the Marines successfully landed 13,000 troops at Inchon, suffered only 21 deaths, and moved back into Seoul within 11 days.

As MacArthur's troops drove northward, Truman faced a crucial decision. MacArthur, emboldened by success, urged an all-out war of "liberation" and reunification. Other advisers warned that China would retaliate if U.S. forces approached its border. Cautiously, Truman allowed MacArthur to carry the war into the North but ordered him to avoid antagonizing China.

MacArthur pushed too far, advancing toward the Yalu River on the Chinese-Korean border. China responded by sending troops into North Korea and driving MacArthur back across the 38th parallel. With China now in the war, Truman again faced the question of military goals. When MacArthur's troops regained the initiative, Truman ordered his general to negotiate a truce at the 38th parallel. But MacArthur challenged the president, arguing instead for all-out victory over North Korea—and over China, too. Truman thereupon relieved him of his command in April 1951, pointing out that the Constitution specified that military commanders must obey the orders of the president, the commander in chief.

MacArthur returned home as a war hero. One poll reported that less than 30 percent of the U.S. public supported Truman's actions. The China lobby portrayed MacArthur as a martyr to Truman's "no-win," containment policy. But this outpouring of admiration reflected

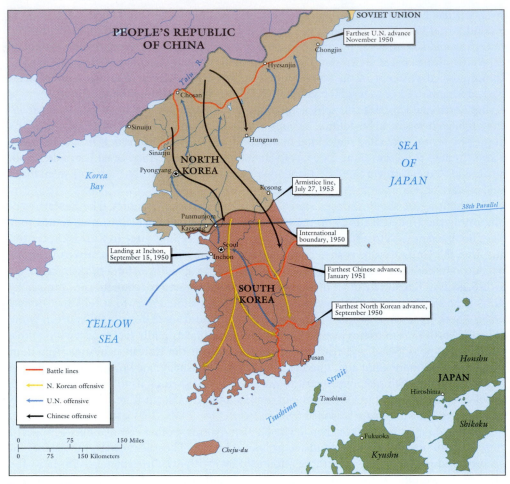

KOREAN WAR

MacArthur's personal charisma rather than any significant public support for a full-scale land war in Asia. During Senate hearings on the general's dismissal, military strategists expressed their opposition to such a war. And most Americans apparently preferred a negotiated settlement in Korea. Truman now set about convincing North Korea and South Korea to meet at the conference table. Eisenhower, the Republican candidate for president in 1952, promised to go to Korea to hasten the peace process. The negotiations that eventually reestablished the borderline at the 38th parallel emerged as a major foreign policy task for the new Eisenhower administration in 1953.

KOREA AND CONTAINMENT

The Korean War justified the global offensive that NSC-68 had recommended. The United States announced a plan to rearm West Germany, scarcely five years after Germany's defeat, and increased NATO's military forces. In 1951 the United States signed a formal peace treaty with Japan, and a Japanese-American security pact granted the United States a base on Okinawa and permission for U.S. troops to be stationed in Japan. The United States also acquired bases in Saudi Arabia and Morocco. In 1950 direct military aid to Latin American governments, which had been voted down in the past, slid through Congress. In French Indochina, Truman provided assistance to strengthen French efforts to put down a communist-led movement that was fighting for independence. In the Philippines, the United States stepped up military assistance for the suppression of the leftist Huk rebels. And in 1951 the ANZUS collective security pact linked the United States strategically to Australia and New Zealand. Throughout the world, economic pressure, covert activities by the CIA, and propaganda campaigns helped to forge anticommunist alliances. Truman's global "Campaign of Truth," an intensive informational and psychological offensive, used mass media and cultural exchanges to counter Soviet claims with pro-American perspectives.

While the Truman administration fortified America's strategic position throughout the world, U.S. military budgets increased. Strategic priorities linked Washington to ongoing weapons research and production. The Atomic Energy Commission had been created in 1946 to succeed the Manhattan Project in overseeing development of nuclear power; aviation had received special government funding for the first time in the 1946 budget; the Army had joined with aircraft manufacturers in an effort to develop surface-to-surface missiles. And to coordinate global strategy with the development of long-range weapons, a new "think tank"—RAND, an acronym for Research and Development—was created. Expensive contracts for the manufacture of military materials worried cost-conscious members of Congress, but the prospect that the contracts would create new jobs in their home districts muted their opposition. The Cold War thus brought what the historian Michael Sherry has called "the militarization of American life": a steady military buildup and an intermingling of military and economic policies.

As the emphasis on anticommunism intensified, U.S. policymakers became more suspicious of any movement that was left-leaning in its political orientation. The U.S. occupation government in Japan, for example, increasingly restricted the activities of labor unions and barred communists from government offices and universities. As in Germany, the United States tried to contain communism by strengthening industrial elites and promoting economic growth.

In Africa, as well, anticommunism shaped U.S. policies, bringing the United States into an alliance with South Africa. In 1948 the all-white (and militantly anticommunist) Nationalist Party instituted a legal system based on elaborate rules of racial separation and subordination of blacks (apartheid). Some State Department officials warned that supporting apartheid in South Africa would damage U.S. prestige, but the Truman administration decided to cement an alliance with South Africa nonetheless.

Containment relied on a rhetoric of defensiveness: The term "national security" replaced "national interest"; the "War Department" became the "Department of Defense." Yet the United States extended its power into the former British sphere of influence of Iran, Greece, and Turkey; initiated the Marshall Plan and NATO; transformed its former enemies—Italy, Germany, and Japan—into anti-Soviet bulwarks; assumed control of hundreds of Pacific islands; launched research for the development of the hydrogen bomb; winked at apartheid in order to win an anticommunist ally in South Africa; solidified its sphere of influence in Latin America; acquired bases around the globe; and devised a master plan for using military, economic, and covert action to achieve its goals. Beginning with the Truman Doctrine of 1947, the United States staked out global interests.

CONTAINMENT AT HOME

Although containment abroad generally gained bipartisan support, a strident debate over how best to counter alleged communist influences in the United States raged from the late 1940s through the middle 1950s. Conservative members of Congress and private watchdog groups, taking their cue from Truman's anticommunist rhetoric, launched their own search for evidence of internal communist subversion. Civil libertarians complained that a "witch-hunt" was being conducted against people whose only sins were dissent from the Truman administration's anticommunist measures or support for a leftist political agenda at home. Indeed, witch-hunters increasingly charged Truman's own anticommunist administration with harboring people who were disloyal or "soft" on communism. In time, even devoted anticommunists began to complain that wild-goose chases after unlikely offenders were hampering the search for authentic Soviet agents. Still, the search for supposed subversives continued, affecting many areas of postwar life. A particularly vitriolic group of anticommunists emerged in Congress.

ANTICOMMUNISM AND THE LABOR MOVEMENT

The labor movement became an obvious target for anticommunist legislators. After the end of the Second World War, militant workers had struck for increased wages and for a greater voice over workplace routines and production decisions. Strikes had brought both the auto industry and the electronics industry to a standstill. In Stamford, Connecticut, and Lancaster, Pennsylvania, general strikes had led to massive work stoppages that later spread to Rochester, Pittsburgh, Oakland, and other large cities. By 1947, however, labor militancy had begun to subside as Truman took a hard line. He threatened to seize mines and railroads that had been shut down by strikes and ordered the strikers back to work.

Still, in 1947 congressional opponents of organized labor effectively tapped anticommunist sentiment to help pass the Labor-Management Relations Act, popularly known as the Taft-Hartley Act. The law negated some of the gains that unions had made during the 1930s by limiting a union's power to conduct boycotts, to compel employers to accept "closed shops" in which only union members could be hired, and to conduct any strike that the president judged against the national interest. In addition, the law required that union officials sign affidavits stating that they did not belong to the Communist Party or to any other "subversive" organization. A union that refused to comply was effectively denied protection under national labor laws. Truman vetoed Taft-Hartley, but Congress swiftly overrode him.

The place of communists in the labor movement was becoming a national security issue. Anticommunist unionists had long charged that communists were more loyal to their party than to their unions; now they charged communists with disloyalty to the nation itself. Differences over whether to support the Democratic Party or Henry Wallace's third-party effort in 1948 heightened tensions within many unions, and in the years following Truman's victory the Congress of Industrial Organizations (CIO) expelled 13 unions. Meanwhile, many workers found their jobs at risk because of their political ideas. By the end of the

Truman era, some type of loyalty-security check had been conducted on about 20 percent of the American workforce. People who were especially outspoken on behalf of labor radicalism risked being labeled as pro-Communist.

HUAC and the Loyalty Program

Anticommunists carefully scrutinized the Hollywood film industry. In 1947 the House Committee on Un-American Activities (popularly known as HUAC) opened hearings in Hollywood to expose alleged communist infiltration. Basking in the glare of newsreel cameras, its members seized on the refusal of 10 screen writers, producers, and directors who had been or still were Communist Party members to testify about their own political affiliations and those of other members of the film community. Known as "the Hollywood Ten," this group claimed that the First Amendment shielded their political activities from official scrutiny. But the federal courts upheld HUAC's inquisitional powers, and the Hollywood Ten eventually went to prison for contempt of Congress because of their defiance of HUAC.

Meanwhile, studio heads secretly drew up a "blacklist" of so-called subversives who could no longer work in Hollywood. By the mid-1950s hundreds of people in Hollywood and in the fledgling television industry were unable to find jobs unless they would agree to appear before HUAC and ritualistically name people whom they had seen at some "communist meeting" some time in the past.

Ronald Reagan and Richard Nixon first attracted the political spotlight through the HUAC hearings. Reagan, who was president of the Screen Actors Guild and also a secret informant for the FBI (identified as "T-10"), decried the presence of subversives in the movie industry. Nixon, then an obscure member of Congress from California, began his climb to national prominence in 1948 when Whittaker Chambers, a journalist who had once been active in the Communist Party, came before HUAC to charge Alger Hiss, a prominent liberal Democrat who had a long career in government, with having also been a party member and with passing classified documents to Soviet agents in the late 1930s.

The Hiss-Chambers-Nixon affair set off a raging controversy. Hiss maintained that he had been framed in an elaborate FBI plot, alleging that the Bureau rigged his typewriter so it would appear to be the source of incriminating evidence. Legal technicalities prevented Hiss from being prosecuted for espionage, but he was charged with lying to Congress about his activities and went to prison. To Nixon and other leaders of the anticommunist campaign, the exposure of Hiss proved the need to search out subversion with more vigor than was being shown by the Truman administration. But to civil libertarians, the cases of the Hollywood Ten and Alger Hiss suggested the consequences of overzealous witch-hunting. Debates over whether the Hiss case was an example of high-level espionage or anticommunist hysteria would continue for decades.

Meanwhile, the Truman administration continued to pursue its own hard-line policies. Under the president's loyalty program, hundreds of government employees were dismissed. Attorney General Tom Clark authorized J. Edgar Hoover, head of the FBI, to draw up his own list of alleged subversives and to detain them, without any legal hearing, in the event of a national security emergency. Clark's successor, Howard McGrath, proclaimed that communist subversives were lurking "in factories, offices, butcher stores, on street corners, in private business."

At the same time, the FBI was also accumulating dossiers on a wide range of artists and intellectuals, particularly prominent African Americans. Richard Wright (author of the novel

Native Son), W. E. B. Du Bois (the nation's most celebrated African American intellectual), and Paul Robeson (one of America's most prominent entertainer-activists) became special targets. Robeson and Du Bois were harassed by State Department and immigration officials because of their ties to the Communist Party and their identification with anti-imperialist and anti-racist struggles throughout the world.

Concern that people with subversive political affiliations and ideas might emigrate to the United States produced a new immigration law. In 1952 Congress passed the McCarran-Walter Act, which placed restrictions on immigration from areas outside northern and western Europe and on the entry of people who immigration officials suspected might threaten national security.

TARGETING DIFFERENCE

Homosexuals became special targets. During the Second World War more visible and assertive gay and lesbian subcultures had begun to emerge. After the war, Dr. Alfred Kinsey's research on sexual behavior—the first volume, on male sexuality, was published in 1948—claimed that homosexual behavior could be found throughout American society. At about the same time, gays themselves formed the Mattachine Society (in 1950) and lesbians founded the Daughters of Bilitis (in 1955), organizations that cautiously began to push for recognition of rights for homosexuals. The *Kinsey Report*'s implicit claim that homosexuality was a normal form of sexuality that should be tolerated, together with the discreet militancy among gays and lesbians, produced a backlash that became connected to the broader antisubversion crusade. The fact that several founders of the Mattachine Society had also been members of the Communist Party, coupled with a belief that homosexuals could be blackmailed by Soviet agents more easily than heterosexuals, helped to link homosexuality with subversion.

A connection between antihomosexual and anticommunist rhetoric developed. Radical political ideas and homosexuality were both portrayed as "diseases" that could be spread throughout the body politic by people who often looked no different from "ordinary" Americans. According to this logic, homosexuality was an acceptable basis for denying people government employment.

THE ROSENBERG CASE AND "THE GREAT FEAR"

Harry Truman's last years as president were played out against a backdrop of public anxiety that the historian David Caute has called "the Great Fear." Foreign policy events of 1949 and 1950 highlighted the issue of whether subversives were at work in the most sensitive recesses of the U.S. government. Suspicions arose about the loyalty of foreign policy personnel, and stories about Soviet agents having stolen U.S. nuclear secrets spread rapidly. In early 1950, Great Britain released evidence that a spy ring had been operating in the United States since the mid-1940s. Shortly afterward, the U.S. Justice Department arrested several alleged members of this ring, including two members of the Communist Party, Julius and Ethel Rosenberg.

The Rosenberg case became a Cold War melodrama. The trial, the verdicts of guilty, the sentences of death at Sing Sing prison, the numerous legal appeals, the worldwide protests, and the executions in 1953—all provoked intense controversy. Were the Rosenbergs guilty of having been involved in the theft of important nuclear secrets? And even so, were their death sentences on the charge of espionage the constitutionally appropriate punishment? To their supporters, the Rosenbergs (who steadfastly maintained their innocence) had fallen victim to the Great Fear. Many believed that the government seemed more intent on punishing scapegoats than in conducting a fair trial. To others, the evidence showed that information had been channeled to the Soviets.

More than 45 years after the Rosenbergs' deaths, debates still rage over their case. Intelligence reports from the Cold War era not released until the 1990s strongly suggest that Julius Rosenberg had been engaged in espionage and that Ethel Rosenberg, though not directly involved, may have known of his activities. Yet, the government declined to prosecute others who almost certainly, according to a 1997 report, "were atomic spies." Only Julius and Ethel Rosenberg were charged with a crime that carried the death penalty.

The manner in which the courts responded to the anticommunist crusade sparked controversy. During the Justice Department's 1949 prosecution of Communist Party leaders for sedition, for example, the trial judge allowed the government a wide latitude to introduce evidence against the defendants. In effect, he accepted the claim that, by definition, the American Communist Party was simply the arm of an international conspiracy. Its Marxist ideology and its theoretical publications, even in the absence of any proof of subversive *acts* against national security, justified convictions against the party's leaders. In contrast, civil libertarians insisted that the government lacked any evidence that the publications and speeches of Communist Party members, by themselves, posed any "clear and present danger" to national security. In this view, the Communist Party's abstract political beliefs, which should enjoy the protection of the First Amendment, were unconstitutionally put on trial.

When the convictions of the Communist Party leaders were appealed to the Supreme Court, in the case of *Dennis* v. *U.S.* (1951), civil libertarians renewed their arguments that this prosecution violated constitutional guarantees for the protection of speech. The Supreme Court, however, modified the "clear and present danger" doctrine and upheld the lower court. The defendants, a majority of the Court declared, had been constitutionally convicted.

By 1952, the Truman administration itself became a primary target of anticommunist zealots. In Congress, Republicans and conservative Democrats condemned the administration's handling of anticommunist initiatives and introduced their own legislation, the McCarran Internal Security Act of 1950. It authorized the detention, during any national emergency, of alleged subversives in special camps, and created the Subversive Activities Control Board (SACB) to investigate organizations suspected of being affiliated with the Communist Party and to administer the registration of organizations allegedly controlled by communists.

The Truman administration responded ambiguously to the McCarran Act. Although the president vetoed the law, a futile response that Congress quickly overrode, his administration secretly allowed Hoover to plan a covert detention program. Still, Truman could never defuse the charges leveled at his own administration.

McCARTHYISM

Republican Senator Joseph McCarthy of Wisconsin became Truman's prime accuser. Charging in 1950 that communists were at work in Truman's State Department, McCarthy put the administration on the defensive. The nation was in a precarious position, according to McCarthy, "not because our only powerful potential enemy has sent men to invade our shores, but rather because of the traitorous actions of those who have been treated so well by this Nation." Among those people, McCarthy named Alger Hiss, Secretary of State Dean Acheson, and former Secretary of State George C. Marshall.

Truman's efforts to contain McCarthy failed. Although McCarthy never substantiated his charges, he lacked neither imagination nor targets. The main targets of McCarthy and his imitators were former members of the Communist Party of the United States and people associated with "communist front" organizations, supposedly legitimate political groups secretly manipulated by communists. In most of the cases McCarthy cited, the affiliations had been perfectly legal. He also made vague charges against the entertainment industry and academic institutions. And despite his claims that hundreds of communist subversives were working in the State Department, he produced no credible evidence to support his case.

Nevertheless, McCarthy seemed unstoppable. In the summer of 1950, a subcommittee of the Senate Foreign Relations Committee, after examining State Department files in search of the damning material, concluded that McCarthy's charges amounted to "the most nefarious campaign of half-truths and untruths in the history of this republic." McCarthy simply charged that the files had been "raped," and he broadened his mudslinging to include Millard Tydings, the Maryland senator who had chaired the subcommittee. In the November 1950 elections, Tydings was defeated, in part, because of a fabricated photo that linked him to an alleged Communist Party member.

Despite McCarthy's recklessness, influential people tolerated, even supported, his crusade. Conservative, anticommunist leaders of the Roman Catholic Church endorsed McCarthy, himself a Catholic. Leading Republicans welcomed McCarthy's attacks on their Democratic rivals. As head of a special Senate Subcommittee on Investigations, popularly known as the "McCarthy committee," McCarthy enjoyed broad subpoena power and legal immunity from libel suits. He bullied witnesses and encouraged self-styled "experts" to offer outlandish estimates of a vast Red Menace.

In the long run, growing concern about national security subtly altered the nation's constitutional structure. Except for the Twenty-second and the Twenty-third Amendments (adopted in 1951 and 1961, respectively), which barred future presidents from serving more than two terms and allowed the District of Columbia a vote in presidential elections, there were no formal modifications of the written Constitution during these years. But legislative enactments, especially the National Security Act of 1947, and the growing power of the executive branch of government, particularly of agencies like the CIA and the FBI, brought important informal changes to the nation's unwritten constitution. As the Truman administration sought to contain communism and conduct a global foreign policy, older ideas about a constitutional structure of limited governmental powers gave way to the idea that broader executive authority was necessary to protect national security.

DOMESTIC POLICY: TRUMAN'S FAIR DEAL

Although the Truman administration placed its greatest priority on containment, it also reconstructed the domestic legacy of Franklin Roosevelt. Many supporters of FDR's New Deal still endorsed the "Second Bill of Rights" that FDR had proclaimed in his State of the Union address of 1944. According to this vision, all Americans had the "right" to a wide range of substantive liberties, including employment, food and shelter, education, and health care. Whenever people were unable to obtain these "rights," the national government was responsible for providing access to them. Such governmental largesse required constant economic and social planning—and government spending—for the general welfare.

Talk about government planning and increased spending proved highly controversial. Even before the Second World War, the pace of domestic legislation had begun to slow, and throughout the war critics had assailed economic planning as meddlesome interference in private decision making. Government programs, Republicans charged, were an unconstitutional intrusion into people's private affairs and posed a threat to individual initiative and responsibility.

During Truman's presidency, opposition to dramatic innovations in social policymaking hardened. The National Association of Manufacturers (NAM) warned that new domestic programs would destroy the private, free enterprise system. Southern Democrats in Congress joined Republicans in blocking new programs that they feared might weaken white supremacy in their region. Even before Truman succeeded Roosevelt, these conservative forces had succeeded in abolishing several New Deal agencies that might have contributed to economic planning after the war, and had flatly rejected FDR's Second Bill of Rights.

THE EMPLOYMENT ACT OF 1946 AND THE PROMISE OF ECONOMIC GROWTH

Faced with such intense opposition to FDR's 1944 agenda, Truman needed to find a different approach to domestic policymaking. The 1946 debate over the Full Employment Bill helped identify one. The Full Employment Bill, as initially conceived, would have increased government spending and empowered Washington to intervene aggressively in the job market, so as to ensure employment for all citizens seeking work. To the bill's opponents, these provisions and the phrase "full employment" resembled socialism.

As the effort to enact the bill stalled, a scaled-down vision of domestic policymaking gradually emerged. The law that Congress finally passed, renamed the Employment Act of 1946, called for "maximum" (rather than "full") employment and specifically acknowledged that private enterprise, not government, bore primary responsibility for economic decision making. The act nonetheless recognized that the national government would play an ongoing role in economic management. It created a new executive branch body, the Council of Economic Advisers, to help formulate long-range policy recommendations and signaled that government policymakers would assume some responsibility for the performance of the economy.

A crucial factor in the gradual acceptance of Washington's new role was a growing faith that *advice* from economic experts, as an alternative to government *planning*, could help guarantee a constantly expanding economy. An influential group of theorists, many of them disciples of the British economist John Maynard Keynes, insisted that the United States no longer needed to endure the boom-and-bust cycles that had afflicted the nation during the 1920s and 1930s. Instead of leaving the economy to the uncoordinated decisions of private individuals and business firms, policymakers and citizens alike were urged to trust in the theoretical expertise of economists. They would advise government and private business on the policies most likely to produce uninterrupted economic growth.

The promise of economic growth as a permanent condition of American life dazzled postwar business and government leaders. Corporate executives viewed economic growth as a guarantee of social stability. Members of the Truman administration embraced the idea that the government should encourage economic growth not through centralized governmental planning but by updating, through measures such as the Employment Act of 1946, the cooperative relationship with both big business and organized labor that the Roosevelt administration had introduced during the Second World War.

In fact, Truman's closest advisers believed that such cooperation would actually make domestic policymaking easier. Economic growth would produce increased tax revenues and, in turn, give Washington the money to fund domestic programs. Using the relatively new measure of a "gross national product" (or GNP), postwar experts could actually calculate the nation's growing economic bounty. Developed in 1939, the concept of GNP—defined as the total dollar value of all the goods and services produced in the nation during a given year—became the standard gauge of economic health.

By the end of 1948 Truman and his advisers were preaching the gospel of economic growth. Indeed, that ideal fitted nicely with their foreign policy programs, such as the Marshall Plan, which were designed to create markets and investment opportunities overseas. Economic growth at home was linked to development in the world at large—and to the all-pervasive concern with national security.

TRUMAN'S FAIR DEAL

In his inaugural address of January 5, 1949, Truman unveiled a domestic agenda he labeled the "Fair Deal." He called for the extension of popular New Deal programs such as Social Security and minimum wage laws; enactment of civil rights and national health care legislation; federal aid for education; and repeal of the Taft-Hartley Act of 1947. Charles Brannan, Truman's secretary of agriculture, proposed an ambitious new plan for supporting farm prices by means of additional governmental subsidies, and the president himself urged substantial spending on public housing projects.

Two prominent government programs suggested the approach to domestic policymaking that dominated the Fair Deal years. The first, the so-called GI Bill (officially entitled the Serviceman's Readjustment Act of 1944), had always enjoyed strong support in Congress. After previous wars, Congress had simply voted veterans cash pensions or bonuses. But, this time, Congress worked out a comprehensive program of benefits for the several million men and the 40,000 women who had served in the armed forces. The GI Bill encompassed several different programs, including immediate financial assistance for college and job-training programs for veterans of the Second World War. In other provisions, veterans received preferential treatment when applying for government jobs; generous terms on loans when purchasing homes or businesses; and, eventually, comprehensive medical care in veterans' hospitals. The Veterans' Readjustment Assistance Act of 1952, popularly known as the "GI Bill of Rights," extended these programs to veterans of the Korean War.

Meanwhile, Social Security, the most popular part of Roosevelt's New Deal, expanded under Truman's Fair Deal. Fighting a rearguard attack by conservatives, the Social Security Administration defended its program, which also included support for the disabled and the blind, as a system that simply provided "income security" that older people had themselves earned through years of work and monetary contributions that had been withheld from their paychecks.

Under the Social Security Act of 1950 the level of benefits was increased significantly; the retirement portions of the program were expanded; and coverage was extended to more than 10 million people, including agricultural workers.

The more expansive (and expensive) Fair Deal proposals either failed or were scaled back. For instance, Truman's plan for a comprehensive national health insurance program ran into strong opposition. The American Medical Association (AMA) and the American Hospital Association (AHA) blocked any government intervention in the traditional fee-for-service medical system. Opinion polls suggested that most voters, many of whom were enrolling in private health insurance plans such as Blue Cross and Blue Shield, were simply apathetic, or confused, about Truman's national health proposals.

Because of the continued shortage of affordable housing in urban areas, polls showed greater support for home-building programs, another part of Truman's Fair Deal. Private construction firms and realtors welcomed extension of federal home loan guarantees, such as those established under the GI Bill and through the Federal Housing Administration, but they lobbied against publicly financed housing projects. Yet even conservatives recognized the housing shortage and supported the Housing Act of 1949. This law authorized construction of 810,000 public housing units and provided federal funds for "urban renewal" zones, areas to be cleared of run-down dwellings and built up again with new construction. The Housing Act of 1949 set forth relatively bold goals but provided only modest funding for its public housing program.

Domestic policymaking during the Truman era, then, ultimately focused on specific groups, such as veterans of the Second World War and older Americans, rather than on more extensive programs for all, such as a national health care plan and a large-scale commitment to government-built, affordable housing projects. Opponents of economic planning and greater spending by government considered the broader proposals of the Fair Deal to be "welfare," and the Truman administration found it easier to defend more narrowly targeted programs, which could be hailed as economic "security" measures for specific groups.

CIVIL RIGHTS

During his 1948 presidential campaign, Truman had strongly endorsed proposals that had been advanced by a civil rights committee he established in 1946. The committee's report called for federal legislation against lynching; a special civil rights division within the Department of Justice; antidiscrimination initiatives in employment, housing, and public facilities; and desegregation of the military. Although these proposals prompted many white southern Democrats to bolt to the short-lived Dixiecrat Party, they won Truman significant support from African Americans.

The Dixiecrat Party episode, a reaction to Truman's stance on civil rights, portended significant political change among southern whites who had voted overwhelmingly Democratic since the late 19th century. Strom Thurmond, the Dixiecrats' presidential candidate, denounced Truman for offering a "civil wrongs" program. Although Thurmond insisted that southern Democrats did not oppose all civil rights measures, he also argued that the Constitution required this kind of legislation to come from state governments and not from Washington. Moreover, white southern Democrats pledged to fight any effort to end racial segregation. Thurmond carried only four states in 1948, but his candidacy showed that, because of the issue of race, lifelong southern Democrats were willing to desert the party in national presidential elections.

Despite discord within his own party, Truman generally supported the efforts of the civil rights movement. When successive Congresses failed to enact any civil rights legislation—including an antilynching law and a ban on the poll taxes that prevented most southern blacks from voting—the movement turned to a sympathetic White House and to the federal courts. After A. Philip Randolph threatened to organize protests against continued segregation in the military, Truman issued an executive order calling for desegregation of the armed forces. Truman also endorsed the efforts of the Fair Employment Practices Commission (FEPC) to end racial discrimination in federal hiring.

Meanwhile, Truman's Justice Department regularly appeared in court on behalf of litigants who were contesting government-backed segregation of public schools and "restrictive covenants" (legal agreements that prevented racial or religious minorities from acquiring real estate). In 1946, the Supreme Court declared restrictive covenants illegal and began chipping away at the "separate but equal" principle that had been used since *Plessy* v. *Ferguson* (1898) to justify segregated schools. In 1950, the Court ruled that under the Fourteenth Amendment racial segregation in state-financed graduate and law schools was unconstitutional. In light of these decisions, all the traditional legal arguments that had been used since *Plessy* to legitimate racial segregation in all public schools seemed open to successful challenge—which would finally come in 1954 (see Chapter 28).

In summary, the years immediately after the Second World War marked a turning point in domestic policymaking. The New Deal's hope for comprehensive socioeconomic planning gave way to a view of social policy based on the assumption that the nation could expect uninterrupted economic growth. Henceforth, Washington could reap, through taxation, its own steady share of a growing economy, so the government could finance a set of targeted programs to assist specific groups. As one supporter of this new approach argued, postwar policymakers were sophisticated enough to embrace "partial remedies," such as the GI Bill, rather than to wait for fanciful "cure-alls," such as FDR's Second Bill of Rights.

SOCIAL CHANGE AND CONTAINMENT

The postwar years brought dramatic changes in the daily life of most Americans. Encouraged by the advertising industry, most people seemed, at one level, to believe that virtually any kind of change automatically meant "progress." Yet at another level the pace and scope of social change during these years brought a feeling of uneasiness into American life, prompting many people to try to contain the impact of new developments. Containment abroad sometimes paralleled a similar stance toward containing social innovation at home.

JACKIE ROBINSON AND THE BASEBALL "COLOR LINE"

The interplay between these two forces could be seen in the integration of organized baseball during the 1940s and 1950s. In 1947, major league baseball's policy of racial segregation finally changed when Jackie Robinson, who had played in the Negro National League, became the Brooklyn Dodgers' first baseman. A number of players, including several on Robinson's own club, had talked about boycotting any game in which Robinson appeared. Baseball's leadership, aware of the steady stream of African American fans coming out to the parks, crushed the opposition by threatening to suspend any player who refused to play with Robinson.

The pressure to integrate the national pastime became inexorable. Several months after Robinson's debut, the Cleveland Indians signed center fielder Larry Doby, and a number of other African American stars quickly left the Negro leagues for the American and National circuits. Eventually, the talent of Robinson—named Rookie of the Year in 1947 and the National League's Most Valuable Player in 1949—and of the other African American players carried the day. By 1960 every major league team fielded black players, and some had begun extensive recruiting in Puerto Rico and in the nations of the Caribbean. In 1997, the 50th anniversary of Robinson's debut, Major League Baseball staged elaborate memorial ceremonies

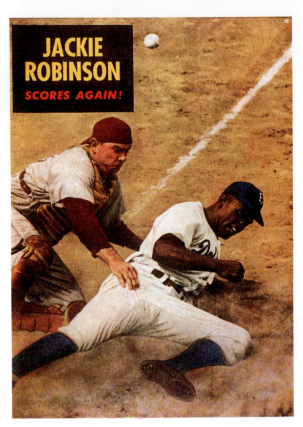

JACKIE ROBINSON   In 1947 Jackie Robinson joined the Brooklyn Dodgers and became the first African American since the 19th century to play Major League baseball. He had served as a lieutenant in the Army during the Second World War. The racial integration of the national pastime of baseball became a powerful symbol of progress in race relations, and Robinson himself was a favorite of fans, both white and black.

for Robinson, who had died in 1972—and congratulated the sport for having led the fight against racial prejudice during the Cold War years.

Yet, during the late 1940s and early 1950s, baseball's leaders had worked to contain the participation of African Americans. Several teams waited for years before fielding any black players, claiming they could find no talented prospects. More commonly, teams restricted the number of nonwhite players they would take on and kept their managers, coaches, and front-office personnel solidly white.

THE POSTWAR SUBURBS

Suburbia was another place where the celebration of change and efforts to contain its effects were both constant themes. Suburban living had long been a feature of the "American dream." The new Long Island, New York, suburb of Levittown, which welcomed its first residents in October 1947, seemed to make that dream a reality, at affordable prices, for middle-income families.

Nearly everything about Levittown seemed unprecedented. A construction company that had mass-produced military barracks during the Second World War, Levitt & Sons could complete a five-room bungalow every 15 minutes. Architectural critics sneered at these "little boxes," but potential buyers stood in long lines hoping to get one. By 1950, Levittown consisted of more than 10,000 homes and 40,000 residents. By then, bulldozers and construction crews were sweeping into other suburban developments across the country.

To help buyers purchase their first home, the government offered an extensive set of programs. The Federal Housing Administration (FHA), which had been established during the New Deal, helped private lenders extend credit to mass-production builders, who could then sell the houses they built on generous financing terms. Typically, people who bought FHA-financed homes needed only 5 percent of the purchase price as a down payment; they could then finance the rest with a long-term, government-insured mortgage. Millions of war veterans enjoyed even more favorable terms under the GI loan program operated by the Veterans Administration. These government programs made it cheaper to buy a new house in the average suburb than to rent a comfortable apartment in most cities. Moreover, families could deduct from their federal income tax the interest they paid on their mortgages. This deduction was a disguised form of governmental subsidy.

Suburban homes promised greater privacy and more amenities than crowded city neighborhoods. Builders soon began to offer larger houses, including the sprawling, one-level "ranch style" model. The joys of "easy and better" living often came with the house. Levitt homes, for

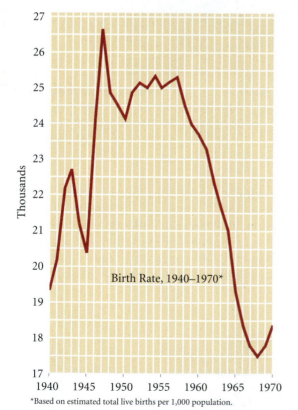

THE BABY BOOM

Birth Rate, 1940–1970*

*Based on estimated total live births per 1,000 population.

example, contained an automatic washer and a built-in television set. By being attached to the house itself, even the TV qualified as a "structural" component and could be financed under federally guaranteed loan programs.

Suburbs enjoyed the reputation for being ideal places in which to raise children, and families were having babies in much larger numbers. After the war, a complex set of factors, including early marriages and rising incomes, helped produce a "baby boom" that would last well into the next decade. With houses generally occupying only about 15 percent of suburban lots, large lawns served as private playgrounds. Nearby schools were as new as the rest of the neighborhood, and suburban school boards used the lure of modern, well-equipped buildings to attract both skilled teachers and middle-income families.

In many respects, the new suburban lifestyle epitomized an optimistic spirit of new possibilities, confidence in the future, and acceptance of change. In other respects, though, it represented an effort to contain some of the effects of rapid change by creating a material and psychological refuge. Most obviously, buying a new suburban home seemed a way of cushioning the impact of social and demographic changes. With African American families leaving the rural South in search of work in northern cities, "white flight" to suburbia quickened.

Government and private housing policies helped to structure and maintain the segregationist pattern of white suburbs and increasingly nonwhite urban neighborhoods. Federal laws allowed local groups to veto public housing projects in their communities. Although land and building costs would have been cheaper in the suburbs, public housing projects were concentrated on relatively expensive, high-density urban sites. More important, the lending industry channeled government loan guarantees away from most urban neighborhoods, and private lenders generally denied credit to nonwhites seeking new suburban housing.

No one in the postwar housing industry admitted intentional complicity in these discriminatory patterns. William Levitt might identify his private housing projects with the public crusade against communism. He held himself blameless, however, for racial issues. He could help solve the nation's housing problem, but he deceptively claimed that his "private" construction had nothing to do with the public issue of race.

Similarly, the architects of suburbia saw nothing problematic with postwar gender patterns. The lending industry made loan guarantees available only to men. Single women simply could not obtain FHA-backed loans, a policy that the agency justified on the grounds that women rarely made enough money to qualify as good credit risks.

THE SUBURBAN FAMILY AND GENDER ISSUES

Because the new suburbs generally lacked mass transit facilities, life revolved around the automobile. But if the male breadwinner needed the "family" car to commute to work, the wife spent the day at home. Until car ownership expanded in the mid-1950s, even a trip to the supermarket could prove difficult.

Still, wives and mothers found plenty of work at home. New appliances and conveniences— automatic clothes washers, more powerful vacuum cleaners, frozen foods, and home freezers—eased old burdens but created new ones. Contrary to what the ads promised, women were actually spending as much time on housework after the war as their grandmothers had spent at the turn of the century. The time spent on domestic tasks was reallocated but not reduced. Moreover, because child care facilities were not generally available in the new suburbs, mothers spent a great deal of time taking care of their children.

Daily life in the suburbs fell into a fairly rigid pattern of "separate spheres"—a public sphere of work and politics dominated by men and a private sphere of housework and child care reserved for women. Because few jobs of any kind initially were available in postwar suburbia, the distance between home and the workplace became greater for suburban men, and women who wanted to work found nearby job opportunities about as scarce as child care facilities.

Without mothers and grandmothers living close by, suburban mothers increasingly turned to child care manuals for advice. Dr. Benjamin Spock's *Baby and Child Care,* first published in 1946, sold millions of copies. Like earlier manuals, Spock's book assigned virtually all child care duties to women and underscored the importance of their nurturing role by stressing the need constantly to oversee a child's psychological growth. Other manuals picked up where Dr. Spock left off and counseled mothers on the care and feeding of teenagers. The alarmist tone of many of these books reflected—and also helped to generate—widespread concern over "juvenile delinquency."

The crusade against an alleged increase in juvenile crime soon attracted the attention of government officials. J. Edgar Hoover, director of the FBI, and Attorney General Tom Clark coupled their pleas for containing communism with pleas for containing juvenile delinquency. In a 1953 report, Hoover claimed that the first of the war babies were about to enter their teenage years, "the period in which some of them will inevitably incline toward juvenile delinquency and, later, full-fledged criminal careers."

How could this threat be contained? Many authorities suggested cures that focused on the individual family. Delinquents, according to one study in the early 1950s, sprang from a "family atmosphere not conducive to development of emotionally well-integrated, happy youngsters, conditioned to obey legitimate authority." It was up to parents, especially mothers, to raise good kids. The ideal mother, according to most advice manuals, did not work outside the home but devoted herself to rearing her own segment of the baby boom generation. Women who sought careers outside the home risked being labeled as lost, maladjusted, guilt-ridden, man-hating, or all of the above.

Even the nation's prestigious women's colleges offered instruction that was assumed to lead to marriage, not to work or careers. In his 1955 commencement address at Smith, a women's college, Adlai Stevenson, the Democratic Party's urbane presidential candidate in 1952 and 1956, told the graduates that it was the duty of each to keep her husband "truly purposeful, to keep him whole." Postwar magazines, psychology, and popular culture were filled with concerns about the reintegration and stability of returned war veterans.

Discussions about the ideal postwar family did not always offer such a one-dimensional view of gender relationships. When interviewed by researchers, most men reported they did not want a "submissive, stay-at-home" wife. Even popular TV shows, such as *Father Knows Best* or *Leave It to Beaver,* suggested a hope that middle-class fathers would become more involved in family life than their own fathers had been. And although experts on domestic harmony still envisioned suburban men earning their family's entire income, they also urged them to be "real fathers" at home. Literature on parenting emphasized "family togetherness," and institutions like the YMCA began to offer courses on how to achieve it.

In another sense, the call for family togetherness was a reaction against what some cultural historians have seen as an incipient "male revolt" against "family values." Hugh Hefner's *Playboy* magazine, which first appeared in 1953, preached that men who neglected their own happiness in order to support a wife and children were not saints but suckers. In *Playboy's* very first issue, Hefner proclaimed: "We aren't a 'family magazine.'" In Hefner's version of the good life, the man rented a "pad" rather than owned a home; drove a sports car rather than a sedan or a station wagon; and courted the Playmate of the Month rather than the Mother of the Year.

WOMEN'S CHANGING ROLES

Despite all of the media images that depicted the "average woman" as a homebound wife and mother, economic realities were propelling more and more women into the job market. Female employment rose steadily during the late 1940s and throughout the 1950s. Moreover, increasing numbers of married women were entering the labor force, many of them as part-time workers in the expanding clerical and service sectors. In 1948, about 25 percent of married mothers had jobs outside the home; at the end of the 1950s, nearly 40 percent did.

If more women were holding jobs outside their homes, their employment opportunities nevertheless remained largely contained within well-defined, sex-segregated areas. In 1950, for example, more than 90 percent of all nurses, telephone operators, secretaries, and elementary school teachers were women. As low-paid jobs for women expanded, professional opportunities actually narrowed. Medical and law schools and many professional societies admitted few, if any, women; the number of women on college faculties shrank back even from the low levels of the 1920s and 1930s.

Although the notion of the "family wage" was still invoked in order to excuse the disparity of pay and opportunity based on gender, more and more women were trying to support a family on their paychecks. This was especially true for women of color; by 1960 slightly more than 20 percent of black families were headed by women. Recognizing that stereotypical images of domesticity hardly fit the experience of African American women, *Ebony* magazine celebrated women who were able to combine success in parenting and in work. One story, for example, highlighted the only female African American mechanic at American Airlines.

Postwar magazines targeted to white women also carried somewhat ambiguous messages about domesticity. Although pursuing activities outside the home was stigmatized by some social commentators as "unnatural," magazines that depended on a broad, popular readership generally gave more positive portrayals of women who were participating in public life. Women's magazines, while being deferential to the dominant ideal of domesticity, still published articles that sensitively chronicled the difficulties of running a home and raising children and often ran stories on prominent career women.

The great fear of communism during the years from 1947 to 1954 accentuated pressures for conformity and often made it difficult to advocate significant social change. Yet, despite efforts to "contain" change at home, demographic shifts, new expectations stemming from the war, and robust prosperity inevitably transformed many social and cultural patterns. The everyday lives of Americans were inexorably changing.

FROM TRUMAN TO EISENHOWER

Emphasis on anticommunism and containment continued into the presidency of Republican Dwight D. Eisenhower. The election of 1952 marked few fundamental shifts in either foreign

FEMMES FATALES FROM FILM NOIR

During the 1940s and 1950s Hollywood released a cycle of motion pictures that came to be called film noir. These movies, nearly always filmed in black-and-white and often set at night in large cities, peeked into the dark corners of postwar America. They hinted at deep-seated anxieties and fears, especially about the possibility of men and women living together happily and harmoniously.

Many film noir pictures featured alluring femmes fatales: beautiful but dangerous women who challenged the prevailing social order. The femme fatale represented the opposite of the nurturing, safely contained wife and mother. Usually unmarried and childless, she posed a threat to both men and other women. In *The File on Thelma Jordan* (1949), for instance, the title character, played by Barbara Stanwyck, cynically destroys the marriage of a young, weak-willed district attorney. She initiates an illicit affair with him not because of love, or even lust, but as part of a complicated plot

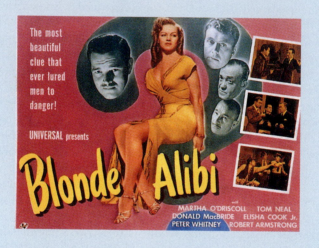

or domestic policies. Containing communism overseas and at home continued to be central issues, especially during the first two years of the Eisenhower presidency.

THE ELECTION OF 1952

By 1952, Harry Truman and the Democrats were on the defensive. Denunciations of the communist threat remained the order of the day. Adlai Stevenson of Illinois, the Democratic presidential candidate, denounced Joseph McCarthy but used McCarthy-like rhetoric in his anticommunist pronouncements: "Soviet secret agents and their dupes" had "burrowed like moles" into governments throughout the world. Stevenson approved of the prosecution of the Communist Party's leaders and the dismissal of schoolteachers who were party members.

to use him in manipulating the criminal justice system. The postwar era's most prominent female stars—such as Stanwyck, Joan Crawford, Rita Hayworth, and Lana Turner—achieved both popular and critical acclaim by playing such roles.

What is the significance of the many femme fatale characters in postwar film culture? It is tempting, of course, to view them as nothing more than negative symbols, part of a Cold War culture that exalted family life and stressed the subordination of women to male heads-of-households. Film noir features, however, developed a loyal audience among women, and some students of Hollywood films have suggested that the femme fatale—who sought independence and power—might have provided an exaggerated symbol of repressed dissatisfaction among female filmgoers with tightly contained women's roles.

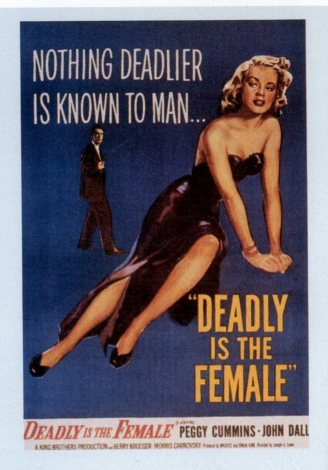

But a strong anticommunist stance was not enough to save Stevenson or the Democratic Party in 1952. The GOP's vice presidential candidate, Senator Richard Nixon, called Stevenson "Adlai the appeaser." Democrats faced criticism over Truman's handling of the Korean War and over revelations about favoritism and kickbacks on government contracts. The Republicans' successful election formula could be reduced to a simple equation, "K^1C^2": "Korea, corruption, and communism."

For their presidential candidate the Republicans turned to the hero of the Second World War, Dwight David Eisenhower, who was popularly known as "Ike." Eisenhower had neither sought elective office nor even been identified with a political party before 1952, but nearly a half-century of military service had made him a skilled politician. Ike grew up in Kansas; graduated from West Point; rose through the Army ranks under the patronage of General George

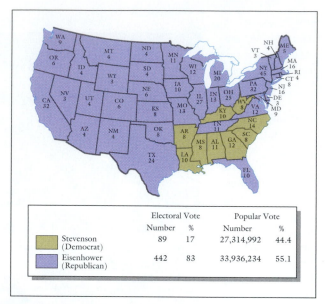

		Electoral Vote		Popular Vote	
		Number	%	Number	%
	Stevenson (Democrat)	89	17	27,314,992	44.4
	Eisenhower (Republican)	442	83	33,936,234	55.1

PRESIDENTIAL ELECTION, 1952

Marshall; directed the Normandy invasion of 1944 as Supreme Allied Commander; served as Army Chief of Staff from 1945 to 1948; and, after an interim period as president of Columbia University, returned to active duty as the commander of NATO, a post he held until May 1952.

Eisenhower seemed an attractive candidate. Although his partisan affiliations were vague, he finally declared himself a Republican. Initially reluctant to seek the presidency, he became convinced that Robert Taft, his main GOP rival, leaned too far to the right on domestic issues and might abandon Truman's aggressive containment policies. Perceived as a middle-of-the-roader, Ike seemed able to lead the nation through a Cold War as firmly as he had during a hot one.

In the 1952 election, the Eisenhower-Nixon ticket received almost 7 million more popular votes than the Democrats and won in the Electoral College by a margin of 442 to 89. The Republican Party itself made less spectacular gains. The GOP gained only a one-vote majority in the Senate and an eight-vote majority in the House of Representatives. The electoral coalition Franklin Roosevelt had put together during the 1930s still survived, even though it showed signs of fraying, especially in the South. There, many of the white votes that had gone to the Dixiecrats in 1948 began swinging over to the Republicans.

EISENHOWER TAKES COMMAND

Eisenhower's "moderate Republicanism" initially brought few fundamental changes in either foreign or domestic policies. Eisenhower honored his campaign pledge to travel to Korea as a means of bringing an end to U.S. military involvement there. However, armistice talks stalled when an impasse developed over whether North Korean and Chinese prisoners of war who had asked to remain in the South should be forcibly returned to North Korea and China. Hoping to end the diplomatic stalemate, Eisenhower began to threaten, in vague messages that

CHRONOLOGY

1946	Baruch plan for atomic energy proposed • Employment Act passed • Republicans gain control of Congress in November elections • Dr. Benjamin Spock's *Baby and Child Care* published
1947	Truman Doctrine announced • HUAC begins hearings on communist infiltration of Hollywood • George Kennan's "Mr. X" article published • National Security Act passed (CIA and NSC established) • Marshall Plan adopted • Truman's loyalty order announced • Taft-Hartley Act passed over Truman's veto • Jackie Robinson and Larry Doby break major league baseball's color line
1948	Berlin Airlift begins • Truman wins reelection • The *Kinsey Report* published
1949	NATO established • "Fall" of China to communism occurs • NSC-68 drafted • Soviet Union explodes atomic device • Truman outlines his Fair Deal
1950	Korean War begins • Senator Joseph McCarthy charges communist infiltration of state department • McCarran Internal Security Act passed
1951	Truman removes General MacArthur as commander in Korea
1952	GI Bill of Rights passed • Dwight Eisenhower elected president
1953	Korean War ends • Julius and Ethel Rosenberg executed • *Playboy* magazine debuts
1954	Joseph McCarthy censured by U.S. Senate • Communist Control Act passed

quickly reached China and North Korea, the use of nuclear weapons if negotiations failed. Talks resumed, and on July 27, 1953, both sides signed a truce that established a special commission of neutral nations to rule on the POW cases. (The POWs themselves were subsequently allowed to determine whether they wished to be repatriated.) So finally ended the fighting in which more than 2 million Asians, mostly noncombatants, and 33,000 Americans had died. A formal peace treaty remained unsigned, however, and the 38th parallel remained one of the most heavily armed borders in the world.

In both foreign and domestic policy, Eisenhower stood near the center. This strategy not only helped Eisenhower pursue his foreign policies but eventually allowed him to wrest control of the issue of national security at home from Senator McCarthy and the other extreme anticommunists in Congress. The Republican-controlled Congress did pass the Communist Control Act of 1954, which barred the Communist Party from entering candidates in elections and extended the registration requirements established by the McCarran Act of 1950. But with a Republican administration now in charge, many members of the GOP began to see McCarthy more as a liability than an asset.

McCarthy finally careened out of control when he claimed that the U.S. Army was harboring subversives within its ranks. During the spring of 1954, a televised Senate committee investigation into McCarthy's fantastic claim finally brought him down. Under the glare of TV lights during the Army-McCarthy hearings, the senator appeared as a crude, desperate bully who was flinging slanders in every direction. In December 1954 a majority of McCarthy's colleagues voted to censure him for conduct "unbecoming" a member of the Senate.

With McCarthyism discredited, Eisenhower could proceed with the expansion of the national security state. Following the excesses of McCarthyism, Ike's low-key approach seemed eminently reasonable. Indeed, the demonstrated unreliability of Congress's anticommunist zealots strengthened Eisenhower's own position when he claimed the constitutional privilege to withhold from Congress secret information on national security matters. Relatively free from congressional oversight, the Eisenhower administration quietly proceeded to extend Truman's earlier programs of domestic surveillance, wiretapping, and covert action overseas.

Many historians now see Eisenhower as a skilled leader who increased the power of the executive branch while seeming to do the opposite. According to one scholar, the crafty Eisenhower conducted a "hidden hand presidency." Mindful of how the mercurial Truman had become personally linked to unpopular policies, Ike tried to stay in the background and to project an air of calm steadiness. On matters of foreign policy, he usually had John Foster Dulles take center stage; on domestic issues, he let people assume that White House policies were being shaped by George Humphrey, his secretary of the treasury, and by Sherman Adams, his chief of staff.

Eisenhower's presidency helped to lower the pitch of the shrill anticommunist crusade that characterized American domestic and international policy from 1946 to 1954. With Eisenhower's presidency symbolizing tranquillity, a new sense of calm was settling over life in the United States in the middle 1950s—or so it seemed on the surface.

CONCLUSION

Efforts at "containing" communism dominated both domestic and foreign policy during the years after the Second World War. As worsening relations between the United States and the Soviet Union reached the stage of a Cold War, the Truman administration pursued policies that expanded the power of the government to counter the threat. The militarization of foreign policy intensified when the United States went to war in Korea in 1950. At home, anticommunism focused on containing the activities and ideas of alleged subversives. These initiatives raised difficult issues about how to protect the liberty of those who were suspected of being subversives or of simply being insufficiently zealous anticommunists.

Within this Cold War climate, struggles to achieve greater equality still emerged. Truman's Fair Deal promised that new economic wisdom would be able to guarantee economic growth and thereby provide the tax revenue to expand domestic programs. Truman himself pressed for national measures to end racial discrimination.

The election of a Republican president, Dwight D. Eisenhower, in 1952 brought few immediate changes in the Cold War climate. A moderate on most issues and a skillful political strategist, Eisenhower projected the image of an elder statesperson who kept above day-to-day partisan battles. In time, his style of presidential leadership helped to lower the shrillness of anticommunist rhetoric and to offer the prospect of calmer times.

AFFLUENCE AND ITS DISCONTENTS, 1954–1963

Beginning in 1954 the Cold War tensions that had prevailed since 1947 began to abate. President Dwight Eisenhower lowered the pitch of superpower rivalry. Yet he and his successor, John F. Kennedy, still directed a determined anticommunist foreign policy. At home, Eisenhower's relaxed presidential style and Kennedy's youthful charisma helped them cautiously extend some of the domestic programs initiated during the Roosevelt and Truman eras. The economic growth of the late 1950s and early 1960s encouraged talk about an age of affluence.

Nevertheless, the era's general affluence also generated apprehension about a presumed conformity, the emergence of a "youth culture," and the impact of a mass commercial culture. At the same time, a broad-based movement against racial discrimination and new attention to economic inequities prompted renewed debate over the meaning of liberty, how to achieve equality, and the use of governmental power.

FOREIGN POLICY, 1954–1960

By 1954 the shrill anticommunist rhetoric associated with McCarthyism and the Korean War era was beginning to subside. The dominant assumption of Cold War policy—that the United States had to protect the "free world" and fight communism everywhere—remained unchanged, but the focus of that policy shifted. Bipolar confrontations between the United States and the Soviet Union over European issues gave way to greater reliance on nuclear deterrence and to more subtle and complex power plays in the "Third World"—the Middle East, Asia, Latin America, and Africa.

THE NEW LOOK AND SUMMITRY

One reason for this shift was a change of leadership in Moscow after the death of Joseph Stalin in 1953. Nikita Khrushchev, the new Soviet leader, talked of "peaceful coexistence." Seeking to free up resources to produce more consumer goods, Khrushchev began reducing Soviet armed forces.

The political climate in the United States also was changing. In December 1953, Admiral Arthur Radford, chairman of the Joint Chiefs of Staff, called for a reduction of the military budget and a revision of defense strategy. Radford's "New Look" reflected Eisenhower's belief that massive military expenditures would eventually impede the nation's economic growth. The new strategy would rely less on expensive ground forces and more on airpower, advanced nuclear capabilities, and covert action.

According to the Eisenhower administration's doctrine of "massive retaliation," the threat of U.S. atomic weaponry would hold communism in check. To make America's nuclear umbrella more effective worldwide, Eisenhower expanded NATO to include West Germany in 1955 and added two other mutual defense pacts with noncommunist nations in Central and Southeast Asia. The Southeast Asia Treaty Organization (SEATO), formed in 1954, was a mutual defense pact among Australia, France, Great Britain, New Zealand, Pakistan, the Philippines, and Thailand. The weakly bonded Central Treaty Organization (CENTO), formed in 1959, linked Pakistan, Iran, Turkey, Iraq, and Britain.

The Eisenhower administration also elevated psychological warfare and "informational" programs into major Cold War weapons. The government-run Voice of America extended its radio broadcasts globally and programmed in more languages. Covertly, the government also funded Radio Free Europe, Radio Liberation (directly to the Soviet Union), and Radio Asia. In 1953 Eisenhower persuaded Congress to create the United States Information Agency (USIA) to coordinate anticommunist informational and propaganda campaigns.

In an effort to improve relations, the superpowers resumed high-level "summit" meetings. In May 1955 an agreement was reached to end the postwar occupation of Austria and to transform that country into a neutral state. Two months later the United States, the Soviet Union, Britain, and France met in Geneva. In the fall of 1959, to soothe a crisis that had developed over Berlin, Khrushchev toured the United States, met with Eisenhower, and paid well-publicized visits to farmers in Iowa and to Disneyland in California. But a summit scheduled for 1960 in Paris was canceled after the Soviets shot down an American U-2 spy plane over their territory. Still, the tone of Cold War rhetoric had grown less strident.

The superpowers even began to consider arms limitation. In Eisenhower's "open skies" proposal of 1955, the president proposed that the two nations verify disarmament efforts by reconnaissance flights over each other's territory. The Soviets refused. But some progress was made in limiting atomic tests. Responding to worries about the health hazards of atomic fallout, both countries slowed their above-ground testing and discussed some form of test-ban agreement. For many Americans, concerns about the impact of nuclear testing came too late. Government documents declassified in the 1980s finally confirmed what antinuclear activists had long suspected: Many people who had lived "downwind" from rural nuclear test sites during the 1940s and 1950s had suffered an unusual number of atomic-related illnesses. Worse, in the 1990s it was revealed that Washington had conducted tests with radioactive materials on American citizens, who had no knowledge of these experiments.

Events in Eastern Europe accentuated American policymakers' caution about being drawn into a military confrontation with the Soviet Union. There, the reluctant satellites of the Soviet Union were chafing under the managed economy and police-state control imposed by the Soviets. Seizing on the post-Stalin thaw, Poland's insurgents staged a three-day rebellion in

June 1956 and forced the Soviets to accept Wladyslaw Gomulka, an old foe of Stalin, as head of state. Hungarians then began to demonstrate in support of Imre Nagy, an anti-Stalinist communist, who formed a new government and pledged a multiparty democracy. Hungarian revolutionaries appealed for American assistance, but the United States could hardly launch a military effort so close to Soviet power. Soviet armies crushed the uprising and killed thousands of Hungarians, including Nagy.

COVERT ACTION AND ECONOMIC LEVERAGE

Increasingly, the focus of the U.S. battle against communism began to shift from Europe to the Third World, with covert action and economic leverage replacing overt military confrontation as primary diplomatic tools. These techniques were less expensive than military action and provoked less public controversy because they were less visible.

In 1953 the CIA helped to bring about the election of the anticommunist leader Ramón Magsaysay as president in the Philippines. That same year, the CIA helped execute a coup to overthrow Mohammad Mossadegh's constitutional government in Iran, restoring to power Shah Reza Pahlavi. The increasingly dictatorial Shah remained a firm ally of the United States and a friend of American oil interests in Iran until his ouster by Moslem fundamentalists in 1979. In 1954 the CIA, working closely with the United Fruit Company, helped topple President Jacobo Arbenz Guzmán's elected government in Guatemala. Officials of the Eisenhower administration and officers of the fruit company regarded Arbenz as a communist because he sought to nationalize and redistribute large tracts of land, including some owned by United Fruit itself.

After these "successes" the CIA, under the direction of John Foster Dulles's brother Allen, grew in influence and power. In 1954 the National Security Council widened the CIA's mandate, and by 1960 it had approximately 15,000 agents deployed around the world.

Eisenhower also employed economic strategies—trade and aid—to fight communism and win converts in the Third World. Those strategies were aimed at opening more opportunities for American enterprises overseas, discouraging other countries from adopting state-directed economic systems, and encouraging expansion of commerce. New governmental assistance programs offered economic aid to friendly nations, and military aid rose sharply as well. Under the Mutual Security Program and the Military Assistance Program, the United States spent $3 billion a year, and 225,000 representatives from nations around the world were trained in anticommunism and police tactics. The buildup of military forces in friendly Third World nations strengthened anticommunist forces but also contributed to the development of military dictatorships.

AMERICA AND THE THIRD WORLD

In applying these new anticommunist measures, the Eisenhower administration employed a very broad definition of "communist." In many countries, communist political parties had joined other groups in fighting to bring about changes in labor laws and land ownership that would benefit the poor. Meanwhile, U.S. companies doing business abroad joined forces with local elites to resist the redistribution of power that such programs implied. Consequently, the

United States often found itself supporting "anticommunist" measures that simply suppressed political and social change.

LATIN AMERICA

In Latin America, Eisenhower talked about encouraging democracy but regularly supported dictatorial regimes as long as they welcomed U.S. investment and suppressed leftist movements. Eisenhower awarded the Legion of Merit to unpopular dictators in Peru and Venezuela and privately confessed his admiration for the anticommunism of Paraguay's General Alfredo Stroessner, who sheltered ex-Nazis and ran his country as a private fiefdom. The CIA established a training program for Cuban dictator Fulgencio Batista's repressive security forces.

Such policies offended many Latin Americans, and "yankeephobia" spread. Events in Cuba dramatized the growing anti-American hostility. After Fidel Castro overthrew Batista in 1959 and tried to curtail Cuba's dependence on the United States, the Eisenhower administration imposed an economic boycott of the island. Castro turned to the Soviet Union, declared himself a communist, and pledged to support leftist insurgencies throughout Latin America. At the same time the Eisenhower administration ordered a review of the policies that had sparked such ill will throughout Latin America. The review recommended that policymakers should place more emphasis on democracy, human rights, and economic growth.

NASSERISM AND THE SUEZ CRISIS OF 1956

In the Middle East, distrust of nationalism, neutralism, and social reform also influenced U.S. policy. In 1954, when Gamal Abdel Nasser overthrew a corrupt monarchy and took power in Egypt, he promised to rescue Arab nations from imperialist domination and guide them toward "positive neutralism." Nasser strengthened Egypt's economic and military power. Then he purchased advanced weapons from communist Czechoslovakia and extended diplomatic recognition to communist China. Those actions prompted the United States to cancel loans for the building of the huge Aswan Dam, a project designed to improve agriculture along the Nile River and provide power for new industries. Nasser retaliated in July 1956 by nationalizing the British-controlled Suez Canal. Suez was of major economic and symbolic importance to Britain, and the British government, joined by France and Israel, attacked Egypt in October to retake the canal.

Although Eisenhower distrusted Nasser, he decried Britain's blatant attempt to retain its imperial position. Denouncing the Anglo-French-Israeli action, Eisenhower threatened to destabilize the British currency unless the invasion was terminated. In the end, a plan supported by the United States and the United Nations allowed Nasser to retain the Suez Canal. But American prestige and power in the area suffered as the Soviet Union took over financing of the Aswan Dam.

With Nasser-style nationalism now more closely aligned with the Soviets, the Eisenhower administration feared the spread of "Nasserism" throughout the oil-rich Middle East. In the spring of 1957, his "Eisenhower Doctrine" pledged to defend Middle Eastern countries "against overt armed aggression from any nation controlled by international communism." When elites in Lebanon and Jordan, fearful of revolts by forces friendly to Nasser, asked the United States and Britain to stabilize their countries, Eisenhower sent U.S. marines to set up an anti-Nasser government in Beirut, and Britain simultaneously restored King Hussein to the throne in Jordan. These actions were part of Eisenhower's policy to support friendly, conservative governments in the Middle East, but Western military intervention also intensified Arab nationalism and anti-Americanism.

The Eisenhower administration tried to thwart revolutionary political movements elsewhere in the world. In 1958 the president approved a plan for the CIA to support an uprising against Achmed Sukarno, the president of Indonesia, who drew support from Indonesia's large Communist Party. But when the rebellion failed, the United States abandoned its Indonesian allies, and Sukarno tightened his grip on power. In the next few years, CIA activities included various schemes to assassinate Fidel Castro (these efforts failed) and Patrice Lumumba, a popular black nationalist in the Congo (Lumumba was killed in 1961, although the degree of CIA involvement in his death is still debated by scholars).

VIETNAM

Eisenhower's strategy of thwarting communism and neutralism in the Third World set the stage for U.S. involvement in Vietnam, where communist-nationalist forces led by Ho Chi Minh were fighting for independence from France. Ho Chi Minh had studied in France and in the Soviet Union before returning to lead his country's anticolonial insurgency. At the end of the Second World War, Ho Chi Minh appealed in vain to the United States to support Vietnamese independence rather than allow the return of French colonial administration. But U.S. leaders backed France and its ally in the South, the government of Bao Dai. Ho Chi Minh went to war against the French who, after a major defeat at Dien Bien Phu in 1954, decided to withdraw. The subsequent Geneva Peace Accords of 1954 ended French control over all of Indochina and divided it into Laos, Cambodia, and Vietnam. Vietnam itself was split into two jurisdictions—North Vietnam and South Vietnam—until an election could be held to unify the country under one leader.

Eisenhower's advisers felt that Ho Chi Minh's powerful communist-nationalist appeal might set off a geopolitical chain reaction. The Eisenhower administration took the position that "the loss of any of the countries of Southeast Asia to Communist aggression" would ultimately "endanger the stability and security of Europe" and of Japan. This became known as the "domino theory." As Ho Chi Minh's government established itself in North Vietnam, Eisenhower supported a noncommunist government in the South.

Colonel Edward Lansdale, who had directed CIA efforts against a leftist insurgency in the Philippines from 1950 to 1953, arrived in Saigon, capital of the South, in 1954. Lansdale was to mastermind the building of a pro-U.S. government in South Vietnam under Ngo Dinh Diem, an anticommunist Catholic. Diem's government, with U.S. concurrence, denounced the Geneva Peace Accords and refused to take part in elections to create a unified government for Vietnam. It extended control over the South, redistributed land formerly owned by the French, built up its army, and launched a program of industrialization. But Diem alienated much of South Vietnam's predominantly Buddhist population and, as time passed, grew more and more isolated from his own people and almost totally dependent on the United States. By 1960 the United States had sent billions of American dollars and 900 advisers to prop up Diem's government.

The opposition to Diem in the South coalesced in the National Liberation Front (NLF). The NLF, formed in December 1960, was an amalgam of nationalists who resented Diem's dependence on the United States, communists who demanded more extensive land reform, and politicians who decried Diem's corruption and cronyism. It was allied with the Viet Minh communists of the North, from which it gradually received more and more supplies.

Although Eisenhower warned that military intervention in Indochina would be a "tragedy," he committed more and more aid and national prestige to South Vietnam and tied America's honor to Diem's diminishing political fortunes. The decision of whether to turn these commitments into a large-scale military intervention would fall to Eisenhower's successors in the White House.

In his farewell address of 1961, Eisenhower warned that the greatest danger to the United States was not communism but the nation's own "military-industrial complex." Despite his desire to limit militarism and lower the pitch of Cold War rivalries, however, Eisenhower and Secretary of State Dulles had nevertheless directed a resolutely anticommunist foreign policy that helped fuel the nuclear arms race and accelerate superpower contests in the Third World.

AFFLUENCE—A "PEOPLE OF PLENTY"

Writing in 1954, the historian David Potter called Americans a "people of plenty." The 1950s marked the midpoint of a period of generally steady economic growth that began during the Second World War and continued until the early 1970s. Corporations turned out vast quantities of consumer goods and enjoyed rising rates of profit. Investments and business ventures overseas boosted corporate profits at home. The domestic economy intersected with an international marketplace that was dominated by firms based in the United States. National security policies helped to keep the economy growing by facilitating access to raw materials and energy from the Third World.

Newer industries, such as chemicals and electronics, became particularly dominant in the world market. The Corning Glass Company reported that most of its sales in the mid-1950s came from products that had not even existed in 1940. General Electric proclaimed that "progress is our most important product." Government spending on national security pumped money into the general economy and stimulated specific industries.

HIGHWAYS AND WATERWAYS

Eisenhower was a fiscal conservative. His administration kept nonmilitary spending under tight control. After 1955 even the Pentagon's budget was reduced; and for several years, the federal government itself ran a balanced budget.

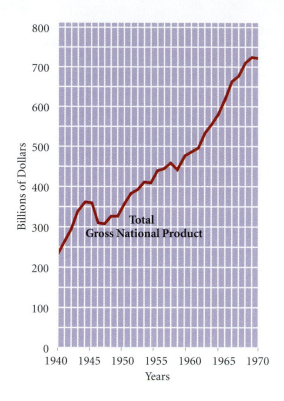

STEADY GROWTH OF GROSS NATIONAL PRODUCT, 1940–1970

Eisenhower did, however, support the Highway Act of 1956. Financed by a national tax on gasoline and other highway-related products, the Highway Act provided funds for the construction of a national system of limited-access, high-speed expressways. Touted as the largest public works project in the history of the world, this program provided steady work for construction firms and boosted the interstate trucking business. It was the first centrally planned transportation system in the nation's history.

By the mid-1950s, U.S. highways were crowded with automobiles that rivaled suburban homes as symbols of abundance. Automakers touted their annual model changes and their increasingly larger engines. Detroit's auto industry helped to support other domestic industries such as steel. In 1956 the steel industry could boast of being three and a half times more efficient than its fledgling Japanese rival.

The Eisenhower administration also supported river-diversion projects in the Far West. The Army Corps of Engineers and the Bureau of Reclamation spent billions of dollars on dams, irrigation canals, and reservoirs. Irrigation turned desert into crop land, and elaborate pumping systems even allowed rivers to flow uphill. By 1960, the western states had access to trillions of gallons of water per year, and the basis for new economic growth in Texas, California, and Arizona was established.

These water projects came at a high price. Technologically complicated and costly, they generated similarly complex and expensive bureaucracies to sustain them. As a consequence, ordinary people lost power to government agencies and private entrepreneurs. Increasingly, large corporate-style operations pushed out smaller farmers and ranchers. In addition, American

Indians found portions of their tribal lands being flooded or being purchased by agribusinesses or by large ranching interests. Finally, the vast water projects laid the basis for ecological problems. Plans to divert surface waters, to tap into groundwater tables, and to dot the West with dams and reservoirs began to take their toll upon the land. Worse, the buildup of salt byproducts in the water and the soil was accompanied by the disastrous overuse of pesticides such as DDT.

LABOR-MANAGEMENT ACCORD

Most corporate leaders, having accepted the kind of government involvement required to build interstate highways and water projects, were learning to live with labor unions as well. The auto industry led the way.

Closer cooperation with corporate management, labor leaders reasoned, could guarantee employment stability and political influence for their unions. Taking their cue from the United Auto Workers, labor dropped the demand for greater union involvement in corporate decision making. In exchange for recognizing "management prerogatives" over crucial issues—such as the organization of the daily work routine, the introduction of new technologies, and investment priorities—union leaders could still bargain aggressively for wages and fringe benefits.

Moreover, union leaders guaranteed management that rank-and-file workers would abide by the terms of their union contracts and disavow the wildcat tactics used in the 1930s and 1940s. To police this new labor-management détente, both sides looked to the federal government's National Labor Relations Board (NLRB). Meanwhile, in 1955, the AFL and the CIO merged—another sign of declining militancy within the labor movement.

Business leaders regarded this labor-management accord as a substantial victory. *Fortune* magazine noted that General Motors had paid a price in terms of more costly employee benefit packages and higher wages in the 1950s, but that "it got a bargain" in terms of labor peace. To safeguard their control over management functions, corporations regularly expanded their supervisory staffs. That practice drove up consumer prices and deprived workers of active participation in planning the work process. This accord may also have helped to divide industrial workers from one another, as those who worked in the more prosperous sectors of the economy, such as the auto industry, were able to bargain more effectively than those who worked in peripheral areas.

Most workers, however, did make economic gains. During the 1950s and early 1960s, real wages (what workers make after their paychecks are adjusted for inflation) steadily rose; the rate of industrial accidents dropped; fringe benefits (what workers receive in terms of health insurance, paid vacation time, and pension plans) improved; and job security was generally high.

Economic growth had made the United States the envy of the world. Widespread ownership of kitchen appliances, television sets, and automobiles supported the claim that American consumers were enjoying a culture of abundance. Harvard's celebrated economist John Kenneth Galbraith had simply entitled his 1952 study of the economy *American Capitalism;* his 1958 follow-up was *The Affluent Society,* a book that topped the best-seller lists for nearly six months.

Although Galbraith's second study was actually much more critical of economic affairs than his first, the term "affluence" fit nicely with the vision of constant economic growth. It also directed attention away from the deeply rooted inequalities that persisted in American society. Talking about affluence, for example, meant that one could avoid using the word "wealth," which might suggest its opposite, "poverty," a term seldom used in economic analyses of the mid-1950s. And by shifting the focus from what people *actually owned*— their accumulated wealth—to their affluence—what they could, with the aid of generous credit terms, *consume*—observers found that the "American way of life" was constantly improving.

POLITICAL PLURALISM

Many observers also credited economic affluence with giving rise to a new political structure. Galbraith, for example, suggested that unions, consumer lobbies, farm organizations, and other noncorporate groups could exert effective "countervailing power" against corporations. Only a few mavericks, such as the sociologist C. Wright Mills, disagreed. Mills saw corporate leaders as members of a small "power elite" that dominated American life. He claimed that this elite had made all of the big decisions on foreign and domestic policy in the decade since the Second World War.

In Mills's critique, the nation's Cold War policies represented an unwise, potentially disastrous, extension of government power at home and overseas. And in the vaunted affluent society, work was becoming more regimented and jobs were bringing little satisfaction. Although Mills anticipated and inspired critics of the 1960s and early 1970s, most of his contemporaries dismissed his power elite thesis as a simplistic conspiracy theory.

To those who subscribed to the dominant view, called "pluralism," no power elite could ever dominate the political process. According to pluralist accounts, public policymaking proceeded from wide participation in public debate by a broad range of different interest groups. Short-term conflicts over specific issues would obviously continue to arise, but as a professor at Harvard Law School put it, constant economic growth meant that "in any conflict of interest," it was "always possible to work out a solution" because affluence guaranteed that all interests would be "better off than before." Pluralists praised postwar leaders for finding "realistic" solutions to difficult problems.

A RELIGIOUS PEOPLE

The celebration of political pluralism dovetailed with an exaltation of the role of religion in American life. Congress emphasized religious values by constructing a nondenominational prayer room on Capitol Hill; by adding the phrase "under God" to the Pledge of Allegiance; and declaring the phrase "In God We Trust" the official national motto.

The emphasis on a pluralistic, transdenominational religious faith was not simply a product of anticommunism. Intense religious commitments, most analysts insisted, no longer divided people as much as in the past. President Eisenhower urged people to practice their own religious creed, whatever it might be. "Our government makes no sense," he declared "unless it is founded in a deeply felt religious faith—and I don't care what it is."

Religious leaders echoed this theme. Will Herberg's *Protestant-Catholic-Jew* (1955) argued that these three faiths were really "'saying the same thing' in affirming the 'spiritual ideals' and 'moral values' of the American Way of Life." Rabbi Morris Kretzer, head of the Jewish Chaplain's Organization, reassured Protestants and Catholics that they and their Jewish neighbors shared "the same rich heritage of the Old Testament . . . the sanctity of the Ten Commandments, the wisdom of the prophets, and the brotherhood of man." Religious commentators increasingly talked about the "Judeo-Christian traditon."

Individual religious leaders became national celebrities. Norman Vincent Peale, a Protestant minister who emphasized the relationship between religious faith and "peace of mind," sold millions of books declaring that belief in a Higher Power could reinvigorate daily life "with health, happiness, and goodness." His *The Power of Positive Thinking* (1952) remained a best-seller throughout the 1950s. The Catholic Bishop Fulton J. Sheen hosted an Emmy-winning, prime-time, TV program called *Life Is Worth Living*. Oral Roberts and Billy Graham—two younger, more charismatic TV ministers—began to spread their fiery brand of Protestant evangelism during the 1950s.

Peale, Sheen, Roberts, and Graham identified themselves with conservative, anticommunist causes, but an emphasis on religious faith was hardly limited to the political right. Dorothy Day, who had been involved in grass-roots activism since the early 1930s, continued to crusade for world peace and for a program aimed at redistributing wealth at home through the pages of *The Catholic Worker*. Church leaders and laypeople from all of the three major denominations supported the antidiscrimination cause and came to play important roles in the civil rights movement. Even so, the revival of religious faith during the 1950s remained closely identified with the culture of affluence.

DISCONTENTS OF AFFLUENCE

Alongside the celebrations of economic affluence, political pluralism, and religious faith, the 1950s still produced a good deal of social criticism—especially about conformity, youth, mass culture, discrimination, and inequality.

CONFORMITY IN AN AFFLUENT SOCIETY

In *The Organization Man* (1956), the sociologist William H. Whyte Jr. indicted the business corporation for contributing to one of the problems produced by affluence: conformity. Whyte saw middle-class corporate employees accepting the values of their employers, at the expense of their own individuality. The security of knowing what the corporate hierarchy wanted outweighed the organization man's concerns about a loss of individuality, Whyte argued.

In *The Lonely Crowd* (1950), David Riesman, another sociologist, wrote of a shift from an "inner-directed" society, in which people looked to themselves and to their immediate families for a sense of identity and self-worth, to an "other-directed" society, in which people looked to peer groups for approval and measured their worth against mass-mediated models. To illustrate the subtle manner in which conformist values were taught to children, Riesman pointed to *Tootle the Engine,* a popular children's book of the 1950s. When Tootle showed a preference for frolicking in the fields beside the tracks, people came to him to exert peer pressure on him as a means of getting him to conform. If Tootle stayed on tracks laid down by others, they assured him, he would grow up to be a powerful and fast-moving streamliner. This message of unprotesting adjustment to peer expectations, Riesman argued, contrasted vividly with the conflict-filled fairy tales, such as *Little Red Riding Hood,* on which earlier generations of young people had been raised.

The critique of conformity reached a broad audience through the best-selling books of journalist Vance Packard. *The Hidden Persuaders* (1957) argued that advertising produced conformity. The book, Packard wrote his publisher, was designed to show "how to achieve a creative life in these conforming times" when so many people "are left only with the roles of being consumers or spectators."

Critics such as Whyte, Riesman, and Packard wrote primarily about the plight of middle-class men, but other writers, such as Betty Friedan, claimed to find a similar psychological malaise among many women. Corporation managers, for example, were criticized for expecting the wives of their male executives to help their husbands deal with the demands of corporate life, including the need for frequent relocation. The organization man, it was said, found that his ascent up the corporate ladder depended on how well his wife performed her informal corporate duties in an equally conformist social world.

YOUTH CULTURE

Concerns about young people also intensified during the 1950s. Many criminologists linked burgeoning sales of comic books to an alleged rise in juvenile delinquency. The psychologist Frederick Wertham, in *The Seduction of the Innocent* (1954), blamed comics displaying sex and violence for "mass-conditioning" children and for stimulating juvenile unrest. Responding to local legislation and to calls for federal regulation, the comic book industry resorted to self-censorship. Publishers who adhered to new guidelines for the portrayal of violence and deviant behavior could display a seal of approval, and the great comic book scare soon faded away.

Critics of the youth culture, however, easily found other worrisome signs. In 1954 Elvis Presley, a former truck driver from Memphis, rocked the pop music establishment with a string of hits on the tiny Sun record label. Presley's sensual, electric stage presence thrilled his youthful admirers and outraged critics. Presley ("The King") and other youthful rock stars—such as Buddy Holly from West Texas, Richard Valenzuela (Richie Valens) from East Los Angeles, and Frankie Lymon from Spanish Harlem—crossed cultural and ethnic barriers and shaped new musical forms from older ones, especially African American rhythm and blues (R&B) and the "hillbilly" music of southern whites.

The first rock 'n' rollers inspired millions of fans and thousands of imitators. They sang about the joys of "having a ball tonight"; the pain of the "summertime blues"; the torment of being "a teenager in love"; and the hope of deliverance, through the power of rock, from "the days of old." Songs such as "Roll over Beethoven" by Chuck Berry became powerful teen anthems.

Guardians of older, family-oriented forms of mass culture found rock 'n' roll music even more frightening than comic books. They denounced its sparse lyrics, pulsating guitars, and screeching saxophones as an assault on the very idea of music. Religious groups condemned it as the "devil's music"; red-hunters detected a communist plan to corrupt youth; and segregationists found it to be part of a sinister plot to mix the races. The dangers of rock 'n' roll were abundantly evident in *The Blackboard Jungle* (1955), a film in which a racially mixed gang of high school students terrorized teachers and mocked adult authority.

Some rock 'n' roll music looked critically at daily life in the 1950s. The satirical song "Charley Brown" contrasted pieties about staying in school with the bleak educational opportunities open to many students. Chuck Berry sang of alienated teenagers riding around "with no particular place to go." This kind of implied social criticism, which most older listeners failed to decode, anticipated the more overtly rebellious rock music of the 1960s.

But rock music and the larger youth culture gradually merged into the mass-consumption economy of the 1950s. Top-40 radio stations and the producers of 45-rpm records identified middle-class teenagers as a market worth targeting. By 1960, record companies and disk jockeys promoted songs and performers exalting the pursuit of "fun, fun, fun" with the help of clothes, cars, and rock 'n' roll records. Rock music had come to celebrate the ethic of a people of plenty.

THE MASS CULTURE DEBATE

Criticism of conformity and of youth culture merged into a wider debate over the effects of mass culture. Much of the anxiety about the decline of individualism and the rise of rock 'n' roll could be traced to fears that "hidden persuaders" were now conditioning millions of people.

Custodians of culture decried mass-marketed products. According to the cultural critic Dwight MacDonald, "bad" art—such as rock music and Mickey Spillane's best-selling "Mike Hammer" series—was driving "good" art from the marketplace and making it difficult for people to distinguish between them. MacDonald and other critics of mass culture argued that entrepreneurs, by treating millions of consumers as if they were all the same, obscured difficult social issues with a blur of pleasant, superficial imagery.

Television became a prominent target. Evolving out of network radio, television was dominated by three major corporations (NBC, CBS, and ABC) and sustained by advertisers. Picturing millions of seemingly passive viewers gathered around "the boob tube," critics decried both the quality of mass-produced programming and its impact on the public. Situation comedies, such as *Father Knows Best,* generally featured middle-class, consumption-oriented suburban families. At the same time, network television responded to pressure from advertisers and avoided programs with contemporary themes in favor of ones that, according to TV's critics, encouraged retreat into unrealities such as the mythical, heroic Old West.

These critics also worried about how mass culture seemed to be transforming the fabric of everyday life. Architects were calling for the rearrangement of living space within middle-class homes so that the television set could become the new focal point for family life. Entire new lines of products—such as the frozen TV dinner and the influential magazine *TV Guide*—became extensions of the new televisual culture. The TV set itself became an important symbol of postwar affluence.

The Limits of the Mass Culture Debate

Most critics of mass culture acknowledged that mass culture was closely linked to the economic system. Was it really possible to cure the ills of mass culture while still enjoying the benefits of affluence? Convinced that the nation was on the right track, critics of mass culture refused to question the distribution of political and economic power in the United States. Radical critiques of industrial capitalism, heard so often during the 1930s, were no longer in vogue during the 1950s.

Moreover, the most obvious cures for the disease of mass culture clashed with the critics' own commitment to an open, pluralistic society. If, on the one hand, Congress were encouraged to legislate against "dangerous" cultural products, censorship might end up curtailing freedom of expression. On the other hand, if local communities were to step in, the results might be even worse. The prospect of southern segregationists censoring civil rights literature or of local censorship boards banning movies produced in Hollywood or books published in New York City hardly appealed to the cosmopolitan critics of mass culture.

Meanwhile, amid the concern about mass culture, a number of other questions about the direction of postwar life were beginning to emerge. Americans remained especially divided over issues related to race and to the role of government.

The Fight against Discrimination, 1954–1960

Following the death in 1953 of Chief Justice Fred Vinson, Eisenhower rejected more conservative candidates to replace him on the Supreme Court and chose Earl Warren, a former governor of California. Under Warren, the Court would come to play an important role in the civil rights struggle, the most significant movement for change in the postwar period.

BROWN V. BOARD

In 1954 Warren wrote the Court's unanimous opinion in *Brown* v. *Board of Education of Topeka,* which declared that segregation of public schools violated the constitutional right of African American students to equal protection of the law. Although it technically applied only to educational facilities, *Brown* implied that all segregated public facilities, not simply schools, were open to legal challenge.

The job of carrying out the broader implications of *Brown* tested the nation's political and social institutions. The crusade against racial discrimination had long centered on the South, but demographic changes meant that national leaders could no longer treat the issue as simply a regional one.

The 1950s marked the beginning of a period in which the South was becoming more like the rest of the country. New cultural forces, such as network television, were linking the South more closely with a nationally based culture. Economic forces were also at work. Machines were replacing the region's predominantly black field workers, and the absence of strong labor

"THE PROBLEM WE ALL LIVE WITH"   Eighty years after federal troops withdrew from enforcement of Reconstruction in southern states in 1877, they returned to enforce school desegregation against resistance by southern whites. This 1960 painting by Norman Rockwell shows a young black girl being escorted by U.S. marshals to a newly desegregated school in New Orleans, while an unseen mob screams obscenities and threats. Despite the affluence enjoyed by most of U.S. society in the decade following the Korean War, some members of the population were still fighting for their most basic rights.

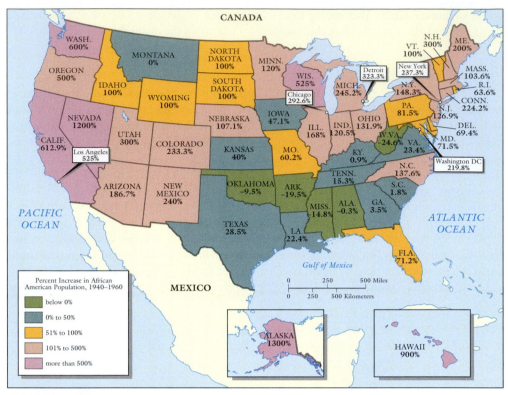

SHIFTS IN AFRICAN AMERICAN POPULATION PATTERNS, 1940–1960

unions and the presence of favorable tax laws were attracting national chain stores, business franchises, and northern-based industries to the South.

At the same time, the racial composition of cities in the West, Midwest, and Northeast was becoming more like that of the South. Accelerating the pattern begun during the Second World War, African Americans left the rural South and settled in cities like Los Angeles, Chicago, New York, and Cleveland during the late 1940s and early 1950s. In the mid-1950s this demographic shift helped to quicken "white flight" to the suburbs and to transform political alignments. With African American voters becoming increasingly important in the North, for example, urban Democrats came to support the drive to end racial discrimination. Meanwhile, the Republicans were making small electoral gains in what had long been the Democratic Party's "solid South." Most important, African Americans themselves mounted a new attack on segregation and racial discrimination in the South.

The battle against racial discrimination was coming to dominate domestic politics. Segregationists in the South pledged "massive resistance" to the Supreme Court ruling in *Brown* v. *Board of Education.* This strategy seemed to be succeeding when in 1955 the Supreme Court ruled that school desegregation should proceed with "all deliberate speed." In the following year, 100 members of the U.S. House and Senate signed a "Southern Manifesto" in which they promised to support any state that intended "to resist forced integration by any lawful means."

ROSA PARKS IGNITES DESEGREGATION CAMPAIGN   Rosa Parks's refusal to sit at the back of a segregated bus in 1955 sparked a campaign to integrate public transit in Montgomery, Alabama. Here, following a successful boycott, Rosa Parks rides in the front seat on the first day of desegregated bus travel.

Defiance went beyond the courtroom. Vigilantes donned the white robes of the Ku Klux Klan, which was joined by new racist organizations, such as the White Citizens Council. As a result, antidiscrimination activists constantly risked injury and death. In August 1955 two white Mississippians murdered 14-year-old Emmett Till, a visitor from Chicago, for acting "disrespectful" to a white woman. Mamie Till Bradley demanded that her son's maimed corpse be displayed publicly for "the whole world to see" and that young Till's killers be punished. When their case came to trial, an all-white jury found the killers—who would subsequently confess their part in the murder—not guilty.

THE MONTGOMERY BUS BOYCOTT AND MARTIN LUTHER KING JR.

In response to the uncertainty of judicial remedies, African Americans began supplementing legal maneuvering with aggressive campaigns of direct action. In Montgomery, Alabama, Rosa Parks, a member of the local NAACP, was arrested in 1955 for refusing to obey a state segregation law that required black passengers to give up their seats to whites and sit at the back of the bus. Montgomery's black community responded to her arrest by boycotting public transportation. The resulting financial losses convinced the city's public transit system to reconsider its segregationist policy.

The Montgomery boycott vaulted the Reverend Martin Luther King Jr., one of its leaders, into the national spotlight. King followed up the victory in Montgomery by joining with other black ministers to form the Southern Christian Leadership Conference (SCLC). In addition to pressing for the desegregation of public facilities, the SCLC launched an effort to register

African American voters throughout the South. More activist than the NAACP, the SCLC served to spread King's broad vision of social change—integration forced by passive civil disobedience—throughout the nation. The purpose of civil disobedience, according to King, was to persuade people of the moral evil of racial discrimination. Aided by the national media, especially network television, King's powerful presence and religiously rooted rhetoric carried the message of the antidiscrimination movement in the South to the entire nation.

THE POLITICS OF CIVIL RIGHTS

But political institutions in Washington responded very slowly. The Supreme Court expanded its definition of civil rights but generally backed away from mandating the sweeping institutional changes needed to make these rights meaningful. Congress, meanwhile, remained deeply divided on racial issues. With southern segregationists, all of them members of the Democratic majority, holding key posts on Capitol Hill, antidiscrimination legislation faced formidable obstacles.

Even so, Congress passed its first civil rights measures in more than 80 years. The Civil Rights Act of 1957 set up a procedure for expediting lawsuits by African Americans who claimed their right to vote had been abridged. It also created a permanent Commission on Civil Rights to study alleged violations and recommend new remedies. In 1960, another act promised additional federal support for blacks who were being barred from voting in the South. These civil rights initiatives, which became law against fierce opposition from southern Democrats, dramatized the difficulty of getting even relatively limited antidiscrimination measures through Congress.

President Eisenhower appeared largely indifferent to the issue of racial discrimination. When liberal Republicans urged him to take action, he did nothing. He regarded the fight against discrimination as primarily a local matter, and he publicly doubted that any federal civil rights legislation could change the attitudes of people opposed to the integration of public facilities or job sites.

Indeed, Eisenhower's grasp of domestic issues seemed to grow more uncertain during his second term as president. In the election of 1956, he achieved another landslide victory over Democrat Adlai Stevenson, but his personal appeal did relatively little to help his party. In 1956 the Republicans failed to win back control of Congress from the Democrats. In fact, in this presidential election and in the off-year races of 1958, the GOP lost congressional seats as well as state legislatures and governors' mansions to the Democrats. Meanwhile, Eisenhower, who had suffered a mild heart attack prior to the 1956 election, seemed progressively enfeebled, physically as well as politically. He appeared especially weak in his handling of racial issues.

In 1957, however, Eisenhower was forced to act. Orval Faubus, the segregationist governor of Arkansas, ordered his state's National Guard to block enforcement of a federal court order mandating integration of Little Rock's Central High School. Responding to this direct challenge to national authority, Eisenhower put the Arkansas National Guard under federal control and augmented it with members of the U.S. Army. Black students, escorted by armed troops, then were able to enter the high school.

AMERICAN INDIAN POLICY

The Eisenhower administration also lacked coherent policies on issues affecting American Indians. It attempted to implement two programs, "termination" and "relocation," that had been

proposed during the Truman years. The termination policy called for the national government to end its oversight of tribal affairs and to treat American Indians as individuals rather
than as members of tribes. Its long-term goals were to abolish reservations, to liquidate assets
of the tribes, and to end the kinds of federal services offered by the Bureau of Indian Affairs
(BIA). In 1954, one year after this general policy had received congressional approval, six bills
of termination were enacted, affecting more than 8,000 Native Americans.

Under the relocation program, Indians were encouraged to leave their rural reservations
and take jobs in urban areas. In 1954 the BIA intensified its earliest relocation efforts, with
Minneapolis, St. Louis, Dallas, and several other cities joining Denver, Salt Lake City, and Los
Angeles as relocation sites. This program, like the termination policy, encouraged American
Indians to migrate to urban areas and become assimilated into the social mainstream.

Both programs were deeply flawed. As several more termination bills were enacted during
the Eisenhower years, almost 12,000 people lost their status as tribal members, and the bonds
of communal life for many Indians grew weaker. At the same time, nearly 1.4 million acres of
tribal lands were lost, often falling into the hands of real estate speculators. Indians from terminated tribes lost both their exemptions from state taxation and the social services provided
by the BIA and gained almost nothing in return. Most terminated Indians sank into even
deeper poverty. Relocation went no better. Most of the relocated Indians found only low-
paying, dead-end jobs and racial discrimination. In the mid-1950s, Indian children who had
been relocated from reservations found it difficult even to enter *segregated,* let alone integrated, public schools in some cities. Despite its problems, the program nevertheless continued throughout the Eisenhower years.

Gradually, however, both Indians and civil rights activists mobilized against the termination and relocation policies. By 1957 the BIA had scaled back its initial timetable for liquidat-
ing every tribe within five years, and in 1960 the party platforms of both the Republicans and
Democrats repudiated the termination policy entirely. In 1962 this disastrous policy was itself terminated. Meanwhile, however, the relocation program continued, and by 1967 almost

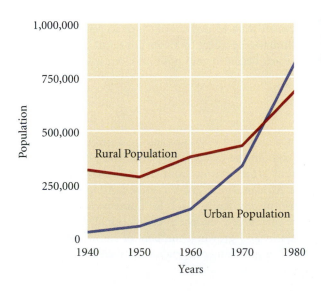

**TOTAL URBAN AND RURAL INDIAN
POPULATION IN THE UNITED
STATES, 1940–1980**

half of the nation's Indians were living in relocation cities. The policy hardly touched the deeply rooted problems that many Indians confronted, including a life expectancy only two-thirds that of whites, nor did it ever provide significantly better opportunities for employment or education.

THE GROWTH OF SPANISH-SPEAKING POPULATIONS

The millions of new Spanish-speaking people, many of whom had recently arrived in the United States, also highlighted the issue of discrimination. In the 1950s Puerto Ricans began moving to the mainland in large numbers. Finding only low-paying jobs and settling in older urban neighborhoods, these new arrivals were U.S. citizens but often spoke only Spanish. In 1960 New York City's Puerto Rican community was nearly 100 times greater than it had been before the Second World War.

Meanwhile, large numbers of Spanish-speaking people from Mexico were moving into the Southwest, where they joined already sizable Mexican American communities. Beginning during the Second World War and continuing until 1967, the U.S. government sponsored the *bracero* (or farmhand) program, which brought nearly 5 million Mexicans northward to serve as agricultural laborers. Many of the *braceros* remained in the United States after their contracts expired. Joining them were legal immigrants from Mexico and growing numbers of people who illegally filtered across the border. The illegal Mexican immigrants, derisively labeled "wetbacks" because they supposedly swam across the Rio Grande, became the target of a government dragnet called "Operation Wetback." During the early 1950s, the government rounded up and deported to Mexico nearly 4 million people.

Leaders in long-established Mexican American communities mobilized to fight discrimination. Labor organizers sought higher wages and better working conditions in the factories and fields, although the FBI labeled many of these efforts as "communist-inspired" and harassed unions that had large Mexican American memberships. Middle-class organizations, such as the League of United Latin American Citizens (LULAC) and the Unity League, also sought to desegregate schools, public facilities, and housing in southern California and throughout the Southwest. In 1940 Mexican Americans had been the most rural of all the major ethnic groups; by 1950, in contrast, more than 65 percent of Mexican Americans were living in urban areas, a figure that would climb to 85 percent by 1970. As a result of this fundamental demographic shift, Mexican Americans began to gain political clout in many southwestern cities.

URBAN ISSUES

The growth of new, largely white, suburban areas in the 1950s was accompanied by new urban issues, many of them related to race. Throughout the 1950s, both public and private institutions were shifting money and construction projects away from the cities, especially away from neighborhoods in which Latinos and African Americans had settled. Adopting a policy called "redlining," many banks and loan institutions denied funds for home buying and business expansion in neighborhoods that were considered "decaying" or "marginal" because they contained aging buildings, dense populations, and growing numbers of nonwhites. Meanwhile, the Federal Housing Authority and other government agencies channeled most of their funds toward the new suburbs.

"Urban renewal" programs, authorized by the Housing Act of 1949 (see Chapter 27), often amounted to "urban removal." Although federal housing laws called for "a feasible method for the temporary relocation" of persons displaced by urban renewal projects, developers often ignored the housing needs of the people they displaced. People with low-income jobs were evicted so that their apartments and homes could be replaced by office buildings and freeways.

Public housing projects, which had been designed to provide affordable housing for low- and moderate-income families, proved an especially grave disappointment. Although the suburbs, where land was abundant and relatively inexpensive, seemed an obvious place in which to build public housing, middle-income suburbanites blocked such construction. Consequently, the few public projects built were in the cities, where population density was high and land was expensive. Originally conceived as a temporary alternative for families who would rather quickly move out to their own homes, public housing facilities became stigmatized as "the projects," housing of last resort for people with little prospect for economic advancement.

By the end of the 1950s, the urban policies of both the Fair Deal and the Eisenhower era were widely regarded as failures. Urban renewal projects not only disrupted housing patterns but also helped to dislocate industries that had long provided entry-level jobs for unskilled workers. Both major presidential candidates in 1960 pledged to create a new cabinet office for urban affairs and to expand the federal government's role.

DEBATES OVER GOVERNMENT'S ROLE IN THE ECONOMY

Controversy over urban issues was related to larger debates over the role that government should play in economic life. Although Eisenhower sometimes hinted to conservative Republicans that he wanted to roll back the New Deal and the Fair Deal, he lacked both the will and the political support to do so. Actually, Eisenhower presided over an expanded Social Security system, higher minimum wages, better unemployment benefits, and a new Department of Health, Education, and Welfare (HEW). Still, as his stance on urban and racial issues showed, he took few steps to enlarge governmental power. His popularity seemed to rest on his personality rather than on the specifics of his policies.

EISENHOWER AND THE NEW CONSERVATIVES

As a result of his centrist position on most domestic issues, Eisenhower attracted the ire of a growing group of political conservatives. Eisenhower, of course, was the first Republican president since Herbert Hoover, but did his administration really represent basic GOP principles?

Not to Arizona's Barry Goldwater. A fervent anticommunist, Goldwater was elected to the U.S. Senate in 1952. In his book *Conscience of a Conservative* (1960), Goldwater criticized postwar U.S. leaders, including Eisenhower, for failing to take stronger military measures against the Soviet Union. At the same time, Goldwater decried almost all domestic programs, especially civil rights legislation, as grave threats to individual liberty.

While Goldwater was working to push the GOP to the right of Eisenhower's moderate Republicanism, William F. Buckley Jr. was trying to reshape a broader right-wing message for the country at large. Buckley, a devout Roman Catholic, first gained national attention while still in his twenties with a 1952 book, *God and Man at Yale*, that detected a "collectivist" and antireligious tilt in American higher education. Three years later, Buckley helped found the

National Review, a magazine that attracted a talented group of writers. The *National Review* moved away from extremist positions, particularly the hysterical anticommunism of groups such as the John Birch Society. Although this "new conservatism" began amid considerable doubts about its immediate prospects for success, Buckley's own *Up from Liberalism* (1959), Goldwater's *Conscience of a Conservative,* and other books looked to a long-term strategy for building a right-of-center movement.

ADVOCATES OF A MORE ACTIVE GOVERNMENT

While the new conservatives were criticizing the Eisenhower administration for failing to break decisively with the policies of the Roosevelt and Truman years, liberals were grumbling that it was failing to address pressing public issues through the more active use of government power. They were especially critical of Eisenhower's relatively passive approach to questions involving racial discrimination. Moreover, critics ridiculed Eisenhower's commitment to a balanced budget as evidence of his 19th century approach. After Eisenhower suffered a second heart attack and a mild stroke during his second term, many critics talked about the need for more vigorous presidential leadership. Liberal advocates of greater governmental intervention in the economy urged deficit spending by Washington as a way to stimulate continued economic expansion.

Other critics recommended dramatic increases in spending for national security. The 1957 Gaither Report, prepared by prominent people with close ties to defense industries, warned that the Soviet Union's GNP was growing even more quickly than that of the United States and that much of this expansion came in the military sector. It urged an immediate increase of about 25 percent in the Pentagon's budget and long-term programs for building fallout shelters, for developing intercontinental ballistic missiles (ICBMs), and for expanding conventional military forces.

Eisenhower reacted cautiously. Although he agreed to accelerate the development of ICBMs, he opposed any massive program for building fallout shelters or for fighting limited, nonnuclear wars around the globe. In fact, he reduced the size of several Army and Air Force units and kept his defense budget well below the levels his critics were proposing. Eisenhower could confidently take such steps because secret flights over the USSR by U-2 surveillance planes, which had begun in 1956, revealed that the Soviets were lagging behind, rather than outpacing, the United States in military capability.

Concerns about national security and calls for greater governmental spending also surfaced in the continuing controversy over education. Throughout the 1950s, some critics complained that schools were emphasizing "life adjustment" skills—getting along with others and accommodating to social change—instead of teaching the traditional academic subjects. Rudolf Flesch's best-selling book of 1955 wondered *Why Johnny Can't Read.* Other books suggested that Johnny and his classmates couldn't add or subtract very well either and that they lagged behind their counterparts in the Soviet Union in their mastery of science. These arguments gained new intensity when, in October 1957, the Soviets launched the world's first artificial satellite, a 22-inch sphere called *Sputnik.*

Using the magical phrase "national security," school administrators and university researchers sought and won more federal dollars. The National Defense Education Act of 1958 funneled money to college-level programs in science, engineering, foreign languages, and the social sciences. This act marked a milestone in the long battle to overcome congressional opposition to federal aid to education.

Other critics urged the Eisenhower administration to seek increased federal spending for social welfare programs. Writing in 1958, in *The Affluent Society,* John Kenneth Galbraith found a dangerous tilt in the "social balance," away from "public goods." Affluent families could travel in air-conditioned, high-powered automobiles, Galbraith observed, but they must pass "through cities that are badly paved, made hideous by litter, blighted buildings," and billboards. While the researcher who develops a new carburetor or an improved household cleanser is well rewarded, the "public servant who dreams up a new public service is [labeled] a wastrel."

Galbraith's musings seemed mild in comparison to the jeremiads of Michael Harrington. In 1959, *Commentary,* one of several influential magazines that featured social criticism during the late 1950s, published an article in which Harrington argued that the problem of economic inequality remained as urgent as it had been during the 1930s. At least one-third of the population was barely subsisting in a land of supposed affluence. Avoiding statistics and economic jargon, Harrington told dramatic stories about the ways in which poverty could ravage the bodies and spirits of people who had missed out on the affluence of the 1940s and 1950s.

During the early 1960s, when domestic policymaking became a priority of John F. Kennedy and Lyndon Baines Johnson, critics such as Galbraith and Harrington became political celebrities. But their critique should be seen as a product of the political culture of the late 1950s. The Kennedy presidency of 1961–1963 would be firmly rooted in the critique of both foreign and domestic policymaking that had emerged during the Eisenhower years.

THE KENNEDY YEARS: FOREIGN POLICY

John Fitzgerald Kennedy had been groomed for the White House by his politically ambitious father. After his graduation from Harvard in 1940, Kennedy pursued a life devoted to public service. After winning military honors while serving in the U.S. Navy during the Second World War, Kennedy entered politics. In 1946 he won election from Massachusetts to the House of Representatives, and in 1952 he captured a seat in the Senate. In Washington, Kennedy gradually gained a national political reputation, largely on the basis of his charm and youthful image. He was aided by his 1953 marriage to Jacqueline Bouvier. In 1956, he narrowly missed winning the Democratic vice presidential nomination.

THE ELECTION OF 1960

Between 1956 and 1960, Kennedy barnstormed the country, speaking at party functions and rounding up supporters for a presidential bid. This early campaigning, along with his talented political advisers and his family's vast wealth, helped Kennedy overwhelm his primary rivals, including the more liberal Senator Hubert Humphrey of Minnesota and Lyndon Johnson.

Richard Nixon remained on the defensive throughout the campaign of 1960. Nixon seemed notably off balance during the first of several televised debates in which political pundits credited the cool, tanned Kennedy with a stunning victory over the pale, nervous Nixon. Despite chronic and severe health problems, which his loyal staff effectively concealed, Kennedy projected the image of a youthful, vigorous leader.

During the 1960 campaign, Kennedy stressed four issues that together made up what he called his "New Frontier" proposals. On civil rights and social programs, he pledged support for antidiscrimination efforts. In an important symbolic act, he sent his aides to Georgia to

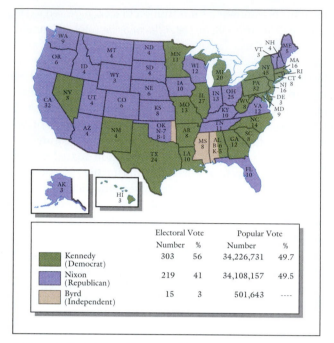

PRESIDENTIAL ELECTION, 1960

		Electoral Vote		Popular Vote	
		Number	%	Number	%
■ (green)	Kennedy (Democrat)	303	56	34,226,731	49.7
■ (purple)	Nixon (Republican)	219	41	34,108,157	49.5
■ (tan)	Byrd (Independent)	15	3	501,643	----

assist Martin Luther King Jr., who had been sentenced to six months in jail for a minor traffic violation. Moreover, Kennedy endorsed the sort of social programs that liberals had been advocating. Although his proposals remained vague, he did mention greater federal spending to rebuild rural communities, to increase educational opportunities, and to improve urban conditions.

Kennedy also highlighted two other issues that had provoked debate during the 1950s: stimulating greater economic growth and conducting a more aggressive foreign policy. He surrounded himself with advisers who spoke of stimulating the economy by means of tax cuts and deficit spending measures. On Cold War issues, he criticized Eisenhower for failing to rid the hemisphere of Castro in Cuba and for allowing a "missile gap" to develop in U.S. defenses against the Soviet Union. By spending heavily on defense, he claimed, he would create a "flexible response" against communism, especially in the Third World.

The 1960 election defied easy analysis. Kennedy defeated Nixon by only about 100,000 popular votes and won the electoral votes of several states, including Illinois, by a razor-thin margin. Apparently hurt by his Catholicism, especially in the South, Kennedy won a smaller percentage of the popular vote than most other Democrats running for lesser offices. Clearly, his victory owed a great deal to his vice presidential running mate, Lyndon Johnson, whose appeal to southern whites helped the ticket carry the Deep South and Johnson's home state of Texas.

From the outset, the president and his wife Jacqueline riveted media attention on the White House. They hobnobbed with movie stars and brought prominent intellectuals into the administration. In his inaugural address, Kennedy challenged people to "ask not what your country can do for you; ask what you can do for your country." The "best and the brightest," the hard-driving people who joined Kennedy's New Frontier, promised to launch exciting new crusades, even to the ultimate frontier of outer space.

KENNEDY'S FOREIGN POLICY GOALS

In foreign policy, Kennedy boasted of making a break with the past to wage the Cold War more vigorously. Military assistance programs, propaganda agencies, and covert action plans all received strong support from the White House. In one of his most popular initiatives, the president created the Peace Corps, a new program that sent Americans to nations around the world to work on development projects that were supposed to undercut the appeal of communism.

Kennedy, however, also built upon many of Eisenhower's policies. Eisenhower's last-minute efforts to reorient Latin American policies away from reliance on dictators and toward support of more progressive programs were elaborated on and repackaged as Kennedy's "Alliance for Progress." Proposed in the spring of 1961 as a way to prevent the spread of anti-Americanism and communist insurgencies, the Alliance offered $20 billion in loans over a 10-year period to Latin American countries that would undertake land reform and democratic development measures. The Alliance, based on a naive assessment of the obstacles to social and economic development, rapidly failed.

CUBA AND BERLIN

The worst fiasco of the Kennedy presidency, a daring but ill-conceived CIA mission against Cuba, also had its roots in the Eisenhower administration. The CIA was planning a secret invasion to topple Fidel Castro, Cuba's revolutionary leader. On April 17, 1961, when U.S.-backed and trained forces (mainly anticommunist Cuban exiles) landed at the Bahia de Cochinas (the Bay of Pigs) on the southern coast of Cuba, however, the expected popular uprising against Castro did not occur. The invaders were quickly surrounded and imprisoned. Kennedy refused to provide the air support that Cuban exiles had been led to expect and at first even tried to deny that the United States had been involved in the invasion, but the CIA's role quickly became public, and anti-Yankee sentiment mounted in Latin America. Castro tightened his grip over Cuba and strengthened his ties with the Soviet Union. "I have made a tragic mistake," Kennedy told Clark Clifford, an adviser. Yet, stung by the failed invasion, the Kennedy administration continued to target Castro with a covert program called Operation Mongoose, which consisted of economic destabilization activities and futile assassination plots.

Another dramatic confrontation loomed in Berlin. In June 1961, Nikita Khrushchev and Kennedy met in Vienna, where Khrushchev proposed ending the Western presence in Berlin and reuniting the city as part of East Germany. His proposal was motivated by the steady flow of immigrants from East Germany into West Berlin, a migration that was both embarrassing and economically draining to the German communist regime. Kennedy was forceful in his refusal to abandon West Berlin, but the East German government continued to press Khrushchev to help solve their problems. On August 13, 1961, the communist regime began to erect a wall to separate East from West Berlin. East Germans attempting to escape into the West were shot. The Berlin Wall became a symbol of communist repression. Kennedy's assertion, "*Ich bin ein Berliner*" ("I am a Berliner"), delivered in front of the wall to a massive crowd, became one of the most memorable lines of his presidency.

THE CUBAN MISSILE CRISIS   During the Cuban Missile Crisis of October 1962, these Cuban refugees, like most people, were riveted to their television sets to obtain the latest update from President Kennedy. In this nuclear confrontation, the fate of the world seemed at stake.

Superpower confrontation escalated to its most dangerous level during the Cuban Missile Crisis of 1962. The Soviet Union, responding to Castro's request, sent sophisticated weapons to Cuba. In October, after spy-plane flights confirmed the existence of missile launching sites there, the Kennedy administration publicly warned that it would not allow nuclear warheads to be installed so close to American shores. Kennedy demanded that the Soviets dismantle the missile silos they had already prepared and turn back some supply ships that were heading for Cuba. After dramatic meetings with his top advisers, Kennedy rejected an outright military strike. Instead, he ordered the U.S. Navy to "quarantine" the island. The Strategic Air Command was put on full alert for possible nuclear war. Meanwhile, both sides engaged in complicated, secret diplomatic maneuvers to prevent a nuclear confrontation.

The maneuvers succeeded. On October 28, 1962, Khrushchev ordered the missiles dismantled and the Soviet supply ships brought home; Kennedy promised not to invade Cuba and secretly assured Khrushchev that he would complete the previously ordered withdrawal of U.S. Jupiter missiles from Turkey. In the mid-1990s, with the opening of some Soviet archives, Americans learned that the crisis had been even more perilous than they had imagined. Unknown to Kennedy's circle at the time, the Soviets already had tactical nuclear weapons in Cuba that could have been launched.

After the Cuban Missile Crisis, both superpowers seemed to recognize the perils of direct conflict. A direct phone line was established between Moscow and Washington to ensure the kind of communication that might forestall a nuclear confrontation or an accident in the future. And both nations became a bit more cautious.

SOUTHEAST ASIA AND "FLEXIBLE RESPONSE"

In Southeast Asia, Kennedy followed Eisenhower's policy of trying to build South Vietnam into a viable, noncommunist state. After the Bay of Pigs disaster, in which the attempt to overthrow an already established pro-communist government had failed, Kennedy decided that the U.S. must put down communist-led "wars of national liberation" before they succeeded.

Kennedy viewed Vietnam as a test case for "flexible response," which aimed at implementing a variety of methods to combat the growth of communist movements. Elite U.S. special forces known as Green Berets were trained in "counterinsurgency" tactics to use against communist guerrillas; cadres of social scientists charged with "nation building" were sent as advisers. When these efforts brought nothing but greater corruption and a deeper sense of isolation to the Diem regime, the CIA gave the South Vietnamese army the green light to orchestrate Diem's overthrow. Just weeks before Kennedy himself would be assassinated, Diem was run out of his palace and murdered. The coup against Diem brought a military leader to power, but this seemed only to breed even greater political instability.

THE KENNEDY YEARS: DOMESTIC POLICY

Despite his campaign promises, Kennedy was slow to depart from Eisenhower's cautious fiscal policies. He was fearful of running federal budget deficits greater than those of the Eisenhower years. Relations with corporate leaders nevertheless turned ugly in 1962, when Kennedy publicly clashed with the president of U.S. Steel over that company's decision to raise prices beyond the guidelines suggested by the administration.

POLICYMAKING UNDER KENNEDY

Eventually, though, Kennedy endorsed tax breaks as a means of promoting economic growth. According to prevailing theory, lower tax rates for everyone and special deductions for corporations that invested in new plants and equipment would free up money for investment. In 1962 he urged Congress to change the complex tax code. Despite opposition from those who thought the tax breaks would unfairly benefit corporations and the wealthy, the bill seemed headed for passage in the fall of 1963.

On matters of social welfare, the Kennedy administration advanced policies that had been initiated by the Fair Deal of the 1940s—namely, a higher minimum wage and continuation of urban renewal programs. It also lent its support to the Area Redevelopment Bill of 1961, which called for directing federal grants and loans to areas that had missed out on the general economic prosperity of the postwar years. Meanwhile, under the urban renewal programs begun during the 1940s, bulldozers were still razing large parts of urban America so that low-income housing continued to be replaced by business and freeway construction projects aimed at middle- and upper-income people. Finally, the Kennedy administration made the fight against organized crime a top priority—much more so (at least initially) than the fight for racial equality.

THE CIVIL RIGHTS CRUSADE, 1960–1963

Although JFK talked about new civil rights legislation, he tried to placate segregationist Democrats by doing little to press the issue for nearly the first two years of his presidency. Meanwhile, the president and his brother Robert, the attorney general, listened sympathetically to complaints from J. Edgar Hoover, director of the FBI, about the allegedly suspicious political activities of Martin Luther King Jr. and his associates. To keep tabs on King's activities and gather information that it might use against him, the FBI used surveillance and, ultimately, illegal wiretaps of his private conversations.

Rising dissatisfaction over the slow pace of the campaign against racial discrimination, however, gradually forced the Kennedy administration to consider new initiatives. In early 1960 young African American students at North Carolina A & T College in Greensboro sat down at a dimestore lunch counter, defied state segregation laws, and asked to be served in the same manner as white patrons. It was the beginning of the "sit-in" movement, a new phase in the civil rights movement in which groups of young activists challenged legal segregation by demanding equal access to hitherto segregated public facilities. All across the South, demon-

RACIAL CONFLICT IN BIRMINGHAM   Images such as this 1963 photograph of a confrontation in Birmingham, Alabama, in which segregationists turned dogs on youthful demonstrators, helped rally public support for civil rights legislation. Events in Birmingham, however, also presaged the increasingly violent clashes that would punctuate the efforts to end racial discrimination.

strators staged nonviolent sit-in demonstrations at restaurants, bus and train stations, and other public facilities.

The courage and commitment of the demonstrators gave the antidiscrimination movement new momentum. With songs such as "We Shall Overcome" and "Oh Freedom" inspiring solidarity, young people pledged their talents and resources—indeed their lives—to the civil rights struggle. In 1961 interracial activists from the Congress of Racial Equality (CORE) and the Student Non-Violent Coordinating Committee (SNCC), a student group that had grown out of the sit-in movement, risked racist retaliation in "freedom rides" across the South; the freedom riders were determined that a series of federal court decisions, which had declared segregation on buses and in waiting rooms to be unconstitutional, would not be ignored by southern officials.

The new grass-roots activism forced the Kennedy administration to respond. In 1961 it sent federal marshals into the South in order to protect freedom riders. In 1962 and again the following year, it called on National Guard troops and federal marshals to prevent segregationists from stopping racial integration at several educational institutions in the Deep South, including the universities of Mississippi and Alabama. In November 1962, Kennedy issued a long-promised executive order that banned racial discrimination in housing financed by the national government. In February 1963, Kennedy sent Congress a moderate civil rights bill, which focused on providing faster trial procedures in voting rights cases.

But events were outpacing Kennedy's policies. Racial conflict convulsed Birmingham, Alabama, in 1963. White police officers used dogs and high-power water hoses on young African Americans who were demanding an end to segregation in the city. Four children were later murdered (and 20 injured) when racists bombed Birmingham's Sixteenth Street Baptist Church, a center of the antisegregation campaign. When thousands of blacks took to the streets in protest—and two more children were killed, this time by police officers—the Kennedy administration finally took more vigorous action.

During the last six months of the Kennedy presidency, civil rights issues dominated domestic politics. Kennedy himself made an emotional plea on television for a national commitment to the cause of antidiscrimination. However, the administration still hoped to shape the direction and pace of change by passing new laws to get demonstrators "off the streets and into the courts." Thus, it supported stronger civil rights legislation, including a ban on racial discrimination in all public facilities and housing and new federal laws to guarantee the vote to millions of African Americans who were being kept from polls in the South.

On August, 28, 1963, an integrated group of more than 200,000 people marched through the nation's capital. Leaders of the march endorsed Kennedy's new civil rights bill, but they also pressed a broader agenda. In addition to more effective civil rights legislation, the marchers' formal demands included a higher minimum wage and a federal program to guarantee new jobs. Standing in front of the Lincoln Memorial, Martin Luther King Jr. delivered his eloquent "I Have a Dream" speech. The march on Washington, which received favorable coverage from the national media, put considerable pressure on the White House and Congress to offer new legislative initiatives.

WOMEN'S ISSUES

The seeds of a resurgent women's movement were also being sown, although more quietly, during the Kennedy years. All across the political spectrum, women were speaking out on contemporary issues. The new conservative movement benefited from the energy of women

CHRONOLOGY

1954	*Brown v. Board of Education of Topeka* decision • SEATO formed • Arbenz government overthrown in Guatemala • Elvis Presley releases first record on Sun label • Geneva Peace Accords in Southeast Asia
1955	Montgomery bus boycott begins • *National Review* founded
1956	Suez Crisis • Anti-Soviet uprisings occur in Poland and Hungary • Federal Highway Act passed • Eisenhower reelected
1957	Eisenhower sends troops to Lebanon • Eisenhower sends troops to Little Rock • Congress passes Civil Rights Act, first civil rights legislation in 80 years • Soviets launch *Sputnik* • Gaither Report urges more defense spending
1958	National Defense Education Act passed by Congress • *The Affluent Society* published
1959	Khrushchev visits United States • Castro overthrows Batista in Cuba
1960	Civil Rights Act passed • U-2 incident ends Paris summit • Kennedy elected president • Sit-in demonstrations begin
1961	Bay of Pigs invasion fails • Berlin Wall erected • Freedom rides begin in the South • Kennedy announces Alliance for Progress
1962	Cuban Missile Crisis • Kennedy sends troops to University of Mississippi to enforce integration
1963	Civil rights activists undertake march on Washington • Betty Friedan's *The Feminine Mystique* published • Kennedy assassinated (November 22); Lyndon Johnson becomes president

such as Phyllis Schlafly, whose book *A Choice, Not an Echo* (1964) became one of the leading manifestos of the Republican Party's right wing. African American activists such as Bernice Johnson Reagon (whose career with the Freedom Singers combined music and social activism) and Fannie Lou Hamer (who helped to organize an integrated Mississippi Freedom Democratic Party) fought discrimination based on both race and gender. And during Kennedy's final year in office, 1963, Betty Friedan published *The Feminine Mystique*. Generally credited with helping to spark a new phase of the feminist movement, Friedan's book articulated the dissatisfactions that many middle-class women felt about the narrow confines of domestic life and the lack of public roles available to them.

To address women's issues, Kennedy appointed the Presidential Commission on the Status of Women, chaired by Eleanor Roosevelt. Negotiating differences between moderate and more militant members, the commission issued a report that documented discrimination against women in employment opportunities and wages. Kennedy responded with a presidential order designed to eliminate gender discrimination within the federal civil service system. His administration also supported the Equal Pay Act of 1963, which made it a federal crime for employers to pay lower wages to women who were doing the same work as men.

THE ASSASSINATION OF JOHN F. KENNEDY

By the fall of 1963 the Kennedy administration was preparing initiatives on civil rights and economic opportunity. Then, on November 22, 1963, John F. Kennedy was shot down as his presidential motorcade moved through Dallas, Texas. Police quickly arrested Lee Harvey Oswald as the alleged assassin. Oswald had ties to the Marcello crime family, had once lived in the Soviet Union, and had a bizarre set of political affiliations, especially with groups interested in Cuba. Oswald declared his innocence, but he was never brought to trial. Instead, Oswald himself was killed, while in the custody of the Dallas police, by Jack Ruby, a nightclub owner who also had links to powerful crime figures. A lengthy but flawed investigation by a special commission headed by Chief Justice Earl Warren concluded that both Oswald and Ruby had acted alone—but these claims came under increasing scrutiny. In 1978 a special panel of the House of Representatives claimed that Kennedy might have been the victim of an assassination plot, perhaps involving organized crime.

A variety of other theories about Kennedy's assassination sprang up, including one, which pointed toward the CIA, advanced in Oliver Stone's film, *JFK* (1991). Although most historians ridiculed Stone's scenario, his film reignited controversy over the report issued by the Warren commission. In response, Congress created the Assassinations Records Review Board as a means of preserving from destruction information about Kennedy's death.

CONCLUSION

After 1954, the Cold War fears associated with McCarthyism began to abate. Presidents Dwight Eisenhower and John F. Kennedy cautiously eased tensions with the Soviet Union, especially after Kennedy found himself on the brink of nuclear war over the presence of Soviet weapons in Cuba in 1962. Even so, both presidents continued to pursue anticommunist foreign policies that focused on the buildup of nuclear weapons, economic pressure, and covert activities. Developments in the Third World, particularly in Cuba and Southeast Asia, became of growing concern.

At home, the period from 1954 to 1963 was one of generally steady economic growth. A cornucopia of new consumer products encouraged talk about an age of affluence but also produced apprehension about conformity, mass culture, and the problems of youth. At the same time, the concerns of racial minorities and other people who were missing out on this period's general affluence increasingly moved to the center of public debates over the meaning of liberty and equality. The Eisenhower administration, many critics charged, seemed too reluctant to use the power of government to fight segregation or to create economic conditions that would distribute the benefits of affluence more widely.

Although Kennedy did not rush to deal with domestic issues, the press of events gradually forced his administration to use government power to confront racial discrimination and advance the cause of equality at home. When Kennedy was killed in November 1963, a new kind of insurgent politics, growing out of the battle against racial discrimination in the Deep South, was beginning to transform political life in the United States.

In the post-Kennedy era, debates would become riveted around issues related to the government's exercise of power: Was the U.S. spreading liberty in Vietnam? Was it sufficiently active in pursuing equality for racial minorities and the poor? Lyndon Johnson's troubled presidency would grapple with these questions.

29

AMERICA DURING ITS
LONGEST WAR, 1963–1974

THE GREAT SOCIETY ～ ESCALATION IN VIETNAM

THE WAR AT HOME ～ THE NIXON YEARS, 1969–1974

FOREIGN POLICY UNDER NIXON AND KISSINGER

THE WARS OF WATERGATE

Lyndon Baines Johnson promised to finish what John F. Kennedy had begun. Ultimately though, Johnson's troubled presidency bore little resemblance to John Kennedy's thousand days of "Camelot."

In Southeast Asia, Johnson faced a crucial decision: Should the United States introduce its own forces and weaponry in order to prop up its South Vietnamese ally? If Johnson did this, what would be the consequences?

At home, Johnson enthusiastically mobilized the federal government's power in order to promote greater equality. But could federal action produce the Great Society that Johnson envisioned?

Many Americans, particularly young people, began to dissent from Johnson's foreign and domestic policies. As a result of a war overseas and dissent at home, the late 1960s and early 1970s became a time of increasingly sharp political and cultural polarization. Richard Nixon's presidency contributed to this polarization. By the end of America's longest war and the Watergate crisis that caused Nixon's resignation, the nation's political culture and social fabric differed significantly from what Johnson had inherited from Kennedy in 1963.

THE GREAT SOCIETY

Johnson lacked Kennedy's charisma, but he possessed political assets of his own. As a member of the House of Representatives during the late 1930s and early 1940s and majority leader of the U.S. Senate in the 1950s, the gangling Texan became the consummate legislative horse trader. Few issues, Johnson believed, defied consensus. Nearly everyone could be flattered, cajoled, even threatened into lending him their support. During his time in Congress, LBJ's wealthy Texas benefactors gained valuable oil and gas concessions and lucrative construction contracts, while Johnson himself acquired a personal fortune. At the same time, the growth of Dallas, Houston, and other cities and the economic boom throughout the Southwest owed much to Johnson's skill in pushing measures such as federally funded irrigation and space-exploration projects through Congress.

Kennedy's death gave Johnson the opportunity to fulfill his dreams of transforming the nation, just as he had transformed Dallas and Houston. Confident that he could use the tactics he had employed in the Senate to build a national consensus for the expansion of government power, Johnson began by urging Congress to honor JFK's memory by passing legislation that Kennedy's administration had originated.

COMPLETING KENNEDY'S INITIATIVES

More knowledgeable in the ways of Congress than Kennedy, Johnson quickly completed the major domestic goals of JFK's New Frontier. Working behind the scenes, Johnson secured passage of Kennedy's proposed $10 billion tax cut, a measure intended to stimulate the economy. Although historians differ on how much this tax cut contributed to the economic boom of the mid-1960s, it *appeared* to work. GNP rose 7 percent in 1964 and 8 percent the following year; unemployment dropped to about 5 percent; and consumer prices rose by less than 3 percent.

Johnson also built on Kennedy-era plans for addressing the problem of poverty. In his January 1964 State of the Union address, Johnson announced that his administration was declaring "an unconditional war on poverty in America." In August 1964 Congress created the Office of Economic Opportunity (OEO) to coordinate the various elements of a multifaceted program. The Economic Opportunity Act of 1964, in addition to establishing OEO, mandated loans for rural and small-business development; established a program of work training called the Jobs Corps; created a domestic version of the Peace Corps program, called VISTA; provided low-wage jobs, primarily in urban areas, for young people; began a work-study plan to assist college students; and, most important, authorized the creation of additional federally funded social programs that were to be designed in concert with local community groups.

Finally, Johnson secured passage of civil rights legislation. In 1964 he helped push an expanded version of Kennedy's civil rights bill through Congress. Championing the bill as a memorial to Kennedy, he nevertheless recognized that southern segregationists in the Democratic Party would try to delay and dilute the measure. Consequently, he successfully lobbied key Republicans for their support. Passed in July 1964 after lengthy delaying tactics by southerners, the Civil Rights Act of 1964, administered by a new Equal Employment Opportunity Commission (EEOC), strengthened federal remedies for fighting job discrimination. It also prohibited racial discrimination in public accommodations connected with interstate commerce, such as hotels and restaurants. Moreover, Title VII, a provision added to the bill during the legislative debates, barred discrimination based on sex, a provision that became extremely important to the women's movement.

THE ELECTION OF 1964

Civil rights legislation was also a testimony to the moral power of civil rights workers. During the summer of 1964 a coalition of civil rights organizations enlisted nearly a thousand volunteers to help register voters in Mississippi—an operation they called "Freedom Summer." During that violent summer, six volunteers were murdered by segregationists, but their fellow civil rights workers pressed forward, only to see their political work frustrated at the Democratic national convention. Pressured by Johnson, who used the FBI to gather information on dissidents, party leaders seated Mississippi's "regular" all-white delegates rather than members of the alternative (and racially diverse) "Freedom Democratic Party."

After this rebuff, civil rights activists recalled their earlier suspicions about Lyndon Johnson and the national Democratic Party. Johnson did seem more committed to change than John Kennedy had been, but would LBJ—and Hubert Humphrey, Johnson's personal choice for his vice presidential running mate—continue to press for antidiscrimination measures after the election? This question became all the more important once it became apparent that Johnson would win the 1964 presidential race.

The Republicans nominated Senator Barry Goldwater of Arizona to oppose Johnson. Goldwater's strategists believed that an unabashedly conservative campaign would attract the millions of voters who were thought to be dissatisfied with both Democratic liberalism and moderate Republicanism. Goldwater denounced Johnson's foreign policies as too timid and Johnson's domestic programs as destructive of individual freedoms. Goldwater, one of eight Republican senators who had voted against the Civil Rights Act of 1964, had criticized the measure as a dangerous extension of power by the national government.

Goldwater's penchant for blurting out ill-considered opinions allowed critics to picture him as fanatical, unpredictable, and reactionary. Goldwater suggested that people who feared nuclear war were "silly and sissified." U.S. weapons were so accurate, he once quipped, that the military could target the men's room in the Kremlin. Reinforcing his "radical-right" image, Goldwater declared in his acceptance speech at the 1964 Republican convention that "extremism in the pursuit of liberty is no vice" and "moderation in the pursuit of justice is no virtue."

Even many Republican voters came to view Goldwater as too extreme, and he led the GOP to a crushing defeat in November. Johnson carried 44 states and won more than 60 percent of the popular vote; in addition, Democrats gained 38 new seats in Congress. Most political pundits immediately hailed the 1964 election as a triumph for Johnson's vision of domestic policymaking.

In retrospect, however, the 1964 election presaged significant political changes that would eventually erode support for Johnson. During the Democratic primaries, for example, Alabama's segregationist governor, George Wallace, had run strongly against the president in several northern states. An opponent of civil rights legislation, Wallace attacked federal "meddling" in local affairs and demonstrated the potential of a "white backlash" movement. The 1964 election was the last time the Democratic Party would capture the White House by hewing to the New Deal–Fair Deal tradition of urging expanded use of governmental power at home.

Goldwater's defeat seemed to invigorate his conservative supporters. His youthful campaign staff had pioneered several innovative stratagems such as direct mail fund-raising. By refining these tactics in future campaigns, conservative strategists helped to make the 1964 election the beginning, not the end, of the Republican Party's movement to the right. Moreover, Goldwater's stand against the Civil Rights Act of 1964 helped him carry five southern states, and these victories convinced Republicans that opposition to antidiscrimination measures by Washington would continue to attract white voters in the South who had once been solidly Democratic.

The Goldwater effort also propelled an attractive group of conservative leaders into national politics. Ronald Reagan, the actor and corporate spokesperson, proved such an effective campaigner in 1964 that conservative Republicans began to groom him for a political career. Other prominent conservatives such as William Rehnquist also entered national politics through the 1964 campaign. In the immediate aftermath of Goldwater's defeat, however, the prospect that a President Ronald Reagan would one day nominate William

Rehnquist to be Chief Justice of the United States seemed beyond any conservative's wildest dream (see Chapter 31).

LYNDON JOHNSON'S GREAT SOCIETY

Lyndon Johnson wanted to capitalize quickly on his electoral victory. Enjoying broad support in Congress, Johnson announced his plans for a "Great Society," an array of programs funded by the national government, that he envisioned would bring economic opportunity to all the people who had missed the prosperity of the 1950s and early 1960s. Some of the Great Society programs fulfilled the dreams of Johnson's Democratic predecessors. Nationally funded medical coverage for the elderly (Medicare) and for low-income citizens (Medicaid) culminated efforts begun during the New Deal and revived during the Fair Deal. Similarly, an addition to the president's cabinet, the Department of Housing and Urban Development (HUD), built upon earlier plans for coordinating urban revitalization programs. Finally, the Voting Rights Act of 1965, which mandated federal oversight of elections in the South, seemed to cap federal efforts begun during the 1930s to end racial discrimination in political life.

The array of initiatives developed under Johnson's "War on Poverty" heartened his supporters and appalled his conservative critics. The "Model Cities Program" was intended to demonstrate how to reconstruct cities without the inequality that had marked the urban renewal efforts of the 1950s; rent supplements were designed to help low-income families maintain and eventually upgrade their living conditions; the expanded Food Stamp program was aimed at improving nutritional levels; Head Start was to help preschool youngsters from low-income families climb the educational ladder; a variety of other federally financed educational programs would upgrade classroom instruction throughout the nation, especially in low-income neighborhoods; and a legal services program would provide legal advice and access to the court system for those who could not afford private attorneys. These initiatives were intended to build services, funded by federal tax dollars, to help people fight their own way out of economic distress.

The Great Society's Community Action Program (CAP) also promised to empower grassroots activists. It encouraged citizens, working through local organizations, to design community-based projects that would be financed from Washington. By promoting "maximum feasible participation" by citizens themselves, CAP was supposed to spark the kind of community-based democracy that could transform the entire political system.

EVALUATING THE GREAT SOCIETY

Why did the Great Society become so controversial? Most obviously, Johnson's dramatic extension of Washington's power rekindled old debates about the proper role of the national government. In addition, the president's extravagant rhetoric, with its promise of an "unconditional" victory over poverty, raised expectations that could not be met in one presidency, or even in one generation. Most important, the faith that economic growth would generate the tax revenues needed to fund expanding social programs simply collapsed with the onset of economic problems during the late 1960s. In 1964 Lyndon Johnson assumed that continued prosperity would allow him to build a consensus for the Great Society; worsening economic conditions, however, made greater federal spending for domestic programs a highly divisive policy.

Historians have evaluated Lyndon Johnson's Great Society programs in a variety of ways. Conservatives have subjected them to harsh criticism. Charles Murray's influential *Losing*

Ground (1984) set the tone by charging that massive government expenditures during the Johnson years had encouraged antisocial behavior. Lured by welfare payments, he argued, many people with low incomes had abandoned the goals of marrying, settling down, and seeking jobs. According to this view, the Great Society's spending had also created huge government deficits that slowed economic growth. Had the nation's economic structure not been weakened by the Great Society, virtually everyone in America could have come to enjoy a middle-class lifestyle. This conservative argument condemned Johnson's program as the cause, not the remedy, for persistent economic inequality in America.

Historians more sympathetic to Johnson's approach have vigorously rejected the conservative argument. They find scant evidence for the claim that low-income people preferred welfare to meaningful work. Spending on the military sector far outstripped that for social programs and seemed the principal cause of burgeoning government deficits. Moreover, they note, expenditures on Great Society programs neither matched Johnson's promises nor commanded the massive amounts claimed by conservatives.

Historians on the left have criticized the Great Society's failure to challenge the prevailing distribution of political and economic power. The Johnson administration, they argue, remained closely wedded to large-scale bureaucratic solutions for problems that had many local variations. In addition, they point out, the Great Society never sought a redistribution of wealth and income. For these critics, the Great Society was a noble ideal that was never seriously implemented.

Although historians evaluate the impact of the Great Society in very different ways, there is broad agreement that Johnson's domestic agenda left its mark on American life. It represented the first significant new outlay of federal dollars for domestic social programs since the New Deal. Spending on such programs increased more than 10 percent in every year of Johnson's presidency. Within a decade of the beginning of the Great Society, programs such as Medicaid, legal services, and job training provided low-income individuals with some of the services more affluent Americans had long taken for granted.

The Great Society, by extending the reach of the welfare state that had begun to appear in the United States during the 1930s, ignited increasingly intense public debate over how best to use the power and resources of the national government. In seeking to extend tangible assistance to the poor, how could policymakers follow the distinction between people who seemed to deserve assistance and those who seemed to be, in Lyndon Johnson's own formulation, seeking a "hand-out" rather than a "hand-up"? Partisan debates over government's social welfare policies would continue throughout the rest of the century.

ESCALATION IN VIETNAM

Johnson's crusade to build a Great Society at home had its counterpart in an ambitious extension of U.S. power abroad. The escalation of the war in Vietnam demanded increasingly more of the administration's energy and resources. Eventually, it alienated many Americans, especially the young, and divided the entire nation.

THE TONKIN GULF RESOLUTION

Immediately after John Kennedy's assassination in November 1963, Johnson had avoided widening the war in Vietnam. But he did not wish to appear "soft" on communism. Seeing no alternative to backing the government in South Vietnam, he accepted his military advisers' recommendation to forestall enemy offensives in the South by staging air strikes against the North. He prepared a congressional resolution authorizing such an escalation of hostilities.

Events in the Gulf of Tonkin, off the coast of North Vietnam, provided him with a rationale for taking the resolution to Congress. On August 1, 1964, the U.S. destroyer *Maddox* exchanged fire with North Vietnamese torpedo boats while conducting an intelligence-gathering mission. Three days later, the *Maddox* returned with the destroyer *Turner Joy* and, amid severe weather conditions, reported a torpedo attack. Although the *Maddox*'s commander radioed that the "attack" might have been a false report, Johnson proclaimed that U.S. forces had been the target of "unprovoked aggression." He rushed the resolution to Congress, where he received overwhelming approval to take "all necessary measures to repel armed attack." Johnson subsequently used this Tonkin Gulf Resolution as tantamount to a congressional declaration of war.

Despite his moves in the Gulf of Tonkin, the president was still able to position himself as a cautious moderate during the presidential campaign of 1964. When Goldwater urged stronger measures against North Vietnam and mentioned the possible use of tactical nuclear weapons, Johnson's campaign managers portrayed Goldwater as a threat to the survival of civilization. A TV commercial depicted a little girl picking the petals from a daisy as a nuclear bomb exploded onscreen. The implication was that a Goldwater victory would bring nuclear holocaust. Johnson promised not to commit American troops to fight a land war in Asia.

Soon after the election, however, Johnson further escalated the war. The 1963 coup against Diem (see Chapter 28) had left a political vacuum in the South. The incompetence of the South's new military-led government sparked growing discontent. Soldiers deserted at an alarming rate. In January 1965, the regime fell, and factionalism prevented any stable government from emerging in its wake.

Without any credible or effective government in South Vietnam, Johnson increasingly worried over his options. Should the pursuit of anticommunism turn the Vietnamese struggle into "America's war"? What would be the public backlash against a possible communist victory? Could the United States escalate and win the war without provoking a deadly clash with China or even the Soviet Union?

Johnson's advisers offered conflicting views. National Security Adviser McGeorge Bundy predicted inevitable defeat unless the United States sharply escalated its military role. Walt Rostow assured Johnson that a determined effort would bring a clear-cut victory. If all routes to victory are denied the enemy, he advised, they will give up. Undersecretary of State George Ball, by contrast, warned that greater Americanization of the war would bring defeat, not victory. "The South Vietnamese are losing the war," he wrote, and "no one has demonstrated that a white ground force of whatever size can win a guerrilla war . . . in jungle terrain in the midst of a population that refuses cooperation to the white forces." The Joint Chiefs of Staff, afflicted by interservice rivalries, provided differing military assessments and no clear advice.

Although privately doubting the long-term prospects for success, Johnson nonetheless feared the immediate political hazards of a U.S. pullout from Vietnam. Domestic criticism of a communist victory in South Vietnam, he believed, would certainly endanger his Great Society programs. Moreover, to those who argued that Vietnam had little strategic importance to the United States, Johnson countered that U.S. withdrawal would set off a "domino effect": encouraging Castro-style insurgencies in Latin America, increasing pressure on West Berlin, and damaging American credibility around the world.

Swayed by political calculations, Johnson decided on a sustained campaign of bombing in North Vietnam, code-named "Rolling Thunder." While the bombing was going on, he deployed

U.S. ground forces to regain territory in the South, expanded covert operations, and stepped up economic aid to the beleaguered Saigon government. Only six months into his new term, with both civilian and military advisers divided in their recommendations, Johnson committed the United States to full-scale war against North Vietnam.

THE WAR WIDENS

The war grew more intense throughout 1965. U.S. military commanders called for an all-out effort to escalate the number of casualties inflicted. Accordingly, the administration authorized the use of napalm, a chemical that charred both foliage and people, and allowed the Air Force to bomb new targets. Additional combat troops arrived to secure enclaves in the South. Each escalation seemed to make further escalation inevitable. North Vietnam's rejection of an unrealistic "peace plan," outlined by Johnson in a speech in April 1965, became a pretext for again raising the levels of U.S. military spending and action. North Vietnam's leader, Ho Chi Minh, was playing the same game of escalation and attrition, convinced that Johnson commanded meager public and congressional support for continuing the costly war.

In April 1965, Johnson brought his anticommunist crusade closer to home. Prompted by exaggerated reports of a communist threat in the Dominican Republic, Johnson sent American troops to unseat a left-leaning, elected president and to install a government favorable to U.S. economic interests. This U.S. incursion violated a long-standing, "good neighbor" pledge not to intervene militarily in the Western Hemisphere. Although the action was criticized throughout Latin America, the seemingly successful military ouster of a leftist regime boosted the administration's determination to hold the line against communism in Vietnam.

During the spring of 1965, as the fifth government since Diem's death took office in Saigon, U.S. strategists were still puzzling over how to prop up its South Vietnamese ally. The commander in charge of the American effort, General William Westmoreland, recommended moving U.S. forces out of their enclaves and sending them on "search and destroy" missions. In July, Johnson dispatched 50,000 additional troops to Vietnam. He also approved saturation bombing of the countryside in the South and intensified bombing of the North.

Some of his advisers urged Johnson to admit candidly to the public that the scope of the war was being steadily enlarged. They also recommended either an outright declaration of war or emergency legislation that would formally put the United States on a wartime footing, so that the president could wield the economic and informational controls that past administrations had used in conflicts of this magnitude. But Johnson feared that assuming the formal status of a belligerent would provoke the Soviet Union or China. He also worried about arousing greater protests from Congress and the public. Rather than risk open debate that might reveal his shallow political support, Johnson decided to stress the administration's efforts to negotiate and to pretend that the war was not a war.

Over the next three years, the number of American troops increased from 50,000 to 535,000. Operation RANCHHAND scorched South Vietnam's crop lands and defoliated half its forests in an effort to eliminate the natural cover for enemy troop movements. Bombs leveled North Vietnamese cities and pummeled the villages and inhabitants of "free-fire zones" (designated areas in which anything was considered a fair target) in the South. Still, Johnson was careful to avoid bombing too close to the Chinese border or doing anything else that might provoke either Chinese or Soviet entry into the war.

The weekly body count of enemy dead became the measure by which the Johnson administration gauged the war's progress. Estimates that a kill ratio of 10 to 1 would force the North to

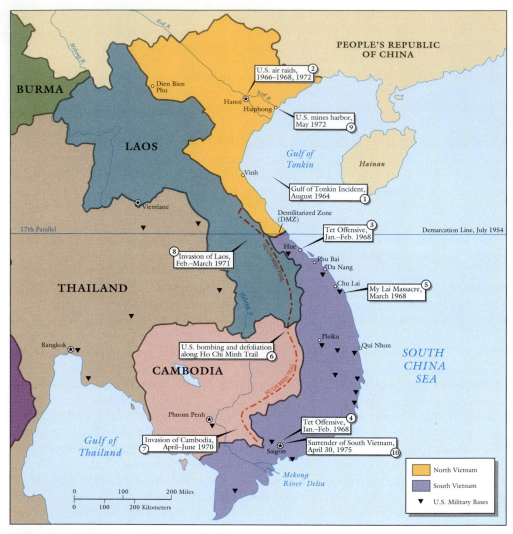

VIETNAM WAR

surrender encouraged the military to inflate body count figures and to engage in indiscriminate killing. Johnson welcomed figures suggesting that "victory was around the corner." Actually, North Vietnam was controlling its losses by concealing troops under the jungle canopy that remained. The North was able to channel a constant flow of supplies into the South through a shifting network of jungle paths called the Ho Chi Minh Trail. The war had reached a stalemate, but few members of Johnson's administration would admit it.

The extent of the destruction wreaked by the U.S. effort gave North Vietnamese leaders a decided propaganda advantage. Critics around the world condemned the escalation of American attacks. The Soviet Union and China increased their aid to Ho Chi Minh. Both at home and abroad, Johnson administration officials were hounded by protesters almost everywhere they went.

Meanwhile, the government in Saigon was reeling under the devastation of its countryside, the destabilizing effect of the flood of U.S. dollars on its economy, and the corruption of its politicians. So-called "pacification" and "strategic hamlet" programs, which brought Vietnamese farmers together in tightly guarded villages, sounded viable in Washington but caused further chaos by uprooting one in four South Vietnamese from their villages and ancestral lands. Buddhist priests persistently demonstrated against foreign influence. When Generals Nguyen Van Thieu and Nguyen Cao Ky, who had led the government since 1965, held elections in 1967 to legitimate their regime, their narrow margin of victory merely highlighted their weakness.

THE MEDIA AND THE WAR

Criticism against the war continued to mount. In most earlier wars, Congress had imposed strict controls on what journalists could report to the public. Because the Vietnam War was undeclared, Johnson had to resort to informal ways of managing information. With television coverage making Vietnam a "living room war," Johnson kept three TV sets playing in his office in order to monitor the major networks. Sometimes he would phone the news anchors after their broadcasts and castigate them for their stories. Increasingly sensitive to criticism, Johnson equated any question or doubt about his policy in Vietnam with a lack of patriotism.

Antiwar activists were equally disturbed by what they regarded as the media's uncritical reporting on the war. Most of the reporters, they claimed, relied on official handouts for their stories and took pains to avoid offending anyone at the White House. Indeed, especially in the early years, few reporters filed hard-hitting stories. In time, however, news coverage and its impact became more critical. The unrelenting images of destruction on the nightly news turned people against the war. In addition, a few journalists forthrightly expressed their opposition. Harrison Salisbury of *The New York Times* sent reports from Vietnam that dramatized the destructiveness of U.S. bombing missions. Gloria Emerson wrote reports picturing the war as a class-based effort in which the United States used poor and disproportionately nonwhite fighting forces, while rich men with draft-exempt sons raked in war profits.

As the war dragged on, Americans became polarized into "hawks" and "doves." Johnson insisted that he was merely following the policy of containment favored by Eisenhower and Kennedy. Secretary of State Dean Rusk spoke of the dangers of "appeasement." But influential senators warned of misplaced priorities and an "arrogance of power." Meanwhile, antiwar protestors began to challenge the structure of American society itself.

THE WAR AT HOME

Millions came to oppose the war in Southeast Asia, and backing eroded for the Great Society at home. Tensions that had been slowly building over recent years appeared to be reaching a critical point.

THE RISE OF THE NEW LEFT

During the early 1960s small groups of young people, many of them college students, came to reject the welfare-state policies of the postwar years. In 1962, two years after activists on the right had formed Young Americans for Freedom (YAF), insurgents on the left established a political organization called Students for a Democratic Society (SDS). Although SDS endorsed familiar causes, especially the fight against racial discrimination, its founding "Port Huron Statement" also spoke of new issues: the "loneliness, estrangement, isolation" of postwar society.

SDS became part of a new political initiative, popularly known as the "New Left," that tried to distance itself from both the welfare-state policies of the Great Society and the "old" communist-inspired Left. By confronting the dominant culture, which allegedly valued bureaucratic expertise over citizen engagement and conspicuous consumption over meaningful work, members of the New Left sought to create an alternative social vision. They called for "participatory democracy," grass-roots politics responsive to the wishes of local communities rather than the preferences of national elites.

During the early 1960s, many young, white college students found inspiration from the antidiscrimination movement in the Deep South. Risking racist violence, they went to the South where they forged bonds of community with African American activists. Some stayed in the South or moved on to political projects in northern neighborhoods. Others returned to their college campuses and joined protests against both the war in Southeast Asia and social conditions at home.

These dissenting students denounced the nation's prestigious colleges and universities as part of a vast "establishment" that resisted significant change. Giant universities, they claimed, seemed oblivious to the social and moral implications of their war-related research. Student dissidents charged faculty and administrators with ignoring the relevant issues of the day in favor of traditional, required courses. Moreover, restrictions on personal freedoms, such as student dress codes and mandatory dormitory hours, were labeled as relics of an authoritarian past in which colleges and universities acted *in loco parentis* (in place of parents). During the Berkeley "student revolt" of 1964 and 1965, students and sympathetic faculty protested the university administration's restrictions on political activity on campus and then moved on to broader issues such as Vietnam and racism.

By 1966 the war in Vietnam had come to dominate the agenda of student protesters. For young men, the antiwar movement became, in part, a matter of self-interest; when they reached age 18 they were required by federal law to register for possible military service. Local draft boards usually granted men who were attending college a student deferment, but these expired upon graduation. The burning of draft cards, as a symbolic protest against both the war and universal military service for men, became a central feature of many antiwar protests.

Meanwhile, many campuses became embroiled in bitter strife. At "teach-ins," supporters and opponents of the war presented their positions and debated the morality of the involvement of universities in national security policies. Teach-ins soon gave way to less-structured demonstrations. As antiwar sentiments grew more intense, campus supporters of the war claimed that *their* right to free speech was being threatened. Conservatives, along with many moderates, pressured college administrators to crack down on "troublemakers" and made opposition to campus protests a prominent part of their new agenda.

THE COUNTERCULTURE

Accompanying the spread of New Left politics was the rise of an antiestablishment "counterculture." Even though only a relatively small percentage of young people fully embraced countercultural values, they came to symbolize the youthful ferment of the late 1960s. Ridiculing

AMERICAN ATTITUDES TOWARD THE VIETNAM WAR   Responses to the question: "Do you think that the United States made a mistake in sending troops to fight there?"

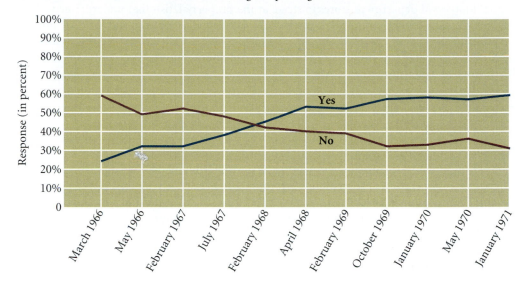

traditional attitudes on such matters as clothing, hair styles, and sexuality, devotees of the counterculture sought an open and experimental approach to daily life. Caricatured as "hippies," they dabbled with mind-altering drugs, communal living arrangements, and new forms of folk-rock music. Bob Dylan's "Like a Rolling Stone" (1965) exploded onto the Top 40 chart of AM radio. Although Dylan never sought the role, members of the counterculture and the media cast him as the musical prophet for an entire generation.

The trappings of the counterculture soon found a ready market among middle-class consumers. Impressed by the success of hippie bands like San Francisco's Grateful Dead and the Jefferson Airplane, the mass culture industry welcomed the youth rebellion. The Rolling Stones made big money with their ode to a "Street Fighting Man" (1968). The Beatles made even more money and attracted critical acclaim with *Sgt. Pepper's Lonely Hearts Club Band* (1967) and *The White Album* (1968). Hollywood tapped the youth culture market with *The Graduate* (1967) and *Bonnie and Clyde* (1967) and followed up with films, such as *Easy Rider* (1969) and *Wild in the Streets* (1968), that portrayed adult authority figures as vampirish ravagers of youth.

A lively debate arose over the media's coverage of the counterculture. Critics of the youth culture charged the media with spreading dangerous, antisocial images. According to conservative critics, the media's extensive coverage of demonstrations in which young radicals and countercultural musicians joined with older opponents of the war helped to exaggerate the strength of the antiwar movement. At the same time, ironically, veterans of earlier New Left protests claimed that the media's unrelenting attention to the counterculture actually undercut antiwar politics.

The media's coverage of an antiwar march on the Pentagon in 1967 crystallized this debate. Rejecting political speeches and the ritualistic burning of draft cards as too dull, some of the marchers amused themselves by trying to levitate the Pentagon. Abbie Hoffman, self-proclaimed leader of the fictitious Youth International Party (the "Yippies"), facetiously urged "loot-ins at department stores to strike at the property fetish that underlies genocidal war" in Vietnam. Although the Pentagon march played well as a media spectacle, its impact on political events was uncertain. At best, dramatic television clips conveyed the passion of dissenters; at worst, a colorful mélange of media-conscious demonstrators helped to fuel polarization throughout American society.

FROM CIVIL RIGHTS TO BLACK POWER

A similar debate developed over media images of the increasingly militant protests against racial discrimination. Early on, leaders in the fight against discrimination, notably Dr. Martin Luther King Jr., had recognized the benefits to be derived from media coverage. During King's 1965 drive to win access to the ballot box for African Americans, TV pictures of the racist violence in Selma, Alabama, helped to galvanize support for federal legislation. President Johnson used television to dramatize his support for voting-rights legislation.

At the same time, the media became the forum for fierce debates over what was increasingly being called a "racial crisis." Conservatives argued that subversive agitators were provoking conflict and violence and that only a good dose of law and order would ease urban racial tensions. Social activists argued that a complex mix of racism, lack of educational and

VIOLENCE IN DETROIT, 1967   Outbreaks of violence, rooted in economic inequality and racial tension, swept through many U.S. cities between 1965 and 1969. The 1967 violence in Detroit, which federal troops had to quell, left many African American neighborhoods in ruin.

employment opportunities, and inadequate government responses were producing the frustration and despair that burst forth in sporadic racial violence. This debate intensified in 1965 in the wake of a devastating racial conflict in Los Angeles. A confrontation between a white Highway Patrol officer and a black motorist escalated into six days of urban violence, centered in the largely African American community of Watts in South-Central Los Angeles. Thirty-four people died; hundreds of businesses and homes were burned; the National Guard patrolled the streets of Los Angeles; and TV cameras framed the conflagration as an ongoing media spectacle. Violence erupted in many other U.S. cities during the remainder of the decade.

Meanwhile, a radical "Black Power" movement emerged. A charismatic preacher named Malcolm X had heralded its arrival. A spokesperson for the Nation of Islam, Malcolm X preached a message fundamentally at odds with that of the leaders of the civil rights movement. He proclaimed that integration was unworkable. Although he never called for violent confrontation, he did endorse self-defense "by any means necessary."

Malcolm X offered more than angry rhetoric. He called for renewed pride in the African American heritage and for vigorous efforts at community reconstruction. In order to revitalize their contemporary institutions, he urged African Americans to "launch a cultural revolution to unbrainwash an entire people." Seeking to forge a broader movement, Malcolm X eventually broke from the Nation of Islam and established his own Organization of Afro-American Unity. Murdered in 1965 by political enemies from the Nation of Islam, Malcolm X remained a powerful symbol of both militant politics and a renewed pride in African American culture.

A new generation of African Americans picked up the mantle of Malcolm X. Disdaining the older integrationist agenda, the youthful militants embraced the word "black." "Black power" advocates soon caught the media's attention and began to gain support within African American communities. "Black Is Beautiful" became the watchword. James Brown captured this new spirit. His "Say It Loud, I'm Black and Proud" encapsulated the cultural message of the Black Power movement.

The Black Power crusade raised philosophical and tactical disagreements within the antidiscrimination movement. Angered by the slow pace of civil rights litigation, some younger African Americans, including Stokely Carmichael, who became head of the Student Non-Violent Coordinating Committee (SNCC) in 1966, and members of the Black Panther Party, escalated attacks on the gradualist and nonviolent methods of the established civil rights organizations such as King's Southern Christian Leadership Conference. A Black Panther manifesto, for example, called for community "self-defense" groups as protection against police harassment, the release from jail of all African American prisoners (on the assumption that none had received fair trials in racist courts), and guaranteed employment for all citizens. Although opinion surveys suggested that the vast majority of African Americans still supported the integrationist agenda, the new modes of insurgency were unraveling the established civil rights alliance.

Within this social context, the Civil Rights Act of 1968 passed Congress. One provision of this omnibus law, popularly known as the Fair Housing Act, sought to eliminate racial discrimination in housing. But in response to charges that antidiscrimination legislation could illegally infringe on the rights of landlords and real estate agents, the act provided certain exemptions that rendered the law's enforcement provisions weak. Moreover, another section in the law made it a crime to cross state lines in order to incite a "riot." This antiriot provision was widely understood to be aimed at using the power of the federal government against radical political activists, particularly those connected with the Black Power movement.

1968: THE VIOLENCE OVERSEAS

In 1968, several shocking and violent events worsened political polarization. The first came in Vietnam. At the end of January, during a truce in observance of Tet, the lunar new year celebration, troops of the National Liberation Front (NLF) joined North Vietnamese forces in a series of coordinated surprise attacks throughout South Vietnam. During two weeks of intense fighting, they suffered heavy casualties and made no significant military gains. But Tet turned out to be a serious psychological defeat for the United States because it suggested that Johnson's claims about an imminent South Vietnamese–United States victory were not to be trusted. When General Westmoreland asked for 206,000 additional troops, most of Johnson's closest advisers urged that South Vietnamese troops be required to assume more of the military burden. Johnson accepted these arguments, realizing that such a large troop increase would have fanned antiwar opposition at home. In a way, Tet contributed to the beginning of a policy that would later be referred to as the "Vietnamization" of the war.

Although some analysts blamed the media for turning the Tet "victory" into a "defeat" by exaggerating the effect of the early attacks and by ignoring the heavy losses suffered by the NLF and the North Vietnamese, others pointed out that communist strength had caught the U.S. off guard. Faced with revolt in his own party, led by Senator Eugene McCarthy of Minnesota, Johnson suddenly declared on March 31, 1968, that he would not run for reelection. He halted the bombing of North Vietnam and promised to devote his remaining time in office to seeking an end to the war. McCarthy, campaigning on a peace platform, continued his election bid against Johnson's vice president and party stalwart, Hubert H. Humphrey.

1968: THE VIOLENCE AT HOME

One person who rejoiced at Johnson's withdrawal was Martin Luther King Jr. King hoped that the Democratic Party would now turn to an antiwar candidate, preferably Senator Robert Kennedy of New York, who could advance King's new vision of economic transformation for the United States. But on an April 4, 1968, trip to Memphis, Tennessee, in support of a strike by African American sanitation workers, King was assassinated, allegedly by a lone gunman named James Earl Ray.

As news of King's assassination spread, violence swept through black neighborhoods around the country. More than 100 cities and towns witnessed outbreaks; 39 people died; 75,000 regular and National Guard troops were called to duty. When Johnson proclaimed Sunday, April 7, as a day of national mourning for the slain civil rights leader, parts of Washington, D.C., were still ablaze.

Meanwhile, Robert Kennedy had entered the race for the Democratic presidential nomination. Campaigning at a feverish pace, Kennedy battled McCarthy in a series of primary elections, hoping to gain a majority of the convention delegates that had not already been pledged to Hubert Humphrey by the party's old-line bosses such as Richard J. Daley, mayor of Chicago. Then, on June 5, Kennedy fell victim to an assassin's bullets. Kennedy's nationally televised funeral was a disturbing reminder of King's recent murder and the assassination of his own brother nearly five years earlier.

The violence of 1968 continued. During the Republican national convention in Miami, as presidential candidate Richard Nixon was promising to restore "law and order," racial violence in that city killed four people. Later that summer, in Chicago, thousands of antiwar demonstrators converged on the Democratic Party's convention to protest the expected nomination of Humphrey, who was still supporting Johnson's policy in Vietnam. Responding to acts of provocation by demonstrators who seemed to welcome confrontation, members of the Chicago police department struck back with indiscriminate violence. Hubert Humphrey easily captured the Democratic nomination, but controversy over Johnson's Vietnam policies and the response to the antiwar demonstrations left the Democratic Party badly divided.

THE ELECTION OF 1968

Both Humphrey and Nixon faced a serious challenge from the political right, spearheaded by Alabama's George Wallace. After running successfully in several northern Democratic primaries, Wallace decided to seek nationwide support as a third-party candidate. A grass-roots campaign eventually placed his American Independent Party on the presidential ballot in every state. Because Wallace's opposition to racial integration was well established, he could concentrate his fire on other controversial targets, particularly the counterculture and the antiwar movement. Moreover, Wallace recognized that many voters were beginning to lose faith in welfare-state programs and to see themselves as victims of an aloof, tax-and-spend bureaucracy in Washington.

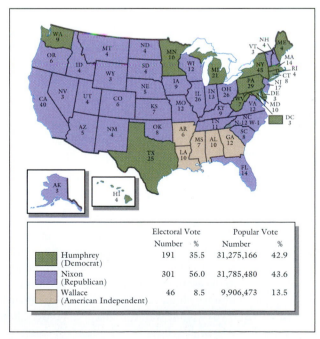

	Electoral Vote		Popular Vote	
	Number	%	Number	%
Humphrey (Democrat)	191	35.5	31,275,166	42.9
Nixon (Republican)	301	56.0	31,785,480	43.6
Wallace (American Independent)	46	8.5	9,906,473	13.5

PRESIDENTIAL ELECTION, 1968

Wallace's candidacy exacerbated the political polarization of 1968. By threatening to prevent either major-party candidate from winning a majority of the electoral votes, it raised the possibility that the choice of the nation's president would rest with the House of Representatives and that Wallace himself could act as a power broker between Democrats and Republicans. In order to capitalize on right-wing dissent against U.S. foreign policy, Wallace chose the hawkish Air Force General Curtis LeMay as his running mate. LeMay quickly inflamed political passions when he complained that too many Americans had a "phobia" about the use of nuclear weapons. Political pundits immediately labeled Wallace and LeMay the "Bombsey Twins."

Nixon narrowly prevailed in November. Although he won 56 percent of the electoral vote, he out-polled Humphrey in the popular vote by less than 1 percent. Humphrey had benefited when Johnson ordered a pause in the bombing of North Vietnam and pledged to begin peace talks in Paris; and he helped his own cause with a belated decision to distance himself from Johnson's Vietnam policies. Still, Humphrey carried only Texas in the South. George Wallace picked up 46 electoral votes, all from the Deep South, and 13.5 percent of the popular vote. Nixon won five key southern states. Hinting that he had a plan for ending the war in Vietnam, he claimed to be the candidate most likely to restore tranquillity to the domestic front. But soon after taking office, Nixon embraced policies that proved every bit as divisive as those of Lyndon Johnson.

THE NIXON YEARS, 1969–1974

Raised in a modest Quaker home in southern California, Richard Nixon graduated from Whittier College, a small Quaker school near his hometown. Three years at Duke Law School, a hitch in the Navy during the Second World War, and a job in Franklin Roosevelt's wartime bureaucracy gave Nixon a taste of new, cosmopolitan worlds. After the war, however, he returned to his small-town California law practice before beginning a meteoric political career that took him to the House of Representatives in 1946, the Senate in 1950, and the vice presidency in 1952.

Nixon seemed to thrive on seeking enemies, at home and abroad, and on confronting a constant series of personal challenges. He titled an early memoir of his political life *Six Crises*. Devastated by his narrow defeat by Kennedy in 1960, Nixon seemed crushed politically when, in 1962, he failed to win the governorship of California. At a postelection press conference, a bitter Nixon announced his political retirement. But Barry Goldwater's 1964 defeat and Johnson's problems helped to revive his political fortunes. During his presidency (1969–1974) the "new" Nixon seemed increasingly like the old Nixon in his ability to inflame, rather than to calm, political passions.

THE ECONOMY

Nixon's presidency coincided with a series of economic problems unthinkable only a decade earlier. No simple cause can account for these difficulties, but most analyses begin with the war in Vietnam. This expensive military commitment, along with fundamental changes in the world economy, brought an end to the economic growth of the previous two decades.

Lyndon Johnson, determined to stave off defeat in Indochina without cutting Great Society programs, had concealed the rising costs of the war from his own advisers. Johnson bequeathed Nixon a deteriorating (though still favorable) balance of trade and a rising rate of inflation. Between 1960 and 1965, consumer prices had risen on average only about 1 percent a year; by 1968, the rate exceeded 4 percent.

Nixon pledged to cut war costs by reducing troop levels, but this strategy continued to drain economic resources. Moreover, although Nixon spoke of reducing domestic spending, he soon discovered that many federal programs still enjoyed support in the Democrat-controlled Congress and among voters. During his first years in office, the percentage of federal funds spent on domestic programs increased steadily.

Meanwhile, unemployment soared, topping 6 percent by 1971. According to conventional wisdom, expressed in a technical economic concept called "the Phillips curve," when unemployment rises, prices should remain constant or even decline. Yet *both* unemployment and inflation were rising. Economists invented the term "stagflation" to describe this puzzling, unprecedented convergence of economic stagnation and price inflation. Along with stagflation, U.S. exports were becoming less competitive in international markets, and in 1971, for the first time in the 20th century, the United States ran a trade deficit, importing more products than it exported.

Long identified as an opponent of government regulation of the economy but fearful of the political consequences of stagflation and the trade deficit, Nixon searched for a cure for the nation's economic ills. Suddenly he proclaimed himself a believer in greater government management of the economy. In August 1971 he announced a "new economic policy" that mandated a 90-day freeze on any increase in wages and prices, to be followed by government monitoring to detect "excessive" increases in either.

To try to reverse the trade deficit, Nixon also revised the U.S. relationship to the world monetary structure. Ever since the 1944 Bretton Woods agreement (see Chapter 26), the value of the dollar had been tied to the value of gold at $35 for every ounce. This meant that the United States was prepared to exchange U.S. dollars for gold at that rate if any other nation's central bank requested it to do so. Other countries had fixed their own exchange rates against the dollar. But U.S. trade deficits undermined the value of the American dollar, enabling foreign banks to exchange dollars for gold at highly favorable rates. Consequently, in August 1971 the Nixon administration abandoned the fixed gold-to-dollar ratio, announcing that the dollar would be free to "float" against the prevailing market price of gold and against all other currencies. In 1973, the Nixon administration devalued the dollar, cheapening the price of American goods in foreign markets in order to make them more competitive. The strategy fundamentally altered the international economic order but did little to arrest the deterioration of U.S. trade balances.

SOCIAL POLICY

At the urging of Daniel Patrick Moynihan, a Democrat who became Nixon's chief adviser on domestic policy, Nixon began to consider a drastic revision of the nation's welfare programs. After heated debates within his inner circle, Nixon unveiled his Family Assistance Plan (FAP) during a TV address in August 1969. The centerpiece of this complex policy package was the replacement of most welfare programs, including the controversial Aid to Families with Dependent Children (AFDC), with a guaranteed annual income for all families. AFDC provided government payments to cover basic costs of care for low-income children who had lost the support of a bread-winning parent. By 1970, half of all persons in families headed by women were receiving AFDC payments.

Under Nixon's proposal, the government would guarantee a family of four an annual income of $1,600, with the possibility of further assistance depending on how much income the family earned. In one bold stroke, FAP would replace the post–New Deal welfare system, which provided services and assistance *only* to those in particular circumstances, such as low-income mothers with small children or people who were unemployed, with a system that offered government aid to *all* low-income families.

Conservatives blasted FAP, especially its provisions for supplementing the income of families that had a regularly employed, though low-paid, wage earner. In contrast, proponents of more generous government assistance programs criticized its guaranteed income of $1,600 as too miserly. The House of Representatives approved a modified version of FAP in 1970, but a curious alliance of senators to the right and to the left of Nixon blocked its passage.

Some changes in domestic programs were enacted during the Nixon years, however. For example, Congress passed the president's revenue-sharing plan, which provided for the return of a certain percentage of federal tax dollars to state and local governments in the form of "block grants." Instead of Washington specifying how the funds were to be used, the block grant concept left the state and local governments free, within broad limits, to spend the funds as they saw fit.

Congress stitched together a revised welfare program in the early 1970s. It included rent subsidies for people at the lowest income levels and Supplementary Security Insurance (SSI) payments for those who were elderly, blind, or disabled. The Medicare and Medicaid programs, established under Johnson's Great Society, were gradually expanded during Nixon's presidency. In 1972 Social Security benefits were "indexed," which meant they would rise with the rate of inflation. More cautious than Nixon's FAP proposals, these congressional initiatives substantially extended the nation's income-support programs, albeit only for specific groups. Between 1970 and 1980 the federal government's spending for social welfare rose from 40.1 percent of total government outlays to slightly over 53 percent.

CONTROVERSIES OVER RIGHTS

These legislative initiatives came against the backdrop of a much broader debate over how to define the federal government's responsibility to protect basic constitutional rights. The struggle to define those rights embroiled the U.S. Supreme Court in controversy. Under the leadership of Chief Justice Earl Warren and Associate Justice William Brennan, both appointees of Dwight Eisenhower, an "activist" majority that was devoted to recognizing a broad range of constitutionally protected rights had dominated the Court during the 1960s. Although nearly all the Warren Court's rights-related decisions drew critical fire, the most emotional cases involved the rights of persons accused of violent crime. In *Miranda* v. *Arizona* (1966), the Court's activists held that the Constitution required police officers to advise people arrested for a felony offense of their constitutional rights to remain silent and to consult an attorney. While civil libertarians defended decisions such as *Miranda* as the logical extension of settled principles, the Court's numerous critics attacked the activist justices for allegedly inventing new rights that could not be found in the text of the Constitution. Amid rising public concern over crime, conservatives made *Miranda* a symbol of the judicial "coddling" of criminals.

Richard Nixon had campaigned for president in 1968 as an opponent of the Warren Court's activist stance. Before the election, Chief Justice Warren had announced his resignation, and incoming President Nixon was therefore able to appoint a moderately conservative Republican, Warren Burger, as Chief Justice. Pledged to select only judges who would interpret rights claims narrowly, Nixon also appointed three new associate justices to the Supreme Court during his presidency—Harry Blackmun, William Rehnquist, and Lewis Powell. The Supreme Court, meanwhile, continued to face controversial new cases involving the issue of rights.

Considerable discussion focused on the constitutional status of social welfare programs. Activist lawyers argued that access to adequate economic assistance from the federal government should be recognized as a national right. Many observers expected that the Court might soon take this step. In 1970, however, in *Dandridge* v. *Williams,* the Court rejected the argument that laws capping the amount a state would pay to welfare recipients violated the Constitution's requirement that the government must extend equal protection of the laws to all citizens. The Court drew a sharp distinction between the government's responsibility to respect the individual liberties of all citizens, such as the right to vote and freedom of speech, and its discretionary ability to make distinctions in the administration of spending programs such as AFDC. In short, the Court refused to hold that welfare was a national right.

Another controversial aspect of the rights debate involved issues of health and safety. A vigorous consumer rights movement, which had initially drawn inspiration from Ralph Nader's exposé about auto safety, titled *Unsafe at Any Speed* (1965), attracted immediate political support. Under Nader's leadership, consumer advocates lobbied for federal legislation to protect the right to safety in the workplace, the right to safe consumer products, and the right to a healthy environment. This effort found expression in such legislation as the Occupational Safety Act of 1973, stronger consumer protection laws, and new environmental legislation (see Chapter 30).

At the same time, a newly energized women's rights movement pushed its own set of issues. The National Organization for Women (NOW), founded in 1966, backed an Equal Rights Amendment (ERA) that would explicitly guarantee women the same legal rights as men. After having been passed by Congress in 1972 and quickly ratified by more than half the states, the ERA suddenly emerged as one of the most divisive domestic issues of the early 1970s. Conservative women's groups, such as Phyllis Schlafly's "Stop ERA," charged that equal rights would undermine traditional "family values." As a result of such opposition, the ERA, which once seemed assured of passage, failed to attain approval from the three-quarters of states needed for ratification. Ultimately, women's groups abandoned the ERA effort in favor of urging the courts to recognize equal rights on a case-by-case, issue-by-issue basis.

One of these specific issues, involving a woman's right to a safe and legal abortion, became even more controversial than the ERA. In *Roe* v. *Wade* (1973), the Supreme Court ruled that a state law making abortion a criminal offense violated a woman's right of privacy. The *Roe* decision outraged conservatives. Rallying under the "Right to Life" slogan and focusing on the rights of the unborn fetus, antiabortion groups labeled *Roe* v. *Wade* as another threat to family values, and in 1976 they succeeded in persuading Congress to ban the use of federal funds to finance abortions for women with low incomes. Feminist groups made the issue of individual choice in reproductive decisions a principal rallying point.

Nixon had promised an administration that, in contrast to Johnson's, would "bring us together." Instead, bitter divisions over economic policies, government spending programs, and the meaning of basic constitutional guarantees made the Nixon presidency a period of increasing, rather than decreasing, polarization.

FOREIGN POLICY UNDER NIXON AND KISSINGER

While attempting to deal with divisive domestic concerns, the Nixon administration was far more preoccupied with international affairs. Nixon appointed Henry Kissinger, a political scientist from Harvard, as his national security adviser. Under Kissinger, the National Security

Council (NSC) emerged as the most powerful shaper of foreign policy within the government. In 1973 Kissinger was appointed Secretary of State, a position that he continued to hold until 1977. With Nixon, Kissinger orchestrated a grand strategy for foreign policy: détente with the Soviet Union, normalization of relations with China, and disengagement from direct military involvement in Southeast Asia and other parts of the world.

DÉTENTE

Although Nixon had built his political career on hard-line anticommunism, the Nixon-Kissinger team mapped a foreign policy that aimed at easing tensions with the two major communist nations, the Soviet Union and China. Kissinger surmised that, as both nations began to seek favor with the United States, they might ease up on their support for North Vietnam, facilitating America's ability to withdraw from the war that was dividing the nation.

Arms control talks took top priority in U.S.-Soviet relations. In 1969 the two superpowers opened the Strategic Arms Limitation Talks (SALT), and after several years of high-level diplomacy they signed an agreement (SALT I) that limited further development of both antiballistic missiles (ABMs) and offensive intercontinental ballistic missiles (ICBMs). The impact of SALT I on the arms race was negligible because it did not limit the number of warheads that could be carried by each missile. Still, the very fact that the Soviet Union and the United States had concluded high-level discussions on arms control signaled a shift.

Nixon's overtures toward the People's Republic of China brought an even more dramatic break with the Cold War past. Tentative conversations arranged through the embassies of both countries in Poland led to a slight easing of U.S. trade restrictions against China in early 1971 and then to an invitation from China for Americans to compete in a Ping-Pong tournament. This celebrated exhibition became a prelude to more significant exchange. In 1972 Nixon himself visited China. Relations between the two countries remained difficult, especially over the status of Taiwan, which the United States still recognized as the legitimate government of China. A few months after Nixon's visit, however, the United Nations admitted the People's Republic as the representative of China, and in 1973 the United States and China exchanged informal diplomatic missions.

VIETNAMIZATION

Meanwhile, the Nixon administration continued to wage war in Vietnam. Nixon and Kissinger decided to start the withdrawal of U.S. ground forces (the policy called "Vietnamization") while stepping up the air war and intensifying diplomatic efforts to reach a settlement. In July of 1969 the president publicly announced the "Nixon Doctrine," which pledged that the United States would provide military assistance to anticommunist governments in Asia but would leave it to them to provide their own military forces.

The goal of Vietnamization was to withdraw U.S. ground troops without accepting compromise or defeat. While officially adhering to Johnson's 1968 bombing halt over the North, Nixon and Kissinger accelerated both the ground war and the air war by launching new offensives in the South and approving a military incursion into Cambodia, an ostensibly neutral country.

The move set off a new wave of protest at home. Campuses exploded in anger, and bomb threats led many colleges to close early for the 1970 summer recess. White police officers killed two students at the all-black Jackson State College in Mississippi, and National Guard troops

IMAGES THAT SHOCKED   The war in Indochina produced a spiral of violence that also found its way back to the United States. In the photo at left, a military officer in the South Vietnamese Army summarily executes a prisoner suspected of being a member of the Viet Cong. At right, an anguished antiwar activist bends over the body of a college student killed by Ohio National Guard troops at Kent State University in 1970.

at Kent State University in Ohio fired on demonstrators and killed four students. As growing numbers of protestors took to the streets, moderate business and political leaders became alarmed by how Vietnam was dividing the country. Disillusionment with the war also grew from revelations that, a month after Tet, troops led by U.S. Lieutenant William Calley had entered a small hamlet called My Lai and shot more than 200 people, mostly women and children. This massacre of South Vietnamese civilians had become public in 1969; in 1971 a military court convicted Calley and sentenced him to life imprisonment.

The Cambodian incursion of 1970 was part of a widening secret war in Cambodia and Laos. Although the U.S. government denied that it was waging any such war, large areas of those rich agricultural countries were disrupted by American bombing. As the number of Cambodian refugees swelled and food supplies dwindled, the communist guerrilla force in Cambodia—the Khmer Rouge—grew into a well-disciplined army. The Khmer Rouge would later seize the government and, in an attempt to eliminate potential dissent, turn Cambodia into a "killing field." While peace negotiations with North Vietnam proceeded in Paris, the Vietnam War actually broadened into a war that destabilized the entire region of Indochina.

Even greater violence was yet to come. In the spring of 1972 a North Vietnamese offensive approached within 30 miles of Saigon. Nixon responded by resuming the bombing of North Vietnam and by mining its harbors. Just weeks before the 1972 election, Kissinger again promised peace and announced a cease-fire. After the election, however, the United States unleashed even greater firepower. In the so-called Christmas bombing of December 1972, B-52 bombers pounded North Vietnamese military and civilian targets around the clock.

By this time, however, much of the media, Congress, and the public had become sickened by the violence. In response, Nixon proceeded with full-scale Vietnamization of the war. In January 1973 North Vietnam and the United States signed peace accords in Paris that provided for the withdrawal of U.S. troops. As U.S. troops pulled out, the South Vietnamese government, headed by Nguyen Van Thieu, continued to fight, though it was growing increasingly demoralized and disorganized.

In the spring of 1975, South Vietnam's army was no longer able to withstand the advance of North Vietnam's skilled general Nguyen Giap. Thieu's government collapsed, North Vietnamese armies entered Saigon, and U.S. helicopters scrambled to airlift the last remaining officials out of the besieged U.S. embassy.

THE AFTERMATH OF WAR

Between 1960 and 1973, approximately 3.5 million American men and women served in Vietnam: 58,000 died; 150,000 were wounded; 2,000 remain missing. In the aftermath of the long, costly war, many Americans struggled to find meaning. Why had their country failed to

THE VIETNAM WAR MEMORIAL   This memorial, a kind of wailing wall that bears the names of all Americans who were killed in action in Vietnam, was dedicated on the Mall in Washington, D.C., in 1982.

prevail over a small, barely industrialized nation? Conservatives blamed the uncensored and irresponsible media, the coddling of dissenters, and the "failure of will" in Congress. The goals of the war, they believed, were laudable; politicians, setting unrealistic limits on the war, had denied the military the means to attain victory. By contrast, those who had opposed the war stressed the misguided belief that the United States was unbeatable, the deceitfulness of governmental leaders, and the incompetence of bureaucratic processes. For them, the war was in the wrong place and waged for the wrong reasons; and the human costs to Indochina outweighed any possible gain.

Regardless of their positions on the war, most Americans could agree on one proposition: There should be "no more Vietnams." The United States should not undertake future military involvements unless there were clear and compelling political objectives, demonstrable public support, and the provision of adequate means to accomplish the goal.

THE NIXON DOCTRINE

In molding foreign policy, Henry Kissinger relied increasingly on pro-U.S. anticommunist allies to police their own regions of the world. Kissinger made it clear that the United States would not dispatch troops to oppose revolutionary insurgencies but would give generous assistance to anticommunist regimes or factions that were willing to fight the battle themselves.

During the early 1970s, America's Cold War strategy came to rely on supporting staunchly anticommunist regional powers: nations such as Iran under Shah Reza Pahlavi, South Africa with its apartheid regime, and Brazil with its repressive military dictatorship. All of these states built large military establishments trained by the United States. U.S. military assistance, together with covert CIA operations, also incubated and protected anticommunist dictatorships in South Korea, in the Philippines, and in much of Latin America. In one of its most controversial foreign policies, the Nixon administration employed covert action against the elected socialist government of Salvador Allende Gossens in Chile. In 1973 Allende was overthrown by the Chilean military, who immediately suspended democratic rule and began a policy of political repression.

Critics charged that the United States, in the name of anticommunism, had too often wedded its diplomatic fortunes to such questionable covert actions and unpopular military governments. In 1975 Senator Frank Church conducted widely-publicized Senate hearings into abuses by the CIA. But supporters of the Nixon Doctrine applauded the administration's strengthening of a system of allies and its tough anticommunism. In many circles, Nixon received high marks for a pragmatic foreign policy that combined détente toward the communist giants with strong containment against the further global spread of revolutionary regimes.

THE WARS OF WATERGATE

Nixon's presidency ultimately collapsed as a result of horrendous decisions made in the president's own Oval Office. From the time Nixon entered the White House, he had been deeply suspicious of nearly every person and institution in Washington. Such suspicions centered on antiwar activists and old political opponents but even extended to likely allies, such as J. Edgar Hoover, the staunchly conservative director of the FBI. Isolated behind a close-knit group of advisers, Nixon ultimately set up his own secret intelligence unit.

During the summer of 1971 Daniel Ellsberg, a dissident member of the national security bureaucracy, leaked to the press a top-secret history of U.S. involvement in the Vietnam War, subsequently known as the "Pentagon Papers." Nixon responded by seeking, unsuccessfully, a court injunction to stop publication of the study and, more ominously, by unleashing his secret intelligence unit, now dubbed "the plumbers," to stop the leaking of information to the media. Looking for materials that might discredit Ellsberg, the plumbers burglarized his psychiatrist's office. Thus began a series of "dirty tricks" and outright illegalities, often financed by funds illegally solicited for Nixon's 1972 reelection campaign, that would culminate in the political scandal and constitutional crisis known as "Watergate."

THE ELECTION OF 1972

As the 1972 election approached, Nixon's political strategists worried that economic troubles and the war might deny the president reelection. Creating a campaign organization separate from that of the Republican Party, with the ironic acronym of CREEP (Committee to Re-Elect the President), they secretly raised millions of dollars, much of it from illegal contributions.

As the 1972 campaign proceeded, Nixon's chances of reelection dramatically improved. An assassin's bullet crippled George Wallace. Meanwhile, Democratic Senator Edmund Muskie of Maine made a series of blunders (some of them precipitated by Republican "dirty tricksters") that derailed his campaign. Eventually, Senator George McGovern of South Dakota, an outspoken opponent of the Vietnam War, won the Democratic nomination.

During the campaign, McGovern called for higher taxes on the wealthy, a guaranteed minimum income for all Americans, amnesty for Vietnam War draft resisters, and the decriminalization of marijuana—positions significantly to the left of the views of many traditional Democrats. In foreign policy, McGovern called for deep cuts in defense spending and for vigorous efforts to achieve peace in Vietnam—positions that Nixon successfully portrayed as signs of weakness.

Nixon won an easy victory in the November elections. The president received the Electoral College votes of all but one state and the District of Columbia, won more than 60 percent of the popular vote, and carried virtually every traditional Democratic bloc except the African American vote. His margin of victory was one of the largest in U.S. history.

NIXON PURSUED

In achieving that victory, however, the president's team left a trail of corruption that cut short Nixon's second term. In June 1972 a surveillance team with links to both CREEP and the White House had been arrested while adjusting some eavesdropping equipment that it had installed earlier in the Democratic Party's headquarters in Washington's Watergate office complex. In public, Nixon's spokespersons dismissed the Watergate break-in as an insignificant "third-rate burglary"; privately, Nixon and his closest aides immediately launched an illegal cover-up. They paid hush money to the Watergate burglars and had the CIA falsely warn the FBI that any investigation into the break-in would jeopardize national security.

While reporters from *The Washington Post* took the lead in pursuing the taint of scandal, members of Congress and the federal judiciary sought evidence on possible violations of the law. In January 1973 Judge John Sirica, a Republican appointee who was presiding over the trial of the Watergate burglars, refused to accept their claim that neither CREEP nor the White House had been involved in the break-in. While Sirica pushed for more information, Senate leaders convened a special Watergate Committee, headed by North Carolina's conservative Democratic Senator Sam Ervin, to investigate the 1972 campaign. Meanwhile, federal prosecutors uncovered evidence that seemed to link key administration and White House figures, including John Mitchell, Nixon's former attorney general and later the head of CREEP, to illegal activities.

Nixon's political and legal difficulties grew steadily worse during 1973. In March, under unyielding pressure from Judge Sirica, one of the Watergate burglars finally broke his silence. By May, he joined other witnesses who testified before the Senate's Watergate Committee about various illegal activities committed by CREEP and the White House. Nixon's closest aides were soon called before the committee. John Dean, who had been Nixon's chief legal counsel, gave testimony that linked the president himself to an elaborate Watergate cover-up and to other illegal activities.

Along the way, Senate investigators discovered that a voice-activated taping machine had recorded every conversation held in Nixon's Oval Office. Now it was possible to determine whether the president or John Dean was lying. Nixon claimed an "executive privilege" to keep the tapes from being released to other branches of government, but Judge Sirica, Archibald Cox (who had been appointed as a special, independent prosecutor in the Watergate case), and Congress all launched legal moves to gain access to them.

If Nixon's own problems were not enough, his vice president, Spiro Agnew, resigned in October 1973 after pleading "no contest" to income tax evasion. He agreed to a plea-bargain arrangement in order to avoid prosecution for having accepted illegal kickbacks while he was in Maryland politics. Acting under the Twenty-fifth Amendment (ratified in 1967), Nixon appointed—and both houses of Congress confirmed—Representative Gerald Ford of Michigan, a Republican Party stalwart, as the new vice president.

Nixon's Final Days

By the early summer of 1974, the nation's legal-constitutional system was closing in on Nixon, and the president's inept attempts to sidetrack his pursuers only redounded against him. During the previous autumn, for example, Nixon had clumsily orchestrated the firing of Archibald Cox. When this rash action was greeted by a public outcry—the affair came to be known as Nixon's "Saturday Night Massacre"—the president was obliged to appoint another independent prosecutor, Leon Jaworski. Similarly, Nixon's own release of edited, and occasionally garbled, transcripts of a series of Watergate-related conversations merely prompted people to demand the original tape recordings. Finally, by announcing that he would only obey a "definitive" Supreme Court decision on the tapes' legal status, Nixon was all but inviting the justices to reach a unanimous decision. And on July 24, 1974, the Court did just that in the case of *U.S. v. Nixon.* By this time, Nixon was in desperate straits. While the Supreme Court was unanimously ruling that Nixon's claim of "executive privilege" over the tapes could not justify his refusal to release evidence needed in a criminal investigation, the Judiciary Committee of the House of Representatives was already moving toward a vote on impeachment.

At the end of July, after nearly a full week of televised deliberations, a majority of the House Judiciary Committee voted three formal articles of impeachment against the president for

CHRONOLOGY

1963	Johnson assumes presidency and pledges to continue Kennedy's initiatives
1964	Congress passes Kennedy's tax bill, the Civil Rights Act of 1964, and the Economic Opportunity Act • Gulf of Tonkin Resolution gives Johnson authority to conduct undeclared war • Johnson defeats Barry Goldwater in presidential election
1965	Johnson announces plans for the Great Society • Malcolm X assassinated • U.S. intervenes in Dominican Republic • Johnson announces significant U.S. troop deployments in Vietnam • Congress passes Voting Rights Act • Violence rocks Los Angeles and other urban areas
1966	Black Power movement emerges • *Miranda* v. *Arizona* decision guarantees rights of criminal suspects • U.S. begins massive air strikes in North Vietnam
1967	Large antiwar demonstrations begin • Beatles release *Sgt. Pepper's Lonely Hearts Club Band*
1968	Tet offensive (January) • Martin Luther King Jr. assassinated (April) • Robert Kennedy assassinated (June) • Violence at Democratic national convention in Chicago • Civil Rights Act of 1968 passed • Vietnam peace talks begin in Paris • Richard Nixon elected president
1969	Nixon announces "Vietnamization" policy • Pictures of My Lai massacre become public
1970	U.S. troops enter Cambodia • Student demonstrators killed at Kent State and Jackson State
1971	"Pentagon Papers" published; White House "plumbers" formed • Military court convicts Lieutenant Calley for My Lai incident
1972	Nixon crushes McGovern in presidential election
1973	Paris peace accords signed • *Roe* v. *Wade* upholds women's right to abortion • Nixon's Watergate troubles begin to escalate
1974	House votes impeachment, and Nixon resigns • Ford assumes presidency
1975	Saigon falls to North Vietnamese forces

obstruction of justice, violation of constitutional liberties, and refusal to produce evidence requested during the impeachment process. Nixon boasted that he would fight these accusations before the Senate, the body authorized by the Constitution (Article I, Section 3) to render a verdict of guilty or innocent after the House votes impeachment.

Nixon's closest aides, however, were already making ready for his departure. One of his own attorneys had discovered that a tape Nixon had been withholding contained the long-sought "smoking gun": a 1972 conversation confirming that Nixon himself had agreed to a plan by which the CIA would advance the fraudulent claim of national security in order to stop the FBI from investigating the Watergate burglary. At this point, Nixon's secretary of defense ordered all military commanders to ignore any order from the president unless it was countersigned by the secretary. Abandoned by almost every prominent Republican and about to confront a Senate prepared to vote him guilty on the impeachment charges, Nixon went on television on August 8, 1974, to announce that he would resign from office. On August 9, Gerald Ford became the nation's 38th president.

In 1974, most people believed that Watergate was one of the gravest crises in the history of the republic. As time passed, though, the public's recollection and knowledge of the Watergate illegalities and Nixon's forced resignation faded. Opinion polls conducted on the 20th anniversary of Nixon's resignation suggested that most Americans retained only a dim memory of Watergate.

One reason may be that although nearly a dozen members of the Nixon administration were convicted of criminal activities, the president himself escaped punishment. Only a month after Nixon's resignation, Gerald Ford granted Nixon an unconditional presidential pardon. The nation was spared the spectacle of witnessing a former president undergoing a lengthy, perhaps divisive trial; but it was also denied an authoritative accounting, in a court of law, of the full range of Nixon's misdeeds.

Another reason for the fading memory of Watergate may be the popular penchant for linking it to nearly every political scandal of the post-Nixon era. The suffix "-gate" became attached to grave constitutional episodes (such as Ronald Reagan's "Iran-Contragate" affair) and to the most trivial of political events (such as the brief "Nannygate" controversy that eliminated one of President Bill Clinton's nominees for attorney general in 1993). By the end of the 20th century, popular political discourse, it seemed, framed the dramatic events of 1973 and 1974 as another example of routine political corruption rather than as a unique, serious constitutional crisis.

Finally, what the historian Stanley Kutler has called the "wars of Watergate" may have been overshadowed by the enormity of the turmoil and loss Americans experienced as a result of America's longest war. In this sense, Watergate tends to blend into a broader pattern of political, social, economic, and cultural turmoil that emerged during the lengthy, increasingly divisive war in Southeast Asia.

CONCLUSION

The power of the national government expanded during the 1960s. Lyndon Johnson's Great Society created a blueprint for an expanding welfare state and a War on Poverty. The Great Society, however, was quickly overshadowed by the escalation of the war in Vietnam, a struggle that consumed increasingly more of the nation's wealth in order to prevent communism from gaining a victory in Southeast Asia.

This growth of governmental power—both the enlargement of domestic social programs and the waging of war abroad—prompted divisive debates that polarized the country. Johnson left the presidency a broken man. And his Republican successor, Richard Nixon, in trying to control the divisions at home, let loose an abuse of power that ultimately drove him from office in disgrace. The exalted hopes of the early 1960s—that the U.S. government would be able to enhance liberty and equality both in America and throughout the rest of the world—ended in frustration and defeat.

The era of America's longest war was a time of high political passions, of generational and racial conflict, of differing definitions of patriotism. It saw the slow convergence of an antiwar movement, along with the emergence of a youthful counterculture, of "Black Power," of "women's liberation," and of a variety of contests over what constituted basic rights for Americans. Different groups assigned different causes to explain the failures of both the Great Society and the war, and the polarization from these years shaped the fault lines of politics for years to come. Nearly all Americans, however, became much more reserved, many even cynical, about further enlarging the power of the federal government in the name of expanding liberty and equality.

30

AMERICA IN TRANSITION: ECONOMICS, CULTURE, AND SOCIAL CHANGE IN THE LATE 20TH CENTURY

A CHANGING PEOPLE ∾ ECONOMIC TRANSFORMATIONS
THE ENVIRONMENT ∾ MEDIA AND CULTURE ∾ SOCIAL ACTIVISM
RACE, ETHNICITY, AND SOCIAL ACTIVISM ∾ THE NEW RIGHT

At the end of the 20th century historians tried to assess several decades of remarkable economic and cultural changes. The 1960s—fraught with political assassinations, a lengthy foreign war, and domestic dissent—had once seemed a period peculiar for its upheavals. In fact, the decades that followed brought even more far-reaching, although less violent, changes. Increasing immigration, urbanization, and movement of people southward and westward altered the demographics of American life. A transformation from manufacturing to postindustrial employment swept the economy. A digital revolution transfigured systems of information and entertainment. And social movements associated with environmentalism, women's rights, gay pride, racial and ethnic solidarity, and the New Right affected both politics and the ways that Americans defined themselves.

A CHANGING PEOPLE

In demographic terms, the post-1970 period marked a watershed in American life. The population was becoming older, more urban, and more ethnically and racially diverse. Moreover, the nation's center of power was shifting away from the Northeast and toward the South and West.

AN AGING POPULATION

After about 1970 the birth rate slowed dramatically. During the 1970s and 1980s, even with a wave of new immigration and longer life expectancy, the growth rate was only about 1 percent a year. Most young people were delaying marriage until well into their twenties, and the number of women in their mid-thirties who had never married tripled between 1970 and 1990 to 16 percent.

As a result of declining birth rates, rising life expectancy, and the aging of the baby boom generation, the median age of the population rose steadily. Advertising agencies and TV serials turned to midlife appeals. As aging baby boomers pondered retirement, policymakers grew concerned that the projected payouts in Social Security and Medicare benefits would bequeath a staggering cost burden to the smaller post–baby boom generation of workers. During the 1990s, halting the rise of health care costs, revamping health payment systems, and guaranteeing Social Security benefits became major public policy issues.

THE RISE OF THE SUNBELT

Not only did population growth slow in the 1970s and 1980s, but the regional pattern of population distribution began to shift political and economic power within the country. Between 1970 and 1990, 90 percent of the nation's population growth came in the South and the West. The census of 1980 revealed that for the first time more Americans were living in the South and the West than were living in the North and the East.

The population shift profoundly reshaped national politics. In the late 1960s, Republican political analyst Kevin Phillips looked at the region extending from Florida to California—the Sunbelt—and predicted that its voters would join together in a conservative coalition. It was

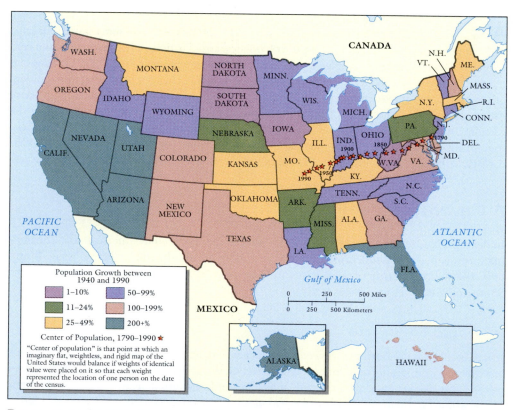

POPULATION SHIFTS TOWARD THE "SUNBELT"

just such a coalition that elected Californian Ronald Reagan president in 1980. The South, once solidly Democratic, finally developed a two-party system. And in the reapportionment of seats in the House of Representatives during the early 1990s, California gained seven seats, Florida gained four, New York lost three, and several other northeastern states lost two.

There were many reasons for this demographic shift. One was the availability of affordable air-conditioning for homes and offices. Another was the rise of tourism and the proliferation of new retirement communities in Nevada, California, Arizona, and Florida. Also, lower labor costs and the absence of strong unions prompted manufacturers to build new plants and relocate old ones in the Sunbelt. Equally important was the growth of high-tech industries with their economic fortunes tied to military-industrial spending. Those industries attracted highly skilled engineers and scientists. Silicon Valley in Santa Clara County near San Francisco, for example, had been a rural area until 1940. From then on, it doubled its population every decade. This spectacular growth was triggered by the new semiconductor industry and its network of electronics-related suppliers.

Government spending on the space program also helped shift research and technology to the Sunbelt. After the Soviet Union's launch of its *Sputnik* satellite in 1957, the United States stepped up its own space program under the newly formed National Aeronautics and Space Administration (NASA). In 1961 President Kennedy announced plans for the Apollo program, promising a manned mission to the moon by 1970. In July 1969 astronauts Neil Armstrong and Edwin ("Buzz") Aldrin stepped from their spacecraft onto the moon, planted the American flag, and gathered 47 pounds of lunar rocks for later study.

In the 1980s NASA began launching a series of "space shuttles," manned rockets that served as scientific laboratories and could be flown back to earth for reuse. This progression of ever more innovative, and costly, advances in space technology spurred economic development in the Sunbelt states.

NEW IMMIGRATION

Another reason for the sharp rise in the population of the Sunbelt was a dramatic increase in immigration. During the 1970s and 1980s, 10 million immigrants from Asia and Latin America arrived in the United States, six times the number of European immigrants arriving over the same period. (If illegal immigrants were included, the count would be far higher.)

The largest number of non-European immigrants came from Mexico. Many Americans of Mexican ancestry, of course, were not recent immigrants. Immigration became significant in the 20th century, spurred by the Mexican revolution after 1910 (see Chapter 24) and responding to U.S. labor shortages during the First World War, the Second World War, and the Korean War. In every decade of the postwar period, immigration from Mexico rose substantially. Many migrants came as seasonal agricultural workers; many others formed permanent communities. Ninety percent of all Mexican Americans lived in the Southwest.

Although Mexican Americans comprised the majority of the Spanish-speaking population across the country in the late 20th century, Puerto Ricans were more numerous on the East Coast. The United States annexed Puerto Rico after the Spanish-American War of 1898 (see Chapter 22) and in 1917 granted U.S. citizenship to its inhabitants. Puerto Ricans, therefore, were not really immigrants but could come and go freely from island to mainland. Before the Second World War, the Puerto Rican population in the United States was small and centered in New York City. After the war, however, immigration rose significantly (see Chapter 28). By

NEW AMERICANS   These new Americans, who are taking the oath of citizenship, are part of the upsurge in immigration that began in the mid-1960s. Before obtaining citizenship, applicants must demonstrate knowledge of basic English and pass a test on public rights and responsibilities.

the 1970s, more Puerto Ricans were living in New York City than in San Juan, Puerto Rico's capital. Sizable Puerto Rican communities also developed in Chicago and in industrial cities in New England and Ohio. By 1990 the Puerto Rican population had grown to over 2 million.

Cubans comprised the third most numerous Spanish-speaking group in the U.S. population. In 1962 congressional action designated Cubans who were fleeing Fidel Castro's regime as refugees eligible for admittance. Over the next 30 years, 800,000 Cubans quickly established themselves in South Florida. By 1990 Cubans comprised one-third of the population in Miami.

The Immigration Act of 1965 sharply altered national policy. Since the 1920s, rates of immigration had been determined by quotas based on national origins (see Chapter 24). The 1965 act ended these quotas and laid the basis not only for a resumption of high-volume immigration but also for a substantial shift in region of origin. The law placed a ceiling of 20,000 immigrants for every country, gave preference to those with close family ties in the United States, and accorded priority to those with special skills and those classified as "refugees." Under the new act, large numbers of people immigrated from Korea, China, the Philippines, the Dominican Republic, Colombia, and countries in the Middle East. In the aftermath of the Vietnam War, Presidents Ford and Carter ordered the admittance of many Vietnamese, Cambodians, Laotians, and Hmong (an ethnically distinct people who inhabited lands extending across the borders of all three countries) who had assisted the United States during the war.

In response to the surge in number of refugees, Congress passed the Refugee Act of 1980. It specified that political refugees would be admitted but that refugees who were seeking simply to improve their economic lot would be denied entry. In practice, the terms "political" and "economic" tended to be applied in such a way that people fleeing communist regimes were usually admitted but those fleeing right-wing oppression were turned away. For example,

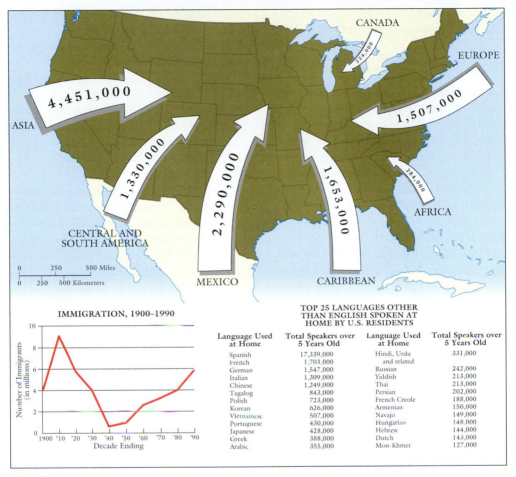

IMMIGRATION, 1900–1990

TOP 25 LANGUAGES OTHER
THAN ENGLISH SPOKEN AT
HOME BY U.S. RESIDENTS

Language Used at Home	Total Speakers over 5 Years Old	Language Used at Home	Total Speakers over 5 Years Old
Spanish	17,339,000	Hindi, Urdu and related	331,000
French	1,703,000	Russian	242,000
German	1,547,000	Yiddish	213,000
Italian	1,309,000	Thai	213,000
Chinese	1,249,000	Persian	202,000
Tagalog	843,000	French Creole	188,000
Polish	723,000	Armenian	150,000
Korean	626,000	Navajo	149,000
Vietnamese	507,000	Hungarian	148,000
Portuguese	430,000	Hebrew	144,000
Japanese	428,000	Dutch	143,000
Greek	388,000	Mon-Khmer	127,000
Arabic	355,000		

NEW IMMIGRANTS, 1970–1990

Cubans and Soviet Jews were admitted, but Haitians were often denied immigrant status. Many Guatemalans and Salvadorans, trying to escape the repressive military governments backed by the United States during the 1980s, stood little chance of being admitted as legal immigrants. Some of them, however, were helped into the U.S. and then harbored by a church-based "sanctuary movement" that opposed U.S. policies in Central America.

As illegal immigration became a major political issue in the mid-1980s, Congress passed another immigration law. The Immigration Reform and Control Act of 1987 imposed penalties on businesses employing illegal aliens and granted residency to workers who could prove that they had been living in the United States since 1982. Although this law may have temporarily reduced the number of illegal aliens entering the country, it became increasingly ineffective during the 1990s.

Los Angeles became a microcosm of world cultures. By the mid 1990s, fewer than half of the schoolchildren in Los Angeles were proficient in English, and some 80 different languages were spoken in homes there. The slogan "A City Divided and Proud of It" described Los Angeles's ambivalence about the issue of separate versus common identities.

URBANIZATION AND SUBURBANIZATION

Urban-suburban demographics were also in a state of flux. By 1990 nearly 80 percent of Americans were living in metropolitan areas. As those areas continued to expand, the suburbs melded into "urban corridors," metropolitan strips often running between older cities, as between Los Angeles and San Diego, Washington and Baltimore, Seattle and Tacoma, or into "edge cities," former suburban areas such as the Galleria area west of Houston, the Perimeter Center south of Atlanta, and Tysons Corner near Washington, D.C.

Meanwhile, central cities became centers primarily of financial, administrative, and entertainment activity. During the 1970s and 1980s, the percentage of upper- and middle-income residents within city boundaries fell, and tax bases declined at the same time that an influx of low-income populations placed greater demands on public services. Higher rates of homelessness and crime, together with deteriorating schools and urban infrastructures (such as sewer and water systems), plagued most large cities. Although many central cities began to revive during the mid-1990s—as a result of general economic growth, lower crime rates, better

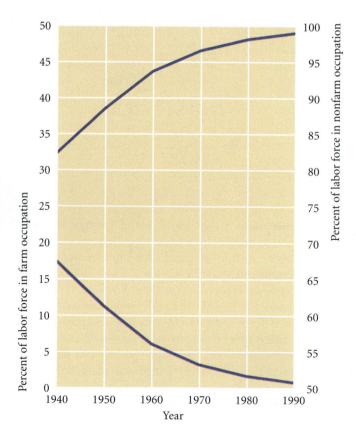

DECREASING NUMBER OF FARMERS, 1940–1990

During the late 20th century, Americans continued to leave farms and small towns for cities and suburbs. In 1990 only a few states retained a preponderance of rural population.

policing, and the renewed desire to enjoy the amenities of an urban lifestyle—the population growth of urban corridors continued to outpace that of traditional cities.

ECONOMIC TRANSFORMATIONS

A typical American adult of the 1990s would likely awake to a digital alarm clock, pop breakfast into a microwave oven, work at a desktop computer, and relax with a movie or TV program taped earlier on the VCR, while the children amused themselves with Nintendo or surfed the Internet. None of these products or activities had been known in the early 1960s. The pace of technological change had brought an astonishing transformation in consumer products, production processes, and the structure of the labor force.

NEW TECHNOLOGIES

The most noteworthy technological advances were made in biotechnology, high-performance computing, and communications systems. As scientists deepened their understanding of DNA and genetic engineering, they devised new techniques of gene transfer, embryo manipulation, tissue regeneration, and even cloning. Those techniques led the way to possible breakthroughs in cancer treatment, alteration of genetically inherited diseases, new and improved crops, waste conversion, and toxic cleanup. But biotechnology, especially genetic engineering, also raised fears about the decline in the variety of biological organisms, what scientists called "biodiversity," and prompted ethical questions about the role of science in manipulating reproduction.

The computer revolution, which began after the Second World War, entered a new phase during the 1970s, when the availability of microchips boosted the capability and reduced the size and cost of computer hardware. Sales of home computers soared. High-performance computers with powerful memory capabilities and "parallel processors," which allow many operations to run simultaneously, began to transform both industry and information systems. Computerized factories and robotics streamlined business operations. "Artificial intelligence" capabilities emerged, along with voice interaction between people and machines.

The computer revolution, enhanced by new communications technologies such as fiber-optic networks and satellite transmission, fueled an "information revolution." Libraries replaced card catalogs with computer networks. Electronic mail, fax transmissions, voice mail, and the World Wide Web rapidly came to supplement posted (sometimes called "snail") mail and telephone conversations. Cellular phones became widespread. The variety of ways in which people could speedily communicate with other people or with information-bearing machines changed the patterns of human interaction and work. "Telecommuting" from home became common as electronic networks made it less necessary for workers to appear in person at an office.

BIG BUSINESS

Computerized communications helped transform ways of doing business by enabling the growth of electronic banking, far-flung business franchising, and huge globalized industries.

Although buying on credit had been widespread in the United States since the 1920s, Bank of America's introduction of its Visa credit card lifted credit-buying to new levels. From the

1970s on, use of bank-issued credit cards mounted. Private debt and personal bankruptcies also soared, and the rate of personal savings fell. Other innovations in electronic banking—automatic teller machines (ATMs), checking (or debit) cards, automatic depositing, and electronic bill-paying—moved Americans closer to a cashless economy where electronic impulses would substitute for currency.

Franchising and chain stores also changed the way consumer products were bought and sold. McDonald's and Holiday Inn pioneered nationwide standardization in the fast-food and travel industries during the 1950s. Other chain restaurants soon copied the McDonald's model, and some even showed that franchise food need not be inexpensive. Similarly, Starbuck's parlayed a simple dietary staple, coffee, into a pricey designer commodity. And Sam Walton's success in building his Wal-Mart chain symbolized the transformation that was engulfing the entire retailing industry. By the late 20th century, books, videotapes, records, electronics equipment, shoes, groceries, travel accommodations, and just about every other consumer item were made available by chains that brought a greater array of merchandise and lower prices—but often offered only low-wage or part-time jobs. Amazon.com became the darling of another innovation—e-commerce (buying over the Internet).

American chain businesses expanded overseas as well as at home. Especially after the collapse of communist regimes in the Soviet Union and Eastern Europe, they rushed to supply consumers with long-denied, American-style goods and services. McDonald's opened to great fanfare in Moscow and Budapest, while the Hilton chain opened new hotels in Eastern European capitals. Pepsi and Coke carried on with their "cola wars" for dominance in foreign markets.

Production, as well as consumption, turned international. U.S. automakers, for example, moved many of their production and assembly plants outside of the United States. Moreover, the trend toward "privatization" (the sale of government-owned industries to private business) in many economies worldwide provided American companies with new opportunities for acquisition. Foreign interests also purchased many U.S. companies and real estate holdings. So many industrial giants had become globalized by the late 20th century that it was difficult to define what constituted an American or a foreign company.

POSTINDUSTRIAL RESTRUCTURING

New technologies and economic globalization brought structural changes to American business and the workforce. Many companies cut their workforces and trimmed their management staffs. In the 1970s more than a dozen major steel plants closed, and the auto industry laid off thousands of workers. The Chrysler Corporation managed to survive only after the federal government took the unprecedented step of guaranteeing loans to the company. The steel and auto industries regained profitability in the 1980s and 1990s, but other giant corporations also began to "downsize." As employment in traditional manufacturing and extractive sectors decreased, jobs in service, high-technology, and the information-entertainment sector increased. By the end of the 1990s, the unemployment rate was at its lowest point in several decades, but the kinds of jobs held by Americans had shifted. Computing and other high-tech jobs brought high salaries, but jobs in the expanding service sector—clerks, servers, cleaners—tended to remain low-paid.

Union membership, always highest in the manufacturing occupations, fell to under 15 percent of the labor force by the late 1990s. While union membership rolls and political power steadily slipped, efforts to expand the base of the union movement into new sectors of the

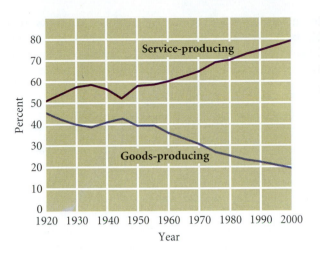

PERCENTAGES OF GOODS-PRODUCING AND SERVICE-PRODUCING U.S. JOBS, 1920–2000

SOURCE: U.S. Census Bureau.

economy initially met with little success. For example, some union locals around the country attempted to organize restaurant and hotel workers, a sector that employed many women. But businesses adamantly fought unionization, claiming that it would raise labor costs.

Cesar Chavez's efforts during the late 1960s and early 1970s to organize agricultural workers also dramatized the difficulties of expanding the base of the union movement. Chavez, a charismatic leader, vaulted the United Farm Workers (UFW) into public attention. As the union president, Chavez instituted several well-publicized consumer boycotts of lettuce and grapes as means of pressuring growers to bargain with the UFW. He won a major contract victory in 1970. During the late 1970s and the 1980s, however, the UFW steadily lost ground. Strong stands by growers to keep out union organizers and the continued influx of new immigrants eager for work undercut the UFW's efforts.

The major growth for organized labor came among government employees and workers in the health care industry. But these gains did not offset the losses in union membership in the old industrial sectors.

Some economists warned that the shift to a "postindustrial" economy was "deskilling" the labor force and worsening technological unemployment—people out of work because the jobs for which they were trained no longer exist. Critics of the new trends expressed alarm over statistics revealing that well over half the new jobs created in the U.S. economy during the 1980s paid less than $7,000 per year. Some analysts warned that the widening gulf between highly paid, highly skilled positions and minimum-wage jobs might ultimately undermine the middle-class nature of American society. By the late 1990s, the labor movement was trying to redress this trend.

More optimistic observers pointed out that internationalization and corporate downsizing might temporarily mean lost jobs for some people but that gains in productivity would eventually translate into lower consumer prices and rising living standards. Indeed, real wages did begin to rise in the 1990s. Moreover, new technologies promised to create business opportunities for future generations. New high-tech businesses turned many computer mavens into millionaires. Product innovation paved a broad avenue of upward economic mobility for those with computer-age skills.

These revolutionary changes in technology and the economy had profound effects on the lives of Americans. Skilled workers of earlier generations had tended to stick to one profession or place of employment throughout their working life. But by the end of the 20th century, even middle-income professionals were likely to switch occupations several times before retiring.

THE ENVIRONMENT

The modern environmental movement began during the 1970s, but its roots reached back to the earlier conservation and preservation movements. During the first four decades of the 20th century, the conservation movement promoted "wise use" of water, forests, and farm-lands by urging government to promote scientific resource management and to designate areas as national parks and forests (see Chapter 21). A preservation movement—led by the Sierra Club, the Audubon Society, the Wilderness Society, and others—was primarily concerned with the aesthetics of nature and wanted to protect and enjoy the natural environment in a state as pristine as possible. Landmark legislation during the 1960s—the Wilderness Act of 1964, the National Wild and Scenic Rivers Act of 1968, and the National Trails Act of 1968—set aside new areas, protecting them from development.

ENVIRONMENTAL ACTIVISM AND GOVERNMENT POLICY

The conservation and preservation movements broadened into an "environmental move-ment." In 1962 Rachel Carson had published *Silent Spring,* which warned that the pesticides used in agriculture, especially DDT, threatened bird populations. Air pollution in major cities such as Los Angeles became so bad that simply breathing urban air was equivalent to smoking several packs of cigarettes a day. Industrial processes polluted water systems, and fears of over-exposure to radiation mounted as a result of the testing of atomic weapons and the prolifera-tion of nuclear power plants. In response to these concerns, environmentalists tried to focus national attention on toxic chemicals and the adverse impact of industrial development on air, water, and soil quality. The Environmental Defense Fund, a private organization formed in 1967, took the crusade against DDT and other dangerous toxins to the courts. And in 1970 ac-tivitists came together for Earth Day, organized largely by college students, to raise awareness about environmental degradation.

During the 1970s combating environmental hazards and maintaining ecological balances emerged as major concerns of public policy. During Richard Nixon's presidency, the federal government established the Environmental Protection Agency (EPA) in 1970 and enacted major pieces of environmental legislation: the Resources Recovery Act of 1970 (dealing with waste management), the Clean Air Act of 1970, the Water Pollution Control Act of 1972, the Pesticides Control Act of 1972, and the Endangered Species Act of 1973. National parks and wilderness areas were further expanded, and a new law required that "environmental impact statements" be prepared in advance of any major government project. Administering environ-mental policies became a complex task requiring sophisticated research and negotiations among conflicting interest groups. It also prompted heated public debates. Environmentalist groups grew in size, resources, and expertise, while businesses opposed to these types of bu-reaucracies attacked government regulation and branded environmentalism an elitist cause that destroyed jobs and impeded economic growth.

New standards brought some significant improvements. The Clean Air Act's restrictions on auto and smokestack emissions, for example, reduced the amount of six major airborne pollutants by one-third in a single decade. The emission of lead into the atmosphere declined by 95 percent. But the remedies could also create new problems. Requiring higher smokestacks to eliminate smog helped to clear city skies but also elevated pollutants into the atmosphere, where they produced damaging "acid rain."

In the late 1970s families living at Love Canal, a housing development near Buffalo, New York, learned that the soil under their homes was contaminated by chemical wastes produced 30 years earlier. The finding explained why residents of the area suffered from high levels of cancer and had children with genetic defects. The costs of resettlement and cleanup of wastes prompted Congress to create a cleanup "Superfund" to be financed by taxes imposed on polluting industries. The most heavily contaminated areas, designated as Superfund sites, were slated for special cleanup efforts.

Environmental legislation prompted a backlash. President Ronald Reagan denounced the environmental regulations of the 1970s. James Watt, Reagan's first secretary of the interior, angered environmentalists by supporting the "sagebrush rebellion," in which western states demanded fewer restrictions on the use of public land within their borders. Emotional battles broke out during the 1980s over private use of resources in federal wilderness areas and over whether protection of endangered species should take priority over economic activities.

The acrimony of environmental debates lessened somewhat during the 1990s. Alternative approaches to environmental management sought to promote change through incentives rather than penalties. In 1997, for example, the Conservation Reserve Program, a farm subsidy program that previously paid farmers to remove land from tillage, now stipulated payment to farmers who would restore wetlands on their properties in order to decrease polluted runoff into streams and preserve wildlife habitat.

The U.S. government itself, however, turned out to be one of the country's most flagrant polluters. In 1988 Secretary of Energy John Harrington admitted that the government's nuclear facilities had been lax on safety measures and estimated that cleanup would cost more than $1 billion. The revelation of hazardous conditions at sites where atomic weapons had been produced shocked nearby residents, who feared that they might have been victims of radiation poisoning. Medical records, long suppressed by the government, revealed that people living downwind of nuclear test sites in the 1940s and 1950s had experienced an abnormally high incidence of cancer, leukemia, and thyroid disorders. In 1993 President Bill Clinton's energy secretary, Hazel O'Leary, finally released records relating to radiation testing and experimentation and promised programs to inform and compensate victims.

The environmental movement increasingly focused on international, as well as national, ecological dangers. Those hazards included global warming (the "greenhouse effect"); holes in the ozone layer caused by chlorofluorocarbons (CFCs); massive deforestation and desertification; pollution of the oceans; and the rapid decline of biological diversity. Solutions to these global problems required worldwide cooperation. International meetings on environmental issues became more frequent. Conventions in Vienna in 1985, Montreal in 1987, London in 1990, and Kyoto in 1997 worked toward establishing international standards on emissions of CFCs and greenhouse gases. A so-called Earth Summit was held in Brazil in 1992, and a conference in Cairo in 1994 took up global population issues. Fear that environmental restrictions could harm economic growth and the lack of mechanisms to enforce internationally agreed-on targets, however, slowed the progress of the international environ-mental crusade.

ENERGY

The problem of global warming stemmed largely from patterns of energy use. The United States obtained 90 percent of its energy from the burning of fossil fuels, a major source of the carbon dioxide that creates the greenhouse effect. The nation's dependence on fossil fuels aroused serious public concern during the 1970s. Part of the concern was simply economic. In 1973 and again in 1976 the Organization of Petroleum Exporting Countries (OPEC), a cartel dominated by the oil-rich nations of the Middle East, sharply raised the price of oil and pre-cipitated acute shortages in the industrialized world. As Americans wearied of high prices and long lines at gas stations, President Jimmy Carter (1976–1980) promised to make the United States less dependent on imported fossil fuel. He created a new cabinet-level Department of Energy in 1977 and gave some support to conservation efforts and to the development of re-newable energy sources.

But Carter also continued to support the use of nuclear power generated by giant reactors. Boosters of the nation's atomic research program had promised that nuclear reactors would provide a cheap, almost limitless supply of energy. The cost of building and maintaining the reactors, however, far exceeded the original estimates, and critics charged that the reactors posed a grave safety risk. The danger was illustrated in 1979 by a malfunction at a reactor at Three Mile Island in Pennsylvania that nearly produced a nuclear meltdown. In response to growing public alarm, power companies canceled orders for new nuclear reactors. During the 1980s, expansion of the nuclear power industry halted.

Meanwhile, the cost of OPEC oil was skyrocketing, helping to boost U.S. inflation rates during Carter's presidency. On taking office as president in 1981, Ronald Reagan promised to break OPEC's oil monopoly by encouraging the development of new sources of supply. Rea-gan and his successor George Bush followed a "cheap oil" energy policy throughout the 1980s. The tapping of new supplies of oil, together with rivalries among OPEC members, weakened OPEC's hold over the world market and reduced energy costs. But little progress was made in breaking U.S. reliance on fossil fuels, and the United States government assumed little leader-ship in pushing for international standards on carbon dioxide emissions.

MEDIA AND CULTURE

Innovations in electronic technologies transformed America's culture as well as its economy. By 1995 virtually every residential unit in the country had at least one TV, 99 percent had a VCR, and about 80 percent had a personal computer. More than one-third of the population needed a computer in their daily work, and more than half of all schoolchildren used one in the classroom. The video screen seemed the preeminent symbol of the nation's mass culture.

THE VIDEO REVOLUTION

Video monitors were everywhere. Visitors to museums and historical sites could access infor-mation about a particular display simply by pressing spots on an interactive video screen.

Sports bars lined their walls with video monitors, enabling patrons to follow favorite teams. Meanwhile, TV screens were replacing last year's magazines in doctors' waiting rooms and auto repair shops. Air travelers could catch the latest news updates and weather conditions by watching a special Airport Channel.

The kind of specially targeted programming found in many airports highlighted the increasingly fragmented nature of cultural production. The 1970s represented the last decade in which the three major television networks—CBS, NBC, and ABC—were able to command the daily attention of a nation of loyal viewers.

At the beginning of the 1970s, the three major TV networks still offered a range of general-interest programming that was designed to attract a mass audience. A typical 30-minute episode of a top-rated situation comedy might draw more viewers in a single evening than a hit motion picture attracted over an entire year. The networks could promise advertisers that a cross section of the American public would be watching their sales pitches. Various ratings devices, including the venerable Nielsen system, tracked the number of viewers who were tuning in.

The networks began to modify this mass-market strategy during the 1970s. Early in the decade, CBS jettisoned a number of highly rated programs and targeted shows at younger urban and suburban viewers. This shift in strategy, CBS assured potential advertisers, would allow them concentrate on the consumers most likely to spend money on new products.

In line with this strategy of targeting specific groups, CBS began using its comedy lineup to offer more controversial programming. *All in the Family,* a sitcom that highlighted generational conflict within a blue-collar family from Queens, allowed Archie Bunker, the show's bigoted protagonist, to serve as a lightning rod for controversial issues involving race and gender. Although *The Mary Tyler Moore Show* rarely took positions that seemed overtly "feminist," this popular sitcom featured a woman who worked in a fictional TV newsroom. It portrayed the personal politics of working women of the 1970s. TV critics joined viewers in applauding new CBS shows, such as *M*A*S*H,* for integrating comedy with social commentary. NBC soon joined the trend; in 1975 *Saturday Night Live* brought the barbed humor of the 1960s counterculture to network television.

Choosing a strategy different from that of CBS or NBC, ABC cultivated the teenage audience. Aware that young people generally controlled at least one of the family's TV sets, ABC increased its ratings with sex-and-action programs *(Charlie's Angels),* mildly risqué sitcoms *(Three's Company),* fast-paced police shows *(Kojak),* and a variety of upbeat programs such as the nostalgic *Happy Days* and the escapist *Fantasy Island.*

All three networks enjoyed rising profits during the 1970s. At the end of the decade, 9 of every 10 TV sets were still tuned to a network program during prime-time viewing hours.

During the 1980s, however, the networks began to confront a slow yet steady loss of viewers. One reason was that programmers found it increasingly difficult to create successful prime-time programs. Although NBC found great success with *The Bill Cosby Show,* which featured an affluent African American family, and *Cheers,* a sitcom set in a Boston tavern where "everybody knows your name," most of its other offerings had significantly less audience appeal. NBC, like the other networks, adjusted by slashing budgets and spicing its prime-time programs with sexually oriented themes.

Meanwhile, independent stations began to compete in local markets. At a time when the number of daily newspapers was steadily shrinking, 200 independent TV stations went on the air during the 1980s. Lacking access to new network programs, these independents targeted small but lucrative markets by strategically scheduling Hollywood films, sporting events, and reruns of canceled network programs.

Capitalizing on the rise of the independents, Rupert Murdoch's Fox television network debuted in 1988. Fox broke new ground by offering a limited program schedule to previously independent stations. One of its first hit series, *The Simpsons,* a cartoon send-up of the venerable family sitcom, became a mass-marketing bonanza. Fox gradually expanded its nightly offerings and in 1993 shocked the TV industry by outbidding CBS for the rights to carry the National Football League's NFC conference games. In the 1990s, two other communication conglomerates, Paramount and Time-Warner, set up networks based on the Fox model and aimed much of their prime-time programming at younger, urban viewers.

New technologies were also undermining the monopoly of the major networks. At the simplest level, the remote-control device gave rise to a new TV aesthetic, called "zapping" or "channel surfing," in which viewers rapidly switch from program to program, usually during commercial breaks. The mass-marketing of VCRs also gave people new control over their television viewing habits.

But the greatest impact on viewing patterns came from the growth of cable television (CATV). By 1995 nearly 65 percent of the nation's homes were wired for CATV. Capable of carrying scores of different programs, most of which were aimed at very specific audiences, CATV further fragmented TV viewership. Ted Turner, one of the first to recognize the potential of CATV with his "Superstation" WTBS, later added Cable News Network (CNN), and several movie channels before his communications empire merged with that of Time-Warner. Cable operations—whether they featured news, cartoons, sports, public affairs, commercial-free movies, round-the-clock weather, or home shopping programs—steadily expanded. By 1998, the percentage of television viewers watching programs on ABC, CBS, and NBC had fallen to less than 60 percent.

HOLLYWOOD AND THE "MTV AESTHETIC"

The new media environment affected nearly every aspect of mass culture. With movie ticket sales remaining about the same in 1980 as they had been in 1960, Hollywood studios raised the price of each ticket and concentrated on turning out a handful of blockbuster epics, such as *Star Wars* (1977), and an occasional surprise hit, such as Sylvester Stallone's original *Rocky* (1976). But for every *Star Wars* or *Rocky,* Hollywood moguls seemed equally able to produce expensive box-office duds like *Waterworld* (1995). Thus, filmmakers increasingly tended to play it safe and use the kind of story lines and special effects that had made money in the past. Classic TV series, such as *Batman* and *Leave It to Beaver,* became motion pictures. Blockbuster hits such as *Jurassic Park* (1993) spawned sequels such as *Lost World* (1996). And following ABC's TV strategy, Hollywood also made teenagers a major target for films such as *The Breakfast Club* (1985), *Ferris Bueller's Day Off* (1986), and *Clueless* (1995). CATV and VCRs did, however, provide Hollywood with new sources of revenue. Although huge multiplex movie theaters opened in suburban shopping areas throughout the 1980s and early 1990s, video rental stores surpassed them in number, and VCR sales soared. During the late 1990s, most of the smaller video stores faced often-fatal competition from giant chains like Blockbuster and from corner gas-marts and convenience stores. More and more people were using VCRs and the various all-movie CATV channels to convert their TV sets into home movie theaters.

CATV and VCRs helped to transform the pop music industry as well. Music Television (MTV), initially offering a 24-hour supply of rock videos, was launched in 1981. Critics charged it with consistently portraying women as sex objects and with excluding artists of color. Eventually, however, MTV defused complaints—especially after airing Michael Jackson's 29-minute video based on his hit single "Thriller" (1983). Several years later, Madonna used MTV to create a new relationship between music and visual image. A decade later, Madonna's first MTV videos migrated to VH-1, the CATV channel whose musical format catered to older, post-MTV viewers. By the late 1990s, the entertainment industry was releasing VHS and CD-ROM musical packages, as well as singles and albums on tape and compact disc (CD), and was introducing new mini-disk and DVD technologies.

The New Mass Culture Debate

Mass commercial culture generated controversy. In 1975 the Federal Communications Commission (FCC) ordered the TV networks to dedicate the first 60 minutes of prime time each evening to "family" programming free of violence or "mature" themes. Several TV production companies challenged this requirement, and a federal court ruled that it was a violation of the First Amendment's guarantee of free speech. Demands that the government regulate rock lyrics and album covers also ran afoul of complaints that this constituted illegal censorship. Although governmental efforts faltered, private organizations were more successful in pressing media companies to practice self-censorship. In 1992 pressure on Time-Warner resulted in the withdrawal of a song titled "Cop Killer" by the African American rap artist Ice-T; television networks subsequently adopted a rating system designed to inform parents about the amount of violence and sexual content in prime-time programs.

Meanwhile, a new generation of writers, reviewers, and university professors were paying serious attention to mass culture. Unlike the critics of the 1950s, who dismissed mass culture as trivial and condemned its effects on American life, the critics of the 1980s and 1990s often became fans of the cultural products they were reviewing. Instead of comparing mass culture to "high" culture (the so-called classical works of Western civilization), many abandoned the distinction between lowbrow and highbrow. They insisted that music of the Beatles should be studied along with that of Beethoven and argued that the lyrics of Chuck Berry and Bob Dylan merited academic analysis.

These new analysts also studied the ways in which consumers integrated the products of mass culture into their daily lives. Again rejecting the cultural criticism of the 1950s, they stressed ordinary people's creative interaction with mass culture. Much of this analysis came from professors in the new field of "cultural studies," who focused on how people reworked images from the mass media. Scholarly studies of *Star Trek,* for example, explored the ways in which loyal fans had kept this popular TV series of the 1960s alive in syndication and had subsequently prompted a succession of Hollywood motion pictures and several new *Star Trek* television series. Moreover, through conventions, self-produced magazines (called "fanzines"), and Web sites, fans of *Star Trek* ("Trekkies") and of shows such as *Xena* created a grass-roots subculture that used TV programs as vehicles for discussing social and political issues, especially ones that touched on race, gender, and sexuality. Those who advocated cultural studies argued that students should study such popular phenomena and also that they should be exposed to a range of works by women, people of color, and political outsiders.

Political and social conservatives condemned the introduction of cultural studies into the college curriculum and viewed such teaching as evidence of "the closing of the American mind" (which became the title of a best-selling 1987 book by Allan Bloom) and of the "opening" of students' minds only to what was trendy and "politically correct" (or "PC"). They

TV's Family Values

Television sitcoms have always provided visual representations of the "typical" family. During the 1940s, when most viewers resided in urban areas, TV families also lived in cities and often held blue-collar jobs. Chester A. Riley, played by Jackie Gleason and later William Bendix, worked in an aircraft factory on *The Life of Riley.* Ralph Kramden, also portrayed by Gleason, drove a bus on *The Honeymooners.* By the mid-1950s, however, most sitcom families had moved to the suburbs and upward on the socioeconomic scale. Ward Cleaver of *Leave It to Beaver* and Jim Anderson of *Father Knows Best* were prosperous professionals who provided their wives and children with all of the amenities appropriate to the age of affluence. Other sitcom families—such as those portrayed on *I Love Lucy, The Adventures of Ozzie and Harriet,* and *Make Room for Daddy*—featured a husband who worked in show business and a wife who dominated home life from her command post in the kitchen.

Although most of these classic sitcom families continued to appear on television during the 1980s and 1990s through syndication to local stations or on cable channels such as NICK-at-

Nite, they were joined by a new and very different generation of TV families. The Huxtables (Bill Cosby and Phylicia Rashad), although as middle-class and affluent as the Andersons or Cleavers, represented a successful African American family that was coheaded by two well-educated professionals. The title character of *Murphy Brown* (Candice Bergen) worked in the media, but her family was composed of coworkers rather than a spouse. When the unmarried Murphy gave birth to a baby, Dan Quayle, the vice president of the United States, condemned her for endangering family values. The resultant flap only increased *Murphy Brown*'s ratings.

The Simpsons also drew critical fire from defenders of the traditional sitcom family. Although Homer and Marge were married with children, *The Simpsons,* especially during its early years, drew humor by portraying a dysfunctional family. Bart was "an underachiever—and proud of it," and Homer spent more time at Moe's Tavern than with his children. Gradually, the show gained cult status, particularly as viewers came to appreciate the subtle ways in which it playfully parodied TV and movie conventions.

charged that such fascination with mass culture represented a debasement of intellectual life that was also spreading beyond the classroom.

THE DEBATE OVER MULTICULTURAL EDUCATION

Debates over mass culture often merged with controversies over educational policies. Cultural studies, multiculturalism, and political correctness became fighting words. During the late 1970s, the government-funded National Endowment for the Humanities (NEH) and the National Endowment for the Arts (NEA) began to provide financial backing for projects that focused on America's cultural diversity and on politically sensitive reinterpretations of traditional works. In the 1980s conservative Republicans launched a counterattack. Ronald Reagan's secretary of education, William Bennett, used his office to crusade against multicultural education, while Lynn Cheney, head of the NEH, championed traditional programs. Seeking to placate conservatives such as North Carolina's Senator Jesse Helms, President George Bush's administration pressured the NEA to cancel grants to controversial artistic projects, especially those relating to feminism or homosexuality. Controversies over the funding, and even the continued survival, of the NEA and the NEH continued through the 1990s. On college campuses, meanwhile, faculty and students heatedly debated the value of multicultural curricula.

Conservative pressure groups mounted a parallel critique of educational practices in public schools. This phase of the conservative movement, which had initially begun in response to the Supreme Court decisions of the 1960s that barred state-sponsored prayers and Bible-reading in public schools, argued that cultural and educational innovations were manifestations of an antireligious philosophy they called "secular humanism." In the 1950s and 1960s, liberal opponents of Bible-reading and prayer in public schools had insisted that students should not be forced to participate in religious activities. In the 1980s conservatives adapted this argument for their cause and insisted that children should not be coerced into participating in secular-humanist activities that contradicted the religious teachings of their families and churches.

Originating in a complex and electronically mediated environment, the controversy over mass culture extended from the White House to the local schoolhouse. During the 1992 presidential campaign, Bill Clinton eagerly appeared on MTV. The Republican Party's national platform, in contrast, strongly attacked the new cultural climate. Meanwhile, in communities across the country, militant conservatives mobilized to elect school boards that opposed multicultural curricula and other educational changes. As the United States became the home to increasingly fragmented and highly politicized cultures, people debated the complex meanings of multiculturalism and tolerance for difference.

SOCIAL ACTIVISM

The legacy of activism from the 1960s became deeply embedded in American life and rippled through the decades that followed. The mass demonstration remained a tool of social activists representing all kinds of causes. Washington, D.C., continued to provide a favorite stage where huge rallies could attract the attention of national lawmakers and the media, but activists also mounted smaller rallies and protests that recalled the demonstrations of the 1960s. In the early 1980s the Clamshell Alliance mounted a campaign of civil disobedience against a nuclear reactor being built in Seabrook, New Hampshire. Women's groups staged annual "Take Back the Night" marches in major cities to protest the rising tide of sexual assaults, and both pro-choice and anti-abortion groups sponsored demonstrations in Washington, D.C., and in local communities. In October 1995, the "Million Man March" in Washington, D.C., sought to mobilize African American men behind a campaign of social reconstruction in black communities, and two years later an evangelical men's group called the "Promise Keepers" filled Washington's Mall.

Mass demonstrations, however, had lost much of their power to attract media attention by the end of the 20th century. During a period of violence in May 1991 in Los Angeles, 30,000 Korean Americans staged a march for peace. Although it was the largest demonstration ever conducted by any Asian American group, even the local media ignored it.

WOMEN'S ISSUES

Older ideologies of domesticity increasingly clashed with the situations in which millions of women found themselves. More and more women were working outside the home, postponing marriage, remaining single, or getting divorced. Moreover, the development of the birth-control pill gave women more control over reproduction and significantly changed the nature of sexual relationships.

As they pursued activities outside their homes, women came to realize the extent of gender discrimination and to ask new questions about the gender-based division of both public and private power arrangements. Even many of the men who were involved in movements for social change saw no contradiction between women's second-class status and men's positions of authority and leadership. Some male leaders of these movements expected female members to provide secretarial or sexual services and complained that raising issues of sexual equality "interfered" with the movements' primary tasks of redirecting racial and foreign policies. As a result, struggles for gender equality emerged within various older insurgency movements. African American women advocated black feminism; Chicana groups coalesced within Mexican American organizations; radical feminists split off from the antiwar movement; other women challenged the ethics of capitalism by forming new, female-directed cooperatives.

Throughout the 1970s groups of women came together in "consciousness-raising" sessions to discuss issues and share perspectives. These discussions produced a growing conviction that women's larger *political* concerns about the maldistribution of power in the United States could not be separated from the very *personal* power relationships that shaped their own lives. "The personal is political" became the watchword for this new generation of feminists.

Economic self-sufficiency became a pressing issue for many women. Although women increasingly entered the professions and gained unionized positions, the average female worker throughout the 1970s and 1980s continued to earn about 60 cents for every dollar earned by the average male worker. During the 1960s, social welfare benefits for single mothers with children had been boosted by higher AFDC payments and by the Food Stamp program. But in the 1970s and 1980s, the real monetary value of these benefits, measured in constant dollars, steadily decreased. Homeless shelters, which once catered primarily to single men, increasingly had to address the needs of women and children. Throughout the 1970s and 1980s, this "feminization of poverty," and the growing number of children raised in low-income, female-headed families, became a fact of life.

Feminism grew into a highly diverse movement. Women from all sectors of society built new institutions to address needs that had been long ignored by male leaders. American life was greatly influenced by an explosion of female-oriented organizations: battered-women's shelters, clinics specializing in women's medicine, rape crisis centers, economic development counseling for women-owned businesses, union-organizing efforts led by women, women's studies programs in colleges and universities, and academic journals devoted to research on women.

Pressure to end gender discrimination changed existing institutions as well. Previously all-male bastions, such as country clubs and service organizations, were pressured into admitting women. Most mainline Protestant churches and Reform Jewish congregations were challenged to accept women into the ministry. Educational institutions began to adopt "gender-fair" hiring practices and curricula. The everyday lives of most American women by the end of the 20th century took place in an institutional environment very different from that of their mothers a generation earlier.

Sexual harassment, to take only one of the new concerns, became a significant issue among women. Some feminists argued that to focus on sexual harassment would tend to identify feminism with a kind of sexual puritanism that the women's movement had once promised to end. Others, however, continued to push government organizations and private employers to ban behavior that demeaned women and exploited their lack of power vis-à-vis male supervisors and coworkers. In 1986 the U.S. Supreme Court ruled that sexual harassment constituted a form of discrimination covered under the 1964 Civil Rights Act.

In 1991 the issue of sexual harassment attracted national attention when Clarence Thomas, an African American nominee for the Supreme Court, was accused by Anita Hill, an African American law professor, of sexually harassing her when both had worked for the Office of Economic Opportunity. Feminists were angered when the all-male Senate Judiciary Committee seemed unable to understand the issues raised by Hill's charges. When the Senate confirmed Thomas's nomination, women's groups gained new converts to their views on sexual harassment. In addition, political observers credited anger over the Thomas-Hill hearings with helping to mobilize female voters to elect four women to the U.S. Senate in 1992.

Sexual harassment also became a controversial issue within the U.S. military. The service academies began accepting female cadets, and women seemed to be finding places within the military establishment. Front-page revelations about harassment and even sexual assaults against female naval officers by their male comrades at the 1991 "Tailhook" convention, however, highlighted problems. Attempts by Navy officials to cover up the incident provoked outrage, and several high-ranking officers were forced to step down.

SEXUAL POLITICS

Debates over gender and sexuality became extremely divisive when it came to issues involving gays and lesbians. Some homosexuals had already begun to claim rights on the basis of their sexuality in the 1950s (see Chapter 27). A new spirit of insurgence and self-assurance emerged toward the end of the 1960s. In 1969, New York City police raided the Stonewall Inn, a gay bar in Greenwich Village. "Stonewall" marked a turning point in homosexual politics. Within a decade after Stonewall, thousands of gay and lesbian advocacy groups sprang up, and many homosexuals came "out of the closet," proudly proclaiming their sexual orientation.

Soon, newspapers, theaters, nightspots, and religious groups identifying themselves with the homosexual community became part of daily life in cities and large towns. Specific forms of popular entertainment, such as the disco craze of the 1970s, became closely identified with the gay and lesbian subcultures. As a cultural movement, homosexuality benefited significantly at the end of the 20th century from a general relaxation of legal and cultural controls over the portrayal and practice of *all* forms of explicit sexuality.

Homosexuals pressured state and local governments to enact laws prohibiting discrimination in housing and jobs on the basis of sexual preference. Moreover, they demanded that the police treat attacks on homosexuals no less seriously than they treated other forms of violent crime. By the 1990s gays and lesbians had gained some political power. Activism by homosexuals, however, was also met with either indifference or determined opposition, especially by conservatives.

In addition to battling traditional forms of discrimination, broadly labeled as "homophobia," gays faced a new issue: acquired immunodeficiency syndrome (AIDS), a fatal and contagious condition that attacks a person's immune system. First identified in the early 1980s, AIDS quickly became an intensely emotional and often misunderstood medical and political issue. Epidemiologists correctly recognized AIDS as a health problem for the general public. The disease could be transmitted through the careless use of intravenous drugs, tainted blood supplies, and "unprotected" heterosexual intercourse. At first, however, its incidence in the United States was limited almost solely to gay men. As a consequence of this association, gay activists charged, the Reagan and Bush administrations placed a low priority on medical efforts to check the spread of AIDS or to find a cure for it. The controversy over AIDS and medical funding galvanized gay and lesbian activists to assert their concerns more forcefully.

RACE, ETHNICITY, AND SOCIAL ACTIVISM

The emphasis on group identity as the basis for activism grew especially strong among various racial and ethnic communities in the late 20th century. Groups emphasized pride in their distinctive traditions and declared that cultural differences among Americans should be celebrated rather than simply tolerated. Especially with the influx of new immigrants, multiculturalism became a contentious issue.

DEBATES WITHIN AFRICAN AMERICAN CULTURE

African Americans had developed a strong sense of cultural identity during the 1960s (see Chapters 28 and 29). Battles against discrimination continued in the post-Vietnam era. Controversies over future directions, however, also emerged.

During the 1970s a movement called "Afrocentrism" began to attract a number of African American intellectuals and professionals. In contrast to the cold rationality of "Eurocentrists," it was argued, African Americans understood people and knowledge in broader, more empathetic ways. Afrocentrists encouraged blacks to take pride in heroic figures from the recent past, especially Malcolm X (see Chapter 29). A trend that one African American writer called "Malcolmania" accelerated with the appearance of Spike Lee's film *Malcolm X* (1992). The stress on racial pride was also prominent in rap and hip-hop music. By 1990 more than 300 private schools and even some public systems were offering black students an "Afrocentric" curriculum.

Pride in racial identity and an African heritage became a complex, contested proposition. African American women who identified with feminist issues tended to view Afrocentrism and some male rap music as infected with misogyny. Queen Latifah sang songs like "Ladies First," which criticized what she saw to be the gender stereotyping and the romanticizing of a mythical African past in many rap lyrics. African American women's groups organized to pressure record companies and radio stations to censor some rap music, especially "gangsta rap," which they considered misogynistic.

Similarly in academia, most programs in African American studies veered away from a strict Afrocentric approach in order to acknowledge the diversity and complexity of a heritage that stemmed from a multiplicity of African and American cultural influences. African American scholars such as Henry Lewis Gates Jr., who became head of Harvard's Afro-American studies department in 1991, made pride in the black experience one part of a larger multicultural vision. Gates urged that African American authors, such as Toni Morrison (who won the Nobel Prize for Literature in 1993) and Alice Walker, be viewed as writers who take "the blackness of the culture for granted, as a springboard to write about those human emotions that we share with everyone else, and that we have always shared with each other." Although African American cultures could be seen as unique and different, said Gates, they should not be considered apart from their interaction with American culture generally.

This issue of whether African Americans should cultivate separateness or seek more interaction with the broader American culture surfaced at the NAACP convention in 1997. Leaders opened for debate the possibility that the NAACP should no longer adhere to its long-standing agenda favoring school integration. Although the organization did not change its stance, the very discussion of returning to separatist schools illustrated both frustration over the test scores of African American children in integrated public education and the impact of Afrocentric influences.

Other developments underscored the fact that a broad spectrum of views existed among African Americans. The controversy over the appointment of Clarence Thomas to the U.S. Supreme Court divided African Americans, just as it divided whites. Some, especially African American feminists, saw Anita Hill's testimony against Thomas as evidence of pervasive sexism within black culture, but many other African Americans remained focused on race. No white nominee, they argued, would ever have faced the kind of personal scrutiny that Thomas confronted.

The 1996 trial of sports star O. J. Simpson raised another important debate about the place of African Americans in American life. On this issue, African Americans were less divided. In the "trial of the century," Simpson was prosecuted for two brutal murders, including that of his former wife. Simpson's defense team, headed by the African American attorney Johnnie Cochran Jr., successfully refocused the trial on alleged misconduct by racist officers within the Los Angeles police department, and a largely black jury returned a verdict of not-guilty. Opinion polls indicated a significant division along racial lines: Whites were solidly convinced of Simpson's guilt, and African Americans overwhelmingly believed he was innocent. Quite apart from whatever the trial proved about Simpson's guilt or innocence, it indicated an enormous gulf between whites and African Americans because of the distrust of police and the legal system in African American communities.

AMERICAN INDIANS

American Indians pursued a variety of strategies for social change from the 1970s to the 1990s. In 1969 activists began a two-year sit-in, designed to dramatize a history of broken

INDIAN GAMING AT MYSTIC LAKE CASINO IN MINNESOTA   By the mid-1990s, legal gambling had become one of the nation's leading recreational enterprises. Native Americans saw casinos as an important way to generate jobs and capital on Indian reservations.

treaty promises over land claims, at the former federal prison on Alcatraz Island in San Francisco harbor. Expanding on this tactic, the American Indian Movement (AIM), which had been created in 1968 by young activists from several Northern Plains tribes, adopted a confrontational approach. Clashes erupted in early 1973 on the Pine Ridge Reservation in South Dakota. In response, the FBI and federal prosecutors targeted members of AIM for illegal surveillance and criminal prosecutions.

Many American Indians, like other ethnic groups, emphasized building a stronger sense of identity through traditional cultural practices. To forestall the disappearance of their languages, Indian activists urged bilingualism and the revival of traditional rituals. AIM denounced the use of stereotypical Indian names in amateur and professional sports. Teams that had long called themselves "Chiefs" or "Redskins" were pressured to seek new names.

Meanwhile, important legal changes were taking place. The omnibus Civil Rights Act of 1968 contained six sections that became known as the "Indian Bill of Rights." In these, Congress finally extended most of the provisions of the constitutional Bill of Rights to reservation Indians while still upholding the legitimacy of tribal laws. Federal legislation and several Supreme Court decisions in the 1970s subsequently reinforced the broad principle of tribal self-determination.

Many tribes used the courts to press demands derived from old treaties with the U.S. government and the unique status of tribal nations. Some tribal representatives insisted that their traditional fishing and agricultural rights be restored, a demand that often provoked resentment among non-Indians. Indians also sued to protect tribal water rights and traditional religious ceremonies (some of which include the ritual use of drugs such as peyote) and to secure repatriation of Native American skeletal remains from museums across the country. Pressure from Indian rights groups led several states and finally Congress to pass laws that provided for the repatriation of both Indian remains and sacred religious artifacts.

Claiming exemption from state gaming laws, Indians opened bingo halls and then full-blown gambling casinos. In 1988 the Supreme Court ruled that states could not prohibit gambling operations on tribal land, and Congress soon passed the Indian Gaming Regulatory Act, which gave a seal of approval to their casino operations. In states such as Connecticut, Minnesota, and Wisconsin, Indian gaming establishments became a major source of employment for Indians and non-Indians alike. Vividly underscoring the contradictions within Indian culture, the glitzy postmodernism of Las Vegas–style casinos existed alongside tribal powwows and efforts to revive older tribal practices.

SPANISH-SPEAKING AMERICANS

The media proclaimed the 1980s the "decade of the Hispanics." (Many Spanish-speaking people preferred the term "Latino.") Whether "Hispanic" or "Latino," the designation signified a population that soon would comprise America's largest minority group. Beneath this designation and a common language, however, was enormous diversity. For example, Cuban Americans generally enjoyed greater access to education and higher incomes than did other Latinos. Émigrés from Puerto Rico were already U.S. citizens and focused some of their political energies on the persistent "status" question—that is, whether Puerto Rico should hope for independence, strive for statehood, or retain a "commonwealth" connection to the mainland. Immigrants from the Dominican Republic and Central America generally were the most recent and most impoverished newcomers.

Mexican Americans comprised the oldest and most numerous Spanish-speaking group in the United States. Among them, a spirit of *Chicanismo*, a populistic pride in a heritage that could be traced back to the ancient civilizations of Middle America, emerged in the late 1960s. Young activists made "Chicano," once a term of derision, a rallying cry. In cities in the Southwest, advocates of *Chicanismo* gained considerable cultural influence. Attempts by the police to crack down on Chicano activism during the 1970s backfired, and increasing numbers of young Mexican Americans came to identify with the new insurgent spirit.

The La Raza Unida movement, founded in 1967, began to win local elections in the Southwest during the early 1970s. At the same time, *Chicanismo* continued to stimulate a cultural flowering. Catholic priests opened their churches to groups devoted to ethnic dancing, mural painting, poetry, and literature. And Spanish-language newspapers, journals, and Chicano studies programs reinforced the growing sense of pride.

In the 1970s Ernesto Cortes Jr. took the lead in founding COPS (Communities Organized for Public Service), a group that focused on achieving concrete, tangible changes that touched the everyday lives of ordinary citizens. In San Antonio, a city with a large Mexican American population, this strategy meant that Mexican American activists worked with Anglo business leaders and with Democratic politicians like Henry Cisneros, who became the city's mayor in 1981. COPS brought many Mexican Americans, particularly women, into the public arena for the first time.

By the 1990s Mexican American politics was becoming increasingly diverse. La Raza Unida continued its activities during the 1980s but never became a national force. Instead, the Mexican American Legal Defense and Educational Fund (MALDEF) emerged as the most visible national group ready to lobby or litigate on behalf of Mexican Americans. At the local level, organizations formed on the model of COPS, such as UNO (United Neighborhood Organization) in Los Angeles, continued to work on community concerns. Meanwhile, as the U.S. economy of the 1990s offered expanding employment and educational opportunities, many Mexican Americans were encouraged to pursue their own career advancement. For example, the National Network of Hispanic Women, founded in the 1970s, represented Chicanas who had obtained positions in the professions and business corporations. Linda Chavez, who had moved from the business world to the Reagan administration and then to a prominent public-policy institute, symbolized the possibility of mobility for Mexican American professionals and businesspeople.

ASIAN AMERICANS

Diverse people with ancestral roots in Asia increasingly used the term "Asian American" as a way of signifying a new ethnic consciousness. Especially at colleges and universities on the West Coast, courses and then programs in Asian American studies were established during the 1970s. By the early 1980s political activists were gaining influence, and a number of Asian American politicians were elected to office during the late 1980s and early 1990s. During the 1970s, older Japanese Americans finally began to talk about their experiences in internment camps during the Second World World (see Chapter 26). Talk eventually turned to political action, and in 1988 Congress issued a formal apology and voted a reparations payment of $20,000 to every living Japanese American who had been confined in the camps.

The new Asian American vision encouraged Americans of Chinese, Japanese, Korean, Filipino, and other backgrounds to join together in a single pan-Asian movement. Organizations such as the Asian Pacific Planning Council (APPCON) lobbied to obtain government funding for projects that benefited Asian American communities. The Asian Law Caucus and the Committee Against Anti-Asian Violence mobilized to fight a wide range of legal battles. And in 1997, the National Asian Pacific American Network Council began to lobby on issues related to immigration and education.

Emphasis on ethnic identity, however, raised problems of inclusion and exclusion. Activists who were Filipino American, the second largest Asian American group in the United States in 1990, often resisted the Asian American label because they felt that Chinese Americans and Japanese Americans dominated groups such as APPCON. As a result of complex pressures from different ethnic groups, the federal government finally decided to designate "Asian or Pacific Islanders" (API) as a single pan-ethnic category in the 1990 census, but it also provided nine specifically enumerated subcategories (such as Hawaiian or Filipino) and allowed other API groups (such as Hmong and Thai) to write in their respective ethnic identifications.

Socioeconomic differences also divided Asian Americans. Although in the late 1980s and early 1990s many Asian American groups showed remarkable upward mobility, others struggled to find jobs that paid more than the minimum wage. Thus, the term "Asian American" both reflected and was challenged by the new emphasis on ethnic identity.

DILEMMAS OF ANTIDISCRIMINATION EFFORTS

The assertion of racial and ethnic solidarity raised difficult questions about the meaning of equality. Between the end of the Second World War and about 1970, the antidiscrimination movement had demanded that the government not be permitted to categorize people according to group identities based on race or ethnicity. On matters such as education, housing, or employment, the law must remain "color-blind," and government should strike down discriminatory laws and practices and enact measures that effectively secure equality of opportunity for all individuals.

In the 1960s this agenda began to be modified as ethnic groups embraced the politics of group identity. With people taking new pride in their ethnic heritage, there was a shift of emphasis in social programs away from individual advancement and toward ethnic-group interests. By the 1970s this shift helped to produce a new vision of antidiscrimination in which government was to move beyond simply eliminating discriminatory barriers to *individual* opportunity. Social justice, according to the new antidiscrimination credo, required government to take "affirmative action" so that *groups* that had historically faced discrimination would now receive an equitable share of the nation's jobs, public spending, and educational programs. Affirmative action, supporters argued, would help compensate for historic discrimination and hidden racial attitudes that continued to disadvantage members of minority groups.

Affirmative action sparked fierce controversy. Many people who had supported previous policies against discrimination found affirmative action a dangerous form of racialist thought. Setting aside jobs or openings in educational institutions for certain racial or ethnic groups smacked of racist "quotas," they charged. Moreover, was not affirmative action *on behalf of* some groups inevitably also "reverse discrimination" *against* others? The issue of reverse discrimination became particularly emotional when members of one ethnic group received jobs or entry to educational institutions despite lower scores on admissions exams. Even some beneficiaries of affirmative action programs began to claim that the "affirmative action" label devalued their individual talents.

Meanwhile, courts found it difficult to square affirmative action programs with already mandated antidiscrimination policies. As a general rule, courts tended to strike down plans that seemed to contain inflexible ethnic quotas but to uphold plans that intended to remedy past patterns of discrimination and to make ethnicity only one of several criteria in hiring or educational decisions.

But the movement to scale back affirmative action plans gained momentum during the 1990s. In 1996, voters in California passed Proposition 209, which aimed at ending most affirmative action measures in California by abolishing racial or gender "preference" in state hiring, contracting, and college admissions. The number of African Americans and Latinos admitted to the state's most prestigious law and medical schools precipitously dropped, and proponents of affirmative action immediately challenged Proposition 209 as discriminatory.

Ironically, the late 20th century debates over identity politics and affirmative action coincided with a rise in racial and ethnic intermarriage. In the 1990s, growing numbers of people identified themselves as "mixed race." In 1997, the media hailed Eldrick ("Tiger") Woods as the first African American golfer to win the prestigious Masters tournament. But Woods, whose mother was from Thailand, fiercely resisted being assigned any particular ethnic identification. In an official statement to the media, he said he was "EQUALLY PROUD" to be "both African American and Asian!" But he hoped that he could also "be just a golfer and a human being."

THE NEW RIGHT

The most successful social and cultural movement to emerge during the late 20th century was a newly militant conservatism, "the New Right." Beginning in the mid-1970s, a diverse coalition mobilized on behalf of the conservative reconstruction of American life. By the 1980s and 1990s this new conservative vision had captured the imagination of millions.

Several different constituencies comprised the New Right. Older activists contributed continuity (see Chapter 28). Espousing anticommunism and denouncing domestic spending programs, they also spoke out on an ever wider range of social issues. Phyllis Schlafly assumed a prominent role in mobilizing opposition to ratification of the Equal Rights Amendment, and William F. Buckley's broad-ranging *Firing Line* became one of public television's most successful programs.

NEOCONSERVATIVES

These established activists were joined by a group of intellectuals called the "neoconservatives." Many had been anticommunist liberals during the 1950s and early 1960s. They had criticized the Democratic Party for retreating from an anticommunist foreign policy. In 1968 most had still supported Democrat Hubert Humphrey over Republican Richard Nixon, but the left-leaning candidacy of George McGovern in 1972 prompted a rush to the right.

Although neoconservatives remained true to their Cold War roots, many simultaneously renounced their support of domestic social programs. Their lively essays denounced any movement associated with the 1960s, especially affirmative action. Neoconservatives offered intellectual sustenance to a new generation of conservative thinkers who worked to reinvigorate the nation's anticommunist foreign policy and celebrate its capitalist economic system.

A new militancy among conservative business leaders contributed to this movement. They advocated that the United States rededicate itself to "economic freedom." Generous funding by corporations and philanthropic organizations helped to staff conservative research institutions (such as the American Enterprise Institute and Heritage Foundation) and to finance new lobbying organizations (such as the Committee on the Present Danger). Conservatism also gained considerable ground on college campuses.

THE NEW RELIGIOUS RIGHT

The New Right of the 1970s also attracted much grass-roots support from Protestants who belonged to fundamentalist and evangelical churches. The Supreme Court's abortion decision in *Roe* v. *Wade* (1973) mobilized fundamentalist and evangelical leaders. Since the 1920s, fundamentalist and evangelical Protestants had generally stayed clear of partisan politics. Now they formed the core of this "New Religious Right" and united with Catholic conservatives over opposition to abortion and other social and cultural issues. Leaders of the New Religious Right also embarked on a lengthy legal battle to prevent the Internal Revenue Service from denying tax-exempt status to private Christian colleges and academies, particularly in the South, that allegedly discriminated against students of color.

CONSERVATIVE POLITICS

Political developments of the 1970s also contributed to the emergence of the New Right. The declining political fortunes of George Wallace left many conservatives looking for new leadership. The end of Richard Nixon's presidency in 1974 intensified the desire for a "real" conservative leader. This desire became a crusade after Nixon's successor, Gerald Ford, selected the standard-bearer of Republican liberalism, Nelson Rockefeller, as his vice president.

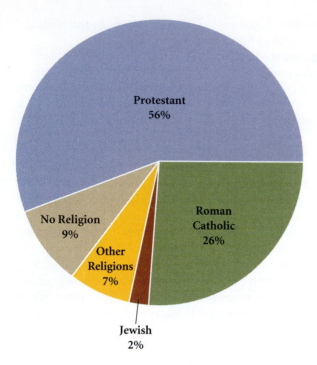

RELIGIOUS PREFERENCES IN
THE UNITED STATES (PERSONS
18 YEARS OF AGE AND OLDER)

SOURCE: *Statistical Abstract,* 1995.

Protestant
56%

No Religion
9%

Other
Religions
7%

Jewish
2%

Roman
Catholic
26%

George Wallace's campaigns had indicated that conservative politics could excite millions of voters. Eventually, activists organized the National Conservative Political Action Committee in 1975, the first of a number of organizations, including the Conservative Caucus, The Committee for the Survival of a Free Congress, and the Moral Majority. Although these organizations initially focused on lobbying in Washington and electing conservative Republicans, they also had broader cultural and social goals.

Increasingly, this crusading spirit became phrased in terms of defending "family values" and of opposing what the religious right considered to be "degenerate lifestyles," particularly those espoused by feminists and homosexuals. Jerry Falwell's *Listen America!* (1980) suggested that the nation's military establishment was "under the complete control of avid supporters of the women's liberation movement." Because homosexuality was "one of the gravest sins condemned in the Scriptures," argued Paul Weyrich, the issue of gay and lesbian rights was not a matter of private lifestyles but a "question of morality which . . . affects the society as a whole." American institutions, particularly the male-headed nuclear family, needed protection. Similarly, parents needed to be able to protect their children from educational "experiments." School boards and liberal educators, religious conservatives argued, were not only challenging Biblical precepts by teaching evolution but were advancing dangerous new ideas such as multiculturalism and gender-fair educational curricula.

The New Right proved adept in publicizing its crusade. Conservative foundations funded conferences and radio and TV programs. The New Religious Right mastered the media, and

CHRONOLOGY

1965	Congress passes Immigration Act of 1965
1968	Indian Bill of Rights extends most provisions of the Constitution's Bill of Rights to Native Americans
1970	First Earth Day observed • Environmental Protection Act passed • Clean Air Act passed
1973	*Roe* v. *Wade* decision upholds women's right to abortion • Endangered Species Act passed • Sudden rise in oil prices as result of OPEC action
1981	MTV debuts
1986	Supreme Court holds that sexual harassment qualifies as "discrimination"
1987	Immigration Reform and Control Act toughens laws against illegal aliens
1992	"Earth Summit" held in Brazil
1995	Million Man March takes place in Washington, D.C.
1996	O. J. Simpson tried and acquitted of murder • California's Proposition 209 curtails affirmative action

preachers such as Pat Robertson capitalized on the expansion of CATV in the 1970s and early 1980s. Robertson built a multimedia empire that included the 24-hour Christian Broadcasting Network (later renamed "The Family Channel"). During the 1980s, scandals and financial problems overtook some religious broadcasters, but Robertson's *700 Club*, a program that adapted his conservative evangelicalism to the talk-show and morning-news formats, grew steadily. At the same time, broadcasters associated with the New Right used talk-radio programs at both the local and national levels to spread the conservative message.

On its fringes, the New Right attracted support from ultralibertarian paramilitary groups who denounced gun control laws, taxes, and the federal government. Violent confrontations between such groups and federal authorities, especially the government's assault on the Branch Davidian group in Texas (in which 78 people were killed), left supporters of paramilitary politics feeling besieged. Any symbol of the federal government, one paramilitary leader claimed, could be considered a *"strategic military target."* In April 1995, on the second anniversary of the government's attack on the Branch Davidians, the Alfred P. Murrah Federal Building in Oklahoma City became such a target. A powerful bomb ripped through the building and killed 168 people. This bombing, for which a paramilitary loner named Timothy McVeigh was convicted and sentenced to death in 1997 (and for which accomplice Terry Nichols was convicted of conspiracy), discredited the extremist, antigovernment movement. Conservatives and liberals alike denounced the violent tendencies of paramilitary groups.

The New Right, a coalition of disparate parts, became a powerful force in American culture and, increasingly, in American politics. After the middle of the 1970s, the many strains of the new conservatism helped to challenge New Deal–Great Society liberalism and to remap the ways in which the nation's political system dealt with questions of liberty and power.

CONCLUSION

Sweeping changes occurred in demographics, economics, culture, and society during the last quarter of the 20th century. The nation aged, and more of its people gravitated to the Sunbelt. Sprawling "urban corridors" and "edge cities" challenged older central cities as sites for commercial, as well as residential, development. Rapid technological change fueled the growth of globalized industries, restructuring the labor force to fit a "postindustrial" economy. Americans also developed a new environmental consciousness.

In American mass culture, the most prominent development was the proliferation of the video screen. Television and motion pictures increasingly targeted specific audiences, and the fragmented nature of cultural reception was exemplified by the rise of new, particularistic media ventures such as CNN and MTV.

Meanwhile, American society itself also seemed to fragment. Social activism often organized around sexual, ethnic, and racial identities: the women's movement, gay and lesbian pride, Afrocentrism, Indian rights, and movements that represented people of Latino and Asian ancestry. Multiculturalists celebrated this fragmentation while another activist movement, the New Right, argued that it was dividing the nation. The New Right's stress on conservative social values and the necessity for limiting the power of government increasingly came to set the terms for political debate during the 1980s and 1990s.

31

WINDS OF CHANGE: POLITICS AND FOREIGN POLICY FROM FORD TO CLINTON

THE FORD PRESIDENCY ∽ THE CARTER PRESIDENCY: DOMESTIC ISSUES

THE CARTER PRESIDENCY: FOREIGN POLICY

REAGAN'S "NEW MORNING IN AMERICA" ∽ RENEWING THE COLD WAR

FROM REAGAN TO BUSH ∽ FOREIGN POLICY UNDER BUSH

TOWARD THE 21ST CENTURY

The power of the national government continually expanded during the three decades after the Second World War. Most people supported augmenting the government's military and intelligence capabilities so that the United States could play a dominant role in world affairs. They also generally endorsed the use of government power to cushion against economic downturns and to assist needy families.

The Vietnam War and the Watergate scandals (see Chapter 29), however, shook faith in government. Disillusionment with secrecy, corruption, and bloated budgets bred cynicism about the use of government power. Social and economic changes bred a feeling that the national government no longer operated effectively.

In this environment, divisive debates punctuated political life. How might a stagnating economy and a beleaguered welfare system be reshaped? Should there be more governmental activism in addressing persistent problems of poverty and inequality, or would conditions improve if government's role were reduced?

Disagreements also focused on foreign policy. Should the United States set aside anticommunism to pursue other goals, or should it wage the Cold War even more vigorously? Then, in 1989, the Cold War came to an unexpected end, and the United States faced the task of reorienting its foreign policy in a world without a Soviet threat.

The post–Cold War environment also affected domestic politics. Americans still debated the proper relationship of government power to the preservation of liberty and equality, but as the economy strengthened during the mid-1990s, domestic issues seemed less divisive than they had been only a decade earlier.

THE FORD PRESIDENCY

Gerald Ford, the first person to become vice president and then president without having been elected to either office, promised to mend the divisions that had split the nation during the 1960s and early 1970s. But Ford's ability to "heal the land," as he put it, proved limited. A genial, unpretentious person, Ford could not shake the impression that he was a weak, indecisive chief executive.

DOMESTIC ISSUES UNDER FORD

Ford quickly ran into trouble. Needing to appoint a new vice president (subject to congressional approval), Ford picked New York's Nelson Rockefeller. The choice of Rockefeller, one of the GOP's most liberal figures, infuriated conservatives within the Republican Party. Granting a presidential pardon to former President Nixon, in September 1974, proved even more controversial, and Ford's approval rating sharply plummeted.

Economic problems soon dominated the domestic side of Ford's presidency. Focusing on rising prices, rather than on increasing unemployment, Ford touted a program he called "Whip Inflation Now" (WIN). It offered a one-year income tax surcharge and cuts in federal spending as solutions to inflation. But escalating prices were accompanied by a sharp recession. As both prices and unemployment continued to rise, creating the condition known as "stagflation," Ford abandoned WIN.

Meanwhile, Ford and the Democratic-controlled Congress differed over how to deal with stagflation. Ford vetoed 39 spending bills during his brief presidency. He eventually acquiesced to an economic program that included a tax cut, an increase in unemployment benefits, an unbalanced federal budget, and a limited set of controls over oil prices.

FOREIGN POLICY UNDER FORD

While struggling with economic problems at home, Ford steered the nation through its final involvement in the war in Southeast Asia. Upon assuming office, Ford assured South Vietnam that the United States would renew its military support if the government in Saigon ever became directly menaced by North Vietnamese troops. The antiwar mood in Congress and throughout the country, however, made fulfilling this commitment impossible. North Vietnam's armies, sensing final victory, moved rapidly through the South in March 1975, and Congress refused to reintroduce U.S. military power. In early April, Khmer Rouge forces in Cambodia drove the American-backed government from the capital of Phnom Phen, and on April 30, 1975, North Vietnamese troops overran the South Vietnamese capital of Saigon, renaming it Ho Chi Minh City. The final defeat reignited the debate over U.S. policy in Indochina: Former "doves" lamented the lives lost and money wasted, while former "hawks" derided their country's "failure of will."

Within this charged atmosphere, Ford immediately sought to demonstrate that the United States could still conduct an assertive foreign policy. In May 1975, the Khmer Rouge boarded a U.S. ship, the *Mayaguez,* and seized its crew. Secretary of State Henry Kissinger convinced Ford to order a mission to rescue the *Mayaguez*'s crew and bombing strikes against Cambodia. This military response, along with pressure on the Khmer Rouge from China, secured the release of the *Mayaguez* and its crew. The president's approval ratings briefly shot up, but the incident did little to allay growing doubts about Ford's ability to handle complex foreign policy issues. The president's other foreign policy initiatives, which included extending Nixon's policy of détente with the Soviet Union and pursuing a peace treaty for the Middle East, achieved little.

THE ELECTION OF 1976

Conservative Republicans rallied behind Ronald Reagan, the former governor of California. Reagan's campaign initially floundered, but it suddenly caught fire when his advisers urged him to forgo specific proposals and to highlight his image as a true conservative who, unlike Ford, was not beholden to Washington insiders. By this time, however, Ford had already won just enough delegates in the early primaries to eke out a narrow, first-ballot victory at the Republican Party's national convention.

The Democrats turned to an outsider, James Earl (Jimmy) Carter, the former governor of Georgia. Carter had graduated from the Naval Academy with a degree in nuclear engineering and had worked on the nuclear submarine program. His military career had been cut short in the early 1950s, when he returned to Plains, Georgia, to run his family's peanut farming business following the death of his father. Later, Carter had entered state politics, gaining the reputation of being a moderate on racial issues and a fiscal conservative. When he announced his intention to run for the presidency in 1976, few people took him seriously; no governor had captured the White House since Franklin Roosevelt in 1932.

Carter campaigned as a person of many virtues. He emphasized his personal character and the fact that most of his life had been spent outside of politics. Highlighting his small-town roots, he pledged to "give the government of this country back to the people of this country." A devout Baptist, Carter campaigned as a born-again Christian. He also touted his record as a successful governor. In order to counterbalance his own status as a Washington outsider, he picked a member of the Senate, Walter Mondale, as his running mate. Although economic conditions seemed to be improving, it was not enough to secure Ford's reelection. In November, Carter won a narrow victory over Ford.

Carter owed his election to a diverse, transitory coalition. Capitalizing on his regional appeal, he carried every southern state except Virginia. He ran well among southern whites, but his victory in the South rested on a strong turnout among African Americans. Meanwhile, Carter courted the youth vote by promising to pardon most of the young men who had resisted the draft during the Vietnam War. Mondale's appeal to traditional Democrats helped Carter narrowly capture three key states—New York, Pennsylvania, and Ohio. Even so, Carter won by less than 2 million popular votes, and by the close margin of 297 to 241 in the electoral vote.

THE CARTER PRESIDENCY: DOMESTIC ISSUES

Jimmy Carter's lack of a popular mandate and his image as an outsider proved serious handicaps. Powerful constituencies, including both labor unions and multinational corporations, feared that Carter might prove to be an unpredictable leader. Moreover, many Democratic members of Congress stressed their independence from the White House, even though it was now occupied by a president from their own party. Carter also failed to develop the aura of a national leader. Although he brought some people with long experience in government into his cabinet, he relied mainly on the Georgians on his White House staff, a small cadre of advisers whom the Washington press corps dubbed the "Georgia Mafia."

WELFARE AND ENERGY

In trying to frame his agenda, Carter found himself caught between those who claimed that the power of the national government had already expanded too much and those who argued that Washington was doing too little to address social and economic problems. Unlike Richard Nixon, who had unveiled a bold Family Assistance Plan (FAP) in 1969 (Chapter 29), Carter temporized on what to do about social welfare policy. His advisers were divided between those who favored a more complicated version of FAP, which would have granted greater monetary assistance to low-income families, and those who thought the national government should create several million new public service jobs. Carter, while opposing any increase in the federal budget, asked Congress for a program that included both additional cash assistance and more jobs. He presented his proposal to Congress in 1977, where it quickly died in committee.

Carter pushed harder on energy issues. In response to soaring Middle East oil prices (see Chapter 30), he delegated James Schlesinger to develop a sweeping energy plan. Schlesinger, Carter's secretary of energy, came up with a set of ambitious goals: a decrease in U.S. reliance on foreign oil and natural gas; the expansion of domestic energy production through new tax incentives and the repeal of regulations on the production of natural gas; the levying of new taxes to discourage use of gasoline; the fostering of conservation by encouraging greater reliance on energy-saving measures; and the promotion of alternative sources of energy, especially coal and nuclear power. Neither Carter nor Schlesinger consulted Congress. Instead, Carter went on national television, in April 1977, to announce the new energy plan.

Congress quickly rejected the plan. Legislators from oil-producing states opposed the proposal for higher taxes on gasoline, and critics of the big oil companies blocked the idea of rapid deregulation of oil and natural gas production. Meanwhile, environmentalists opposed any increase in coal production. And most Americans simply ignored Carter's claim that the nation's struggle with its energy problems amounted to "the moral equivalent of war."

ECONOMIC POLICY

Carter had no greater success with economic policy. He inherited the economic problems—especially stagflation—that had bedeviled Nixon and Ford. He pledged to lower both unemployment and inflation, to stimulate greater economic growth, and to balance the federal budget. Instead, by 1980 the economy had almost stopped expanding, unemployment (after dipping to a rate of under 6 percent in 1979) was beginning to rise again, and inflation topped 13 per cent. Most voters believed that economic conditions were deteriorating.

The economic difficulties of the 1970s were not limited to individuals. New York City, beset by long-term economic and social problems and short-term fiscal mismanagement, faced bankruptcy. It could neither meet its financial obligations nor borrow money through the usual channels. Finally, private bankers and public officials collaborated on congressional legislation to provide the nation's largest city with federal loan guarantees. New York's troubles were symptomatic of a broader urban crisis. According to one estimate, New York City lost 600,000 manufacturing jobs in the 1970s; Chicago lost 200,000. As a consequence, increasing

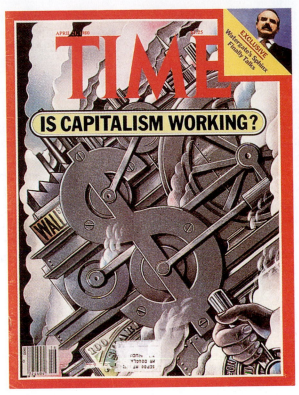

"IS CAPITALISM WORKING?"   In 1980 *Time* magazine wondered about the future of the United States. Unprecedented economic problems—in particular, high rates of inflation and unemployment—dominated the Ford and Carter presidencies.

numbers of people living in central cities could find only low-paying, short-term jobs that carried no fringe benefits. Many found no jobs at all. Rising crime rates and deteriorating downtown neighborhoods afflicted most American cities, just when the impact of inflation further eroded city budgets.

What went wrong? Tax cuts and increased spending on public works projects had temporarily lowered the unemployment rate. And the Federal Reserve Board had permitted a growth in the supply of money. Those very measures, which were designed to stimulate recovery, fueled price inflation. Meanwhile, the continued rise in international oil prices triggered a series of increases for gasoline and home heating fuel that rippled through the economy. Inflation and high interest rates choked off productivity and economic growth.

Conservative economists and business groups argued that the domestic programs favored by most congressional Democrats also contributed to the spiral of rising prices. By increasing the minimum wage and by vigorously enforcing safety and antipollution regulations, conservatives argued, the national government had driven up the cost of doing business and had forced companies to pass on this increase to consumers in the form of higher prices. During the last two years of his presidency, Carter himself seemed to agree with some of this analysis when he reduced spending for a variety of social programs, supported a law that reduced the capital gains taxes paid by wealthier citizens, and began a process of deregulating transportation industries.

THE CARTER PRESIDENCY: FOREIGN POLICY

In foreign policy, as in domestic policy, Carter promised a significant change of direction. On his first day in office, he extended amnesty to those who had resisted the draft in the Vietnam War. After four years, however, his foreign policy initiatives were in disarray. Carter himself, although skillful in handling small-group negotiations, had little experience working with long-term foreign policy issues. Furthermore, his top policy advisers—Cyrus Vance as secretary of state and Zbigniew Brzezinski as national security adviser—often had contradictory approaches to policymaking. Brzezinski favored a hard-line, anti-Soviet policy with an emphasis on military muscle; Vance preferred avoiding public confrontations and emphasized the virtues of quiet diplomacy. Pulled in divergent directions, Carter's policy often seemed to waffle. Still, Carter set some important new directions, emphasizing negotiation in particular trouble spots of the world and elevating a concern for human rights into a foreign policy priority.

NEGOTIATIONS IN PANAMA AND THE MIDDLE EAST

One of the first concerns of the Carter administration involved the Panama Canal treaties. U.S. ownership of the canal, a legacy of turn-of-the-century imperialism, had sparked growing anti-Yankee sentiment throughout Latin America. Moreover, Carter argued, the canal was no longer the economic and strategic necessity it had once been. Despite strong opposition, Carter adroitly managed public and congressional relations to obtain ratification of treaties that granted Panama increasing jurisdiction over the canal, with full control after the year 2000.

Carter's faith in negotiations, and in his personal skill as a facilitator, again emerged in the Camp David peace accords of 1978. Relations between Egypt and Israel had been strained ever since the Yom Kippur War of 1973. Reviving Henry Kissinger's earlier efforts to mediate Arab-Israeli conflicts, Carter brought Menachem Begin and Anwar Sadat, leaders of Israel and Egypt, respectively, to the Camp David presidential retreat. After 13 days of bargaining, the three leaders announced the framework for a negotiating process and a peace treaty. Although Middle East tensions hardly vanished, the Camp David accords kept high-level discussions alive, lowered the level of acrimony between Egypt and Israel, and bound both sides to the United States through its promises of economic aid.

In Asia and Africa, the Carter administration also emphasized accommodation. Building on Nixon's initiative, Carter expanded economic and cultural relations with China and finally established formal diplomatic ties with the People's Republic on New Year's Day 1979. In Africa, Carter abandoned Kissinger's reliance on white colonial regimes and supported the transition of Zimbabwe (formerly Rhodesia) to a government run by the black majority.

HUMAN RIGHTS POLICY

Carter's foreign policy became best known for its emphasis on human rights. Cold War alliances with anticommunist dictatorships, Carter believed, were undermining U.S. influence in the world. In the long run, Carter's policy helped to raise consciousness around the world about human rights issues. The trend toward democratization that occurred in many nations during the 1980s and 1990s was partially triggered by the rising awareness associated with Carter's stress on human rights.

The immediate impact of the human rights policy, however, was ambiguous. Because Carter applied the policy inconsistently, many of America's most repressive allies, such as Ferdinand Marcos in the Philippines, felt little pressure to change their ways. Moreover, Carter's rhetoric about human rights helped spark revolutionary movements against America's long-standing dictator-allies in Nicaragua and Iran. These revolutions brought anti-American regimes to power and presented Carter with thorny policy dilemmas. In Nicaragua, for example, the Sandinista revolution toppled dictator Anastasio Somoza, whom the United States had long supported. The Sandinistas, initially a coalition of moderate democrats and communists, quickly drifted toward a more militant Marxism and began to expropriate property. Carter opposed Nicaragua's movement to the left but could not change the revolution's course. The president's Republican critics charged that his policies had given a green light to communism in Central America and pledged that they would work to oust the Sandinista government.

THE HOSTAGE CRISIS IN IRAN

Events in Iran dramatically eroded Carter's standing. Shah Reza Pahlavi had regained his throne with the help of Western intelligence agencies in a 1953 coup, and the United States had subsequently provided him with a steady supply of military hardware. The overthrow of the Shah by an Islamic fundamentalist revolution in January 1979 thus signaled a massive rejection of U.S. influence in Iran. When the Carter administration bowed to political pressure and allowed the deposed and ailing Shah to enter the United States for medical treatment in November 1979, a group of Iranians took 66 Americans hostage at the U.S. embassy compound in Teheran; they demanded the return of the Shah in exchange for the release of the hostages.

As the hostage incident gripped the country, Carter's critics cited it as evidence of how weak and impotent the United States had become. Carter talked tough; levied economic reprisals against Iran; and sent a military mission to rescue the hostages. But the mission proved an embarrassing failure, and Carter never managed to resolve the situation. After his defeat in the 1980 election, diplomatic efforts finally brought the hostages home, but the United States and Iran remained at odds.

Meanwhile, criticism of Carter intensified when the Soviet Union invaded Afghanistan in December 1979. Many Americans interpreted the invasion as a simple sign that the Soviets now dismissed the United States as too weak to contain their expansionism. Carter could never shake the charge that he was afflicted with "post-Vietnam syndrome," a failure to act strongly in foreign affairs. Carter halted grain exports to the Soviet Union, organized a boycott of the 1980 Olympic Games in Moscow, withdrew a new Strategic Arms Limitation Treaty (SALT) from the Senate, and revived registration for the military draft. Still, conservatives charged Carter with presiding over a decline of American power and prestige, and Ronald Reagan made constant reference to Iran and Afghanistan as he prepared for the 1980 elections.

THE ELECTION OF 1980

For a time, when Senator Edward Kennedy of Massachusetts entered the party's 1980 presidential primaries, it seemed that the Democrats might not even allow Carter to run for a second term. Kennedy's campaign underscored Carter's vulnerability and popularized anti-Carter themes that Republicans gleefully embraced. "It's time to say no more hostages, no more high interest rates, no more high inflation, and no more Jimmy Carter," went one of Kennedy's stump speeches. More than one-third of the people who supported Kennedy in the final eight Democratic primaries (five of which Kennedy won) were conservative Democrats who told pollsters they would likely vote Republican in the general election. As Carter entered the fall campaign against the Republicans, he seemed a likely loser.

Republican challenger Ronald Reagan exuded confidence. He stressed his opposition to federal social programs and his support for a stronger national defense. His successful primary campaign highlighted an optimistic vision of a rejuvenated America. To remind voters of the alleged failures of the Carter presidency, he asked repeatedly, "Are you better off now than you were four years ago?" He quickly answered his own question by invoking what he called a "misery index," which added the rate of inflation to the rate of unemployment.

Reagan's optimism allowed him to seize an issue that Democrats had long regarded as their own: economic growth. Reagan promised that tax cuts would bring back the kind of economic expansion the nation had enjoyed during the 1950s and 1960s. During a crucial television debate, when Carter tried to criticize Reagan's promises for their lack of specificity, a smiling Reagan spotlighted Carter's apparent pessimism by repeatedly quipping, "There you go again!"

Reagan won the November presidential election with only slightly more than 50 percent of the popular vote. (Moderate Republican John Anderson, who ran an independent campaign for the White House, won about 7 percent.) But Reagan's margin over Carter in the Electoral College was overwhelming: 489 to 49. Moreover, Republicans took 12 Senate seats away from Democrats, gaining control of the Senate for the first time since 1954.

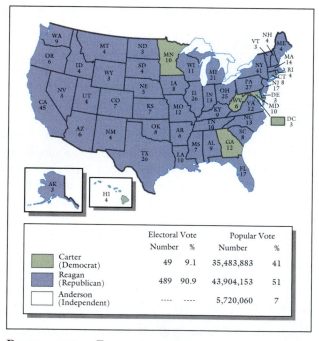

	Electoral Vote		Popular Vote	
	Number	%	Number	%
Carter (Democrat)	49	9.1	35,483,883	41
Reagan (Republican)	489	90.9	43,904,153	51
Anderson (Independent)	----	----	5,720,060	7

PRESIDENTIAL ELECTION, 1980

Noting Reagan's slim majority in the popular vote, many Democrats portrayed 1980 as more of a defeat for Carter than a victory for the Republicans. By reducing expenditures for domestic programs and lowering taxes on capital gains, according to this analysis, Carter had alienated traditional Democratic voters. Moreover, Reagan's sophisticated media campaign was credited with temporarily misleading voters; in due course, these Democrats claimed, Reagan would be unmasked as a media-manufactured president.

Democrats, however, failed to recognize that their own domestic agenda had been steadily losing support. The real income of the average American family, which had risen at an annual rate of just under 3 percent per year between 1950 and 1965, rose only 1.7 percent a year between 1965 and 1980. In such a stagnant economic climate, middle-income taxpayers found Democratic social welfare programs far less palatable than they had found them in more prosperous times.

During the 1970s, then, the United States had entered a new, more conservative era in social policymaking. Liberals continued to talk about how to improve welfare-state initiatives. But conservatives advocated a radical reduction in government spending programs, denouncing AFDC (Aid to Families with Dependent Children) and food stamps as socially debilitating for their recipients and a drag on the national economy. More and more voters came to identify with the position championed by Ronald Reagan.

REAGAN'S "NEW MORNING IN AMERICA"

Tapping anxieties about declining national power and eroding living standards, Reagan promised a "new morning in America," especially in the area of taxation. A taxpayer revolt, which had emerged in California in the late 1970s, provided a model for Reagan's attack on federal spending for domestic programs. Across the country, people responded to Reagan's tax-reduction message.

In addition, Reagan courted the New Right with opposition to abortion, support for prayer in school, and the endorsement of traditional "family values." Conservative religious figures, including Jerry Falwell and Pat Robertson, onetime Democrats, joined Reagan's new Republican coalition. Reagan also found a way to reach white (especially male) voters, who were upset over affirmative action, while avoiding being charged with making racial appeals. Reagan himself proclaimed a commitment to "color-blind" social policies. "Guaranteeing equality of treatment is the government's proper function," Reagan proclaimed at one of his first presidential press conferences.

REAGAN'S FIRST TERM: ECONOMIC ISSUES

To justify cutting taxes, Reagan touted a theory called "supply-side economics." This theory held that tax reductions would stimulate the economy by putting more money in the hands of investors and consumers, thereby reversing the economic stagnation of the 1970s. Reagan pushed his tax plan through Congress during the summer of 1981. The new law significantly reduced taxes for people who earned high incomes and already possessed significant wealth. Taxes on businesses were also slashed to encourage investment in new facilities and equipment. At the same time, the Federal Reserve Board pursued a policy of keeping interest rates high in order to drive down inflation.

After a severe recession in 1981 and 1982, the worst since the Great Depression of the 1930s, the economy rebounded and entered a period of noninflationary growth. By 1986, the GNP was steadily climbing, while the rate of inflation had plunged to less than 2 percent; unemployment figures, however, stubbornly refused to drop. Still, Reagan's supporters called the turnaround an "economic miracle" and hailed the "Reagan Revolution."

The economic revival of the 1980s sparked debate over the cumulative impact of annual federal budget deficits and the consequences of the economic expansion. On the first issue—budget deficits—Reagan's critics pointed out that his tax cuts had not been matched by budget reductions. Although Reagan constantly inveighed against budget deficits and big spenders, during his presidency the annual deficits tripled to nearly $300 billion. To finance such spending, the United States borrowed abroad and piled up the largest foreign debt in the world. Reagan's "Revolution," critics charged, brought short-term recovery for some people by courting a long-term budget crisis that would harm people with low incomes, who relied on government programs, and would imperil future generations, who would have to pay for the soaring government debt.

On the second issue—the soundness of the U.S. economy—critics complained that Reagan's policies were creating a "Swiss-cheese" economy, one that was full of holes. Farmers in the Midwest were especially battered during the recession of 1981–1982, as falling crop prices made it difficult for them to make payments on the high-interest loans contracted during the inflation-ridden 1970s. A series of mortgage foreclosures hit farm states, and the ripple effect decimated many small-town businesses. At the same time, urban families, who were struggling to get by on low-paying jobs and declining welfare benefits, were also puzzled by talk about a "Reagan boom." Many of the jobs created in the 1980s offered relatively low wages and few, if any, fringe benefits. The minimum wage, when measured in constant dollars, fell throughout Reagan's presidency.

In communities of color, this uneven pattern was especially glaring. From the late 1960s on, people of color with educational credentials and marketable skills had made significant economic gains. The number of African American families making a solid middle-class income more than doubled between 1970 and 1990. African American college graduates could expect incomes comparable to those of white college graduates. Many persons of color, therefore, could afford to move away from inner-city neighborhoods. But the story of mobility was very different for an "underclass" of people who persistently unemployed and trapped in declining urban centers. At the end of the 1980s, one-third of all black families lived in poverty. In inner cities, less than half of African American children were completing high school, and more than 60 percent were unemployed. Throughout America, the gap between rich and poor widened significantly.

IMPLEMENTING A CONSERVATIVE AGENDA

Meanwhile, Reagan made changes in other areas. In 1981 he fired the nation's air traffic controllers when their union refused to halt a nationwide strike. Overall, union membership continued to decline, as both the Reagan administration and many large businesses pursued aggressive antiunion strategies during the 1980s. The percentage of non-farmworkers who were unionized fell to just 16 percent by the end of Reagan's presidency. Workers, who recognized that the balance of power was tilting against them, increasingly turned away from strikes as an economic weapon.

Reagan also placed a conservative stamp on the federal court system. Almost immediately, he was able to nominate a Supreme Court justice, Sandra Day O'Connor, the first woman to sit on the High Court. During Reagan's first term, when the Republican Party controlled the Senate, Reagan also named other prominent conservative jurists, such as Robert Bork and Antonin Scalia, to lower federal courts. Conservatives welcomed the influx of judges from the political right. Civil libertarians complained that the federal courts were becoming less hospitable to legal claims made by criminal defendants, labor unions, and political dissenters. Because of the retirement of a number of older judges, by 1989 about 50 percent of the federal judiciary had been nominated and confirmed during Ronald Reagan's presidency.

In his non-judicial appointments, Reagan also looked for staunch conservatives. He filled the Justice Department with lawyers who were eager to end the "rights revolution" and affirmative action programs. He appointed James Watt, an outspoken critic of environmental legislation, as secretary of the interior. Reagan's first two appointees to the Department of Energy actually proposed eliminating the department they headed—an idea that Congress successfully blocked. Finally, having staffed most of the administrative agencies with conservatives, Reagan sought to ease regulations on businesses by relaxing enforcement of safety and environmental laws. The administration also eased the enforcement of affirmative action laws, in line with Reagan's call for a "color-blind" approach on racial issues.

In addition, Reagan eliminated some social welfare programs, most notably the Comprehensive Employment and Training Act (CETA), and reduced funding for others, such as food stamps. Nevertheless, he pledged that Washington would still maintain a "safety net" for those who were really in need of governmental assistance.

Critics complained, however, about the number of people whose total package of income and government benefits still fell below what economists considered the "poverty" level. Conditions would have been worse if the nation's most popular welfare program, Social Security, had not been redesigned in the 1970s so that its benefits automatically increased along with the rate of inflation (an arrangement called "indexing"). Rising Social Security payments, along with Medicare benefits, enabled millions of older Americans who might otherwise have fallen below the official poverty line to hold their own economically during the Reagan years. The burden of the growing poverty, then, fell disproportionately on female-headed households and especially on children. By the end of the 1980s, one of every five children was being raised in a household whose total income fell below the official poverty line.

Amid the controversies over the growing budget deficit and the inequalities in wealth, Reagan became known as the "Teflon president." No matter what problems beset his administration, nothing negative ever seemed to stick to Reagan himself. His genial optimism seemed unshakable. He even appeared to rebound quickly after being shot by a would-be assassin in March 1981.

THE ELECTION OF 1984

Democrats continued to underestimate Reagan's popular appeal—a miscalculation that doomed their 1984 presidential campaign. Walter Mondale, Jimmy Carter's vice president from 1976 to 1980, ran on a platform that called for "the eradication of discrimination in all aspects of American life" and for an expansion of domestic spending programs by the national government. Mondale's running mate, Representative Geraldine Ferraro of New York, was the first woman ever to run for president or vice president on a major-party ticket. Convinced that Reagan's "economic miracle" would eventually self-destruct, Mondale stuck to his basic themes. Reagan would soon have to raise taxes to cover the burgeoning federal deficit, Mondale bravely declared, and "so will I. He won't tell you; I just did."

The Republicans ran a textbook-perfect campaign. The president labeled Mondale's support by labor and civil rights groups as a vestige of the old politics of "special interests" and denounced Mondale's tax proposal as a reminder of the "wasteful tax-and-spend policies" that he claimed had precipitated the stagflation of the 1970s. Mondale's selection of Ferraro was criticized as another example of his kowtowing to special interests. Reagan himself continued to sketch the picture of a bright, conservative future for America. In his campaign films, the United States appeared as a glowing landscape of bustling small towns and lush farmland. His campaign slogan was "It's Morning Again in America." The 1984 presidential election ended with Mondale carrying only his home state of Minnesota and the District of Columbia.

Reagan and his conservative supporters succeeded in giving new meaning to many traditional political terms. "Liberal" no longer meant a set of government programs that would stimulate the economy and help people to buy new homes and more consumer goods. Instead, Republicans made "liberalism" a code word for supposedly wasteful social programs devised by a bloated federal government that gouged hardworking people and gave their dollars to people who were undeserving and lazy. The term "conservative," as used by Republicans, came to mean economic growth through limited government and support for traditional social-cultural values.

RENEWING THE COLD WAR

Reagan quickly established foreign policy themes that dominated both of his terms in office. Under Carter, he claimed, the nation's power had been eroded by the "Vietnam syndrome" of passivity and "loss of will." Reagan promised to reverse that trend. Although he did not repudiate Carter's human rights policy, he called it into the service of a renewed Cold War against the Soviet Union, highlighting the Soviet Union's mistreatment of its Jewish population and ethnic minorities.

THE DEFENSE BUILDUP

The United States, Reagan claimed, had "unilaterally disarmed" during the 1970s, while the Soviets were staging a massive military buildup. He called for a new battle against what he called the "evil empire" of the Soviet Union. Closing what Reagan called America's "window of vulnerability" against Soviet military power, however, would be expensive. Although his tax cuts would inevitably reduce government revenues, Reagan nonetheless asked Congress for dramatic increases in military spending. The Pentagon launched programs to enlarge the Navy and to modernize strategic nuclear forces, concentrating especially on missile systems. It also deployed new missiles throughout Western Europe.

In 1984 Reagan surprised even his closest advisers by proposing the most expensive defense system in history—a space-based shield against incoming missiles. The Strategic Defense Initiative (SDI) soon had its own agency in the Pentagon that projected a need for $26 billion over five years, just for start-up research. Critics dubbed the program "Star Wars," and many members of Congress shuddered at its astronomical costs. Although most scientists considered the project impractical, Congress voted appropriations for SDI, and throughout his presidency Reagan clung to the idea of a defensive shield. SDI dominated both the strategic debate at home and arms talks with the Soviet Union.

Greater defense spending had another strategic dimension. Secretary of Defense Caspar Weinberger suggested that, as the Soviets increased the burden on their own faltering economy in order to compete in the accelerating arms race, the Soviet Union itself might collapse under the economic strain. This had been an implicit goal of the containment policy since NSC-68 was drafted in 1949 (see Chapter 27).

MILITARY ACTIONS IN LEBANON, GRENADA, NICARAGUA, AND LIBYA

In waging the renewed Cold War, Reagan promised vigorous support to "democratic" revolutions around the globe. Reagan's UN representative, Jeane Kirkpatrick, wrote that "democratic" forces included almost any movement, no matter how autocratic, that was noncommunist. The United States thus funded opposition movements in countries that were aligned with the Soviet Union: Ethiopia, Angola, South Yemen, Cambodia, Grenada, Cuba, Nicaragua, and Afghanistan. Reagan called the participants in such movements "freedom fighters," although few had any visible commitment to liberty or equality.

The Reagan administration also displayed a new willingness to unleash U.S. military power. The first occasion was in southern Lebanon, where Israeli troops were facing off against Lebanese Moslems supported by Syria and the Soviet Union. Alarmed by the gains the Moslems were achieving, the Reagan administration in 1982 convinced Israel to withdraw and sent 1,600 American marines as part of a "peacekeeping force" to restore stability. But Moslem fighters then turned their wrath against the Americans. After a suicide commando mission into a U.S. military compound killed 241 marines, Reagan pulled out U.S. troops and disengaged from the conflict.

Although the debacle in Lebanon raised questions about Reagan's policies, another military intervention restored his popularity. In October 1983 Reagan sent 2,000 U.S. troops to the tiny Caribbean island of Grenada, whose socialist leader was forging ties with Castro's Cuba. U.S. troops overthrew the government and installed one friendly to American interests. Tight military control over news coverage shielded the administration from criticism and allowed it to declare Grenada a complete foreign policy victory.

Buoyed by events in Grenada, the Reagan administration fixed its sights on the Central American country of Nicaragua. The socialist government, led by the Sandinista Party, was trying to build ties with Cuba. The United States augmented its military forces in neighboring Honduras and conducted training exercises throughout the area. But Reagan decided to use covert means to topple the Sandinista regime. The United States tightened its economic stranglehold on Nicaragua and launched a propaganda offensive to discredit the Sandinistas. These measures were designed to give the United States time to train and equip an opposition military force of Nicaraguans, the *contras*. Meanwhile, the administration supported murderous dictatorships in nearby El Salvador and Guatemala to prevent other leftist insurgencies from gaining ground in Central America.

U.S. initiatives in Central America became the most controversial aspect of Reagan's foreign policy. U.S. backed regimes were clearly implicated in abuses of human rights. Mounting evidence of the brutality and corruption of the Nicaraguan *contras* brought growing public criticism. In 1984, the Democratic-controlled Congress denied further military aid to the *contras*.

The Reagan administration quickly sought ways around the congressional ban. One solution was to encourage wealthy U.S. conservatives and other governments to donate money to the *contras*. In June 1984, at a top secret meeting of the National Security Planning Group, Reagan and his top advisers discussed the legality of pressing "third parties" to contribute to the *contra* cause.

Meanwhile, violence continued to escalate throughout the Middle East. Militant Islamic groups stepped up the use of terrorism against Israel and Western powers; bombings and the kidnapping of Western hostages became more frequent. Apparently, such activities were being encouraged by Libyan leader Muammar al-Qaddafi as well as by Iran. In the spring of 1986 the United States launched an air strike into Libya aimed at Qaddafi's personal compound. The bombs did serious damage and killed Qaddafi's young daughter, but Qaddafi and his government survived. Despite some public criticism of this action, Americans generally approved of using strong measures against sponsors of terrorism and hostage-taking.

OTHER INITIATIVES

Reagan's foreign policy included initiatives other than military incursions. In a new "informational" offensive, the administration funded a variety of conservative groups around the world and established Radio Martí, a Florida radio station beamed at Cuba and designed to discredit Fidel Castro. When the United Nations agency UNESCO criticized the global dominance of the U.S. media and called for a "New World Information Order" that would reduce the overwhelming influence of U.S.-originated news and information, Reagan cut off U.S. contributions to UNESCO and demanded changes in the organization and operation of the UN. Reagan also championed free markets, urging other nations to minimize tariffs and restrictions on foreign investment. His Caribbean Basin Initiative, for example, rewarded with U.S. aid those small nations in the Caribbean region that adhered to free-market principles.

THE IRAN-CONTRA AFFAIR

In November 1986, a magazine in Lebanon reported that the Reagan administration was selling arms to Iran as part of a secret deal to secure the release of Americans being held hostage by Middle Eastern factions friendly to Iran's government. The story quickly became front-page news in the United States because such a deal would be in clear conflict with the Reagan administration's stated policies that it would not sell arms to Iran and that it would not reward hostage-taking by negotiating for the release of any captives.

As Congress began to investigate the arms-for-hostages story, matters turned even more bizarre. Profits from secret arms sales to Iran had been channeled to the *contra* forces in Nicaragua as a means of circumventing the congressional ban on U.S. military aid. Oliver North, a lieutenant colonel who worked in the office of the national security adviser, had directed the effort. Responsibility for carrying out the deal had been entrusted to a secret unit in the National Security Council, shadowy international arms dealers, and private go-betweens. North had been running a covert operation that violated both the stated policy of the White House and the ban legislated by Congress.

The arms-for-hostages idea dovetailed with Reagan's foreign policy priorities. During the 1980 campaign, Reagan had made hostages a symbol of U.S. weakness under Carter; as Iranian-backed groups continued to kidnap Americans, Reagan began to worry that the hostage issue might be as disastrous for his presidency as it had been for Carter's. Meanwhile, Iran was waging a prolonged war with Iraq. Although the United States allowed arms sales to Iraq, it had organized a ban on the sale of arms to Iran by Western powers because of Iran's connection with hostage-taking. The arms-for-hostages deal thus evolved out of mutual interests and fears: Despite the public enmity between the two nations, Iran needed arms to fight its war with Iraq, and the United States needed to show that it could bring hostages home. The secret deal satisfied both countries. Even better, the Reagan administration could use the profits from the sale secretly to fund other projects—such as the *contra* cause—that had to be hidden from Congress and the public.

This scheme seemed to cut at the heart of democratic processes, but everyone involved escaped accountability. Reagan maintained that he could not remember any details about either the release of the hostages or the funding of the *contras*. His management style might deserve criticism, he admitted, but no legal issues were involved. Vice President George Bush also escaped censure by claiming ignorance. Oliver North and National Security Adviser John Poindexter were convicted of felonies, including falsification of documents and lying to Congress, but their convictions were overturned on appeal. Six years later George Bush pardoned six former officials who had been involved in the Iran-*Contra* affair.

The Beginning of the End of the Cold War

Although Reagan's first six years in office had revived the Cold War confrontation, his last two years saw a sudden thaw in U.S.-Soviet relations and a movement toward détente. The economic cost of superpower rivalry was burdening both nations. Moreover, changes within the Soviet Union were eliminating the reasons for confrontation. Mikhail Gorbachev, who became general secretary of the Communist Party in 1985, was a new style of Soviet leader. He realized that his isolated country was facing economic stagnation and an environmental crisis brought on by decades of poorly planned industrial development. To redirect his country's course, he withdrew Soviet troops from Afghanistan, reduced commitments to Cuba and Nicaragua, proclaimed a policy of *glasnost* ("openness"), and began to implement *perestroika* ("economic liberalization") at home.

Soon Gorbachev was pursuing policies that stirred winds of change throughout the Soviet empire. He began summit meetings with the United States on arms control. At Reykjavik, Iceland, in October 1986, Reagan shocked both Gorbachev and his own advisers by proposing a wholesale ban on nuclear weapons. In December 1987 Reagan and Gorbachev signed a major arms treaty that reduced the number of intermediate-range missiles held by each nation and allowed for on-site verification, something the Soviets had never before permitted. The next year, Gorbachev scrapped the policy that forbade any nation under Soviet influence from renouncing communism. In effect, Gorbachev was declaring an end to the Cold War. And within the next few years, the Soviet sphere of influence—and then the Soviet Union itself—would cease to exist.

From Reagan to Bush

Even before the Iran-*Contra* affair, Reagan's image and influence were beginning to fade. Members of the New Right came to criticize the president for failing to support their agendas vigorously enough, while economic problems—especially the growing federal deficit—sparked broader-based calls for more assured leadership from the White House.

DOMESTIC POLICY DURING REAGAN'S SECOND TERM

During Reagan's second term, the White House and Congress began to address two long-term domestic issues: reduction of the federal budget and reform of the welfare system. First, the Gramm-Rudman-Hollings Act of 1985 mandated a balanced federal budget by 1991, but neither Congress nor the Reagan administration seemed eager to implement that goal. Second, the Family Support Act of 1988 required states to inaugurate work training programs and to move people off the welfare rolls. But this law did little to guarantee that people would actually find—and then keep—jobs. Without a plan to create new employment opportunities, the Family Support Act seemed to have more to do with the desire to cut domestic programs and less to do with finding actual alternatives to the existing welfare system. Yet, despite their limitations, Gramm-Rudman-Hollings and the Family Support Act set policymakers on a course of action that would culminate in a comprehensive budget-reduction and welfare-reform package nearly a decade later.

Meanwhile, many of Reagan's supporters became disappointed by domestic developments during his second term. In 1986, following the resignation of Warren Burger, the Senate confirmed William Rehnquist as chief justice of the Supreme Court and Antonin Scalia, another staunch conservative, to replace Rehnquist as associate justice. But in 1987 the Senate rebuffed Reagan's attempt to elevate Robert Bork, another conservative, to the Court. Bork's rejection sparked discord among conservatives, many of whom blamed Reagan for not working hard enough to secure his confirmation. Members of the Religious Right chafed at what they considered Reagan's tepid support for their antiabortion crusade, while his massive spending for military programs undermined the conservative dream of decreasing the federal budget.

Reagan's second term was also marked by charges of mismanagement and corruption. The process of banking deregulation became linked to malfeasance in financial circles and to risky speculation. Problems in the savings and loan industry reached crisis proportions. During a period of lax oversight by federal regulators, many savings and loan institutions (S&Ls) had extended too much money to risky ventures and had incurred financial obligations far beyond their means. As hundreds of S&Ls fell insolvent, the people and the businesses to whom they had lent money also faced financial disaster. The agency that regulated S&Ls predicted an impending crisis as early as the spring of 1985, but the Reagan administration and most members of Congress dismissed the warning.

Finally, in 1989 Congress enacted an expensive bailout plan, designed to save some institutions and to provide a means of transferring the assets of failed S&Ls to those that were still solvent. Even as taxpayers began paying for the plan, corruption plagued its execution; large, well-connected commercial banks purchased the assets of bankrupt S&Ls at bargain prices. By the time the Treasury Department stepped in, early in 1994, most of the larger S&Ls had already been sold.

THE ELECTION OF 1988

Despite the growing criticism of Reagan's leadership at home, Cold War détente boosted the 1988 presidential prospects of his heir-apparent, Vice President George Bush, who easily gained the Republican nomination. Part of a prominent Republican family from Connecticut, Bush had gone to Texas and entered the oil business as a young man. He had served in the House of Representatives and as director of the CIA. Bush chose as his running mate Senator J. Danforth Quayle, a staunch conservative. The selection of Quayle delighted political comedians, who found the bumbling Quayle a rich source for new comic material.

Governor Michael Dukakis of Massachusetts emerged from the primaries as the Democratic presidential candidate. Dukakis avoided talk of new domestic programs and higher taxes. Instead, he pledged to bring competence and honesty to the White House and boasted of how he had mobilized private experts to help streamline the government and stimulate the economy of Massachusetts. By running a cautious campaign and avoiding controversial domestic issues, Dukakis gambled that he could defeat Bush, who was burdened by Reagan's domestic failures.

The election of 1988 was dominated by negative campaigning, especially on behalf of George Bush. Pro-Bush television commercials usually presented Dukakis bathed in shadows and always showed him with a frown on his face. In the campaign's most infamous ad, Dukakis was linked to Willie Horton, an African American prison inmate who had committed a rape while on furlough from a Massachusetts prison. Clearly designed to play on racial fears, the ad also implied that Dukakis was soft on crime. Rising rates of violent crime during the late 1980s alarmed Americans across the country. As one pundit put it, the Bush campaign made it seem that Willie Horton was Dukakis's running mate.

Bush won a solid majority in both the popular vote and the Electoral College. Yet, he carried so many states by such small margins that relatively minor shifts in voter turnouts could have given the victory to Dukakis. Dukakis did better in 1988 than Mondale had done in 1984, winning 111 electoral votes. Outside the South, which went heavily for Bush, Dukakis carried more than 500 counties that had supported Reagan in 1984. Overall, voter turnout was the lowest it had been in any national election since 1924.

Although conservatives hoped Bush would build on the Reagan presidency, many doubted his commitment to their cause. Might not his campaign pledge of a "kinder, gentler America" be meant as a veiled criticism of Reagan's domestic policies? Bush angered many conservatives by agreeing to an increase in the minimum wage and by failing to veto the Civil Rights Act of 1991, a law they wrongly claimed set up quotas for the preferential hiring of women and people of color in business and government. Most important, in 1990 he broke his campaign promise of "no new taxes" and accepted a tax increase as a means of dealing with the rising federal deficit.

Meanwhile, there was a growing popular perception that the national government, divided between a Democratic-controlled Congress and a Republican-occupied White House, was suffering from "gridlock." Little seemed to be getting done on domestic issues. Moreover, the economic growth of the Reagan years was slowing, and the budget deficit was expanding. George Bush's chances for a second term would depend on his record in foreign, rather than domestic, policy.

FOREIGN POLICY UNDER BUSH

During Bush's presidency Soviet communism collapsed. As communist states fell like dominoes, the international order underwent its greatest transformation since the end of the Second World War.

THE END OF THE COLD WAR

Beginning in 1989, political change swept through Eastern and Central Europe. In Poland, the anticommunist labor party, Solidarity, ousted the pro-Soviet regime. The pro-Soviet government in East Germany fell in November 1989, and Germans from both West and East hacked down the Berlin Wall. Divided since the Second World War, Germany began the difficult process of reunification. In Czechoslovakia, Hungary, Romania, and Bulgaria, public demonstrations forced out communist governments. Yugoslavia disintegrated, and warfare ensued as ethnic groups tried to re-create the separate states of Slovenia, Serbia, Bosnia, and Croatia. The Baltic countries of Latvia, Lithuania, and Estonia, which had been under Soviet control

COLLAPSE OF THE SOVIET BLOC

since the Second World War, declared their independence. And most dramatic, the major provinces that had comprised the Soviet Union itself assumed self-government. The president of the new state of Russia, Boris Yeltsin, put down a coup by hard-line communists in August 1991, and his popularity rapidly eclipsed that of Mikhail Gorbachev. Yeltsin urged that the Soviet Union be abolished and replaced with 11 republics, loosely joined in a Commonwealth of Independent States. In December 1991, the Russian Parliament ratified that plan.

As the map of Europe changed, the United States faced the task of establishing diplomatic relations with many new and reconfigured countries. In December 1991 Congress authorized $400 million to help the Soviet Union's successor states dismantle their nuclear weaponry, and it allotted an equivalent amount the next year for promoting democracy in the new European republics. Critics charged that these sums for peace-building were minuscule compared to the funds that had been appropriated for military containment. But Bush, who feared being charged with slighting domestic problems, felt reluctant to press for more assistance.

Meanwhile, the international economic picture was improving. In the mid-1980s, huge debts that Third World nations owed to U.S. banks had threatened to shake the international banking system, but by the end of the decade most of these obligations had been renegotiated. Free-market economies began to emerge in the former communist states, and Western Europe moved toward economic integration. The nations of the Pacific Rim continued to prosper, and Bush pressed for a North American Free Trade Agreement (NAFTA) that would bring Canada, the United States, and Mexico together to form the largest free-market zone in the world.

As the likelihood of armed conflict with the Soviet Union faded, the Bush administration set about redefining "national security." In Central America, the Sandinistas were voted out of office in Nicaragua and became just another political party in a multiparty state. Supported by the United States, the United Nations began to assist both El Salvador and Guatemala in charting a course that would turn armed conflicts into electoral ones. The Pentagon thus began to consider new missions for its military forces. Future action, its planners predicted, would take the form of rapid, sharply targeted strikes rather than lengthy campaigns. Military troops might even be used to fight a "war against drugs." In Latin America, the Bush administration sponsored missions to destroy drug crops and interdict drug shipments.

Panama, whose government was headed by General Manuel Noriega, was deeply involved in the drug trade. The Reagan administration had secured an indictment in the United States against Noriega for drug trafficking and had tried to force him from power through economic pressure. But this had only deepened Noriega's reliance on drug revenues. Deciding how to deal with Noriega was a significant problem for U.S. policymakers. First, there was the embarrassing fact that Noriega had been recruited as a CIA "asset" in the mid-1970s, when Bush himself was the agency's director. In addition, the United States needed a friendly, responsible government in Panama in order to complete the transfer of the Panama Canal to Panamanian sovereignty by the end of the century. Bush finally decided to topple Noriega. In a military incursion called "Operation Just Cause," U.S. marines landed in Panama in December 1989, pinpointed Noriega's whereabouts, and put him under siege. Soon he surrendered and was extradited to stand trial in Florida. In April 1992 he was convicted of cocaine trafficking and imprisoned.

Seizing the leader of a foreign government in this manner raised questions of international law, and the resort to military force in a region long sensitive to U.S. intervention sparked controversy. Still, this military action, which involved 25,000 troops but only about two dozen U.S. casualties, boosted Bush's popularity at home. It also provided a new model for post–Cold War military action. The Pentagon firmed up plans for phasing out its older military bases, particularly in Germany and the Philippines, and for creating highly mobile, rapid-deployment forces. A test of this new strategy came in the Persian Gulf War.

THE PERSIAN GULF WAR

On August 2, 1990, President Saddam Hussein of Iraq ordered his troops to occupy the small neighboring emirate of Kuwait. Within a day, Iraq's forces had taken control of Kuwait, a move that caught the United States off guard. Although Iraq had been massing troops on Kuwait's border and denouncing Kuwaiti oil producers, U.S. intelligence forecasters had doubted that it was about to take over the country. Now, however, they warned that Iraq might make Saudi Arabia its next target.

Moving swiftly, Bush convinced the Saudi government to accept a U.S. military presence. Four days after Iraq's invasion of Kuwait, Bush launched operation "Desert Shield" by sending 230,000 troops to protect Saudi Arabia. After consulting with European leaders, he took the matter to the United Nations. The UN denounced Iraqi aggression, ordered economic sanctions against Saddam Hussein's regime, and authorized the United States to lead an international force to restore the government of Kuwait if Saddam Hussein had not withdrawn his troops by January 15, 1991. Bush assembled an international coalition and persuaded Congress to approve a resolution backing the use of force. Although Bush claimed a moral obligation to rescue Kuwait, his policymakers spoke frankly about the economic peril Hussein's aggression posed for the United States and other oil-dependent economies.

Just after the January 15 deadline passed, the United States launched an air war on Iraq. "Pools" of journalists, whose movements were carefully controlled by the military, focused mainly on new military technology, especially the antimissile missile called the "Patriot." The media also highlighted the new role that women played in America's modernized military. After six weeks of devastating aerial bombardment and economic sanctions against Iraq, General Colin Powell ordered a ground offensive on February 24. Over the next four days Saddam Hussein's armies were shattered. The United States, with its control of the skies, kept its casualties relatively light (148 deaths in battle). Estimates of Iraq's casualties ranged from 25,000 to 100,000 deaths. Although the conflict had lasted scarcely six weeks, the destruction of highways, bridges, communications, and other infrastructure in both Iraq and Kuwait was enormous.

In a controversial decision, Bush decided not to force Saddam Hussein's ouster. Instead, the United States, backed by the UN, maintained its economic pressure, worked to dismantle Iraq's nuclear and bacteriological capabilities, and enforced a "no-fly" zone over northern Iraq to protect the Kurdish population, which was being persecuted by Saddam Hussein. The government of Iraq survived, still headed by Saddam Hussein. Even so, the Persian Gulf War boosted George Bush's popularity and seemed to assure his reelection.

The end of the Cold War had eliminated some foreign policy issues, but new ones emerged. Turmoil broke out in some of the former Soviet provinces, and Russia struggled to develop a private-property, free-market economy. Full-scale warfare erupted among the states of the former Yugoslavia, with Serbians launching a brutal campaign against Bosnian Muslims. In the Far East, Japan's economic strength prompted Americans to grumble about unfair competition. In Africa, when severe famine struck the country of Somalia, Bush ordered American troops to establish humanitarian supply lines, but the American public remained wary of this military mission.

In confronting such diverse global issues, Bush met with mixed success. He could claim significant foreign policy accomplishments: He had assembled and held together an international coalition against Iraq, had constructively assisted the transition in Russia and Eastern Europe at the end of the Cold War, and had begun a process of trade liberalization. But when Bush spoke about creating a "new world order," neither he nor his advisers could explain just what that meant. The old reference points that had defined national security, especially containment of the Soviet enemy, had disappeared, and Bush never effectively articulated a new vision that could firmly establish his reputation as a foreign policy leader.

TOWARD THE 21ST CENTURY

The unraveling of George Bush's presidency and the meteoric rise of Democrat Bill Clinton in 1992 was followed, in congressional elections two years later, by a surprising Republican triumph. These abrupt swings suggested, among other things, a suspicion of national political leaders and a declining loyalty to political parties, particularly among people who had come to oppose many of the domestic policies that had been championed by the Democratic Party since the 1930s.

THE ELECTION OF 1992

The inability to portray a coherent vision of either foreign or domestic policy threatened Bush's reelection and forced him to make concessions to the New Right. Dan Quayle returned as his running mate, and the president allowed conservative activists to dominate the 1992 Republican national convention. They talked about "a religious war" for "the soul of America" and pictured Democrats as the enemies of "family values." But conservative Democrats and independents found this rhetoric no substitute for policies that addressed domestic problems, particularly the sluggish economy.

Bush's Democratic challenger, Governor Bill Clinton of Arkansas, concentrated on economic issues, pledging to increase government spending for job creation and long-term economic growth. Addressing a concern that apparently cut across partisan lines, Clinton promised a comprehensive revision of the nation's health care system. On other domestic issues, Clinton almost sounded like a Republican. "It's time to end this [welfare] system as we know it," Clinton insisted. He claimed to be a "new Democrat" who would reduce taxes for middle-class Americans, cut the federal deficit, and shrink the size of government. Clinton, in short, highlighted economic issues while making it difficult for Bush to label him as a "big government" liberal.

This focus on economics also helped to deflect attention from social-cultural issues on which Clinton appeared vulnerable. As a college student in the 1960s, he had not only avoided service in Vietnam but also had participated in antiwar demonstrations while in England as a Rhodes Scholar. When Bush, a decorated veteran of the Second World War, challenged Clinton's patriotism, Clinton countered by emphasizing, rather than repudiating, his roots in the Vietnam War generation. He became the first presidential candidate to campaign on MTV. In addition, he chose Senator Albert Gore, who had served in Vietnam, as his running mate. And when Clinton's personal life drew fire, Bill and Hillary Rodham Clinton defended their marriage as an effective, ongoing partnership. Hillary Rodham Clinton's

BILL CLINTON PLAYS THE SAXOPHONE   During the 1992 presidential campaign, Clinton eagerly identified himself as a baby boomer who had grown up with rock 'n' roll.

career as a lawyer and advocate for children's issues, the couple insisted, would be an asset to a Clinton presidency.

The 1992 presidential campaign was enlivened by the third-party candidacy of Ross Perot, a billionaire from Texas. A blunt, folksy speaker, Perot claimed that political insiders in Washington, both Republicans and Democrats, had created a "mess" that satisfied only special interests. If people would only come together in the 1990s as they had done in the 1940s, he argued, they could "take back our country." After suddenly dropping out of the presidential race in July, the unpredictable Perot returned in October with a media blitz that apparently hurt Bush more than Clinton.

Clinton won by a comfortable margin. He garnered 43 percent of the popular vote and won 370 electoral votes. Perot gained no electoral votes but did attract 19 million popular votes. Bush won a majority only among white Protestants in the South. In contrast, Clinton carried the Jewish, African American, and Latino vote by large margins, and he even gained a plurality among people who had served in the Vietnam War. He also ran very well among independents, voters whom Reagan and Bush had carried during the 1980s and on whom Perot had counted in 1992. Perhaps most surprising, about 55 percent of eligible voters went to the polls, a turnout that reversed 32 years of steady decline in voter participation.

CLINTON'S DOMESTIC POLICIES

Bill Clinton, the first Democratic president in 12 years, brought an emphasis on youth, vitality, and cultural diversity to Washington. The African American author Maya Angelou delivered a poem especially commissioned for his inauguration, and there were different inaugural balls for different musical tastes. Clinton's first cabinet included three African Americans and two Latinos; three cabinet posts went to women. As his first nomination to the Supreme Court, he chose Ruth Bader Ginsburg, only the second woman to sit on the Court. And as representative to the United Nations, Clinton named Madeleine Albright, who would become the country's first female secretary of state during his second term.

On social issues, Clinton claimed several victories during his first term. He ended the Reagan era's ban on abortion counseling in family planning clinics; pushed a family leave program for working parents through Congress; established a program, Americorps, that allowed students to repay their college loans through community service; and secured passage of the Brady Bill, which instituted a five-day waiting period for the purchase of handguns.

But health care reform collapsed. Hillary Rodham Clinton led a task force that produced a plan so complex that few understood it; worse, it pleased virtually no one. Republicans used the health care fiasco to paint Clinton as an advocate of "big government" spending. The administration's health care proposal died in Congress.

Meanwhile, Clinton faced problems of his own. Hillary Rodham Clinton's prominent role in the failed heath care effort fueled criticism of her public activities, and the Clintons' joint involvement in financial dealings in Arkansas—particularly those connected to a bankrupt S&L and to a failed land development called "Whitewater"—drew renewed criticism. In August 1994 Kenneth Starr, a Republican, was appointed as an independent prosecutor charged with investigating the allegations. Starr soon negotiated guilty pleas from several people in Arkansas who were connected to Whitewater and pressed forward with an investigation that seemed aimed at securing an indictment against at least one of the Clintons. Conservative talk show hosts leveled a nonstop barrage of criticism against the president.

The 1994 elections brought a dramatic GOP victory. Republicans secured control of both houses of Congress for the first time in 40 years; they won several new governorships; gained ground in most state legislatures; and made significant headway in many city and county elections. Led by Representative Newt Gingrich of Georgia, conservative Republicans hailed these gains as a mandate for their new agenda called the "Contract with America," which aimed at rolling back federal spending and a variety of governmental programs and regulations.

Congressional Republicans, however, overplayed their hand. Opinion polls suggested that people found Gingrich less trustworthy and competent than the president. Moreover, surveys also showed little support for the kind of thoroughgoing "revolution" against federal programs that was being proposed by the conservatives in Congress. When conflict between the Democratic president and GOP Congress over budget issues led to two brief shutdowns of many government agencies (November 14–20, 1995, and December 16, 1995–January 4, 1996), most people blamed the Republicans in Congress, rather than the White House.

Most important, a revived U.S. economy benefited Clinton. As low rates of inflation accompanied steady economic growth, new jobs were created at a rate that surpassed the president's

POLITICS ON THE WEB

Although the World Wide Web has begun to transform many aspects of daily life, especially at colleges and universities, the Web's impact on American politics remains uncertain. Candidates who have tried to use the Internet to distribute information have run into great difficulty because recipients have generally considered e-mail from politicians to be a form of "spam," or junk mail. In some cases, angry constituents have retaliated by flooding the Web servers used by politicians with their own "junk replies."

Political commentary on the World Wide Web has also been slow to develop. Internet sites still suffer from the stigma of disseminating too many rumors and too little verifiable information.

most optimistic predictions. The stock market, buoyed by technology companies, soared to new heights. Although the specific benefits of this general expansion were distributed unequally—the gap between the pay of corporate executives and ordinary workers grew steadily larger and the wealthiest 10 percent of households still owned 90 percent of the nation's stock holdings—many people did see their economic fortunes improve significantly.

During independent prosecutor Kenneth Starr's investigation of President Bill Clinton, the "Drudge Report," an iconoclastic Web site generally viewed as being hostile to the Clinton administration, gained wider attention for daring to publish information that more traditional political publications hesitated to release. But it also attracted a libel suit by one of the president's advisers for posting claims that were later retracted. Similarly, several newspapers posted stories on their Web sites containing rumors that would likely not have been printed in their "hard copies" and that were later withdrawn from the Internet.

As a result of these and other problems, one of the most popular uses of the World Wide Web for politics has been the relatively traditional sites maintained by the Democratic and Republican parties. What effects might the Web revolution have on modern political culture? Visit these two sites and surf others to see for yourself.

A backlash against the budget gridlock of 1995, together with the signs of continued economic growth, inclined both the White House and Congress to cooperate on overhauling the welfare system. The Personal Responsibility and Work Opportunity Reconciliation Act of 1996 represented a series of compromises that pleased conservatives more than liberals. Relatively noncontroversial sections of the law tightened collection of child support payments and reorganized nutrition and child care programs. Clinton, while voicing concern about provisions that cut the Food Stamp program and benefits for recent immigrants, embraced the law's central feature: the replacement of the AFDC program, which had promised a minimum level of funds and social services to poor families headed by single unemployed women, by a flexible system of block grants to individual states. Under the new program, entitled Temporary Assistance to Needy Families (TANF), states were to design their own welfare-to-work programs under broad federal guidelines.

TANF, which effectively ended the welfare system that had been in place since the New Deal, provoked bitter controversy. Its proponents claimed it would encourage states to experiment with new programs that would reduce their welfare costs. Critics worried that its provisions, including those that limited a person to five years of government assistance during his or her lifetime and authorized states to cut off support if recipients did not find employment within two years, ignored the difficulty that people without job skills faced. They also feared the impact that TANF might have on daily lives of children, especially if states provided inadequate child care, nutritional, and medical care programs. Studies showed that one of every five children already lived in poverty. By pushing further debate over such issues into the future, however, the new welfare law helped to remove a number of potential domestic issues from the political campaign of 1996.

CLINTON'S FOREIGN POLICY

For nearly half a century, anticommunism and rivalry with the Soviet Union had shaped policy-making. The United States now had to redefine national security to fit a multipolar world. Clinton often articulated an expansive, internationalist vision: improving relations with the UN, expanding NATO, advancing human rights and democracy abroad, reducing nuclear threats, working on global environmental concerns, and promoting free-market policies. During both of his presidential campaigns, however, Clinton focused primarily on domestic issues, and the public seemed suspicious of new international commitments.

One of the most perplexing issues involved revamping the U.S. military for the post–Cold War world. Under what conditions should U.S. troops participate in "peacekeeping" missions? Some people saw any reluctance to use military power as a "new isolationism." Others cautioned against drifting into long-term, ill-defined commitments.

Several trouble spots sparked debate. In the African country of Somalia, U.S. troops had been assisting a humanitarian effort to provide food and relief supplies since May 1992. Caught in factional fighting, however, U.S. troops suffered well-publicized casualties, and Clinton ordered a pullout during the spring of 1994. In Haiti, Clinton vowed to help reestablish the elected president, Jean-Bertrand Aristide. In September 1994, U.S. troops landed in Haiti, and last-minute negotiations by former president Jimmy Carter persuaded the Haitian military to step aside. After six months, with Aristide in power and political institutions functioning again, U.S. soldiers handed over the responsibility for keeping civil order to UN forces. In the former Yugoslavia, the United States committed troops to halt the massacre of Bosnian Muslims by Bosnian Serbs and to oversee a cease-fire and peace-building process that all parties to the conflict had accepted in the U.S.-brokered Dayton (Ohio) accords of 1995.

In March 1999, President Clinton supported a bombing campaign by NATO in Kosovo, a province of Serbia. NATO leaders and Clinton insisted that this controversial use of military force was necessary to protect Muslims of Albanian descent, who comprised nearly 90 percent of Kosovo's population, from an "ethnic cleansing" program directed by Serbia's president,

Slobodan Milosevic. Although NATO's bombs systematically decimated Serbia's economic infrastructure, Milosevic stepped up his campaign and forced hundreds of thousands of ethnic Albanians to flee from Kosovo into neighboring countries. Finally, in June 1999, after 78 days of bombardment, Serbia agreed to withdraw its forces and permit troops under NATO command to oversee the return of ethnic Albanians to Kosovo.

Meanwhile, other post–Cold War concerns drew Clinton's attention. In February 1994, the CIA was rocked by scandal when a high-ranking official, Aldrich Ames, and his wife were arrested on charges of selling information to the Soviet Union and Russia over the preceding decade, contributing to the deaths of several CIA agents. Ames subsequently pled guilty to espionage and was sentenced to life in prison; his wife received a lesser sentence. A year later, it was revealed that the CIA had maintained connections to death squads in Guatemala. Mindful of calls for reform, the CIA tried to chart new, post–Cold War missions. International drug traffickers and other criminal syndicates posed potential threats. And the CIA also targeted international terrorism. In early 1993, a bomb rocked the World Trade Center in New York City, killing 6 people and injuring nearly 1,000. Investigators arrested four Muslims, who had links to previous terrorist acts.

Clinton also shaped new policies on weapons of mass destruction. He dismantled some of the U.S. nuclear arsenal and tried to curtail the potential danger from other nuclear powers. When the Soviet Union collapsed and its nuclear weapons became dispersed among several independent states, the Clinton administration feared these might be sold on the black market to terrorists. In early 1994 Clinton increased economic aid for Ukraine in return for promises to disarm its 1,600 warheads. In the same year, a highly secret "Project Sapphire" transferred enriched uranium stocks from Kazakhstan to storage facilities in the United States. Jimmy Carter helped negotiate a complicated agreement with North Korea over nuclear weapons, signed in 1994. North Korea agreed to begin dismantling its nuclear program and permit international inspections as soon as the United States helped it construct safer, light-water nuclear reactors for its energy needs. Throughout the rest of the world, the United States successfully pressed many nations to sign a new Nuclear Nonproliferation Treaty in the spring of 1995. In early 1998, Clinton went to the brink of war with Iraq to maintain international inspections of Saddam Hussein's weapons programs, but after enduring punishing air strikes, Iraq expelled the investigators.

A principal goal of Clinton's foreign policy was to lower trade barriers and expand global markets. Building on the Reagan-Bush legacy, Clinton argued that such policies would boost prosperity and foster democracy around the world. His administration consummated several historic trade agreements. Despite opposition from labor unions and other groups, Clinton strongly backed the North American Free Trade Agreement (NAFTA), which projected cutting tariffs and eliminating other trade barriers among the United States, Canada, and Mexico over a 15-year period. After adding new provisions on labor and environmental issues, in December 1993 he muscled the bill through Congress in a close vote. NAFTA took effect on January 1, 1994. Then, in early 1995, Mexico's severe debt crisis and a dramatic devaluation of its peso prompted Clinton to extend a $20 billion loan from America's Exchange Stabilization Fund. Clinton's trade negotiators completed the so-called "Uruguay Round" of the General Agreement on Tariffs and Trade (GATT) in late 1993, and in early 1995 GATT was replaced by a new World Trade Organization (WTO), a group created to enlarge world trade by implementing new agreements and mediating disputes. Clinton also granted China, despite its dismal record on human rights, equal trading status with other nations and in October 1999 agreed to back China's entry into the WTO in exchange for a promise to liberalize its policies toward the United States and other potential trading partners. To justify this action, he argued that increased trade with China

PROTESTS AGAINST THE WORLD TRADE ORGANIZATION   Police used pepper spray and tear gas to clear thousands of protesters from downtown Seattle streets during demonstrations against the World Trade Organization conference on November 30, 1999.

would contribute to long-term pressures for democratization there. Similarly, in February 1994, the United States ended its 19-year-old trade embargo against Vietnam.

Clinton claimed that all of these measures on behalf of market expansion, along with the emergence of free-market economies in Eastern Europe and Latin America, provided the framework for a new era of global prosperity. When Asian economies faltered during 1998, the president strongly supported acting with the International Monetary Fund to provide huge emergency credits to reform and restore financial systems from Korea to Indonesia.

THE ELECTION OF 1996 AND ITS AFTERMATH

The election of 1996 brought few political changes. The special Whitewater prosecutor had failed to secure any new indictments, and corruption in the White House never became a major issue. The Clinton-Gore team, benefiting from the burgeoning economy, defeated the Republican ticket of Bob Dole and Jack Kemp by about the same margin that it had beaten Bush and Quayle in 1992. Clinton and most other Democrats ran particularly well among African Americans, women, and Hispanic voters. Republicans retained control of Congress and gained several new governorships, but Democrats still held a majority of the seats in state legislatures, a sign that many voters found ticket-splitting (voting for both Democrats and Republicans) a desirable course. After the election, Clinton and congressional Republicans re-

CHRONOLOGY

1974	Nixon resigns and Ford becomes president; Ford soon pardons Nixon
1975	South Vietnam falls to North Vietnam • Ford asserts U.S. power in *Mayaguez* incident
1976	Jimmy Carter elected president
1978	Carter helps negotiate Camp David peace accords on Middle East
1979	Soviet Union invades Afghanistan • Sandinista Party comes to power in Nicaragua • U.S. hostages seized in Iran
1980	Reagan elected president
1981	Reagan tax cut passed • U.S. hostages in Iran released
1983	U.S. troops removed from Lebanon • U.S. troops invade Grenada • Reagan announces SDI ("Star Wars") program
1984	Reagan defeats Walter Mondale
1986	Reagan administration rocked by revelation of Iran-*Contra* affair
1988	George Bush defeats Michael Dukakis in presidential election
1989	Communist regimes in Eastern Europe collapse; Berlin Wall falls • Cold War, in effect, ends
1990	Bush angers conservative Republicans by agreeing to a tax increase
1991	Bush orchestrates Persian Gulf War against Iraq
1992	Bill Clinton defeats Bush and third-party candidate Ross Perot in presidential race
1993	Congress approves North American Free Trade Agreement (NAFTA) and the General Agreement on Tariffs and Trade (GATT)
1994	Republicans gain control of both houses of Congress and pledge to enact their "Contract with America"
1995	Special prosecutor Kenneth Starr takes over the investigation of "Whitewater" allegations
1996	Personal Responsibility and Work Opportunity Reconciliation Act becomes first major overhaul of the national welfare system since the 1930s • Clinton defeats Robert Dole in the presidential race
1998	Congress votes two articles of impeachment against Clinton
1999	Impeachment trial in Senate fails to convict the president • NATO bombs Serbia to stop persecution of Albanians in Kosovo

sponded by cooperating to pass legislation that promised broadly distributed tax cuts and phased reductions in the federal deficit. In his 1998 State of the Union address, Clinton proudly proclaimed that the budget deficit would soon move to zero.

After the election of 1996, however, national politics increasingly came to revolve around Kenneth Starr's investigations of the president and his administration. The White House had hoped to focus Clinton's second term on a new "national conversation" about racial issues and on programs to improve education, but the media highlighted a seemingly endless array of legal allegations leveled against the president and his associates. While Starr continued to press forward on matters related to the involvement of the Clintons in the Whitewater land deal, he broadened his inquiry to include claims that the president had made inappropriate sexual advances to female employees and that he had later engaged in an effort to obstruct justice either by committing perjury himself or by pressuring others to offer false accounts of his behavior with a young White House intern, Monica Lewinsky.

Clinton's presidency, though still judged a success by a majority of people in public opinion surveys, came under intense scrutiny. Republicans charged the White House with impeding Starr's investigation and the president of lying, and some began to talk about impeaching the president for obstruction of justice. The president's defenders charged Starr's office with engaging in a partisan vendetta against Clinton, leaking secret testimony to the media, and working in concert with the conservative political action committees that were financing a private lawsuit against the president by Paula Corbin Jones for an incident of sexual harassment that had allegedly occurred while Clinton had been governor of Arkansas. And with economic statistics continuing to show improvement, Clinton's approval rating went up, while that of Starr plummeted. Although the GOP surprisingly lost five seats in the House during the off-year election of 1998, the lame-duck 105th Congress voted, in December 1998, two articles of impeachment against the still-popular president. After a month of proceedings, which concluded on February 12, 1999, Republican senators could not muster the two-thirds vote required by the Consititution (nor even a bare majority) to remove Clinton, only the second president in U.S. history to have faced an impeachment trial in the Senate.

Partisan rancor marked post-impeachment politics as both major parties prepared for the election of 2000. Republicans rebuffed the White House's effort to secure Senate ratification of a nuclear test ban treaty and to expand entitlement spending at home, while Clinton vetoed the GOP's sweeping tax-cut bill. This political stalemate, which was broken only by congressional repeal of New Deal–era regulations that had barred banks from entering the insurance and securities businesses, prevented the two parties from fulfilling earlier promises to overhaul the Social Security and Medicare programs. Meanwhile, the continued revenue surplus, a result of the sustained economic boom and the partisan deadlock over tax policy, meant that the once-massive federal debt, which had been a pressing concern only a decade earlier, was steadily disappearing.

CONCLUSION

Winds of change swept over American life during the final 25 years of the 20th century. In foreign policy, people had to adjust to the trauma of Vietnam, to the sudden end of the Cold War, and to a global environment in which U.S. economic and strategic interests seemed in a state of constant flux. How and where should U.S. military and economic power be exercised?

At home, the Watergate scandal and the economic problems of the 1970s helped to breed cynicism about government. Support for extending the power of the national government in order to address domestic problems slowly eroded. Meanwhile, the "Reagan Revolution" of the 1980s marked the emergence of a new conservative movement. The strength of the Republican Party, which by 1996 could claim nearly as many supporters as the once-dominant Democratic Party, and the presidency of Bill Clinton, a "new Democrat" who declared that the era of "big government" had ended, suggested that many people now rejected the idea that increasing the power of the government meant progress. But how else could a diverse nation confront economic and social problems? As the United States entered the 21st century, Americans continued to debate how to negotiate the difficult balance among liberty, equality, and power.

APPENDIX

CANADA

Mt. Olympus
2424 m
(7954 ft)
Olympia ★

WASHINGTON

Mt. Rainier
4392 m
(14,410 ft)

Cascade Range

Salem ★ Columbia R.

Blue Mts.

Bitterroot Range

ROCKY

Helena ★

MONTANA

GREAT

Missouri R.

NORTH DAKOTA

Bismarck ★

Coast Ranges

Klamath Mts.

OREGON

Columbia Plateau

Snake R.

Boise ★

IDAHO

Absaroka Range

Wind River Range

Bighorn Mts.

WYOMING

Badlands

Black Hills

SOUTH DAKOTA

Pierre ★

Badlands

Sacramento R.

Sierra Nevada

Carson City ★

Great Basin

Lake Tahoe

NEVADA

Great Salt Lake

Salt Lake City

Uinta Mts.

UTAH

Wyoming Basin

M

O

U

N

Cheyenne ★

Denver ●

COLORADO

Sand Hills

NEBRASKA

Platte R.

Smoky Hills

KANSAS

San Francisco ○

Sacramento ★

Central Valley

San Joaquin R.

Mt. Whitney
4418 m
(14,494 ft)

Death Valley

CALIFORNIA

Lake Mead

Lake Powell

Colorado R.

Grand Canyon

Black Mesa

Colorado Plateau

T

A

I

N

Mt. Elbert
4399 m
(14,433 ft)

▲ Pikes Peak
4301 m
(14,110 ft)

Arkansas R.

Point Conception

Channel Islands

Coast Ranges

Los Angeles ●

Mojave Desert

Salton Sea

Colorado R.

ARIZONA

Painted Desert

Santa Fe ★

Sangre de Cristo Mts.

S

NEW MEXICO

Sonoran Desert

Phoenix ★

Oklahoma City ●

OKLAHOMA

Red R.

PACIFIC

OCEAN

Guadalupe Mts.

Llano Estacado

Rio Grande

Stockton Plateau

TEXAS

Austin ★

Austin Cha

Cliffs

Rio Grande

MEXICO

Kauai
Niihau Oahu
Honolulu ★ Molokai
Lanai Maui
Kahoolawe
Hawaii

HAWAII

PACIFIC
OCEAN

0   75   150 Miles
0   75   150 Kilometers

ARCTIC OCEAN

Beaufort Sea

Chukchi Sea

RUSSIA

Brooks Range

Bering Strait

ALASKA

MacKenzie R.

CANADA

St. Lawrence I.

Yukon R.

Mt. McKinley
6194 m
(20,320 ft)

Kuskokwim R.

Alaska Range

Yukon R.

Juneau ★

Bering Sea

Alaska Peninsula

Kodiak I.

Gulf of Alaska

Alexander Archipelago

Aleutian Islands

0   150   300 Miles
0   150   300 Kilometers

UNITED STATES
Physical

Lake of the Woods

Mesabi Range

Lake Superior

Upper Peninsula

Lake Huron

Lower Peninsula

Lake Michigan

NESOTA

WISCONSIN

St. Paul

Mississippi R.

MICHIGAN

Lansing

Madison

MAINE

Augusta

White Mts.

Green Mts.

St. Lawrence R.

Lake Champlain

Montpelier

N.H.

Concord

Gulf of Maine

Adirondack Mts.

VT.

Boston

Cape Cod

MASS.

Albany

Providence

R.I.

Connecticut R.

NEW YORK

Lake Ontario

Niagara Falls

Finger Lakes

Hartford

CONN.

Lake Erie

Long Island

Susquehanna R.

New York

Trenton

Chicago

IOWA

Des Moines

ILLINOIS

Springfield

INDIANA

Indianapolis

OHIO

Columbus

PENN.

Allegheny Front

MOUNTAINS

N.J.

Harrisburg

Dover

MD.

Annapolis

DEL.

Delaware Bay

Washington, D.C.

Jefferson City

St. Louis

Frankfort

Ohio R.

WEST VIRGINIA

Charleston

VIRGINIA

Richmond

Chesapeake Bay

ska

Missouri R.

Kansas City

MISSOURI

KENTUCKY

Kentucky Lake

Cumberland Plateau

APPALACHIAN

Blue Ridge

Piedmont

ATLANTIC

OCEAN

Ozark Plateau

Nashville

Raleigh

NORTH CAROLINA

Boston Mts.

Arkansas R.

Little Rock

Tennessee R.

Great Smoky Mts.

Mt. Mitchell 2037 m (6684 ft.)

TENNESSEE

Columbia

SOUTH CAROLINA

Piedmont

COASTAL

Ouachita Mts.

ARKANSAS

Yazoo Basin

Mississippi R.

ALABAMA

Atlanta

GEORGIA

ATLANTIC

PLAIN

LOUISIANA

MISSISSIPPI

Jackson

Montgomery

Red R.

Tallahassee

Baton Rouge

New Orleans

Houston

GULF COASTAL PLAIN

FLORIDA

Cape Canaveral

Gulf of Mexico

L. Okeechobee

Miami

Florida Keys

Straits of Florida

BAHAMAS

CUBA

Inset

ATLANTIC OCEAN

PUERTO RICO

San Juan

Charlotte Amalie

VIRGIN ISLANDS

| 0 | 50 | 100 Miles |
| 0 | 50 | 100 Kilometers |

| 0 | 150 | 300 Miles |
| 0 | 150 | 300 Kilometers |

Legend

Elevation in feet	Elevation in meters
Over 13,100	Over 4,000
6,600–13,100	2,000–4,000
1,600–6,600	500–2,000
700–1,600	200–500
0–700	0–200
Below sea level	Below sea level

CANADA

Olympia ★

WASHINGTON
(1889)

Columbia R.

Salem ★

**OREGON COUNTRY
(By agreement with
Britain, 1846)**

OREGON
(1859)

Boise ★

IDAHO
(1890)

Snake R.

Helena ★

MONTANA
(1889)

Missouri R.

NORTH DAKOTA
(1889)

Bismarck ★

SOUTH DAKOTA
(1889)

Pierre ★

WYOMING
(1890)

**LOUISIANA PURCHA
(From France, 1803)**

*Great
Salt Lake*

Salt
Lake City ★

Cheyenne ★

NEBRASKA
(1867)

Platte R.

Carson City ★

NEVADA
(1864)

UTAH
(1896)

**MEXICAN CESSION
(1848)**

Sacramento ★

Colorado R.

Denver ★

COLORADO
(1876)

KANSAS
(1861)

Arkansas R.

CALIFORNIA
(1850)

Colorado R.

ARIZONA
(1912)

Phoenix ★

Santa Fe ★

NEW MEXICO
(1912)

OKLAHOMA
(1907)

Oklahoma
City

Red R.

**GADSDEN
PURCHASE
(From Mexico,
1853)**

**PACIFIC
OCEAN**

**TEXAS
(Independent republic,
annexed 1845)**

T E X A S
(1845)

Rio Grande

Austin ★

**HAWAII
(Annexed, 1898)**

Honolulu ★

HAWAII
(1959)

*PACIFIC
OCEAN*

0   75   150 Miles
0   75   150 Kilometers

RUSSIA

ARCTIC   OCEAN

MacKenzie R.

CANADA

Yukon R.

ALASKA
(1959)

**ALASKA PURCHASE
(from Russia, 1867)**

Bering Sea

*Gulf of
Alaska*

Juneau ★

MEXICO

Rio Grande

0   150   300 Miles
0   150   300 Kilometers

UNITED STATES
Territorial Expansion

Lake of the Woods

Lake Superior

St. Lawrence R.

MAINE (1820)
Augusta

MINNESOTA (1858)

Lake Michigan

Lake Huron

VT. (1791)
Montpelier

N.H. (1788)
Concord
Boston

NEW YORK (1788)
Albany

MASS. (1788)

Lake Ontario

Hartford

Providence
R.I. (1790)

CONN. (1788)

St. Paul

WISCONSIN (1848)

Mississippi R.

Madison

MICHIGAN (1837)
Lansing

Lake Erie

N.J. (1787)
Trenton

PENN. (1787)
Harrisburg

1800
MD. (1788)
Dover

1790
DEL. (1787)

IOWA (1846)

Des Moines

**ORIGINAL UNITED STATES
(By treaty with Britain, 1783)**

OHIO (1803)
Columbus

1850

Annapolis

Washington, D.C.

Chesapeake Bay

INDIANA (1816)
Indianapolis

ILLINOIS (1818)
Springfield

1900

Ohio R.

Charleston

VIRGINIA (1788)
Richmond

ORIGINAL THIRTEEN COLONIES

MISSOURI (1821)
Jefferson City

1950

Frankfort

WEST VIRGINIA (1863)

Missouri R.

1990

KENTUCKY (1792)

Raleigh

NORTH CAROLINA (1789)

ATLANTIC OCEAN

Nashville

ARKANSAS (1836)
Little Rock

TENNESSEE (1796)

Arkansas R.

Tennessee R.

SOUTH CAROLINA (1788)
Columbia

Atlanta

Mississippi R.

● Geographical center of population per Census year

ALABAMA (1819)
Montgomery

GEORGIA (1788)

MISSISSIPPI (1817)
Jackson

PUERTO RICO (From Spain, 1898)

ATLANTIC OCEAN

San Juan

Charlotte Amalie

VIRGIN ISLANDS (From Denmark, 1917)

0   50   100 Miles
0   50   100 Kilometers

Red R.

Tallahassee

Baton Rouge

LOUISIANA (1812)

(Seized from Spain, 1810, 1813)

FLORIDA (By treaty with Spain, 1819)

Gulf

of

Mexico

FLORIDA (1845)

Lake Okeechobee

BAHAMAS

0   150   300 Miles
0   150   300 Kilometers

CUBA

THE DECLARATION OF INDEPENDENCE

THE UNANIMOUS DECLARATION OF THE
THIRTEEN UNITED STATES OF AMERICA

When in the Course of human events it becomes necessary for one people to dissolve the political bands which have connected them with another, and to assume among the Powers of the earth, the separate and equal station to which the Laws of Nature and of Nature's God entitle them, a decent respect to the opinions of mankind requires that they should declare the causes which impel them to the separation.

We hold these truths to be self-evident, that all men are created equal, that they are endowed by their Creator with certain unalienable Rights, that among these are Life, Liberty and the pursuit of Happiness. That to secure these rights, Governments are instituted among Men, deriving their just Powers from the consent of the governed. That whenever any Form of Government becomes destructive of these ends, it is the Right of the People to alter or to abolish it, and to institute new Government, laying its foundation on such principles and organizing its Powers in such form, as to them shall seem most likely to effect their Safety and Happiness. Prudence, indeed, will dictate that Governments long established should not be changed for light and transient causes; and accordingly all experience hath shewn, that mankind are more disposed to suffer, while evils are sufferable, than to right themselves by abolishing the forms to which they are accustomed. But when a long train of abuses and usurpations, pursuing invariably the same Object evinces a design to reduce them under absolute Despotism, it is their right, it is their duty, to throw off such Government, and to provide new Guards for their future security. Such has been the patient sufferance of these Colonies; and such is now the necessity which constrains them to alter their former Systems of Government. The history of the present King of Great Britain is a history of repeated injuries and usurpations, all having in direct object the establishment of an absolute Tyranny over these States. To prove this, let Facts be submitted to a candid world.

He has refused his Assent to Laws, the most wholesome and necessary for the public good.

He has forbidden his Governors to pass Laws of immediate and pressing importance, unless suspended in their operation till his Assent should be obtained; and when so suspended, he has utterly neglected to attend to them.

He has refused to pass other Laws for the accommodation of large districts of people, unless those people would relinquish the right of Representation in the Legislature, a right inestimable to them and formidable to tyrants only.

He has called together legislative bodies at places unusual, uncomfortable, and distant from the depository of their Public Records, for the sole Purpose of fatiguing them into compliance with his measures.

He has dissolved Representative Houses repeatedly, for opposing with manly firmness his invasions on the rights of the People.

Text is reprinted from the facsimile of the engrossed copy in the National Archives. The original spelling, capitalization, and punctuation have been retained. Paragraphing has been added.

He has refused for a long time, after such dissolutions, to cause others to be elected; whereby the Legislative Powers, incapable of Annihilation, have returned to the People at large for their exercise; the State remaining in the mean time exposed to all the dangers of invasion from without, and convulsions within.

He has endeavoured to prevent the Population of these States; for that purpose obstructing the Laws for Naturalization of Foreigners; refusing to pass others to encourage their migrations hither, and raising the conditions of new Appropriations of Lands.

He has obstructed the Administration of Justice, by refusing his Assent to Laws for establishing Judiciary Powers.

He has made Judges dependent on his Will alone, for the tenure of their offices, and the amount and payment of their salaries.

He has erected a multitude of New Offices, and sent hither swarms of Officers to harass our People, and eat out their substance.

He has kept among us, in times of peace, Standing Armies without the Consent of our legislatures.

He has affected to render the Military independent of and superior to the Civil Power.

He has combined with others to subject us to a jurisdiction foreign to our constitution, and unacknowledged by our laws; giving his Assent to their Acts of pretended Legislation:

For Quartering large bodies of armed troops among us:

For protecting them, by a mock Trial, from Punishment for any Murders which they should commit on the Inhabitants of these States:

For cutting off our Trade with all parts of the world:

For imposing Taxes on us without our Consent:

For depriving us in many cases, of the benefits of Trial by Jury:

For transporting us beyond Seas to be tried for pretended offences:

For abolishing the free System of English Laws in a neighbouring Province, establishing therein an Arbitrary government, and enlarging its Boundaries so as to render it at once an example and fit instrument for introducing the same absolute rule into these Colonies:

For taking away our Charters, abolishing our most valuable Laws, and altering fundamentally the Forms of our Governments:

For suspending our own Legislatures, and declaring themselves invested with Power to legislate for us in all cases whatsoever.

He has abdicated Government here, by declaring us out of his Protection, and waging War against us.

He has plundered our seas, ravaged our Coasts, burnt our towns, and destroyed the lives of our people.

He is at this time transporting large Armies of foreign Mercenaries to compleat the works of death, desolation and tyranny, already begun with circumstances of Cruelty and perfidy scarcely paralleled in the most barbarous ages, and totally unworthy the Head of a civilized nation.

He has constrained our fellow Citizens taken Captive on the high Seas to bear Arms against their Country, to become the executioners of their friends and Brethren, or to fall themselves by their Hands.

He has excited domestic insurrections amongst us, and has endeavoured to bring on the inhabitants of our frontiers, the merciless Indian Savages, whose known rule of warfare, is an undistinguished destruction of all ages, sexes and conditions.

In every stage of these Oppressions We have Petitioned for Redress in the most humble terms: Our repeated Petitions have been answered only by repeated injury. A Prince, whose character is thus marked by every act which may define a Tyrant, is unfit to be the ruler of a free People.

Nor have We been wanting in attentions to our British brethren. We have warned them from time to time of attempts by their legislature to extend an unwarrantable jurisdiction over us. We have reminded them of the circumstances of our emigration and settlement here. We have appealed to their native justice and magnanimity, and we have conjured them by the ties of our common kindred to disavow thee usurpations, which, would inevitably interrupt our connections and correspondence. They too have been deaf to the voice of justice and of consanguinity. We must, therefore, acquiesce in the necessity, which denounces our Separation, and hold them, as we hold the rest of mankind, Enemies in War, in Peace Friends.

We, THEREFORE, the Representatives of the UNITED STATES of AMERICA, in General Congress, Assembled, appealing to the Supreme Judge of the world for the rectitude of our intentions, do, in the Name, and by Authority of the good People of these Colonies, solemnly publish and declare, That these United Colonies are, and of Right ought to be FREE AND INDEPENDENT STATES; that they are Absolved from all Allegiance to the British Crown, and that all political connection between them and the State of Great Britain, is and ought to be totally dissolved; and that, as Free and Independent States, they have full Power to levy War, conclude Peace, contract Alliances, establish Commerce, and to do all other Acts and Things which Independent States may of right do. And for the support of this Declaration, with a firm reliance on the protection of divine Providence, we mutually pledge to each other our Lives, our Fortunes and our sacred Honor.

THE CONSTITUTION OF THE
UNITED STATES OF AMERICA

We the People of the United States, in Order to form a more perfect Union, establish Justice, insure domestic Tranquility, provide for the common defence, promote the general Welfare, and secure the Blessings of Liberty to ourselves and our Posterity, do ordain and establish this Constitution for the United States of America.

ARTICLE I.

SECTION 1. All legislative Powers herein granted shall be vested in a Congress of the United States, which shall consist of a Senate and House of Representatives.

SECTION 2. The House of Representatives shall be composed of Members chosen every second Year by the People of the several States, and the Electors in each State shall have the Qualifications requisite for Electors of the most numerous Branch of the State Legislature.

No Person shall be a Representative who shall not have attained to the Age of twenty five Years, and been seven Years a Citizen of the United States, and who shall not, when elected, be an Inhabitant of that State in which he shall be chosen.

Text is from the engrossed copy in the National Archives. Original spelling, capitalization, and punctuation have been retained.

Representatives and direct Taxes[1] shall be apportioned among the several States which may be included within this Union, according to their respective Numbers, which shall be determined by adding to the whole Number of free Persons, including those bound to Service for a Term of Years, and excluding Indians not taxed, three fifths of all other Persons.[2] The actual Enumeration shall be made within three Years after the first Meeting of the Congress of the United States, and within every subsequent Term of ten Years, in such Manner as they shall by Law direct. The Number of Representatives shall not exceed one for every thirty Thousand, but each State shall have at Least one Representative; and until such enumeration shall be made, the State of New Hampshire shall be entitled to chuse three; Massachusetts eight; Rhode Island and Providence Plantations one; Connecticut five; New York six; New Jersey four; Pennsylvania eight; Delaware one; Maryland six; Virginia ten; North Carolina five; South Carolina five; and Georgia three.

When vacancies happen in the Representation from any State, the Executive Authority thereof shall issue Writs of Election to fill such Vacancies.

The House of Representatives shall chuse their Speaker and other Officers; and shall have the sole Power of Impeachment.

SECTION 3. The Senate of the United States shall be composed of two Senators from each State, chosen by the Legislature thereof, for six Years; and each Senator shall have one Vote.[3]

Immediately after they shall be assembled in Consequence of the first Election, they shall be divided as equally as may be into three Classes. The Seats of the Senators of the first Class shall be vacated at the Expiration of the second Year, of the second Class at the Expiration of the fourth Year, and of the third Class at the Expiration of the sixth Year, so that one third may be chosen every second Year; and if Vacancies happen by Resignation, or otherwise, during the Recess of the Legislature of any State, the Executive thereof may make temporary Appointments until the next Meeting of the Legislature, which shall then fill such Vacancies.[4]

No Person shall be a Senator who shall not have attained to the Age of thirty Years, and been nine Years a Citizen of the United States, and who shall not, when elected, be an Inhabitant of that State for which he shall be chosen.

The Vice President of the United States shall be President of the Senate, but shall have no Vote, unless they be equally divided.

The Senate shall chuse their other Officers, and also a President pro tempore, in the Absence of the Vice President, or when he shall exercise the Office of President of the United States.

The Senate shall have the sole Power to try all Impeachments. When sitting for that Purpose, they shall be on Oath or Affirmation. When the President of the United States is tried, the Chief Justice shall preside: And no Person shall be convicted without the Concurrence of two thirds of the Members present.

Judgment in Cases of Impeachment shall not extend further than to removal from Office, and disqualification to hold and enjoy any Office of honor, Trust or Profit under the United

---

[1]Modified by the Sixteenth Amendment.
[2]Replaced by the Fourteenth Amendment.
[3]Superseded by the Seventeenth Amendment.
[4]Modified by the Seventeenth Amendment.

States: but the Party convicted shall nevertheless be liable and subject to Indictment, Trial, Judgment and Punishment, according to Law.

SECTION 4. The Times, Places and Manner of holding Elections for Senators and Representatives, shall be prescribed in each State by the Legislature thereof, but the Congress may at any time by Law make or alter such Regulation, except as to the Places of chusing Senators.

The Congress shall assemble at least once in every Year, and such Meeting shall be on the first Monday in December, unless they shall by Law appoint a different Day.[5]

SECTION 5. Each House shall be the Judge of the Elections, Returns and Qualifications of its own Members, and a Majority of each shall constitute a Quorum to do Business; but a smaller Number may adjourn from day to day, and may be authorized to compel the Attendance of absent Members, in such Manner, and under such Penalties as each House may provide.

Each House may determine the Rules of its Proceedings, punish its Members for disorderly Behaviour, and, with the Concurrence of two thirds, expel a Member.

Each House shall keep a Journal of its Proceedings, and from time to time publish the same, excepting such Parts as may in their Judgment require Secrecy; and the Yeas and Nays of the Members of either House on any question shall, at the Desire of one fifth of those Present, be entered on the Journal.

Neither House, during the Session of Congress, shall, without the Consent of the other, adjourn for more than three days, nor to any other Place than that in which the two Houses shall be sitting.

SECTION 6. The Senators and Representatives shall receive a Compensation for their Services, to be ascertained by Law, and paid out of the Treasury of the United States. They shall in all Cases, except Treason, Felony and Breach of the Peace, be privileged from Arrest during their Attendance at the Session of their respective Houses, and in going to and returning from the same; and for any Speech or Debate in either House, they shall not be questioned in any other Place.

No Senator or Representative shall, during the Time for which he was elected, be appointed to any civil Office under the Authority of the United States, which shall have been created, or the Emoluments whereof shall have been encreased during such time; and no Person holding any Office under the United States, shall be a Member of either House during his Continuance in Office.

SECTION 7. All Bills for raising Revenue shall originate in the House of Representatives; but the Senate may propose or concur with Amendments as on other Bills.

Every Bill which shall have passed the House of Representatives and the Senate shall, before it become a Law, be presented to the President of the United States; If he approve he shall sign it, but if not he shall return it, with his Objections to that House in which it shall have originated, who shall enter the Objections at large on their Journal, and proceed to reconsider it. If after such Reconsideration two thirds of that House shall agree to pass the Bill, it shall be sent, together with the Objections, to the other House, by which it shall likewise be reconsidered, and if approved by two thirds of that House, it shall become a Law. But in all such Cases the Votes of both Houses shall be determined by yeas and Nays, and the Names of the Persons

---

[5]Superseded by the Twentieth Amendment.

voting for and against the Bill shall be entered on the Journal of each House respectively. If any Bill shall not be returned by the President within ten Days (Sundays excepted) after it shall have been presented to him, the Same shall be a Law, in like Manner as if he had signed it, unless the Congress by their Adjournment prevent its Return, in which Case it shall not be a Law.

Every Order, Resolution, or Vote to which the Concurrence of the Senate and House of Representatives may be necessary (except on a question of Adjournment) shall be presented to the President of the United States; and before the Same shall take Effect, shall be approved by him, or being disapproved by him shall be repassed by two thirds of the Senate and House of Representatives, according to the Rules and Limitations prescribed in the Case of a Bill.

SECTION **8.** The Congress shall have power To lay and collect Taxes, Duties, Imposts and Excises, to pay the Debts and provide for the common Defence and general Welfare of the United States; but all Duties, Imposts and Excises shall be uniform throughout the United States;

To borrow Money on the credit of the United States;

To regulate Commerce with foreign Nations, and among the several States, and with the Indian Tribes;

To establish an uniform Rule of Naturalization, and uniform Laws on the subject of Bankruptcies throughout the United States;

To coin Money, regulate the Value thereof, and of foreign Coin, and fix the Standard of Weights and Measures;

To provide for the Punishment of counterfeiting the Securities and current Coin of the United States;

To establish Post Offices and post Roads;

To promote the Progress of Science and useful Arts, by securing for limited Times to Authors and Inventors the exclusive Right to their respective Writings and Discoveries;

To constitute Tribunals inferior to the supreme Court;

To define and punish Piracies and Felonies committed on the high Seas, and Offences against the Law of Nations;

To declare War, grant Letters of Marque and Reprisal, and make Rules concerning Captures on Land and Water;

To raise and support Armies, but no Appropriation of Money to that Use shall be for a longer Term than two Years;

To provide and maintain a Navy;

To make Rules for the Government and Regulation of the land and naval Forces;

To provide for calling forth the Militia to execute the Laws of the Union, suppress Insurrections and repel Invasions;

To provide for organizing, arming, and disciplining, the Militia, and for governing such Part of them as may be employed in the Service of the United States, reserving to the States respectively, the Appointment of the Officers, and the Authority of training the Militia according to the discipline prescribed by Congress;

To exercise exclusive Legislation in all Cases whatsoever, over such District (not exceeding ten Miles square) as may, by Cession of particular States, and the Acceptance of Congress, become the Seat of the Government of the United States, and to exercise like Authority over all

Places purchased by the Consent of the Legislature of the State in which the Same shall be, for the Erection of Forts, Magazines, Arsenals, dock-Yards, and other needful Buildings;—And

To make all Laws which shall be necessary and proper for carrying into Execution the foregoing Powers, and all other Powers vested by this Constitution in the Government of the United States, or in any Department or Officer thereof.

SECTION 9. The Migration or Importation of such Persons as any of the States now existing shall think proper to admit, shall not be prohibited by the Congress prior to the Year one thousand eight hundred and eight, but a Tax or duty may be imposed on such Importation, not exceeding ten dollars for each Person.

The Privilege of the Writ of Habeas Corpus shall not be suspended, unless when in Cases of Rebellion or Invasion the public Safety may require it.

No Bill of Attainder or ex post facto Law shall be passed.

No Capitation, or other direct, Tax shall be laid, unless in Proportion to the Census or Enumeration herein before directed to be taken.

No Tax or Duty shall be laid on Articles exported from any State.

No Preference shall be given by any Regulation of Commerce or Revenue to the Ports of one State over those of another: nor shall Vessels bound to, or from, one State, be obliged to enter, clear, or pay Duties in another.

No Money shall be drawn from the Treasury, but in Consequence of Appropriations made by Law, and a regular Statement and Account of the Receipts and Expenditures of all public Money shall be published from time to time.

No Title of Nobility shall be granted by the United States: And no Person holding any Office of Profit or Trust under them, shall, without the Consent of the Congress, accept of any present, Emolument, Office, or Title, of any kind whatever, from any King, Prince, or foreign State.

SECTION 10. No State shall enter into any Treaty, Alliance, or Confederation; grant Letters of Marque and Reprisal; coin Money; emit Bills of Credit; make any Thing but gold and silver Coin a Tender in Payment of Debts; pass any Bill of Attainder, ex post facto Law, or Law impairing the Obligation of Contracts, or grant any Title of Nobility.

No State shall, without the Consent of the Congress, lay any Imposts or Duties on Imports or Exports, except what may be absolutely necessary for executing its inspection Laws: and the net Produce of all Duties and Imposts, laid by any State on Imports or Exports, shall be for the Use of the Treasury of the United States; and all such Laws shall be subject to the Revision and Controul of the Congress.

No State shall, without the Consent of Congress, lay any Duty of Tonnage, keep Troops, or Ships of War in time of Peace, enter into any Agreement or Compact with another State, or with a foreign Power, or engage in War, unless actually invaded, or in such imminent Danger as will not admit of delay.

ARTICLE II.

SECTION 1. The executive Power shall be vested in a President of the United States of America. He shall hold his Office during the Term of four Years, and, together with the Vice President, chosen for the same Term, be elected, as follows:

Each State shall appoint, in such Manner as the Legislature thereof may direct, a Number of Electors, equal to the whole Number of Senators and Representatives to which the State may be entitled in the Congress: but no Senator or Representative, or Person holding an Office of Trust or Profit under the United States, shall be appointed an Elector.

The Electors shall meet in their respective States, and vote by Ballot for two Persons, of whom one at least shall not be an Inhabitant of the same State with themselves. And they shall make a List of all the Persons voted for, and of the Number of Votes for each; which List they shall sign and certify, and transmit sealed to the Seat of the Government of the United States, directed to the President of the Senate. The President of the Senate shall, in the Presence of the Senate and House of Representatives, open all the Certificates, and the Votes shall then be counted. The Person having the greatest Number of Votes shall be the President, if such Number be a Majority of the whole Number of Electors appointed; and if there be more than one who have such Majority, and have an equal Number of Votes, then the House of Representatives shall immediately chuse by Ballot one of them for President; and if no Person have a Majority, then from the five highest on the List the said House shall in like Manner chuse the President. But in chusing the President, the Votes shall be taken by States, the Representation from each State having one Vote; A quorum for this Purpose shall consist of a Member or Members from two thirds of the States, and a Majority of all the States shall be necessary to a Choice. In every Case, after the Choice of the President, the Person having the greatest Number of Votes of the Electors shall be the Vice President. But if there should remain two or more who have equal Votes, the Senate shall chuse from them by Ballot the Vice President.[6]

The Congress may determine the Time of chusing the Electors, and the Day on which they shall give their Votes; which Day shall be the same throughout the United States.

No Person except a natural born Citizen, or a Citizen of the United States, at the time of the Adoption of this Constitution, shall be eligible to the Office of President, neither shall any Person be eligible to that Office who shall not have attained to the Age of thirty five Years, and been fourteen Years a Resident within the United States.

In Case of the Removal of the President from Office, or of his Death, Resignation, or Inability to discharge the Powers and Duties of the said Office, the Same shall devolve on the Vice President, and the Congress may by Law provide for the Case of Removal, Death, Resignation or Inability, both of the President and Vice President, declaring what Officer shall then act as President, and such Officer shall act accordingly, until the Disability be removed, or a President shall be elected.[7]

The President shall, at stated Times, receive for his Services, a Compensation, which shall neither be encreased nor diminished during the Period for which he shall have been elected, and he shall not receive within that Period any other Emolument from the United States, or any of them.

Before he enter on the Execution of his Office, he shall take the following Oath or Affirmation:—
"I do solemnly swear (or affirm) that I will faithfully execute the Office of President of the United States, and will to the best of my Ability, preserve, protect and defend the Constitution of the United States."

SECTION 2. The President shall be Commander in Chief of the Army and Navy of the United States, and of the Militia of the several States, when called into the actual Service of the United States; he may require the Opinion, in writing, of the principal Officer in each of the executive Departments, upon any Subject relating to the Duties of their respective Offices, and he shall have Power to grant Reprieves and Pardons for Offences against the United States, except in Cases of Impeachment.

[6]Superseded by the Twelfth Amendment.
[7]Modified by the Twenty-fifth Amendment.

He shall have Power, by and with the Advice and Consent of the Senate, to make Treaties, provided two thirds of the Senators present concur; and he shall nominate, and by and with the Advice and Consent of the Senate, shall appoint Ambassadors, other public Ministers and Consuls, Judges of the supreme Court, and all other Officers of the United States, whose Appointments are not herein otherwise provided for, and which shall be established by Law; but the Congress may by Law vest the Appointment of such inferior Officers, as they think proper, in the President alone, in the Courts of Law, or in the Heads of Departments.

The President shall have Power to fill up all Vacancies that may happen during the Recess of the Senate, by granting Commissions which shall expire at the End of their next Session.

SECTION 3. He shall from time to time give the Congress Information of the State of the Union, and recommend to their Consideration such Measures as he shall judge necessary and expedient; he may, on extraordinary Occasions, convene both Houses, or either of them, and in Case of Disagreement between them, with Respect to the Time of Adjournment, he may adjourn them to such Time as he shall think proper; he shall receive Ambassadors and other public Ministers; he shall take Care that the Laws be faithfully executed, and shall Commission all the Officers of the United States.

SECTION 4. The President, Vice President and all civil Officers of the United States, shall be removed from Office on Impeachment for, and Conviction of, Treason, Bribery, or other high Crimes and Misdemeanors.

ARTICLE III.

SECTION 1. The judicial Power of the United States, shall be vested in one supreme Court, and in such inferior Courts as the Congress may from time to time ordain and establish. The Judges, both of the supreme and inferior Courts, shall hold their Offices during good Behaviour, and shall, at stated Times, receive for their Services, a Compensation, which shall not be diminished during their Continuance in Office.

SECTION 2. The judicial Power shall extend to all Cases, in Law and Equity, arising under this Constitution, the Laws of the United States, and Treaties made, or which shall be made, under their Authority;—to all Cases affecting Ambassadors, other public Ministers and Consuls;—to all Cases of admiralty and maritime Jurisdiction;—to Controversies to which the United States shall be a Party;—to Controversies between two or more States;—between a State and Citizens of another State;[8]—between Citizens of different States,—between Citizens of the same State claiming Lands under Grants of different States, and between a State, or the Citizens thereof, and foreign States, Citizens or Subjects.

In all Cases affecting Ambassadors, other public Ministers and Consuls, and those in which a State shall be Party, the supreme Court shall have original Jurisdiction. In all the other Cases before mentioned, the supreme Court shall have appellate Jurisdiction, both as to Law and Fact, with such Exceptions, and under such Regulations as the Congress shall make.

The Trial of all Crimes, except in Cases of Impeachment, shall be by Jury; and such Trial shall be held in the State where the said Crimes shall have been committed; but when not committed within any State, the Trial shall be at such Place or Places as the Congress may by Law have directed.

SECTION 3. Treason against the United States, shall consist only in levying War against

[8]Modified by the Eleventh Amendment.

them, or in adhering to their Enemies, giving them Aid and Comfort. No Person shall be convicted of Treason unless on the Testimony of two Witnesses to the same overt Act, or on Confession in open Court.

The Congress shall have Power to declare the Punishment of Treason, but no Attainder of Treason shall work Corruption of Blood, or Forfeiture except during the Life of the Person attainted.

ARTICLE IV.

SECTION 1. Full Faith and Credit shall be given in each State to the public Acts, Records, and judicial Proceedings of every other State. And the Congress may by general Laws prescribe the Manner in which such Acts, Records and Proceedings shall be proved, and the Effect thereof.

SECTION 2. The Citizens of each State shall be entitled to all Privileges and Immunities of Citizens in the several States.

A Person charged in any State with Treason, Felony, or other Crime, who shall flee from Justice, and be found in another State, shall on Demand of the executive Authority of the State from which he fled, be delivered up, to be removed to the State having Jurisdiction of the Crime.

No Person held to Service or Labour in one State, under the Laws thereof, escaping into another, shall, in Consequence of any Law or Regulation therein, be discharged from such Service or Labour, but shall be delivered up on Claim of the Party to whom such Service or Labour may be due.

SECTION 3. New States may be admitted by the Congress into this Union; but no new State shall be formed or erected within the Jurisdiction of any other State, nor any State be formed by the Junction of two or more States, or Parts of States, without the Consent of the Legislatures of the States concerned as well as of the Congress.

The Congress shall have Power to dispose of and make all needful Rules and Regulations respecting the Territory or other Property belonging to the United States; and nothing in this Constitution shall be so construed as to Prejudice any Claims of the United States, or of any particular State.

SECTION 4. The United States shall guarantee to every State in this Union a Republican Form of Government, and shall protect each of them against Invasion; and on Application of the Legislature, or of the Executive (when the Legislature cannot be convened) against domestic Violence.

ARTICLE V.

The Congress, whenever two thirds of both Houses shall deem it necessary, shall propose Amendments to this Constitution, or, on the Application of the Legislatures of two thirds of the several States, shall call a Convention for proposing Amendments, which, in either Case, shall be valid to all Intents and Purposes, as Part of this Constitution, when ratified by the Legislatures of three fourths of the several States, or by Conventions in three fourths thereof, as the one or the other Mode of Ratification may be proposed by the Congress; Provided that no Amendment which may be made prior to the Year One thousand eight hundred and eight shall in any Manner affect the first and fourth Clauses in the Ninth Section of the first Article; and that no State, without its Consent, shall be deprived of its equal Suffrage in the Senate.

ARTICLE VI.

All Debts contracted and Engagements entered into, before the Adoption of this Constitution, shall be as valid against the United States under this Constitution, as under the Confederation.

This Constitution, and the Laws of the United States which shall be made in Pursuance thereof; and all Treaties made, or which shall be made, under the Authority of the United States, shall be the supreme Law of the Land; and the Judges in every State shall be bound thereby, any Thing in the Constitution or Laws of any State to the Contrary notwithstanding.

The Senators and Representatives before mentioned, and the Members of the several State Legislatures, and all executive and judicial Officers, both of the United States and of the several States, shall be bound by Oath or Affirmation, to support this Constitution; but no religious Test shall ever be required as a Qualification to any Office or public Trust under the United States.

ARTICLE VII.

The Ratification of the Conventions of nine States, shall be sufficient for the Establishment of this Constitution between the States so ratifying the Same.

Done in Convention by the Unanimous Consent of the States present the Seventeenth Day of September in the Year of our Lord one thousand seven hundred and Eighty seven and of the Independence of the United States of America the Twelfth. In witness whereof We have hereunto subscribed our Names,

Articles in Addition to, and Amendment of, the Constitution of the United States of America, Proposed by Congress, and Ratified by the Legislatures of the Several States, Pursuant to the Fifth Article of the Original Constitution.

AMENDMENT I[9]

Congress shall make no law respecting an establishment of religion, or prohibiting the free exercise thereof; or abridging the freedom of speech, or of the press; or the right of the people peaceably to assemble, and to petition the Government for a redress of grievances.

AMENDMENT II

A well regulated Militia, being necessary to the security of a free State, the right of the people to keep and bear Arms shall not be infringed.

AMENDMENT III

No Soldier shall, in time of peace, be quartered in any house, without the consent of the Owner, nor in time of war, but in a manner to be prescribed by law.

---

[9]The first ten amendments were passed by Congress September 25, 1789. They were ratified by three-fourths of the states December 15, 1791.

AMENDMENT IV

The right of the people to be secure in their persons, houses, papers, and effects, against unreasonable searches and seizures, shall not be violated, and no Warrants shall issue, but upon probable cause, supported by Oath or affirmation, and particularly describing the place to be searched, and the persons or things to be seized.

AMENDMENT V

No person shall be held to answer for a capital or otherwise infamous crime, unless on a presentment or indictment of a Grand Jury, except in cases arising in the land or naval forces, or in the Militia, when in actual service in time of War or public danger; nor shall any person be subject for the same offence to be twice put in jeopardy of life or limb; nor shall be compelled in any criminal case to be a witness against himself, nor be deprived of life, liberty, or property, without due process of law; nor shall private property be taken for public use, without just compensation.

AMENDMENT VI

In all criminal prosecutions, the accused shall enjoy the right to a speedy and public trial, by an impartial jury of the State and district wherein the crime shall have been committed, which district shall have been previously ascertained by law, and to be informed of the nature and cause of the accusation; to be confronted with the witnesses against him; to have compulsory process for obtaining witnesses in his favor, and to have the Assistance of Counsel for his defence.

AMENDMENT VII

In suits at common law, where the value in controversy shall exceed twenty dollars, the right of trial by jury shall be preserved, and no fact tried by a jury, shall be otherwise reexamined in any Court of the United States, than according to the rules of the common law.

AMENDMENT VIII

Excessive bail shall not be required, nor excessive fines imposed, nor cruel and unusual punishments inflicted.

AMENDMENT IX

The enumeration in the Constitution, of certain rights, shall not be construed to deny or disparage others retained by the people.

AMENDMENT X

The powers not delegated to the United States by the Constitution; nor prohibited by it to the States, are reserved to the States respectively, or to the people.

AMENDMENT XI[10]

The Judicial power of the United States shall not be construed to extend to any suit in law or equity, commenced or prosecuted against one of the United States by Citizens of another State, or by Citizens or Subjects of any Foreign State.

AMENDMENT XII[11]

The Electors shall meet in their respective States and vote by ballot for President and Vice-President, one of whom, at least, shall not be an inhabitant of the same State with themselves; they shall name in their ballots the person voted for as President, and in distinct ballots the person voted for as Vice-President, and they shall make distinct lists of all persons voted for as President, and of all persons voted for as Vice-President, and of the number of votes for each, which lists they shall sign and certify, and transmit sealed to the seat of the government of the United States, directed to the President of the Senate;—The President of the Senate shall, in the presence of the Senate and House of Representatives, open all the certificates and the votes shall then be counted;—The person having the greatest number of votes for President, shall be the President, if such number be a majority of the whole number of Electors appointed; and if no person have such majority, then from the persons having the highest numbers not exceeding three on the list of those voted for as President, the House of Representatives shall choose immediately, by ballot, the President. But in choosing the President, the votes shall be taken by states, the representation from each state having one vote; a quorum for this purpose shall consist of a member or members from two-thirds of the states, and a majority of all the states shall be necessary to a choice. And if the House of Representatives shall not choose a President whenever the right of choice shall devolve upon them, before the fourth day of March next following, then the Vice-President shall act as President, as in the case of the death or other constitutional disability of the President.—The person having the greatest number of votes as Vice-President, shall be the Vice-President, if such number be a majority of the whole number of Electors appointed, and if no person have a majority, then from the two highest numbers on the list, the Senate shall choose the Vice-President; a quorum for the purpose shall consist of two-thirds of the whole number of Senators, and a majority of the whole number shall be necessary to a choice. But no person constitutionally ineligible to the office of President shall be eligible to that of Vice-President of the United States.

AMENDMENT XIII[12]

SECTION 1. Neither slavery nor involuntary servitude, except as a punishment for crime whereof the party shall have been duly convicted, shall exist within the United States, or any place subject to their jurisdiction.

SECTION 2. Congress shall have power to enforce this article by appropriate legislation.

---

[10]Passed March 4, 1794. Ratified January 23, 1795.
[11]Passed December 9, 1803. Ratified June 15, 1804.
[12]Passed January 31, 1865. Ratified December 6, 1865.

AMENDMENT XIV[13]

SECTION 1. All persons born or naturalized in the United States, and subject to the jurisdiction thereof, are citizens of the United States and of the State wherein they reside. No State shall make or enforce any law which shall abridge the privileges or immunities of citizens of the United States; nor shall any State deprive any person of life, liberty, or property, without due process of law; nor deny to any person within its jurisdiction the equal protection of the laws.

SECTION 2. Representatives shall be apportioned among the several States according to their respective numbers, counting the whole number of persons in each State, excluding Indians not taxed. But when the right to vote at any election for the choice of electors for President and Vice-President of the United States, Representatives in Congress, the Executive and Judicial officers of a State, or the members of the Legislature thereof, is denied to any of the male inhabitants of such State, being twenty-one years of age, and citizens of the United States, or in any way abridged, except for participation in rebellion, or other crime, the basis of representation therein shall be reduced in the proportion which the number of such male citizens shall bear to the whole number of male citizens twenty-one years of age in such State.

SECTION 3. No person shall be a Senator or Representative in Congress, or elector of President and Vice-President, or hold any office, civil or military, under the United States, or under any State, who, having previously taken an oath, as a member of Congress, or as an officer of the United States, or as a member of any State legislature, or as an executive or judicial officer of any State, to support the Constitution of the United States, shall have engaged in insurrection or rebellion against the same, or given aid or comfort to the enemies thereof. But Congress may by a vote of two-thirds of each House, remove such disability.

SECTION 4. The validity of the public debt of the United States, authorized by law, including debts incurred for payment of pensions and bounties for services in suppressing insurrection or rebellion, shall not be questioned. But neither the United States nor any State shall assume or pay any debt or obligation incurred in aid of insurrection or rebellion against the United States, or any claim for the loss or emancipation of any slave; but all such debts, obligations, and claims shall be held illegal and void.

SECTION 5. The Congress shall have the power to enforce, by appropriate legislation, the provisions of this article.

AMENDMENT XV[14]

SECTION 1. The right of citizens of the United States to vote shall not be denied or abridged by the United States or by any State on account of race, color, or previous conditions of servitude—

SECTION 2. The Congress shall have power to enforce this article by appropriate legislation.

[13]Passed June 13, 1866. Ratified July 9, 1868.
[14]Passed February 26, 1869. Ratified February 2, 1870.

AMENDMENT XVI[15]

The Congress shall have power to lay and collect taxes on incomes, from whatever source derived, without apportionment among the several States, and without regard to any census or enumeration.

AMENDMENT XVII[16]

The Senate of the United States shall be composed of two Senators from each State, elected by the people thereof, for six years; and each Senator shall have one vote. The electors in each State shall have the qualifications requisite for electors of the most numerous branch of the State legislatures.

When vacancies happen in the representation of any State in the Senate, the executive authority of such State shall issue writs of election to fill such vacancies: *Provided,* That the legislature of any State may empower the executive thereof to make temporary appointments until the people fill the vacancies by election as the legislature may direct.

This amendment shall not be so construed as to affect the election or term of any Senator chosen before it becomes valid as part of the Constitution.

AMENDMENT XVIII[17]

SECTION 1. After one year from the ratification of this article the manufacture, sale, or transportation of intoxicating liquors within, the importation thereof into, or the exportation thereof from the United States and all territory subject to the jurisdiction thereof for beverage purposes is hereby prohibited.

SECTION 2. The Congress and the several States shall have concurrent power to enforce this article by appropriate legislation.

SECTION 3. This article shall be inoperative unless it shall have been ratified as an amendment to the Constitution by the legislatures of the several States, as provided in the Constitution, within seven years from the date of the submission hereof to the States by the Congress.

AMENDMENT XIX[18]

The right of citizens of the United States to vote shall not be denied or abridged by the United States or by any State on account of sex.

Congress shall have power to enforce this article by appropriate legislation.

AMENDMENT XX[19]

SECTION 1. The terms of the President and Vice-President shall end at noon on the 20th day of January, and the terms of Senators and Representatives at noon on the 3d day of January, of

---

[15]Passed July 12, 1909. Ratified February 3, 1913.
[16]Passed May 13, 1912. Ratified April 8, 1913.
[17]Passed December 18, 1917. Ratified January 16, 1919.
[18]Passed June 4, 1919. Ratified August 18, 1920.
[19]Passed March 2, 1932. Ratified January 23, 1933.

the years in which such terms would have ended if this article had not been ratified; and the terms of their successors shall then begin.

SECTION 2. The Congress shall assemble at least once in every year, and such meeting shall begin at noon on the 3d day of January, unless they shall by law appoint a different day.

SECTION 3. If, at the time fixed for the beginning of the term of the President, the President elect shall have died, the Vice-President elect shall become President. If a President shall not have been chosen before the time fixed for the beginning of his term, or if the President elect shall have failed to qualify, then the Vice-President elect shall act as President until a President shall have qualified; and the Congress may by law provide for the case wherein neither a President elect nor a Vice-President elect shall have qualified, declaring who shall then act as President, or the manner in which one who is to act shall be selected, and such person shall act accordingly until a President or Vice-President shall have qualified.

SECTION 4. The Congress may by law provide for the case of the death of any of the persons from whom the House of Representatives may choose a President whenever the right of choice shall have devolved upon them, and for the case of the death of any of the persons from whom the Senate may choose a Vice-President whenever the right of choice shall have devolved upon them.

SECTION 5. Sections 1 and 2 shall take effect on the 15th day of October following the ratification of this article.

SECTION 6. This article shall be inoperative unless it shall have been ratified as an amendment to the Constitution by the legislatures of three-fourths of the several States within seven years from the date of its submission.

AMENDMENT XXI[20]

SECTION 1. The eighteenth article of amendment to the Constitution of the United States is hereby repealed.

SECTION 2. The transportation or importation into any State, Territory, or possession of the United States for delivery or use therein of intoxicating liquors, in violation of the laws thereof, is hereby prohibited.

SECTION 3. This article shall be inoperative unless it shall have been ratified as an amendment to the Constitution by conventions in the several States, as provided in the Constitution, within seven years from the date of the submission hereof to the States by the Congress.

AMENDMENT XXII[21]

No person shall be elected to the office of the President more than twice, and no person who has held the office of President, or acted as President, for more than two years of a term to which some other person was elected President shall be elected to the office of the President more than once.

But this Article shall not apply to any person holding the office of President when this Article was proposed by the Congress, and shall not prevent any person who may be holding the

[20]Passed February 20, 1933. Ratified December 5, 1933.
[21]Passed March 12, 1947. Ratified March 1, 1951.

office of President, or acting as President, during the term within which this Article becomes operative from holding the office of President or acting as President during the remainder of such term.

AMENDMENT XXIII[22]

SECTION 1. The District constituting the seat of Government of the United States shall appoint in such manner as the Congress may direct:

A number of electors of President and Vice President equal to the whole number of Senators and Representatives in Congress to which the District would be entitled if it were a State, but in no event more than the least populous State; they shall be in addition to those appointed by the States, but they shall be considered, for the purposes of the election of President and Vice President, to be electors appointed by the State; and they shall meet in the District and perform such duties as provided by the twelfth article of amendment.

SECTION 2. The Congress shall have power to enforce this article by appropriate legislation.

AMENDMENT XXIV[23]

SECTION 1. The right of citizens of the United States to vote in any primary or other election for President or Vice President, or for Senator or Representative in Congress, shall not be denied or abridged by the United States or any State by reason of failure to pay any poll tax or other tax.

SECTION 2. The Congress shall have power to enforce this article by appropriate legislation.

AMENDMENT XXV[24]

SECTION 1. In case of the removal of the President from office or of his death or resignation, the Vice President shall become President.

SECTION 2. Whenever there is a vacancy in the office of the Vice President, the President shall nominate a Vice President who shall take office upon confirmation by a majority vote of both Houses of Congress.

SECTION 3. Whenever the President transmits to the President pro tempore of the Senate and the Speaker of the House of Representatives his written declaration that he is unable to discharge the powers and duties of his office, and until he transmits them a written declaration to the contrary, such powers and duties shall be discharged by the Vice President as Acting President.

SECTION 4. Whenever the Vice President and a majority of either the principal officers of the executive department or of such other body as Congress may by law provide, transmit to the President pro tempore of the Senate and the Speaker of the House of Representatives their written declaration that the President is unable to discharge the powers and duties of his office, the Vice President shall immediately assume the powers and duties of the office of Acting President

---

[22]Passed June 16, 1960. Ratified April 3, 1961.
[23]Passed August 27, 1962. Ratified January 23, 1964.
[24]Passed July 6, 1965. Ratified February 11, 1967.

Thereafter, when the President transmits to the President pro tempore of the Senate and the Speaker of the House of Representatives his written declaration that no inability exists, he shall resume the powers and duties of his office unless the Vice President and a majority of either the principal officers of the executive department or of such other body as Congress may by law provide, transmit within four days to the President pro tempore of the Senate and the Speaker of the House of Representatives their written declaration that the President is unable to discharge the powers and duties of his office. Thereupon Congress shall decide the issue, assembling within forty-eight hours for that purpose if not in session. If the Congress, within twenty-one days after receipt of the latter written declaration, or, if Congress is not in session, within twenty-one days after Congress is required to assemble, determines by two-thirds vote of both Houses that the President is unable to discharge the powers and duties of his office, the Vice President shall continue to discharge the same as Acting President; otherwise, the President shall resume the powers and duties of his office.

AMENDMENT XXVI[25]

SECTION 1. The right of citizens of the United States, who are eighteen years of age or older, to vote shall not be denied or abridged by the United States or by any State on account of age.

SECTION 2. The Congress shall have power to enforce this article by appropriate legislation.

AMENDMENT XXVII[26]

No law, varying the compensation for the service of the Senators and Representatives, shall take effect, until an election of Representatives shall have intervened.

[25]Passed March 23, 1971. Ratified July 5, 1971.
[26]Passed September 25, 1789. Ratified May 7, 1992

Admission of States

Order of Admission	State	Date of Admission	Order of Admission	State	Date of Admission
1	Delaware	December 7, 1787	26	Michigan	January 26, 1837
2	Pennsylvania	December 12, 1787	27	Florida	March 3, 1845
3	New Jersey	December 18, 1787	28	Texas	December 29, 1845
4	Georgia	January 2, 1788	29	Iowa	December 28, 1846
5	Connecticut	January 9, 1788	30	Wisconsin	May 29, 1848
6	Massachusetts	February 6, 1788	31	California	September 9, 1850
7	Maryland	April 28, 1788	32	Minnesota	May 11, 1858
8	South Carolina	May 23, 1788	33	Oregon	February 14, 1859
9	New Hampshire	June 21, 1788	34	Kansas	January 29, 1861
10	Virginia	June 25, 1788	35	West Virginia	June 20, 1863
11	New York	July 26, 1788	36	Nevada	October 31, 1864
12	North Carolina	November 21, 1789	37	Nebraska	March 1, 1867
13	Rhode Island	May 29, 1790	38	Colorado	August 1, 1876
14	Vermont	March 4, 1791	39	North Dakota	November 2, 1889
15	Kentucky	June 1, 1792	40	South Dakota	November 2, 1889
16	Tennessee	June 1, 1796	41	Montana	November 8, 1889
17	Ohio	March 1, 1803	42	Washington	November 11, 1889
18	Louisiana	April 30, 1812	43	Idaho	July 3, 1890
19	Indiana	December 11, 1816	44	Wyoming	July 10, 1890
20	Mississippi	December 10, 1817	45	Utah	January 4, 1896
21	Illinois	December 3, 1818	46	Oklahoma	November 16, 1907
22	Alabama	December 14, 1819	47	New Mexico	January 6, 1912
23	Maine	March 15, 1820	48	Arizona	February 14, 1912
24	Missouri	August 10, 1821	49	Alaska	January 3, 1959
25	Arkansas	June 15, 1836	50	Hawaii	August 21, 1959

POPULATION OF THE UNITED STATES

YEAR	TOTAL POPULATION	NUMBER PER SQUARE MILE	YEAR	TOTAL POPULATION	NUMBER PER SQUARE MILE	YEAR	TOTAL POPULATION	NUMBER PER SQUARE MILE
1790	3,929	4.5	1817	8,899		1844	19,569	
1791	4,056		1818	9,139		1845	20,182	
1792	4,194		1819	9,379		1846	20,794	
1793	4,332		1820	9,618	5.6	1847	21,406	
1794	4,469		1821	9,939		1848	22,018	
1795	4,607		1822	10,268		1849	22,631	
1796	4,745		1823	10,596		1850	23,261	7.9
1797	4,883		1824	10,924		1851	24,086	
1798	5,021		1825	11,252		1852	24,911	
1799	5,159		1826	11,580		1853	25,736	
1800	5,297	6.1	1827	11,909		1854	26,561	
1801	5,486		1828	12,237		1855	27,386	
1802	5,679		1829	12,565		1856	28,212	
1803	5,872		1830	12,901	7.4	1857	29,037	
1804	5,065		1831	13,321		1858	29,862	
1805	6,258		1832	13,742		1859	30,687	
1806	6,451		1833	14,162		1860	31,513	10.6
1807	6,644		1834	14,582		1861	32,351	
1808	6,838		1835	15,003		1862	33,188	
1809	7,031		1836	15,423		1863	34,026	
1810	7,224	4.3	1837	15,843		1864	34,863	
1811	7,460		1838	16,264		1865	35,701	
1812	7,700		1839	16,684		1866	36,538	
1813	7,939		1840	17,120	9.8	1867	37,376	
1814	8,179		1841	17,733		1868	38,213	
1815	8,419		1842	18,345		1869	39,051	
1816	8,659		1843	18,957		1870	39,905	13.4

Figures are from *Historical Statistics of the United States, Colonial Times to 1957* (1961), pp. 7, 8; *Statistical Abstract of the United States: 1974,* p. 5, Census Bureau for 1974 and 1975; and *Statistical Abstract of the United States: 1988,* p. 7.

Note: Population figures are in thousands. Density figures are for land area of continental United States.

(continued)

YEAR	TOTAL POPULATION	NUMBER PER SQUARE MILE	YEAR	TOTAL POPULATION	NUMBER PER SQUARE MILE	YEAR	TOTAL POPULATION[1]	NUMBER PER SQUARE MILE
1871	40,938		1900	76,094	25.6	1929	121,700	
1872	41,972		1901	77,585		1930	122,775	41.2
1873	43,006		1902	79,160		1931	124,040	
1874	44,040		1903	80,632		1932	124,840	
1875	45,073		1904	82,165		1933	125,579	
1876	46,107		1905	83,820		1934	126,374	
1877	47,141		1906	85,437		1935	127,250	
1878	48,174		1907	87,000		1936	128,053	
1879	49,208		1908	88,709		1937	128,825	
1880	50,262	16.9	1909	90,492		1938	129,825	
1881	51,542		1910	92,407	31.0	1939	130,880	
1882	52,821		1911	93,868		1940	131,669	44.2
1883	54,100		1912	95,331		1941	133,894	
1884	55,379		1913	97,227		1942	135,361	
1885	56,658		1914	99,118		1943	137,250	
1886	57,938		1915	100,549		1944	138,916	
1887	59,217		1916	101,966		1945	140,468	
1888	60,496		1917	103,414		1946	141,936	
1889	61,775		1918	104,550		1947	144,698	
1890	63,056	21.2	1919	105,063		1948	147,208	
1891	64,361		1920	106,466	35.6	1949	149,767	
1892	65,666		1921	108,541		1950	150,697	50.7
1893	66,970		1922	110,055		1951	154,878	
1894	68,275		1923	111,950		1952	157,553	
1895	69,580		1924	114,113		1953	160,184	
1896	70,885		1925	115,832		1954	163,026	
1897	72,189		1926	117,399		1955	165,931	
1898	73,494		1927	119,038		1956	168,903	
1899	74,799		1928	120,501		1957	171,984	

[1]Figures after 1940 represent total population including armed forces abroad, except in official census years.

Year	Total Population[1]	Number per Square Mile	Year	Total Population[1]	Number per Square Mile	Year	Total Population[1]	Number per Square Mile
1958	174,882		1972	208,842		1986	241,596	
1959	177,830		1973	210,396		1987	234,773	
1960	178,464	60.1	1974	211,894		1988	245,051	
1961	183,672		1975	213,631		1989	247,350	
1962	186,504		1976	215,152		1990	250,122	
1963	189,197		1977	216,880		1991	254,521	
1964	191,833		1978	218,717		1992	245,908	
1965	194,237		1979	220,584		1993	257,908	
1966	196,485		1980	226,546	64.0	1994	261,875	
1967	198,629		1981	230,138		1995	263,434	
1968	200,619		1982	232,520		1996	266,096	
1969	202,599		1983	234,799		1997	267,901	
1970	203,875	57.5[2]	1984	237,001		1998	269,501	
1971	207,045		1985	239,283		1999	274,114	

[1]Figures after 1940 represent total population including armed forces abroad, except in official census years.
[2]Figure includes Alaska and Hawaii.

YEAR	NUMBER OF STATES	CANDIDATES[1]
1789	11	**George Washington** John Adams Minor candidates
1792	15	**George Washington** John Adams George Clinton Minor candidates
1796	16	**John Adams** Thomas Jefferson Thomas Pinckney Aaron Burr Minor candidates
1800	16	**Thomas Jefferson** Aaron Burr John Adams Charles C. Pinckney John Jay
1804	17	**Thomas Jefferson** Charles C. Pinckney
1808	17	**James Madison** Charles C. Pinckney George Clinton
1812	18	**James Madison** DeWitt Clinton
1816	19	**James Monroe** Rufus King
1820	24	**James Monroe** John Quincy Adams
1824	24	**John Quincy Adams** Andrew Jackson William H. Crawford Henry Clay
1828	24	**Andrew Jackson** John Quincy Adams

[1]Before the passage of the Twelfth Amendment in 1804, the Electoral College voted for two presidential candidates; the runner-up became vice president. Figures are from *Historical Statistics of the United States, Colonial Times to 1957* (1961), pp. 682–683; and the U.S. Department of Justice.

Parties	Popular vote	Electoral vote	Percentage of popular vote[2]
No party designations		69	
		34	
		35	
No party designations		132	
		77	
		50	
		5	
Federalist		71	
Democratic-Republican		68	
Federalist		59	
Democratic-Republican		30	
		48	
Democratic-Republican		73	
Democratic-Republican		73	
Federalist		65	
Federalist		64	
Federalist		1	
Democratic-Republican		162	
Federalist		14	
Democratic-Republican		122	
Federalist		47	
Democratic-Republican		6	
Democratic-Republican		128	
Federalist		89	
Democratic-Republican		183	
Federalist		34	
Democratic-Republican		231	
Independent Republican		1	
Democratic-Republican	108,740	84	30.5
Democratic-Republican	153,544	99	43.1
Democratic-Republican	46,618	41	13.1
Democratic-Republican	47,136	37	13.2
Democratic	647,286	178	56.0
National Republican	508,064	83	44.0

[2]Candidates receiving less than 1 percent of the popular vote have been omitted. For that reason the percentage of popular vote given for any election year may not total 100 percent.

Year	Number of states	Candidates
1832	24	**Andrew Jackson** Henry Clay William Wirt John Floyd
1836	26	**Martin Van Buren** William H. Harrison Hugh L. White Daniel Webster W. P. Mangum
1840	26	**William H. Harrison** Martin Van Buren
1844	26	**James K. Polk** Henry Clay James G. Birney
1848	30	**Zachary Taylor** Lewis Cass Martin Van Buren
1852	31	**Franklin Pierce** Winfield Scott John P. Hale
1856	31	**James Buchanan** John C. Frémont Millard Fillmore
1860	33	**Abraham Lincoln** Stephen A. Douglas John C. Breckinridge John Bell
1864	36	**Abraham Lincoln** George B. McClellan
1868	37	**Ulysses S. Grant** Horatio Seymour
1872	37	**Ulysses S. Grant** Horace Greeley
1876	38	**Rutherford B. Hayes** Samuel J. Tilden

PARTIES	POPULAR VOTE	ELECTORAL VOTE	PERCENTAGE OF POPULAR VOTE[1]
Democratic	687,502	219	55.0
National Republican	530,189	49	42.4
Anti-Masonic }	33,108	7	2.6
National Republican }		11	
Democratic	765,483	170	50.9
Whig ⎫		73	
Whig ⎬	739,795	26	
Whig ⎪		14	
Whig ⎭		11	
Whig	1,274,624	234	53.1
Democratic	1,127,781	60	46.9
Democratic	1,338,464	170	49.6
Whig	1,300,097	105	48.1
Liberty	62,300		2.3
Whig	1,360,967	163	47.4
Democratic	1,222,342	127	42.5
Free Soil	291,263		10.1
Democratic	1,601,117	254	50.9
Whig	1,385,453	42	44.1
Free Soil	155,825		5.0
Democratic	1,832,955	174	45.3
Republican	1,339,932	114	33.1
American	871,731	8	21.6
Republican	1,865,593	180	39.8
Democratic	1,382,713	12	29.5
Democratic	848,356	72	18.1
Constitutional Union	592,906	39	12.6
Republican	2,206,938	212	55.0
Democratic	1,803,787	21	45.0
Republican	3,013,421	214	52.7
Democratic	2,706,829	80	47.3
Republican	3,596,745	286	55.6
Democratic	2,843,446	2	43.9
Republican	4,036,572	185	48.0
Democratic	4,284,020	184	51.0

[1]Candidates receiving less than 1 percent of the popular vote have been omitted. For that reason the percentage of popular vote given for any election year may not total 100 percent.

[2]Greeley died shortly after the election; the electors supporting him then divided their votes among minor candidates.

YEAR	NUMBER OF STATES	CANDIDATES
1880	38	**James A. Garfield** Winfield S. Hancock James B. Weaver
1884	38	**Grover Cleveland** James G. Blaine Benjamin F. Butler John P. St. John
1888	38	**Benjamin Harrison** Grover Cleveland Clinton B. Fisk Anson J. Streeter
1892	44	**Grover Cleveland** Benjamin Harrison James B. Weaver John Bidwell
1896	45	**William McKinley** William J. Bryan
1900	45	**William McKinley** William J. Bryan John C. Wooley
1904	45	**Theodore Roosevelt** Alton B. Parker Eugene V. Debs Silas C. Swallow
1908	46	**William H. Taft** William J. Bryan Eugene V. Debs Eugene W. Chafin
1912	48	**Woodrow Wilson** Theodore Roosevelt William H. Taft Eugene V. Debs Eugene W. Chafin
1916	48	**Woodrow Wilson** Charles E. Hughes A. L. Benson J. Frank Hanly

Parties	Popular vote	Electoral vote	Percentage of popular vote[1]
Republican	4,453,295	214	48.5
Democratic	4,414,082	155	48.1
Greenback-Labor	308,578		3.4
Democratic	4,879,507	219	48.5
Republican	4,850,293	182	48.2
Greenback-Labor	175,370		1.8
Prohibition	150,369		1.5
Republican	5,477,129	233	47.9
Democratic	5,537,857	168	48.6
Prohibition	249,506		2.2
Union Labor	146,935		1.3
Democratic	5,555,426	277	46.1
Republican	5,182,690	145	43.0
People's	1,029,846	22	8.5
Prohibition	264,133		2.2
Republican	7,102,246	271	51.1
Democratic	6,492,559	176	47.7
Republican	7,218,491	292	51.7
Democratic; Populist	6,356,734	155	45.5
Prohibition	208,914		1.5
Republican	7,628,461	336	57.4
Democratic	5,084,223	140	37.6
Socialist	402,283		3.0
Prohibition	258,536		1.9
Republican	7,675,320	321	51.6
Democratic	6,412,294	162	43.1
Socialist	420,793		2.8
Prohibition	253,840		1.7
Democratic	6,296,547	435	41.9
Progressive	4,118,571	88	27.4
Republican	3,486,720	8	23.2
Socialist	900,672		6.0
Prohibition	206,275		1.4
Democratic	9,127,695	277	49.4
Republican	8,533,507	254	46.2
Socialist	585,113		3.2
Prohibition	220,506		1.2

[1]Candidates receiving less than 1 percent of the popular vote have been omitted. For that reason the percentage of popular vote given for any election year may not total 100 percent.

Year	Number of states	Candidates
1920	48	**Warren G. Harding** James N. Cox Eugene V. Debs P. P. Christensen
1924	48	**Calvin Coolidge** John W. Davis Robert M. La Follette
1928	48	**Herbert C. Hoover** Alfred E. Smith
1932	48	**Franklin D. Roosevelt** Herbert C. Hoover Norman Thomas
1936	48	**Franklin D. Roosevelt** Alfred M. Landon William Lemke
1940	48	**Franklin D. Roosevelt** Wendell L. Willkie
1944	48	**Franklin D. Roosevelt** Thomas E. Dewey
1948	48	**Harry S Truman** Thomas E. Dewey J. Strom Thurmond Henry A. Wallace
1952	48	**Dwight D. Eisenhower** Adlai E. Stevenson
1956	48	**Dwight D. Eisenhower** Adlai E. Stevenson
1960	50	**John F. Kennedy** Richard M. Nixon
1964	50	**Lyndon B. Johnson** Barry M. Goldwater
1968	50	**Richard M. Nixon** Hubert H. Humphrey George C. Wallace

Parties	Popular vote	Electoral vote	Percentage of popular vote[1]
Republican	16,143,407	404	60.4
Democratic	9,130,328	127	34.2
Socialist	919,799		3.4
Farmer-Labor	265,411		1.0
Republican	15,718,211	382	54.0
Democratic	8,385,283	136	28.8
Progressive	4,831,289	13	16.6
Republican	21,391,993	444	58.2
Democratic	15,016,169	87	40.9
Democratic	22,809,638	472	57.4
Republican	15,758,901	59	39.7
Socialist	881,951		2.2
Democratic	27,752,869	523	60.8
Republican	16,674,665	8	36.5
Union	882,479		1.9
Democratic	27,307,819	449	54.8
Republican	22,321,018	82	44.8
Democratic	25,606,585	432	53.5
Republican	22,014,745	99	46.0
Democratic	24,105,812	303	49.5
Republican	21,970,065	189	45.1
States' Rights	1,169,063	39	2.4
Progressive	1,157,172		2.4
Republican	33,936,234	442	55.1
Democratic	27,314,992	89	44.4
Republican	35,590,472	457	57.6
Democratic	26,022,752	73	42.1
Democratic	34,227,096	303	49.9
Republican	34,108,546	219	49.6
Democratic	43,126,506	486	61.1
Republican	27,176,799	52	38.5
Republican	31,785,480	301	43.4
Democratic	31,275,165	191	42.7
American Independent	9,906,473	46	13.5

[1]Candidates receiving less than 1 percent of the popular vote have been omitted. For that reason the percentage of popular vote given for any election year may not total 100 percent.

YEAR	NUMBER OF STATES	CANDIDATES
1972	50	**Richard M. Nixon** George S. McGovern
1976	50	**Jimmy Carter** Gerald R. Ford
1980	50	**Ronald W. Reagan** Jimmy Carter John B. Anderson Ed Clark
1984	50	**Ronald W. Reagan** Walter F. Mondale
1988	50	**George H. Bush** Michael Dukakis
1992	50	**William Clinton** George H. Bush Ross Perot
1996	50	**William Clinton** Robert Dole Ross Perot

Parties	Popular vote	Electoral vote	Percentage of popular vote[1]
Republican	47,169,911	520	60.7
Democratic	29,170,383	17	37.5
Democratic	40,827,394	297	50.0
Republican	39,145,977	240	47.9
Republican	43,899,248	489	50.8
Democratic	35,481,435	49	41.0
Independent	5,719,437		6.6
Libertarian	920,859		1.0
Republican	54,281,858	525	59.2
Democratic	37,457,215	13	40.8
Republican	47,917,341	426	54.0
Democratic	41,013,030	112	46.0
Democratic	44,908,254	370	43.0
Republican	39,102,343	168	37.4
Independent	19,741,065		18.9
Democratic	45,628,667	379	49.2
Republican	37,869,435	159	40.8
Reform	7,874,283	0	8.5

[1]Candidates receiving less than 1 percent of the popular vote have been omitted. For that reason the percentage of popular vote given for any election year may not total 100 percent.

Justices of the U.S. Supreme Court

Name	Term of Service	Years of Service	Appointed By
John Jay	1789–1795	5	Washington
John Rutledge	1789–1791	1	Washington
William Cushing	1789–1810	20	Washington
James Wilson	1789–1798	8	Washington
John Blair	1789–1796	6	Washington
Robert H. Harrison	1789–1790	—	Washington
James Iredell	1790–1799	9	Washington
Thomas Johnson	1791–1793	1	Washington
William Paterson	1793–1806	13	Washington
John Rutledge[1]	1795–	—	Washington
Samuel Chase	1796–1811	15	Washington
Oliver Ellsworth	1796–1800	4	Washington
Bushrod Washington	1798–1829	31	J. Adams
Alfred Moore	1799–1804	4	J. Adams
John Marshall	1801–1835	34	J. Adams
William Johnson	1804–1834	30	Jefferson
H. Brockholst Livingston	1806–1823	16	Jefferson
Thomas Todd	1807–1826	18	Jefferson
Joseph Story	1811–1845	33	Madison
Gabriel Duval	1811–1835	24	Madison
Smith Thompson	1823–1843	20	Monroe
Robert Trimble	1826–1828	2	J. Q. Adams
John McLean	1829–1861	32	Jackson
Henry Baldwin	1830–1844	14	Jackson
James M. Wayne	1835–1867	32	Jackson
Roger B. Taney	1836–1864	28	Jackson
Philip P. Barbour	1836–1841	4	Jackson
John Catron	1837–1865	28	Van Buren
John McKinley	1837–1852	15	Van Buren

Note: Chief Justices appear in bold type.

[1]Acting Chief Justice; Senate refused to confirm appointment.

Name	Term of Service	Years of Service	Appointed By
Peter V. Daniel	1841–1860	19	Van Buren
Samuel Nelson	1845–1872	27	Tyler
Levi Woodbury	1845–1851	5	Polk
Robert C. Grier	1846–1870	23	Polk
Benjamin R. Curtis	1851–1857	6	Fillmore
John A. Campbell	1853–1861	8	Pierce
Nathan Clifford	1858–1881	23	Buchanan
Noah H. Swayne	1862–1881	18	Lincoln
Samuel F. Miller	1862–1890	28	Lincoln
David Davis	1862–1877	14	Lincoln
Stephen J. Field	1863–1897	34	Lincoln
Salmon P. Chase	1864–1873	8	Lincoln
William Strong	1870–1880	10	Grant
Joseph P. Bradley	1870–1892	22	Grant
Ward Hunt	1873–1882	9	Grant
Morrison R. Waite	1874–1888	14	Grant
John M. Harlan	1877–1911	34	Hayes
William B. Woods	1880–1887	7	Hayes
Stanley Matthews	1881–1889	7	Garfield
Horace Gray	1882–1902	20	Arthur
Samuel Blatchford	1882–1893	11	Arthur
Lucius Q. C. Lamar	1888–1893	5	Cleveland
Melville W. Fuller	1888–1910	21	Cleveland
David J. Brewer	1890–1910	20	B. Harrison
Henry B. Brown	1890–1906	16	B. Harrison
George Shiras, Jr.	1892–1903	10	B. Harrison
Howell E. Jackson	1893–1895	2	B. Harrison
Edward D. White	1894–1910	16	Cleveland
Rufus W. Peckham	1895–1909	14	Cleveland

Name	Term of Service	Years of Service	Appointed By
Joseph McKenna	1898–1925	26	McKinley
Oliver W. Holmes, Jr.	1902–1932	30	T. Roosevelt
William R. Day	1903–1922	19	T. Roosevelt
William H. Moody	1906–1910	3	T. Roosevelt
Horace H. Lurton	1910–1914	4	Taft
Charles E. Hughes	1910–1916	5	Taft
Willis Van Devanter	1911–1937	26	Taft
Joseph R. Lamar	1911–1916	5	Taft
Edward D. White	1910–1921	11	Taft
Mahlon Pitney	1912–1922	10	Taft
James C. McReynolds	1914–1941	26	Wilson
Louis D. Brandeis	1916–1939	22	Wilson
John H. Clarke	1916–1922	6	Wilson
William H. Taft	1921–1930	8	Harding
George Sutherland	1922–1938	15	Harding
Pierce Butler	1922–1939	16	Harding
Edward T. Sanford	1923–1930	7	Harding
Harlan F. Stone	1925–1941	16	Coolidge
Charles E. Hughes	1930–1941	11	Hoover
Owen J. Roberts	1930–1945	15	Hoover
Benjamin N. Cardozo	1932–1938	6	Hoover
Hugo L. Black	1937–1971	34	F. Roosevelt
Stanley F. Reed	1938–1957	19	F. Roosevelt
Felix Frankfurter	1939–1962	23	F. Roosevelt
William O. Douglas	1939–1975	36	F. Roosevelt
Frank Murphy	1940–1949	9	F. Roosevelt
Harlan F. Stone	1941–1946	5	F. Roosevelt
James F. Byrnes	1941–1942	1	F. Roosevelt
Robert H. Jackson	1941–1954	13	F. Roosevelt
Wiley B. Rutledge	1943–1949	6	F. Roosevelt
Harold H. Burton	1945–1958	13	Truman

Name	Term of Service	Years of Service	Appointed By
Fred M. Vinson	1946–1953	7	Truman
Tom C. Clark	1949–1967	18	Truman
Sherman Minton	1949–1956	7	Truman
Earl Warren	1953–1969	16	Eisenhower
John Marshall Harlan	1955–1971	16	Eisenhower
William J. Brennan, Jr.	1956–1990	34	Eisenhower
Charles E. Whittaker	1957–1962	5	Eisenhower
Potter Stewart	1958–1981	23	Eisenhower
Byron R. White	1962–1993	31	Kennedy
Arthur J. Goldberg	1962–1965	3	Kennedy
Abe Fortas	1965–1969	4	Johnson
Thurgood Marshall	1967–1994	24	Johnson
Warren E. Burger	1969–1986	18	Nixon
Harry A. Blackmun	1970–1994	24	Nixon
Lewis F. Powell, Jr.	1971–1987	15	Nixon
William H. Rehnquist[2]	1971–	—	Nixon
John P. Stevens III	1975–	—	Ford
Sandra Day O'Connor	1981–	—	Reagan
Antonin Scalia	1986–	—	Reagan
Anthony M. Kennedy	1988–	—	Reagan
David Souter	1990–	—	Bush
Clarence Thomas	1991–	—	Bush
Ruth Bader Ginsburg	1993–	—	Clinton
Stephen G. Breyer	1994–	—	Clinton

[2]Chief Justice from 1986 on (Reagan administration).

~ SUGGESTED READINGS ~

Chapter 17

The most comprehensive and incisive general history of Reconstruction is Eric Foner, *Reconstruction: America's Unfinished Revolution 1863–1877* (1988). For a skillful abridgement of this book, see Eric Foner, *A Short History of Reconstruction* (1990). A more concise survey of this era can be found in James M. McPherson, *Ordeal by Fire: The Civil War and Reconstruction,* 3rd ed. (2000), Part 3. Still valuable are Kenneth M. Stampp, *The Era of Reconstruction, 1865–1877* (1965), and John Hope Franklin, *Reconstruction: After the Civil War* (1961). The essays in Eric Anderson and Alfred A. Moss Jr., eds., *The Facts of Reconstruction: Essays in Honor of John Hope Franklin* (1991), offer important insights. The constitutional issues involved in the era are analyzed by Harold M. Hyman, *A More Perfect Union: The Impact of the Civil War and Reconstruction on the Constitution* (1973).

For the evolution of federal Reconstruction policies during the war and early postwar years, see three books by Herman Belz: *Reconstructing the Union: Theory and Policy during the Civil War* (1969), *A New Birth of Freedom: The Republican Party and Freedmen's Rights* (1976), and *Emancipation and Equal Rights: Politics and Constitutionalism in the Civil War Era* (1978). Also valuable is David Donald, *The Politics of Reconstruction 1863–1867* (1965). Important for their insights on Lincoln and the Reconstruction question are Peyton McCrary, *Abraham Lincoln and Reconstruction: The Louisiana Experiment* (1978), and LaWanda Cox, *Lincoln and Black Freedom: A Study in Presidential Leadership* (1981). A superb study of the South Carolina Sea Islands as a laboratory of Reconstruction is Willie Lee Rose, *Rehearsal for Reconstruction: The Port Royal Experiment* (1964).

JOHNSON VERSUS CONGRESS For the vexed issues of Andrew Johnson, Congress, and Reconstruction from 1865 to 1868, the following are essential: Eric L. McKitrick, *Andrew Johnson and Reconstruction* (1960); LaWanda Cox and John H. Cox, *Politics, Principle, and Prejudice 1865–1866* (1963); William R. Brock, *An American Crisis: Congress and Reconstruction 1865–1867* (1963); Michael Les Benedict, *A Compromise of Principle: Congressional Republicans and Reconstruction* (1974); David Warren Bowen, *Andrew Johnson and the Negro* (1989); and Hans L. Trefousse, *The Radical Republicans: Lincoln's Vanguard for Racial Justice* (1969), *Thaddeus Stevens: Nineteenth-Century Egalitarian* (1997), and *Andrew Johnson: A Biography* (1989). The two best studies of Johnson's impeachment are Michael Les Benedict, *The Impeachment and Trial of Andrew Johnson* (1973), and Hans L. Trefousse, *Impeachment of a President: Andrew Johnson, the Blacks, and Reconstruction* (1975).

THE FOURTEENTH AND FIFTEENTH AMENDMENTS For the political and judicial dimensions of the Fourteenth and Fifteenth Amendments and their enforcement, see Joseph B. James, *The Framing of the Fourteenth Amendment* (1956), and *The Ratification of the Fourteenth Amendment* (1984); Michael Kent Curtis, *No State Shall Abridge: The Fourteenth Amendment and the Bill of Rights* (1986); William E. Nelson, *The Fourteenth Amendment: From Political Principle to Judicial Doctrine* (1988); William Gillette, *The Right to Vote: Politics and Passage of the Fifteenth Amendment* (1965); and Robert J. Kaczorowski, *The Politics of Judicial Interpretation: The Federal Courts, Department of Justice and Civil Rights, 1866–1876* (1985).

RECONSTRUCTION SOCIETY, POLITICS, AND ECONOMICS For the social and political scene in the South during Reconstruction, a good introduction is Howard N. Rabinowitz, *The First New South, 1865–1920* (1991). Dan T. Carter, *When the War Was Over: the Failure of Self-Reconstruction in the South, 1865–1867* (1985), and Michael Perman, *Reunion without Compromise: The South and Reconstruction, 1865–1868* (1973), portray the early postwar years, while Michael Perman, *The Road to Redemption: Southern Politics, 1868–1879* (1984), is a provocative interpretation. Otto H. Olsen, ed., *Reconstruction and Redemption in the South* (1980), contains essays on the Reconstruction process in a half-dozen states. For the role of the Ku Klux Klan and other white paramilitary organizations, see Allen W. Trelease, *White Terror: The Ku Klux Klan Conspiracy and Southern Reconstruction* (1974), and George C. Rable, *But There Was No Peace: The Role of Violence in the Politics of Reconstruction* (1984). For a fresh and intelligent look at the carpetbaggers, see Richard Nelson Current, *Those Terrible Carpetbaggers: A Reinterpretation* (1988). Economic issues are the subject of Mark W. Summers, *Railroads, Reconstruction, and the Gospel of Prosperity: Aid under the Radical Republicans, 1865–1877* (1984), and Terry L. Seip, *The South Returns to Congress: Men, Economic Measures, and Intersectional Relationships, 1868–1879* (1983).

FREEDPEOPLE DURING RECONSTRUCTION Two classics that portray sympathetically the activities of freedpeople during Reconstruction are W. E. Burghardt Du Bois, *Black Reconstruction* (1935), and Leon F. Litwack, *Been in the Storm So Long: The Aftermath of Slavery* (1979). A challenging brief interpretation is provided by Eric Foner, *Nothing but Freedom: Emancipation and Its Legacy* (1983). Howard N. Rabinowitz, *Race Relations in the Urban South, 1865–1890* (1978), and Howard N. Rabinowitz, ed., *Southern Black Leaders of the Reconstruction Era* (1982), add important dimensions to the subject. There are many good studies of black social and political life in various states during Reconstruction; three of the best deal with the state in which African Americans played the most active part: Joel Williamson, *After Slavery: The Negro in South Carolina during Reconstruction 1861–1877* (1965); Thomas Holt, *Black over White: Negro Political Leadership in South Carolina during Reconstruction* (1977); and Laura F. Edwards, *Gendered Strife and Confusion: The Political Culture of Reconstruction* (1997). See also Eric Foner, *Freedom's Lawmakers: A Directory of Black Officeholders during Reconstruction* (1993).

For the evolution of sharecropping and other aspects of freedpeople's economic status, see Roger L. Ransom and Richard Sutch, *One Kind of Freedom: The Economic Consequences of Emancipation* (1977), and William Cohen, *At Freedom's Edge: Black Mobility and the Southern White Quest for Racial Control, 1861–1915* (1991). Two sound studies of the Freedmen's Bureau are George R. Bentley, *A History of the Freedmen's Bureau* (1955), and Donald G. Nieman, *To Set the Law in Motion: The Freedmen's Bureau and the Legal Rights of Blacks 1865–1868* (1979). For the education of freedpeople, see especially William Preston Vaughan, *Schools for All: The Blacks & Public Education in the South 1865–1877* (1974); Joe M. Richardson, *Christian Reconstruction, The American Missionary Association and Southern Blacks, 1861–1890* (1986); and James M. McPherson, *The Abolitionist Legacy: From Reconstruction to the NAACP* (1975).

THE END OF RECONSTRUCTION The national political scene in the 1870s and the retreat from Reconstruction are the subject of William Gillette, *Retreat from Reconstruction: A Political History 1867–1878* (1979). The issues of corruption and civil service reform receive exhaustive treatment in Mark Wahlgren Summers, *The Era of Good Stealings* (1993). The classic analysis of the disputed election of 1876 and the Compromise of 1877 is C. Vann Woodward, *Reunion and Reaction: The Compromise of 1877 and the End of Reconstruction*, rev. ed., (1956); for challenges to aspects of Woodward's thesis see Keith I. Polakoff, *The Politics of Inertia: The Election of 1876 and the End of Reconstruction* (1973), and Michael Les Benedict, "Southern Democrats in the Crisis of 1876–1877: A Reconsideration of Reunion and Reaction," *Journal of Southern History* 46 (1980): 489–524.

Chapter 18

WESTWARD EXPANSION Classic accounts of the post–Civil War West can be found in Walter Prescott Webb, *The Great Plains* (1931), and Wallace Stegner, *Beyond the Hundredth Meridian* (1954). Also valuable are Rodman Paul, *The Far West and the Great Plains in Transition* (1988), and Howard Lamar, *The Far Southwest, 1846–1912* (1970). The best modern general study of the history of the West from the first contact between Europeans and Indians down to the present is Richard White, *"It's Your Misfortune and None of My Own": A History of the American West* (1991).

RAILROADS The role of railroads in westward expansion is treated in Robert R. Riegel, *The Story of the Western Railroads* (1926), and Oscar O. Winther, *The Great Iron Trail: The Story of the First Transcontinental Railroad* (1963).

THE FARMING FRONTIER The farmers' frontier is chronicled in Gilbert C. Fite, *The Farmer's Frontier, 1865–1900* (1966), and Fred Shannon, *The Farmers' Last Frontier, 1860–1897* (1945). The important part played by immigrants in western settlement is treated in Frederick C. Luebke, *Ethnicity on the Great Plains* (1980). Farmers' wives and other frontier women are the subject of Sandra Myres, *Western Women and the Frontier Experience, 1880–1915* (1982); Julie Roy Jeffrey, *Frontier Women: The Trans-Mississippi West,*

1840–1880 (1979); and Christiane Fischer, *Let Them Speak for Themselves: Women in the American West, 1849–90* (1977). The experience of children is discussed in Elliott West, *Growing Up with the Country: Childhood on the Far Western Frontier* (1989).

THE MINING FRONTIER For the mining frontier, the following are valuable: William Greever, *The Bonanza West: The Story of the Western Mining Rushes* (1963); Rodman Paul, *Mining Frontiers of the Far West, 1848–1880* (1963); Richard Lingenfelter, *The Hardrock Miners: A History of the Mining Labor Movement in the American West, 1863–1893* (1974); and Mark Wyman, *Hard Rock Epic: Western Miners and the Industrial Revolution, 1860–1910* (1979).

THE RANCHING FRONTIER The saga of the ranching frontier and the cowboy is the subject of many books, including Lewis Atherton, *The Cattle Kings* (1961); Edward E. Dale, *The Range Cattle Industry*, rev. ed. (1969); Robert Dykstra, *The Cattle Towns* (1968); Ernest S. Osgood, *The Day of the Cattleman* (1929); Joe B. Frantz and Julian Choate, *The American Cowboy: The Myth and Reality* (1955); and William Savage, *The Cowboy Hero: His Image in American History and Culture* (1979). For black cowboys, see William L. Katz, *The Black West* (1971).

INDIANS AND THE WEST The best brief survey of Indians and Indian-white relations in this period is Philip Weeks, *Farewell, My Nation: The American Indian and the United States, 1820–1890* (1990). Other valuable works include Ralph K. Andrist, *The Long Death: The Last Day of the Plains Indians* (1964); and Robert M. Utley, *The Indian Frontier of the American West 1846–1890* (1984), and *The Last Days of the Sioux Nation* (1963). For the reformers and the Dawes Act, see Robert Mardock, *Reformers and the American Indian* (1971), and Leonard A. Carlson, *Indians, Bureaucrats, and Land* (1981). Two books by Francis Paul Prucha contain valuable material on this period: *The Great Father: The United States Government and the American Indians* (1984), and *The Indians in American Society from the Revolutionary War to the Present* (1985).

THE NEW SOUTH The classic study of the New South is C. Vann Woodward, *Origins of the New South, 1877–1913* (1951). It can be supplemented by Paul M. Gaston, *The New South Creed: A Study in Southern Mythmaking* (1970), and Edward L. Ayres, *The Promise of the New South: Life after Reconstruction* (1992). For the economy of the New South, see Gavin Wright, *Old South, New South: Revolutions in the Southern Economy Since the Civil War* (1986); Pete Daniel, *Breaking the Land: The Transformation of Cotton, Tobacco, and Rice Cultures Since 1880* (1985); John F. Stover, *The Railroads of the South, 1865–1900* (1955); Patrick H. Hearden, *Independence and Empire: The New South's Cotton Mill Campaign, 1865–1901* (1982); and David L. Carlton, *Mill and Town in South Carolina, 1880–1920* (1982).

RACE RELATIONS The politics of race in the New South is the subject of Vincent P. DeSantis, *Republicans Face the Southern Question . . . 1877–1897* (1959); Stanley P. Hirshson, *Farewell to the Bloody Shirt: Northern Republicans and the Southern Negro 1877–1893* (1962); and J. Morgan Kousser, *The Shaping of Southern Politics: Suffrage Restriction and the Establishment of the One-Party South 1880–1910* (1974). The rising tide of racism and segregation is treated in C. Vann Woodward, *The Strange Career of Jim Crow*, 3rd rev. ed. (1974); Joel Williamson, *The Crucible of Race: Black-White Relations in the American South Since Emancipation* (1984), which was also published in an abridged edition with the title *A Rage for Order: Black-White Relations in the American South Since Emancipation* (1986); and Howard B. Rabinowitz, *Race Relations in the Urban South 1865–1890* (1978). The horrors of lynching and the convict lease system are analyzed in Fitzhugh Brundage, *Lynching in the New South: Georgia and Virginia, 1880–1930* (1993), and Matthew J. Mancini, *One Dies, Get Another: Convict Leasing in the American South, 1866–1928* (1996). For responses by black leaders to these developments, see August Meier, *Negro Thought in America, 1880–1915* (1963), and Louis R. Harlan, *Booker T. Washington: The Making of a Black Leader, 1856–1901* (1972).

THE POLITICS OF STALEMATE Two useful political narratives of this period are John A. Garraty, *The New Commonwealth, 1877–1890* (1968), and John M. Dobson, *Politics in the Gilded Age* (1972). For the continuing impact of Civil War issues and memories in politics, see Mary R. Dearing, *Veterans in Politics: The Story of the G.A.R.* (1952); Stuart McConnell, *Glorious Contentment: The Grand Army of the Republic, 1865–1900* (1992); and Gaines M. Foster, *Ghosts of the Confederacy: Defeat, the Lost Cause, and the Emergence of the New South* (1987). Other useful studies include Paul Kleppner, *The Third Electoral System, 1853–1892* (1979); Robert Marcus, *Grand Old Party: Political Structure in the Gilded Age* (1971); H. Wayne Morgan, *From Hayes to McKinley* (1969); and Ari Hoogenboom, *Outlawing the Spoils: A History of the Civil Service Reform Movement* (1961).

Chapter 19

For stimulating overviews of this period and the Progressive Era that followed, consult Richard Hofstadter, *The Age of Reform* (1955); Robert H. Wiebe, *The Search for Order 1877–1920* (1967); and Nell Irvin Painter, *Standing at Armageddon: The United States, 1877–1919* (1987).

RAILROADS AND INDUSTRIAL GROWTH For the impact of the railroad on the Gilded Age economy and culture, see George R. Taylor and Irene D. Neu, *The American Railroad Network, 1861–1890* (1956); Albro Martin, *Railroads Triumphant: The Growth, Rejection, and Rebirth of a Vital American Force* (1992); and Alfred D. Chandler Jr., *The Railroads: The Nation's First Big Business* (1965). For the rise of industry and "big business," the following are useful: Glen Porter, *The Rise of Big Business, 1860–1910* (1973); Edward C. Kirkland, *Industry Comes of Age . . . 1860–1897* (1961); Harold G. Vatter, *The Drive to Industrial Maturity: The U.S. Economy, 1865–1914* (1975); Robert Higgs, *The Transformation of the American Economy, 1865–1914* (1971); and Alfred D. Chandler, *The Visible Hand: The Managerial Revolution in American Business* (1977). An old and entertaining (although biased and outmoded) portrait of the financial and industrial leaders of the era is Matthew Josephson, *The Robber Barons: The Great American Capitalists 1861–1901* (1934).

THE RESPONSE TO INDUSTRIALISM The response to industrialism and the rise of a regulatory antitrust movement are treated in Samuel P. Hays, *The Response to Industrialism, 1885–1914* (1957); Sidney Fine, *Laissez Faire and the General Welfare State: A Study of Conflict in American Thought, 1865–1900* (1956); George H. Miller, *Railroads and the Granger Laws* (1971); Gabriel Kolko, *Railroads and Regulation, 1877–1915* (1965); and Ari and Olive Hoogenboom, *A History of the ICC* (1976).

LABOR For the labor movement and labor strife, the following are particularly useful: Melvin Dubofsky, *Industrialism and the American Worker, 1865–1920* (1975); Walter Licht, *Working for the Railroad* (1983); Herbert G. Gutman, *Work, Culture, and Society in Industrializing America* (1976); Bruce Laurie, *Artisans into Workers: Labor in Nineteenth-Century America* (1989); David Montgomery, *The Fall of the House of Labor . . . 1865–1925* (1987); David Montgomery, *Workers' Control in America: Studies in the History of Work, Technology, and Labor Struggles* (1979); Leon Fink, *Workingmen's Democracy: The Knights of Labor and American Politics* (1983); Robert E. Weir, *Beyond Labor's Veil: The Culture of the Knights of Labor* (1996); Stuart Kaufman, *Samuel Gompers and the Origins of the American Federation of Labor* (1973); David Brody, *Steelworkers in America: The Nonunion Era* (1960); Robert V. Bruce, *1877: Year of Violence* (1959); Paul Avrich, *The Haymarket Tragedy* (1984); Leon Wolff, *Lockout, the Story of the Homestead Strike of 1892* (1965); and Almont Lindsey, *The Pullman Strike* (1971).

POPULISM AND THE ELECTION OF 1896 The classic history of the Populist movement, still valuable as a narrative, is John D. Hicks, *The Populist Revolt* (1931). The best modern survey of the movement is Lawrence Goodwyn, *Democratic Promise: The Populist Moment in America* (1976), which was published in an abridged edition with the title *The Populist Moment* (1978). Among the many other fine books about populism, the following are especially useful: C. Vann Woodward, *Tom Watson, Agrarian Rebel* (1938); Peter Argersinger, *Populism and Politics* (1974); Steven Hahn, *The Roots of Southern Populism* (1983); Sheldon Hackney, *Populism to Progressivism in Alabama* (1969); Robert McMath, *Populist Vanguard: A History of the Southern Farmers' Alliance* (1975); and Gerald H. Gaither, *Blacks and the Populist Revolt* (1977). The complexities of the silver issue are unraveled in Allen Weinstein, *Prelude to Populism: Origins of the Silver Issue* (1970).

The politics of the 1890s culminating in the climactic election of 1896 are treated in J. Rogers Hollingsworth, *The Whirligig of Politics: The Democracy of Cleveland and Bryan* (1963); Richard J. Jensen, *The Winning of the Midwest: Social and Political Conflict, 1888–1896* (1971); R. Hal Williams, *Years of Decision: American Politics in the 1890s* (1978); Paul W. Glad, *McKinley, Bryan, and the People* (1964); Stanley Jones, *The Presidential Election of 1896* (1964); and Robert F. Durden, *The Climax of Populism: The Election of 1896* (1965).

Chapter 20

For a general overview of the period, Alan Dawley, *Struggles for Justice: Social Responsibility and the Liberal State* (1991), and Nell Irvin Painter, *Standing at Armageddon: The United States, 1877–1919* (1987), are excellent accounts that are particularly strong on issues of social history.

ECONOMIC GROWTH AND TECHNOLOGICAL INNOVATION On economic growth in the late 19th and early 20th centuries, see Harold G. Vatter, *The Drive to Industrial Maturity: The United States Economy, 1860–1914* (1975); Elliot Brownlee, *Dynamics of Ascent: A History of the American Economy*, 2nd ed. (1979); David Hounshell, *From the American System to Mass Production, 1800–1932: The Development of Manufacturing Technology in the United States* (1984); Nathan Rosenberg, *Technology and American Economic Growth* (1972); Charles Singer et al., eds., *History of Technology*, vol. 5: *The Late Nineteenth Century* (1958); and Harold I. Sharlin, *The Making of the Electrical Age* (1963). David Nye, *Electrifying America: Social Meanings of a New Technology, 1890–1940* (1990), is a fascinating account of the social consequences of technological change. For an older but lively history on this theme, see Frederick Lewis Allen, *The Big Change: America Transforms Itself, 1900–1950* (1952). Robert Conot, *A Streak of Luck* (1979), and Matthew Josephson, *Edison* (1959), assess Thomas Edison's contributions to the electrical revolution.

THE RISE OF THE MODERN CORPORATION Alfred D. Chandler Jr., *The Visible Hand: The Managerial Revolution in American Business* (1977), is the classic work. See also Richard Tedlow, *The Rise of the American Business Corporation* (1991); Naomi Lamoreaux, *The Great Merger Movement in American Business, 1895–1904* (1985); and Glenn Porter, *The Rise of Big Business, 1860–1910* (1973). On the emerging alliance between corporations and science, see David F. Noble, *America by Design: Science, Technology and the Rise of Corporate Capitalism* (1977); Frederick A. White, *American Industrial Research Laboratories* (1961); and Leonard S. Reich, *The Making of Industrial Research: Science and Business at GE and Bell, 1876–1926* (1985). On the legal and political changes that undergirded the corporation's triumph, see Martin J. Sklar, *The Corporate Reconstruction of American Capitalism, 1890–1916: The Market, the Law and Politics* (1988). Olivier Zunz, *Making America Corporate, 1870–1920* (1990), is one of the first social histories to focus on the middle managers who comprised the new corporate middle class. A provocative exploration of the paths to economic development shut off by the triumph of mass production is found in Michael J. Piore and Charles F. Sabel, *The Second Industrial Divide: Possibilities for Prosperity* (1984). For an equally provocative critique of this interpretation, consult Philip Scranton, *Endless Novelty: Specialty Production and American Industrialization, 1865–1925* (1997).

SCIENTIFIC MANAGEMENT Any examination of this topic must start with Frederick Winslow Taylor, *The Principles of Scientific Management* (1911), and Robert Kanigel, *The One Best Way: Frederick Winslow Taylor and the Enigma of Efficiency* (1997). Daniel Nelson, *Frederick W. Taylor and the Rise of Scientific Management* (1980), and David Montgomery, *The Fall of the House of Labor: The Workplace, the State, and American Labor Activism, 1865–1925* (1987), are important. For its broader political ramifications, see Samuel Haber, *Efficiency and Uplift: Scientific Management in the Progressive Era* (1964). Allan Nevins and Frank E. Hill, *Ford* (1954–1963), is still the best biography of Henry Ford, but on Ford's labor policies, Stephen Meyer III, *The Five Dollar Day: Labor Management and Social Control in the Ford Motor Company, 1908–1921* (1981), and Nelson Lichtenstein and Stephen Meyer III, eds., *On the Line: Essays in the History of Auto Work* (1989), are essential reading. For a general perspective on the changes in work and management in this period, consult Sanford M. Jacoby, *Employing Bureaucracy: Managers, Unions, and the Transformation of Work in American Industry, 1900–1945* (1985).

ROBBER BARONS AND THE TURN TO PHILANTHROPY The classic work on the robber barons themselves is Matthew Josephson, *The Robber Barons* (1934). On the industrialists' turn to philanthropy, see Andrew Carnegie, *The Gospel of Wealth* (1889), and *Autobiography* (1920); Robert H. Bremner, *American Philanthropy* (1988); George E. Pozzetta, ed., *Americanization, Social Control and Philanthropy* (1991); Barry D. Karl and Stanley N. Katz, "The American Private Philanthropic Foundation and the Public Sphere, 1890–1930," *Minerva* 19 (Summer 1981): 236–270; and Ellen Condliffe Lagemann, *The Politics of Knowledge: The Carnegie Corporation, Philanthropy, and Public Policy* (1989).

"RACIAL FITNESS" AND SOCIAL DARWINISM On America's growing obsession with physical and racial fitness during this period, see John Higham, "The Reorientation of American Culture in the 1890s," in John Horace Weiss, ed., *The Origins of Modern Consciousness*, pp. 25–48 (1965), and Higham, *Strangers in the Land: Patterns of American Nativism*, rev. ed. (1992). For an assessment of the influence of Darwinist thinking on American culture, see Richard Hofstadter, *Social Darwinism in American Thought*, rev. ed. (1955); Robert Bannister, *Social Darwinism: Science and Myth in Anglo-American Social Thought* (1979); and Carl N. Degler, *In Search of Human Nature: The Decline and Revival of Darwinism in American Social Thought* (1991).

IMMIGRATION: GENERAL HISTORIES The best single-volume history of European immigrants is John Bodnar, *The Transplanted: A History of Immigrants in Urban America* (1985). Maldwyn Allen Jones, *American Immigration*

(1974), and Alan M. Kraut, *The Huddled Masses: The Immigrant in American Society, 1880–1921* (1982), are also useful. Ronald Takaki, *A Different Mirror: A History of Multicultural America* (1993), Roger Daniels, *Coming to America: A History of Immigration and Ethnicity in American Life* (1990), and Leonard Dinnerstein, Roger L. Nichols, and David Reimers, *Natives and Strangers: Ethnic Groups and the Building of America* (1979), integrate the story of European immigrants with that of African, Asian, and Latin American newcomers. Stephan Thernstrom, ed., *Harvard Encyclopedia of American Ethnic Groups* (1980), is indispensable on virtually all questions pertaining to immigration and ethnicity. Frank Thistlewaite, "Migration from Europe Overseas," in Stanley N. Katz and Stanley I. Kutler, eds., *New Perspectives on the American Past* (1969), vol. 2, pp. 152–181, is a pioneering article on patterns of European migration. On European immigrants' encounters with racial patterns in the United States, see Matthew Frye Jacobson, *Whiteness of a Different Color: European Americans and the Alchemy of Race* (1998).

HISTORIES OF PARTICULAR IMMIGRANT GROUPS Irving Howe, *World of Our Fathers: The Journey of the East European Jews to America and the Life They Found and Made* (1976), is the best work on Jewish immigration, although it must be supplemented by Susan A. Glenn, *Daughters of the Shtetl: Life and Labor in the Immigrant Generation* (1990). For work on the Irish, see Kerby A. Miller, *Emigrants and Exiles: Ireland and the Irish Exodus to North America* (1985), and Hasia A. Diner, *Erin's Daughters in America: Irish Immigrant Women in the Nineteenth Century* (1983). Other excellent works on particular ethnic groups include Ewa Morawska, *For Bread with Butter: The Life-Worlds of East Central Europeans in Johnstown, Pennsylvania, 1890–1940* (1985); John J. Bukowczyk, *And My Children Did Not Know Me: A History of Polish Americans* (1987); Virginia Yans-McLaughlin, *Family and Community: Italian Immigrants in Buffalo, 1880–1930* (1977); Yuji Ichioka, *The Issei: The World of the First Japanese Immigrants, 1895–1924* (1988); Sucheng Chan, *Asian Americans: An Interpretive History* (1991); and Mario T. Garcia, *Desert Immigrants: The Mexicans of El Paso, 1880–1920* (1981). Olivier Zunz, *The Changing Face of Inequality: Urbanization, Industrial Development and Immigrants in Detroit, 1880–1920* (1982), and S. J. Kleinberg, *The Shadow of the Mills: Working-Class Families in Pittsburgh, 1870–1907* (1989), compare the experiences of several European American groups in one city.

IMMIGRANT LABOR Essential sources on both immigrant and nonimmigrant labor are Herbert Gutman, *Work, Culture and Society in Industrializing America* (1976); Montgomery, *The Fall of the House of Labor* (previously cited); and Alice Kessler-Harris, *Out of Work: A History of Wage-Earning Women in the United States* (1982). For a brief but incisive survey of working conditions in this period, consult Melvyn Dubofsky, *Industrialism and the American Worker, 1865–1920*, 2nd ed. (1985). Tamara Hareven, *Family Time and Historical Time: The Relationship between the Family and Work in a New England Industrial Community* (1982), and James R. Barrett, *Work and Community in the Jungle: Chicago's Packinghouse Workers, 1894–1922* (1990), are excellent local studies. Leon Stein, *The Triangle Fire* (1962), and John F. McClymer, *The Triangle Strike and Fire* (1998), chronicle that industrial disaster; and Alexander Keyssar, *Out of Work: The First Century of Unemployment in Massachusetts* (1986), offers the best analysis of unemployment in this period.

IMMIGRANTS, AFRICAN AMERICANS, AND SOCIAL MOBILITY Good sources on this topic include Stephan Thernstrom, *The Other Bostonians: Poverty and Progress in the American Metropolis* (1973); Joel Perlman, *Ethnic Differences: Schooling and Social Structure among the Irish, Italians, Jews, and Blacks in an American City, 1880–1935* (1988); Thomas Kessner, *The Golden Door: Italian and Jewish Mobility in New York City, 1880–1915* (1977); Edna Bonacich and John Modell, *The Economic Basis of Ethnic Solidarity: Small Businessmen in the Japanese-American Community* (1980); Stephen Steinberg, *The Ethnic Myth: Race, Ethnicity, and Class in America* (1981); Thomas Sowell, *Ethnic America: A History* (1981); and Stanley Lieberson, *A Piece of the Pie: Blacks and White Immigrants Since 1880* (1980).

IMMIGRANTS, POLITICAL MACHINES, AND ORGANIZED CRIME Steven P. Erie, *Rainbow's End: Irish Americans and the Dilemmas of Urban Machine Politics, 1840–1945* (1988), insightfully examines the benefits and costs of big city machines. See also Harold Zink, *City Bosses in the United States: A Study of Twenty Municipal Bosses* (1930); M. Craig Brown and Charles N. Halaby, "Machine Politics in America, 1870–1945," *Journal of Interdisciplinary History* 8 (1987): 587–612; John M. Allswang, *Bosses, Machines, and Urban Voters* (1977); Alexander B. Callow, ed., *The City Boss in America* (1976); and William L. Riordon, *Plunkitt of Tammany Hall: A Series of Very Plain Talks on Very Practical Politics* (1994). On organized crime, consult Joseph Albini, *The American Mafia* (1971); Humbert Nelli, *The Business of Crime* (1976); and Jenna Weissman Joselit, *Our Gang: Jewish Crime and the New York Jewish Community* (1983). Doris Kearns Goodwin, *The Fitzgeralds and the Kennedys* (1987), chronicles the history of President John F. Kennedy's family.

AFRICAN AMERICANS John Hope Franklin and Alfred A. Moss Jr., *From Slavery to Freedom: A History of Negro Americans*, 7th ed. (1994), offers a masterful overview. Gavin Wright, *Old South, New South: Revolutions in the Southern Economy since the Civil War* (1986), analyzes the southern sharecropping economy, while William H. Harris, *The Harder We Run: Black Workers since the Civil War* (1982), assesses the experiences of black industrial workers, South and North. On black female workers, consult Jacqueline Jones, *Labor of Love, Labor of Sorrow: Black Women, Work and the Family from Slavery to the Present* (1985). Kenneth L. Kusmer, *A Ghetto Takes Shape: Black Cleveland, 1870–1930* (1978), is the best work on the formation of urban black communities in the North prior to the Great Migration (1916–1920), but it should be supplemented with Elizabeth Hafkin Pleck, *Black Migration and Poverty: Boston, 1865–1900* (1979); Allan H. Spear, *Black Chicago: The Making of a Negro Ghetto, 1890–1920* (1967); and Theodore Hershberg et al., *Philadelphia: Work, Space, Family, and Group Experience in the Nineteenth Century* (1981). On the rise of a new black middle class, see Evelyn Brooks Higginbotham, *Righteous Discontent: The Women's Movement in the Black Baptist Church, 1880-1920* (1993), and Kevin K. Gaines, *Uplifting the Race: Black Leadership, Politics, and Culture in the Twentieth Century* (1996).

WORKERS AND UNIONS Indispensable sources are Montgomery, *The Fall of the House of Labor* (previously cited); David Brody, *Workers in Industrial America: Essays on the Twentieth Century Struggle* (1980); and Melvyn Dubofsky, *We Shall Be All: A History of the Industrial Workers of the World* (1969). Samuel Gompers's career can be traced through Stuart Kaufman, *Samuel Gompers and the Origins of the American Federation of Labor* (1973), and Gompers's own *Seventy Years of Life and Labor: An Autobiography*, ed. Nick Salvatore (1984). Michael Kazin, *Barons of Labor: The San Francisco Building Trades and Union Power in the Progressive Era* (1987), is a sterling study of AFL craftsmen at work and in local politics; and Gwendolyn Mink, *Old Labor and New Immigrants in American Political Development: Union, Party, and State, 1875–1920* (1986), offers a provocative interpretation of the AFL's role in national politics. Christopher Tomlins, *The State and the Unions: Labor Relations, Law, and the Organized Labor Movement in America, 1880–1960* (1985), carefully analyzes the effect of law on the labor movement's development.

David A. Corbin, *Life, Work, and Rebellion in the Coal Fields: The Southern West Virginia Miners, 1880–1922* (1981), examines the rise of the United Mine Workers; and Howe, *World of Our Fathers* (previously cited), treats the early years of the ILGWU in New York City. Sterling D. Spero and Abram L. Harris, *The Black Worker: The Negro and the Labor Movement* (1931), and James R. Grossman, *Land of Hope: Chicago, Black Southerners, and the Great Migration* (1989), analyze AFL attitudes toward black workers. Eric Arnesen, *Waterfront Workers of New Orleans: Race, Class and Politics, 1863–1923* (1991), probes that city's remarkable experiment in biracial unionism. Graham Adams Jr., *Age of Industrial Violence, 1910–1915: The Activities and Findings of the United States Commission on Industrial Relations* (1966), chronicles the Ludlow massacre and other labor-capital confrontations in these years. See also J. Anthony Lukas, *Big Trouble: A Murder in a Small Western Town Sets Off a Struggle for the Soul of America* (1997), a remarkable study of class conflict in the West during the early years of the 20th century.

THE RISE OF MASS CULTURE On the rise of mass culture, see David Nasaw, *Going Out: The Rise and Fall of Public Amusements* (1993); William Leach, *Land of Desire: Merchants, Power, and the Rise of a New American Culture* (1993); Roy Rosenzweig, *Eight Hours for What We Will: Workers and Leisure in an Industrial City, 1870–1920* (1983); and Lewis A. Erenberg, *Steppin' Out: New York Nightlife and the Transformation of American Culture, 1890–1930* (1981). Warren I. Susman, *Culture as History: The Transformation of American Society in the Twentieth Century* (1984), is essential reading for any student of this subject. Excellent studies of the rise of movies are Rosenzweig, *Eight Hours for What We Will* (previously cited); Lary May, *Screening Out the Past: The Birth of Mass Culture and the Motion Picture Industry* (1980); Robert Sklar, *Movie-Made America: A Social History of the American Movies* (1975); and Steven J. Ross, *Working-Class Hollywood: Silent Film and the Shaping of Class in America* (1998).

THE "NEW WOMAN" On the emergence of the "new woman," see Kathy Peiss, *Cheap Amusements: Working Women and Leisure in Turn-of-the-Century New York* (1986); Elaine Tyler May, *Great Expectations: Marriage and Divorce in Post-Victorian America* (1980); Leslie Woodcock Tentler, *Wage-Earning Women: Industrial Work and Family Life in the United States, 1900–1930* (1979); Joanne Meyerowitz, *Women Adrift: Independent Wage-Earners in Chicago, 1870–1930* (1988); and Elizabeth Lunbeck, *The Psychiatric Persuasion: Knowledge, Gender and Politics in Modern America* (1994).

FEMINISM Nancy F. Cott, *The Grounding of Modern Feminism* (1987), is the most important study of the movement's origins. Linda Gordon, *Woman's Body, Woman's Right: A Social History of Birth Control in America*

(1976), and James Reed, *The Birth Control Movement and American Society: From Private Vice to Public Virtue* (1983), are important works on the history of birth control. Also see the following first-rate biographies: David M. Kennedy, *Birth Control in America: The Career of Margaret Sanger* (1970); Alice Wexler, *Emma Goldman: An Intimate Life* (1984); and Christine A. Lunardini, *From Equal Suffrage to Equal Rights: Alice Paul and the National Women's Party, 1912–1928* (1986). For a brief biography of Charlotte Perkins Gilman, see Gary Scharnhorst, *Charlotte Perkins Gilman* (1985). Leslie Fishbein, *Rebels in Bohemia: The Radicals of "The Masses," 1911–1917* (1982), deftly recreates the politics and culture of Greenwich Village.

Chapter 21

No topic in 20th century American history has generated as large and rapidly changing a scholarship as has progressivism. Today, few scholars treat this political movement in the terms set forth by the progressives themselves: as a movement of "the people" against the "special interests." In *The Age of Reform: From Bryan to FDR* (1955), Richard Hofstadter argues that progressivism was the expression of a declining Protestant middle class at odds with the new industrial order. In *The Search for Order, 1877–1920* (1967), Robert Wiebe finds the movement's core in a rising middle class, closely allied to the corporations and bureaucratic imperatives that were defining this new order. Gabriel Kolko, *The Triumph of Conservatism: A Reinterpretation of American History* (1963), and James Weinstein, *The Corporate Ideal in the Liberal State, 1900–1918* (1969), both argue that progressivism was the work of industrialists themselves, who were eager to ensure corporate stability and profitability in a dangerously unstable capitalist economy. Without denying the importance of this corporate search for order, Nell Irvin Painter, *Standing at Armageddon: The United States, 1877–1919,* (1987), and Alan Dawley, *Struggles for Justice: Social Responsibility and the Liberal State* (1991), insist on the role of the working class, men and women, whites and blacks, in shaping the progressive agenda. James T. Kloppenberg, *Uncertain Victory: Social Democracy and Progressivism in European and American Thought, 1870–1920* (1986), and Thomas J. Knock, *To End All Wars: Woodrow Wilson and the Quest for a New World Order* (1992), emphasize the influence of socialism on progressive thought, while Martin J. Sklar, *The Corporate Reconstruction of American Capitalism, 1900–1916: The Market, the Law and Politics* (1988), stresses the role of progressivism in "containing" or taming socialism. Paul Boyer, *Urban Masses and Moral Order in America, 1820–1920* (1978), treats progressivism as a cultural movement to enforce middle-class norms on an unruly urban and immigrant population. Theda Skocpol, *Protecting Soldiers and Mothers: The Political Origins of Social Policy in the United States* (1992), reconstructs the central role of middle-class Protestant women in shaping progressive social policy, while Robert M. Crunden, *Ministers of Reform: The Progressives' Achievement in American Civilization, 1889–1920* (1982), stresses the religious roots of progressive reform. Summaries of some of these various interpretations of progressivism—but by no means all—can be found in Arthur S. Link and Richard L. McCormick, *Progressivism* (1983).

MUCKRAKERS, SETTLEMENT HOUSES, AND WOMEN REFORMERS On the muckrakers, see Walter M. Brasch, *Forerunners of Revolution: Muckrakers and the American Social Conscience* (1990); Harold S. Wilson, *McClure's Magazine and the Muckrakers* (1970); and Justin Kaplan, *Lincoln Steffens* (1974). On the settlement houses and women reformers, consult Jane Addams, *Twenty Years at Hull House* (1910); Kathryn Kish Sklar, *Florence Kelley and the Nation's Work: The Rise of Women's Political Culture, 1830–1900* (1995); Allen F. Davis, *Spearheads for Reform: The Social Settlements and the Progressive Movement, 1890–1914* (1967); Mina Julia Carson, *Settlement Folk: Social Thought and the American Settlement Movement, 1885–1930* (1990); and Rivka Shpak Lissak, *Pluralism and the Progressives: Hull House and the New Immigrants, 1890–1919* (1989). Ruth Borden, *Women and Temperance* (1980), is useful on the role of women in the prohibition movement. Paula Baker, "The Domestication of Politics: Women and American Political Society, 1780–1920," *American Historical Review* 89 (June 1984): 620–647, and Robyn Muncy, *Creating a Female Dominion in American Reform, 1890–1935* (1991), are important for understanding women's political activism in the years before they gained the vote.

SOCIALISM For general histories, see James Weinstein, *The Decline of Socialism in America, 1912–1925* (1967), and Irving Howe, *Socialism in America* (1985). Mari Jo Buhle, *Women and American Socialism, 1870–1920* (1981), expertly analyzes the experiences of women who became socialists. Nick Salvatore, *Eugene V. Debs: Citizen and Socialist* (1982), is a superb biography of the charismatic Debs; Melvyn Dubofsky, *We Shall Be All: A History of the Industrial Workers of the World* (1969), offers the most thorough treatment of the IWW. James R. Green, *Grass-Roots Socialism: Radical Movements in the Southwest, 1895–1943* (1978), and Elliott Shore,

Talkin' Socialism: J. A. Wayland and the Role of the Press in American Radicalism, 1890–1912 (1988), analyze socialist movements in the Southwest.

POLITICAL REFORM IN THE CITIES Melvin Holli, *Reform in Detroit: Hazen S. Pingree and Urban Politics* (1969), is an exemplary study of a progressive mayor. On efforts to reform municipal governments, see David C. Hammack, *Power and Society: Greater New York at the Turn of the Century* (1982); Bradley R. Rice, *Progressive Cities: The Commission Government Movement in America, 1901–1920* (1977); and Martin J. Schiesl, *The Politics of Efficiency: Municipal Administration and Reform in America* (1977).

REFORM IN THE STATES Richard L. McCormick, *The Party Period and Public Policy* (1986), is indispensable on the roots of state reform. Thomas E. Cronin, *Direct Democracy: The Politics of Initiative, Referendum and Recall* (1989), examines the various movements to limit the power of party bosses and private interests in state politics. David P. Thelen, *The New Citizenship: Origins of Progressivism in Wisconsin, 1885–1900* (1972) and *Robert M. La Follette and the Insurgent Spirit* (1976), offer the best introduction to Wisconsin progressivism. For New York progressivism, consult Richard L. McCormick, *From Realignment to Reform: Political Change in New York State, 1893–1910* (1981); J. Joseph Huthmacher, *Senator Robert F. Wagner and the Rise of Urban Liberalism* (1971); Oscar Handlin, *Al Smith and His America* (1958); and Irvin Yellowitz, *Labor and the Progressive Movement in New York State* (1965). On social and economic reform movements more generally, see John D. Buenker, *Urban Liberalism and Progressive Reform* (1973). George E. Mowry, *The California Progressives* (1951), and Michael Kazin, *Barons of Labor: The San Francisco Building Trades and Union Power in the Progressive Era* (1987), examine the complexities of progressivism in California. On progressivism in the South, consult Sheldon Hackney, *Populism to Progressivism in Alabama* (1969); Jack Temple Kirby, *Darkness at the Dawning: Race and Reform in the Progressive South* (1972); and Dewey Grantham, *Southern Progressivism: The Reconciliation of Progress and Tradition* (1983).

RECONFIGURING THE ELECTORATE AND THE REGULATION OF VOTING On progressive efforts to reform and reconfigure the electorate, see Michael E. McGerr, *The Decline of Popular Politics: The American North, 1865–1928* (1986); L. E. Fredman, *The Australian Ballot: The Story of an American Reform* (1968); Paul Kleppner, *Who Voted? The Dynamics of Electoral Turnout, 1870–1980* (1982); and John Francis Reynolds, *Testing Democracy: Electoral Behavior and Progressive Reform in New Jersey, 1880–1920* (1988). J. Morgan Kousser, *The Shaping of Southern Politics: Suffrage Restriction and the Establishment of the One-Party South, 1880–1910* (1974), is indispensable on black disfranchisement. On the campaign for woman suffrage, see Anne Firor Scott and Andrew MacKay Scott, *One Half the People: The Fight for Woman Suffrage* (1982); Aileen Kraditor, *Ideas of the Woman Suffrage Movement* (1965); David Morgan, *The Suffragists and Democrats: The Politics of Woman's Suffrage in America* (1972); and Christine Lunardini, *From Equal Suffrage to Equal Rights: Alice Paul and the National Women's Party, 1912–1920* (1986).

CIVIL RIGHTS On the renewed campaign for black civil rights, see Charles F. Kellogg, *NAACP: The History of the National Association for the Advancement of Colored People* (1967); Louis R. Harlan, *Booker T. Washington: Wizard of Tuskegee, 1901–1915* (1983); David Levering Lewis, *W. E. B. Du Bois: Biography of a Race, 1868–1919* (1993); and Nancy Weiss, *The National Urban League, 1910–1940* (1974).

NATIONAL REFORM George E. Mowry, *The Era of Theodore Roosevelt* (1958), and Arthur Link, *Woodrow Wilson and the Progressive Era* (1954), are comprehensive overviews of progressivism at the national level. On the conservation movement, see Samuel P. Hays, *The Gospel of Efficiency: The Progressive Conservation Movement, 1890–1920* (1962); Stephen R. Fox, *The American Conservation Movement: John Muir and His Legacy* (1981); and Alfred Runte, *National Parks: The American Experience* (1979). On conflicts within the Republican Party, consult Horace S. Merrill and Marion G. Merrill, *The Republican High Command* (1971). On the Federal Reserve Act, see Robert T. McCulley, *Banks and Politics during the Progressive Era: The Origins of the Federal Reserve System* (1992), and James Livingston, *Origins of the Federal Reserve System: Money, Class and Corporate Capitalism, 1890–1913* (1986). On Louis Brandeis, consult Phillippa Strum, *Louis D. Brandeis* (1984), and Melvin Urofsky, *Louis D. Brandeis and the Progressive Tradition* (1981).

THEODORE ROOSEVELT Good biographies of Roosevelt include Henry F. Pringle, *Theodore Roosevelt* (1931); William H. Harbaugh, *The Life and Times of Theodore Roosevelt* (1975); G. Wallace Chessman, *Theodore Roosevelt and the Politics of Power* (1969); Robert V. Friedenberg, *Theodore Roosevelt and the Rhetoric of Militant*

Decency (1990); and H. W. Brands, *TR: The Last Romantic* (1997). John M. Blum, *The Republican Roosevelt* (1954), is a brief but interpretively significant account of Roosevelt's career, and Edmund Morris, *The Rise of Theodore Roosevelt* (1979), is a lively account of Roosevelt's early years.

WILLIAM HOWARD TAFT The fullest biography is still Henry F. Pringle, *The Life and Times of William Howard Taft*, 2 vols. (1939). For more critical views of Taft, see Paolo E. Coletta, *The Presidency of Taft* (1973), and Donald E. Anderson, *William Howard Taft* (1973). On the Pinchot-Ballinger affair, consult James Penich Jr., *Progressive Politics and Conservation: The Ballinger-Pinchot Affair* (1968), and Harold T. Pinkett, *Gifford Pinchot: Private and Public Forester* (1970).

WOODROW WILSON The premier biography and chronicle of Wilson's life from birth until the First World War is Arthur S. Link, *Woodrow Wilson,* 5 vols. (1947–1965). Other important biographies include Arthur Walworth, *Woodrow Wilson,* 2 vols. (1958); John M. Blum, *Woodrow Wilson and the Politics of Morality* (1962); August Heckscher, *Woodrow Wilson* (1991); Kendrick A. Clements, *The Presidency of Woodrow* Wilson (1992); and John Milton Cooper Jr., *The Warrior and the Priest: Woodrow Wilson and Theodore Roosevelt* (1983).

Chapter 22

General works on America's imperialist turn in the 1890s and early years of the 20th century include John Dobson, *America's Ascent: The United States Becomes a Great Power, 1880–1914* (1978); H. Wayne Morgan, *America's Road to Empire* (1965); David F. Healy, *U.S. Expansionism: Imperialist Urge in the 1890s* (1970); Ernest R. May, *Imperial Democracy: The Emergence of America as a Great Power* (1961); Robert L. Beisner, *From the Old Diplomacy to the New, 1965–1900* (1986); and Walter LaFeber, *The Cambridge History of Foreign Relations: The Search for Opportunity, 1865–1913* (1993).

MOTIVES FOR EXPANSION Patricia Hill, *The World Their Household: The American Woman's Foreign Mission Movement and Cultural Transformation, 1870–1920* (1984), and Jane Hunter, *The Gospel of Gentility: American Women Missionaries in Turn-of-the-Century China* (1984), are very good on the overseas work of female Protestant missionaries. William Appleman Williams, *The Tragedy of American Diplomacy,* rev. ed. (1972), is still indispensable on the economic motives behind imperialism, but it should be supplemented with Emily Rosenberg, *Spreading the American Dream: American Economic and Cultural Expansion, 1890–1945* (1982). For an important critique of Frederick Jackson Turner's notion that the year 1890 marked the end of the frontier, consult Patricia Nelson Limerick, *The Legacy of Conquest: The Unbroken Past of the American West* (1987). William E. Livezey, *Mahan on Sea Power* (1981), analyzes Admiral Mahan's strategy for transforming the United States into a world power, and Walter R. Herrick, *The American Naval Revolution* (1966), examines the emergence of a "Big Navy" policy. Julius W. Pratt, *Expansionists of 1898* (1936), is an important account of mounting jingoist fever in the 1890s.

THE SPANISH-AMERICAN WAR David F. Trask, *The War with Spain in 1898* (1981), is a comprehensive study of the Spanish-American War, but it should be supplemented with Philip S. Foner, *The Spanish-Cuban-American War and the Birth of American Imperialism,* 2 vols. (1972). See also James E. Bradford, *Crucible of Empire: The Spanish-American War and Its Aftermath* (1993). Joyce Milton, *The Yellow Journalists* (1989), discusses the role of the press in whipping up war fever, and Michael Blow, *A Ship to Remember: The Maine and the Spanish-American War* (1992), analyzes the battleship sinking that became the war's catalyst. Graham A. Cosmas, *An Army for Empire: The United States Army in the Spanish-American War* (1971), examines the achievements and failures of the army. Edmund Morris, *The Rise of Theodore Roosevelt* (1979), captures the daring of Roosevelt's Rough Riders and their charge up Kettle Hill, while William B. Gatewood Jr., *"Smoked Yankees": Letters from Negro Soldiers, 1898–1902* (1971), examines the important and unappreciated contributions of black soldiers. Gerald F. Linderman, *The Mirror of War: American Society and the Spanish-American War* (1974), brilliantly recaptures the shock that overtook Americans who discovered that their Cuban allies were black and the Spanish enemies were white.

BUILDING AN EMPIRE Julius W. Pratt, *America's Colonial Empire* (1950), analyzes steps the United States took to build itself an empire in the wake of the Spanish-American War. The annexation of Hawaii can be followed in Merze Tate, *The United States and the Hawaiian Kingdom* (1965), and William A. Russ Jr., *The Hawaiian*

Republic, 1894–1898, and Its Struggle to Win Annexation (1961). The acquisition of Guam and Samoa is examined in Paul Carano and Pedro Sanchez, *A Complete History of Guam* (1964), and Paul M. Kennedy, *The Samoan Tangle* (1974). The anti-imperialist movement is analyzed in E. Berkeley Tompkins, *Anti-Imperialism in the United States, 1890–1920: The Great Debate* (1970); Robert L. Beisner, *Twelve against Empire: The Anti-Imperialists, 1898–1900* (1968); and Daniel B. Schirmer, *Republic or Empire? American Resistance to the Philippine War* (1972). Richard E. Welch Jr., *Response to Imperialism: The United States and the Philippine War, 1899–1902* (1979), and Stuart Creighton Miller, *"Benevolent Assimilation": The American Conquest of the Philippines, 1899–1903* (1982), analyze the Filipino-American war, while Peter Stanley, *A Nation in the Making: The Philippines and the United States, 1899–1921* (1974), examines the fate of the Philippines under the first 20 years of U.S. rule. James H. Hitchman, *Leonard Wood and Cuban Independence, 1898–1902* (1971), and Louis A. Perez, *Cuba under the Platt Amendment, 1902–1934* (1986), analyze the extension of U.S. control over Cuba, while Raymond Carr, *Puerto Rico: A Colonial Experiment* (1984), examines the history of Puerto Rico following its annexation by the United States. For the unfolding of the Open Door policy toward China, consult Marilyn B. Young, *The Rhetoric of Empire: American China Policy, 1895–1901* (1968); Warren I. Cohen, *America's Response to China* (1971); and Thomas J. McCormick, *China Market: America's Quest for Informal Empire, 1890–1915* (1971).

THEODORE ROOSEVELT Howard K. Beale, *Theodore Roosevelt and the Rise of America to World Power* (1956), is still a crucial work on Roosevelt's foreign policy, although it should be supplemented with David H. Burton, *Theodore Roosevelt: Confident Imperialist* (1968), and Frederick Marks III, *Velvet on Iron: The Diplomacy of Theodore Roosevelt* (1979). Richard H. Collin, *Theodore Roosevelt's Caribbean: The Panama Canal, the Monroe Doctrine and the Latin American Context* (1990), examines Roosevelt's Caribbean policy. Of the many books written on the Panama Canal, two stand out: Walter LaFeber, *The Panama Canal* (1978), and David McCullough, *The Path between the Seas* (1977), a lively account of the canal's construction. See also Michael L. Conniff, *Black Labor on a White Canal: Panama, 1904–1981* (1985). For Roosevelt's policy in East Asia, consult Akira Iriye, *Pacific Estrangement: Japanese and American Expansion, 1897–1911* (1972); Charles Neu, *An Uncertain Friendship: Theodore Roosevelt and Japan, 1906–1909* (1967); and Charles Neu, *The Troubled Encounter* (1975). On the treatment of the Japanese in California, see Jules Becker, *The Course of Exclusion, 1882–1924: San Francisco Newspaper Coverage of the Chinese and Japanese in the United States* (1991).

WILLIAM HOWARD TAFT Ralph E. Minger, *William Howard Taft and American Foreign Policy* (1975), and Walter V. Scholes and Marie V. Scholes, *The Foreign Policies of the Taft Administration* (1970), are the standard works on William Howard Taft's foreign policies. For a comprehensive look at his "dollar diplomacy" and its effects on the Caribbean, see Dana G. Munro, *Intervention and Dollar Diplomacy in the Caribbean, 1900–1920* (1964). See also Emily Rosenberg, *Financial Missionaries to the World: The Politics and Culture of Dollar Diplomacy, 1900–1930* (1999).

WOODROW WILSON Two books by Arthur Link, *Wilson the Diplomatist* (1957) and *Woodrow Wilson: Revolution, War, and Peace* (1979), sympathetically treat Wilson's struggle to fashion an idealistic foreign policy. These works must be supplemented with Thomas J. Knock, *To End All Wars: Woodrow Wilson and the Quest for a New World Order* (1992). Lloyd C. Gardner, *Safe for Democracy: The Anglo-American Response to Revolution, 1913–1923* (1984), offers a more critical appraisal of Wilson's policies. On U.S. responses to the Mexican Revolution, see John S. D. Eisenhower, *Intervention: The United States and the Mexican Revolution, 1913–1917* (1993); Peter Calvert, *The Mexican Revolution, 1910–1914* (1968); Kenneth J. Grieb, *The United States and Huerta* (1969); and Robert E. Quirk, *An Affair of Honor: Woodrow Wilson and the Occupation of Veracruz* (1962).

Chapter 23

On the factors leading to the outbreak of war in Europe in 1914, see James Joll, *The Origins of the First World War* (1984), and Fritz Fisher, *Germany's War Aims in the First World War* (1972). On the horrors of trench warfare, see John Keegan, *The Face of Battle* (1976), and Erich Maria Remarque's classic novel, *All Quiet on the Western Front* (1929). Paul Fussell, *The Great War and Modern Memory* (1973), is indispensable for understanding the effects of the First World War on European culture.

AMERICAN NEUTRALITY AND INTERVENTION On American neutrality, see Arthur S. Link, *Woodrow Wilson: Revolution, War and Peace* (1979); John Milton Cooper Jr., *The Vanity of Power: American Isolationism and the*

First World War, 1914–1917 (1969); and Ernest R. May, *The World War and American Isolation, 1914–1917* (1959). Roland C. Marchand, *The American Peace Movement and Social Reform, 1898–1918* (1972), reconstructs the large and influential antiwar movement, while Ross Gregory, *The Origins of American Intervention in the First World War* (1971), analyzes the events that triggered America's intervention. Daniel R. Beaver, *Newton D. Baker and the American War Effort, 1917–1919* (1966), and John W. Chambers, *To Raise an Army: The Draft Comes to Modern America* (1987), analyze efforts to raise a multimillion-man fighting machine. Russell Weigley, *The American Way of War* (1973), examines the combat experiences of the American Expeditionary Force, while David F. Trask, *The AEF and Coalition Warmaking, 1917–1918* (1973), looks at relations between the AEF and the Allied armies. On the soldiers themselves, consult J. Garry Clifford, *The Citizen Soldiers* (1972), and A. E. Barbeau and Florette Henri, *The Unknown Soldiers: Black American Troops in World War I* (1974). Frank E. Vandiver, *Black Jack: The Life and Times of John J. Pershing* (1977), chronicles the life of the AEF's commander. Daniel H. Kevles, "Testing the Army's Intelligence: Psychologists and the Military in World War I," *Journal of American History* 55 (December 1968): 565–582, examines the military's use and misuse of IQ tests.

THE HOME FRONT David Kennedy, *Over Here: The First World War and American Society* (1980), is a superb account of the effects of war on American society, but it should be supplemented with Robert H. Ferrell, *Woodrow Wilson and World War I, 1917–1921* (1985), and Ronald Schaffer, *America in the Great War: The Rise of the War Welfare State* (1991). On industrial mobilization, see Robert D. Cuff, *The War Industries Board: Business-Government Relations during World War I* (1973), and the pertinent sections of Jordan Schwarz, *The Speculator* (1981), an excellent biography of Bernard Baruch. Efforts to secure labor's cooperation are examined in Valerie J. Connor, *The National War Labor Board* (1983); Keith Grieves, *The Politics of Manpower, 1914–1918* (1988); and Frank L. Grubb, *Samuel Gompers and the Great War* (1982). On the migration of African Americans to northern industrial centers and the movement of women into war production, see Florette Henri, *Black Migration: Movement North, 1900–1920* (1975); Joe William Trotter Jr., ed., *The Great Migration in Historical Perspective: New Dimensions of Race, Class, and Gender* (1991); James R. Grossman, *Land of Hope: Chicago, Black Southerners, and the Great Migration* (1989); and Maurine W. Greenwald, *Women, War and Work* (1980). David Montgomery, *The Fall of the House of Labor: The Workplace, the State, and American Labor Activism, 1865–1925* (1987), expertly reconstructs the escalation of labor-management tensions during the war, but it should be read alongside Joseph A. McCartin, *Labor's Great War: The Struggle for Industrial Democracy and the Origins of Modern Labor Relations, 1912–1921* (1997). Charles Gilbert, *American Financing of World War I* (1970), is indispensable on wartime tax and bond policies. See also Sidney Ratner, *Taxation and Democracy in America* (1967), and Dale N. Shook, *William G. McAdoo and the Development of National Economic Policy, 1913–1918* (1987).

GOVERNMENT PROPAGANDA AND REPRESSION Stephen Vaughn, *Holding Fast the Inner Lines: Democracy, Nationalism, and the Committee on Public Information* (1980), is an important account of the CPI, the government's central propaganda agency. See also George Creel, *How We Advertised America* (1920); John A. Thompson, *Reformers and War: Progressive Publicists and the First World War* (1987); and Walton Rawls, *Wake Up, America! World War I and the American Poster* (1987). The government's turn to repression as a way of achieving social unity can be followed in Zechariah Chafee Jr., *Free Speech in the United States* (1941); Harry N. Scheiber, *The Wilson Administration and Civil Liberties, 1917–1921* (1960); Harold C. Peterson and Gilbert Fite, *Opponents of War, 1917–1918* (1968); and William Preston Jr., *Aliens and Dissenters: Federal Suppression of Radicals, 1903–1933* (1966). John Higham, *Strangers in the Land: Patterns of American Nativism, 1865–1925* (1955), and Frederick C. Luebke, *Bonds of Loyalty: German-Americans and World War I* (1974), analyze the effects of this repression on European ethnic communities. Carol S. Gruber, *Mars and Minerva: World War I and the Uses of Higher Learning in America* (1975), discusses the effect of war on universities.

WOODROW WILSON AND THE LEAGUE OF NATIONS The best introduction is Thomas J. Knock, *To End All Wars: Woodrow Wilson and the Quest for a New World Order* (1992). For a more critical view of Wilson's motives, however, consult Arno Mayer, *The Politics and Diplomacy of Peacemaking: Containment and Counterrevolution at Versailles, 1918–1919* (1967); N. Gordon Levin Jr., *Woodrow Wilson and World Politics: America's Response to War and Revolution* (1968); and Lloyd C. Gardner, *Safe for Democracy: The Anglo-American Response to Revolution, 1913–1923* (1984). On Republican opposition to the League of Nations, see Ralph Stone, *The Irreconcilables: The Fight against the League of Nations* (1970), and William C. Widenor, *Henry Cabot Lodge and the Search for an American Foreign Policy* (1980).

Postwar Strikes and Radicalism Nell Irvin Painter, *Standing at Armageddon: The United States, 1877–1919* (1987), offers a good overview of the class and racial divisions that convulsed American society in 1919. Consult Dana Frank, *Purchasing Power: Consumer Organizing, Gender, and the Seattle Labor Movement, 1919–1929* (1994), on the Seattle general strike; Francis Russell, *A City in Terror* (1975), on the Boston police strike; and David Brody, *Labor in Crisis: The Steel Strike of 1919* (1965), on the steel strike. James Weinstein, *The Decline of Socialism in America, 1912–1925* (1967), and Theodore Draper, *The Roots of American Communism* (1957), analyze the effects of the Bolshevik Revolution on American socialism. On the Red Scare, consult Robert K. Murray, *Red Scare: A Study in National Hysteria* (1955); Stanley Coben, *A. Mitchell Palmer: Politician* (1963); and Richard Polenberg, *Fighting Faiths: The Abrams Case, the Supreme Court, and Free Speech* (1987). Roberta Strauss Feuerlicht, *Justice Crucified* (1977), and Francis Russell, *Tragedy in Dedham* (1962), offer divergent interpretations of the Sacco-Vanzetti affair. Paul Avrich, *Sacco-Vanzetti: The Anarchist Background* (1991), reconstructs the anarchist milieu from which Sacco and Vanzetti emerged.

Race Riots and Black Nationalism William Tuttle Jr., *Race Riot: Chicago in the Red Summer of 1919* (1970), and Elliott M. Rudwick, *Race Riot at East St. Louis* (1964), examine the two most notorious race riots of 1919. On the emergence of Marcus Garvey and the Universal Negro Improvement Association, see Judith Stein, *The World of Marcus Garvey: Race and Class in Modern Society* (1986), and David Cronon, *Black Moses* (1955).

Chapter 24

Overviews See William Leuchtenberg, *The Perils of Prosperity, 1914–1932* (1958); Geoffrey Perrett, *America in the Twenties* (1982); and Ellis Hawley, *The Great War and the Search for a Modern Order: A History of the American People and Their Institutions, 1917–1933* (1979). Frederick Lewis Allen, *Only Yesterday* (1931), remains the most entertaining account of the Jazz Age.

Prosperity and a Consumer Society George Soule, *Prosperity Decade: From War to Depression, 1917–1929* (1947), offers a thorough analysis of the decade's principal economic developments. Alfred D. Chandler Jr., *Strategy and Structure: Chapters in the History of the American Enterprise* (1962), and Adolph A. Berle Jr. and Gardiner F. Means, *The Modern Corporation and Private Property* (1932), examine changes in the structure and management of corporations. Important works on the consumer revolution include Robert S. Lynd and Helen Merrell Lynd, *Middletown: A Study in Modern American Culture* (1929); Warren I. Susman, *Culture as History: The Transformation of American Society in the Twentieth Century* (1984); Stewart Ewen, *Captains of Consciousness: Advertising and the Social Roots of the Consumer Culture* (1976); Roland Marchand, *Advertising the American Dream: Making Way for Modernity, 1920–1940* (1985); Richard Wightman Fox and T. J. Jackson Lears, eds., *The Culture of Consumption: Critical Essays in American History, 1880–1980* (1983); Kathy Lee Peiss, *Hope in a Jar: The Making of America's Beauty Culture* (1998); and Jackson Lears, *Fables of Abundance: A Cultural History of Advertising in America* (1994). The ways in which consumer ideals reshaped gender roles and family life can be followed in Ruth Schwartz Cowan, *More Work for Mother* (1982); William Chafe, *The American Woman: Her Changing Social, Economic, and Political Role* (1972); Dorothy M. Brown, *Setting a Course: American Women in the 1920s* (1987); Paula S. Fass, *The Damned and the Beautiful: American Youth in the 1920s* (1977); and Ben B. Lindsay and Wainright Evans, *The Companionate Marriage* (1927).

Republican Politics John D. Hicks, *Republican Ascendancy, 1921–1933* (1960), and Arthur M. Schlesinger Jr., *The Crisis of the Old Order* (1957), are excellent introductions to national politics during the 1920s. On Harding, see Robert K. Murray, *The Politics of Normalcy: Governmental Theory and Practice in the Harding-Coolidge Era* (1973), and Eugene Trani and David Wilson, *The Presidency of Warren G. Harding* (1977). William Allen White, *A Puritan in Babylon* (1939), is a colorful portrait of Calvin Coolidge; but see also Donald McCoy, *Calvin Coolidge: The Quiet President* (1967), and Thomas B. Silver, *Coolidge and the Historians* (1982). On Hoover's efforts to substitute "associational" politics for laissez-faire, two indispensable sources are Ellis Hawley, ed., *Herbert Hoover as Secretary of Commerce: Studies in New Era Thought and Practice* (1974), and Joan Hoff Wilson, *Herbert Hoover: Forgotten Progressive* (1975); see also David Burner, *Herbert Hoover: A Public Life* (1979). On Republican foreign policy, see Thomas Buckley, *The United States and the Washington Conference* (1970); Dexter Perkins, *Charles Evans Hughes and American Democratic Statesmanship* (1953); Joan Hoff Wilson, *American Business and Foreign Policy, 1920–1933* (1971); Warren I. Cohen, *Empire without Tears* (1987); Derek A. Aldcroft, *From Versailles to Wall Street, 1919–1929* (1977); and Robert H. Ferrell, *Peace in Their Time* (1952).

AGRICULTURAL DISTRESS AND PROHIBITION On agricultural distress and protest, see Gilbert Fite, *George Peek and the Fight for Farm Parity* (1954), and Theodore Saloutos and John D. Hicks, *Twentieth Century Populism: Agricultural Discontent in the Middle West, 1900–1939* (1951). For an examination of the economic and social effects of Prohibition, consult Andrew Sinclair, *The Era of Excess* (1962); Norman Clark, *Deliver Us from Evil: An Interpretation of American Prohibition* (1976); Mark Thornton, *The Economics of Prohibition* (1991); and John C. Burnham, *Bad Habits: Drinking, Smoking, Taking Drugs, Gambling, Sexual Misbehavior, and Swearing in American History* (1993).

NATIVISM, KU KLUX KLAN, AND IMMIGRATION RESTRICTION John Higham, *Strangers in the Land: Patterns of American Nativism, 1865–1925* (1955), remains the best work on the spirit of intolerance that gripped America in the 1920s. On the 1920s resurgence of the Ku Klux Klan, consult David Chalmers, *Hooded Americanism: The History of the Ku Klux Klan* (1965); Kenneth Jackson, *The Ku Klux Klan in the City* (1965); Nancy MacLean, *Behind the Mask of Chivalry: The Making of the Second Ku Klux Klan* (1994); Leonard J. Moore, *Citizen Klansmen: The Ku Klux Klan in Indiana, 1921–1928* (1991); Katherine M. Blee, *Women of the Klan: Racism and Gender in the 1920s* (1991); and Shawn Lay, ed., *The Invisible Empire in the West: Toward a New Historical Appraisal of the Ku Klux Klan of the 1920s* (1992). The movement for immigration restriction is examined in William S. Bernard, *American Immigration Policy: A Reappraisal* (1950); Robert A. Divine, *American Immigration Policy* (1957); and Henry B. Leonard, *The Open Gates: The Protest Against the Movement to Restrict Immigration, 1896–1924* (1980).

LIBERAL AND FUNDAMENTALIST PROTESTANTISM Ferenc Morton Szasz, *The Divided Mind of Protestant America, 1880–1930* (1982), expertly analyzes the split in Protestant ranks between liberals and fundamentalists. On the fundamentalist movement itself, consult George S. Marsden, *Fundamentalism in American Culture* (1980); Norman Furniss, *The Fundamentalist Controversy, 1918–1931* (1954); and William G. McLoughlin, *Modern Revivalism* (1959). Ray Ginger, *Six Days or Forever? Tennessee versus John Thomas Scopes* (1958), is a colorful account of the Scopes trial, while Lawrence Levine, *Defender of the Faith: William Jennings Bryan: The Last Decade, 1915–1925* (1965), offers a sympathetic portrait of Bryan during his final years. For a provocative reading of the Scopes trial, see Garry Wills, *Under God: Religion and American Politics* (1990).

INDUSTRIAL WORKERS Irving Bernstein, *The Lean Years: A History of the American Worker, 1920–1933* (1960), remains the most thorough examination of 1920s workers, but it should be supplemented with Robert H. Zeiger, *American Workers, American Unions, 1920–1985* (1986); Melvyn Dubofsky and Warren Van Tine, *John L. Lewis: A Biography* (1977); Leslie Tentler, *Wage-Earning Women* (1979); and Jacquelyn Hall et al., *Like a Family: The Making of a Southern Cotton Mill World* (1987). Siegfried Giedion, *Mechanization Takes Command: A Contribution to Anonymous History* (1948), is an insightful account of the effects of mechanization.

EUROPEAN AMERICAN ETHNIC COMMUNITIES On ethnic communities and Americanization in the 1920s, see Gary Gerstle, *Working-Class Americanism: The Politics of Labor in a Textile City, 1914–1960* (1989); Lizabeth Cohen, *Making a New Deal: Industrial Workers in Chicago, 1919–1939* (1990); and Stephen J. Shaw, *The Catholic Parish as a Way-Station of Ethnicity and Americanization: Chicago's Germans and Italians, 1903–1939* (1991). Leonard Dinnerstein, *Antisemitism in America* (1994), analyzes the resurgence of antisemitism in the 1920s and the use of quotas by universities to limit the enrollment of Jews. On the growing political strength of European American ethnics, see David Burner, *The Politics of Provincialism* (1967); Oscar Handlin, *Al Smith and His America* (1958); Paula Elder, *Governor Alfred E. Smith: The Politician as Reformer* (1983); and Kristi Andersen, *The Creation of a Democratic Majority, 1928–1936* (1979).

AFRICAN AMERICANS Good studies of the African American experience in the 1920s include Gilbert Osofsky, *Harlem: The Making of a Ghetto: Negro New York, 1890–1930* (1963); Kenneth L. Kusmer, *A Ghetto Takes Shape: Black Cleveland, 1870–1930*; Joe William Trotter Jr., *Black Milwaukee: The Making of an Industrial Proletariat, 1915–1945* (1985); and August Meier and Elliott Rudwick, *Black Detroit and the Rise of the UAW* (1979). Kathy H. Ogren, *The Jazz Revolution: Twenties America and the Meaning of Jazz* (1989), offers a probing analysis of jazz's place in 1920s culture. On the Harlem Renaissance, see Nathan Huggins, *Harlem Renaissance* (1971); Cary D. Mintz, *Black Culture and the Harlem Renaissance* (1988); and Jervis Anderson, *This Was Harlem: A Cultural Portrait, 1900–1950* (1981). Arnold Rampersand, *The Life of Langston Hughes*, 2 vols. (1986–1988), and Robert E. Hemenway, *Zora Neale Hurston: A Literary Biography* (1977), are important biographical works on two leading African American literary figures.

MEXICAN AMERICANS On the 1920s experience of Mexican immigrants and Mexican Americans, see George J. Sánchez, *Becoming Mexican American: Ethnicity, Culture and Identity in Chicano Los Angeles, 1900–1945* (1993); David Montejano, *Anglos and Mexicans in the Making of Texas, 1836–1986* (1987); Ricardo Romo, *East Los Angeles: History of a Barrio* (1983); Mark Reisler, *By the Sweat of Their Brow: Mexican Immigrant Labor in the United States, 1900–1940* (1976); and Manuel Gamio, *The Life Story of the Mexican Immigrant* (1931).

THE "LOST GENERATION" AND DISILLUSIONED INTELLECTUALS Malcolm Cowley, *Exiles Return* (1934), is a marvelous account of the writers and artists who comprised the "lost generation." See also Arlen J. Hansen, *Expatriate Paris* (1990), and William Wiser, *The Great Good Place: American Expatriate Women in Paris* (1991). On the southern "Agrarians," see John Stewart, *The Burden of Time* (1965), and Paul K. Conkin, *Southern Agrarians* (1988). Frederick J. Hoffman, *The Twenties: American Writing in the Postwar Decade,* rev. ed. (1962), is a fine sampler of the decade's best fiction. For biographical treatments of some of the decade's notable writers, consult Cleanth Brooks, *William Faulkner: The Yoknapathwapha County* (1963); Joel Williamson, *William Faulkner and Southern History* (1993); Carlos Baker, *Hemingway: The Writer as Artist* (1965); Kim Townshend, *Sherwood Anderson* (1987); and Virginia S. Carr, *Dos Passos: A Life* (1984). For a provocative interpretation of the intertwined character of white and black literary cultures in 1920s New York, see Ann Douglas, *Terrible Honestry: Mongrel Manhattan in the 1920s* (1995).

POLITICAL THOUGHT Robert Crunden, *From Self to Society: Transition in American Thought, 1919–1941* (1972), and Roderick Nash, *The Nervous Generation: American Thought, 1917–1930* (1969), are superior analyses of intellectual thought during the decade. On Mencken, see George H. Douglas, *H. L. Mencken* (1978), and Edward A. Martin, *H. L. Mencken and the Debunkers* (1984). Ronald Steel, *Walter Lippmann and the American Century* (1980), and Robert Westbrook, *John Dewey and American Democracy* (1991), are the best biographies of these two critical thinkers. On the new reform vanguard that began to form around Sidney Hillman, Franklin Roosevelt, and others, see Steven Fraser, *Labor Will Rule: Sidney Hillman and the Rise of American Labor* (1991), and Kenneth S. Davis, *FDR: The New York Years, 1928–1933* (1985).

Chapter 25

T. H. Watkins, *The Great Depression: America in the 1930s* (1993), provides a broad overview of society and politics during the 1930s. No work better conveys the tumult and drama of that era than Arthur M. Schlesinger Jr.'s three-volume *The Age of Roosevelt: The Crisis of the Old Order* (1957), *The Coming of the New Deal* (1958), and *The Politics of Upheaval* (1960).

CAUSES OF THE GREAT DEPRESSION On causes of the depression, consult John Kenneth Galbraith, *The Great Crash* (1955); Milton Friedman and Anna J. Schwartz, *The Great Contraction, 1929–1933* (1965); Michael A. Bernstein, *The Great Depression: Delayed Recovery and Economic Change in America, 1929–1939* (1987); Charles Kindelberger, *The World in Depression* (1973); and John A. Garraty, *The Great Depression* (1986).

HERBERT HOOVER On Hoover's failure to restore prosperity and popular morale, see Albert U. Romasco, *The Poverty of Abundance: Hoover, the Nation, the Depression* (1965), and David Burner, *Herbert Hoover: A Public Life* (1979). Roger Daniels, *The Bonus March* (1971), analyzes the event that became a symbol of Hoover's indifference to the depression's victims. More sympathetic treatments of Hoover's efforts to cope with the depression can be found in Harris G. Warren, *Herbert Hoover and the Great Depression* (1959); Joan Hoff Wilson, *Herbert Hoover: Forgotten Progressive* (1975); and Martin L. Fausold, *The Presidency of Herbert C. Hoover* (1985). Hoover offered his own spirited defense of his policies and a critique of the New Deal in his *Memoirs: The Great Depression* (1952).

FRANKLIN D. ROOSEVELT AND ELEANOR ROOSEVELT No 20th century president has attracted more scholarly attention than Franklin Roosevelt. The most detailed biography is Frank Freidel, *Franklin D. Roosevelt* (1952–1973), four volumes that cover Roosevelt's life from birth through the Hundred Days of 1933. The most complete biography, and one that is remarkably good at balancing Roosevelt's life and times, is Kenneth S. Davis, *FDR* (1972–1993), also in four volumes. Anyone interested in Roosevelt's youth and prepresidential career should consult Geoffrey Ward's *Before the Trumpet: Young Franklin Roosevelt, 1882–1905* (1985) and *A*

First-Class Temperament: The Emergence of Franklin Roosevelt (1989). James McGregor Burns, *Roosevelt: The Lion and the Fox* (1956), offers an intriguing portrait of Roosevelt as president.

On Eleanor Roosevelt, see Lois Scharf, *Eleanor Roosevelt: First Lady of American Liberalism* (1987); Joseph P. Lash, *Eleanor and Franklin* (1981); and, most importantly, Blanche Wiesen Cook, *Eleanor Roosevelt*, vol. 1 (1992), which chronicles her life from birth until she moved into the White House in 1933.

NEW DEAL OVERVIEWS William E. Leuchtenberg, *Franklin D. Roosevelt and the New Deal, 1932–1940* (1963), is still an authoritative account of the New Deal, although it should be supplemented with Robert S. McElvaine, *The Great Depression* (1984). Both books treat the New Deal as a transformative moment in American politics and economics. For more critical interpretations of the New Deal, stressing the limited nature of the era's reforms, see Barton J. Bernstein, "The New Deal: The Conservative Achievements of Liberal Reform," in Barton J. Bernstein, ed., *Toward a New Past: Dissenting Essays in American History* (1968); Paul K. Conkin, *The New Deal* (1975); and Anthony J. Badger, *The New Deal: The Depression Years, 1933–1940* (1989). Barry D. Karl, *The Uneasy State: The United States from 1915–1945* (1983), and the essays in Steve Fraser and Gary Gerstle, eds., *The Rise and Fall of the New Deal Order, 1930–1980* (1989), offer new perspectives on the achievements and limitations of the New Deal.

FIRST NEW DEAL See Susan E. Kennedy, *The Banking Crisis of 1933* (1973), and Michael Parrish, *Securities Regulation and the New Deal* (1970), on the First New Deal's efforts to restructure the nation's financial institutions. On New Deal relief efforts, consult George T. McJimsey, *Harry Hopkins: Ally of the Poor and Defender of Democracy* (1987); John Salmond, *The Civilian Conservation Corps, 1933–42* (1967); Percy H. Merrill, *Roosevelt's Forest Army: A History of the Civilian Conservation Corps, 1933–1942* (1981); and Bonnie Fox Schwartz, *The Civilian Works Administration: The Business of Emergency Employment in the New Deal 1933–1934* (1984). James T. Patterson, *America's Struggle against Poverty, 1900–1980* (1981), contains a substantial section on New Deal poor relief. For the New Deal's role in rebuilding the nation's infrastructure, see T. H. Watkins, *Righteous Pilgrim: The Life and Times of Harold Ickes, 1874–1952* (1990), and James S. Olson, *Saving Capitalism: The Reconstruction Finance Corporation and the New Deal, 1933–1940* (1988). Albert V. Romasco, *The Politics of Recovery: Roosevelt's New Deal* (1983), provides a useful overview of the First New Deal's efforts to restore prosperity.

FIRST NEW DEAL, AGRICULTURAL POLICY Van Perkins, *Crisis in Agriculture* (1969), and Theodore M. Saloutos, *The American Farmer and the New Deal* (1982), examine efforts to revive agriculture; David E. Conrad, *The Forgotten Farmers: The Story of Sharecroppers in the New Deal* (1965), and Paul Mertz, *The New Deal and Southern Rural Poverty* (1978), focus on groups ignored by New Deal programs. Donald Worster, *Dust Bowl: The Southern Plains in the 1930s* (1979), and James N. Gregory, *American Exodus: The Dust Bowl Migration and Okie Culture in California* (1989), are indispensable on the crisis in plains agriculture and the ensuing "Okie" migration.

FIRST NEW DEAL, INDUSTRIAL POLICY Ellis Hawley, *The New Deal and the Problem of Monopoly* (1966), is essential to understand the First New Deal's industrial policy. See also Bernard Bellush, *The Failure of the NRA* (1975); Michael Weinstein, *Recovery and Redistribution under the NRA* (1980); and Donald R. Brand, *Corporatism and the Rule of Law: A Study of the National Recovery Administration* (1988). On the TVA alternative, see Thomas K. McCraw, *TVA and the Power Fight, 1933–1939* (1971), and Walter L. Creese, *TVA's Public Planning: The Vision, the Reality* (1990).

POPULAR UNREST On populist critics of the New Deal, see Alan Brinkley, *Voices of Protest: Huey Long, Father Coughlin and the Great Depression* (1982); Michael Kazin, *The Populist Persuasion: An American History* (1995); and Abraham Holtzman, *The Townsend Movement* (1963). For the rebirth of the labor movement, consult Irving Bernstein, *The Turbulent Years: A History of the American Worker, 1933–1941* (1969); Lizabeth Cohen, *Making a New Deal: Industrial Workers in Chicago, 1919–1939* (1990); Gary Gerstle, *Working-Class Americanism: The Politics of Labor in a Textile City, 1914–1960* (1989); Jacquelyn Hall et al., *Like a Family: The Making of a Southern Cotton Mill World* (1987); Bruce Nelson, *Workers on the Waterfront: Seamen, Longshoremen, and Unionism in the 1930s* (1988); and Joshua B. Freeman, *In Transit: The Transport Workers Union in New York City, 1933–1966* (1989).

RADICAL POLITICS Richard M. Vallely, *Radicalism in the States: The Minnesota Farmer-Labor Party and the American Political Economy* (1989), and Greg Mitchell, *The Campaign of the Century: Upton Sinclair's EPIC Race for Governor of California and the Birth of Media Politics* (1992), analyze the upheaval in state politics that followed closely upon labor's resurgence. Irving Howe and Lewis Coser, *The American Communist Party: A Critical History, 1919–1957* (1957), is still the best single-volume history of the Communist Party during the 1930s. On the work of communists among the nation's dispossessed, see Mark Naison, *Communists in Harlem during the Depression* (1983); Robin D. G. Kelley, *Hammer and Hoe: Alabama Communists during the Great Depression* (1990); Dorothy Ray Healey and Maurice Isserman, *California Red: A Life in the American Communist Party* (1990); and Vicki Ruiz, *Cannery Women/Cannery Lives: Mexican Women, Unionization, and the California Food Processing Industry, 1930–1950* (1987).

THE SECOND NEW DEAL   Steven Fraser, *Labor Will Rule: Sidney Hillman and the Rise of American Labor* (1991), is indispensable for understanding the ideology, programs, and personalities of the Second New Deal. On the forging of the 1936 Democratic coalition, see Kristi Andersen, *The Creation of a Democratic Majority, 1928–1936* (1979), and Nancy J. Weiss, *Farewell to the Party of Lincoln: Black Politics in the Age of FDR* (1983). Roy Lubove, *The Struggle for Social Security* (1968), and J. Joseph Huthmacher, *Senator Robert Wagner and the Rise of Urban Liberalism* (1968), provide in-depth analyses of the Social Security Act, Wagner Act, and other crucial pieces of Second New Deal legislation. For critical perspectives on these reforms that stress their limitations as well as their achievements, consult Christopher Tomlins, *The State and the Unions: Labor Relations, Law and the Organized Labor Movement in America, 1880–1960* (1985), and Mark Leff, *The Limits of Symbolic Reform: The New Deal and Taxation, 1933–1939* (1984). Important for understanding the role of capitalists and money in the New Deal coalition are Jordan A. Schwarz, *The New Dealers: Power Politics in the Age of Roosevelt* (1993); Robert A. Caro, *The Years of Lyndon Johnson: The Path to Power* (1981); and Colin Gordon, *New Deals: Business, Labor, and Politics in America, 1920–1935* (1994).

NEW DEAL MEN, NEW DEAL WOMEN   On the political and cultural style of New Deal men, see Peter H. Irons, *The New Deal Lawyers* (1982); Samuel I. Rosenman, *Working with Roosevelt* (1952); Joseph P. Lash, *Dealers and Dreamers: A New Look at the New Deal* (1988); and Katie Louchheim, ed., *The Making of the New Deal: The Insiders Speak* (1983). On New Deal women, consult Susan Ware, *Beyond Suffrage: Women in the New Deal* (1981), and *Partner and I: Molly Dewson, Feminism and New Deal Politics* (1987); also see Linda Gordon, *Pitied but Not Entitled: Single Mothers and the History of Welfare, 1890–1935* (1994). On feminist weakness and male anxiety during the depression, see Lois Scharf, *To Work and to Wed: Female Employment, Feminism, and the Great Depression* (1980); Winifred Wandersee, *Women's Work and Family Values, 1920–1940* (1981); and Alice Kessler-Harris, *Out to Work: A History of Wage-Earning Women in the United States* (1982). Elizabeth Faue, *Community of Suffering and Struggle: Women, Men, and the Labor Movement in Minneapolis, 1915–1945* (1991), is illuminating on the strident masculinism that dominated 1930s labor and popular culture.

LABOR AND THE CIO   Melvyn Dubofsky and Warren Van Tine, *John L. Lewis: A Biography* (1977), is important on the birth of the CIO and labor's growing power in 1936 and 1937. Sidney Fine, *Sit-Down: The General Motors Strike of 1936–1937* (1967), is the most complete study of that pivotal event, but Nelson Lichtenstein, *"The Most Dangerous Man in Detroit": Walter Reuther and the Fate of American Labor* (1995), should be consulted for the broader industrial and union context in which it occurred. The best work on the centrality of labor and the "common man" to literary and popular culture in the 1930s is that of Michael Denning, *The Cultural Front: The Laboring of American Culture in the Twentieth Century* (1996); see also Richard H. Pells, *Radical Visions and American Dreams: Culture and Social Thought in the Depression Years* (1973). On the government's role in supporting public art through the WPA and other federal agencies, see William F. McDonald, *Federal Relief Administration and the Arts* (1968); Richard D. McKinzie, *The New Deal for Artists* (1973); and Barbara Melosh, *Engendering Culture: Manhood and Womanhood in New Deal Public Art and Theater* (1991).

MINORITIES AND THE NEW DEAL   Harvard Sitkoff, *A New Deal for Blacks* (1978), is a wide-ranging examination of the place of African Americans in New Deal reform. See also John B. Kirby, *Black Americans in the Roosevelt Era: Liberalism and Race* (1980); Robert L. Zangrando, *The NAACP Crusade against Lynching, 1909–1950* (1980); and James Goodman, *Stories of Scottsboro* (1994). Abraham Hoffman, *Unwanted Mexican Americans in the Great Depression: Repatriation Pressures, 1929–1939* (1974), is the best introduction to the repatriation campaign. George J. Sánchez, *Becoming Mexican American: Ethnicity, Culture and Identity in Chicano Los Angeles, 1900–1945* (1993), reconstructs the experience of the largest Mexican urban settlement in 1930s America; and Cletus E. Daniel, *Bitter Harvest: A History of California Farmworkers, 1870–1941* (1981), shows how little Chicanos and other groups of agricultural laborers benefited from New Deal reform. On Native Americans, consult Francis Paul Prucha, *The Great Father: The United States Government and the American Indians* (1984), and Christine Bolt, *American Indian Policy and American Reform* (1987). The importance of John Collier and the Indian Reorganization Act are treated well in Lawrence C. Kelly, *The Assault on Assimilation: John Collier and the Origins of Indian Policy Reform* (1983), and Graham D. Taylor, *The New Deal and American Indian Tribalism: The Administration of the Indian Reorganization Act, 1934–1945* (1980). For more detailed examinations of particular tribes' encounters with the New Deal, see Donald L. Parman, *The Navajos and the New Deal* (1976), and Harry A. Kersey Jr., *The Florida Seminoles and the New Deal, 1933–1942* (1989).

EBBING OF NEW DEAL James T. Patterson, *Congressional Conservatism and the New Deal* (1967), expertly analyzes the growing congressional opposition to the New Deal in the late 1930s. See also Frank Freidel, *FDR and the South* (1965). Leonard Baker, *Back to Back: The Duel between FDR and the Supreme Court* (1967), chronicles the court-packing fight. Alan Brinkley, *The End of Reform: New Deal Liberalism in Recession and War* (1995), provocatively examines the efforts of New Dealers to adjust their beliefs and programs as they lost support, momentum, and confidence in the late 1930s.

Chapter 26

U.S ENTRY INTO THE SECOND WORLD WAR The U.S entry into the Second World War is analyzed in Arnold A. Offner, *The Origins of the Second World War: American Foreign Policy and World Politics, 1917–1941* (1975); Waldo H. Heinrichs, *Threshold of War: Franklin D. Roosevelt and American Entry into World War II* (1988); Michael A. Barnhart, *Japan Prepares for Total War: The Search for Economic Security* (1987); Robert Dallek, *Franklin D. Roosevelt and American Foreign Policy, 1932–1945* (1979); Robert Divine, *The Reluctant Belligerent: American Entry into World War II* (1965); Akira Iriye, *The Origins of the Second World War in Asia and the Pacific* (1987); Ralph E. Schaffer, ed., *Towards Pearl Harbor: The Diplomatic Interchange between Japan and the United States, 1899–1941* (1991); and Sabura Ienaga, *The Pacific War: World War II and the Japanese* (1978). On isolationism, see Manfred Jonas, *Isolationism in America, 1935–1941* (1966); Wayne S. Cole, *Roosevelt and the Isolationists, 1932–45* (1983); and Goeffrey S. Smith, *To Save a Nation: American "Extremism," the New Deal, and the Coming of World War II* (1992).

PEARL HARBOR Pearl Harbor itself is the subject of several books by Gordon N. Prange, including *At Dawn We Slept: The Untold Story of Pearl Harbor* (1981); and *December 7, 1941: The Day the Japanese Attacked Pearl Harbor* (1988). See also John Toland, *Infamy: Pearl Harbor and Its Aftermath* (1982), and Michael Slackman, *Target–Pearl Harbor* (1990).

CONDUCT AND DIPLOMACY OF THE WAR The conduct and diplomacy of the war can be surveyed in Alastair Parker, *The Second World War: A Short History* (1997); Gerhard L. Weinberg, *A World at Arms: A Global History of World War II* (1994); and Stephen E. Ambrose, *The American Heritage New History of World War II* (rev. ed., 1997) and *Citizen Soldiers* (1997). Other important studies include Martin Gilbert, *The Second World War: A Complete History* (1989); John Ellis, *Brute Force: Allied Strategy and Tactics in the Second World War* (1990); Michael J. Lyons, *World War II: A Short History* (1989); Gary R. Hess, *The United States at War, 1941–1945* (1986); Gaddis Smith, *American Diplomacy during the Second World War* (2nd ed., 1985); John Keegan, *The Second World War* (1989); Robert A. Divine, *Roosevelt and World War II* (1969) and *Second Chance: The Triumph of Internationalism in America during World War II* (1967); Mark Stoler, *The Politics of the Second Front: American Military Planning and Diplomacy in Coalition Warfare, 1941–1943* (1977); Ronald Schaffer, *Wings of Judgment: American Bombing in World War II* (1985); Michael S. Sherry, *The Rise of American Air Power: The Creation of Armageddon* (1987); D. Clayton James, *A Time for Giants: Politics of the American High Command in World War II* (1987); and Nathan Miller, *War at Sea: A Naval History of World War II* (1995). David Wyman, *The Abandonment of the Jews: America and the Holocaust, 1941–1945* (1984), and William B. Rubinstein, *The Myth of Rescue: Why the Democracies Could Not Have Saved More Jews from the Nazis* (1997), offer very different views of U.S. policy toward the Holocaust. See also Eric Markusen and David Kopf, *The Holocaust and Strategic Bombing: Genocide and Total War in the Twentieth Century* (1995), and Verne W. Newton, ed., *FDR and the Holocaust* (1996). Paul Fussell, *Wartime: Understanding and Behavior in the Second World War* (1989), examines life in the military, and David R. Segal, *Recruiting for Uncle Sam: Citizenship and Military Manpower Policy* (1989), discusses the selective service.

WAR IN THE PACIFIC On the war in the Pacific, see Christopher Thorne, *Allies of a Kind: The United States, Britain, and the War against Japan, 1941–1945* (1978); Ronald Lewin, *The American Magic: Codes, Ciphers, and the Defeat of Japan* (1983); Ronald H. Spector, *Eagle against the Sun: The American War with Japan* (1985); John Dower, *War without Mercy: Race and Power in the Pacific War* (1986); Akira Iriye, *Power and Culture: The Japanese-American War, 1941–1945* (1981); Michael Schaller, *The U.S. Crusade in China, 1938–1945* (1979) and *Douglas MacArthur: The Far Eastern General* (1989); Sheldon H. Harris, *Factories of Death: Japan's Biological Warfare 1932–45 and the American Cover-Up* (1994); Edward J. Drea, *MacArthur's ULTRA: Code Breaking and the War against Japan* (1992); Bartlett E. Kerr, *Flames over Tokyo* (1991); Kenneth P. Werrell, *Blankets of Fire: U.S. Bombers over Japan during World War II* (1996); John D. Chappell, *Before the Bomb: How America Approached the End of the Pacific War* (1997); and Gunter Bischof and Robert L. Dupont, eds., *The Pacific War Revisited* (1997).

INDIVIDUAL POLICYMAKERS Individual policymakers are treated in Warren Kimball, *The Juggler: Franklin Roosevelt as Wartime Statesman* (1991); Forrest C. Pogue, *George C. Marshall*, vols. 2 and 3 (1966, 1973); Stephen E. Ambrose, *Eisenhower* (1983); Michael Schaller, *Douglas MacArthur: The Far Eastern General* (1989); and James Hershberg, *James B. Conant: Harvard to Hiroshima and the Making of the Nuclear Age* (1993).

THE HOME FRONT The home front receives attention in John Morton Blum's *V Was for Victory: Politics and American Culture during World War II* (1976); William L. O'Neill, *A Democracy at War: America's Fight at Home and Abroad in World War II* (1993); Richard Polenberg's *War and Society: The United States 1941–1945* (1972); Allan M. Winkler, *Home Front U.S.A.: America during World War II* (1986); Gerald D. Nash, *The Great Depression and World War II: Organizing America, 1933–1945* (1979); William Tuttle, *Daddy's Gone to War: The Second World War in the Lives of America's Children* (1993); Michael C. C. Adams, *The Best War Ever: America and World War II* (1994); and John W. Jeffries, *Wartime America: The World War II Home Front* (1996). Geoffrey Perret, *Days of Sadness, Years of Triumph: The American People, 1939–1945* (1973), remains good reading; Studs Terkel, *"The Good War": An Oral History of World War II* (1984), is a classic. Helpful works on the economy and labor include Paul A. C. Koistinen, *The Military-Industrial Complex: A Historical Perspective* (1980); Stephen B. Adams, *Mr. Kaiser Goes to War* (1998); James B. Atleson, *Labor and the Wartime State: Labor Relations and Law during World War II* (1998); Nelson Lichtenstein, *Labor's War at Home: The CIO in World War II* (1982); Bartholomew H. Sparrow, *From the Outside In: World War II and the American State* (1996); and George Lipsitz, *Rainbow at Midnight: Labor and Culture in the 1940s* (1994).

CHANGING GENDER RELATIONS ON THE HOME FRONT Major studies on the changing gender relations on the home front include Leila J. Rupp, *Mobilizing Women for War: German and American Propaganda, 1939–1945* (1978), a comparative study of the United States and Germany; Karen Anderson, *Wartime Women: Sex Roles, Family Relations, and the Status of Women during World War II* (1981); D'Ann Campbell, *Women at War with America: Private Lives in a Patriotic Era* (1984); Susan Hartman *The Home Front and Beyond: American Women in the 1940s* (1982); Ruth Milkman, *Gender at Work: The Dynamics of Job Segregation during World War II* (1987); and Sherna Berger Gluck, *Rosie the Riveter Revisited: Women, the War, and Social Change* (1988). See also Glen Jeansonne, *Women of the Far Right: The Mothers' Movement and World War II* (1996). Judy Barrett Litoff and David C. Smith, eds., *Since You Went Away: World War II Letters from American Women on the Home Front* (1991), is a moving compilation. John Costello, *Virtue under Fire: How World War II Changed Our Social and Sexual Attitudes* (1985), and Allan Berube, *Coming Out Under Fire: The History of Gay Men and Women in World War II* (1990), discuss changing sexual politics.

RACE AND THE HOME FRONT On issues of race and the home front, see Peter Irons *Justice at War* (1993); Roger Daniels, *Concentration Camps U.S.A.: Japanese Americans and World War II* (1989); Mauricio Mazon, *The Zoot-Suit Riots: The Psychology of Symbolic Annihilation* (1984); Neil Wynn, *The Afro-American and the Second World War* (1993); Dominic J. Capeci Jr. and Martha Wilkerson, *Layered Violence: The Detroit Rioters of 1943* (1991); Alison Bernstein, *American Indians and World War II: Toward a New Era in Indian Affairs* (1991); Clete Daniel, *Chicano Workers and the Politics of Fairness* (1991); and Merl E. Reed, *Seedtime for the Modern Civil Rights Movement: The President's Committee on Fair Employment Practice, 1941–1946* (1991).

THE PEACE MOVEMENT AND PACIFISM The peace movement and pacifism are examined in Lawrence Wittner, *Rebels against War: The American Peace Movement, 1941–1960* (1969); Cynthia Eller, *Conscientious Objectors and the Second World War: Moral and Religious Arguments in Support of Pacifism* (1991); Heather T. Frazier and John O'Sullivan, *"We Have Just Begun to Not Fight": An Oral History of Conscientious Objectors in Civilian Public Service during World War II* (1996); and Rachel Waltner Goosen, *Women against the Good War* (1998).

CULTURE DURING THE WAR On culture during the war, see Lewis A. Erenberg and Susan E. Hirsch, eds., *The War in American Culture: Society and Consciousness during World War II* (1996), and Lawrence Samuel, *Pledging Allegiance: American Identity and the Bond Drive of World War II* (1997). Thomas Patrick Doherty, *Projections of War: Hollywood, American Culture, and World War II* (1993), Clayton Koppes and Gregory D. Black, *Hollywood Goes to War; How Politics, Profits & Propaganda Shaped World War II Movies* (1987), and John Whiteclay Chambers II and David Culbert, *World War II, Film, and History* (1996), concentrate on film. Allan M. Winkler, *The Politics of Propaganda: The Office of War Information, 1942–1945* (1978), covers propaganda; Frank W. Fox, *Madison Avenue Goes to War* (1975), describes wartime advertising; and Robin Winks *Cloak and Gown: Scholars in the Secret War, 1939–1961* (1987), describes academic ties to government policy. Karl Ann Marling and John Wetenhall, *Iwo Jima: Monuments, Memory, and the American Hero* (1991), and George H. Roeder Jr., *The Censored War: American Visual Experience during World War II* (1993), both deal with the popular memory of the war.

WARTIME DIPLOMACY AND POSTWAR SETTLEMENTS On wartime diplomacy and postwar settlements, see Gabriel Kolko, *The Politics of War: The World and the United States Foreign Policy, 1943–1945* (1990); Remi Nadeau, *Stalin, Churchill and Roosevelt Divide Europe* (1990); Randall B. Woods and Howard Jones, *Dawning of the Cold War: The United States' Quest for Order* (1991); Diane S. Clemens, *Yalta* (1970); Randall B. Woods, *A Changing of the Guard: Anglo-American Relations, 1941–1946* (1990); and Michael Schaller, *The American Occupation of Japan: The Origins of the Cold War in Asia* (1985).

DROPPING OF THE ATOMIC BOMB The dropping of the atomic bomb has attracted a large and impressive literature. Good starting places for understanding the various controversies are Michael J. Hogan, ed., *Hiroshima in History and Memory* (1996); Edward J. Linenthal and Tom Engelhardt, *History Wars: The Enola Gay and Other Battles for the American Past* (1996); and J. Samuel Walker, *Prompt and Utter Destruction: Truman and the Use of Atomic Bombs against Japan* (1997). Major works on this topic, from various perspectives, include Martin Sherwin, *A World Destroyed: The Atomic Bomb and the Grand Alliance* (1975); Barton J. Bernstein, *The Atomic Bomb: The Critical Issues* (1976); Michael Mandelbaum, *The Nuclear Revolution: International Politics before and after Hiroshima* (1981); John Ray Skates, *The Invasion of Japan: Alternative to the Bomb* (1994); Peter Wyden, *Day One: Before Hiroshima and After* (1984); Richard Rhodes, *The Making of the Atomic Bomb* (1986); Gar Alperovitz, *The Decision to Use the Bomb and the Architecture of an American Myth* (1995); Robert Jay Lifton, *Hiroshima in America: Fifty Years of Denial* (1995); and Ronald Takaki, *Hiroshima: Why America Dropped the Atomic Bomb* (1995).

VIDEOS There are many video sources on the Second World War. *How Hitler Lost the War* (1990) and *The Call to Glory* (1991) are useful. The original "Why We Fight" series, produced by Frank Capra during the war, remains an important primary source. *WW II—The Propaganda Battle* is a fascinating entry in the "Walk through the 20th Century" series, hosted by Bill Moyers. *Rosie the Riveter* (1980) is a documentary of women workers during the war. *Without Due Process* (1991) is a video account of the evacuation of Japanese Americans. On the development of the atomic bomb, see *Day after Trinity* (1980) and *J. Robert Oppenheimer: Father of the Atomic Bomb* (1995). *The Promised Land* (1995) is a three-part documentary on the African American migration from the Deep South to Chicago.

Chapter 27

U.S. FOREIGN POLICY AND THE ORIGINS OF THE COLD WAR For overviews of U.S. foreign policy and the origins of the Cold War, see Thomas G. Paterson, *Meeting the Communist Threat: Truman to Reagan* (1988); Thomas J. McCormick, *America's Half-Century: United States Foreign Policy in the Cold War and After* (2nd ed., 1995); Warren I. Cohen, *America in the Age of Soviet Power* (1993); Fraser J. Harbutt, *The Iron Curtain: Churchill, America, and the Origins of the Cold War* (1986); John Lewis Gaddis, *Strategies of Containment: A Critical Appraisal of Postwar American National Security Policy* (1982), his *The Long Peace: Inquiries into the History of the Cold War* (1987), and his *We Now Know: Rethinking Cold War History* (1997); Thomas G. Paterson, *On Every Front: The Making and Unmaking of the Cold War* (rev. ed., 1992); Walter LaFeber, *America, Russia, and the Cold War, 1945–1992* (7th ed., 1993); Stephen Ambrose, *Rise to Globalism: American Foreign Policy since 1938* (8th ed., 1997); H. W. Brands, *The Devil We Knew: Americans and the Cold War* (1993); Melvin Leffler, *The Specter of Communism* (1994); Deborah Welch Larson, *Anatomy of Mistrust: U.S.-Soviet Relations during the Cold War* (1997); and Ronald E. Powaksi, *The Cold War: The United States and the Soviet Union, 1917–1991* (1998).

Specific Issues and Incidents of the Cold War Era For the history of specific issues and incidents of the Cold War era, see Gregg Herken, *The Winning Weapon: The Atomic Bomb in the Cold War, 1945–1950* (1980); Walter Hixson, *George F. Kennan: Cold War Iconoclast* (1989); Bruce R. Kuniholm, *The Origins of the Cold War in the Near East: Great Power Conflict and Diplomacy in Iran, Turkey, and Greece* (1980); Michael Schaller, *The American Occupation of Japan: The Origins of the Cold War in Asia* (1985); Frank Ninkovich, *Germany and the United States: The Transformation of the German Question since 1945* (1988); Robert A. Pollard, *Economic Security and the Origins of the Cold War, 1945–1950* (1985); Michael J. Hogan, *The Marshall Plan: America, Britain, and the Reconstruction of Western Europe, 1949–52* (1987); Louis Liebovich, *The Press and the Origins of the Cold War, 1944–1947* (1988); Howard Jones, *"A New Kind of War": America's Global Strategy and the Truman Doctrine in Greece* (1989); Sallie Pisani, *The CIA and the Marshall Plan* (1991); Lawrence S. Wittner, *One World or None: A History of the World Nuclear Disarmament Movement through 1953* (1993); Steven Hugh Lee, *Outposts of Empire: Korea, Vietnam, and the Origins of the Cold War in Asia, 1949–84* (1995); Robert Accinelli, *Crisis and Commitment: United States Policy toward Taiwan, 1950–55* (1996); Michael L. Krenn, *The Chains of Interdependence: U.S. Policy toward Central America, 1945–1954* (1996); Richard Rhodes, *Dark Sun: The Making of the Hydrogen Bomb* (1995); and Justus D. Doenecke, *Not to the Swift: The Old Isolationists in the Cold War Era* (1979). A superb political history of the early Cold War years is James T. Patterson, *Grand Expectations: The United States, 1945–74* (1996).

National Security Policy On national security policy during the late 1940s and early 1950s consult Daniel Yergin, *Shattered Peace: The Origins of the Cold War and the National Security State* (1977); Melvyn Leffler, *A Preponderance of Power: National Security, the Truman Administration, and the Cold War* (1992); and Michael S. Sherry, *In the Shadow of War: The United States since the 1930s* (1995). See also Walter Isaacson and Evan Thomas, *The Wise Men: Six Friends and the World They Made: Acheson, Bohlen, Harriman, Kennan, Lovett, McCloy* (1986), and Evan Thomas, *The Very Best Men: Four Who Dared; The Early Years of the CIA* (1995).

Cultural Interpretations of National Security Policies For cultural interpretations of national security policies see the relevant chapters of Richard Slotkin, *Gunfighter Nation: The Myth of the Frontier in Twentieth-Century America* (1992), and Robert J. Corber, *In the Name of National Security: Hitchcock, Homophobia, and the Political Construction of Gender in Postwar America* (1993). For broader views of the cultural climate of the early Cold War see Lary May, ed., *Recasting America: Culture and Politics in the Age of the Cold War* (1989); Stephen J. Whitfield, *The Culture of the Cold War* (2nd ed., 1996); William Graebner, *The Age of Doubt: American Thought and Culture in the 1940s* (1991); Paul Boyer, *By the Bomb's Early Light* (1985); Tom Englehardt, *The End of Victory Culture: Cold War America and the Disillusioning of a Generation* (1994); Guy Oakes, *The Imaginary War: Civil Defense and American Cold War Culture* (1994); Mark Jancovich, *Rational Fears: American Horror in the 1950s* (1996); Alan Nadel, *Containment Culture: American Narrative, Postmodernism, and the Atomic Age* (1995); and Margot A. Henriksen, *Dr. Strangelove's America: Society and Culture in the Atomic Age* (1997).

President Truman Harry Truman enjoys a number of good biographical treatments. See Robert H. Ferrell, *Harry S Truman and the Modern American Presidency* (1983) and *Harry S. Truman: A Life* (1994); Donald R. McCoy, *The Presidency of Harry S. Truman* (1984); William E. Pemberton, *Harry S. Truman: Fair Dealer and Cold Warrior* (1988); David G. McCullough, *Truman* (1992); Alonzo L. Hamby, *Man of the People: A Life of Harry S. Truman* (1995); and Sean J. Savage, *Truman and the Democratic Party* (1998). Michael J. Lacey, ed., *The Truman Presidency* (1989), offers interpretive essays, while Alonzo L. Hamby, *Beyond the New Deal: Harry S Truman and American Liberalism* (1973), remains a useful look at Truman's Fair Deal that should be supplemented by the relevant chapter of the same author's *Liberalism and Its Challengers: Liberalism from FDR to Bush* (2nd ed., 1992). Steve Fraser and Gary Gerstle, eds., *The Rise and Fall of the New Deal Order, 1930–1980* (1989), takes a longer view of postwar themes.

Domestic Policymaking during the Fair Deal On domestic policymaking during the Fair Deal, see R. Alton Lee, *Truman and Taft-Hartley: A Question of Mandate* (1966); Kevin Boyle, *The UAW and the Heyday of American Liberalism, 1945–1968* (1997); Allen J. Matusow, *Farm Policies and Politics in the Truman Years* (1967); Richard O. Davies, *Housing Reform during the Truman Administration* (1966); Susan M. Hartmann, *Truman and the 80th Congress* (1971); Monte M. Poen, *Harry S. Truman versus the Medical Lobby: The Genesis of Medicare* (1979); Andrew J. Dunar, *The Truman Scandals and the Politics of Morality* (1984); the relevant chapters of Edward D. Berkowitz, *America's Welfare State: From Roosevelt to Reagan* (1991); and Sheryl R. Tynes, *Turning Points in Social Security: From "Cruel Hoax" to "Sacred Entitlement"* (1996).

ANTICOMMUNISM Anticommunism is the subject of M. J. Heale, *American Anticommunism: Combating the Enemy Within, 1880–1970* (1990), and Richard Gid Powers, *Not without Honor: The History of American Anticommunism* (1995), both of which take the long view. Fred Inglis, *The Cruel Peace: Everyday Life in the Cold War* (1991), offers an international perspective. Allen Weinstein's *Perjury: The Hiss Chambers Case* (rev. ed., 1997) is an important, once controversial study which is now bolstered by, among other recent works, Joseph Albright and Marcia Kunstel, *Bombshell: The Secret Story of America's Unknown Atomic Spy Conspiracy* (1997); Sam Tanenhaus, *Whittaker Chambers: A Biography* (1997); and *Secrecy: Report of the Commission on Protecting and Reducing Government Secrecy* (1997). Richard M. Fried, *Nightmare in Red: The McCarthy Era in Perspective* (1990), and Ellen Schrecker, *The Age of McCarthyism: A Brief History with Documents* (1994), are solid syntheses, but David Caute's *The Great Fear: The Anti-Communist Purge under Truman and Eisenhower* (1978) remains the most detailed account. See also Michael R. Belknap, *Cold War Political Justice: The Smith Act, the Communist Party, and American Civil Liberties* (1977); Stanley I. Kutler, *The American Inquisition: Justice and Injustice in the Cold War* (1982); Marjorie Garber and Rebecca L. Walkowitz, eds., *Secret Agents: The Rosenberg Case, McCarthyism, and Fifties America* (1995); and John F. Neville, *The Press, the Rosenbergs, and the Cold War* (1995).

SOCIAL CHANGES OF THE EARLY COLD WAR YEARS The social changes of the early Cold War years have drawn the attention of many recent historical works. For an interesting view, see Wendy Kozol, *Life's America: Family and Nation in Postwar Photojournalism* (1994). The baby boom is the focus of Richard A. Easterlin, *Birth and Fortune: The Impact of Numbers on Personal Welfare* (2nd ed., 1987), and Landon Y. Jones, *Great Expectations: America and the Baby Boom Generation* (1980). See also the relevant chapters of John Modell, *Into One's Own: From Youth to Adulthood in the United States, 1920–1975* (1989). On women's issues, see the final chapters of Susan Strasser, *Never Done: A History of American Housework* (1982); Alice Kessler-Harris, *Out to Work: A History of Wage-Earning Women in the United States* (1982); Jacqueline Jones, *Labor of Love, Labor of Sorrow: Black Women, Work and the Family, from Slavery to the Present* (1985); Eugenia Kaledin, *Mothers and More: American Women in the 1950s* (1984); Leila Rupp and Verta Taylor, *Survival in the Doldrums: The American Women's Rights Movement, 1945 to the 1960s* (1990); and Cynthia Harrison, *On Account of Sex: The Politics of Women's Issues, 1945–68* (1988). Family and gender issues are nicely tied to Cold War culture in Elaine Tyler May, *Homeward Bound: American Families in the Cold War Era* (1989), and in Stephanie Coontz, *The Way We Never Were: American Families and the Nostalgia Trip* (1992). On issues related to sexuality and gender, see the relevant chapters of John D'Emilio and Estelle B. Freedman, *Intimate Matters: A History of Sexuality in America* (1988); Wini Breines, *Young, White, and Miserable: Growing Up Female in the Fifties* (1992); Graham McCann, *Rebel Males: Clift, Brando and Dean* (1993); and Joanne Meyerowitz, ed., *Not June Cleaver: Women and Gender in Postwar America, 1945–1960* (1994).

SUBURBAN AND URBAN ISSUES On suburban and urban issues, see Robert A. Caro, *The Power Broker: Robert Moses and the Fall of New York* (1974); Mark Gelfand, *A Nation of Cities: The Federalist Government and Urban America, 1933–1945* (1975); Herbert Gans, *The Levittowners: Ways of Life and Politics in a New Suburban Community* (2nd ed., 1982); the relevant chapters of Kenneth T. Jackson, *Crabgrass Frontier: The Suburbanization of the United States* (1985); Barbara M. Kelly, *Expanding the American Dream: Building and Rebuilding Levittown* (1993); and Rob Kling, Spencer Olin, and Mark Poster, *Postsuburban California: The Transformation of Orange County since World War II* (1991). See also John M. Findlay, *Magic Lands: Western City Scapes and American Culture after 1940* (1992); David L. Kirp, John P. Dwyer, and Larry A. Rosenthal, *Our Town: Race, Housing and the Soul of Suburbia* (1995); John R. Gillis, *A World of their Own: Myth, Ritual, and the Quest for Family Values* (1996); Jon C. Teaford, *The Rough Road to Renaissance: Urban Revitalization in America, 1940–85* (1990) and *Post-Suburbia: Government and the Politics in the Edge Cities* (1997); Alan Ehrenhalt, *The Lost City: Discovering the Forgotten Virtues of Community in the Chicago of the 1950s* (1995); Michael F. Logan, *Fighting Sprawl and City Hall: Resistance to Urban Growth in the Southwest* (1995); and James Hudnut-Beumler, *Looking for God in the Suburbs: the Religion of the American Dream and Its Critics, 1945–1965* (1994). Thomas J. Sugrue, *The Origins of the Urban Crisis: Race and Inequality in Postwar Detroit* (1996), is a recent, award-winning study.

THE KOREAN WAR On the Korean War, Burton I. Kaufman, *The Korean War: Challenges in Crisis, Credibility, and Command* (1986), is a brief synthesis. More detailed analyses may be found in several volumes by Bruce Cumings: *The Origins of the Korean War* (1981); *Child of Conflict: The Korean-American Relationship, 1943–53* (1983), a series of essays that he edited; and *Korea: The Unknown War* (coauthored with Jon Halliday) (1988). See also William Stueck, *The Korean War: An International History* (1995); Chen Jian, *China's Road to the Korean War: The Making of the Sino-American Confrontation* (1994); Shu Guang Zhang, *Mao's Military Romanticism:*

China and the Korean War, 1950–1953 (1995); and William T. Bowers, William M. Hammond, and George L. MacGarrigle, *Black Soldier, White Army: The 24th Infantry Regiment in Korea* (1996).

THE EISENHOWER YEARS The Eisenhower years received an early scholarly synthesis in Charles C. Alexander, *Holding the Line: The Eisenhower Era, 1952–1960* (1975), which can be updated with Chester Pach Jr. and Elmo Richardson, *The Presidency of Dwight D. Eisenhower* (rev. ed., 1991); Robert F. Burk, *Dwight David Eisenhower* (1986); William B. Pickett, *Dwight David Eisenhower and American Power* (1995); the relevant chapter of Hamby, *Liberalism and Its Challengers* (2nd ed., 1992); and Jeff Broadwater, *Eisenhower and the Anti-Communist Crusade* (1992). Stephen E. Ambrose's massive two-volume study *Eisenhower* (1983, 1984) contains a wealth of information. *Adlai Stevenson and American Politics: The Odyssey of a Cold War Liberal* (1994), by Jeff Broadwater, is a solid biography of the man twice defeated by Eisenhower for the presidency. Fred I. Greenstein, *The Hidden-Hand Presidency: Eisenhower as Leader* (rev. ed., 1994) helped to begin the trend toward a new view of Eisenhower's presidency.

VIDEOS *March of Time: American Lifestyles* (1987) is a five-video compilation taken from newscasts of the period. *Post-War Hopes, Cold War Fears*, from the "Walk through the 20th Century" series, offers an interesting overview. For a visual recounting of the beginning of U.S. involvement in the Vietnam War, see *The First Vietnam War* (1946–1954), a one-hour video documentary in the series "Vietnam: A Television History." *The Rise of J. Edgar Hoover* (1991) is a superb video documentary in the "American Experience" series. *The Forgotten War* (1987) is a three-part video documentary on Korea. *Truman* (1997) and *Ike*, formally titled *Eisenhower* (1993), are solid entries in PBS's "The White House Collection." *George Marshall and the American Century* (1993) offers a sweeping overview of Eisenhower's important military benefactor, while *The Marshall Plan: Against All Odds* (1997) covers Marshall's most important Cold War initiative. *Adlai Stevenson: The Man from Libertyville* (1992) is a video portrait of the Democrat who was twice defeated by Eisenhower for the presidency. *Seeing Red* (1993) looks, with considerable compassion, on the people who supported the Communist Party. The anticommunist crusade in Hollywood is the subject of *Hollywood on Trial* (1976) and *Legacy of the Hollywood Blacklist* (1987). *Point of Order: A Documentary of the Army-McCarthy Hearings* (1964) is a classic documentary on the congressional hearings that marked the beginning of McCarthy's demise.

Chapter 28

EISENHOWER'S FOREIGN POLICY Robert Divine, *Eisenhower and the Cold War* (1981), and Blanche Wiesen Cook, *The Declassified Eisenhower* (1981), offer differing interpretations of Eisenhower's foreign policies. See also Joann P. Krieg, ed., *Dwight D. Eisenhower: Soldier, President and Statesman* (1987), and H. W. Brands, *Cold Warriors: Eisenhower's Generation and American Foreign Policy* (1988). See also the many works on Eisenhower which are cited in Chapter 27.

SPECIALIZED STUDIES ON FOREIGN POLICY More specialized studies on foreign policy include Robert Divine, *Blowing in the Wind: The Nuclear Test-Ban Debate* (1978) and *The Sputnik Challenge: Eisenhower's Response to the Soviet Satellite* (1993); Allan M. Winkler, *Life under a Cloud: American Anxiety about the Atom* (1993); Stuart W. Leslie, *The Cold War and American Science: The Military-Industrial-Academic Complex at MIT and Stanford* (1993). Regional studies include Stephen G. Rabe, *Eisenhower and Latin America: The Foreign Policy of Anticommunism* (1988); Zhang Shu Guang, *Deterrence and Strategic Culture Culture: Chinese-American Confrontations, 1949–1958* (1992); Robert J. McMahon, *The Cold War on the Periphery: The United States, India and Pakistan* (1994); Kenton J. Clymer, *Quest for Freedom: The United States and India's Independence* (1995); Isaac Alteras, *Eisenhower and Israel: U.S.-Israeli Relations, 1953–1960* (1993); Thomas G. Paterson, *Contesting Castro: The United States and the Triumph of the Cuban Revolution* (1994); Bonnie F. Saunders, *The United States and Arab Nationalism: The Syrian Case, 1953–1960* (1996); Saki Dockrill, *Eisenhower's New-Look National Security Policy, 1953–61* (1996); G. Wyn Rees, *Anglo-American Approaches to Alliance Security, 1955–60* (1996); and Cole C. Kingseed, *Eisenhower and Suez Crisis of 1956* (1995). The growing importance of intelligence agencies in foreign policy is examined in Stephen Ambrose and Richard H. Immerman, *Ike's Spies: Eisenhower and the Espionage Establishment* (1981) and *The CIA in Guatemala: The Foreign Policy of Intervention* (1982); Michael R. Beschloss, *Mayday: Eisenhower, Khrushchev, and the U-2 Affair* (1986); Rhodri Jeffreys-Jones, *The CIA and American Democracy* (1989); Loch K. Johnson, *America's Secret Power: The CIA in a Democratic Society* (1989); Thomas F. Troy, *Donovan and the CIA: A History of the Establishment of the Central Intelligence Agency* (1981);

John Prados, *President's Secret Wars: CIA and Pentagon Covert Operations since World War II* (1986); Audrey R. Kahin and George McT. Kahin, *Subversion as Foreign Policy: The Secret Eisenhower and Dulles Debacle in Indonesia* (1995); and Nicholas Cullather, *Operation PSSUCCESS: The United States and Guatemala 1952–54* (1997). African Americans and foreign policy are discussed in Brenda Gayle Plummer, *Rising Wind: Black Americans and U.S. Foreign Affairs, 1935–1960* (1996), and Penny M. Von Eschen, *Race against Empire: Black Americans and Anticolonialism, 1937–1957* (1997). On cultural diplomacy, see especially Walter L. Hixson, *Parting the Curtain: Propaganda,Culture, and the Cold War, 1945–1961* (1997), and Robert H. Haddow, *Pavilions of Plenty: Exhibiting American Culture Abroad in the 1950s* (1997).

U.S. INVOLVEMENT IN VIETNAM On the deepening U.S. involvement in Vietnam, see David L. Anderson, *Trapped by Success: The Eisenhower Administration and Vietnam, 1953–1961* (1991); George Herring, *America's Longest War: The United States and Vietnam, 1950–1975* (1986); Andrew J. Rotter, *The Path to Vietnam: Origins of the American Commitment to Southeast Asia* (1987); Lloyd C. Gardner, *Approaching Vietnam: From World War II through Dien Bien Phu* (1988); James Arnold, *The First Domino: Eisenhower, the Military, and America's Intervention in Vietnam* (1991); and Melanie Billings-Yun, *Decision against War: Eisenhower and Dien Bien Phu, 1954* (1988).

DOMESTIC POLITICS Domestic politics are treated in Mark Rose, *Interstate: Express Highway Politics, 1941–1956* (1979); R. Alton Lee, *Eisenhower and Landrum Griffin: A Study in Labor-Management Politics* (1990); Richard Kluger, *Simple Justice: The History of* Brown *v.* Board of Education *and Black America's Struggle for Equality* (1975); Austin Sarat, ed., *Race, Law, and Culture: Reflections on* Brown *v.* Board of Education (1996); and Tom Lewis, *Divided Highways: Building the Interstate Highways, Transforming American Life* (1997). Clarence G. Lasby, *Eisenhower's Heart Attack: How Ike Beat Heart Disease and Held on to the Presidency* (1996), is an interesting account.

POSTWAR MASS CULTURE For overviews of postwar mass culture, see Andrew Ross, *No Respect: Intellectuals and Popular Culture* (1989); W. T. Lhamon Jr., *Deliberate Speed: The Origins of a Cultural Style in the American 1950s* (1990); Karal Ann Marling, *As Seen on TV: The Visual Culture of Everyday Life in the 1950s* (1994); and James L. Baughman, *The Republic of Mass Culture: Journalism, Filmmaking, and Broadcasting in America since 1941* (2nd ed., 1996). The debates over mass culture in the 1950s can be sampled in Bernard Rosenberg and David Manning White, *Mass Culture* (1957) and *Mass Culture Revisited* (1971). James Gilbert, *A Cycle of Outrage: America's Reaction to the Juvenile Delinquent in the 1950s* (1986), critiques this debate and relates it to an emerging youth culture. On TV, see Cecelia Tichi, *The Electronic Hearth* (1991), and Michael Curtin, *Redeeming the Wasteland: Television Documentary and Cold War Politics* (1995). On rock music, see Greil Marcus, *Mystery Train: Images of America in Rock n' Roll* (3rd ed., 1990); Charley Gillet, *Sound of the City: The Rise of Rock and Roll* (rev. ed., 1984); and Nelson George, *The Death of Rhythm and Blues* (1988). On the diversity of the youth culture, see William Graebner, *Coming of Age in Buffalo: Youth and Authority in the Postwar Era* (1989).

SOCIAL ISSUES On social issues, see Michael Harrington's classic *The Other America: Poverty in the United States* (1962); James T. Patterson, *America's Struggle against Poverty, 1900–1980* (1981); Doug McAdam, *Political Process and the Development of Black Insurgency, 1930–1970* (1982); Harvard Sitkoff, *The Struggle for Black Equality, 1954–1992* (1993); Larry Burt, *Tribalism in Crisis: Federal Indian Policy, 1953–1961* (1982); Donald L. Fixico, *Termination and Relocation: Federal Indian Policy, 1945–1960* (1986); Manuel Alers-Montalvo, *The Puerto Rican Migrants of New York* (1985); David Garrow, *Bearing the Cross: Martin Luther King, Jr., and the Southern Christian Leadership Conference* (1986); Joseph P. Fitzpatrick, *Puerto Rican Americans: The Meaning of Migration to the Mainland* (2nd ed., 1987); Taylor Branch, *Parting the Waters: America in the King Years, 1954–1963* (1988); Steven J. Whitfield, *A Death in the Delta: The Story of Emmett Till* (1988); Mario Garcia, *Mexican-Americans: Leadership, Ideology, Identity, 1930–1960* (1989); Ricardo Romo, *East Los Angeles: History of a Barrio* (1989); Armstead L. Robinson and Patricia Sullivan, eds., *New Directions in Civil Rights Studies* (1991); the relevant chapters of Jacqueline Jones, *The Dispossessed: America's Underclass from the Civil War to the Present* (1992); Mark V. Tushnet, *Making Civil Rights Law: Thurgood Marshall and the Supreme Court, 1936–1961* (1993); James F. Findlay, *Church People in the Struggle: The National Council of Churches and the Black Freedom Movement, 1950–1970* (1993); Maria Cristina Garcia, *Havana USA: Cuban Exiles and Cuban Americans in South Florida, 1959–1994* (1996); and David G. Gutierrez, *Walls and Mirrors: Mexican Americans, Mexican Immigrants, and the Politics of Ethnicity* (1995). Clayborne Carson, ed., *The Papers of Martin Luther King, Jr.* (vol 3, 1997) focuses on struggles during the Montgomery bus boycott; see also Richard Lischer, *The*

Preacher King: Martin Luther King, Jr. and the Words that Moved America (1995); and Glenn T. Eskew, *But for Birmingham: The Local and National Movements in the Civil Rights Struggle* (1997). On civil rights issues during the Kennedy years, see Howard Zinn, *SNCC: The New Abolitionists* (1965); William Chafe, *Civilities and Civil Rights: Greensboro, North Carolina and the Black Struggle for Freedom* (1980); John Walton Cotman, *Birmingham, JFK, and the Civil Rights Act of 1963* (1989); Kenneth O'Reilly, *Racial Matters: The FBI's Secret Files on Black America, 1960–72* (1989); Mark Stern, *Calculating Visions: Kennedy, Johnson, and Civil Rights* (1992); and many of the works listed in Chapter 29.

JOHN F. KENNEDY Garry Wills, *Nixon Agonistes: The Crisis of the Self-Made Man* (rev. ed., 1980) and *The Kennedy Imprisonment: A Meditation on Power* (1983) offer critical viewpoints on John F. Kennedy, as does Thomas C. Reeves, *A Question of Character: A Life of John F. Kennedy* (1991). Seymour M. Hersh, *The Dark Side of Camelot* (1997), is an attempt to obliterate the Kennedy mystique. More favorable, though not uncritical, is David Burner, *John F. Kennedy and a New Generation* (1988). James N. Giglio's *The Presidency of John F. Kennedy* (1991) provides a reliable overview. For more detail, see Herbert J. Parmet's two volumes: *Jack: The Struggle of John F. Kennedy* (1980) and *JFK: The Presidency of John F. Kennedy* (1983). There are many sympathetic accounts of Kennedy's presidency by close associates; by far the best is Arthur Schlesinger Jr., *A Thousand Days* (1965). Specific policy decisions are the subject of Jim F. Heath, *John Kennedy and the Business Community* (1969); Victor Navasky, *Kennedy Justice* (1971); Carl M. Brauer, *John F. Kennedy and the Second Reconstruction* (1977); James R. Williamson, *Federal Antitrust Policy during the Kennedy-Johnson Years* (1995).

KENNEDY'S FOREIGN POLICY On Kennedy's foreign policy, see Thomas G. Paterson, ed., *Kennedy's Quest for Victory: American Foreign Policy, 1961–1963* (1989); Michael R. Beschloss, *The Crisis Years: Kennedy and Khrushchev, 1960–1963* (1991); and Noam Chomsky, *Rethinking Camelot: JFK, the Vietnam War, and U.S. Political Culture* (1993). A huge literature on the missile crisis in Cuba includes Graham T. Allison, *Essence of Decision: Explaining the Cuban Missile Crisis* (1971); Trumbell Higgins, *The Perfect Failure: Kennedy, Eisenhower, and the CIA at the Bay of Pigs* (1989); Dino A. Brugioni, *Eyeball to Eyeball: The Inside Story of the Cuban Missile Crisis* (1991); James Blight, *Cuba on the Brink: Castro, the Missile Crisis, and the Soviet Challenge* (1993); Mark J. White, *The Cuban Missile Crisis* (1996); John C. Ausland, *Kennedy, Khrushchev, and the Berlin-Cuba Crisis, 1961–1964* (1996); Timothy Naftali and Aleksandr Fursenko, *"One Hell of a Gamble": Khrushchev, Castro, and Kennedy, 1958–1964* (1997); and Ernest R. May and Philip D. Zelikow, eds., *The Kennedy Tapes: Inside the White House during the Cuban Missile Crisis* (1997).

KENNEDY'S DEATH Events surrounding Kennedy's death have attracted almost as much attention as his life. Michael J. Kurtz, *The Crime of the Century: The Kennedy Assassination from an Historian's Perspective* (1982), tries to offer historical grounding, while Barbie Zelizer, *Covering the Body: The Kennedy Assassination, the Media, and the Shaping of Collective Memory* (1992), is a superb cultural study. Theories of the assassination itself include Peter Dale Scott, *Deep Politics and the Death of JFK* (1993), which is critical of the Warren Commission's findings, and Gerald L. Posner, *Case Closed: Lee Harvey Oswald and the Assassination of JFK* (1993), which defends them. See also John Newman, *Oswald and the CIA* (1995).

VIDEOS *Eisenhower* (1993) is an excellent documentary in the "American Experience" series. *America's Mandarin (1954–1967)* is a one-hour video documentary of U.S. involvement in Vietnam, from Eisenhower to Johnson, in the series "Vietnam: A Television History" (1983). *The Quiz Show Scandal* (1991) and *That Rhythm, Those Blues* (1988) are solid entries in the "American Experience" series. The multipart documentary series "Eyes on the Prize" (1987) provides a dramatic, visual representation of the struggle for African American civil rights. *The Road to Brown* (1990) offers a a more limited, but still important, view. See also, *Dr. Martin Luther King Jr.: A Historical Perspective* (1993) and *Southern Justice: The Murder of Medger Evers* (1994). *The Kennedys* (1992) is a four-hour video documentary in the "American Experience" series. *Spy in the Sky* (1996) is the story of the U.S. reconnaissance program during the Eisenhower years. *Crisis: Missiles in Cuba* (1989) offers a brief, 30-minute overview.

Chapter 29

LYNDON JOHNSON On Lyndon Johnson see Paul K. Conkin, *Big Daddy from the Pedernales: Lyndon Baines Johnson* (1986); Robert Caro, *The Path to Power* (1982) and *Means of Ascent* (1990); Robert J. Dallek, *Lone Star Rising:*

Lyndon Johnson and His Times, 1908–1960 (1991); and Irving Bernstein, *Guns or Butter: The Presidency of Lyndon Johnson* (1996). Other titles include Vaughn Davis Bornet, *The Presidency of Lyndon Baines Johnson* (1993), which is relatively sympathetic, and Doris Kearns Goodwin, *Lyndon Johnson and the American Dream* (1976). Joseph A. Califano Jr., *The Triumph and Tragedy of Lyndon Johnson: The White House Years* (1991), is an interesting memoir, and Michael R. Beschloss, ed., *Taking Charge: The Johnson White House Tapes, 1963–1964* (1997), offers fascinating insights. On the Warren Court see Morton J. Horwitz, *The Warren Court and the Pursuit of Justice* (1998).

CIVIL RIGHTS Civil rights issues are treated in David Garrow, *Protest at Selma: Martin Luther King, Jr., and the Voting Rights Act of 1965* (1980); Clayborne Carson, *In Struggle: SNCC and the Black Awakening of the 1960s* (1981); Doug McAdam, *Freedom Summer* (1988); Emily Stoper, *The Student Non-Violent Coordinating Committee: The Growth of Radicalism in a Civil Rights Organization* (1989); Mark Stern, *Calculating Visions: Kennedy, Johnson, and Civil Rights* (1992); William L. Van Deburg, *New Day in Babylon: The Black Power Movement and American Culture, 1965–1975* (1992); Gerald Horne, *Fire This Time: The Watts Uprising and the 1960s* (1995); David J. Armor, *Forced Justice: School Desegregation and the Law* (1995); Richard Griswold del Castillo and Richard A. Garcia, *Cesar Chavez: A Triumph of Spirit* (1995); Louis A. DeCaro Jr., *On the Side of My People: A Religious Life of Malcolm X* (1996); Michael Eric Dyson, *Making Malcolm: The Myth and Meaning of Malcolm X* (1995); Charles M. Payne, *I've Got the Light of Freedom: The Organizing Tradition and the Mississippi Freedom Struggle* (1995); and Taylor Branch, *Pillar of Fire: America in the King Years, 1963–65* (1998).

THE GREAT SOCIETY AND THE WAR ON POVERTY The Great Society and the War on Poverty receive a critical assessment in Alan J. Matusow, *The Unraveling of America: A History of Liberalism in the 1960s* (1984). The most influential analysis from the right of Great Society liberalism has been Charles Murray's *Losing Ground: American Social Policy, 1950–1980* (1984), which can be compared with Christopher Jencks, *Rethinking Social Policy: Race, Poverty and the Underclass* (1992). A recent overview is Gareth Davies, *From Opportunity to Entitlement: The Transformation and Decline of Great Society Liberalism* (1996). See also Michael L. Gillette, *Launching the War on Poverty: An Oral History* (1996).

JOHNSON'S FOREIGN POLICIES Johnson's foreign policies are treated in Bernard Firestone and Robert C. Vogt, eds., *Lyndon Baines Johnson and the Uses of Power* (1988); Warren I. Cohen and Nancy Bernkopf Tucker, eds., *Lyndon Johnson Confronts the World: American Foreign Policy, 1963–1968* (1994); and Diane Kunz, ed., *The Diplomacy of the Crucial Decade: American Foreign Relations during the 1960s* (1994). On the Dominican intervention see Bruce Palmer Jr., *Intervention in the Caribbean: The Dominican Crisis of 1965* (1989), and Abraham F. Lowenthal, *The Dominican Intervention* (1995).

JOHNSON'S POLICIES IN VIETNAM Johnson's policies in Vietnam have attracted an immense literature. Representative titles include George Herring, *America's Longest War: The United States and Vietnam, 1950–1975* (1986); Marilyn Blatt Young, *The Vietnam-American Wars, 1945–1990* (1991); David L. DiLeo, *George Ball, Vietnam, and the Rethinking of Containment* (1991); Melvin Small, *Johnson, Nixon, and the Doves* (1988); Larry Berman, *Lyndon Johnson's War: The Road to Stalemate in Vietnam* (1989); Marilyn Young and Jon Livingston, *The Vietnam War: How the United States Intervened in the History of Southeast Asia* (1990); Gabriel Kolko, *Anatomy of War: Vietnam, The United States, and the Modern Historical Experience* (1994); Lloyd C. Gardner, *Approaching Vietnam: From World War II through Dien Bien Phu* (1988); George McT. Kahin, *Intervention: How America Became Involved in Vietnam* (1986); R. B. Smith, *An International History of the Vietnam War* (1983); James J. Wirtz, *The Tet Offensive: Intelligence Failure in War* (1991); Ronald Spector, *After Tet: The Bloodiest Year in Vietnam* (1993); David M. Barrett, *Uncertain Warriors: Lyndon Johnson and His Vietnam Advisors* (1993); David L. Anderson, ed., *Facing My Lai: Moving beyond the Massacre* (1997); Michael Hunt, *Lyndon Johnson's War: America's Cold War Crusade in Vietnam, 1945–1968* (1996); Robert Buzzanco, *Masters of War: Military Dissent and Politics in the Vietnam Era* (1996); Richard A. Hunt, *Pacification: The American Struggle for Vietnam's Hearts and Minds* (1995); Edwin Moise, *Tonkin Gulf and the Escalation of the Vietnam War* (1996); Roger Warner, *Back Fire: The CIA's Secret War in Laos and Its Link to the Vietnam War* (1995); and Robert D. Schulzinger, *A Time for War: The United States and Vietnam, 1941–1975* (1997).

CULTURAL DEBATES GENERATED BY THE WAR IN VIETNAM For cultural debates generated by the war in Vietnam, see Loren Baritz, *Backfire: A History of How American Culture Led Us into Vietnam and Made Us Fight the Way We Did* (1985); Kathleen Turner, *Lyndon Johnson's Dual War: Vietnam and the Press* (1985); Susan Jeffords, *The*

Remasculinization of America: Gender and the Vietnam War (1989); Albert Auster and Leonard Quart, *How the War Was Remembered: Hollywood and Vietnam* (1988); John Carlos Rowe and Rick Berg, eds., *The Vietnam War and American Culture* (1991); Michael Gregg, ed., *Inventing Vietnam: The War in Film and Television* (1991); David W. Levy, *The Debate over Vietnam* (2nd ed., 1995); and Fred Turner, *Echoes of Combat: The Vietnam War in American Memory* (1996).

POLITICAL INSURGENCY OF THE 1960s On the political insurgency of the 1960s see W. J. Rorbaugh, *Berkeley at War: The 1960s* (1989); Barbara Tischler, ed., *Sights on the Sixties* (1992); David Chalmers, *And the Crooked Place Made Straight: The Struggle for Social Change in the 1960s* (1996); Timothy Miller, *The Hippies and American Values* (1991); Peter Collier and David Horowitz, *Destructive Generation: Second Thoughts about the Sixties* (1996); Paul Berman, *A Tale of Two Utopias: The Political Journey of the Generation of 1968* (1998); David Farber, ed., *The Sixties: From Memory to History* (1994); Alexander Bloom and Wini Breines, eds., *"Takin It to the Streets": A Sixties Reader* (1995); Paul Lyons, *New Left, New Right, and the Legacy of the Sixties* (1996); Jonah Raskin, *For the Hell of It: The Life and Times of Abbie Hoffman* (1996); and David Burner, *Making Peace with the Sixties* (1996). The conservative insurgency is the subject of Mary C. Brennan, *Turning Right in the Sixties: The Conservative Capture of the GOP* (1995); Robert Alan Goldberg, *Barry Goldwater* (1995); and John A. Andrew III, *The Other Side of the Sixties: Young Americans for Freedom and the Rise of Conservative Politics* (1997).

OPPOSITION TO THE WAR On opposition to the war, see Charles De Benedetti, *An American Ordeal: The Anti-War Movement of the Vietnam Era* (1990); Melvin Small and William D. Hoover, eds., *Give Peace a Chance* (1992); Kenneth J. Heineman, *Campus Wars: The Peace Movement at American State Universities in the Vietnam Era* (1993); Amy Swerdlow, *Women Strike for Peace: Traditional Motherhood and Radical Politics in the 1960s* (1993); Tom Wells, *The War Within: America's Battle over Vietnam* (1993); and Adam Garfinkle, *Telltale Hearts: The Origins and Impact of the Vietnam Antiwar Movement* (1995). Todd Gitlin indicts the media for speeding the fall of opposition efforts in *The Whole World Is Watching: Mass Media in the Making and Unmaking of the New Left* (1980), while Maurice Isserman's *If I Had a Hammer: The Death of the Old Left and the Birth of the New Left* (1987) looks at the general conflict among radicals. See also Wini Breines, *Community and Organization in the New Left, 1962–1968* (1982); Jim Miller, *Democracy Is in the Streets: From Port Huron to the Siege of Chicago* (1987); Todd Gitlin, *The Sixties: Years of Hope, Days of Rage* (1987); and Douglas Knight, *Streets of Dreams: The Nature and Legacy of the 1960s* (1989). On the politics of 1968 see Lewis Gould, *1968: The Election That Changed America* (1993).

RICHARD NIXON AND HIS POLICIES On Richard Nixon and his policies, see Garry Wills, *Nixon Agonistes* (rev. ed., 1980); Bruce Odes, ed., *From the President: Richard Nixon's Secret Files* (1989); Stephen Ambrose, *Nixon* (1989); Roger Morris, *Richard Milhous Nixon: The Rise of an American Politician* (1990); Joan Hoff, *Nixon Reconsidered* (1994); and Terry Terriff, *The Nixon Administration and the Making of U.S. Nuclear Strategy* (1995). On economic policy see Diane B. Kunz, *Butter and Guns: America's Cold War Economic Policy* (1997), and Allen J. Matusow, *Nixon's Economy: Booms, Busts, Dollars, and Votes* (1997).

WATERGATE On Watergate and the broader ethos of secret government, see Peter Schrag, *Test of Loyalty: Daniel Ellsberg and the Rituals of Secret Government* (1974); Theodore White, *Breach of Faith: The Fall of Richard Nixon* (1975); Athan Theoharis, *Spying on Americans: Political Surveillance from Hoover to the Huston Plan* (1978); Frank J. Donner, *The Age of Surveillance: The Aims and Methods of America's Surveillance System* (1980); L. H. LaRue, *Political Discourse: A Case Study of the Watergate Affair* (1988); Stanley I. Kutler, *The Wars of Watergate: The Last Crisis of Richard Nixon* (1990) and *Abuse of Power: The New Nixon Tapes* (1998); and Michael Schudson, *Watergate in American Memory: How We Remember, Forget, and Reconstruct the Past* (1992).

VIDEOS *LBJ* (1991) is a four-hour video documentary in the "American Experience" series; *Chicago, 1968* (1995) is a solid, one-hour entry in the same series. There are a number of video accounts of Malcolm X, including *Malcolm X: Make It Plain* (1993) and *The Real Malcolm X: An Intimate Portrait of the Man* (1992). On civil rights, also consult the appropriate one-hour segments in the longer "Eyes on the Prize" series. On the political insurgency of the 1960s, see *Making Peace with the Sixties* (1991), a three-part series, and the more limited, but more insightful, *Berkeley in the Sixties* (1990). *Watergate* (1994) is a multipart documentary produced in Great Britain.

Chapter 30

SOCIAL, ECONOMIC, AND DEMOGRAPHIC DEVELOPMENTS On social, economic, and demographic developments, see Raymond Mohl, ed., *Searching for the Sunbelt: Historical Perspectives on a Region* (1990); Mike Davis, *City of Quartz: Excavating the Future in Los Angeles* (1990); Alejandro Portes and Alex Stepick, *City on the Edge: The Transformation of Miami* (1993); Merry Ovnick, *Los Angeles: The End of the Rainbow* (1994); Nathan Glazer, ed., *Clamor at the Gates: The New American Immigration* (1985); Michael D'Innocenzo and Josef P. Sirefman, eds., *Immigration and Ethnicity* (1992); Alejandro Portes and Ruben G. Rumbaut, *Immigrant America: A Portrait* (1996); Norman L. Zucker and Naomi Flink Zucker, *Desperate Crossings: Seeking Refuge in America* (1996); Robert J. Samuelson, *The American Dream in the Age of Entitlement, 1945–1995* (1996); Steven P. Dandaneau, *A Town Abandoned: Flint, Michigan, Confronts Deindustrialization* (1996); Ruth Milkman, *Farewell to the Factory: Auto Workers in the Late Twentieth Century* (1997); Charles Noble, *Welfare as We Knew It: A Political History of the American Welfare State* (1997); and Allen J. Scott and Edward W. Soja, *The City: Los Angeles and Urban Theory at the End of the Twentieth Century* (1996).

CHANGES IN TECHNOLOGY AND THE ENVIRONMENT On changes in technology and the environment, see Robert Reich, *The Work of Nations: Preparing Ourselves for 21st Century Capitalism* (1991); Kirkpatrick Sale, *The Green Revolution: The Environmental Movement* (1993); James W. Cortada, *The Computer in the United States: From Laboratory to Market, 1930–1960* (1993); Daniel Yergin, *The Prize: The Epic Quest for Oil, Money, and Power* (1991) and *The Commanding Heights: The Battle between Government and the Marketplace That Is Remaking the Modern World* (1998); Samuel P. Hays, *Beauty, Health, and Permanence: Environmental Politics in the United States, 1955–1985* (1987); Craig E. Coltren and Peter N. Skinner, *The Road to Love Canal: Managing Industrial Waste before the EPA* (1996); Michele Stenehjem Gerber, *On the Home Front: The Cold War Legacy of the Hanford Nuclear Site* (1992); Terence Kehoe, *Cleaning Up the Great Lakes: From Cooperation to Confrontation* (1997); Ann Markusen et al., *The Rise of the Gunbelt: The Military Remapping of Industrial America* (1991); and Philip Shabecoff, *A Fierce Green Fire: The American Environmental Movement* (1993).

CHANGES IN THE MEDIA ENVIRONMENT AND MASS CULTURE On changes in the media environment and mass culture, see Todd Gitlin, *Inside Prime Time* (1983); John Fiske, *Television Culture* (1987); Mark Crispin Miller, *Boxed-In: The Culture of TV* (1988); Robert Kolker, *Cinema of Loneliness: Penn, Kubrick, Scorcese, Spielberg, Altman* (rev. ed., 1988); Marsha Kinder, *Playing with Power in Movies, Television, and Video Games* (1991); Elizabeth G. Traube, *Dreaming Identities: Class, Gender, and Generation in the 1980s Hollywood Movies* (1992); Andrew Goodwin, *Dancing in the Distraction Factory: Music Television and Popular Culture* (1992); Henry Jenkins, *Textual Poachers: Television Fans & Participatory Culture* (1992); Anne Friedberg, *Window Shopping: Cinema and the Postmodern* (1993); Jane Feuer, *Seeing through the Eighties: Television and Reaganism* (1995); Alan Nadel, *Flatlining on the Field of Dreams: Cultural Narratives in the Films of President Reagan's America* (1997); Henry A. Giroux, *Channel Surfing: Race Talk and the Destruction of Today's Youth* (1997); and Joseph Turow, *Breaking Up America: Advertisers and the New Media World* (1997).

CONTINUATION OF POLITICAL INSURGENCY On the continuation of political insurgency, begin with Barbara Epstein, *Political Protest and Cultural Revolution: Non-Violent Direct Action in the 1970s* (1991). See also Paul Chaat Smith and Robert Allen Warrior, *Like a Hurricane: The Indian Movement from Alcatraz to Wounded Knee* (1996). Sara Evans, *Personal Politics: The Roots of Women's Liberation in the Civil Rights Movement and the New Left* (1979); Alice Echols, *Daring to Be Bad: Radical Feminism in America, 1967–1975* (1989); and Nancy Whittier, *Feminist Generations: the Persistence of the Radical Women's Movement* (1995), seek to trace the emergence of a new feminism out of the male-dominated ethos of the New Left and the counterculture and to suggest that the 1960s did not represent a sudden end to insurgent movements. See also Jane J. Mansbridge, *Why We Lost the Era* (1986); Mary Frances Berry, *Why ERA Failed: Politics, Women's Rights, and the Amending Process of the Constitution* (1986); Johnnetta B. Cole, ed., *All American Women: Lines That Divide, Ties That Bind* (1986); Catherine MacKinnon, *Feminism Unmodified: Discourses on Life and Law* (1988); Susan Staggenborg, *The Pro-Choice Movement: Organization and Activism in the Abortion Conflict* (1991); and the relevant chapters of Leslie Reagan, *When Abortion Was a Crime: Women, Medicine, and Law in the United States, 1867–1973* (1997). On the gay and lesbian rights movement, see John D'Emilio and Estelle B. Freedman, *Intimate Matters: A History of Sexuality in America* (1988); Randy Shilts, *And the Band Played On: Politics, People, and the AIDS Epidemic* (1987); and Steven Epstein, *Impure Science: AIDS, Aids Activism, and the Politics of Science* (1996).

RACE AND MULTICULTURALISM On the dilemmas of race and multiculturalism see Russell Ferguson et al., eds., *Out There: Marginalization and Contemporary Cultures* (1990); Toni Morrison, ed., *Race-ing Justice, En-Gendering Power: Essays on Anita Hill, Clarence Thomas, and the Construction of Social Reality* (1992); Andrew Hacker, *Two Nations: Black and White, Separate, Hostile, and Unequal* (1992); bell hooks, *Black Looks: Race and Representation* (1992); Michael Eric Dyson, *Reflecting Black: African-American Cultural Criticism* (1993); Cornel West, *Race Matters* (1993) and *Beyond Eurocentrism and Multiculturalism* (1993); Celeste Olalquiaga, *Megalopolis: Contemporary Cultural Sensibilities* (1992); James Davison Hunter, *Culture Wars: The Struggle to Define America* (1991); Henry Louis Gates Jr., *Loose Canons: Notes on the Culture Wars* (1992); Patricia Turner, *I Heard It through the Grapevine: Rumor in African-American Culture* (1993); Russell A. Potter, *Spectacular Vernaculars: Hip-Hop and the Politics of Postmodernism* (1995); David A. Hollinger, *Post-Ethnic America: Beyond Multiculturalism* (1995); Robert C. Smith, *Racism in the Post–Civil Rights Era; Now You See It, Now You Don't* (1995); Roger Waldinger, *Still the Promised City? African-Americans and New Immigrants in Postindustrial New York* (1996); Mattias Gardell, *In the Name of Elijah Muhammed: Louis Farrakhan and the Nation of Islam* (1996); Michael Eric Dyson, *Between God and Gangsta Rap: Bearing Witness to Black Culture* (1996); Jennifer L. Hochschild, *Facing Up to the American Dream: Race, Class, and the Soul of the Nation* (1995); Toni Morrison ed., *Birth of a Nation 'Hood: Gaze, Script, and Spectacle in the O. J. Simpson Case* (1997); Elaine Bell Kaplan, *Not Our Kind of Girl: Unravelling the Myths of Black Teenage Motherhood* (1997); Pyong Gap Min, *Caught in the Middle: Korean Merchants in America's Multiethnic Cities* (1996); Fergus M. Bordewich, *Killing the White Man's Indian: Reinventing Native Americans at the End of the Twentieth Century* (1996); Ambrose I. Lane Sr., *Return of the Buffalo: The Story behind America's Indian Gaming Explosion* (1995); Raymond Tatalovich, *Nativism Reborn? The Official English Language Movement and the American States* (1995); Gary Y. Okihiro, *Margins and Mainstreams: Asians in American History and Culture* (1994); John William Sayer, *Ghost Dancing and the Law: The Wounded Knee Trials* (1997); Joane Nagel, *American Indian Ethnic Revival: Red Power and the Resurgence of Identity and Culture* (1996); Rennard Strickland, *Tonto's Revenge: Reflections on American Indian Culture and Policy* (1997); and Pierrette Hondagneu-Sotelo, *Gendered Transitions: Mexican Experiences of Immigration* (1994). Alan Klein, *Baseball on the Border: A Tale of Two Laredos* (1997), offers a unique look, through the American pastime, of multiculturalism.

CONSERVATIVE POLITICS The growth of the "new conservatism" may be traced in David Reinhard, *The Republican Right since 1945* (1983); Jerome Himmelstein, *To the Right: The Transformation of American Conservatism* (1990); Walter Capps, *The New Religious Right: Piety, Patriotism, and Politics* (1990); Walter Hixson, *Searching for the American Right* (1992); Michael Lienesch, *Redeeming America: Piety and Politics in the New Christian Right* (1993); Mary C. Brennan, *Turning Right in the Sixties: The Conservative Capture of the GOP* (1995); Robert Alan Goldberg, *Barry Goldwater* (1995); Dan T. Carter, *The Politics of Rage: George C. Wallace, the Origins of the New Conservatism, and the Transformation of American Politics* (1995); Catherine McNicol, *Stock, Rural Radicals: Righteous Rage in the American Grain* (1996); James D. Tabor and Eugene V. Gallagher, *Why Waco? Cults and the Battle for Religious Freedom in America* (1995); Mark J. Rozell and Clyde Wilcox, *Second Coming: The New Christian Right in Virginia Politics* (1996); Raymond Wolters, *Right Turn: William Bradford Reynolds, the Reagan Administration, and Black Civil Rights* (1996); and Didi Herman, *The Antigay Agenda: Orthodox Vision and the Christian Right* (1997).

VIDEOS *DreamWorlds II: Desire, Sex, and Power in Music Video* (1996) is an award-winning critique of the images in rock videos, while Michael Eric Dyson's *Material Witness: Race, Identity and the Politics of Gangsta Rap* (1996) offers a more complex view. *The Myth of the Liberal Media* (1994) is a three-part critique, by Noam Chomsky and Edward Herman, of how the U.S. media shape popular understandings.

Chapter 31

GENERAL SURVEYS OF RECENT POLITICAL TRENDS General surveys of recent political trends include Martin T. Wattenberg, *The Decline of American Political Parties, 1952–1980* (1984); Ryan Barilleaux, *The Post-Modern Presidency: The Office after Ronald Reagan* (1988); Kathleen Hall Jamieson, *Packaging the Presidency: A History and Criticism of Presidential Campaign Advertising* (3rd ed., 1996); William Greider, *Who Will Tell the People: The Betrayal of American Democracy* (1992); Thomas Byrne and Mary D. Edsall, *Chain Reaction: The Impact of Race, Rights, and Taxes on American Politics* (1992); Kevin Phillips, *Boiling Point: Republicans, Democrats, and the Decline of Middle Class Prosperity* (1993); William C. Berman, *America's Right Turn: From Nixon to Bush* (1994); Ronald Radosh, *Divided They Fell: The Demise of the Democratic Party, 1964–1996* (1996); and Philip John Davies, *An American Quarter Century: U.S. Politics from Vietnam to Clinton* (1995).

FOREIGN POLICY On general trends and specific episodes in foreign policy, see Paul Kennedy, *The Rise and Fall of the Great Powers: Economic Change and Military Conflict from 1500 to 2000* (1987); Walter LaFeber, *Inevitable Revolutions: The United States in Central America* (1983); Raymond Garthoff, *Detente and Confrontation: American-Soviet Relations from Nixon to Reagan* (1985); Gaddis Smith, *Morality, Reason, and Power: American Diplomacy in the Carter Years* (1986) and *The Last Years of the Monroe Doctrine, 1945–1993*; Herbert D. Rosenbaum and Alexej Ugrinsky, eds. *Jimmy Carter: Foreign Policy and Post-Presidential Years* (1994); Richard C. Thornton, *The Carter Years: Toward a New Global Order* (1991); David Skidmore, *Reversing Course: Carter's Foreign Policy, Domestic Politics, and the Failure of Reform* (1996); Timothy P. Maga, *The World of Jimmy Carter: U.S. Foreign Policy, 1977–1981* (1994); Joanna Spear, *Carter and Arms: Implementing the Carter Administration's Arms Transfer Restraint Policy* (1995); John Dumbrell, *American Foreign Policy: Carter to Clinton* (1996); Robert A. Pastor, *Whirlpool: U.S. Foreign Policy toward Latin America and the Caribbean* (1992); Raymond Garthoff, *The Great Transition: America-Soviet Relations and the End of the Cold War* (1994); Keith L. Nelson, *The Making of Detente: Soviet-American Relations in the Shadow of Vietnam* (1995); Michael R. Beschloss and Strobe Talbott, *At the Highest Levels: The Inside Story of the End of the Cold War* (1993); Theodore Draper, *A Very Thin Line: The Iran-Contra Affairs* (1991); Gary Sick, *October Surprise: America's Hostages in Iran and the Election of Ronald Reagan* (1991); Morris H. Morley, ed., *Crisis and Confrontation: Ronald Reagan's Foreign Policy* (1988); H. Bruce Franklin, *War Stars: The Superweapon and the American Imagination* (1988); John Lewis Gaddis, *The United States and the End of the Cold War: Implications, Reconsiderations, Provocations* (1991) and *We Now Know* (1997); and Michael Hogan, ed., *The End of the Cold War: Its Meaning and Implications* (1992).

THE GULF WAR For the Gulf War, specifically, see Lawrence Freedman and Efraim Karsh, *The Gulf Conflict, 1990–1991: Diplomacy and War in the New World Order* (1993); Dilip Hiro, *Desert Shield to Desert Storm: The Second Gulf War* (1992); Douglas Kellner, *The Persian Gulf TV War* (1992); Richard Hallion, *Storm over Iraq: Air Power and the Gulf War* (1992); Susan Jeffords and Lauren Rabinovitz, eds., *Seeing through the Media: The Persian Gulf War* (1994); and Frank N. Schubert and Theresa L. Kraus, *The Whirlwind War: The United States Army in Operations Desert Shield and Desert Storm* (1995).

THE BRIEF FORD PRESIDENCY On the brief Ford presidency, see Edward L. and Frederick H. Schapsmeier, *Gerald R. Ford's Date with Destiny: A Political Biography* (1989); James Cannon, *Time and Chance: Gerald Ford's Appointment with History* (1994); John R. Greene, *The Presidency of Gerald R. Ford* (1995); and John F. Guilmartin Jr., *A Very Short War: The Mayaguez and the Battle of Koh Tang* (1995).

THE CARTER YEARS On the Carter years, see Burton I. Kaufman, *The Presidency of James Earl Carter Jr.* (1993); Betty Glad, *Jimmy Carter: In Search of the Great White House* (1980); Erwin C. Hargrove, *Jimmy Carter as President* (1988); Garland Haas, *Jimmy Carter and the Politics of Frustration* (1992); Kenneth Morris, *Jimmy Carter: American Moralist* (1996); Anthony S. Campagna, *Economic Policy in the Carter Administration* (1995); and Gary M. Fink and Hugh Davis Graham, *The Carter Presidency: Policy Choices in the Post–New Deal Era* (1998).

THE REAGAN ERA On the Reagan era, see Sidney Blumenthal and Thomas Byrne Edsall, eds., *The Reagan Legacy* (1988); Robert Dallek, *Ronald Reagan: The Politics of Symbolism* (1984); Garry Wills, *Reagan's America: Innocents at Home* (1987); Robert E. Denton Jr., *The Primetime Presidency of Ronald Reagan* (1988); Michael Schaller, *Reckoning with Reagan* (1992); James E. Combs, *The Reagan Range: The Nostalgic Myth in American Politics* (1993); William Pemberton, *Exit with Honor: The Life and Presidency of Ronald Reagan* (1997); John Lofand, *Polite Protesters: The American Peace Movement of the 1980s* (1993); Raymond Wolters, *Right Turn: William Bradford Reynolds, the Reagan Administration, and Black Civil Rights* (1996); Diane Vaughan, *The Challenger Launch Decision: Risky Technology, Culture and Deviance at NASA* (1997); and Beth A. Fischer, *The Reagan Reversal: Foreign Policy at the End of the Cold War* (1998).

THE BUSH PRESIDENCY On the Bush presidency see Michael Duffy and Dan Goodgame, *Marching in Place: The Status Quo Presidency of George Bush* (1992); David Mervin, *George Bush and the Guardian Presidency* (1996); John Podhoretz, *Hell of a Ride: Backstage at the White House Follies 1989–1993* (1993); Charles Kolb, *White House Daze: The Unmaking of Domestic Policy in the Bush Years* (1994); and Herbert S. Parmet, *George Bush: The Life of a Lone Star Yankee* (1997).

POLITICS OF THE 1990S On the politics of the 1990s, see Jack W. Germond and Jules Witcover, *Mad as Hell: Revolt at the Ballot Box 1992* (1993); David Maraniss, *First in His Class: A Biography of Bill Clinton* (1995); Bob

Woodward, *The Agenda: Inside the Clinton White House* (1994); Michael Lienesch, *Redeeming America: Piety and Politics in the New Christian Right* (1993); James Gibson, *Warrior Dreams: Paramilitary Culture in Post Vietnam America* (1994); Sara Diamond, *Roads to Dominion: Right-Wing Power and Political Power in the United States* (1995); Catherine McNicol Stock, *Rural Radicals: Righteous Rage in the American Grain* (1996); Kathryn S. Olmsted, *Challenging the Secret Government: The Post-Watergate Investigations of the CIA and the FBI* (1996); Theda Skocpol, *Boomerang: Clinton's Health Security Effort and the Turn against Government in U.S. Politics* (1996); Jacob S. Hacker, *The Road to Nowhere: The Genesis of President Clinton's Plan for Health Security* (1997); John Hohenberg, *Reelecting Bill Clinton: Why America Chose a "New" Democrat* (1997); and Robert Reich, *Locked in the Cabinet* (1997).

VIDEOS The A&E "Biography" series contains a number of videos appropriate for these years, including *Jimmy Carter: To the White House and Beyond* (1995). The Gulf War is covered in *A Line in the Sand* (1990); *Desert Triumph* (1991), a three-part series; and *The Gulf War* (1997), also a three-part series. *Rush to Judgment: The Anita Hill Story* (1997) offers interviews with both advocates and critics of Justice Clarence Thomas's chief accuser. *The War Room* (1994) provides a candid, behind-the-scenes look at the 1992 Clinton campaign. *An American Journey: The Great Society to the Reagan Revolution* (1998) is a five-part overview of the period.

❦ CREDITS ❦